SWARM ROBOTICS

Swarm Robotics

Andrew Gun
Samuel Katich

Kruger Brentt
Publishers
2026

Kruger Brentt Publishers UK. LTD.
Company Number 9728962

Regd. Office: 68 St Margarets Road, Edgware, Middlesex HA8 9UU

ISBN: 978-1-78715-629-6

For information on all our publications visit our website at http://krugerbrentt.com/

PREFACE

Swarm Robotics explores the design, development, and application of multi-robot systems inspired by collective behaviors observed in nature, such as those of ants, bees, and birds. Unlike traditional robotics, swarm robotics emphasizes decentralized control, scalability, robustness, and flexibility, enabling groups of simple robots to achieve complex tasks collectively. This book is intended for students, researchers, and professionals in robotics, artificial intelligence, computer science, and engineering who seek a comprehensive understanding of swarm robotics principles, methodologies, and applications.

The book begins by introducing the fundamental concepts of swarm intelligence and its biological inspirations. It then delves into system design, communication protocols, control strategies, and coordination mechanisms that enable efficient collaboration among multiple robots. Key topics include distributed algorithms, self-organization, task allocation, path planning, and collective decision-making.

A major focus of the text is on practical applications, including search and rescue, environmental monitoring, agricultural automation, surveillance, and warehouse logistics. The book also addresses simulation techniques, hardware implementation, performance evaluation, and challenges such as robustness, fault tolerance, and energy efficiency in swarm systems.

Case studies and real-world examples illustrate successful implementations of swarm robotic systems, demonstrating how the integration of theory, algorithms, and hardware can solve complex problems efficiently. The book also highlights emerging trends and future research directions, including human-swarm interaction, autonomous swarm systems, and AI-enhanced swarm coordination.

We hope that Swarm Robotics will serve as a valuable resource for learners and practitioners, providing both theoretical foundations and practical insights to develop, analyze, and implement efficient multi-robot systems.

Andrew Gun

Samuel Katich

CONTENTS

1 Chapter — SWARM ROBOTICS: AN INTRODUCTION

1.1 SWARM ROBOTICS

Swarm Robotics is a dynamic and rapidly evolving subfield of robotics that takes inspiration from the collective behaviour observed in social insects such as ants, bees and termites. These natural systems demonstrate how large groups of simple individuals, with no global awareness or centralized leadership, can work together to solve complex problems efficiently. Swarm robotics applies these principles to artificial agents—typically small, autonomous robots—that operate cooperatively to perform tasks through local interactions. Each robot in the swarm is limited in sensing, computation and communication abilities, but when combined with many similar units, the group as a whole exhibit intelligent, coordinated behaviour. This is known as emergent behaviour, where global patterns arise from simple, local rules. The central idea behind swarm robotics is decentralization. There is no central controller or leader robot; instead, each unit acts independently based on its local environment and communication with nearby peers. This approach makes the system inherently scalable and fault-tolerant. Swarm robotic systems are capable of self-organization, meaning they can adapt to changing conditions, recover from failures and reconfigure themselves without human intervention. The robots may communicate directly (e.g., using infrared, Bluetooth, or radio signals) or indirectly (e.g., through environmental changes—a process called stigmergy). Applications of swarm robotics are wide-ranging and impactful. They include search and rescue missions in disaster zones, environmental monitoring, agricultural automation, military reconnaissance, warehouse automation and even space exploration. These systems are ideal for scenarios were deploying a single, complex robot would be too expensive, risky, or impractical. By mimicking the robustness, flexibility and efficiency found in nature, swarm robotics offers a new paradigm for designing robotic systems that are autonomous, collaborative and resilient. As technology continues to advance, swarm robotics holds the potential to transform how we think about intelligent machines working in teams to solve real-world problems (Fig.-1).

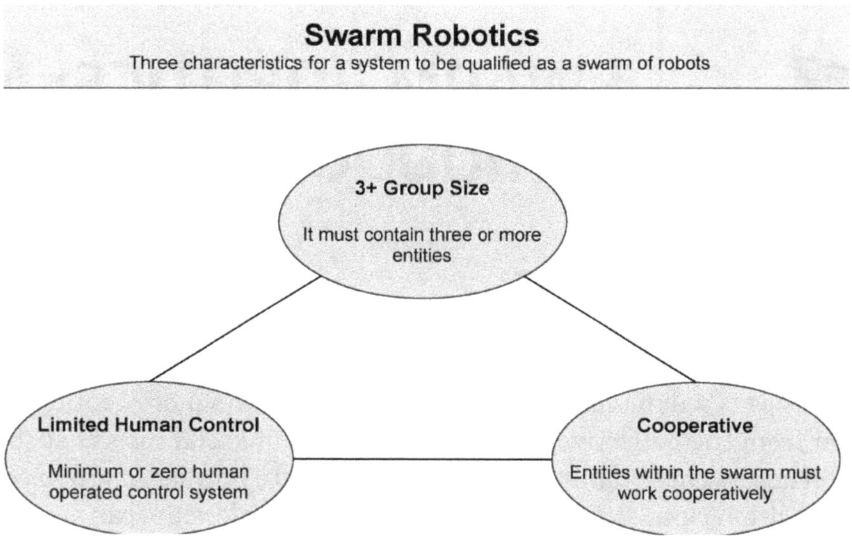

Fig. 1 Swarm Robotics in a Nutshell

Below is a detailed head wise breakdown:

1.1.1 Definition

Swarm Robotics involves the use of multiple autonomous robots that collaborate to complete tasks. The system relies on:

- **Decentralization:** No single robot leads the group.
- **Local Interactions:** Robots make decisions based on information from nearby robots and the environment.
- **Emergent Behaviour:** Complex global patterns and behaviours emerge from simple local rules.

1.1.2 Inspiration from Nature

Swarm robotics is inspired by biological swarms, such as:

- **Ant Colonies:** Ant colonies are a remarkable example of decentralized intelligence and cooperative behaviour. Individual ants have very limited perception and communication abilities, yet collectively, they are able to construct complex nests, forage over vast distances and adapt to environmental changes. One of the most well-known behaviours in ant colonies is their use of pheromone trails for pathfinding. When an ant finds a food source, it deposits a chemical trail as it returns to the nest. Other ants detect this trail and follow it, reinforcing it further if they also find food at the end. Over time, the most efficient (shortest and quickest) path becomes the strongest trail, while longer or less useful paths fade away. This indirect form of communication, known as stigmergy, allows the colony to self-organize and solve optimization problems without any central control. In swarm robotics, this behaviour has inspired path optimization and task allocation algorithms, such as Ant Colony Optimization (ACO). Robots can leave digital signals, light cues, or environmental markers to guide one another, enabling the group to collectively explore, map and complete tasks more efficiently—much like their insect counterparts.

- **Bee Swarms:** Bee swarms, especially honeybees, demonstrate an advanced form of collaborative decision-making that directly influences robotic swarm design. When a bee colony becomes too large, it splits and a swarm must find a new home. Scout bees venture out to evaluate potential nest sites and return to the swarm to report their findings through the waggle dance—a movement pattern that conveys the direction, distance and quality of a location. Initially, many different sites may be proposed, but over time, bees begin to support the best option more frequently. This leads to a natural consensus, as more scouts are recruited to promote the optimal location. This decision-making process occurs without a leader and relies solely on local interactions and repeated signalling. In swarm robotics, this behaviour has been adapted into algorithms for distributed consensus, resource selection and group decision-making. Robots can simulate the waggle dance behaviour using signal broadcasts or shared information to promote specific actions or locations. The result is a system capable of reaching collective agreement in uncertain environments—ideal for scenarios like exploration, deployment and disaster response, where centralized planning is not feasible.
- **Bird Flocks or Fish Schools:** Bird flocks and fish schools are iconic examples of emergent collective motion. Despite lacking a central leader, these groups move in tight, synchronized formations with remarkable fluidity and speed. Each bird or fish follows three basic local rules: alignment (match the direction of nearby individuals), cohesion (stay close to the group) and separation (avoid collisions). These rules enable the group to navigate as a cohesive unit, quickly responding to predators, obstacles, or changes in direction without chaos. This behaviour is incredibly efficient, adaptable and scalable. In swarm robotics, similar flocking algorithms are used to coordinate groups of robots—such as drones or underwater vehicles—so they can move together through space, avoid collisions and maintain formations without needing a central controller. These principles are especially valuable in open or hostile environments, where robots must work together to map terrain, carry payloads, or survey large areas. The elegance of such simple interaction rules leading to complex group dynamics makes flocking and schooling behaviours powerful models for robotic coordination in real-world tasks (Table-1).

Table-1: Concise summary of the Inspiration from Nature

Biological Swarm	Key Behaviours	Robotic Inspiration
Ant Colonies	- Decentralized intelligence - Pheromone trails for pathfinding (stigmergy) - Complex nest building and foraging	- Path optimization algorithms (Ant Colony Optimization) - Task allocation via digital/ environmental markers - Self-organization without central control
Bee Swarms	- Collaborative decision-making - Waggle dance to communicate location & quality of sites - Consensus through repeated signalling	- Distributed consensus algorithms - Resource selection - Group decision-making via local interactions and broadcasts
Bird Flocks / Fish Schools	- Emergent collective motion - Three local rules: alignment, cohesion, separation - Synchronized group movement and obstacle avoidance	- Flocking algorithms for coordinated group navigation - Collision avoidance - Formation control in drones and underwater vehicles

These natural systems are:

- Robust (can tolerate individual failures),
- Scalable (can function with many or few members),
- Flexible (can adapt to changing environments or tasks).

1.1.3 Characteristics Features

- **Scalability:** Scalability is a defining feature of swarm robotic systems, allowing them to expand or contract seamlessly based on task requirements. This characteristic ensures that the swarm can handle increased workloads simply by adding more robots, without the need for architectural changes. Whether scaling up to thousands of units or down to a minimal team, the system maintains its performance. Communication protocols are typically lightweight and local, preventing bottlenecks even in large-scale deployments. Swarms can efficiently cover large areas or perform complex distributed tasks by spreading out or concentrating as needed. This flexibility supports diverse applications, from search and rescue to environmental monitoring. Moreover, the modular nature of the robots facilitates easy integration. As new units are introduced, they self-organize with existing ones through shared behavioural rules. There's no need for manual reprogramming or network reconfiguration. This makes swarm robotics highly cost-effective and future-proof in dynamic environments.
- **Robustness:** Swarm robotics excels in robustness, meaning that the system can tolerate the failure of individual units without significant

degradation of performance. This is achieved through redundancy—many robots perform similar roles, so losing a few doesn't halt the mission. Each robot contributes incrementally and the swarm's collective intelligence compensates for any lost capabilities. Fault tolerance is inherent in the design, as no single robot is critical to system success. Even if several robots break down, the rest can adapt and redistribute the workload. This is crucial in hazardous environments where robot attrition is expected. The system's ability to self-heal or reconfigure its behaviour without external input enhances resilience. Real-time sensing and local communication help robots identify and adapt to failures quickly. As a result, swarm systems are more reliable than traditional centralized systems. This robustness reduces maintenance demands and extends operational lifespans.

- **Flexibility:** Flexibility is a cornerstone of swarm robotic systems, enabling them to perform a wide range of tasks and operate in varied environments. The behavioural algorithms guiding each robot are typically simple and general-purpose, allowing them to adapt quickly to new goals. Whether navigating rough terrain, exploring unknown spaces, or rearranging into different formations, swarms demonstrate dynamic versatility. Their decentralized nature allows rapid re-tasking without the need for extensive reprogramming. Robots can shift roles in response to environmental cues or task demands. For instance, a surveillance swarm could transform into a search party after detecting movement. Flexibility is further enhanced by their ability to learn from local interactions and evolve behaviour over time. This makes swarm systems ideal for unpredictable or changing conditions. Their modularity allows new capabilities to be added easily. As a result, flexible swarm robotics can be used across industries without redesigning from scratch for each application.

- **Decentralization:** Decentralization is fundamental to the design of swarm robotic systems, where no single robot governs the others. Each unit operates autonomously, making decisions based on local information and interactions. This eliminates the need for a central controller, reducing the risk of single points of failure. Decentralized systems are inherently more scalable and robust, as the behaviour of the swarm emerges from collective actions. Communication is often peer-to-peer and local, minimizing bandwidth and complexity. Decisions emerge organically from the swarm's distributed intelligence, not from top-down commands. This approach mimics biological systems like ant colonies or bird flocks, where simple individual rules lead to complex group behaviour. It also enables swarms to function effectively in environments where centralized control would be impractical or impossible, such as underwater or extraterrestrial missions. The autonomy of each robot also makes the system more resilient to disruptions or dynamic changes. Overall, decentralization enhances adaptability, reliability and performance (Table-2).

Table 2 : Characteristic features of swarm robotics

Characteristic	Description	Key Benefits
Scalability	Swarm systems can easily expand or contract by adding or removing robots without changing architecture. Lightweight local communication avoids bottlenecks, allowing swarms to cover large areas or concentrate as needed. Modular robots self-organize via shared rules.	Efficient workload handling; cost-effective; future-proof; supports diverse applications like search and rescue, environmental monitoring.
Robustness	The system tolerates failure of individual units due to redundancy. No single robot is critical and the swarm redistributes tasks automatically. Self-healing and local communication enable quick adaptation to failures.	High fault tolerance; reliable operation in hazardous environments; reduced maintenance; longer operational lifespan.
Flexibility	Simple, general-purpose behavioural algorithms enable robots to adapt to new tasks and environments quickly. Decentralized control allows role switching and dynamic re-tasking without extensive reprogramming. Swarms can learn and evolve behaviours over time.	Versatile across tasks and industries; handles unpredictable, changing conditions; easy integration of new capabilities.
Decentralization	Robots operate autonomously using local information and peer-to-peer communication, without a central controller. Swarm behaviour emerges from collective actions and mimics natural biological systems.	Eliminates single points of failure; enhances scalability and robustness; enables operation in complex or remote environments; improves adaptability and reliability.

1.1.4 Communication Methods

Effective communication is vital for coordinating behaviour in swarm robotics. Swarm robots primarily use local communication, where each unit exchanges information with nearby peers through short-range technologies like infrared, Bluetooth, or radio frequency. This enables real-time coordination without needing a global network. Additionally, swarm robots employ indirect communication, also known as stigmergy, which involves leaving cues in the environment that influence others' behaviour. These cues can take the form of chemical trails, light patterns, or sound pulses. Inspired by social insects like ants or termites, stigmergy allows asynchronous coordination, where robots respond to environmental changes rather than direct commands. This dual communication approach—local and stigmergic—supports decentralized decision-making and increases fault tolerance. It also enhances the swarm's ability to adapt to dynamic environments and unknown scenarios. Since communication is lightweight and distributed, the system remains scalable and robust, even with hundreds or thousands of robots in operation.

Swarm robots communicate using:

- **Local Communication:** Local communication is a core method used by swarm robots to coordinate actions with their nearby peers. This typically involves short-range technologies such as infrared, Bluetooth, or radio frequency (RF), allowing robots to exchange information within a limited spatial range. The advantage of this approach is its simplicity and efficiency, enabling real-time decision-making without relying on a central controller. Robots can share data about their position, task status, or environmental observations, helping to maintain coordination in dynamic settings. Because the communication range is short, interference is minimized and the system scales well as more robots are added. This method mimics natural systems, such as birds or fish, which communicate through local interactions to maintain flocking or schooling behaviour. Local communication is also energy-efficient, as it reduces the need for high-powered transmissions. Additionally, the localized nature ensures that any malfunction in one robot doesn't disrupt the entire swarm. This decentralized, peer-to-peer model enhances robustness, responsiveness and adaptability.
- **Indirect Communication (Stigmergy):** Stigmergy is a unique form of indirect communication in swarm robotics, where robots interact not with each other directly, but by modifying the environment to leave signals or markers. These cues—such as light patterns, sound pulses, pheromone-like chemicals, or physical alterations—serve as information that other robots can detect and respond to. This method allows asynchronous coordination, meaning robots don't need to be present at the same time to collaborate. Inspired by social insects like ants leaving pheromone trails, stigmergy supports the emergence of complex behaviours from simple actions. It reduces the need for complex communication protocols and enables distributed problem-solving. For example, robots might mark paths to efficient resources, guiding others without direct contact. Stigmergy is especially useful in large or unstructured environments where constant communication is impractical. It increases the swarm's scalability, as signals in the environment persist beyond the presence of the signaling robot.

Overall, stigmergy enhances coordination, robustness and environmental awareness.

1.1.5 Components of a Swarm Robot

Each robot in a swarm is a compact, autonomous unit equipped with essential components that enable it to perceive, act and collaborate within a group. Sensors play a crucial role in detecting environmental features, obstacles and the presence of other robots, enabling real-time responsiveness. Actuators, such as wheels, servos, or robotic arms, allow the robot to move or interact with objects in its environment. A processor, often a microcontroller or onboard computer, serves as the brain, executing algorithms that govern behaviour and decision-making. The communication module, using infrared, Bluetooth, or RF, enables robots to exchange information with nearby peers or leave environmental signals for stigmergic coordination. A power source, usually a rechargeable battery or sometimes a solar panel, provides energy for all operations. Together, these components ensure the robot can operate independently while contributing to the swarm's collective goal. Their modular design allows easy replication and scaling. Despite their simplicity, these units combine to form highly intelligent and adaptable systems.

Each robot in the swarm typically includes:

- **Sensors:** Sensors are the eyes and ears of a swarm robot, enabling it to perceive both its environment and fellow robots. These can include infrared, ultrasonic, proximity, light, temperature and vision sensors depending on the task. By interpreting data from these inputs, a robot can avoid obstacles, follow lines, map surroundings, or detect signals left by other units. Sensors also allow robots to assess terrain or identify objects of interest. In swarm settings, proximity sensors help maintain spacing and avoid collisions. Environmental sensors contribute to stigmergic communication by detecting changes in the shared space. The accuracy and responsiveness of the robot's behaviour depend heavily on sensor quality. Efficient sensor fusion ensures reliable, real-time decision-making. Ultimately, sensors enable autonomy and adaptability—critical traits in unpredictable environments.
- **Actuators:** Actuators allow swarm robots to perform physical actions, most commonly movement. These typically include motors, wheels, servos, or even legs, depending on the design. Through actuators, a robot can navigate terrain, manipulate objects, or reposition itself within the swarm. Precision in actuator response is vital for maintaining formations or executing coordinated group behaviours. In some robots, specialized actuators may

control grippers or arms for interacting with the environment. Their efficiency directly impacts energy consumption and operational duration. Combined with sensor input, actuators help create closed-loop control systems that support real-time navigation and task execution. Actuators also allow robots to respond quickly to changes, maintaining the swarm's overall cohesion. Without effective actuation, sensing and communication have little impact.

- **Processor:** The processor acts as the decision-making core of the robot, interpreting sensor data and executing programmed behaviours. Typically, a microcontroller (like an Arduino or Raspberry Pi), it runs algorithms that govern how the robot reacts to its environment and coordinates with the swarm. It manages input/output operations, processes communication signals and determines movement commands for the actuators. Efficient processing is essential for real-time responsiveness, especially in dynamic and uncertain environments. In a decentralized system, each robot makes autonomous decisions, so the processor must balance simplicity with reliability. Some robots may include onboard AI or machine learning modules for more adaptive behaviour. The processor is also responsible for implementing energy-saving strategies and fault handling. Overall, it enables the robot to function as an intelligent, independent unit within the swarm.
- **Communication Module:** The communication module allows each robot to share information with its peers, a critical capability for swarm coordination. Depending on the design, this may include infrared transmitters, Bluetooth chips, RF modules, or even Wi-Fi. Short-range communication ensures that each robot interacts with only nearby units, supporting scalability and avoiding network congestion. These modules transmit data such as position, task progress, or environmental changes. In some designs, robots also receive and interpret stigmergic cues like sound or light signals. Effective communication enables collective behaviours like formation control, task allocation, or dynamic role switching. The reliability of this module impacts the entire swarm's performance, especially in real-time collaborative missions. By decentralizing information flow, the communication module supports fault tolerance and flexibility. It is essential for achieving emergent, group-level intelligence.
- **Power Source:** The power source fuels all of a swarm robot's functions, from processing and sensing to movement and communication. Most commonly, robots use rechargeable batteries such as lithium-ion or lithium-polymer due to their high energy density. Some designs may incorporate solar panels for extended outdoor operation or energy autonomy. Power efficiency is

crucial, as it directly affects mission duration and task effectiveness. Robots may include power management circuits to conserve energy during idle periods or low-activity phases. Designers often face trade-offs between size, weight and battery capacity, especially in micro-robots. A depleted power source not only halts a robot's functions but can also disrupt the swarm if it occurs unpredictably. Therefore, monitoring battery levels and planning energy-aware behaviours are important strategies. In swarm applications, robust power design ensures sustained and distributed operation without frequent recharging interruptions.

1.1.6 Applications of Swarm Robotics:

Swarm robotics is useful in areas where single large robots are impractical or too risky:

- **Search and Rescue Operations:** Swarm robotics is particularly effective in search and rescue missions, where speed, adaptability and safety are critical. Small autonomous robots can rapidly deploy into disaster zones—such as collapsed buildings, earthquake areas, or hazardous industrial sites—without risking human responders. Their compact size allows access to tight or unstable spaces that are unreachable for larger robots. By working cooperatively, swarm robots can map environments, locate victims and relay information in real time. Their decentralized nature ensures that if one unit fails, others can continue the mission uninterrupted. Swarms can dynamically spread out to cover wide areas or concentrate in locations of interest. They can also be equipped with sensors for detecting heat, sound, or gas leaks. Their ability to self-organize and adapt makes them invaluable in unpredictable, life-threatening conditions. Ultimately, they reduce response times and enhance safety for both victims and human rescuers (Fig. 2).

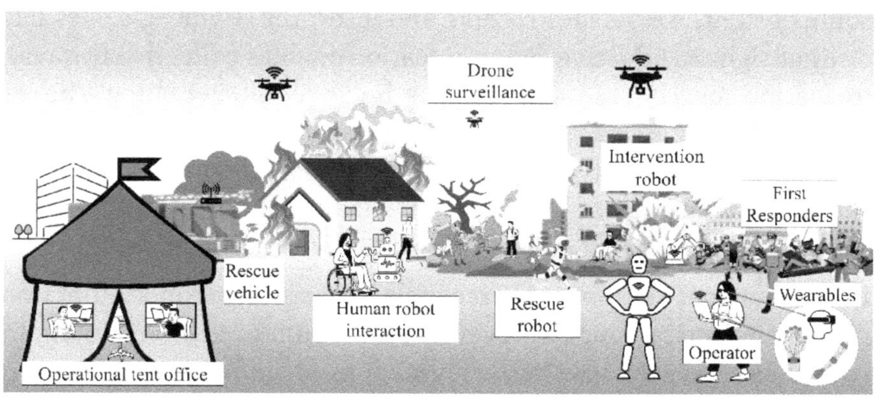

Fig.2 Swarm robotics in Search and Rescue Operations

- **Agriculture:** In modern agriculture, swarm robotics offers an efficient and scalable solution for precision farming. Swarms of small robots can monitor large fields autonomously, collecting data on soil quality, moisture levels and plant health using various sensors. This enables farmers to make data-driven decisions about irrigation, fertilization and pest control. Additionally, these robots can assist with planting seeds, removing weeds, or applying treatments selectively, reducing waste and environmental impact. The collaborative behaviour of swarm robots ensures thorough coverage without overlap or missed areas. Their lightweight and distributed design minimizes soil compaction compared to heavy machinery. Swarms can also adapt to field conditions and adjust their behaviour in real time. This technology reduces labour dependency and enhances productivity, especially in large-scale or remote farming areas. As demand for sustainable practices grows, swarm robotics provides a smart, low-impact alternative to traditional agricultural methods (Fig.-3).

Fig. 3. Swarm robotics in Agriculture

- **Environmental Monitoring:** Swarm robots are well-suited for environmental monitoring tasks across land, air and water. Equipped with appropriate sensors, they can collect data on pollution levels, climate conditions, or biodiversity across large areas efficiently and autonomously. Their distributed operation allows for high-resolution sampling that fixed stations or individual drones cannot match. For instance, a swarm of aquatic robots can measure water quality in lakes or oceans, while aerial swarms can track air pollution or forest health. They can also detect hazardous substances, such as chemical spills or radiation and report them without endangering human lives. Swarm behaviour allows for adaptive coverage, reacting to areas of concern by clustering or dispersing as needed. Data collected can feed into real-time environmental models and long-term studies. Their mobility and flexibility make them ideal for both routine monitoring and emergency response. This supports better-informed environmental management and policy-making (Fig.-4).

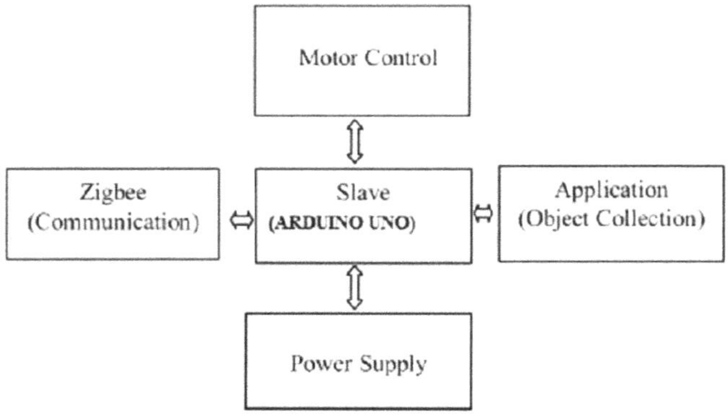

Fig.4. Swarm robotics in Marine Environmental Monitoring

- **Military Surveillance:** In defence applications, swarm robotics offers stealthy, adaptable and resilient surveillance capabilities. Small, agile robots can infiltrate enemy territory or monitor borders without being easily detected. Their decentralized operation makes them hard to disable; if a few units are compromised, the rest continue the mission. Swarms can cover vast areas or focus on high-interest zones, dynamically shifting in response to changing conditions. Equipped with cameras, microphones, or signal interceptors, they gather real-time intelligence without exposing human soldiers. Their low cost and easy deployment make them attractive for both strategic and tactical operations. Additionally, swarm robots can perform decoy functions or distract enemy defences. Advanced algorithms allow them to coordinate movements, share findings and even identify threats autonomously. As warfare increasingly incorporates technology, swarm robotics offers a scalable, low-risk solution for reconnaissance and battlefield awareness (Fig.-5).

Fig. 5. Swarm robotics in the Military

- **Space Exploration:** Swarm robotics is revolutionizing space exploration by enabling collaborative, autonomous missions on planetary surfaces. Unlike single, large, expensive rovers, swarms of smaller robots offer redundancy, flexibility and greater area coverage. They can be deployed simultaneously to map terrain, collect samples, or search for signs of life. If one robot fails due to harsh conditions, the others can continue independently. Their decentralized nature allows them to adapt to unpredictable obstacles or environmental changes. Swarms can also work together to construct habitats or deploy sensors, supporting long-term missions. Their compact size makes them easier and cheaper to transport via spacecraft. They can communicate locally and relay data back to orbiters or Earth through a mesh network. This approach improves reliability and efficiency in the harsh, remote environments of space. Ultimately, swarm robotics enhances our ability to explore, understand and even colonize extraterrestrial worlds (Fig.-6).

Fig. 6. Swarm robotics in the Space Exploration

1.1.7 Challenges in Swarm Robotics

Despite the numerous advantages and promising applications of swarm robotics, the field faces several technical and theoretical challenges that must be addressed to enable widespread adoption and real-world deployment. Key challenges include coordination complexity, communication reliability, energy efficiency, hardware limitations and algorithm design. Despite its potential, swarm robotics faces several challenges:

- **Coordination Complexity:** One of the biggest challenges in swarm robotics is achieving reliable and predictable group behaviour from robots that follow simple, individual rules. Since there's no central controller, coordination must emerge from local interactions, which can be unpredictable. Designing behaviour that scales well with the number of robots while maintaining cohesion is complex. Small changes in initial conditions or the environment can lead to unexpected outcomes. Ensuring that the swarm acts coherently—even in the presence of delays, failures, or external disturbances—requires robust control strategies. Developers must also account for group-level objectives, like pattern formation or collective decision-making, through decentralized logic. Fine-tuning these algorithms involves extensive simulation and real-world testing. Synchronization, task allocation and spatial awareness must be carefully managed to avoid chaos. Ultimately, successful coordination is key to realizing the full potential of swarm systems in real applications.

- **Communication Reliability:** Swarm robots rely on local communication to share information, but this method faces challenges related to reliability and consistency. Wireless signals like infrared, Bluetooth, or radio frequency can be disrupted by environmental obstacles, interference, or noise. In dynamic or cluttered settings, robots may lose contact with one another, leading to gaps in coordination. Message collisions, signal fading, or hardware malfunctions can also affect communication quality. Furthermore, limited communication range restricts information flow to nearby peers only, which can delay swarm-wide updates. Ensuring redundancy in communication protocols—such as repeated messages or multi-hop relaying—adds complexity but improves robustness. Developers must balance bandwidth usage and power consumption while maintaining real-time responsiveness. Testing under realistic conditions is critical to validate communication reliability. Without dependable inter-robot communication, swarm behaviour may degrade or become unpredictable.
- **Energy Efficiency:** Energy efficiency is a critical concern in swarm robotics due to the small size and mobility demands of individual robots. Most swarm robots are powered by compact batteries that limit operational time, especially when performing tasks like sensing, movement, or communication. Efficient power usage is essential to prolong mission durations and reduce downtime for charging. Designing low-power electronics and optimizing algorithms to minimize unnecessary movement or communication can help. Swarm-level strategies, like rotating active and resting robots or task scheduling based on battery levels, further conserve energy. Solar or kinetic energy harvesting can be considered, but adds complexity and weight. Real-time power monitoring is necessary to prevent sudden failure during operation. Energy constraints also limit onboard computation and sensing capabilities, reinforcing the need for

simple but effective behaviours. Long-lasting swarms require a holistic approach to hardware, software and behaviour design that prioritizes power conservation.

- **Hardware Limitations:** Swarm robots are typically small and lightweight, which restricts the types and quality of hardware that can be included. Their size limits the use of high-resolution cameras, powerful processors, or complex sensor arrays. As a result, perception accuracy and computational capabilities are often reduced compared to larger autonomous systems. These limitations affect how well robots can understand their environment, detect other robots, or perform sophisticated tasks. Additionally, miniaturized components are more prone to damage, wear and environmental interference. To compensate, designers must develop algorithms that work with limited, low-fidelity input. Storage capacity, actuator strength and energy reserves are also constrained by hardware size. These trade-offs require creative engineering and system-level optimization. Balancing affordability with functionality is a constant challenge, especially for large-scale deployments. Despite these constraints, effective swarm behaviour must still emerge from minimal, cost-efficient designs.
- **Algorithm Design:** Developing the right algorithms for swarm behaviour is one of the most complex and research-intensive aspects of swarm robotics. The goal is to create simple, local rules for individual robots that result in intelligent, coordinated and purposeful group behaviour—known as emergence. However, predicting and controlling emergent behaviour is notoriously difficult. Designers must consider factors like scalability, fault tolerance, adaptability and robustness when crafting these algorithms. The rules must also accommodate real-world imperfections, such as sensor noise, communication loss and robot failures. Simulations are used to test behaviours before deployment, but transferring results to physical robots introduces additional challenges. Algorithm design often draws inspiration from nature, such as ant foraging or bird flocking, but adapting biological behaviours to robots requires abstraction and engineering judgment. Continuous learning or adaptive behaviours add further complexity. Ultimately, effective swarm algorithms must balance simplicity with the ability to handle complex, dynamic tasks.

1.1.8 Future Scope

The field of swarm robotics is rapidly advancing, driven by breakthroughs in multiple areas of technology and research. As the demand for intelligent, flexible and scalable robotic systems grows across industries, the potential applications and capabilities of swarm robotics continue to expand. Future developments are expected to overcome current limitations and unlock new possibilities, making swarms more autonomous, efficient and adaptive. Key areas such as artificial intelligence, miniaturization and advanced swarm intelligence algorithms are at the forefront of this progress. Together, these innovations promise to elevate swarm robotics from experimental setups to widespread, practical solutions that can address complex challenges in dynamic environments.

The future of swarm robotics is promising with advancements in:

- **AI and Machine Learning:** Artificial Intelligence (AI) and Machine Learning (ML) are poised to transform swarm robotics by enabling smarter, more adaptive behaviour at both the individual and collective levels. With ML, swarm robots can learn from past experiences and environmental data, improving performance over time without explicit reprogramming. Techniques such as reinforcement learning and neural networks allow robots to optimize their decision-making in complex or unfamiliar scenarios. AI can help manage real-time task allocation, path planning and cooperative problem-solving, even in dynamic or uncertain conditions. Furthermore, distributed learning systems could allow individual robots to share learned knowledge with others, accelerating adaptation across the swarm. By leveraging onboard intelligence, swarms will become less reliant on predefined rules and more capable of autonomous innovation. This greatly enhances scalability, fault tolerance and mission success. As AI technology matures, swarms will increasingly behave like intelligent, goal-driven agents rather than reactive machines.
- **Miniaturization:** Miniaturization plays a critical role in the evolution of swarm robotics, enabling the design of smaller, cheaper and more capable robotic units. Advances in microelectronics, MEMS (Micro-Electro-Mechanical Systems) and nanotechnology are making it possible to embed complex sensors, processors and power systems into increasingly compact forms. This reduction in size allows robots to operate in confined or delicate environments such as inside the human body, narrow pipes, or ecological habitats without causing disruption. Smaller robots also reduce manufacturing costs, making large-scale deployments more economically feasible. Despite their size, these robots can perform sophisticated tasks by leveraging improved hardware and collective behaviour. Miniaturized robots require less power, are easier to transport and can function in swarms of hundreds or thousands. As technology continues to shrink while increasing capability, swarm robotics will become even more practical, flexible and accessible for industries ranging from medicine to environmental monitoring.

- **Swarm Intelligence Algorithms:** The future of swarm robotics relies heavily on the development of advanced swarm intelligence algorithms—sets of local rules that produce complex, coordinated behaviours at the group level. These algorithms are becoming more efficient, scalable and resilient, enabling robots to work together seamlessly in dynamic and unpredictable environments. Inspired by nature (e.g., ant colonies, bee swarms, bird flocks), future algorithms will incorporate adaptive and learning-based mechanisms, allowing the swarm to self-organize, self-heal and dynamically allocate tasks. Researchers are also exploring hybrid models that combine rule-based systems with AI-driven learning to achieve more nuanced and context-aware behaviour. Improved algorithms will better handle obstacle avoidance, formation control, exploration and distributed decision-making. Robustness against communication failure and robot loss will be enhanced through redundancy and local autonomy. As these algorithms evolve, they will allow swarms to tackle increasingly complex missions with minimal human intervention, pushing the boundaries of autonomous robotics.

1.2 ORIGINS: FROM SWARM INTELLIGENCE TO ROBOTIC SWARMS

Swarm Robotics finds its origins in the interdisciplinary field of Swarm Intelligence (SI), a concept that studies the collective behaviour of decentralized and self-organizing systems—both in nature and artificial environments. Swarm Intelligence draws inspiration from the observation of natural systems, such as flocks of birds, schools of fish, colonies of ants and swarms of bees. These biological entities demonstrate remarkable coordination and adaptability despite the lack of centralized control, often achieving complex tasks such as foraging, navigation, nest building and defence through simple local interactions. The concept of SI gained momentum in the late 20th century, primarily through the development of computational algorithms like Ant Colony Optimization (ACO) and Particle Swarm Optimization (PSO). These algorithms mimic the natural behaviours of swarms to solve complex optimization problems in engineering, logistics and artificial intelligence. Such models revealed that even rudimentary agents, when following a few simple rules and interacting locally, could produce emergent behaviour at the system level. The transition from theoretical models to physical systems gave rise to Swarm Robotics. Researchers began to explore whether the principles governing biological swarms could be applied to groups of robots, enabling them to operate autonomously in unstructured environments. Unlike traditional robotic systems that often rely on centralized processing or detailed global knowledge, swarm robotic systems are designed to be scalable, fault-tolerant and robust. These characteristics make them ideal for applications in search and rescue, environmental monitoring, agricultural automation and military surveillance (Fig.-7).

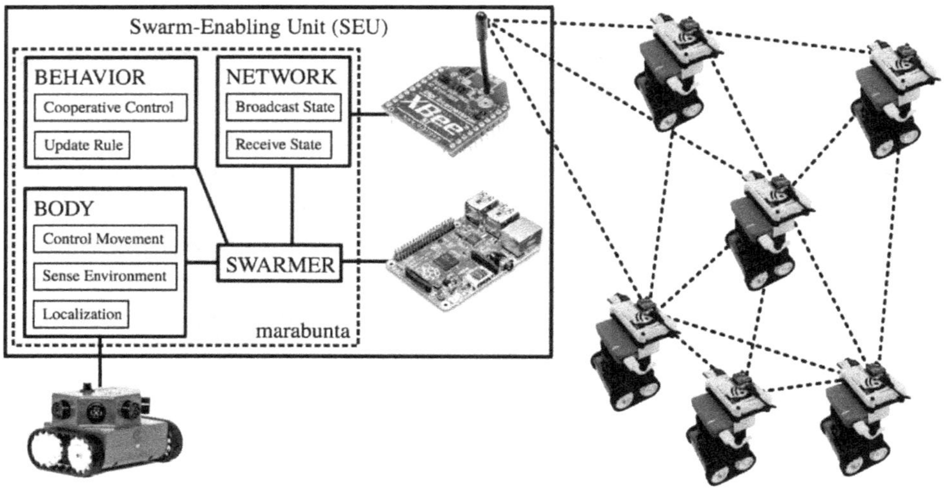

Fig. 7. Swarm-Enabling Technology for Multi-Robot Systems

The appeal of swarm robotics lies in its simplicity, scalability and adaptability. By minimizing the complexity of individual units and leveraging the power of local interactions, engineers and scientists aim to develop robotic swarms that can dynamically respond to changing environments, recover from individual failures and function effectively without supervision. Early experimental platforms, such as Kilobots and e-puck robots, were instrumental in demonstrating the feasibility of these ideas in real-world hardware. These robots, though limited in individual capability, collectively displayed behaviours such as aggregation, dispersion, flocking and task allocation—mirroring their natural counterparts. The development of such platforms also led to innovations in communication protocols, localization methods and coordination algorithms tailored for swarm settings. In essence, swarm robotics represents a convergence of biology, computer science and engineering. It builds upon our understanding of how nature solves problems collectively and applies those principles to robotic systems. The journey from observing ant trails and bird flocks to programming collaborative robots marks a significant shift in how intelligence, control and autonomy are conceived in modern robotics. As technology advances, the vision of large-scale robotic swarms working seamlessly in complex tasks is becoming increasingly realistic, pushing the boundaries of what autonomous systems can achieve.

1.2.1 Swarm Intelligence (SI)

Swarm Intelligence (SI) is a subfield of artificial intelligence that investigates how the collective behaviour of simple, autonomous agents—interacting locally with one another and their environment—can lead to the emergence of complex, intelligent global behaviour. The central idea behind SI is that individual agents, even with limited capabilities and no centralized control, can collectively solve difficult problems through coordination and cooperation (Fig.-8).

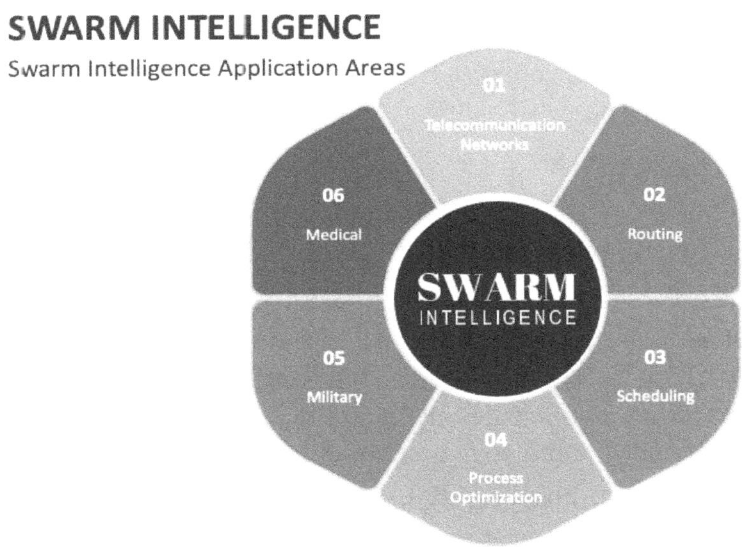

Fig. 8. Swarm Intelligence

The concept of SI originated from the study of natural systems, where groups of organisms demonstrate sophisticated behaviour without any single individual leading the group. These natural inspirations include:

- **Ant Colonies:** Ants exhibit remarkable problem-solving abilities, particularly in foraging and path optimization. Through pheromone trails and simple decision-making rules, ant colonies can efficiently discover and exploit food sources—an idea that led to the development of the Ant Colony Optimization algorithm.
- **Bee Hives:** Bees demonstrate advanced swarm behaviour through tasks such as nest-site selection and collective foraging. The waggle dance used by scout bees to communicate the location of food sources showcases how simple agents can share information effectively to guide group decisions.
- **Flocks of Birds:** Bird flocks exhibit graceful, synchronized movement by following a few simple rules such as alignment, separation and cohesion. These rules allow each bird to adjust its direction and speed based on its neighbours, enabling the group to navigate as a coherent unit.
- **Schools of Fish:** Fish schools display highly coordinated movement that helps them evade predators and explore their environment. Similar to bird flocks, fish follow local interaction rules that result in globally optimized patterns of motion and defence.

Swarm Intelligence leverages these biological principles to design algorithms and systems that are robust, scalable and adaptable. Applications span a wide range of fields, including robotics, optimization, data clustering, network routing and collective decision-making. By emulating nature's decentralized strategies, SI provides innovative solutions to problems that are otherwise challenging for traditional, centralized approaches.

Swarm Intelligence Concepts:

Swarm Intelligence is built upon several foundational principles that collectively enable the emergence of complex, intelligent group behaviour from simple individual components:

- **Self-Organization:** This refers to the ability of a system to spontaneously organize itself without external or centralized control. In swarm systems, individual agents follow simple rules and adapt to local conditions, leading to the formation of coordinated structures or behaviours over time.
- **Decentralized Control:** Unlike traditional systems that rely on a central controller, swarm systems operate without a single point of authority. Each agent functions independently, making decisions based on local information. This decentralization enhances the system's robustness and scalability.
- **Local Interactions:** Agents in a swarm interact primarily with their immediate neighbours or local environment. They exchange information, adjust their behaviour and influence one another only within a limited range. Despite this limited scope, the accumulation of these interactions drives the overall system's dynamics.
- **Emergent Behaviour:** Perhaps the most fascinating aspect of swarm systems is emergent behaviour—complex global patterns or functions that arise from the collective actions of many simple agents. These behaviours are not explicitly programmed but emerge naturally from the rules governing individual agents and their interactions.

These systems display intelligence without any central planning—solutions arise from simple individual actions (Table-3).

Table: 3. Concise Summary of Swarm Intelligence concepts

Concept	Description
Self-Organization	Ability of the system to organize itself spontaneously without centralized control. Individual agents follow simple rules and adapt to local conditions, resulting in coordinated group behaviour over time.
Decentralized Control	No single central controller; each agent makes decisions independently based on local information, enhancing robustness and scalability.
Local Interactions	Agents interact only with nearby neighbours or their immediate environment, exchanging information and adjusting behaviour within a limited range. These local interactions collectively drive system dynamics.
Emergent Behaviour	Complex global patterns or functions arise naturally from the collective actions of simple agents, without explicit programming or central planning.

1.2.2 Biological Inspiration

Swarm Intelligence is built upon several foundational principles that collectively enable the emergence of complex, intelligent group behaviour from simple individual components:

- **Self-Organization:** This refers to the ability of a system to spontaneously organize itself without external or centralized control. In swarm systems, individual agents follow simple rules and adapt to local conditions, leading to the formation of coordinated structures or behaviours over time.
- **Decentralized Control:** Unlike traditional systems that rely on a central controller, swarm systems operate without a single point of authority. Each agent functions independently, making decisions based on local information. This decentralization enhances the system's robustness and scalability.
- **Local Interactions:** Agents in a swarm interact primarily with their immediate neighbours or local environment. They exchange information, adjust their behaviour and influence one another only within a limited range. Despite this limited scope, the accumulation of these interactions drives the overall system's dynamics.
- **Emergent Behaviour:** Perhaps the most fascinating aspect of swarm systems is emergent behaviour—complex global patterns or functions that arise from the collective actions of many simple agents. These behaviours are not explicitly programmed but emerge naturally from the rules governing individual agents and their interactions.

These natural swarms exhibit:

- Resilience to failure
- Adaptive behaviours
- Collective decision-making

Such properties became foundational for designing artificial swarm systems.

1.2.3 Computational Models of Swarm Intelligence

Before the emergence of physical swarm robotic systems, the principles of Swarm Intelligence (SI) were first explored and implemented through computational algorithms. These early models demonstrated that collective behaviour inspired by nature could be harnessed to solve complex problems in digital environments with remarkable efficiency and adaptability ((Fig.-9).

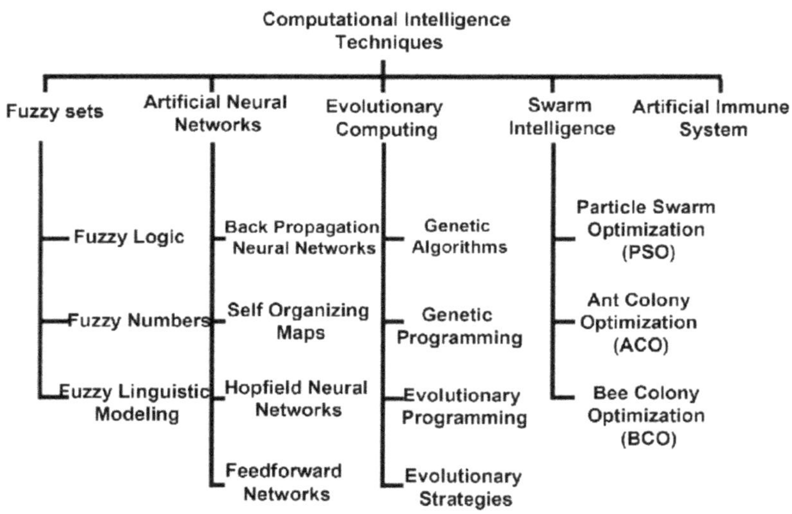

Fig.9. Type of computational intelligence

Two of the most influential algorithms include:

- **Ant Colony Optimization (ACO):** Inspired by the foraging behaviour of real ants, ACO is a probabilistic technique used to solve pathfinding and combinatorial optimization problems, such as the Traveling Salesman Problem or network routing. In these models, artificial "ants" simulate the laying and following of pheromone trails, gradually reinforcing shorter or more optimal paths through positive feedback. ACO has proven highly effective in logistics, network design and scheduling tasks.
- **Particle Swarm Optimization (PSO):** Modelled after the flocking and schooling behaviour observed in birds and fish, PSO involves a population

(swarm) of particles that explore a solution space to find the optimal solution. Each particle adjusts its position based on its own experience and that of its neighbours, balancing individual exploration with collective learning. PSO is widely used in optimizing mathematical functions, machine learning model tuning and engineering design problems.

These algorithms showcased how simple agents—without central coordination—could work together to solve highly complex and computationally demanding problems. They validated the effectiveness of swarm-based logic in artificial settings and laid the groundwork for transferring these principles from virtual agents to real-world physical systems in the form of swarm robotics.

1.2.4 Transition to Swarm Robotics

The shift from theoretical Swarm Intelligence (SI) to its physical embodiment in swarm robotics began in the late 1990s and early 2000s. Building on the success of swarm-based algorithms like ACO and PSO, researchers began exploring whether similar principles could be applied to real-world, autonomous robotic systems. The goal was to create groups of simple robots capable of collectively performing tasks without the need for centralized control.

- **Multiple Mobile Robots:** Researchers deployed groups of small, wheeled robots to simulate real-world swarm behaviour. These robots acted as physical agents in controlled environments, mimicking digital swarms.
- **Simple Sensing and Communication:** Instead of relying on complex sensors or high-bandwidth communication, the robots used minimalistic components—such as infrared sensors, LEDs, or Bluetooth—to detect obstacles, identify neighbours and share basic information.
- **Local Rules:** Just like in natural swarms, each robot followed simple, pre-defined rules based only on local information. This allowed the group to function cohesively and adaptively, even in the presence of noise, delays, or individual robot failures.

Follow trails using light or despite their simplicity, these robotic swarms were able to demonstrate impressive behaviours. They could:

- chemical markers (e.g., mimicking pheromone trails).
- Avoid obstacles through local sensing and reactive navigation.
- Collaborate effectively to perform tasks such as object transport, area coverage and collective decision-making—all without any central controller or global knowledge.

Key projects and platforms that played a foundational role in this transition include:

- **E-puck Robots:** Designed for educational and research use, these robots were equipped with various sensors and used in a wide range of experiments related to swarm behaviour, coordination and evolution.
- **Kilobot Platform:** Developed at Harvard, Kilobots are small, low-cost robots specifically created to test and demonstrate swarm algorithms on a large scale (hundreds to thousands of units). They provided a practical platform to study real-world emergent behaviours.
- **Pioneering Researchers:** Scientists such as Marco Dorigo, known for both ACO and swarm robotics research; James McLurkin, who explored distributed algorithms in robot swarms; and Gerardo Beni, one of the first to coin the term Swarm Intelligence, were instrumental in transforming theoretical insights into tangible robotic systems.

This transition marked a critical step in the evolution of swarm robotics—from nature-inspired theory to real-world engineering—laying the foundation for today's advanced multi-robot systems used in research, industry and beyond.

1.2.5 Early Experiments in Swarm Robotics

The foundational years of swarm robotics were marked by a series of focused experiments designed to test whether simple, decentralized robots could emulate the complex group behaviours observed in nature. Drawing directly from Swarm Intelligence (SI) principles, researchers designed robotic systems with minimal individual capabilities but high potential for collective problem-solving. These early experiments served not only as proofs of concept but also as critical stepping stones toward the development of scalable, robust and autonomous multi-robot systems. One of the primary tasks explored in early swarm robotics was foraging, modelled after the behaviour of ant colonies. In these experiments, robots were tasked with locating and retrieving objects (representing food) from an environment and transporting them back to a central location (the nest). Without a central controller or prior knowledge of the environment, the robots relied on local sensing, basic communication and simple behavioural rules. Success in these trials demonstrated that coordinated group behaviour could emerge through positive feedback mechanisms, similar to pheromone trails in ants. Another area of focus was pattern formation, where swarms of robots were programmed to arrange themselves into specific geometric shapes or structures. This required precise local interactions and adjustments, proving that even without centralized planning, robots could collectively achieve organized spatial configurations. Such behaviour has direct applications in fields like construction, surveillance and environmental monitoring. Flocking and aggregation behaviours were also widely studied, inspired by the natural movement of birds and fish. Using basic alignment, cohesion and separation rules, robots were able to maintain group formation, avoid collisions and move collectively toward goals. These behaviours were particularly important in developing swarm mobility and navigation in dynamic environments. These pioneering experiments validated a central hypothesis of swarm robotics: that complex, coordinated behaviours can emerge from the interaction of simple agents governed by local rules. Despite their limited processing power, sensing and communication, these early robot swarms demonstrated the feasibility and power of distributed intelligence. This laid the groundwork for more advanced research into scalable algorithms, fault tolerance and real-world swarm deployment.

Some of the earliest robotic swarm experiments focused on:

- **Foraging Tasks (Similar to Ant Behaviour):** Foraging was one of the earliest and most foundational tasks explored in swarm robotics, modelled directly after the behaviour of ants searching for and retrieving food. In robotic foraging experiments, multiple simple robots were deployed in an environment to locate scattered objects—typically symbolic representations of food—and return them to a designated area or "nest." These robots used basic sensors to detect objects and navigate their surroundings, often without any map or centralized guidance. Communication between robots was typically limited or entirely absent, mimicking how ants rely on local interactions and indirect coordination through pheromone trails. Instead of chemical trails, robots would simulate pheromones using markers, lights, or wireless signals. Through repeated trial and error, paths to resources would become reinforced, allowing the group to improve efficiency over time. The success of these early experiments demonstrated that collective intelligence could emerge from local behaviours, confirming that complex tasks like resource collection could be achieved using decentralized strategies. Foraging tasks remain a cornerstone in testing swarm algorithms, especially in environments where unpredictability and lack of global knowledge are key challenges.
- **Pattern Formation (Robots Forming Specific Shapes):** Pattern formation tasks tested whether a group of robots could organize themselves into structured, recognizable configurations—such as lines, circles, grids, or even dynamic shapes—without central control. These experiments were inspired by natural systems like cells forming tissues or birds arranging in flight formations. Each robot was programmed with simple local rules for positioning based on the relative location of its neighbours. Robots used basic distance sensors or short-range communication to assess their surroundings and adjust their position accordingly. Despite the lack of global oversight, the group would self-organize into the desired pattern through

repeated local adjustments. Some studies also integrated virtual stigmergy, where robots shared indirect cues about shape formation, enhancing their coordination. These experiments proved that spatial organization and collective structure could be achieved through self-organization, a key breakthrough for applications like automated construction, distributed sensing and perimeter monitoring. Pattern formation not only showcased the potential of decentralized control systems but also highlighted the importance of robustness and adaptability in real-world robotic swarms.

- **Flocking and Aggregation:** Flocking and aggregation experiments were inspired by natural swarms like bird flocks, fish schools and insect clusters, where individuals move or group together based on simple behavioural cues. In robotics, flocking referred to the coordinated movement of a group of robots, while aggregation involved their ability to gather into a shared location. Both behaviours were modelled using basic rules such as alignment (matching direction with neighbours), cohesion (moving toward nearby robots) and separation (avoiding collisions). Robots relied on local sensing and short-range communication to detect nearby units and adjust their movement in real time. These behaviours enabled the group to move as a cohesive unit, adapt to obstacles and respond to dynamic changes in the environment. Aggregation also served as a precursor to more complex tasks like group decision-making and spatial task allocation. The success of these early experiments showed that emergent coordination could be achieved without explicit leadership or external commands. Flocking and aggregation remain essential in areas like multi-robot navigation, exploration and search-and-rescue missions, where staying together enhances robustness and efficiency.

These experiments validated the core hypothesis: simple robots using swarm intelligence principles can achieve complex, coordinated behaviours.

1.2.6 Milestones in the Development

The development of swarm robotics has followed a rich and dynamic trajectory, shaped by key breakthroughs in both theory and technology. Its origins are deeply rooted in the concept of Swarm Intelligence (SI), a term first coined in 1989 by Gerardo Beni and Jing Wang in the context of cellular robotic systems. Their pioneering work laid the conceptual foundation for studying how large groups of simple agents could exhibit complex, collective behaviour through local interaction and decentralized control. Throughout the late 1990s and early 2000s, research laboratories began experimenting with multi-robot systems, translating theoretical SI principles into physical implementations. During this period, small groups of robots were used to perform basic cooperative tasks such as foraging, aggregation and pattern formation. These early successes demonstrated that coordination could emerge without centralized planning, marking a turning point in robotics research. By the mid-2000s, the field advanced significantly with the development of specialized swarm hardware platforms. Notable among these were the Kilobot, designed at Harvard to enable low-cost, large-scale swarm experiments and SwarmBot, which focused on modular, self-reconfiguring robot collectives. These platforms made it possible to test algorithms on dozens or even hundreds of real robots, moving the field from theory and simulation to tangible experimentation. In the present day, swarm robotics is no longer confined to academic settings. Real-world applications are rapidly emerging in diverse domains. In agriculture, swarms of drones and ground robots are being used for crop monitoring and precision farming. In disaster response, robotic swarms can search rubble, map unsafe terrain and assist in locating survivors. In planetary exploration, robotic swarms are being proposed for autonomous missions to explore the Moon, Mars and beyond—where decentralization and adaptability are critical. These milestones represent the evolution of swarm robotics from a theoretical construct into a viable, impactful field of engineering. The journey reflects an ongoing fusion of biology, computation and hardware innovation, promising a future where swarms of autonomous robots work together to solve some of the world's most complex challenges.

- **1989- Gerardo Beni and Jing Wang Coined the Term "Swarm Intelligence":** The foundation of swarm robotics began with the introduction of the term Swarm Intelligence by Gerardo Beni and Jing Wang in 1989. They coined it while studying cellular robotic systems, where simple agents could collectively perform complex tasks. Their insight drew inspiration from natural swarms—such as ant colonies and bird flocks—and proposed that intelligence could emerge from decentralized, local interactions. This marked a pivotal conceptual shift in artificial intelligence and robotics. Rather than relying on a central controller, systems could now be designed to self-organize and adapt dynamically. Their work laid the groundwork for a new research direction focused on collective robotic behaviour and distributed problem-solving.
- **1999–2000s- Emergence of Multi-Robot Systems and Robotic Swarms in Labs:** During the late 1990s and early 2000s, theoretical ideas about swarm behaviour began to materialize in robotics laboratories. Researchers built multi-robot systems to study how groups of physical robots could cooperate using local rules and minimal communication. Tasks such as foraging, obstacle avoidance and formation control were among the first to be tested. These experiments showed that even robots with limited sensors and computing power could achieve coordinated outcomes when

interacting as a group. This era marked the transition from simulation to real-world testing, validating many foundational assumptions of swarm intelligence. The results also sparked broader interest in scalability, fault tolerance and robustness in distributed robotic systems.

- **2004+ Development of Swarm Hardware Platforms (e.g., Kilobots, SwarmBots):** After 2004, the field progressed rapidly with the development of dedicated swarm robotic platforms. Notable systems like Kilobots (developed at Harvard) enabled researchers to test swarm algorithms on hundreds of tiny, low-cost robots. Another major initiative was Swarm-bots, a European project focused on self-assembling robotic units that could physically link together and adapt their structure. These platforms offered standardized tools for large-scale experimentation, helping to bridge the gap between theory and real-world application. By allowing repeatable, scalable testing, these hardware innovations accelerated research, enabling deeper exploration into emergent behaviour, distributed coordination and adaptive control.
- **Present Day-Swarm Robotics in Agriculture, Disaster Zones and Planetary Exploration:** Today, swarm robotics is moving beyond the lab and entering real-world applications across various domains. In agriculture, robotic swarms are used for crop monitoring, weed detection and precision spraying. In disaster response, swarms of drones or ground robots are being developed to navigate rubble, locate victims and map dangerous areas where human access is risky. Additionally, agencies like NASA are exploring the use of swarm robotics in planetary exploration, where decentralized, autonomous systems could operate in remote or unknown terrains without real-time human control. These applications highlight the strength of swarm systems in unstructured, dynamic environments, showcasing their potential to transform industry and science alike.

1.2.7 The Importance of Swarm Intelligence in Robotics

Swarm Intelligence (SI) has become a fundamental paradigm in robotics due to its ability to address some of the most pressing challenges in designing multi-robot systems. One of the main reasons robotics adopted SI is simplicity: swarm robots are typically small, low-cost units built with minimal hardware and limited computational power. This simplicity makes them affordable and easy to manufacture in large quantities, enabling researchers and industries to deploy vast numbers of robots for complex tasks. Moreover, the principle of scalability inherent in SI allows swarms to grow or shrink seamlessly by adding or removing individual robots without disrupting the overall system. This flexibility is crucial for adapting to dynamic task requirements or changing environments. Another key advantage is fault tolerance. Unlike traditional systems that can fail if a central controller or a critical robot breaks down, swarm robotic systems are inherently robust. The collective behaviour continues even if multiple units malfunction or are lost, ensuring uninterrupted operation. This resilience is particularly valuable in hazardous or unpredictable settings such as disaster zones or extraterrestrial exploration. Finally, efficiency is greatly enhanced through parallelism—multiple robots working simultaneously can complete tasks faster and more effectively than a single, complex robot. This distributed workload enables quicker coverage, exploration, or resource gathering. Together, these attributes highlight why swarm intelligence offers a promising approach for advancing robotics, enabling the development of versatile, adaptive and reliable multi-robot systems for real-world challenges.

Why did robotics adopt swarm intelligence?

- **Simplicity- Low-Cost Robots with Minimal Complexity:** One of the greatest strengths of swarm robotics lies in the simplicity of its individual units. Each robot is designed to be inexpensive and built with minimal hardware and computational complexity. This simplicity reduces manufacturing and maintenance costs, making it feasible to deploy large numbers of robots in a swarm. Simple robots rely on basic sensors and straightforward algorithms, which lowers energy consumption and enhances reliability. Rather than investing in a few highly sophisticated machines, swarm robotics leverages many modest agents working collectively. This approach also facilitates easier repair or replacement of malfunctioning units. Ultimately, simplicity enables scalability and accessibility, opening the door to a wide range of applications where cost-effectiveness and robustness are critical.
- **Scalability- Easy to Add or Remove Units from the Swarm:** Swarm robotics inherently supports scalability, which is a key advantage over traditional robotic systems. The decentralized nature of swarms means that individual robots operate based on local information without requiring global coordination. This design allows new robots to be added or existing ones removed without disrupting the swarm's overall functionality. Scalability offers flexibility to tailor the swarm size to specific tasks or environments, whether it's deploying a handful of robots for a small area or thousands for extensive coverage. This dynamic adjustability is especially valuable in unpredictable or evolving scenarios, such as disaster response or environmental monitoring. Furthermore, scalable swarms can optimize resource usage and operational costs by scaling the workforce to meet real-time demands.

- **Fault Tolerance- System Remains Functional Despite Individual Robot Failure:** Fault tolerance is a critical feature of swarm robotics that stems from its decentralized architecture. Since no single robot controls the entire system, the failure or loss of individual units does not compromise the swarm's overall operation. The collective behaviour emerges from the interactions of many simple robots, so the system can adapt and reorganize dynamically when some members malfunction or drop out. This resilience makes swarm robotics highly suitable for harsh or unpredictable environments where damage is likely, such as search-and-rescue missions, military operations, or space exploration. Fault tolerance reduces the need for constant human intervention and enables sustained mission success even under adverse conditions, ensuring robustness and reliability.
- **Efficiency- Parallel Task Execution Improves Performance:** Swarm robotics excels in efficiency through parallelism, where multiple robots perform tasks simultaneously, significantly speeding up completion times. Instead of a single robot handling an entire workload sequentially, a swarm divides the task among its members, working concurrently to explore, gather resources, or build structures. This distributed execution enhances performance, especially in large or complex environments that would be time-consuming for an individual robot. Parallelism also increases robustness because if one robot is slowed or hindered, others can continue unaffected. Moreover, the swarm can dynamically allocate resources to different parts of the task as needed, optimizing overall productivity. Such efficiency gains make swarm systems ideal for time-sensitive operations like environmental monitoring, agriculture and disaster response.

1.3 BIOLOGICAL INSPIRATION: ANTS, BEES, BIRDS AND FISH

Swarm robotics draws heavily from the study of collective behaviour in biological systems, where decentralized agents cooperate to perform complex tasks without central control. Among the most well-studied and inspiring examples are ants, bees, birds and fish—organisms that exhibit sophisticated group behaviours despite each individual having limited sensing, memory and processing capabilities. These animals rely on local interactions and simple behavioural rules, yet their colonies, flocks and schools accomplish feats that surpass what a single individual could do alone. Ant colonies, for instance, demonstrate remarkable coordination in foraging, nest building and Défense (Fig.-10).

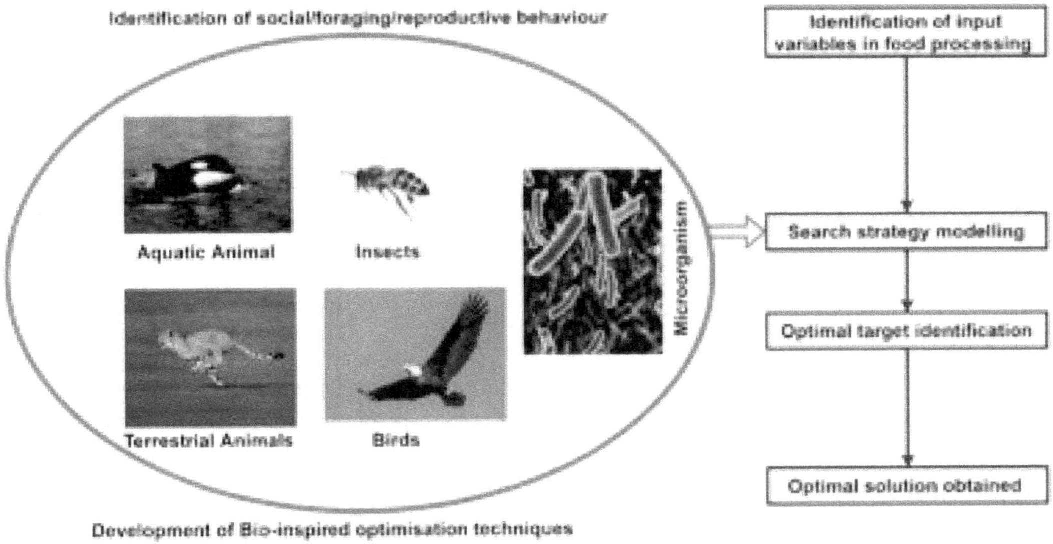

Fig.10. Biological Inspiration

They use a form of indirect communication called stigmergy, where chemical pheromones left in the environment guide the actions of other ants. This allows them to find the shortest path to food, respond to changes in the environment and adjust roles dynamically—all without any ant understanding the colony's full structure. Bees offer another model of intelligent group behaviour. In addition to foraging and colony maintenance, honeybee swarms perform collective decision-making during nest relocation. Scout bees explore potential sites and communicate their findings through the waggle dance, a symbolic movement that conveys distance and direction. Over time, through repetition and quorum sensing, the colony converges on the best site. This decentralized voting mechanism has inspired swarm robotics systems that require consensus without central oversight. Birds, particularly in flocks, exhibit synchronized flight known as flocking behaviour. Each bird follows three simple rules: maintain separation, align with neighbours and stay close to the group. These rules result in stunningly fluid group movements that respond in real time to obstacles or predators. Such behaviours have led to the development of flocking algorithms in robotics that allow swarms of drones or ground robots to move as a cohesive unit while avoiding collisions and maintaining formation. Fish also display similar collective dynamics in the form of schooling. Individual fish react quickly to changes in the movements of their nearest neighbours, enabling the group to evade predators or navigate through complex environments with minimal delay. This type of emergent coordination has inspired reactive behaviours in robotic swarms that must operate in unpredictable, high-risk settings like disaster zones or underwater exploration. What unites all these biological systems is their decentralized architecture, robustness to individual failure and capacity for emergent problem-solving. These traits are central to the design philosophy of swarm robotics. By mimicking nature's strategies, engineers can create robotic systems that are adaptive, scalable and efficient. Whether the goal is to map unknown terrain, conduct surveillance, or perform distributed sensing, the behavioural principles observed in ants, bees, birds and fish provide powerful blueprints for innovation. These systems demonstrate that simple parts, when correctly organized, can generate highly intelligent and reliable group behaviour.

1.3.1 Ant Colonies

Ant colonies serve as one of the most powerful natural models for decentralized coordination and indirect communication. Despite having no central leader, ants perform highly organized and efficient group behaviours through local interactions and environmental cues. Their success lies in simplicity, adaptability and cooperation—qualities that have deeply inspired swarm robotics. Key behaviours such as foraging with pheromones show how ants share information indirectly, guiding others to food sources by reinforcing chemical trails. Similarly, task allocation occurs dynamically, with ants shifting roles based on real-time needs without top-down control. Perhaps most striking is their collective ability in shortest path finding, where optimal routes emerge from repeated local decisions and feedback. These natural mechanisms directly inform robotic systems. Using principles like stigmergy, robotic swarms can replicate ant-like coordination through digital markers or signals, achieving scalability, robustness and autonomy. By studying ants, researchers have developed powerful algorithms and decentralized strategies that allow simple robots to solve complex tasks—efficiently, flexibly and collectively (Fig.-11).

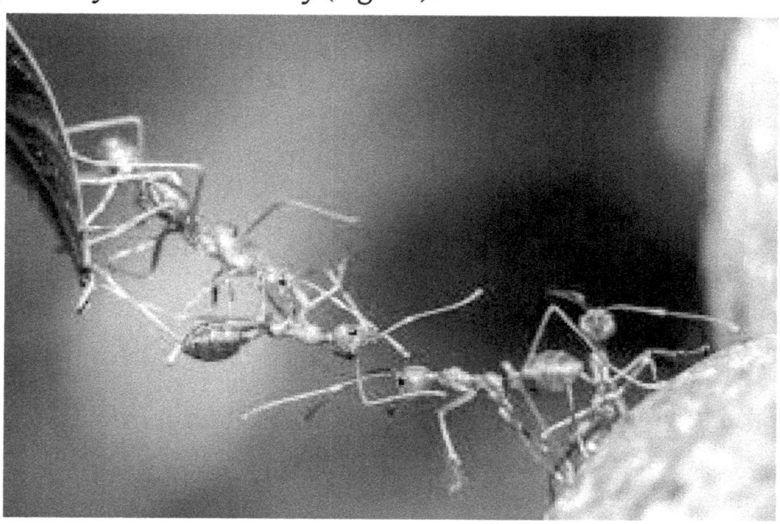

Fig.11. Ant colonies

Key Behaviours:

- **Foraging with Pheromones:** Ants display remarkable efficiency in locating and exploiting food sources through pheromone-based foraging. When a forager ant finds food, it deposits a pheromone trail on its return journey to the nest. Other ants detect this trail and are more likely to follow it, reinforcing the path if they also find food. Over time, stronger trails indicate more reliable food sources, guiding more ants efficiently. This process allows ants to discover and converge on optimal routes without centralized coordination. In robotics, similar behaviour can be replicated through digital signals or environmental markers, enabling simple robots to find and share resource locations through indirect communication.
- **Task Allocation:** In ant colonies, task allocation is a fluid and decentralized process where individuals take on roles such as foragers, caretakers, or builders based on the colony's current needs. There's no central manager assigning tasks—instead, ants respond to local cues like pheromone levels or colony congestion. For example, a shortage of food may cause more ants to leave the nest and forage. This self-organized role switching ensures adaptability and resource efficiency. Robotic swarms adopt similar mechanisms, enabling robots to switch between tasks like mapping, exploring, or transporting materials based on real-time feedback, improving responsiveness to changing mission demands.
- **Shortest Path Finding:** Ants are known for their ability to find the shortest path between their nest and a food source. Initially, they explore randomly, but over time, shorter routes accumulate more pheromone due to faster round trips. As more ants follow these efficient trails, the colony naturally converges on the optimal path. This emergent optimization does not require any individual to "know" the shortest route—it arises from local interactions and feedback loops. In robotics and network design, this principle inspired algorithms where agents or data packets dynamically find the most efficient routes, adjusting to environmental changes and obstacles.

Robotic Inspiration:

- **Staggery:** Stigmergy is a form of indirect communication where agents influence each other by altering their environment. In ants, pheromone trails act as stigmergic signals that guide the colony's collective behaviour. In swarm robotics, this concept translates into using light, sound, or digital signals as virtual pheromones. Robots can leave cues for others to follow, creating a shared, evolving map of information. This technique is especially useful in decentralized systems, where direct robot-to-robot communication is limited. Stigmergy supports scalability, robustness and adaptability, making it ideal for tasks like exploration, search-and-rescue and distributed construction.

- **Path Optimization Algorithms:** The natural behaviours of ants inspired the development of Ant Colony Optimization (ACO), a bio-inspired algorithm used in solving complex problems like route planning, network design and scheduling. ACO simulates virtual "ants" that explore potential solutions and leave artificial pheromones to reinforce better options. Over time, the algorithm converges toward optimal or near-optimal solutions. In robotics, ACO enables swarms to efficiently explore environments, navigate to goals, or distribute tasks. Its strength lies in adaptive learning and robustness, allowing robotic systems to respond flexibly to dynamic or uncertain conditions, much like their biological counterparts.

1.3.2 Honeybee Colonies

Honeybee colonies are extraordinary examples of collective intelligence and cooperative behaviour in nature. Despite each bee having limited individual capability, the colony as a whole can make complex, adaptive decisions without any central leadership. Bees communicate, coordinate and respond to environmental challenges through highly structured social interactions and efficient communication systems. One of the most fascinating aspects of honeybee behaviour is their method of collective decision-making, especially during nest-site selection. Through a process involving the waggle dance, bees share information about potential sites, evaluate options and gradually reach a consensus that reflects the best available choice. This decentralized voting-like mechanism ensures the colony selects optimal solutions through consensus, not command. Honeybees also demonstrate task allocation, switching between roles such as foraging, nursing and guarding depending on the hive's needs. These behaviours have inspired robotic systems that aim to replicate such flexibility and distributed decision-making. Studying bees has led to advances in swarm algorithms, enabling robots to share information, evaluate options and adapt cooperatively, just as bees do in nature (Fig. -12).

Fig. 12 Honey Bee: An Overview

Key Behaviours:

- **Waggle Dance:** The waggle dance is a unique and sophisticated form of communication used by honeybees to share information about the location of food sources. When a bee discovers a nectar-rich flower patch, it returns to the hive and performs a figure-eight-shaped dance. The angle of the waggle run relative to the vertical indicates the direction of the food source in relation to the sun, while the duration of the waggle conveys distance. This form of symbolic communication allows other bees to accurately locate the same food source without direct guidance. In swarm robotics, this behaviour has inspired indirect information sharing, enabling robots to broadcast directional data through encoded signals or environmental markers, promoting efficient group exploration and resource discovery.
- **Nest Site Selection:** When a honeybee colony needs a new home, scout bees are sent out to evaluate potential nest sites. Each scout inspects a site and returns to the swarm to perform a waggle dance promoting its quality. The more favourable the site, the more vigorous and frequent the dance. Other bees observe these dances and may visit the sites themselves, repeating the process. Over time, a consensus emerges as more bees support the best site, leading the entire colony to relocate. This decentralized voting mechanism has inspired swarm algorithms where autonomous agents make collective decisions by amplifying good solutions through repetition, enabling robotic swarms to select paths, goals, or locations without centralized control.
- **Division of Labor:** In a honeybee colony, tasks are distributed among individuals through a self-organizing system known as division of labour. Bees take on different roles—such as nursing, foraging, guarding, or cleaning—based largely on age and environmental stimuli. Younger bees

often work inside the hive, while older bees become foragers. This dynamic role assignment ensures that all colony needs are met efficiently without central management. In swarm robotics, similar principles are applied to enable robots to autonomously switch tasks based on local feedback, energy levels, or group status. This flexible task distribution enhances adaptability and ensures system-wide balance across changing mission requirements.

Robotic Inspiration:

- **Distributed Decision-Making:** One of the most powerful lessons from honeybee colonies is their method of distributed decision-making, which has directly inspired robotic swarms. In bees, decision-making happens through a decentralized process: scout bees promote potential nest sites via waggle dances and others gradually shift support toward the best option. This voting-like mechanism requires no leader yet consistently leads to optimal outcomes. In swarm robotics, similar strategies allow robots to evaluate multiple options—such as locations, paths, or resources—and share preferences through indirect communication or digital signals. As more robots "vote" for better options, those become reinforced and selected by the swarm. This approach ensures flexibility and collective intelligence, especially in environments where centralized control is impractical or risky. Robots can adapt in real time, handling uncertainty, failure, or changing goals much like a bee swarm. By mimicking bees' consensus-building, robot teams can reach robust group decisions, making this model ideal for search and rescue, environmental monitoring, or planetary exploration. Task Assignment: Algorithms for dynamic task allocation in robotic teams.
- **Task Assignment:** In a honeybee colony, division of labour is dynamic—bees switch roles based on age, need, or environmental stimuli. This self-organized task allocation model has been effectively translated into algorithms for robotic teams. Rather than assigning roles manually or using a central controller, swarm robots can autonomously decide which task to perform based on local observations or internal states. For example, if too few robots are exploring an area, idle robots can detect this and begin exploring; if transporting materials is prioritized, robots adapt accordingly. These mechanisms enhance the swarm's ability to balance workloads, respond to environmental changes and recover from failure. Inspired by bees, robotic systems achieve resilience and efficiency by decentralizing task management and allowing individuals to adjust behaviour based on group dynamics. This enables large-scale cooperation in tasks like area coverage, surveillance, construction and logistics—especially in unpredictable or hazardous environments where flexibility is essential.

1.3.3 Bird Flocks

Bird flocks are captivating examples of natural collective behaviour, where hundreds or even thousands of birds move in seamless, synchronized formations. Despite the apparent complexity of these movements, each bird follows a simple set of local rules—aligning with nearby neighbours, avoiding collisions and staying close to the group. There is no leader or central coordination; instead, the flock's fluid motion emerges from real-time local interactions among individuals. This decentralized strategy allows the group to adapt quickly to predators, obstacles, or environmental changes while maintaining cohesion and direction. The elegance and efficiency of flocking behaviour have inspired researchers in swarm robotics, particularly for coordinating groups of autonomous agents. By mimicking bird-like movement patterns, robotic swarms can navigate dynamic environments, maintain formations and distribute themselves evenly across a space. Applications range from drone swarms for surveillance to underwater robots for exploration. Studying bird flocks helps engineers design systems where simple agents, using minimal communication, can achieve highly coordinated and robust group behaviours—a key goal of intelligent multi-robot systems (Fig.-13).

Fig.13. Bird flocks

Key Behaviours:

- **Alignment:** Alignment refers to the tendency of each bird in a flock to match the direction and speed of its nearby neighbours. This behaviour ensures that the entire group moves as a cohesive unit, often forming visually striking patterns in the sky. Birds don't follow a leader—they simply adjust based on local observations. In robotics, this principle is used to coordinate swarm movement, allowing drones or ground robots to maintain synchronized heading without central control. By continuously aligning with their neighbours, robotic agents can smoothly adjust to changes in direction and avoid fragmentation of the group. Alignment supports group cohesion and coordinated navigation in dynamic or unknown environments.

- **Separation:** Separation ensures that birds within a flock maintain a safe distance from one another to prevent collisions. Each bird monitors the proximity of nearby individuals and subtly adjusts its position to avoid crowding. This local behaviour contributes to the smooth, non-chaotic flow of the entire flock. In swarm robotics, separation is critical for collision avoidance among agents, especially in tight formations or cluttered environments. Robots equipped with simple sensors can detect nearby units and adjust their paths in real time to maintain safe spacing. Implementing this principle allows robotic swarms to operate safely and autonomously without centralized spacing control.
- **Cohesion:** Cohesion refers to the behaviour of individual birds steering toward the centre of their local group to remain part of the flock. This ensures that no bird strays too far and the group remains unified. Cohesion balances the effects of separation and alignment, keeping the flock both safe and connected. In robotic swarms, cohesion helps maintain group integrity—robots stay within operational range of each other and work cooperatively. This behaviour is especially useful in tasks like exploration, where maintaining communication and collaboration is vital. Cohesion enables distributed systems to function as a unified whole, even when facing unpredictable or changing conditions.

Robotic Inspiration:

- **Boid Model:** The Boid model, developed by Craig Reynolds in 1986, is a foundational algorithm for simulating flocking behaviour in virtual agents. It operates on three simple rules: alignment, separation and cohesion. Each "boid" (bird-oid object) uses local information about its neighbours to decide how to move, resulting in fluid and lifelike group motion. This model has been directly applied in swarm robotics to coordinate the movement of multiple robots. Using the same three principles, robots can autonomously adjust their position and heading without global instructions. The Boid model is especially effective in applications like drone swarms, autonomous vehicles and underwater robot groups, allowing them to navigate together while avoiding collisions and maintaining formation. It demonstrates how complex group dynamics can emerge from simple, decentralized rules, making it an essential tool for designing collective robotic behaviour in real-world environments.
- **Formation Control:** Inspired by bird flocking, formation control is a technique in swarm robotics that enables a group of robots to move in coordinated patterns while maintaining a specific shape or spatial arrangement. Whether in a V-formation, line, or circular pattern,

formation control allows robots to traverse cluttered or unpredictable environments as a unified group. This approach is especially useful in tasks such as search-and-rescue, surveillance and environmental monitoring, where coordination and coverage are critical. Robots rely on local sensing and relative positioning to maintain their place within the formation, adjusting dynamically as obstacles appear or group size changes. By mimicking how birds collectively avoid predators and maintain structure mid-flight, robotic swarms can stay organized and effective in real-world missions. Formation control enhances robustness, scalability and adaptability, key qualities for autonomous multi-robot systems.

1.3.4 Fish Schools

Fish schools are remarkable examples of coordinated group motion and rapid collective response in nature. Thousands of fish can swim together in tight formations, turning, splitting and regrouping almost instantly—all without any apparent leader. Each fish adjusts its speed and direction based on the movements of nearby individuals, creating an agile, synchronized group that can evade predators or navigate obstacles with astonishing precision. This high-speed responsiveness is driven by local interaction rules, not centralized commands. In swarm robotics, fish-inspired models help design systems where robots react quickly and cohesively to dynamic environments. Just as fish scatter and regroup when sensing danger, robot swarms can adapt in real time to obstacles, failures, or sudden changes in mission goals. These natural strategies support robustness, flexibility and fault tolerance—essential traits for robotic applications like autonomous underwater vehicles (AUVs), aerial drones, or search-and-rescue swarms. Studying fish schools offers valuable insights into creating robotic systems that are both highly reactive and deeply cooperative (Fig.-14).

Fig. 14. Fish schools

Key Behaviours:

- **Predator Avoidance- Collective Turning and Dispersion When Threatened:** One of the most striking behaviours in fish schools is their instantaneous, collective reaction to predators. When threatened, fish do not wait for a signal from a leader—instead, each individual rapidly responds to changes in the movement of nearby fish. This results in a dramatic, synchronized turn or sudden dispersion that confuses predators and enhances group survival. In swarm robotics, this behaviour has inspired algorithms that allow robots to detect danger or disruption based on local cues and immediately trigger group-level evasive actions. Such responsiveness is particularly valuable in dynamic or hazardous environments were quick, autonomous decisions can prevent failure or damage.
- **Hydrodynamic Efficiency- Reduces Drag and Conserves Energy:** Fish swimming in schools benefit from hydrodynamic efficiency—a physical advantage that reduces energy expenditure. By positioning themselves strategically within the group, fish take advantage of the water currents created by their neighbours, reducing drag and swimming with less effort. This principle has inspired the design of underwater robotic swarms, where maintaining certain formations can improve overall energy efficiency and battery life. It also informs the development of aerial drone formations that minimize air resistance. By emulating this natural mechanism, robots can conserve energy, extend mission durations and operate more sustainably in both marine and aerial environments.
- **Decentralized Control- Each Fish Reacts Only to Its Nearest Neighbours:** Fish schools operate entirely through decentralized control. Each fish monitors only a handful of its closest neighbours and adjusts its motion accordingly—there's no central leader or global awareness required. This approach ensures flexibility, fault tolerance and scalability, as the group can continue functioning even if some individuals drop out or change direction. In robotics, this principle allows swarms of robots to self-organize and coordinate without needing a central processor or constant communication with all units. Decentralized control makes it possible for large robotic systems to scale up easily, adapt to local changes and continue functioning reliably in unpredictable environments.

Robotic Inspiration:

- **Swarm Reactivity- Rapid Adaptation to Environmental Changes:** Fish schools are renowned for their remarkable reactivity—their ability to swiftly and collectively respond to sudden changes in their environment, such as the appearance of a predator or shifts in currents. This rapid adaptation emerges from local interactions where each fish reacts to the movements of its nearest neighbours. Inspired by this, robotic swarms are designed to be highly responsive and flexible, enabling them to adjust their behaviours in real time without waiting for centralized commands. Such reactivity is critical in dynamic and unpredictable settings like disaster zones, underwater exploration, or crowded urban environments. Robots equipped with similar principles can alter formation, change direction, or switch tasks instantly in response to new obstacles, sensor inputs, or mission requirements. This ability enhances the swarm's robustness and resilience, ensuring mission success even under adverse or rapidly evolving conditions.

- **Obstacle Avoidance- Dynamic Group Motion Inspired by Fish Schools:** Fish schools demonstrate sophisticated obstacle avoidance techniques that allow the entire group to navigate safely through cluttered environments. When faced with a threat or barrier, fish smoothly change their collective direction while maintaining group cohesion, minimizing collisions both with obstacles and with each other. Robotic swarms leverage this behaviour by implementing group motion algorithms that dynamically adjust to obstacles, much like fish avoiding predators. Each robot uses local sensing to detect hazards and coordinates its movements with neighbours to flow around barriers efficiently, avoiding bottlenecks or crashes. This decentralized, real-time obstacle avoidance is essential for applications such as autonomous vehicle fleets, aerial drone swarms and underwater robot teams operating in complex terrains. Emulating fish schooling allows robotic swarms to maintain fluid, safe and coordinated navigation, even in uncertain and cluttered environments.

1.3.5 Common Principles Extracted

Across diverse species such as ants, bees, birds and fish, researchers have identified a set of fundamental principles that underpin their remarkable collective behaviours. These principles form the foundation of swarm robotics, enabling groups of relatively simple robots to perform complex, coordinated tasks without centralized control. One of the most important concepts is decentralization—just as no single ant or bird leads the entire group, robot swarms operate without a central commander, relying instead on distributed decision-making. Alongside this, local sensing and interaction allow individuals to respond dynamically to their immediate neighbours or environment, fostering flexible and robust group behaviour. The concept of stigmergy, inspired by ants, involves indirect communication through environmental changes—robots can leave digital markers to influence the actions of others. From bees, we learn the power of consensus decision-making, where simple voting or promotion strategies help groups agree on the best course of action. The visually stunning coordinated movements of birds and fish have given rise to algorithms that enable flocking and schooling, guiding robot swarms to move smoothly and avoid collisions. Finally, adaptive role assignment, drawn from the task-switching flexibility of ants and bees, allows robotic teams to dynamically shift roles based on current needs, improving efficiency and resilience. Together, these principles have revolutionized multi-robot systems, allowing swarms to tackle complex challenges in unpredictable environments, ranging from agriculture and search-and-rescue to space exploration. Across all these species, we find recurring principles that have directly influenced swarm robotics design (Table-4).

Table-4: Recurring principles that have directly influenced swarm robotics design

Principle	Biological Source	Application in Robotics
Decentralization	All	No central controller in robot swarms
Local Sensing & Interaction	All	Robots use only nearby information
Stigmergy	Ants	Indirect communication via environment
Consensus Decision-Making	Bees	Collective voting algorithms
Flocking & Schooling	Birds, Fish	Coordinated group movement algorithms
Adaptive Role Assignment	Ants, Bees	Dynamic task switching in robotic teams

1.3.6 Concise Summary

Biological systems have evolved simple yet powerful mechanisms for collaboration, adaptability and problem-solving. These mechanisms are observed in nature across a wide variety of species—ants, bees, birds and fish—all of which operate without centralized control yet achieve complex and coordinated behaviour. In an ant colony, for example, individuals follow pheromone trails and local rules to efficiently find food and construct elaborate nests. Bees communicate through dances to choose optimal nesting sites, relying on a consensus that emerges without a designated leader. Similarly, flocks of birds and schools of fish maintain group cohesion and avoid predators through a few instinctive rules based on the position and movement of neighbours. These behaviours are not pre-programmed in a traditional sense; they emerge from simple, local interactions that lead to sophisticated group outcomes. This natural efficiency, resilience and adaptability are the foundation of what is called swarm intelligence. Scientists and engineers have studied these systems closely and translated their principles into artificial agents like swarm robots. Swarm robotics mimics these decentralized strategies to solve real-world problems. The beauty of this approach lies in its minimal reliance on complex computation or high-level communication. Instead, robustness and efficiency emerge from the simplicity of each agent's behaviour. These biologically inspired systems are inherently scalable and fault-tolerant. They can operate in unknown, dynamic, or hazardous environments with minimal oversight. Whether in search and rescue, agriculture, environmental monitoring, or space exploration, the lessons learned from natural swarms offer elegant and reliable engineering solutions. In essence, nature's collective intelligence—honed over millions of years—provides a blueprint for building autonomous robotic systems that are both efficient and resilient, even in the face of uncertainty and change. These mechanisms are directly mapped into swarm robotic systems to achieve:

- **Robustness:** Robustness refers to the ability of a system to continue functioning effectively even when parts of it fail. In swarm robotics, this is a critical feature derived from nature, especially insect colonies, where the failure or death of individual members does not halt the operation of the group. Similarly, robotic swarms are designed to tolerate failures of individual robots without significant performance loss. This is possible due to the distributed and decentralized nature of control in such systems. Since no single robot is in charge, the failure of one unit does not affect the entire swarm. Robots can dynamically adjust to losses by reallocating tasks among remaining members. For example, if several robots in a foraging swarm break down, others simply continue the operation. The swarm compensates by increasing the activity of the functioning robots. Algorithms used in swarm robotics are built with fault tolerance in mind. This makes them suitable for high-risk environments such as space exploration or disaster zones. Robustness also includes resilience to external disturbances, such as signal noise or physical obstacles. The redundancy in large numbers supports graceful degradation rather than catastrophic failure. Even communication loss between members can be handled locally. This self-sustaining behaviour increases mission success rates. Ultimately, robustness ensures that the system performs reliably, even under unpredictable or harsh conditions.
- **Flexibility:** Flexibility in swarm robotics means the ability to adapt to different tasks, environments, or goals without requiring extensive reprogramming. Inspired by biological swarms like ants or bees, swarm robots can switch between roles or behaviours based on context. This quality is essential in environments where tasks and conditions change frequently. For instance, a robot swarm can shift from exploration to rescue without human intervention. Each robot operates using simple, modular rules that can be modified or combined for new tasks. This modularity allows the swarm to handle both structured and unstructured environments. Flexibility also applies to the configuration of the swarm

itself. Robots can join or leave the swarm, or switch positions and the overall system continues functioning. This adaptability makes swarm robotics ideal for dynamic applications such as environmental monitoring or military surveillance. Real-time data and local decisions drive behaviour changes, ensuring responsiveness. Robots can also adjust behaviour based on limited energy, obstacles, or task complexity. The swarm can divide into subgroups to address multiple objectives simultaneously. Flexible swarms also allow incremental deployment—new robots can be introduced during missions. This removes the need for stopping and restarting operations. By mimicking the behavioural plasticity seen in natural swarms, robotic swarms gain operational versatility. Overall, flexibility makes swarm robotics highly applicable in scenarios where change is constant and unpredictability is high.

- **Scalability:** Scalability refers to the ability of a system to maintain performance and efficiency as the number of agents (robots) increases or decreases. In swarm robotics, scalability is a foundational principle, allowing swarms to grow or shrink depending on mission needs. This characteristic comes from biological systems like ant colonies, where thousands of ants work together seamlessly. Robotic swarms follow similar decentralized algorithms that are inherently scalable. Each robot uses only local sensing and communication, meaning the addition of more robots does not create bottlenecks. The control rules do not depend on swarm size, so performance remains stable across different scales. When more robots are added, the system can cover larger areas or perform more tasks in parallel. This is crucial for missions like search and rescue, where coverage is essential. Conversely, reducing the number of robots doesn't require changes in control logic. The system continues operating effectively with minimal adjustments. This is different from traditional centralized systems, where performance often degrades with size. Scalability ensures the system remains efficient even with hundreds or thousands of robots. Moreover, it allows resource optimization; only as many robots as needed are deployed. This saves energy and reduces wear. Scalability also enhances reusability—the same algorithm can run on swarms of different sizes. Overall, scalability ensures that swarm robotics systems are future-proof, adaptable and resource-efficient across a wide range of applications.
- **Efficiency:** Efficiency in swarm robotics refers to the optimal use of resources—time, energy, computation and manpower—to achieve tasks effectively. This principle is influenced by the natural efficiency seen in insect swarms, like ants finding the shortest paths to food or bees selecting the best nest site. In robotic swarms, efficiency is achieved through simple,

distributed algorithms that guide behaviour without excessive computation or communication. Each robot performs lightweight processing, reducing the need for complex central coordination. Tasks are shared and parallelized across robots, which increases throughput and reduces completion time. For example, in an agricultural setting, multiple robots can scan and treat crops simultaneously. Energy is conserved because robots only respond to local information, minimizing unnecessary movement. Communication is also efficient, relying on nearby signalling rather than global broadcasting. This reduces interference and latency. Efficient path planning, task allocation and area coverage help minimize redundant actions. Robots can dynamically adapt to changing task demands, reallocating roles to maintain balanced workload distribution. Moreover, swarm robotics systems can scale operations up or down without losing efficiency. Maintenance is simplified, as individual robots can be small and easy to replace. Hardware costs are lower due to the simplicity of each unit, making large deployments more feasible. Overall, efficiency in swarm robotics ensures high productivity, cost-effectiveness and energy savings, making these systems viable for large-scale, real-world applications. Nature continues to be the ultimate guide for designing intelligent, cooperative robotic systems that can operate autonomously in complex environments.

1.4 CHARACTERISTICS: SCALABILITY, ROBUSTNESS, DECENTRALIZATION

Swarm robotics is an emerging field of robotics that draws its inspiration from the collective behaviour of social animals such as ants, bees, birds and fish. At its core, swarm robotics is built on several foundational principles that make it highly effective in dynamic, uncertain and large-scale environments. Among these principles, scalability, robustness and decentralization stand out as the most critical characteristics that define and distinguish swarm-based systems from traditional robotic systems. These characteristics not only enable a swarm to function efficiently but also make it adaptable, resilient and highly autonomous. Scalability refers to the swarm's ability to maintain functionality and performance as the number of robots increases or decreases. A well-designed swarm system can operate effectively with just a handful of robots or scale up to thousands without requiring any change in the underlying algorithms or control strategies. This is possible because each robot follows simple, local rules and does not depend on global knowledge or centralized coordination. As a result, new robots can be added to or removed from the system on the fly, without disrupting overall behaviour. This feature is particularly useful in large-area applications such as environmental monitoring, agricultural automation, or planetary exploration, where different swarm sizes may be needed at different stages. Robustness is another key trait of swarm robotics, ensuring the system remains operational even when individual robots fail or encounter unexpected challenges. In contrast to centralized systems, where the failure of a single controller could collapse the entire operation, swarm robotics relies on distributed intelligence (Fig.-15).

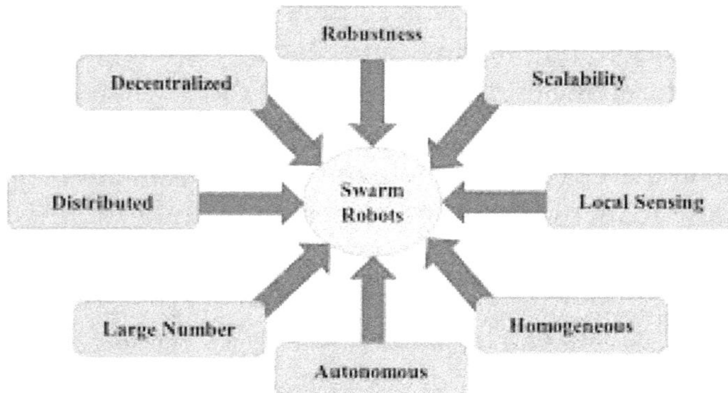

Fig. 15. Characteristics of Swarm robotics

Each robot is autonomous and capable of making decisions based on its local environment and neighbour interactions. This means that the loss or malfunction of one or more robots has minimal impact on the swarm's overall performance. The system dynamically adapts to such failures, redistributing tasks or modifying paths to maintain efficiency. Robustness also implies resistance to environmental disturbances, communication breakdowns, or sensor errors, all of which are common in real-world deployments. Decentralization forms the backbone of swarm behaviour. In a decentralized system, no single unit has complete control or knowledge of the entire operation. Instead, each robot operates independently, communicating only with nearby robots or using indirect signals, such as environmental cues. This decentralized approach reduces the computational and communication overhead, making swarm systems more scalable and energy-efficient. More importantly, it supports emergent behaviour—where complex, global patterns arise from simple local interactions. Such behaviour enables swarms to perform advanced tasks like exploration, mapping, search and rescue, or cooperative transport without requiring centralized planning or coordination. Decentralization also enhances fault tolerance, as there is no single point of failure. Together, scalability, robustness and decentralization form a synergistic triad that gives swarm robotics its unique power. These characteristics enable a swarm to be more than the sum of its parts—exhibiting intelligent, flexible and adaptive behaviour with minimal complexity at the individual level. As technology progresses and the demand for autonomous, resilient systems increases, swarm robotics offers a highly promising solution for future applications across industries and environments. From coordinated drone fleets to autonomous underwater vehicles, the principles of scalability, robustness and decentralization will continue to shape the design of the next generation of intelligent multi-robot systems.

1.4.1. Scalability

Scalability in swarm robotics refers to the system's ability to function efficiently and maintain performance regardless of the number of robots involved. Whether the swarm consists of a dozen or thousands of robots, the same behavioural rules and coordination mechanisms can be applied without major changes. This is made possible because each robot operates based on local information and interactions, without depending on global knowledge or a central controller. As a result, adding or removing robots does not disrupt the system. In fact, increasing the swarm size can enhance coverage, speed up task completion and improve redundancy. Scalability makes swarm robotics highly adaptable for diverse applications, from small indoor inspection tasks to large-scale environmental monitoring or disaster response. This property also enables modular design, where additional robots can be deployed as needed, depending on task complexity or area size.

1.4.2. Robustness

Robustness refers to the system's ability to tolerate faults, failures, or unpredictable conditions without losing overall functionality. In swarm robotics, the failure of individual robots—due to battery depletion, mechanical malfunction, or environmental hazards—does not halt or crash the entire operation. This is because the system is decentralized and each robot acts independently yet cooperatively. The swarm can quickly reallocate tasks or adjust formations in response to these failures. This is similar to biological swarms, where the loss of a few individuals does not impact the colony's survival. Robustness also includes the ability to adapt to dynamic environments. For example, if a path becomes blocked, the swarm can redirect itself or reconfigure the strategy without external instructions. Such resilience is critical for real-world applications in unpredictable or dangerous conditions, such as exploration, military missions, or search and rescue.

1.4.3 Decentralization

Decentralization is a core characteristic of swarm robotics, meaning that no single robot has global control or oversight over the group. Each unit operates autonomously, using local sensing, limited communication and simple rules to make decisions. These local interactions, when combined across the swarm, give rise to emergent global behaviours—complex patterns or task-solving capabilities that are not explicitly programmed. Decentralization reduces system complexity and enhances fault tolerance since there is no central point of failure. It also enables faster decision-making and higher system responsiveness, especially in large-scale or dynamic environments. Communication in decentralized systems is often limited to neighbouring robots or indirect methods (like leaving markers in the environment). This minimal communication lowers bandwidth needs and simplifies coordination. Overall, decentralization enhances the flexibility, robustness and scalability of swarm robotic systems, making them ideal for autonomous and distributed operations.

2 Chapter THEORETICAL FOUNDATIONS

2.0 INTRODUCTION: AN OVERVIEW

Swarm robotics is a multidisciplinary field grounded in several key theoretical foundations that span across biology, computer science, engineering and mathematics. At its core, swarm robotics draws inspiration from the collective behaviour observed in natural systems, particularly in social insects like ants, bees and termites, as well as in flocking birds, schooling fish and even human crowds. These systems exhibit remarkable levels of coordination, adaptability and problem-solving without any centralized control or global knowledge. By understanding and formalizing the underlying principles of these biological systems, researchers have developed a framework for designing artificial swarms—groups of relatively simple robots that can cooperate to achieve complex goals. The theoretical backbone of swarm robotics consists of concepts such as self-organization, decentralized control, local communication, emergent behaviour and stigmergy. These principles explain how large groups of agents can function effectively using only limited, local information and interactions. Unlike traditional robotic systems, where individual units are designed to perform tasks independently or rely on a central controller, swarm systems leverage simple rules and indirect coordination to create intelligent group behaviour. This decentralization not only improves robustness and scalability but also makes the system more adaptable to dynamic or unpredictable environments. Mathematical models and computational algorithms play a critical role in shaping swarm behaviour. Tools such as finite state machines, graph theory, probabilistic models and optimization algorithms provide the necessary language and structure to model interactions and predict outcomes. Additionally, simulation environments are extensively used to test and refine swarm behaviours before they are deployed in physical systems. Bio-inspired algorithms like Particle Swarm Optimization (PSO), Ant Colony Optimization (ACO) and Artificial Bee Colony (ABC) are examples of how natural intelligence has been abstracted into functional tools for robotics and distributed problem-solving (Fig. 1).

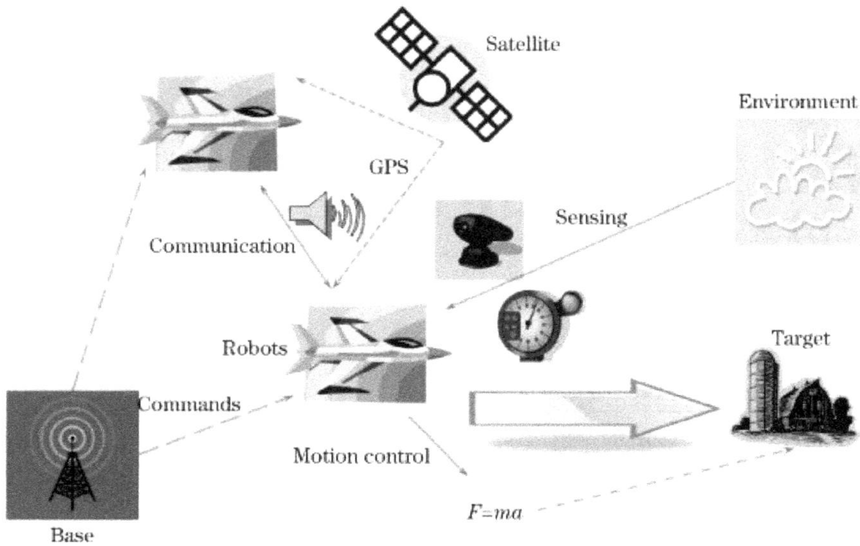

Fig.1 Swarm robotics is a multidisciplinary field grounded in several key theoretical foundations

Another important component of swarm theory is collective decision-making, where swarms reach consensus or choose optimal paths through local feedback and majority mechanisms. These methods are not only efficient but also fault-tolerant—if some agents fail or give incorrect input, the system can still make accurate decisions. Similarly, task allocation in swarms is guided by local perception and self-assigned roles, allowing swarms to divide labour effectively without a planner. The field also considers the challenges of real-world implementation, including issues such as noise, latency, limited sensing capabilities and communication constraints. To address these, robust control strategies and adaptive behaviours are designed, ensuring reliable performance under uncertainty. Furthermore, theories of collective motion, swarm stability and convergence help researchers predict and ensure the desired system-level outcomes over time. As a field still under rapid development, swarm robotics benefits from ongoing research in machine learning, distributed systems, control theory and even philosophy of mind. The interplay between theory and application is especially critical here: while the theoretical models guide the development of swarm behaviours, real-world challenges help refine and evolve these theories. This constant feedback loop is essential for pushing the boundaries of what swarm systems can achieve. The theoretical foundations of swarm robotics provide a structured and interdisciplinary approach to understanding how simple agents can collectively perform complex tasks. By integrating principles from nature with formal computational models, researchers can design intelligent, resilient and scalable robotic systems. This foundation not only advances academic understanding but also fuels practical innovations across sectors like healthcare, defence, agriculture, environmental monitoring and space exploration. The following sections will explore these foundational theories in detail, highlighting the key concepts, models and algorithms that drive the field forward.

2.1 PRINCIPLES OF SWARM INTELLIGENCE

Swarm Intelligence (SI) is the collective behaviour of decentralized, self-organized systems, typically made up of simple agents interacting locally with each other and with their environment. These principles are inspired by natural phenomena like bird flocking, fish schooling and ant colonies.

Below are the key principles of swarm intelligence explained in detail:

2.1.1 Decentralization

Decentralization is a fundamental principle of swarm intelligence, where there is no central authority or control system directing the actions of individual agents. Instead, each agent operates independently, relying solely on local information gathered from its environment or nearby agents. This approach is inspired by biological systems like ant colonies, where no single ant directs the others, yet the colony achieves complex tasks such as finding the shortest path to food. Each ant follows simple rules and reacts to environmental cues like pheromone trails, resulting in effective coordination at the group level. Similarly, in bird flocking or fish schooling, no leader dictates the movement; each individual aligns its motion based on its neighbours, leading to cohesive and agile group movement. The absence of a central controller makes decentralized systems highly robust. If a few agents fail or are removed from the swarm, the system continues functioning with little or no degradation in performance. This fault tolerance is critical in environments where reliability and adaptability are essential, such as disaster recovery, space exploration, or military operations. Moreover, decentralization supports scalability; the system can grow by adding more agents without the need for complex reconfiguration or overload of a central unit. This design also reduces communication overhead, as agents only need to share information locally. Ultimately, decentralization enables swarm systems to be flexible, efficient and resilient, capable of solving complex problems through the collective behaviour of simple, autonomous units.

2.1.2 Self-Organization

Self-organization is a key principle of swarm intelligence where structured and coordinated group behaviour emerges from simple local interactions among agents, without any external control or centralized planning. In self-organizing systems, individual agents operate based on basic rules and their immediate surroundings, yet collectively they produce complex and intelligent outcomes. This natural process is widely observed in biological systems like bird flocking, fish schooling and ant foraging, where no single member dictates the group's actions, but the group still functions in a highly coordinated way. The emergence of self-organization is driven by three primary mechanisms. Positive feedback reinforces successful behaviours, such as when ants follow and strengthen pheromone trails to food sources, leading more ants to do the same. Negative feedback helps control excessive behaviours by dampening actions that may cause instability, such as trail evaporation in ants to prevent overexploitation. Fluctuations, or random variations in agent behaviour, allow the system to explore new solutions and introduce diversity, which is vital for adapting to dynamic conditions. As a result of these mechanisms, the system is capable of adapting to changes in the environment and task demands. For example, when an obstacle appears on a known path, ants can quickly find and reinforce a new route. Self-organization thus makes swarm-based systems highly adaptable, resilient and efficient, particularly in unpredictable or complex environments.

2.1.3 Local Interactions

Local interactions are a foundational aspect of swarm intelligence, where each agent in the system communicates or responds only to its nearby agents or to immediate environmental cues, rather than having access to global information. This principle allows for simplicity at the individual level but leads to the emergence of highly coordinated and intelligent behaviour at the group level. Agents do not need to know the entire structure or state of the system; they rely solely on local data and predefined behavioural rules to act. The mechanism behind this involves simple, rule-based interactions such as alignment, separation and cohesion. For instance, in bird flocking, each bird adjusts its position and velocity by observing only the closest neighbours to avoid collisions, match speed and stay with the group. These minimal interactions ensure the flock moves as a single, synchronized unit, changing direction almost instantly without a leader. This approach is both efficient and scalable. Because agents don't require complex communication or centralized guidance, systems can expand easily by adding more agents. Moreover, local interactions enhance robustness, as the failure of a few agents doesn't disrupt the overall functioning of the swarm. Through such mechanisms, simple local behaviours give rise to complex and often optimal global solutions, which is a key reason why local interaction models are widely used in swarm robotics, sensor networks and distributed AI systems.

2.1.4 Flexibility and Adaptability

Flexibility and adaptability are essential characteristics of swarm intelligence that allow swarms to function effectively in dynamic and unpredictable environments.

The core idea is that the swarm does not rely on a rigid, predefined plan but instead can change its behaviour in real time based on current conditions. This capability stems from the decentralized nature of the swarm and its reliance on local interactions and feedback mechanisms. The mechanism behind this adaptability involves continuous monitoring of the environment by individual agents. Each agent gathers real-time information from its surroundings and adjusts its behaviour accordingly. As agents interact with one another and respond to environmental cues, the entire swarm can shift its strategy or reorganize its formation to handle new challenges or achieve changing goals. This feedback loop enables the swarm to be highly responsive and self-adjusting. A practical application of this principle is seen in swarm robotics, particularly in search and rescue missions. In such scenarios, conditions on the ground may change rapidly due to factors like collapsing structures, fire, or blocked pathways. A robot swarm can adapt by rerouting, reallocating agents to new areas, or focusing efforts where survivors are more likely to be found. Unlike a centrally controlled system that might be slow to respond or vulnerable to single points of failure, a swarm system continues operating effectively even as the environment evolves. This ability to adapt and remain functional despite uncertainty makes swarm intelligence a powerful model for real-world applications in disaster recovery, environmental monitoring, agriculture and even space exploration.

2.1.5 Scalability

Scalability refers to the ability of a swarm system to maintain or even improve its performance as the number of agents increases. This is one of the most powerful features of swarm intelligence. In a scalable system, adding more agents does not cause communication overload or coordination issues. Instead, it enhances the swarm's capacity to explore, cover more ground and provide more diverse solutions to a problem. For example, in a drone surveillance swarm, adding more drones improves the area coverage and allows for faster data collection, without the need for a central controller to manage the entire system. The decentralized and local-interaction-based design ensures that each agent can contribute effectively, making the system more efficient and capable of handling large-scale tasks.

2.1.6 Robustness

Robustness is the swarm's ability to continue functioning effectively even when individual agents fail or are removed. This resilience comes from two key features: redundancy and distributed control. Since no single agent is critical to the operation of the system, the failure of one or even several agents do not disrupt the overall functioning. For instance, in an ant colony, if some ants die or get lost while foraging, the rest continue their work without centralized redirection. Similarly, in robotic swarms, if a few robots malfunction, others adjust and continue the mission. This built-in fault tolerance makes swarm systems ideal for hazardous or unpredictable environments such as disaster zones or deep-sea exploration.

2.1.7 Emergent Behaviour

Emergent behaviour describes how complex and intelligent group behaviour arises from the simple actions and local interactions of individual agents. The key characteristic of emergent behaviour is that it is not explicitly programmed or directed; instead, it arises naturally as agents follow basic rules. This phenomenon is evident in nature, where ant colonies, through simple behaviours like following pheromone trails, manage to find optimal paths to food sources without a leader or map. Similarly, in artificial swarm systems, emergent behaviour allows for intelligent outcomes such as efficient area coverage, pattern formation, or problem solving without central control. It is this self-organized intelligence that makes swarm systems both powerful and unpredictable in a useful way.

2.1.8 Stigmergy

Stigmergy is a form of indirect coordination used in swarm systems, where agents communicate by modifying their environment instead of direct messaging. This allows for asynchronous and distributed interaction, making the system more flexible and less reliant on constant agent-to-agent communication. A classic example is found in ants that lay down pheromone trails as they move. These chemical trails inform other ants of paths to food or danger, influencing their behaviour. In artificial systems, similar concepts are used in virtual environments or robotics, where markers or signals left in the environment can guide the behaviour of other agents. Stigmergy supports efficient, low-overhead coordination among large numbers of agents in dynamic tasks.

2.1.9 Diversity of Agents

Diversity of agents within a swarm enhances both robustness and innovation. While many swarm systems involve identical agents, introducing slight variations in roles or behaviours can improve the overall performance. Diversity ensures that the swarm is not limited to one strategy or stuck in a local optimum. For example, in bee swarms, some bees act as scouts, venturing into unknown areas to find new nesting sites, while others stay behind to evaluate the findings. This division of roles increases adaptability and leads to better collective decision-making. In engineered systems, diverse agents can perform specialized tasks, complement each other's functions and ensure the swarm can tackle a broader range of challenges.

2.1.10 Goal-Oriented Behaviour

Goal-oriented behaviour means that, despite operating under decentralized control, the swarm collectively works toward achieving a common objective. This is achieved by aligning the simple local rules of each agent with the overarching goal of the system. For example, rules for movement, obstacle avoidance, or target attraction can be designed in such a way that agents eventually accomplish tasks like food retrieval, area mapping, or object transport. In real-world applications, this principle is widely used in swarm robotics for agricultural tasks like crop monitoring, in military operations for area patrolling and in logistics for warehouse automation. The power of goal-oriented behaviour lies in its ability to deliver organized outcomes without centralized coordination.

2.2 DISTRIBUTED SYSTEMS AND CONTROL

A Distributed System is a collection of independent computing entities—referred to as nodes, agents, or processors—that collaborate to achieve a shared goal. These entities are geographically or logically separated but interconnected through a communication network. Unlike centralized systems, a distributed system has no single point of control; instead, control is spread across the entire network. Each node operates autonomously, possessing its own resources, processing power and local memory. Yet, they work together through coordination, cooperation and communication to perform complex tasks that would be difficult or inefficient for a single system to handle alone. Distributed Control refers to how decisions and control actions are distributed among these independent nodes. Rather than having a central authority dictate operations, each node makes decisions based on local data, partial knowledge, or shared messages. This decentralized decision-making enables the system to be more robust, adaptive and scalable. It also enhances fault tolerance—if one node fails, the system can continue to function with minimal disruption because control is not concentrated. This makes distributed systems ideal for critical applications such as cloud computing, sensor networks, swarm robotics, smart grids, autonomous vehicles and IoT ecosystems.

The communication protocols and synchronization mechanisms among the nodes are crucial, ensuring that all components have a consistent and updated view of the task or environment. Redundancy and replication often help in maintaining data integrity and service availability. Moreover, distributed systems are designed to scale seamlessly by simply adding more nodes, without major architectural changes. This elasticity supports dynamic load balancing and real-time response, especially under high-demand or changing conditions. In essence, distributed systems and distributed control bring flexibility, resilience, efficiency and intelligence to modern computing, enabling large-scale, decentralized operations in an increasingly connected world. Below is a components and principles of distributed systems and control:

2.2.1 Decentralization

Decentralization in distributed systems refers to the absence of a central authority managing all operations. Control and decision-making are shared among all nodes or agents in the network. This structure eliminates single points of failure, making the system more robust and reliable. It allows the system to continue functioning even if a component crashes or disconnects. Additionally, decentralization enhances scalability by avoiding bottlenecks caused by central controllers. This design is highly effective in environments requiring high availability, such as cloud computing. In cloud systems, for instance, tasks are distributed across multiple servers. If one server fails, others take over without affecting service delivery. Such a model ensures load distribution, improves fault tolerance and minimizes downtime. Moreover, it simplifies maintenance and reduces dependency on a central node. Systems can adapt and evolve independently. This flexibility is particularly useful in dynamic and large-scale environments. Ultimately, decentralization supports resilience, scalability and efficient operation in modern distributed systems.

2.2.2 Autonomy of Agents

In distributed systems, the autonomy of agents means that each node operates independently and makes decisions based on local data. These agents can sense their surroundings, process information and act accordingly without requiring instructions from a central authority. This local decision-making enhances the system's ability to respond in real time, especially in rapidly changing environments. Autonomy promotes parallelism, where multiple agents work simultaneously on different parts of a task. For instance, in a fleet of delivery drones, each drone navigates and makes route adjustments autonomously. This reduces delays and increases system efficiency. Autonomy also improves fault isolation—if one agent fails, others remain unaffected. The design encourages scalability, as adding new agents doesn't overload a central system. This is crucial for large deployments like sensor networks or robotic swarms. Moreover, autonomous agents can adapt to unexpected situations by relying on real-time feedback. This decentralized intelligence makes the entire system more responsive, flexible and robust.

2.2.3 Communication and Coordination

Communication and coordination are vital in distributed systems to ensure agents work together effectively. Agents must exchange information to synchronize their actions, avoid conflicts and complete tasks cooperatively. There are two main forms of communication: direct, where messages are passed explicitly between agents and indirect, such as stigmergy, where agents leave environmental signals for others to interpret. Effective coordination ensures that tasks are not duplicated and resources are used efficiently. However, communication introduces challenges like latency, limited bandwidth and inconsistency. Agents must handle network delays and incomplete data gracefully. For example, in swarm robotics, robots may signal each other through blinking lights or pheromone-like chemicals to navigate a space collectively. Ensuring communication reliability in large systems is a complex task that requires robust protocols. Coordination strategies also include consensus algorithms and leader election when needed. Despite these complexities, coordinated communication helps the system act as a cohesive unit, achieving goals faster and more efficiently.

2.2.4 Distributed Decision-Making

Distributed decision-making allows each agent in a system to make choices based on its local perspective and available information. This avoids the need for global knowledge or centralized instructions. Decisions made independently by each node contribute to the system's overall behaviour. For example, in a distributed traffic light system, each light adjusts based on local traffic flow, leading to better traffic management across a city. Such a system is more resilient and responsive to real-world conditions. The collective outcome of local decisions often results in efficient and adaptive system-wide behaviour. Decision-making mechanisms may include voting, negotiation, or learning from experience. This principle is particularly useful in environments where real-time action is critical. Moreover, it reduces delays caused by waiting for a central decision and allows for greater scalability. When agents collaborate through shared rules and objectives, their distributed decisions can solve complex problems effectively, making the system intelligent and adaptive.

2.2.5 Scalability

Scalability in distributed systems refers to the ability to expand the system's size or capacity without compromising performance. A scalable system maintains consistent efficiency whether it has 10 agents or 10,000. This is particularly important in modern applications like cloud computing, IoT, or blockchain, where workloads and users can grow unpredictably. Distributed systems achieve scalability by decentralizing tasks and enabling parallel processing. Each agent handles its own responsibilities, reducing the load on any single component. For example, in peer-to-peer networks like BitTorrent, more users improve the speed and availability of shared files. Scalability also means the system can grow in complexity—more sensors, more users, or more regions—without major redesign. This ensures long-term viability and flexibility. Efficient communication protocols, resource allocation and adaptive control mechanisms are key to achieving true scalability. Overall, scalability allows systems to evolve and meet increasing demands while preserving performance and reliability.

2.2.6 Fault Tolerance

Fault tolerance is a critical property of distributed systems that ensures continued operation even when individual components fail. Since no system is immune to hardware crashes, software bugs, or network failures, distributed architectures are designed to detect, isolate and recover from these faults. Redundancy is a common strategy—multiple nodes perform similar tasks so that if one fails, others can take over. For example, in a sensor network, if one sensor stops working, others nearby continue to collect data. Replication of data and services across nodes ensures minimal disruption. Fault-tolerant systems use error detection mechanisms, backup processes and failover strategies. They often include self-healing capabilities where faulty nodes are repaired or restarted automatically. This resilience is vital for applications in healthcare, aviation, or industrial automation. Even under partial failure, the system degrades gracefully rather than collapsing. Ultimately, fault tolerance builds reliability, making distributed systems dependable in real-world, high-stakes scenarios.

2.2.7 Load Balancing

Load balancing in distributed systems ensures that workloads are spread evenly across all nodes to prevent bottlenecks and resource exhaustion. Without load balancing, some nodes might become overloaded while others remain idle, leading to inefficiency and potential system failure. A good load balancing strategy dynamically adjusts task distribution based on current resource usage. In cloud environments, for instance, user requests are distributed among servers to optimize performance and reduce response times. Algorithms like round-robin, least connections, or weighted distribution are often used. Load balancing improves throughput, minimizes latency and enhances the overall user experience. It also plays a role in fault tolerance—if one node is down, its load can be redirected. Furthermore, it supports scalability by accommodating new nodes and redistributing tasks accordingly. Whether it's managing user traffic, processing data, or handling sensor inputs, load balancing ensures efficient, stable and high-performing distributed systems.

2.2.8 Synchronization

Synchronization in distributed systems ensures that all nodes have a consistent view of shared data, time, or events. Without proper synchronization, systems can suffer from race conditions, data inconsistency, or process conflicts. Distributed nodes may be geographically dispersed and operate on independent clocks, so coordination is challenging. Methods like logical clocks, timestamps and consensus algorithms (e.g., Paxos, Raft) help align operations and maintain system integrity. Synchronization is vital in applications like distributed databases or financial systems where exact timing and order of transactions matter. Even in robotics, synchronized movement ensures that swarm robots do not collide or repeat tasks. As systems grow, maintaining synchronization becomes harder due to communication delays or partial failures. However, efficient synchronization protocols can ensure reliable coordination across thousands of nodes. While complete synchronization is sometimes unnecessary, achieving eventual consistency or coordination guarantees is often sufficient for real-world applications.

2.2.9. Security and Privacy

Security and privacy in distributed systems are essential to protect sensitive data, communications and operations from unauthorized access or attacks. As these systems often span open networks, they are vulnerable to threats like data breaches, denial-of-service attacks and node tampering. The distributed nature of such systems increases the number of potential attack points. Ensuring secure communication through encryption, authentication and secure protocols is a fundamental requirement. Privacy is especially important in applications involving user data, such as IoT, healthcare, or finance. Techniques like end-to-end encryption, blockchain-based transparency and access control mechanisms help ensure data confidentiality and integrity. Decentralized systems also face unique challenges like trust establishment between unknown nodes. Solutions include public key infrastructures, consensus-based trust models and anomaly detection systems. Maintaining both security and privacy in large-scale distributed environments requires constant updates, monitoring and adaptive defences strategies.

2.2.10 Applications of Distributed Systems and Control

Distributed systems and control are widely applied across industries due to their flexibility, efficiency and resilience. In swarm robotics, multiple autonomous robots coordinate without a central controller to complete complex tasks like exploration, mapping, or search and rescue. In smart grids, electricity generation and distribution are managed dynamically based on demand and supply, improving energy efficiency. Blockchain technology enables decentralized transaction management, removing the need for centralized verification and ensuring transparency. The Internet of Things (IoT) connects millions of devices—from home thermostats to industrial sensors—that interact locally and make real-time decisions to optimize processes. Other applications include distributed databases, cloud computing, autonomous vehicle fleets and disaster recovery networks. These systems offer scalability, robustness and adaptability, making them ideal for modern, data-driven environments. As technology evolves, distributed control continues to redefine how we design intelligent, connected and autonomous systems (Table-1).

Table: 1 concise summary of the Distributed Systems and Control

Head	Definition/Description	Key Points / Examples
Decentralization	No central authority; control shared among nodes.	Prevents single point failure, improves robustness, scalability; e.g., cloud computing distributing tasks.
Autonomy of Agents	Each node operates independently using local data to make decisions.	Enables real-time response, parallelism, fault isolation; e.g., delivery drones navigating autonomously.
Communication & Coordination	Agents exchange info directly or indirectly to synchronize and avoid conflicts.	Handles latency and bandwidth limits; e.g., swarm robots using signals; requires robust protocols.
Distributed Decision-Making	Local decisions by agents combine to form global behaviour.	Enhances scalability and responsiveness; e.g., traffic lights adapting locally to improve flow.
Scalability	System grows without performance loss by decentralizing tasks and parallel processing.	More nodes increase capacity; e.g., BitTorrent speeds up with more users.
Fault Tolerance	System continues working despite failures via redundancy and replication.	Detects, isolates, recovers faults; e.g., sensor networks functioning despite individual sensor failures.
Load Balancing	Workloads evenly distributed to prevent bottlenecks and optimize resource use.	Dynamic task assignment; e.g., cloud services distribute user requests among servers.
Synchronization	Ensures consistent timing, data, or events across nodes despite independent clocks.	Uses logical clocks, timestamps, consensus; e.g., databases and swarm robotics maintaining coordination.
Security and Privacy	Protects data and operations from unauthorized access in a distributed environment.	Uses encryption, authentication, blockchain; challenges include trust establishment among unknown nodes.
Applications	Distributed control used in robotics, smart grids, blockchain, IoT, cloud computing and more.	Enables coordination, efficiency, robustness across multiple sectors; e.g., aut

2.3 MULTI-AGENT SYSTEMS: COORDINATION AND COOPERATION

Multi-Agent Systems (MAS) consist of multiple autonomous agents that interact within a shared environment to achieve individual or collective goals. These agents are capable of perceiving their surroundings, making decisions and executing actions independently, yet they often need to coordinate and cooperate to solve complex problems that are beyond the capability of any single agent. Coordination ensures that agents' actions are aligned and resources are used efficiently, while cooperation enables them to work together towards common objectives, sharing information and tasks. MAS are inspired by natural systems like ant colonies, bird flocks and human social organizations, where decentralized agents achieve remarkable group behaviours through local interactions. In artificial systems, MAS find applications in robotics, distributed sensor networks, traffic management and collaborative software agents. The challenges in MAS revolve around communication, conflict resolution, task allocation and decision-making under uncertainty. Effective coordination and cooperation mechanisms—such as negotiation, consensus algorithms and shared plans—are essential to enable agents to function harmoniously in dynamic and often unpredictable environments. By leveraging distributed intelligence, MAS offer scalability, robustness and flexibility, making them suitable for real-world problems involving distributed control and complex interactions. Understanding the principles of coordination and cooperation in MAS is crucial for designing systems that can adapt, learn and achieve goals collectively while operating autonomously. This makes MAS a powerful paradigm in both theoretical research and practical implementations in fields like artificial intelligence, robotics and multi-user software environments (Fig. 2).

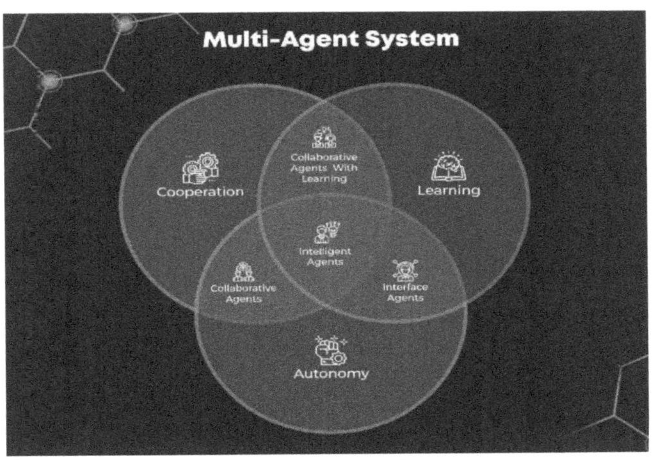

Fig.2 Multi-agent System

2.3.1 Definition of Multi-Agent Systems (MAS)

Multi-Agent Systems (MAS) consist of multiple interacting agents—either physical or virtual—that work together within an environment to achieve individual or collective goals. Each agent is autonomous, capable of perception, decision-making and acting on its own. These agents can represent robots, software processes, or even humans in simulations. MAS are characterized by decentralization, where no single agent has global control. Agents may have incomplete information, yet through interaction, they can solve complex tasks more efficiently than a single agent. MAS are commonly used in domains such as robotics, smart grids, logistics and game AI. Unlike centralized systems, MAS emphasize local knowledge, distributed processing and adaptive behaviour. They are also scalable, meaning more agents can be added without redesigning the system. A key strength is their ability to operate under uncertainty and dynamic conditions. MAS design often incorporates learning, planning and cooperation strategies. Their development draws heavily from artificial intelligence, control theory and distributed computing.

2.3.2 Coordination in MAS

Coordination refers to the process by which agents organize their actions and timing to work harmoniously. It ensures that individual behaviours contribute positively to system-wide objectives, avoiding conflicts and redundancies. Coordination mechanisms can be explicit—such as predefined communication protocols—or implicit, like reacting to environmental changes. A well-coordinated MAS prevents agents from interfering with one another or duplicating effort. For instance, in warehouse automation, robots coordinate to avoid traffic jams or collisions while retrieving items. Coordination may involve scheduling, task allocation, or spatial arrangement strategies. Algorithms like market-based coordination, contract nets, or token-passing are often used. In dynamic environments, coordination must also be flexible, allowing agents to adapt quickly. Time synchronization and shared goals are essential aspects. Effective coordination enhances the MAS's performance, robustness and efficiency. It also lays the groundwork for higher-level behaviours like cooperation and negotiation. As systems scale, coordination becomes more complex, requiring advanced strategies to maintain overall functionality.

2.3.3 Cooperation among Agents

Cooperation in MAS occurs when agents work together to achieve a shared objective that is difficult or impossible for an individual agent to accomplish alone. This goes beyond just avoiding conflict—it involves positive collaboration, resource sharing and joint planning. Cooperative agents may share knowledge, divide tasks and synchronize efforts to complete goals more efficiently. For example, a team of drones cooperating to map a disaster zone will divide the area, share discovered data and update paths accordingly. Cooperation improves the system's problem-solving ability, especially in uncertain and dynamic environments. It requires trust, mutual goals and sometimes negotiation or consensus mechanisms. Agents can be designed to cooperate based on social norms, utility functions, or reinforcement learning. Effective cooperation boosts redundancy and fault tolerance, as agents can support or substitute each other if needed. However, designing cooperative behaviour also introduces complexity in communication and behaviour modelling. Successful cooperation leads to emergent behaviours' that outperform isolated decision-making.

2.3.4 Communication Protocols

Communication is the backbone of coordination and cooperation in MAS. Agents must exchange information to understand intentions, share observations, negotiate roles, or synchronize actions. Communication protocols define the structure, rules and languages used for interaction. These can range from simple signal exchanges to complex semantic messages using agent communication languages (ACLs) like KQML or FIPA-ACL. Efficient communication protocols ensure that information is clear, relevant and timely. Protocols can be categorized as synchronous or asynchronous and centralized or peer-to-peer. In a robotic swarm, for instance, robots might broadcast status updates or send targeted requests. The design of communication protocols must consider limitations like bandwidth, latency, or noise. Protocols also influence agent behaviour—how they respond, escalate, or resolve conflicts. Robust communication enables distributed decision-making, collective learning and cooperative execution. It is essential for scalability and system integrity. As MAS grow in size or operate in volatile environments, communication protocols must evolve to remain efficient and secure.

2.3.5 Task Allocation

Task allocation in a MAS involves distributing work among agents in a way that optimizes efficiency, time, or resource usage. It ensures that each task is handled by the most suitable agent based on its capabilities, location, or workload. Effective task allocation prevents bottlenecks, avoids idle time and balances agent roles. There are centralized and decentralized methods of allocation. In centralized models, a leader assigns tasks, while in decentralized ones, agents negotiate or self-assign tasks. Examples include contract-net protocols, auction-based methods and market-driven strategies. For instance, in a group of cleaning robots, each robot may bid to clean a specific area based on its proximity and energy level. Dynamic task allocation systems adapt to failures or changing priorities. This is crucial in uncertain environments where tasks may evolve or new tasks emerge. Good allocation improves cooperation and system productivity. It also enables specialization, where agents focus on tasks they perform best. Task allocation is key to scalable, autonomous systems.

2.3.6 Negotiation and Conflict Resolution

In a MAS, agents often have overlapping goals or limited resources, leading to conflicts. Negotiation is a mechanism through which agents resolve these conflicts and reach mutually beneficial agreements. It involves offers, counter-offers, preferences and compromises. Conflict resolution ensures that coordination and cooperation are not disrupted. Agents may negotiate over task roles, resource access, or action timing. Various negotiation strategies exist, including bargaining, argumentation, voting and auctions. For example, in a smart grid, energy agents might negotiate energy distribution based on demand and capacity. Agents may also follow predefined conflict resolution rules, such as priority or fairness policies. Intelligent agents can adapt their negotiation strategies based on past experiences or expected outcomes. Effective negotiation increases system robustness, fairness and efficiency. It also promotes trust and long-term collaboration among agents. Designing negotiation mechanisms is complex, requiring clear protocols and logical reasoning capabilities. In dynamic systems, real-time negotiation becomes vital for adaptability and resilience.

2.3.7 Learning in MAS

Learning enables agents in a MAS to improve their behaviour over time based on experience, feedback, or shared knowledge. Learning agents adapt to environmental changes, optimize strategies and enhance cooperation. Various learning methods are used, such as reinforcement learning, supervised learning and multi-agent learning. In reinforcement learning, agents receive rewards or penalties for actions, guiding future decisions. Multi-agent learning focuses on how agents learn both individually and collectively in the presence of other learners. For example, delivery drones may learn optimal routes by interacting with traffic patterns and each other. Learning improves system performance, flexibility and long-term efficiency. It also helps agents deal with uncertainty and incomplete information. Sharing learned knowledge among agents can accelerate learning across the system. However, learning introduces challenges such as non-stationary environments and policy convergence. Balancing exploration (trying new actions) and exploitation (using known successful actions) is also crucial. Ultimately, learning transforms MAS from static systems into adaptive, intelligent networks.

2.3.8 Environment Modelling and Sensing

Agents in a MAS must perceive and interpret their environment to make informed decisions. Environment modelling involves creating a representation—either shared or individual—of the surrounding conditions, objects and other agents. Sensing enables agents to gather data from the environment using physical sensors (in robotics) or software monitoring tools (in virtual agents). Accurate modelling helps agents predict outcomes, navigate spaces and plan actions. Shared environment models improve coordination, as agents operate with similar context awareness. For example, autonomous vehicles in a convoy must sense road conditions and share positioning data to drive safely. Environment models can be static (unchanging) or dynamic (adaptive over time). Sensor data often includes noise, requiring filtering or fusion techniques. Advanced models may also include probabilistic or semantic information for deeper understanding. The quality of environment perception directly affects system performance. It underpins other behaviours like cooperation, learning and planning. In MAS, robust environment modelling ensures agents respond appropriately and effectively to real-world challenges.

2.4 COMPLEX SYSTEMS AND EMERGENT BEHAVIOUR

2.4.1 Complex Systems

Complex systems are composed of many interconnected and interacting components or agents whose collective behaviour cannot be easily inferred from the properties of individual parts. These systems exhibit rich dynamics and can adapt to changes in their environment. Examples include ecosystems, social networks, economies and the brain. The key characteristic of complex systems is that their behaviour emerges from numerous nonlinear interactions rather than from a centralized controller. Because of these interactions, complex systems often show unpredictable, self-organizing and adaptive behaviours. They operate across multiple scales, where small changes at the local level can lead to significant global effects—a property often referred to as sensitivity to initial conditions. Complex systems also tend to have feedback loops, both positive and negative, that influence their evolution. Studying complex systems requires interdisciplinary approaches from physics, biology, computer science and social sciences. Modelling techniques such as agent-based modelling, network theory and dynamical systems help to understand and predict their behaviour. Despite the apparent randomness, complex systems often exhibit patterns, stability, or periodicity. Understanding complex systems is essential for managing real-world problems such as climate change, urban planning and epidemic control, where multiple factors and agents interact dynamically.

2.4.2 Emergent Behaviour

Emergent behaviour refers to complex patterns, structures, or functionalities that arise from simple interactions among system components without any centralized control or explicit programming. This phenomenon means that the whole system exhibits properties and capabilities that individual parts do not possess on their own. For example, the flocking of birds, schooling of fish and formation of traffic jams are emergent behaviours' resulting from local interactions governed by simple rules. Emergence is a hallmark of complex systems and is often unpredictable from the outset. It arises through processes such as self-organization, feedback and adaptation. Positive feedback can amplify certain behaviours', while negative feedback can stabilize the system. Random fluctuations or noise sometimes contribute to diversity and innovation within the system. Emergent behaviours' can be both beneficial, like efficient resource allocation in ant colonies, or problematic, such as cascading failures in power grids. Studying emergence helps in designing decentralized systems like swarm robotics or artificial intelligence.

One challenge is to identify the local rules or mechanisms that give rise to desired emergent outcomes. Emergence underscores the importance of bottom-up design and holistic thinking in understanding and engineering complex systems.

2.5 MATHEMATICAL MODELS FOR SWARM BEHAVIOUR (E.G., CELLULAR AUTOMATA, AGENT-BASED MODELLING)

Mathematical models for swarm behaviour provide essential tools to understand, simulate and predict how individual agents in a swarm interact to produce complex collective phenomena. Swarm behaviour, observed in nature among insects, birds, fish and even human crowds, emerges from simple local interactions following basic rules, without centralized control. To study these phenomena, researchers use mathematical frameworks that capture the dynamics of many interacting agents and how their individual behaviours' lead to coordinated group actions. Two of the most prominent modelling approaches are Cellular Automata (CA) and Agent-Based Modelling (ABM). Cellular Automata use a grid of cells, each representing an agent or state, evolving through discrete time steps based on the states of neighbouring cells. This spatially explicit and rule-based model allows for efficient simulation of pattern formation and propagation phenomena within swarms. Agent-Based Modelling, on the other hand, represents agents as autonomous individuals with distinct behaviours and decision-making capabilities, moving and interacting in continuous or discrete environments. ABM is particularly powerful for capturing heterogeneity among agents, adaptive responses and complex communication patterns. Beyond CA and ABM, other mathematical tools such as differential equations, graph theory and probabilistic models complement the study of swarm systems by addressing various aspects like population dynamics, network structures and uncertainty. Together, these mathematical models provide insights into the principles governing swarm intelligence and guide the design of artificial swarms in robotics, optimization and distributed computing. They help bridge the gap between microscopic agent rules and macroscopic emergent behaviours', enabling the advancement of both theoretical understanding and practical applications of swarm systems (Fig. 3).

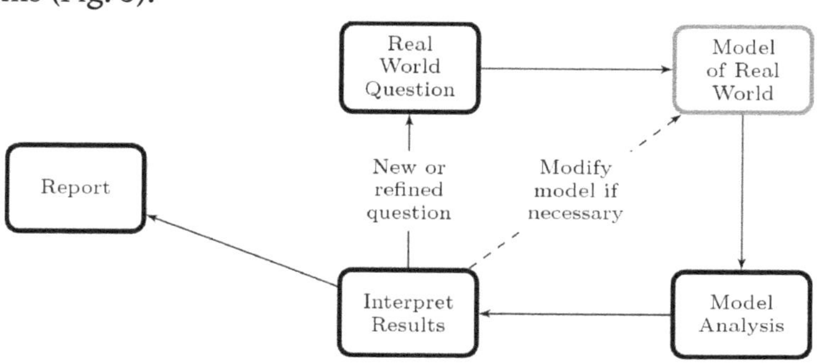

Fig.3 Agent-Based Modelling and Simulation in Mathematics and Biology

2.5.1 Cellular Automata (CA)

Cellular Automata are mathematical models used to simulate complex systems and swarm behaviours through simple, discrete units called cells arranged in a grid. Each cell can be in a finite number of states and the state of each cell evolves over discrete time steps according to a set of local rules based on the states of its neighbouring cells. This local interaction drives the system's overall dynamics, making CA an effective tool for modelling emergent behaviour in swarms. Despite their simplicity, cellular automata can generate highly complex patterns and behaviours', mimicking natural phenomena such as the spread of fire, population dynamics, or traffic flow. CA models emphasize spatial structure and local connectivity, key features of many swarm systems where agents only interact with immediate neighbours. Their discrete nature and rule-based updates allow efficient computer simulation and analysis. However, CA models can be limited by fixed grid structures and synchronous updates, which may not capture all aspects of real-world swarm dynamics. Extensions like asynchronous updates and probabilistic rules help overcome these limitations. Overall, Cellular Automata provide a foundational framework for understanding how local interactions among simple units can produce complex, collective swarm behaviours.

2.5.2 Agent-Based Modelling (ABM)

Agent-Based Modelling is a flexible computational approach that represents swarms as collections of autonomous agents, each with its own set of behaviours', states and decision-making abilities. Unlike cellular automata, agents in ABM are typically free to move in continuous or discrete space and can have heterogeneous characteristics and complex interactions. Each agent perceives its environment and other agents, processes information and acts based on simple local rules or strategies. These interactions lead to emergent swarm behaviour at the system level without central coordination. ABM is widely used for simulating social, biological and engineered swarms because it captures heterogeneity, adaptability and learning capabilities of agents. It enables the study of how individual agent rules influence group dynamics, task allocation and collective decision-making. ABM's flexibility allows incorporation of stochasticity, complex environments and multi-scale interactions. However, large-scale ABMs can be computationally expensive, requiring efficient algorithms and parallel computing. Despite these challenges, Agent-Based Modelling remains one of the most powerful tools for studying and designing swarm systems, offering insights into both natural and artificial collective intelligence.

2.5.3 Other Mathematical Models

Besides Cellular Automata and Agent-Based Models, several other mathematical frameworks help describe swarm behaviour. Differential equations and dynamical systems theory model swarm dynamics continuously over time, capturing population-level trends such as density waves or synchronization. Graph theory represents agents as nodes and their interactions as edges, useful for analysing communication and influence networks in swarms. Markov chains and probabilistic models describe state transitions in stochastic swarm systems, addressing uncertainty and noise. Optimization models, such as particle swarm optimization (PSO), abstract swarm behaviour to solve complex computational problems by simulating cooperative search. Each model offers unique advantages depending on the aspect of swarm behaviour being studied—discrete vs. continuous, deterministic vs. stochastic, or individual vs. population level. Combining multiple models can yield richer and more accurate descriptions of swarm phenomena. The choice of model depends on the goals of the study, computational resources and the biological or engineered system being modelled.

3 Chapter

COMMUNICATION IN SWARM ROBOTICS

3.0 INTRODUCTION: AN OVERVIEW

Swarm robotics is an emerging field inspired by the collective behaviour of social insects such as ants, bees and termites. These natural systems demonstrate how simple agents following basic rules can achieve complex tasks through local interactions and cooperation. Communication plays a pivotal role in enabling such coordination within a swarm. In swarm robotics, communication refers to the transfer of information among individual robots to achieve collective intelligence and synchronized behaviour. Unlike traditional robotic systems that often rely on centralized control, swarm robotics emphasizes decentralized, scalable and robust systems where communication ensures coherence and adaptability across the swarm. The nature of communication in swarm robotics is diverse, encompassing both direct and indirect methods. Robots may share information explicitly through wireless messaging or implicitly via environmental cues—known as stigmergy. The design of communication protocols directly impacts the efficiency, fault tolerance and scalability of swarm systems. It must be lightweight, adaptable and robust to noise, interference and hardware limitations. Furthermore, communication influences task allocation, movement coordination, path planning and group decision-making. As swarm robotics is applied in areas such as search and rescue, environmental monitoring, agriculture and military operations, the communication strategies must also be context-aware and energy-efficient. The study of communication in swarm robotics bridges disciplines like computer science, biology and engineering, aiming to mimic the strengths of natural swarms while overcoming technological constraints. This chapter delves into the mechanisms, challenges and innovations in swarm communication, providing a foundation for understanding its crucial role in enabling autonomous, distributed robotic systems to function effectively (Fig. 1).

Fig. 1 Swarm Robotics Moves Forward – Communications of the ACM

3.1 LOCAL VS. GLOBAL COMMUNICATION:

Local communication in swarm robotics refers to the exchange of information between robots that are within a short physical or communication range, typically in close proximity to one another. This approach is inspired by the behaviour of social insects like ants, bees and termites, which interact with only their immediate neighbours to coordinate group behaviour. It is inherently decentralized, meaning no single robot governs the system; instead, each robot follows simple rules and makes decisions based on local data. This decentralized nature enhances scalability and fault tolerance, as the system doesn't rely on a central controller and can function even if individual robots fail.

Robots using local communication may exchange data via short-range wireless protocols, infrared or ultrasonic sensors, or even visual signals like LEDs or QR codes. Another common method is stigmergy, where robots interact indirectly by modifying their environment—similar to how ants lay pheromone trails. Although local communication can limit a robot's awareness to its immediate surroundings, it enables emergent behaviours through repeated local interactions. Such systems are energy-efficient and suitable for dynamic or unknown environments, where centralized control is impractical. Despite its limitations in global awareness and slower information spread, local communication forms the backbone of robust, adaptive swarm behaviours.

3.1.1 Methods of Local Communication:

- **Wireless Short-Range Communication:** Wireless short-range communication technologies such as Bluetooth, ZigBee and Wi-Fi Direct enable nearby robots to exchange data quickly and efficiently without relying on a central network. These technologies are well-suited for low-power, low-bandwidth scenarios typical of swarm robotics. Bluetooth offers secure, short-distance communication with minimal energy usage, while ZigBee supports mesh networking and is ideal for larger swarms needing decentralized message relaying. Wi-Fi Direct allows peer-to-peer communication with higher data rates, though at the cost of increased energy consumption. These methods are essential for tasks such as real-time coordination, sharing sensor readings, or broadcasting status updates among close-range robots.

- **Infrared (IR) or Ultrasonic Sensors:** Infrared and ultrasonic sensors are commonly used in swarm robotics for proximity detection and simple data transmission. IR sensors allow robots to detect the presence and orientation of nearby robots by emitting and receiving light signals. Ultrasonic sensors, on the other hand, use sound waves to measure distance and detect movement in the surroundings. These sensors are particularly useful in confined or GPS-denied environments, enabling robots to avoid collisions and maintain formations. In some systems, modulated IR signals are also used to encode and transmit small amounts of data between neighbouring units, combining localization and communication in a single sensor.
- **Visual Markers and LED Signaling:** Visual communication using LED lights, QR codes, or other optical markers provides a simple yet effective way for nearby robots to recognize each other and exchange information. LED signalling can be used to indicate a robot's status, direction, or intentions using predefined colour codes or blinking patterns, which can be captured by onboard cameras or light sensors. QR codes or fiducial markers allow more detailed data encoding and can be read visually by other robots during close encounters. This form of communication is intuitive, energy-efficient and particularly advantageous in environments where radio-based communication might be unreliable due to interference.
- **Stigmergy:** Stigmergy is an indirect form of communication where robots leave traces or modifications in the environment that other robots can detect and respond to. This method is inspired by natural systems, such as ants laying pheromone trails to guide others toward food sources. In robotic systems, stigmergy can take the form of digital markers (like RFID tags), light trails, sound signals, or physical markings left on the ground. It enables distributed coordination without requiring direct contact or constant connectivity. Stigmergic communication is especially useful in exploration, mapping, or task allocation scenarios where robots benefit from shared environmental cues rather than explicit data transmission.

Advantages:

- **Scalability:** Local communication enables swarm systems to scale effortlessly to large numbers of robots, since each robot interacts only with nearby peers rather than relying on global connectivity. As the swarm size increases, the communication load per robot remains relatively constant, avoiding bottlenecks or congestion. This makes local communication ideal for applications requiring hundreds or even thousands of robots to operate simultaneously without overwhelming the system infrastructure.
- **Robustness:** Because local communication systems are inherently decentralized, there is no single point of failure. If one or several robots malfunction, the rest of the swarm can continue functioning effectively. This distributed resilience ensures that the overall system remains operational even under dynamic conditions or in the face of hardware or communication failures, making it highly suitable for unpredictable and hazardous environments.
- **Decentralization:** Local communication supports distributed decision-making, where each robot independently evaluates its local environment and interacts with nearby units to determine its actions. This approach fosters emergent behaviours—complex group dynamics arising from simple local rules—and allows the swarm to adapt organically to changing tasks, environments, or obstacles without centralized coordination.
- **Reduced Communication Load:** Since robots only communicate with nearby peers, bandwidth and energy consumption are significantly reduced compared to systems using long-range or global communication. This makes local communication not only more efficient but also more sustainable for battery-powered robots that must operate for extended periods in the field. Lower data transmission requirements also reduce the likelihood of interference or signal collision in dense swarm deployments (Table-1).

Table-1 Concise advantages of local communication in swarm robotics

Advantage	Description
Scalability	Easily supports large swarms as each robot only interacts locally, avoiding network congestion.
Robustness	No central point of failure; the system remains functional even if individual robots fail.
Decentralization	Enables distributed decision-making and emergent behaviors without centralized control.
Reduced Communication Load	Low bandwidth and energy usage due to short-range, peer-to-peer communication; less interference in dense swarms.

Limitations:

- **Limited Awareness:** In local communication systems, each robot can only perceive and interact with its immediate neighbours. This results in limited situational awareness, as individual robots lack a comprehensive view of the entire environment or the state of the swarm. Consequently, they may make decisions based on incomplete or outdated information, which can affect the overall efficiency and coherence of the swarm, especially in large or dynamic environments where global context is important.
- **Slower Propagation of Information:** Because messages or data must pass sequentially from one robot to another, information spreads gradually across the swarm through multiple "hops." This can significantly delay the dissemination of critical updates or discoveries, such as the detection of a target or obstacle. In time-sensitive missions, this latency in information propagation can hinder real-time coordination and responsiveness, especially when robots are sparsely distributed or frequently moving.
- **Coordination Challenges:** Achieving global synchronization or consensus—such as making group decisions, forming global patterns, or executing time-sensitive actions—becomes more challenging in a locally connected system. Without a central authority or global broadcast capability, it is difficult to ensure that all robots receive the same information or act in unison. This can lead to inconsistent behaviour, delays in convergence, or even conflicts in decision-making, particularly in tasks that require tight coordination across the entire swarm (Table:2).

Table:2 Summarizing the limitations of local communication in swarm robotics

Limitation	Description
Limited Awareness	Robots only perceive nearby peers, lacking a global view, which can lead to decisions based on incomplete or outdated information.
Slower Information Spread	Data must pass through multiple robots ("multi-hop"), causing delays in disseminating critical updates across the swarm.
Coordination Challenges	Achieving global consensus or synchronized actions is difficult without centralized communication, potentially leading to inconsistent behaviors.

Example Use Cases:

- Flocking and formation control.
- Foraging tasks where robots share local discoveries.
- Obstacle avoidance through proximity alerts.

3.1.2 Global Communication

Global communication refers to the ability of robots within a swarm to share information across the entire group, regardless of their individual physical locations. Unlike local communication, where interactions are limited to immediate neighbours, global communication allows messages, commands, or data to be broadcast to all or most members of the swarm simultaneously or via long-range transmission networks. This type of communication plays a critical role in tasks that require synchronized actions, centralized monitoring, or rapid dissemination of important updates, such as emergency alerts, path planning, or system-wide reconfiguration. Global communication is typically achieved through technologies such as long-range wireless networks, mesh networking, or centralized servers that coordinate and relay information. These mechanisms ensure that even robots situated at the edge of the environment can access global updates or contribute data for swarm-level decision-making. The use of mesh networks also enables multi-hop communication, extending the effective range of each robot and enhancing connectivity in large-scale environments. The primary advantage of global communication is the speed and consistency with which information can be distributed. It supports real-time awareness of the entire system's state, allowing for faster coordination, centralized control (if needed) and effective global task allocation. For instance, if a robot detects a hazardous area, this information can be instantly broadcasted to the entire swarm, enabling collective avoidance behaviour. However, global communication comes with trade-offs, including higher energy consumption, increased bandwidth requirements and potential vulnerability to network failure or signal congestion. Despite these challenges, it is invaluable in missions where maintaining a shared global state is critical. In many practical implementations, swarm robotic systems adopt a hybrid model, combining the strengths of local and global communication to achieve optimal performance, flexibility and resilience.

Methods of Global Communication:

- **Centralized Server or Base Station:** A centralized server or base station serves as a command center that gathers data from all individual robots and redistributes it back to the swarm. In this model, robots transmit their sensor readings, status updates, or discovered information to the central unit, which processes and analyzes the data. It then makes decisions or generates commands and sends them out to all robots. This architecture ensures a unified global perspective, enabling precise coordination, centralized decision-making and efficient swarm-wide task allocation. It is especially useful in structured environments like factories, warehouses, or controlled outdoor operations. However, this approach introduces a single point of failure—if the base station becomes unreachable due to technical issues or environmental barriers, the entire communication process could collapse. It also increases network traffic and requires higher energy resources for both uplink and downlink data transfers. Despite its limitations, centralized communication is ideal for applications where human supervision, mission-critical decisions, or coordinated strategies are essential.

- **Mesh Networks:** Mesh networks provide a decentralized solution for global communication by allowing robots to relay messages through multiple "hops" until the information reaches distant units. In this setup, each robot acts as both a node and a router, forwarding messages it receives to its neighbours. This creates a self-organizing, robust and flexible communication web that can dynamically adjust to changes in the swarm's structure or environment. Mesh networks are particularly advantageous in large-scale or outdoor applications, such as environmental monitoring or disaster recovery, where maintaining a direct link to a central server is impractical. They improve fault tolerance by rerouting messages through alternate paths if a robot fails or moves out of range. Although data propagation in mesh networks is generally slower than direct broadcasting, the system ensures eventual global dissemination without overloading any single robot. However, network latency, message duplication and synchronization challenges must be carefully managed to ensure reliable performance.
- **Broadcast Systems:** Broadcast systems use high-range wireless technologies—such as Wi-Fi, long-range radio (e.g., LoRa), or cellular networks—to simultaneously transmit messages to all robots in the swarm. This approach enables rapid dissemination of critical information, such as alerts, commands, or environmental data, reaching every robot regardless of its location. Broadcast systems are extremely effective in time-sensitive missions where quick, unified action is required, such as in emergency evacuation scenarios or synchronized swarm reconfiguration. These systems reduce the need for complex routing protocols since all robots receive the same data at once. However, they also demand greater energy consumption and the risk of communication interference or channel congestion increases with swarm density. Additionally, broadcast systems rely heavily on signal strength and network coverage, which may be inconsistent in obstructed or remote environments. Despite these challenges, broadcast communication is an efficient way to maintain real-time global awareness, especially when combined with local methods to filter or interpret data at the individual level.

Advantages:

- **Efficient Information Sharing:** Global communication allows critical information, such as the discovery of a target, hazard, or resource, to be quickly broadcast to all robots in the swarm. This rapid data sharing ensures that every robot is aware of important updates almost simultaneously, minimizing delays in response. Such efficiency is crucial in dynamic or hazardous environments where timely reactions can mean the difference between mission success or failure. By maintaining a constant flow of relevant information across the swarm, robots can adapt their behaviour based on the most current data, improving overall effectiveness and safety. This immediate awareness also prevents redundant efforts, as all robots know which areas have been explored or which tasks have been completed.
- **Improved Coordination:** Global communication enables swarm robots to synchronize their actions effectively, facilitating complex behaviours that require precise timing and cooperation. With shared global data, robots can collectively plan routes, divide tasks, or form formations with high accuracy. This level of coordination is essential for missions that demand unified efforts, such as search and rescue, large-scale mapping, or construction tasks. By having access to a common operational picture, each robot can adjust its movements and decisions in harmony with the swarm, reducing conflicts and inefficiencies. This coordinated approach significantly enhances the swarm's overall performance and ability to handle intricate challenges.
- **Easier Monitoring and Control:** Global communication provides a centralized or networked overview that is invaluable for human supervisors or automated control systems overseeing the swarm. It enables continuous monitoring of individual robots and the swarm's collective status in real time, allowing quick detection of anomalies or failures. Supervisors can issue commands or reassign tasks dynamically based on the global situation, improving mission adaptability and responsiveness. This is particularly important in mission-critical applications such as military operations, disaster response, or industrial automation, where precision and reliability are paramount. The transparency offered by global communication enhances decision-making, reduces uncertainty and ensures safer and more efficient operations.

Limitations:

- **Scalability Issues:** As the number of robots in a swarm grows, global communication systems face significant challenges related to bandwidth limitations, increased latency and processing demands. Transmitting large amounts of data across many robots can saturate communication channels, causing delays and packet loss. Moreover, ensuring timely data delivery and synchronization becomes increasingly complex as the network scales, potentially degrading overall swarm performance. These scalability constraints require sophisticated network management, compression algorithms, or hierarchical communication structures to maintain efficiency in large-scale deployments.

- **Vulnerability:** Centralized global communication architectures are prone to single points of failure, where the malfunction or loss of the central server or base station can disrupt the entire swarm's coordination and information flow. Even in decentralized mesh networks, critical relay nodes may become bottlenecks or failure points, compromising network integrity. This vulnerability increases the risk of mission failure, especially in hostile or unpredictable environments where hardware can be damaged or communication links obstructed. Designing robust fault-tolerant communication protocols and redundant systems is essential to mitigate these risks.
- **Higher Energy Consumption:** Global communication typically demands more power and sophisticated hardware compared to local communication. Long-range transmissions and continuous connectivity require energy-intensive radios and processing units, which can rapidly drain the limited battery life of small robots. Additionally, complex communication protocols and encryption for secure data exchange further increase computational load and energy use. This heightened power consumption restricts the operational duration and mobility of swarm robots, making energy-efficient communication strategies critical for sustainable, long-term missions.

Example Use Cases:

- Mapping large environments collaboratively.
- Coordinated missions where timing and global awareness are critical.
- Task allocation based on global knowledge of robot status and environmental conditions.

The comparative summary of local communication and global communication are depicted in Table-3.

Table-3: Comparative Summary of Local Communication and Global Communication

Feature	Local Communication	Global Communication
Range	Short (neighbors only)	Long (entire swarm)
Architecture	Decentralized	Centralized or distributed
Scalability	High	Limited
Fault Tolerance	High	Lower (esp. with central nodes)
Energy Consumption	Low	High
Speed of Information Spread	Slow (multi-hop)	Fast
Examples	Flocking, formation	Global path planning, mission updates

3.1.3 Hybrid Approaches

In practice, many swarm robotic systems use a hybrid communication strategy that combines both local and global methods to balance scalability, speed and robustness. For example, local communication can manage routine coordination, while global channels are reserved for critical updates or commands from human operators.

The choice between local and global communication in swarm robotics depends on the specific application requirements, environmental constraints and system design goals. While local communication supports decentralized, scalable and fault-tolerant behaviour, global communication offers speed and coordination for complex, mission-critical tasks. A well-designed communication architecture often blends both approaches to leverage their respective strengths.

3.2 IMPLICIT (STIGMERGY) AND EXPLICIT COMMUNICATION

Implicit (Stigmergy) and Explicit Communication: Implicit communication, also known as stigmergy, is an indirect form of interaction where robots influence each other by modifying their shared environment rather than exchanging direct messages.

Mechanism: Robots often utilize physical or digital markers to communicate indirectly with one another, creating a system known as stigmergy. This involves leaving traces in the environment—such as chemical trails, light pulses, heat signatures, sound patterns, or alterations in terrain—that can be detected and interpreted by other robots. These markers guide behaviour, coordination and decision-making without requiring direct communication. For instance, a robot cleaning a floor may leave behind a UV light trail that signals to others where cleaning has already been completed. In swarm robotics, such environmental cues can help distribute tasks efficiently, maintain formation, or signal hazards. This method relies on environmental feedback loops. As robots sense changes or signals in their surroundings, they adjust their behaviour accordingly—perhaps reinforcing a signal or modifying it based on task completion. These loops create dynamic interactions, enabling decentralized systems to adapt and self-organize. Stigmergy reduces the computational load on individual robots, allowing simple agents to contribute to complex, collective behaviours. It's inspired by social insects like ants and termites, whose colonies achieve remarkable coordination through pheromone trails. In robotic applications, this can be replicated digitally, using visual markers or sensor data to simulate chemical trails. Environmental communication is scalable, fault-tolerant and especially suited for unpredictable or unstructured settings. Robots need not maintain constant connectivity; instead, they read the state of the environment to infer what actions to take. This allows for asynchronous collaboration, where agents can come and go without disrupting the overall system. Such methods are crucial for autonomous exploration, disaster response, agriculture and space missions, where centralized control is impractical. Through environmental feedback loops, robot teams achieve emergent intelligence, continuously reshaping their strategies based on shared, indirect signals in the world around them.

Examples:

- Ant-inspired pheromone trails to guide swarm movement or resource collection.
- Robots leaving digital tags or markers in a shared map to indicate explored or hazardous areas.

Advantages:

- Scales naturally with swarm size without increasing communication overhead.
- Robust to failures since communication is embedded in the environment.
- Requires less energy as no direct transmission is needed.

Limitations:

- Slower information propagation as environmental changes take time to be detected and interpreted.
- Difficult to convey complex or time-sensitive information.
- Environmental noise or changes can disrupt stigmergic signals.

Explicit Communication: Explicit communication involves the direct exchange of messages or signals between robots using predefined communication protocols.

Mechanism: Robots communicate by sending and receiving data through various direct communication technologies such as wireless signals (e.g., Wi-Fi, Bluetooth), infrared (IR), radio frequencies, or visual cues like LEDs and screen displays. These methods allow for structured messaging, enabling robots to share precise and complex information such as location, task status, environmental conditions, or commands. Unlike stigmergy, which relies on indirect environmental cues, direct communication involves intentional, real-time data exchange between agents. Wireless networks are particularly useful for long-range, high-bandwidth communication, supporting coordination in distributed systems like warehouse automation or drone fleets. Infrared is often used for short-range line-of-sight data transfer, especially in low-power or indoor environments. Visual signaling—such as color-coded lights or gestures—can be effective in human-robot interaction or for communication in noisy environments where audio signals might fail. These technologies support synchronous or asynchronous messaging, allowing for both one-to-one and broadcast communication.

Structured messages are typically encoded using predefined protocols and data formats, enabling interoperability and error checking. This ensures that robots interpret information consistently, even in diverse or heterogeneous robotic systems. As a result, robots can negotiate roles, divide tasks, avoid collisions, or update each other on environmental changes. Such mechanisms are essential in applications requiring high reliability, like autonomous vehicles, collaborative manufacturing, or robotic surgery. Overall, direct communication enhances coordination, speed and adaptability in complex, multi-robot systems.

Examples:

- Wireless transmission using Bluetooth or Wi-Fi to share sensor data or commands.
- Infrared signals or LED blinking patterns to indicate status or intentions.

Advantages:

- Enables fast and precise information exchange.
- Suitable for complex coordination requiring detailed instructions.
- Easier to implement synchronization and consensus algorithms.

Limitations:

- Requires more energy and bandwidth, especially in large swarms.
- Vulnerable to interference, signal loss, or communication bottlenecks.
- May need sophisticated protocols to avoid collisions and ensure message integrity.

3.3 NETWORK TOPOLOGIES AND CONNECTIVITY

Network Topologies: Network topology refers to the arrangement or structure of communication links between robots in a swarm. The topology determines how information flows within the swarm and affects robustness, efficiency and scalability.

Common Topologies:

- **Star Topology:** In a star topology, one central robot or base station functions as the hub of communication, with all other robots connected directly to this central node. This design is straightforward and easy to manage because all data passes through a single point, simplifying coordination and monitoring. It allows the central hub to quickly gather information and issue commands to the entire swarm. However, the major drawback is the single point of failure—if the central node fails or loses connectivity, the entire communication network collapses, isolating all peripheral robots. This topology is best suited for small swarms or controlled environments where the central unit is highly reliable and well-protected. While it offers low latency between the hub and individual robots, it can become inefficient as the swarm size grows due to the increased load on the central node.
- **Mesh Topology:** Mesh topology is a decentralized communication structure where each robot connects to multiple neighbours, forming an interconnected web of communication links. This arrangement supports multi-hop communication, meaning messages can be relayed through intermediate robots to reach distant members of the swarm. Mesh networks are highly robust because if one node fails or moves out of range, data can be rerouted through alternate paths, ensuring continuous connectivity. This scalability makes mesh topology ideal for large or dynamic swarms operating in unpredictable environments. Additionally, mesh networks can self-organize and adapt to changing conditions without centralized control. However, managing message routing and preventing communication collisions requires sophisticated protocols to maintain efficiency and avoid network congestion.
- **Ring Topology:** In ring topology, robots are arranged in a closed loop where each robot communicates directly with exactly two neighbours—one on either side. This structure ensures equal data flow and simple routing, as messages can travel clockwise or counterclockwise around the ring. The ring topology offers fairness in communication opportunities since every robot has the same number of connections. However, its main weakness lies in vulnerability to failure: if any single robot or communication link breaks, the entire ring can be disrupted, partitioning the swarm into isolated segments. To counteract this, some systems implement dual rings or backup links to maintain connectivity. Ring topologies are best suited

for smaller or more controlled environments where simplicity and equal participation are priorities.

- **Tree Topology:** Tree topology organizes robots hierarchically, resembling a branching tree with parent and child nodes. This structure allows data to flow from leaves (end robots) up to a root node and vice versa, facilitating organized aggregation and distribution of information. It is efficient for tasks requiring hierarchical control or delegation, such as cluster-based swarm management. However, the tree topology is vulnerable to failures at higher-level nodes: if a parent node fails, all its child nodes and their descendants may become disconnected from the network. This dependency makes fault tolerance challenging and requires mechanisms for dynamic restructuring or reassignment of roles. Despite this, tree topologies are effective in scenarios where structured data flow and command hierarchies are necessary.
- **Fully Connected Topology:** In a fully connected topology, every robot maintains a direct communication link with every other robot in the swarm, creating the highest possible level of connectivity. This design maximizes redundancy and ensures the fastest possible data exchange since messages don't need to be relayed through intermediate nodes. Fully connected networks enable seamless coordination, real-time data sharing and collective decision-making. However, the communication overhead grows exponentially as the number of robots increases, making this topology impractical for large swarms due to bandwidth saturation, energy consumption and complexity. It is generally reserved for very small swarms or specialized applications where maximum connectivity and minimal delay are critical.
- **Connectivity:** Connectivity refers to the ability of robots to maintain communication links with one another across the swarm.

Key Aspects:

- **Local Connectivity:** Local connectivity refers to the communication links established between robots that are within a limited physical or communication range of each other. In this setup, each robot only directly exchanges information with its immediate neighbours. To share data beyond their direct range, robots rely on multi-hop forwarding, where messages are relayed from one robot to another until reaching the intended recipient or covering the entire swarm. This approach reduces communication load on individual robots and conserves energy but can introduce delays as information propagates through multiple hops. Local connectivity is fundamental in large, decentralized swarms where maintaining direct global communication is impractical.

- **Global Connectivity:** Global connectivity ensures that any robot in the swarm can communicate with any other robot, either directly or indirectly via intermediate nodes. This level of connectivity guarantees the integrity of the swarm's communication network, enabling coordinated group behaviour and rapid information dissemination. Achieving global connectivity often requires multi-hop communication, network routing protocols, or centralized communication hubs. It is crucial for applications that demand synchronized actions or comprehensive situational awareness across the swarm. Maintaining global connectivity can be challenging in highly dynamic or large-scale environments but is essential for overall swarm coherence.
- **Dynamic Connectivity:** Dynamic connectivity recognizes that the network links between robots change over time due to mobility, environmental obstacles, or failures. Robots continuously move, causing connections to form or break as neighbours come in and out of range. This necessitates adaptive network protocols capable of detecting topology changes and dynamically adjusting routes or communication strategies to maintain network integrity. Dynamic connectivity protocols improve the resilience and flexibility of swarm communication, ensuring that the swarm remains functional despite continuous changes in its configuration or surroundings.
- **Connectivity Metrics:** Connectivity metrics are quantitative measures used to evaluate how well-connected a swarm's communication network is. Important metrics include:
  - **Network Diameter:** The longest shortest path between any two robots, indicating the maximum number of hops a message must traverse.
  - **Average Degree:** The average number of direct neighbours per robot, reflecting network density.
  - **Robustness:** The network's ability to maintain connectivity despite node failures or environmental disturbances.

These metrics help design and optimize swarm networks for better performance, reliability and scalability.

Importance of Topology and Connectivity

- **Robustness:** Robustness refers to the resilience of a swarm's communication network against failures and environmental challenges. Well-designed network topologies ensure that the swarm maintains connectivity even if individual robots malfunction, move out of range, or if obstacles disrupt signal paths. For example, mesh topologies excel in robustness by providing multiple redundant communication routes, allowing messages to be rerouted around failed nodes. This redundancy prevents the network from fragmenting and helps sustain coordinated swarm behaviour. Robust connectivity is crucial in dynamic or hazardous environments where unpredictable conditions can compromise individual units. Additionally, robust networks reduce the risk of mission failure by enabling continuous information flow and collective decision-making despite partial system degradation. Designing for robustness often involves trade-offs with complexity and energy use but is essential for reliable swarm operation.

- **Scalability:** Scalability describes a network topology's ability to efficiently support an increasing number of robots without performance degradation. As swarm size grows, communication overhead can escalate dramatically if not managed properly, causing congestion, delays and energy drain. Efficient topologies like hierarchical trees or decentralized mesh networks distribute communication load evenly across the swarm, preventing bottlenecks and enabling smooth scaling to hundreds or thousands of robots. Scalability also involves adapting protocols to minimize unnecessary transmissions and leveraging local interactions to reduce global message complexity. Poorly scalable topologies, such as star networks, quickly become overwhelmed as more robots join, reducing overall system effectiveness. Ultimately, scalable topologies allow large swarms to operate cohesively without overwhelming communication channels or individual robots' processing capabilities.
- **Latency and Throughput:** Latency and throughput are critical metrics influenced heavily by network topology. Latency measures the delay between sending and receiving messages, while throughput quantifies how much data the network can handle concurrently. Topologies with direct links, like fully connected or star, often have low latency but can suffer from congestion as swarm size increases. Mesh and tree topologies introduce additional hops that can increase latency but improve throughput by balancing communication loads across multiple paths. High throughput is essential for applications that require frequent, large data exchanges, such as environmental monitoring or real-time mapping. Conversely, latency-sensitive tasks like synchronized movements or time-critical decisions demand minimal communication delay. Network design must carefully balance these factors to meet the operational requirements of the swarm while maintaining efficient data flow and timely coordination.
- **Energy Efficiency:** Energy efficiency in swarm communication is vital, especially for battery-powered robots with limited resources. Connectivity strategies directly impact the amount of energy consumed by

communication hardware such as radios or transceivers. Topologies that minimize unnecessary transmissions, such as local connectivity with multi-hop forwarding, conserve energy by restricting communication to nearby neighbours instead of long-range broadcasts. Conversely, fully connected or centralized topologies may require higher transmission power and increased communication frequency, leading to rapid battery depletion. Protocols that implement sleep modes, duty cycling, or adaptive power control further enhance energy efficiency. Energy-aware connectivity design extends the operational lifespan of the swarm, enabling longer missions and reducing the need for frequent recharging or replacement, which is critical for autonomous deployment in remote or hazardous environments.

3.4COMMUNICATIONPROTOCOLSANDBANDWIDTHCONSTRAINTS

Introduction: Effective communication is a cornerstone of swarm robotics, enabling individual robots to coordinate, share information and collectively achieve complex tasks. At the heart of this communication lies the use of well-defined communication protocols, which are sets of standardized rules that govern how data is transmitted, received and interpreted within the swarm. These protocols ensure that messages are exchanged reliably and efficiently despite the decentralized and dynamic nature of swarm systems. Given the typically large number of robots involved, often deployed in unpredictable environments, communication protocols must be robust enough to handle frequent changes in network topology, intermittent connections and potential interference. Additionally, the protocols need to support various communication tasks such as neighbour discovery, message routing, error detection and collision avoidance. One of the key challenges faced in swarm communication is bandwidth constraints, referring to the limited data transmission capacity available to each robot or the network as a whole. Bandwidth limitations arise due to the physical properties of wireless communication channels, hardware capabilities and energy constraints on small, often battery-powered robots (Fig. 2).

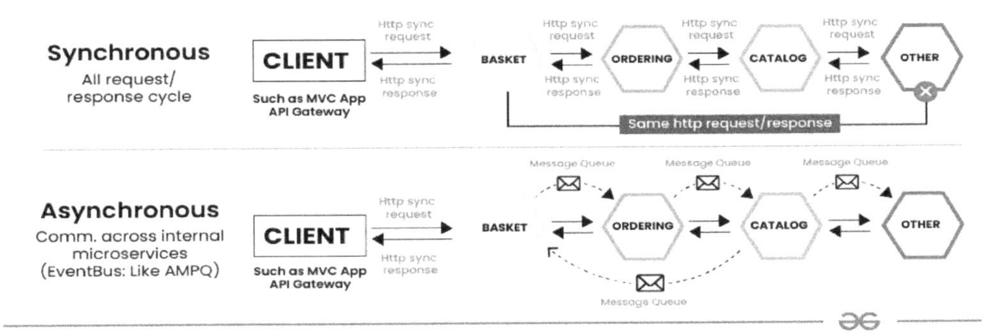

Fig.2 Communication Protocols in System Design

As the swarm size increases, the volume of data exchanged can grow exponentially, potentially overwhelming the available bandwidth. This can result in delays, dropped messages and degraded coordination performance. Therefore, communication protocols must be designed to optimize bandwidth usage by reducing redundant transmissions, compressing data and prioritizing critical messages. Moreover, swarm robotic systems frequently operate in environments with significant noise, interference and obstacles, which further restrict effective bandwidth and complicate reliable communication. Protocols often incorporate adaptive mechanisms to dynamically adjust transmission rates, power levels and routing paths in response to changing network conditions, thereby maintaining connectivity and performance. To address these challenges, different layers of communication protocols—from the physical and data link layers to network and application layers—work in concert, each responsible for managing specific aspects such as signal modulation, medium access control, routing and data formatting. Overall, understanding communication protocols and bandwidth constraints is essential for designing efficient, scalable and resilient swarm robotic systems. By balancing the demands of data exchange with the limitations of hardware and environment, these protocols enable swarms to function cohesively, execute coordinated behaviours and achieve their mission objectives effectively.

3.4.1 Communication Protocols

Communication protocols are sets of rules and conventions that govern the exchange of data between robots in a swarm. These protocols ensure reliable, orderly and efficient transmission of messages.

Types of Protocols:

- **MAC (Medium Access Control) Protocols:** MAC protocols manage how multiple robots access and share a common communication channel to prevent signal collisions and ensure efficient data transfer. These protocols are critical in high-density robotic systems where simultaneous transmissions can cause interference. TDMA (Time Division Multiple Access) divides time into slots, assigning specific time windows to each robot for transmission, ensuring orderly communication. CSMA/CA (Carrier Sense Multiple Access with Collision Avoidance), commonly used in Wi-Fi networks, listens to the channel before transmitting to minimize collisions. MAC protocols also often implement priority schemes, allowing urgent messages to bypass regular scheduling. In robotic swarms, a well-designed MAC layer enhances real-time coordination and conserves energy by minimizing retransmissions. Adaptive MAC protocols can dynamically adjust based on network traffic or robot density.

- **Routing Protocols:** Routing protocols define how data packets navigate through a robotic network, especially when direct communication between sender and receiver is not possible. In multi-hop scenarios, messages may need to pass through several intermediate robots to reach their destination. Proactive protocols like OLSR (Optimized Link State Routing) continuously update routing tables, ensuring fast delivery but at the cost of higher bandwidth usage. Reactive protocols such as AODV (Ad-hoc On-demand Distance Vector) create routes only when needed, conserving resources. Hybrid approaches combine the strengths of both, adapting to dynamic environments like search-and-rescue zones. Efficient routing ensures scalability and resilience in swarm robotics, enabling robust communication even in the presence of node failures or mobility. Load balancing and energy-aware routing are often built into advanced systems to optimize performance.
- **Data Link and Transport Protocols:** These layers ensure reliable data transmission between robots, handling tasks like error detection, correction and data flow regulation. The data link layer adds checksums and headers to detect transmission errors, while the transport layer manages packet sequencing, acknowledgments and retransmissions. Protocols such as TCP (Transmission Control Protocol) provide reliable, ordered delivery but may be too heavy for latency-sensitive robotic applications. Lighter alternatives like UDP (User Datagram Protocol) or custom real-time protocols are often preferred in robotic networks. These layers also manage flow control to prevent overwhelming a receiver with too much data at once. Ensuring data integrity and timely delivery is essential in applications like formation control or synchronized movement. In swarm systems, streamlined transport protocols are vital for balancing reliability with communication overhead.
- **Application Layer Protocols:** At the highest level, application layer protocols define the structure, content and purpose of the messages exchanged between robots. These include formats for task assignments, sensor readings, status reports, control commands, or map updates. Clear protocol definitions ensure interoperability between different robot types or manufacturers. Protocols may use standardized data formats like JSON or XML, or lightweight binary formats for efficiency. In swarm systems, these messages often follow a publish-subscribe model or event-driven structure to reduce unnecessary data exchange. Robust application protocols enable robots to interpret context, collaborate on tasks and adjust behaviour based on real-time updates. Custom protocols can be tailored for specific missions, such as exploration, object transport, or perimeter monitoring.

Overall, this layer connects the technical communication mechanisms with mission-level functionality.

3.4.2 Bandwidth Constraints

Bandwidth refers to the maximum data transfer capacity of the communication channel. In swarm robotics, bandwidth constraints limit how much information can be shared within a given time.

Challenges:

- **Limited Channel Capacity:** Wireless communication channels offer finite bandwidth, meaning only a certain amount of data can be transmitted at a time. In robotic swarms, as the number of robots or message frequency grows, this limited capacity can quickly become saturated. Congestion leads to packet collisions, retransmissions and overall system slowdown. Critical messages may face delays or loss, compromising real-time coordination. To mitigate this, bandwidth-efficient protocols and data compression are often employed. Channel sharing mechanisms, such as dynamic bandwidth allocation or prioritized messaging, help optimize usage. Proper network planning is essential to ensure scalability without sacrificing performance.
- **Interference and Noise:** Wireless communication is highly susceptible to interference from both internal and external sources, such as overlapping frequencies, physical obstructions, or electronic noise. In dense swarm environments, simultaneous transmissions from nearby robots can result in signal collisions and degraded performance. Environmental factors like metallic structures or water can further distort signals. Interference increases error rates, leading to message loss or the need for repeated transmissions. Advanced techniques such as frequency hopping, directional antennas, or error-correction codes help mitigate these issues. Robust swarm systems also include interference-aware routing and channel selection strategies. Overall, managing interference is crucial for maintaining reliable communication in dynamic or harsh environments.
- **Energy Consumption:** Wireless communication, particularly over longer distances or at higher data rates, consumes significant energy—a major concern for battery-powered robots. Transmitting large volumes of data frequently drains power rapidly, shortening mission duration. Listening for incoming messages also consumes energy, especially in always-on receivers. To conserve energy, many systems use sleep-wake cycles, low-power communication modes, or adaptive data transmission based on urgency. Protocols are optimized to reduce redundant transmissions and unnecessary chatter. Energy-aware communication strategies help

balance performance with endurance, enabling longer deployments in field operations. Efficient energy use directly impacts the viability of large-scale swarm robotics.

- **Latency and Throughput Trade-offs:** Limited bandwidth creates a natural trade-off between latency (delay) and throughput (total data transferred). When many robots communicate simultaneously or send large messages, delays increase as packets queue for transmission. High throughput often requires buffering and retransmissions, further increasing latency. This can disrupt time-sensitive tasks such as coordinated movement or obstacle avoidance. To address this, systems may prioritize critical data or use lightweight, real-time protocols. Sometimes, reducing message size or frequency improves responsiveness. Managing this trade-of

Strategies to Address Bandwidth Constraints

- **Data Compression:** Data compression reduces the size of messages before transmission, conserving bandwidth and speeding up communication. By encoding information more efficiently, robots can share the same data using fewer bits. This is especially valuable in swarm systems with limited channel capacity and high message volume. Compression techniques can range from simple encoding schemes to more advanced algorithms like Huffman coding or delta encoding. While compression saves bandwidth, it must be balanced against the computational cost of encoding and decoding. Lightweight compression methods are often preferred in real-time robotic applications. Effective compression enhances scalability and reduces energy consumption in communication-heavy tasks.
- **Selective Communication:** Selective communication focuses on transmitting only essential or aggregated data, rather than sending raw or redundant information. Robots may filter data based on relevance, urgency, or novelty, reducing network load significantly. For example, instead of sharing every sensor reading, a robot may only transmit if a threshold is crossed or a change is detected. Aggregated summaries, such as average values or event counts, also minimize message volume. This approach helps preserve bandwidth, lowers latency and extends battery life. Selective strategies are particularly useful in swarms where constant updates from all units are unnecessary. It ensures efficient communication without overwhelming the system.
- **Hierarchical Communication:** Hierarchical communication structures a swarm into layers, where certain robots act as cluster heads or leaders to aggregate and relay information. Instead of all robots communicating directly with every other unit or the base station, data flows through

designated intermediaries. This reduces overall message traffic and prevents channel congestion. Cluster heads can filter, compress, or prioritize incoming data before forwarding it, improving efficiency. The hierarchy can be fixed or dynamically assigned based on role, location, or energy levels. This method supports scalability, enabling thousands of robots to operate without overwhelming the network. Hierarchical systems also improve fault tolerance and coordination in complex missions.

- **Adaptive Protocols:** Adaptive communication protocols adjust parameters like data rate, transmission power, or frequency based on current network conditions. For instance, if interference is detected, a robot might lower its data rate or switch to a different channel. Similarly, robots can increase communication frequency during critical operations or reduce it when idle to save energy. These protocols allow robots to respond in real-time to congestion, noise, or node failures, maintaining system stability. Adaptivity improves resilience and performance in dynamic environments. Intelligent algorithms can use historical data or predictive models to guide these adjustments. This flexibility is crucial in unpredictable or mission-critical swarm deployments.
- **Frequency and Channel Management:** Managing frequencies and channels efficiently helps avoid congestion and interference in robotic communication networks. By dividing communication across multiple channels or frequency bands, robots can operate in parallel without signal collisions. This is particularly useful in dense swarms or in environments with high external noise. Channel hopping and frequency division multiplexing are common techniques used to spread communication load. Dynamic channel assignment allows robots to switch channels when interference is detected. This enhances both reliability and throughput. Proper frequency management ensures smooth, uninterrupted communication, enabling swarms to perform complex, distributed tasks with minimal disruption..

3.4.3 Importance in Swarm Robotics

In swarm robotics, efficient communication protocols and effective bandwidth management are foundational to the success of coordinated, decentralized behaviour. A swarm's ability to function cohesively depends heavily on timely and accurate information exchange among its members. As swarm size increases, so does the communication load, making scalability a major concern. Without well-optimized protocols, communication channels can become saturated, leading to message collisions, high latency and data loss. These issues can disrupt synchronization, delay task execution, or cause robots to make poor decisions based on outdated or incomplete information. Reliable communication ensures that robots can share sensory inputs, task assignments, environmental updates and status reports without overwhelming the network. Protocols must be designed to prioritize critical messages, support multi-hop routing and adapt to changing network conditions. Bandwidth limitations must be addressed through strategies like data compression, selective communication and hierarchical organization, allowing robots to transmit only essential data. Energy efficiency is another key factor, as excessive communication drains battery-powered robots, shortening their operational lifespan and mission duration. Poor communication design not only affects individual robot performance but can also compromise the behaviour of the swarm as a whole. Failures in task distribution, formation control, or obstacle avoidance often trace back to insufficient communication reliability or excessive bandwidth usage. On the other hand, well-engineered protocols allow the swarm to be robust, flexible and autonomous—even in dynamic, unpredictable environments. Whether exploring unknown terrain, conducting search-and-rescue missions, or managing logistics, a swarm's collective intelligence depends on the efficiency of its internal communication. Therefore, designing lightweight, scalable and adaptive protocols is essential to unlocking the full potential of swarm robotics (Fig. 3).

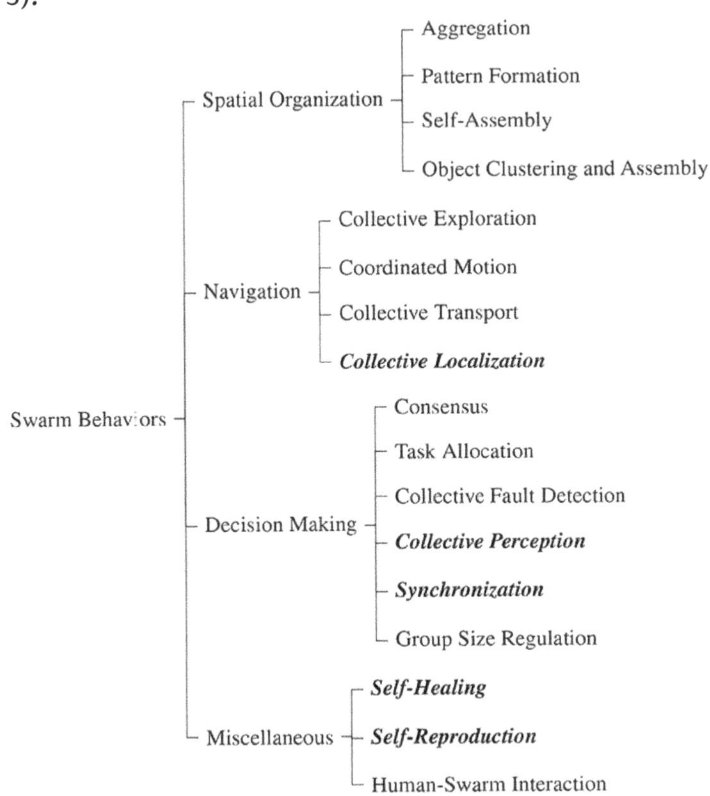

Fig. 3 Swarm Robotics: Applications And Future - Dataconomy

3.5 CHALLENGES: DELAY, NOISE AND SIGNAL LOSS

In modern communication systems, ensuring the reliable transmission of data is a constant challenge. Among the most critical issues that engineers and network designers must address are delay, noise and signal loss. These factors can significantly degrade the performance, efficiency and integrity of communication channels. Delay refers to the time it takes for a signal or data packet to travel from the sender to the receiver. Excessive delay can disrupt real-time applications such as video conferencing and online gaming. Noise, on the other hand, involves unwanted disturbances that interfere with the signal, potentially altering or corrupting the transmitted data. This can lead to errors in reception and the need for retransmission, reducing overall network efficiency. Signal loss, or attenuation, occurs when the strength of a signal decreases as it travels through a medium, such as a cable or air. This phenomenon is particularly problematic over long distances or in environments with physical obstructions. Combined, these challenges impact the quality of service, leading to delays, poor audio or video quality and data loss (Table-4). Improving the reliability of long-range communication against interference for non-line-of-sight conditions in industrial internet of things applications is given in Fig. 4.

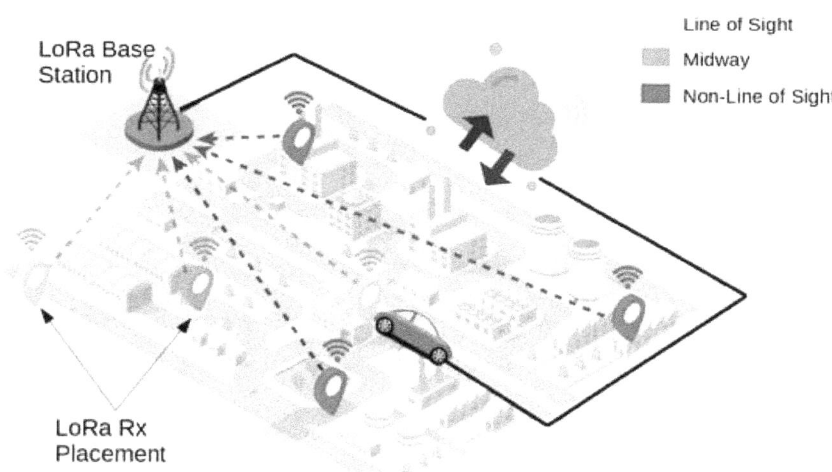

Fig. 4 Improving the Reliability of Long-Range Communication against Interference for Non-Line-of-Sight Conditions in Industrial Internet of Things Applications

Addressing these issues requires sophisticated techniques such as error correction, amplification and optimized routing. As our reliance on fast, clear and stable communication grows, understanding and mitigating these challenges becomes increasingly essential.

3.5.1 Delay

Delay refers to the time lag between sending a message and its successful reception by another robot.

Causes:

- Multi-hop communication where messages must pass through several robots.
- Network congestion causing packet queuing and retransmissions.
- Processing time for encoding, decoding and routing messages.

Impact: Delays can degrade real-time coordination, slow down decision-making and cause outdated information to influence robot behaviours. In time-sensitive missions, such as search-and-rescue, delays can critically impair swarm effectiveness.

Mitigation Strategies:

- Optimizing routing protocols to minimize hops.
- Prioritizing urgent messages.
- Using faster communication hardware.

3.5.2 Noise

Noise refers to unwanted interference or disturbances that corrupt or distort communication signals.

Sources:

- Environmental factors like electromagnetic interference, weather, or obstacles.
- Overlapping transmissions from nearby robots.
- Hardware limitations or malfunctions.

Impact: Noise can cause errors in received messages, requiring retransmissions, which wastes bandwidth and energy. Persistent noise can reduce communication reliability and swarm performance.

Mitigation Strategies:

- Employing error detection and correction codes.
- Using signal filtering and shielding techniques.
- Implementing channel hopping or frequency diversity.

3.5.3 Signal Loss

Signal loss occurs when communication signals weaken or fail to reach the intended recipient.

Causes:

- Distance exceeding communication range.
- Physical obstacles blocking or absorbing signals.
- Multipath fading where signals reflect and interfere destructively.

Impact: Signal loss leads to message dropouts, incomplete data sharing and potential fragmentation of the swarm's communication network, disrupting coordination.

Mitigation Strategies:

- Deploying relay robots to extend communication range.
- Using mesh networking to provide alternate paths.
- Enhancing transmission power or antenna design.

Challenges of Delay, Noise and Signal Loss in communication systems: At a Glance is summarised in Table-4.

Table-4: Challenges of Delay, Noise and Signal Loss in communication systems: At a Glance

Challenge	Description	Causes	Impact	Solutions
Delay	Time lag between data transmission and reception	Long distances, routing hops, processing time, network congestion	Lag in real-time communication (e.g., video calls, online gaming)	Use of faster protocols, low-latency routing, caching and load balancing
Noise	Unwanted disturbances that corrupt the signal	Electromagnetic interference, crosstalk, thermal noise	Data corruption, errors in transmission, reduced signal clarity	Shielded cables, error detection/correction, filtering, digital modulation
Signal Loss	Decrease in signal strength over distance or due to obstacles	Attenuation, distance, physical obstructions, poor transmission media	Weak signals, dropped connections, poor audio/video quality	Signal boosters, repeaters, fiber optics, efficient encoding and modulation

4 Chapter

SENSING, PERCEPTION AND LOCALIZATION

4.0 INTRODUCTION: AN OVERVIEW

In the domain of autonomous systems, robotics and intelligent machines, sensing, perception and localization form the foundational triad that enables machines to interact effectively with the physical world. These three interconnected pillars are essential for transforming raw environmental data into actionable insights and spatial awareness. Sensing refers to the process of collecting data from the environment through various sensors. These may include cameras, LiDARs, radars, ultrasonic sensors, GPS units, inertial measurement units (IMUs) and more. Each sensor type has unique strengths and limitations, which make sensor fusion—combining data from multiple sensors—an effective approach to achieve robust environmental understanding. Perception builds on sensing by interpreting the raw sensor data to identify and classify elements within the environment. Perception modules typically include object detection, tracking, semantic segmentation, lane detection and terrain classification. These capabilities enable an autonomous system to understand its surroundings in a meaningful way, distinguishing between static and dynamic objects and predicting their behaviour over time. Localization is the ability of the system to determine its position and orientation within a known or partially known environment. This process often combines GPS data with inputs from vision, LiDAR, or IMUs using techniques like Kalman filtering, particle filtering, or SLAM (Simultaneous Localization and Mapping). Localization ensures the system knows where it is, which is critical for planning and navigation. Together, sensing, perception and localization empower machines to operate safely and efficiently in dynamic environments. In autonomous vehicles, for example, these modules enable the car to detect road users, traffic signals and obstacles, while also tracking its position relative to the road map. Similarly, in robotics, these systems allow for exploration, manipulation and task execution in complex environments (Fig. 1).

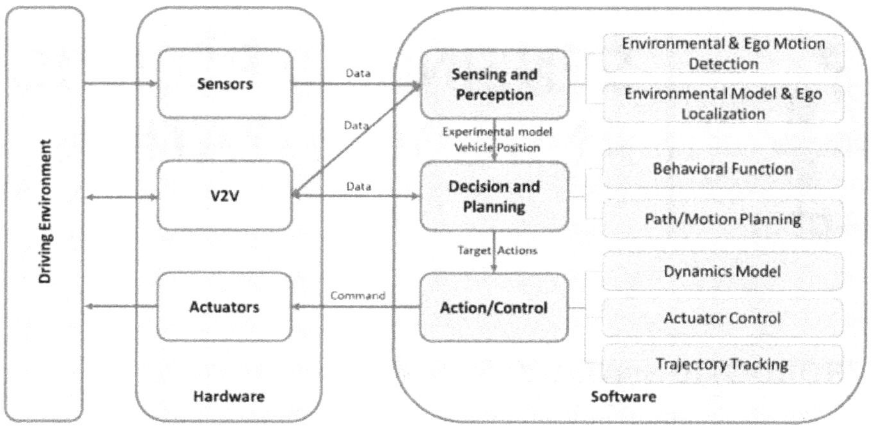

Fig. 1 Sensing, perception, decision, planning and action

The integration of advanced algorithms, real-time data processing and machine learning techniques has significantly enhanced the accuracy and efficiency of these components. Modern systems now achieve human-comparable or even superior capabilities in controlled settings, marking a significant milestone in artificial intelligence and automation. However, challenges remain. Environmental conditions such as lighting, weather, sensor noise and occlusion can degrade performance. The trade-offs between computational cost, accuracy and robustness require careful system design and optimization. Moreover, ensuring real-time performance and fail-safe operation under uncertainty is an ongoing area of research and development. Sensing, perception and localization represent the cognitive framework of autonomous machines. By bridging the physical and digital worlds, they provide the essential tools that enable context-aware, adaptive and intelligent decision-making. This chapter delves deeper into the principles, technologies and current advancements in each of these areas, exploring their roles, challenges and future directions in the evolution of intelligent systems.

4.1 SENSOR TECHNOLOGIES FOR SWARMS

Swarm robotics and autonomous multi-agent systems rely heavily on sensor technologies to enable coordination, communication, navigation and environmental awareness. Each robot within a swarm must independently perceive its surroundings while also interacting with neighbouring agents. The following are the key sensor categories and technologies used in swarm systems:

4.1.1 Proximity Sensors

- **Purpose:** Proximity sensors are used to detect the presence of nearby objects or agents without requiring physical contact. In swarm robotics, they play a crucial role in ensuring collision avoidance and maintaining safe movement within densely packed formations. These sensors allow each agent to sense its immediate surroundings and make reactive navigation decisions. The real-time response enabled by proximity sensors is essential for local-level awareness. This capability ensures smooth group behaviour even in dynamic or cluttered environments. It's especially important when GPS or vision-based systems are unavailable or obstructed. Thus, they form a basic yet essential layer of environmental interaction for swarm systems.

- **Examples:** Common types of proximity sensors include Infrared (IR) sensors and Ultrasonic sensors. IR sensors detect reflected infrared light and are typically used for short-range object detection, while ultrasonic sensors emit sound waves and measure echo times to calculate distances. These technologies are popular due to their simplicity and cost-efficiency. IR sensors are sensitive to ambient lighting but are very compact, while ultrasonic sensors provide more reliable measurements in varied lighting. They are often mounted around the body of swarm robots to enable full coverage. Some systems also use capacitive or inductive proximity sensors in specialized scenarios. Their selection depends on environment type and mission goals.
- **Applications in Swarms:** Proximity sensors are primarily used for obstacle avoidance, a critical requirement for autonomous agents navigating unstructured environments. They help swarm agents maintain safe distances from each other, preventing collisions during movement or while performing group manoeuvres like formation flying or clustering. These sensors also support local behaviour rules in decentralized control architectures—such as "move away when too close"—which are common in bio-inspired swarm strategies. Additionally, proximity data assists in local path planning and trajectory adjustment. In indoor or GPS-denied environments, they provide a vital source of feedback. Their role in maintaining spatial awareness is key to overall swarm stability.
- **Advantages:** Proximity sensors offer several advantages, particularly in cost-sensitive and compact swarm designs. Their small size allows easy integration into small robots or drones. They are power-efficient, making them suitable for battery-operated systems where energy conservation is critical. These sensors offer real-time feedback with fast response times, enabling quick decision-making in dynamic environments. They are also inexpensive compared to more advanced sensors like LiDAR or stereo vision systems, making them ideal for large-scale deployments. Their simplicity reduces system complexity and lowers maintenance needs. Overall, they provide essential functionality without excessive overhead.

- **Limitations:** Despite their benefits, proximity sensors suffer from certain limitations that affect their performance in complex settings. Their short sensing range limits their effectiveness to close-range detection, making them less useful for high-speed navigation or early obstacle detection. Accuracy can degrade in cluttered or noisy environments, especially where reflective or absorptive materials are present. Ultrasonic sensors can produce cross-talk when used in groups and IR sensors are sensitive to ambient lighting, causing false readings. They also lack the ability to distinguish between object types or provide detailed spatial mapping. Hence, they are often supplemented by additional sensors in more advanced swarm systems.

4.1.2 Vision Sensors (Cameras)

- **Purpose:** Vision sensors, commonly known as cameras, are used to capture rich visual data from the environment. This visual input allows agents to perform tasks like object recognition, target tracking, scene interpretation and navigation based on appearance cues. In swarm robotics, vision is essential for enabling behaviours such as recognizing leaders, interpreting visual signals and detecting obstacles or landmarks. Unlike basic proximity sensors, cameras can interpret complex environmental features. Vision enables a more advanced form of perception, often mimicking biological vision. It serves as the foundation for many AI-driven behaviours in modern robotic systems. The use of visual data greatly enhances situational awareness.
- **Types:** Vision sensors come in various configurations suited to different tasks. Monocular cameras use a single lens to capture 2D images, typically used for image-based detection and classification. Stereo cameras use two lenses to perceive depth, allowing for 3D vision and distance estimation. RGB-D cameras (like Intel RealSense or Kinect) provide both colour (RGB) and depth (D) data using active infrared systems. These sensors enable spatial mapping, gesture tracking and surface recognition. Some swarm systems also incorporate fisheye or omnidirectional cameras for wide-angle views. The choice of camera depends on mission requirements, environment and computational resources available to each agent.
- **Applications in Swarms:** Vision sensors enable a wide range of advanced applications in swarm robotics. They are widely used for visual localization, where agents recognize landmarks or match scenes for navigation. Cameras support object detection and tracking, allowing agents to identify targets or monitor other swarm members. They also enable gesture recognition, useful in human-swarm interaction systems. In leader-follower formations,

vision is used to track a leading agent based on visual cues. Swarms may use vision for terrain recognition, QR-code following, or aerial surveying. These capabilities make vision essential for intelligent, adaptable swarm behaviour, especially in dynamic or semi-structured environments.

- **Advantages:** Cameras provide highly detailed and dense information, offering a broad understanding of the environment. Unlike distance-only sensors, vision supports semantic perception, allowing agents to identify object types, interpret symbols, or analyse textures. Cameras are relatively low-cost and lightweight, making them suitable for small swarm agents. When combined with machine learning and computer vision algorithms, they enable advanced perception like facial recognition, anomaly detection and autonomous exploration. Vision systems are scalable and adaptable to a wide variety of tasks. Their data richness makes them ideal for both research and real-world deployment in intelligent robotic swarms.
- **Limitations:** Despite their powerful capabilities, vision sensors come with certain limitations. They are highly sensitive to environmental conditions such as lighting, glare and weather—performance can degrade in fog, darkness, or bright sunlight. Occlusion is another issue, where important objects may be hidden behind others. Vision systems require substantial computational power to process images in real-time, which can be challenging for small or power-constrained agents. Furthermore, camera data can produce false positives or misclassifications without robust algorithms and training. Privacy and ethical concerns also arise in vision-based monitoring. Therefore, vision is often used alongside other sensors for more reliable operation.

4.1.3 LiDAR (Light Detection and Ranging)

- **Purpose:** LiDAR is a powerful remote sensing technology that uses laser pulses to measure distances to surrounding objects and surfaces. It builds highly accurate 3D point clouds, which can be used to model the environment in detail. In swarm systems, LiDAR provides agents with real-time spatial awareness, allowing them to perceive terrain, structures and obstacles with high fidelity. This data enables both reactive and deliberative decision-making processes. LiDAR helps autonomous agents navigate, explore and map unknown environments, particularly in scenarios where vision-based systems may fail. Its geometric precision makes it vital for applications requiring reliable spatial understanding.
- **Applications in Swarms:** In swarm robotics, LiDAR is widely used for 3D mapping and Simultaneous Localization and Mapping (SLAM). Each agent can scan its environment and contribute to building a shared or

distributed map of the area. LiDAR also supports obstacle detection and collision avoidance, even in cluttered environments where other sensors may struggle. It enables autonomous formation control in GPS-denied or unstructured terrains. In aerial and ground-based swarms, LiDAR assists in terrain adaptation, gap detection and spatial coordination. Its high-resolution data is particularly useful in mission-critical operations such as search and rescue, environmental surveying and autonomous infrastructure inspection.

- **Advantages:** One of the greatest strengths of LiDAR is its high spatial accuracy and resolution. It provides detailed geometric information, allowing swarm agents to recognize fine environmental features such as edges, corners and elevation changes. LiDAR is independent of ambient lighting, making it highly effective in low-light or night-time operations where vision sensors underperform. It also offers a large field of view and can detect obstacles at long ranges with great consistency. The data it produces is inherently structured for easy 3D modelling. These features make LiDAR a preferred sensor in systems requiring precise mapping and localization.
- **Limitations:** Despite its advantages, LiDAR comes with some notable drawbacks. It is typically expensive, especially high-end models with long range and high resolution, which can limit its use in cost-sensitive swarm applications. LiDAR units are often power-intensive, making them less ideal for lightweight or battery-constrained platforms like micro-drones. The technology also struggles with reflective or transparent surfaces, such as water, glass, or shiny metals, which can distort readings. In addition, LiDAR systems can generate large volumes of data, requiring significant processing power and bandwidth to handle in real-time. These constraints often necessitate sensor fusion with simpler, cheaper systems for balanced performance.

4.1.4 Inertial Measurement Units (IMUs)

- **Purpose:** Inertial Measurement Units (IMUs) are essential sensors used to measure an agent's orientation, acceleration and angular velocity in space. These measurements allow robotic agents to understand how they are moving and rotating in three-dimensional space without relying on external references like GPS. In swarm systems, IMUs provide real-time feedback on each robot's dynamic state, enabling fast, reactive control. This is particularly useful in fast-moving agents like drones, where instant attitude corrections are critical. IMUs are also crucial for estimating velocity, tilt and fall detection. Their ability to function in any lighting or environmental condition makes them invaluable for both indoor and outdoor missions. As a core internal sensor, IMUs help maintain motion awareness even during communication loss or signal interference.

- **Components:** An IMU typically consists of three main components: an accelerometer, a gyroscope and sometimes a magnetometer. The accelerometer measures linear acceleration along the x, y and z axes. The gyroscope detects angular velocity, allowing for the measurement of pitch, roll and yaw. The magnetometer provides orientation data relative to Earth's magnetic field, often used as a digital compass to correct heading drift. These components work together to capture six or nine degrees of freedom (6-DOF or 9-DOF) motion data. Some advanced IMUs are equipped with onboard processing for sensor fusion and calibration. The integration of these components allows for a holistic view of a robot's motion and orientation in 3D space.
- **Applications in Swarms:** IMUs serve a wide range of functions in swarm robotics. They are commonly used for motion estimation, especially in GPS-denied environments where external positioning is unreliable. IMUs allow agents to estimate their pose and velocity through dead reckoning by integrating acceleration and rotation data. In stability control, IMUs help maintain balance and orientation—especially in flying swarms or legged robots. They are also used to detect collisions, sudden impacts, or falls, which is critical for damage prevention and recovery strategies. IMUs support trajectory planning by providing internal motion feedback, allowing swarm agents to navigate in real-time with greater precision. Their fast-sampling rate makes them ideal for closed-loop control systems in dynamic operations.
- **Advantages:** IMUs offer several advantages that make them well-suited for embedded swarm systems. They are extremely compact and can be easily embedded in small platforms like micro-drones or insect-scale robots. IMUs are also low-power, allowing them to operate continuously without significant energy drain. Since they rely only on internal measurements, they can function independently of external infrastructure—a vital asset in remote or obstructed environments. IMUs have fast response times, typically in the range of microseconds, enabling high-frequency control loops for stability and orientation correction. They are also relatively inexpensive, especially at moderate precision levels, making them ideal for use in large numbers within a swarm. These characteristics support distributed autonomy and decentralized motion sensing.

- **Limitations:** Despite their usefulness, IMUs have some notable limitations. One of the primary issues is drift over time—small measurement errors accumulate during integration, leading to significant inaccuracies if not corrected. Gyroscopes, in particular, are susceptible to bias drift, which can degrade the estimation of orientation. IMUs are also sensitive to vibrations and noise, which can introduce errors in mobile or unstable platforms. To overcome these issues, IMUs are often combined with other sensors (e.g., GPS, vision, or LiDAR) in sensor fusion frameworks. This fusion is computationally demanding and requires well-calibrated models. Moreover, magnetometers can be affected by local magnetic fields, leading to heading errors. While IMUs provide excellent short-term motion sensing, they require continuous correction to maintain long-term accuracy.

4.1.5 GPS (Global Positioning System)

- **Purpose:** The Global Positioning System (GPS) is a satellite-based navigation technology designed to provide global position coordinates in terms of latitude, longitude and altitude. It enables autonomous agents to determine their absolute location anywhere on Earth, as long as there is a clear line of sight to multiple satellites. In swarm robotics, GPS serves as a core technology for outdoor positioning and route planning. It allows each robot or drone in a swarm to know its global position independently and navigate with a shared spatial reference frame. This positioning data is critical for aligning with digital maps, coordinating movements, or maintaining formations. GPS is especially vital in missions such as area coverage, surveying and exploration where global awareness is necessary.
- **Applications in Swarms:** GPS is heavily utilized in outdoor swarm operations that require synchronized movement across wide or distributed areas. In formation control, GPS helps maintain consistent spacing and orientation among agents, ensuring cohesive group behavior during motion. It also supports geofencing, where swarm members are programmed to remain within predefined geographic boundaries for safety or mission-specific constraints. In agricultural robots, drones use GPS to perform tasks like crop spraying or field inspection. For delivery or transport systems, GPS provides route tracking and target localization. Additionally, GPS data can serve as a baseline input for more complex positioning systems, such as GPS-aided SLAM or hybrid localization strategies.
- **Advantages:** One of the main advantages of GPS is that it offers absolute positioning, providing direct access to real-world coordinates without requiring pre-mapped environments or external landmarks. This makes GPS ideal for large-scale navigation, especially in open areas like deserts,

oceans and rural landscapes. It is a well-established, globally supported technology with widespread hardware availability and standardized protocols. Modern GPS receivers are compact and energy-efficient, making them suitable even for small swarm robots. Some modules also support differential GPS (DGPS) or RTK (Real-Time Kinematic) positioning, offering centimeter-level accuracy. This level of precision greatly enhances swarm coordination, positioning reliability and mission execution quality.

- **Limitations:** Despite its benefits, GPS has notable limitations that can restrict its use in certain swarm applications. It is ineffective indoors, underground, or in urban canyons where satellite signals are blocked or reflected, causing positioning errors. This makes GPS unreliable in environments like warehouses, tunnels, forests, or cities with tall buildings. Additionally, GPS signals are susceptible to interference, jamming and spoofing, raising concerns for security and robustness in critical missions. Even in ideal conditions, GPS accuracy can vary based on atmospheric effects and satellite geometry. Moreover, standard GPS lacks the precision required for fine control without augmentation. Therefore, in many swarm systems, GPS is combined with other localization techniques (e.g., vision, IMUs, LiDAR) to achieve reliable and accurate positioning in diverse environments.

4.1.6 Communication Sensors/Modules

- **Purpose:** Communication sensors or modules are critical components in swarm robotics that enable data exchange between individual agents. This communication allows swarm members to share information about their surroundings, status, intentions, or sensory data, which is essential for coordinated group behaviour. Without effective communication, swarms cannot synchronize actions or reach collective decisions. These modules provide the infrastructure for distributed intelligence, where agents cooperate by sharing local observations and processing results collectively. Communication enables real-time updates, dynamic task allocation and flexible response to environmental changes. Ultimately, it supports the emergent behaviours that characterize swarm intelligence.
- **Technologies:** Swarm communication relies on various wireless technologies, each with its own trade-offs in range, bandwidth, power consumption and network topology. Commonly used technologies include Wi-Fi, which offers high data rates but relatively high-power use and moderate range; Bluetooth, suitable for short-range, low-power connections; and ZigBee, which supports mesh networking with low power consumption for moderate distances. RF modules provide flexible options

for custom frequency bands and ranges. LoRa (Long Range) is popular for low-power, long-distance communication in large-scale outdoor swarms but with low bandwidth. Selection depends on the swarm size, mission requirements and environment, balancing communication reliability and energy efficiency.

- **Applications in Swarms:** Communication modules are foundational for numerous swarm applications such as coordination, where agents synchronize movement or tasks. They enable consensus algorithms, allowing agents to agree on shared goals, maps, or environmental interpretations. Communication facilitates behaviour sharing, whereby discoveries by one agent are propagated through the swarm, improving collective knowledge. It also supports distributed decision-making, critical for adapting to dynamic and unpredictable environments without centralized control. For example, in search-and-rescue missions, communication helps agents report obstacles, victims, or hazards. In agricultural swarms, it supports task allocation like pesticide spraying or crop monitoring. Overall, communication underpins swarm robustness and flexibility.
- **Advantages:** The primary advantage of communication sensors is their ability to enable real-time cooperation among swarm agents. This cooperation leads to enhanced efficiency, scalability and resilience. Wireless communication supports decentralized control, reducing single points of failure. It enables swarms to operate in complex environments by pooling sensor data, thereby compensating for individual sensor limitations. Communication also allows for dynamic reconfiguration, where swarm size and behaviour can adapt on the fly. These modules support multi-hop networking, extending communication range beyond direct line-of-sight. Furthermore, communication facilitates human-swarm interaction, allowing operators to monitor and influence swarm behaviour remotely.
- **Limitations:** Despite their essential role, communication modules face several limitations that can impact swarm performance. Bandwidth constraints limit the volume and rate of data that can be shared, especially in large swarms or data-intensive tasks like video streaming. Communication channels are vulnerable to interference from environmental noise, other wireless devices, or physical obstacles, leading to packet loss or delays. Range limitations impose challenges for wide-area operations without relay or mesh networking. Energy consumption for communication can be significant, reducing operational time in battery-powered agents. Additionally, communication protocols must address security concerns to prevent spoofing or hacking, which could disrupt swarm coordination.

Designing robust, scalable communication networks remains an active research challenge.

4.1.7 Sound and Acoustic Sensors

- **Purpose:** Sound and acoustic sensors detect sound waves or use ultrasonic signals for various sensing and communication purposes. Unlike radio-frequency (RF) communication, acoustic signals travel effectively through mediums such as water, soil, or dense vegetation where RF signals attenuate or become unreliable. These sensors can capture environmental sounds, measure distances through echolocation, or facilitate communication between agents via modulated sound waves. In swarm robotics, sound-based sensing allows agents to perceive obstacles, localize themselves relative to others, or synchronize activities. Acoustic sensors thus provide a complementary modality to electromagnetic sensors, especially in environments where RF communication is limited or impossible.
- **Applications in Swarms:** In swarm applications, sound and acoustic sensors are crucial for underwater operations, where RF signals cannot propagate effectively. Underwater swarms rely heavily on acoustic communication to coordinate behaviours, share sensor data and execute collective tasks. Acoustic echolocation techniques enable agents to detect obstacles, map surroundings and estimate distances, similar to sonar. Swarms operating in underground or dense forest environments may also use sound sensors to complement other modalities. Additionally, sound sensors can facilitate gesture or audio-based communication in human-robot interaction scenarios. In air, ultrasonic sensors help with close-range obstacle avoidance and altitude measurement in drones. Overall, acoustic sensing expands swarm capabilities to challenging environments.
- **Advantages:** Acoustic sensors excel in environments where RF signals are limited or unreliable, such as underwater, underground, or inside thick structures. They can operate over moderate distances with relatively low power consumption, making them suitable for long-duration missions. Ultrasonic sensors provide precise range measurements with millimeter-level accuracy for obstacle detection and navigation. Acoustic communication can be directional and less prone to interception compared to RF, offering security benefits in some applications. Furthermore, sound waves travel well in water, enabling swarms to operate in oceans, lakes, or pipes. Acoustic sensing hardware is generally compact, lightweight and cost-effective, facilitating easy integration into diverse swarm platforms.

- **Limitations:** Despite their benefits, sound and acoustic sensors face significant limitations that can restrict their use. Their data transmission rates are much lower than RF-based systems, limiting bandwidth and the amount of information shared. Acoustic signals are vulnerable to ambient noise and reverberations, which can cause interference, signal distortion and reduced accuracy. Environmental factors like temperature, salinity and medium density can affect sound wave propagation unpredictably. Ultrasonic sensors have a limited effective range, typically just a few meters, which restricts their use in large-scale swarms. Additionally, sound-based systems may introduce delays due to slower wave propagation speed compared to RF. These constraints often necessitate combining acoustic sensing with other modalities for robust swarm operation.

4.1.8 Tactile and Force Sensors

- **Purpose:** Tactile and force sensors are designed to detect physical contact, pressure and forces exerted on a robot's surface or manipulative appendages. These sensors mimic the sense of touch in biological organisms, providing critical information about interaction with the environment or other agents. In swarm robotics, tactile sensors help agents detect collisions, determine grip strength and measure forces during cooperative tasks such as carrying or assembling objects. They enable feedback for safe manipulation, preventing damage to both the robot and the objects being handled. These sensors also assist in terrain interaction, allowing ground-based swarms to sense texture, compliance, or obstacles by physical contact, enhancing environmental awareness beyond remote sensing methods.
- **Applications in Swarms:** Within swarm systems, tactile and force sensors are widely used for collision detection to prevent damage during dense group operations or when navigating cluttered environments. They enable cooperative manipulation, allowing multiple agents to grasp, move, or assemble objects collaboratively with precise force control. This is essential in tasks like construction, agriculture, or search and rescue, where physical interaction with the environment is required. Tactile feedback also supports delicate object handling, where excessive force could cause damage. Additionally, tactile sensors help agents maintain stable footing on uneven or slippery surfaces by detecting ground contact forces. These sensors enable swarms to perform complex physical tasks requiring dexterity and real-time touch feedback.
- **Advantages:** The main advantage of tactile and force sensors is their ability to provide direct, contact-based sensing, which complements remote sensing technologies like cameras or LiDAR. This contact sensing is critical

for tasks that involve physical interaction, such as grasping, pushing, or supporting loads. Tactile sensors provide high spatial resolution over the contact surface, allowing detection of pressure distribution and slip, which is vital for adaptive grip and manipulation. They are generally compact and lightweight, making them easy to integrate on small robotic limbs or bodies. These sensors improve safety by enabling collision avoidance through immediate feedback. They also help swarms achieve complex coordinated behaviours that require physical teamwork and environment interaction.

- **Limitations:** Despite their benefits, tactile and force sensors have limitations that can affect their deployment in swarm robotics. Their use is limited to close-range or direct physical contact scenarios, meaning they cannot provide environmental information at a distance. These sensors can be prone to wear and tear, requiring durable materials or regular maintenance, especially in harsh conditions. Tactile sensors often produce large volumes of high-frequency data which require efficient processing and filtering. Integrating tactile sensing with other perception modalities can be challenging, as it demands precise timing and coordination. Additionally, designing sensors sensitive enough to detect subtle forces yet robust enough for rough environments remains complex. Consequently, tactile sensing is typically part of a multi-modal sensing strategy in swarms.

4.1.9 Environmental Sensors

- **Purpose:** Environmental sensors are specialized devices designed to measure various environmental parameters such as temperature, humidity, gas concentrations (e.g., CO2, methane), light intensity and air quality. These sensors provide crucial data about the ambient conditions in which a swarm operates. Understanding the environment allows swarm agents to adapt their behaviour, detect hazardous conditions, or gather scientific data. For instance, temperature and gas sensors help identify fire, toxic leaks, or pollution, while light sensors can aid in day-night cycle detection or shadow avoidance. By integrating environmental sensing, swarms gain context-awareness, enhancing their ability to operate safely and effectively across diverse and potentially hazardous environments.
- **Applications in Swarms:** Environmental sensors are widely used in swarm applications involving environmental monitoring and disaster response. Swarms equipped with these sensors can collectively map pollution levels, track gas leaks, or monitor climate variables over large geographic areas. In hazardous environments such as chemical plants, mines, or forests, they enable early detection of fires, toxic gases, or harmful radiation, prompting rapid swarm adaptation or evacuation. Environmental data also guides

adaptive behaviors, such as changing formation to optimize coverage or retreating from dangerous zones. In agriculture, these sensors help optimize watering, fertilizing and pest control by providing real-time field conditions. These capabilities significantly expand the operational scope and usefulness of robotic swarms.

- **Advantages:** One of the key advantages of environmental sensors is that they are typically lightweight and low-power, making them easy to deploy on small, battery-operated swarm agents. Many environmental sensors are designed to be modular and compact, allowing integration with other sensor systems without significant weight or size penalties. They offer robustness to environmental stressors, functioning reliably in varied weather and terrain conditions. Their low power consumption extends the operational time of swarms during long-term deployments. Additionally, environmental sensors often come at a relatively low cost, enabling large-scale distribution across swarm members. This enables wide-area environmental data collection with high spatial density through swarm cooperation.
- **Limitations:** Environmental sensors generally suffer from slow response times due to the physical and chemical processes involved in sensing, which can limit their effectiveness in fast-changing conditions. Their spatial resolution is often limited, as individual sensors only provide point measurements, requiring many agents to achieve detailed environmental maps. Sensor calibration and drift over time can impact measurement accuracy, especially in harsh or contaminated environments. Environmental factors like dust, moisture, or temperature extremes may degrade sensor performance or lifespan. Moreover, interpreting environmental data often requires complex data fusion and context analysis to avoid false alarms or misinterpretations. These challenges necessitate careful sensor selection and integration strategies in swarm design.

4.1.10 Sensor Fusion in Swarms

- **Purpose:** Sensor fusion is the process of combining data from multiple heterogeneous sensors to create a more accurate, reliable and comprehensive understanding of the environment and the swarm's own state. By integrating complementary information from sources such as vision, LiDAR, IMUs, GPS and environmental sensors, sensor fusion compensates for individual sensor weaknesses and noise. This results in improved perception and localization critical for swarm coordination and decision-making. For example, fusing IMU data with GPS can provide smooth, drift-corrected position estimates, while combining vision and ultrasonic data can enhance obstacle detection. Sensor fusion is thus fundamental to enabling resilient swarm operation in diverse, dynamic and uncertain environments.

- **Techniques:** Several mathematical and computational techniques are employed for sensor fusion; each tailored to different data characteristics and requirements. Kalman filtering is widely used for linear systems and Gaussian noise, allowing recursive estimation of an agent's state (e.g., position, velocity) by optimally blending noisy sensor inputs. For non-linear or more complex fusion problems, Extended Kalman Filters (EKF) or Unscented Kalman Filters (UKF) are used. Bayesian fusion frameworks provide probabilistic models to combine uncertain data and update beliefs based on new sensor readings. More recently, machine learning models like deep neural networks have been applied to learn complex sensor relationships and perform fusion end-to-end, particularly for vision and high-dimensional data. Effective fusion requires synchronization, calibration and sometimes real-time adaptation.
- **Applications in Swarms:** In swarm robotics, sensor fusion enhances many critical functions such as precise localization, enabling agents to know their positions with higher accuracy even when individual sensors fail or are noisy. It supports robust navigation by combining obstacle information from multiple sensors to create reliable maps and safe trajectories. Fusion also improves situational awareness, allowing the swarm to detect and interpret complex environmental cues that single sensors might miss. Additionally, sensor fusion supports fault detection and recovery by cross-validating sensor data to identify anomalies. In cooperative missions, fused data can be shared across agents to build a collective perception that exceeds any single member's capability, fostering intelligent, coordinated behavior.
- **Advantages:** The primary advantage of sensor fusion lies in its ability to improve accuracy and reliability of perception and localization beyond what individual sensors can achieve alone. It reduces uncertainty and noise effects, enabling smoother control and better decision-making in dynamic and cluttered environments. Sensor fusion increases system robustness by mitigating sensor failures or adverse conditions that affect single modalities. It allows swarms to operate in diverse environments — indoors, outdoors, underwater — by leveraging the strengths of different sensor types. Moreover, fusion facilitates higher-level data abstraction, supporting advanced algorithms for mapping, tracking and behaviour prediction. This comprehensive sensing is essential for scalable, autonomous swarm operations.

- **Limitations:** Despite its benefits, sensor fusion introduces significant challenges. One major limitation is the increased computational complexity required to process, align and integrate large volumes of heterogeneous sensor data in real-time, especially on resource-constrained swarm agents. Fusion algorithms often require precise synchronization of sensor measurements, which can be difficult in distributed systems with communication delays. Sensor calibration and error modelling are critical but can be complex to maintain, particularly when sensors degrade or drift over time. Moreover, poorly designed fusion strategies can lead to information conflicts or overconfidence in incorrect data. Developing robust, scalable fusion methods that balance accuracy with efficiency remains an ongoing research challenge in swarm robotics.

4.2 COLLECTIVE PERCEPTION AND SITUATIONAL AWARENESS

Swarm intelligence represents a decentralized and self-organizing approach to problem-solving, inspired by the behaviour of social organisms such as ants, bees, birds and fish. Within this paradigm, multiple autonomous agents operate independently yet cooperatively to achieve complex, large-scale objectives that would be difficult or impossible for a single agent to accomplish alone. At the heart of this collective functionality lies the intertwined concepts of collective perception and situational awareness—two foundational pillars that empower a swarm to sense, interpret and adapt to its environment in a robust, flexible and scalable manner. Unlike traditional centralized systems that rely on a single point of information processing, swarm systems distribute perception and decision-making across all agents, promoting fault tolerance and real-time responsiveness.

Collective perception refers to the mechanism by which a swarm of agents aggregates and integrates individual sensory data to construct a more comprehensive, unified understanding of the environment. Each agent possesses only partial, local observations, but through communication, interaction and data fusion techniques, the swarm achieves a global perspective that transcends individual limitations. This emergent capability allows the swarm to identify environmental features, detect obstacles, monitor changes and localize targets with a level of precision and reliability that no single agent could attain on its own. Situational awareness, on the other hand, extends beyond perception by incorporating cognitive elements—recognizing patterns, predicting outcomes and dynamically responding to changes in the environment or task. It encompasses the swarm's ability to maintain a coherent understanding of the current state of both internal and external conditions, including agent locations, goals, threats and environmental dynamics. Through continuous information exchange and behaviour adaptation, swarm agents collaboratively build a shared mental model of their surroundings. This enables them to make informed decisions, allocate tasks efficiently, synchronize movements and respond to unforeseen events in a coordinated manner. These two processes—collective perception and situational awareness—are not merely beneficial but essential for ensuring resilience, scalability and adaptability in real-world swarm applications such as search and rescue missions, environmental monitoring, autonomous exploration and surveillance. They enable a swarm to operate effectively in dynamic and uncertain environments without the need for central control or global knowledge. Advances in sensor technologies, wireless communication, machine learning and distributed computing have further accelerated the development of sophisticated algorithms that enhance these capabilities, allowing artificial swarms to emulate and, in some cases, surpass the efficiencies observed in natural systems. In essence, collective perception allows agents to see more than they individually can, while situational awareness enables them to understand more together than any one agent ever could. Their synergy is a key enabler for emergent intelligence in swarm systems. Understanding how these two constructs function, interact and evolve within multi-agent systems is crucial to unlocking the full potential of swarm intelligence in increasingly complex, real-time operational scenarios.

4.2.1 Collective Perception

Collective perception refers to the process by which a group of agents shares and integrates sensory data to build a more complete and accurate representation of the environment than what any single agent could perceive individually.

Purpose: It enhances the swarm's capability to detect, recognize and track objects or features in a dynamic environment, even when individual sensors have limited coverage or resolution.

Characteristics:

- **Distributed Data Collection:** In swarm robotics, distributed data collection allows individual agents to independently gather sensor data across a wide area simultaneously. This approach increases coverage and reduces the time required to monitor large or complex environments. Each agent processes local information, enabling efficient and scalable data acquisition. Distributed collection also minimizes the risk of single points of failure, improving overall system robustness. Together, the swarm can build a comprehensive, real-time picture of the environment.
- **Redundant Sensing:** Redundant sensing involves multiple agents or sensors measuring the same environmental variables to increase reliability and accuracy. This redundancy helps detect and correct individual sensor errors or failures by cross-validating data. It also enhances fault tolerance, ensuring that the swarm continues to function even if some sensors degrade.

Redundant sensing improves confidence in critical measurements, which is essential for safety-critical operations. By comparing overlapping data, swarms can filter noise and reduce uncertainty in perception.

- **Information Sharing:** Information sharing is the communication of sensor data, observations, or processed knowledge among swarm agents to create a collective understanding. It enables coordinated decision-making and collective responses to environmental changes or mission goals. Effective sharing requires robust communication protocols that handle delays, bandwidth limits and potential data loss. By pooling data, the swarm leverages the diverse perspectives of multiple agents, enhancing situational awareness. This shared knowledge supports dynamic task allocation and cooperative behaviour.
- **Sensor Fusion Across Agents:** Sensor fusion across agents combines data from multiple swarm members to generate a unified, higher-quality perception of the environment. This inter-agent fusion reduces individual uncertainties and compensates for sensor limitations by leveraging complementary sensing modalities. Distributed fusion algorithms ensure that data integration happens efficiently, even with communication constraints. This collaborative approach enables the swarm to perform complex tasks requiring precise localization and mapping. Cross-agent fusion strengthens robustness, accuracy and adaptability in challenging conditions.

Example Applications:

- Monitoring large areas (e.g., environmental sensing, search and rescue)
- Target tracking with partial views
- Object detection in cluttered or occluded scenes

4.2.2 Situational Awareness in Swarms

Situational Awareness in Swarms refers to the collective capability of a swarm of autonomous agents to not only perceive their environment but also to interpret the contextual relevance of that information and anticipate future developments. This process involves three critical levels: perception of the environment (e.g., detecting obstacles, agents, or dynamic changes), comprehension of the current situation (e.g., understanding mission progress, identifying potential threats or opportunities) and projection of future states (e.g., predicting the movement of targets, estimating resource consumption, or foreseeing environmental shifts). By integrating these layers, the swarm develops a shared, real-time understanding of its operational context, enabling it to make coordinated, adaptive and goal-oriented decisions without centralized control. Situational awareness thus serves as a foundation for intelligent behaviour in swarm systems, supporting functions such as task allocation, path planning, collision avoidance and reconfiguration in response to emerging conditions. It is especially vital in dynamic, unpredictable environments where quick, collective adaptation is key to mission success.

Three Levels (adapted from human-centric SA models):

- **Perception of Elements in the Environment:** This first level involves the basic detection and recognition of key elements such as the positions of swarm agents, obstacles and potential threats within the environment. It relies on raw sensor data to build an initial snapshot of what is happening around the agents. Accurate perception is crucial as it forms the foundation for higher-level understanding. Sensors like cameras, LiDAR and proximity detectors play a central role in this stage. Without reliable perception, subsequent comprehension and projection cannot be effectively achieved.
- **Comprehension of Their Meaning:** At the second level, the swarm processes and interprets perceived data to understand the significance of environmental elements. For example, recognizing that a detected object is blocking a critical path or identifying an intruder entering a restricted zone. This involves integrating sensor inputs and applying contextual knowledge or rules to evaluate the situation. Comprehension enables swarms to distinguish normal conditions from anomalies or threats. It guides decision-making and the selection of appropriate responses based on the current state of the environment.
- **Projection of Future States:** The third level involves anticipating future developments by estimating how the environment and agents will evolve over time. For instance, predicting the path of a moving obstacle or the spread of a hazard. This forward-looking capability supports proactive planning and timely interventions, reducing risks and improving mission success. Projection requires models of dynamics and behaviour, often leveraging machine learning or probabilistic reasoning. Effective projection helps swarms adapt strategies and maintain situational awareness even in rapidly changing conditions.

Importance: Enables real-time decision-making, threat avoidance, efficient task distribution and robust navigation in uncertain environments.

4.2.3 Communication for Shared Awareness

Communication for Shared Awareness is a cornerstone of swarm intelligence, enabling individual agents to transcend their limited local perceptions and contribute to a broader, cohesive understanding of the environment. In a swarm, no single agent possesses complete knowledge of the system's state or the external world. Instead, shared awareness arises through continuous, distributed exchanges of information among agents. This communication—whether explicit through message passing or implicit through observation and interaction—serves as the connective tissue that binds the swarm into a functional whole. It allows agents to synchronize behaviours, align goals, coordinate movements and respond collectively to dynamic changes and emerging threats. Effective communication ensures that situational information—such as the presence of obstacles, discovery of resources, agent status, or environmental changes—is disseminated efficiently across the swarm. This enables agents to maintain an up-to-date, consistent internal model of their operational context. Such shared understanding is crucial for decision-making processes that depend on more than just local data, such as global path planning, formation control, or collaborative task execution. Furthermore, communication allows for emergent behaviours—complex patterns or problem-solving capabilities that arise from the simple interactions of individual agents following basic rules. The design of communication mechanisms in swarm systems must balance several constraints, including bandwidth limitations, energy efficiency, latency and robustness to noise or signal loss. Depending on the application and environment, different communication models may be employed, such as direct peer-to-peer messaging, broadcast schemes, stigmergic interaction (indirect coordination via environmental markers), or bio-inspired signaling techniques. The choice of model significantly affects how well the swarm can achieve shared awareness, especially in large-scale or harsh environments. Importantly, communication in swarms is not just about data exchange—it is about enabling coherent group cognition. It transforms a collection of independent agents into a unified system capable of perceiving, reasoning and acting as one. The richness and reliability of this communication underpin the swarm's ability to adapt, self-organize and succeed in complex, distributed tasks where central control is impractical or impossible. As such, developing scalable, fault-tolerant and adaptive communication strategies remains a vital research focus in advancing the capabilities of swarm robotics, autonomous sensor networks and multi-agent systems in general.

Mechanism: Agents exchange sensory data, object detections, map segments, or processed perceptions via wireless communication (e.g., Wi-Fi, ZigBee, LoRa).

Strategies:

- **Broadcast-Based Sharing:** In broadcast-based sharing, every agent transmits its sensor data or information to all other agents within communication range. This approach maximizes data availability and ensures that every member has access to the most current information. It is simple to implement but can lead to communication congestion and energy drain in large swarms. Despite these challenges, broadcasting supports rapid dissemination of critical data, making it suitable for time-sensitive tasks. Efficient protocols are necessary to manage bandwidth and avoid message collisions.

- **Peer-to-Peer Exchange:** Peer-to-peer exchange involves agents sharing information directly only with their immediate neighbours rather than the entire swarm. This localized communication reduces network load and conserves energy by limiting the data flow to relevant agents. It supports scalability and robustness since failure of one node does not isolate the network. However, it may increase the time required for information to propagate throughout the swarm. Peer-to-peer exchange is ideal for decentralized systems relying on local interactions to achieve global coordination.
- **Leader-Based Aggregation:** In leader-based aggregation, one or more designated leader agents collect data from the swarm, fuse or process it centrally and redistribute the summarized information. This hierarchical approach simplifies data fusion and decision-making by centralizing computation. It reduces redundant transmissions and can improve accuracy by leveraging a more powerful leader node. However, it introduces potential single points of failure and may suffer from communication bottlenecks. Leader-based aggregation is useful in swarms with heterogeneous agents where some have greater processing capabilities.
- **Consensus Algorithms:** Consensus algorithms enable all agents to collectively agree on a shared interpretation of the environment despite individual differences in sensor data or viewpoints. These distributed protocols iteratively exchange information and update estimates to converge on common values such as position, map features, or threat assessments. Consensus ensures consistent swarm behaviour and prevents conflicting decisions. It enhances robustness to sensor noise and communication delays. Though computationally intensive, consensus algorithms are fundamental for cooperative tasks requiring unified swarm understanding (Table-1).

Table 1 : Description of Strategy in summarised form

Strategy	Description	Advantages	Disadvantages	Best Suited For
Broadcast-Based Sharing	All agents send data to all others within range.	Maximizes data availability; fast dissemination; simple to implement.	High communication load; energy-intensive; risk of congestion.	Time-sensitive tasks requiring rapid information spread.

Strategy	Description	Advantages	Disadvantages	Best Suited For
Peer-to-Peer Exchange	Agents share data only with immediate neighbors.	Reduces network load; conserves energy; scalable and robust.	Slower information propagation across swarm.	Decentralized systems using local interactions.
Leader-Based Aggregation	Leader(s) collect, process and redistribute data.	Centralized processing; reduces redundancy; improved accuracy.	Potential single point of failure; communication bottlenecks.	Swarms with heterogeneous agents or centralized decision-making needs.
Consensus Algorithms	Agents iteratively reach agreement on shared data.	Ensures consistent behavior; robust to noise and delays.	Computationally intensive; slower convergence.	Cooperative tasks needing unified swarm understanding.

Challenges:

- **Bandwidth Limitations:** Swarm systems often operate with limited wireless bandwidth, which constrains the volume and frequency of data that can be shared among agents. High data rates from sensors like cameras or LiDAR can quickly saturate the network, leading to dropped packets or delayed transmissions. Efficient data compression, prioritization and scheduling are essential to mitigate bandwidth bottlenecks. Limited bandwidth also restricts scalability, as increasing the number of agents intensifies communication demands. Managing bandwidth is critical to maintaining timely and reliable swarm coordination.
- **Latency and Synchronization Issues:** Communication delays and lack of precise timing synchronization among agents can disrupt the coordination and fusion of sensor data. Latency causes outdated information to circulate, potentially leading to incorrect decisions or collisions. Synchronization challenges arise because agents may operate asynchronously with varying processing speeds and communication intervals. To address this, algorithms must tolerate delays and incorporate time-stamping or predictive models. Minimizing latency and ensuring temporal alignment are vital for real-time swarm responsiveness.
- **Data Consistency Across Agents:** Maintaining consistent and up-to-date information across all swarm members is challenging due to communication losses, network partitioning and asynchronous updates. Inconsistent data can cause agents to have conflicting views of the environment, leading to uncoordinated or unsafe actions. Mechanisms such as consensus algorithms, version control and fault-tolerant protocols are required

to ensure coherence. Data consistency is particularly difficult in large, dynamic swarms with frequent topology changes. Reliable consistency guarantees are foundational for effective collective behaviour.

- **Privacy and Security in Open Networks:** Swarm communications often occur over open or unsecured wireless channels, making them vulnerable to eavesdropping, spoofing and cyber-attacks. Unauthorized access can compromise sensitive mission data or allow malicious agents to disrupt swarm operation. Ensuring privacy and security requires encryption, authentication protocols and intrusion detection mechanisms tailored to resource-constrained swarm agents. Balancing security measures with the limited computational power and energy of agents remains a complex challenge. Robust security is essential to protect the integrity and trustworthiness of swarm systems.

4.2.4 Techniques for Achieving Collective Perception

- **Multi-Agent SLAM (Simultaneous Localization and Mapping):** Multi-Agent SLAM is a cooperative process where multiple autonomous agents work together to build a consistent and unified map of an unknown environment while simultaneously estimating their own positions within it. Unlike traditional SLAM where a single robot incrementally constructs a map using its onboard sensors, multi-agent SLAM distributes this task across a team. Each agent collects local observations of the environment and shares this information with others to collaboratively generate a global representation. Communication is key, as it allows agents to align their individual maps, correct localization errors and minimize redundant exploration. Techniques such as loop closure detection, map merging and transformation alignment help fuse spatial data across agents. This collaborative mapping not only improves accuracy and scalability but also enhances robustness in dynamic or GPS-denied environments. It is especially vital in tasks such as search and rescue, exploration and surveillance where quick and coordinated spatial understanding is required.
- **Distributed Sensor Fusion:** Distributed sensor fusion enables each robot in a swarm to enhance its situational understanding by combining its own sensor data with that received from neighbouring agents. This process allows the swarm to generate more accurate, robust and noise-tolerant estimates of environmental features or system states. Each agent acts as a node in a distributed network, where local computations are performed using probabilistic models such as Kalman filters for linear systems, particle filters for non-linear systems, or Bayesian inference to manage uncertainty. In modern systems, machine learning models like neural networks are also

used to identify patterns across multi-modal sensor inputs. The fusion process does not rely on a central processor, which enhances system resilience and scalability. It reduces the blind spots and sensing limitations of individual agents, allowing the swarm to operate more effectively in complex, cluttered, or partially observable environments.

- **Consensus-Based State Estimation:** Consensus-based state estimation is a distributed approach where agents iteratively exchange and refine their local estimates to reach a shared, consistent view of the environment or system state. Rather than depending on a central coordinator, each agent maintains its own estimate—such as location, velocity, or target position—and updates it by averaging or merging with the estimates of neighbouring agents. Repeated interactions lead to convergence toward a consensus, even in the presence of noisy measurements or limited communication. Algorithms like distributed Kalman consensus filters, average consensus and gossip protocols facilitate this process. This method is particularly powerful in maintaining synchronization, alignment and coordination across the swarm. It also enhances fault tolerance, as the overall estimate does not collapse if a single agent fails or becomes disconnected. Consensus-based estimation is foundational for applications like formation control, cooperative tracking and swarm decision-making.
- **Visual and Object Consensus:** Visual and object consensus involves agents using multiple viewpoints to collaboratively identify and localize objects within a shared environment. Each agent contributes partial visual data—such as images or depth readings—based on its perspective, which may vary due to position, lighting, or occlusion. By combining these different views, the swarm constructs a more complete and accurate representation of an object's identity, shape, size, or pose. Techniques such as multi-view geometry, feature matching and 3D reconstruction are employed to merge visual inputs. Object recognition can be enhanced using deep learning models trained to integrate spatial and semantic information across viewpoints. Consensus mechanisms help filter out inconsistencies and resolve ambiguities, especially in cluttered or dynamic scenes. This approach is critical in tasks like collaborative inspection, object handoff, or target tracking, where reliable perception must emerge from partial, noisy and decentralized data.

4.2.5 Benefits of Collective Perception & Awareness

- **Greater Coverage of Large or Complex Environments:** Swarm-based systems excel at exploring and monitoring vast or intricate environments due to their distributed nature. Multiple agents can be deployed simultaneously, spreading out to maximize spatial coverage and minimize blind spots. This is particularly beneficial in environments that are too hazardous, remote, or complex for centralized systems or single robots. Whether navigating urban ruins, underwater zones, or dense forests, swarms provide scalable and efficient exploration capabilities. Their ability to coordinate locally ensures that agents avoid redundant paths and optimize their trajectories. As a result, mission objectives such as mapping, surveillance, or search and rescue can be achieved more thoroughly and efficiently.

- **Enhanced Accuracy Through Redundancy:** The presence of multiple agents collecting overlapping data ensures that swarm systems benefit from built-in redundancy. When multiple sensors observe the same region or event, their data can be fused to reduce noise, increase precision and validate findings. Redundant observations help correct errors or uncertainties that might arise from individual sensor limitations, such as poor lighting or occlusions. This leads to more robust perception, navigation and decision-making. In localization, for example, multiple viewpoints improve triangulation accuracy. The redundancy not only improves the quality of situational awareness but also boosts system reliability under real-world operational stress.
- **Fault Tolerance (Individual Sensor Failure Doesn't Collapse System):** Swarm systems are inherently fault-tolerant, as their decentralized structure ensures that the failure of a single agent or sensor does not compromise the overall mission. If one-unit malfunctions or is lost, neighbouring agents can compensate by taking over its tasks or extending coverage. This resilience is vital in unpredictable or harsh environments where damage, communication loss, or sensor degradation is likely. The system's performance degrades gracefully rather than catastrophically. Fault detection and recovery strategies can also be implemented collectively, enhancing the swarm's ability to maintain functionality and autonomy even under partial failure conditions.
- **Supports Coordination, Path Planning and Adaptive Behaviours:** Communication and shared situational awareness within the swarm directly support dynamic coordination and path planning. Agents can negotiate roles, avoid collisions and distribute tasks based on real-time information. This allows the swarm to adapt to changing goals or environments—re-routing paths in response to obstacles, redistributing coverage when terrain changes, or reallocating resources as conditions evolve. These adaptive behaviours emerge from local interactions guided by swarm rules

rather than global directives. This flexibility is crucial in time-sensitive or mission-critical applications where pre-programmed strategies are insufficient or infeasible.

- **Enables Emergent Intelligence Without Centralized Control:** Swarm intelligence enables sophisticated group behaviour to emerge from simple, local rules and interactions among agents. Without relying on a central controller, the system collectively perceives, decides and acts in a coherent way. This decentralization reduces communication overhead, increases scalability and improves resilience to single-point failures. Emergent intelligence allows the swarm to solve complex tasks—such as mapping, tracking, or environmental adaptation—that no individual agent could manage alone. It's a hallmark of bio-inspired robotics and a key factor behind the efficiency of natural systems like ant colonies or bird flocks. In artificial swarms, it unlocks powerful, self-organizing capabilities ideal for real-world deployment.

4.2.6 Real-World Applications

- **Autonomous Drone Swarms:** Autonomous drone swarms perform coordinated surveillance by collaboratively covering large areas with overlapping sensor fields. They create detailed terrain maps using onboard cameras and LiDAR, sharing data in real-time to build comprehensive 3D models. These swarms adapt their flight paths dynamically to avoid obstacles and maintain formations. Applications include disaster monitoring, wildlife tracking and agricultural surveys. Their decentralized coordination enhances coverage efficiency and fault tolerance in complex environments.
- **Warehouse Robots:** In modern warehouses, robot swarms work together to manage inventory by maintaining a shared, up-to-date understanding of stock locations and quantities. They track dynamic obstacles such as human workers and moving machinery, adjusting routes to avoid collisions and optimize task efficiency. Communication and sensor fusion enable seamless coordination for tasks like picking, sorting and delivery. This collective intelligence reduces downtime and increases throughput. Scalability and adaptability make warehouse robot swarms a key technology in automated logistics.
- **Underwater Robot Networks:** Underwater robot networks consist of autonomous agents distributed over wide ocean areas to collect oceanographic data like temperature, salinity and currents. Due to limited underwater communication bandwidth, these swarms use efficient data compression and intermittent data exchanges to share sensor readings.

They coordinate movements to maximize spatial coverage and maintain connectivity despite challenging conditions. Applications include environmental monitoring, marine biology research and underwater infrastructure inspection. Their resilience and adaptability make them invaluable in harsh and remote underwater environments.

- **Disaster Response:** Multi-robot swarms are increasingly used for exploring collapsed buildings or hazardous zones where human entry is risky. Equipped with diverse sensors, robots collaboratively map debris, identify survivors and detect dangers like gas leaks or unstable structures. Their ability to communicate and share data in real time enables coordinated search patterns and efficient coverage of complex terrains. These swarms adapt dynamically to changing conditions, overcoming obstacles and sensor limitations. This technology significantly improves the speed, safety and effectiveness of disaster response efforts.

4.2.7 Current Research Challenges

- **Scalability to Hundreds or Thousands of Agents:** One of the biggest challenges in swarm robotics is scaling systems to operate effectively with hundreds or thousands of agents. As swarm size grows, managing communication, computation and coordination becomes exponentially more complex. Ensuring that algorithms remain efficient and that the swarm behaves cohesively without centralized control is critical. Research explores decentralized frameworks and bio-inspired models to maintain performance at large scales. Scalability is key for applications requiring extensive coverage and redundancy.
- **Balancing Local Autonomy with Global Coordination:** Swarms must strike a balance between allowing agents to act independently based on local information and maintaining cohesive global behaviour aligned with mission goals. Too much autonomy can lead to fragmented or conflicting actions, while excessive centralization can reduce adaptability and scalability. Current research focuses on hybrid control architectures that blend local decision-making with global information exchange. Achieving this balance improves robustness and flexibility in complex tasks and environments.
- **Efficient Communication Protocols for Large Swarms:** Developing communication protocols that support reliable, low-latency data exchange across large swarms is an ongoing challenge. Protocols must handle bandwidth constraints, interference and dynamic network topologies caused by agent movement or failures. Research investigates adaptive, event-driven and hierarchical communication schemes to optimize information

flow. Energy efficiency is also crucial, as many swarm agents have limited power resources. Robust protocols enable seamless coordination without overwhelming the network.

- **Robustness in Dynamic and Unpredictable Environments:** Swarms must operate reliably in environments that are constantly changing and often unpredictable, such as disaster zones or urban settings. This requires resilience to sensor noise, communication loss, physical obstacles and unexpected agent failures. Research efforts include fault-tolerant algorithms, redundancy through overlapping sensing and adaptive behaviours that allow swarms to recover and reconfigure autonomously. Enhancing robustness is essential for real-world deployment where uncertainty is the norm.
- **Integrating Machine Learning for Adaptive Perception:** Machine learning techniques are increasingly integrated into swarm systems to enable adaptive perception and decision-making. Learning-based models help swarms interpret complex sensor data, recognize patterns and predict environmental changes. Challenges include training models that can operate efficiently on resource-constrained agents and generalizing across diverse scenarios. Ongoing research aims to combine traditional sensor fusion with learning algorithms for real-time adaptability. This integration promises smarter, more autonomous swarm behaviours.S

4.3 RELATIVE LOCALIZATION AND MAPPING

Relative localization and mapping involve determining the positions of agents within a swarm relative to each other and to local features in the environment, rather than relying solely on absolute global coordinates. This approach is vital for swarm operations in environments where GPS or absolute positioning systems are unavailable or unreliable, such as indoors, underwater, or in urban canyons. By continuously estimating relative positions, agents can maintain formation, avoid collisions and collaboratively explore unknown areas. Relative localization also supports cooperative mapping, enabling the swarm to build a shared representation of the environment that improves navigation and task execution.

4.3.1 Techniques for Relative Localization

Relative localization commonly utilizes onboard sensors such as vision, LiDAR, ultrasonic and IMUs to estimate distances and orientations between swarm agents or between agents and environmental landmarks. Techniques include range-based methods using radio signal strength or time-of-flight measurements, bearing-based approaches using cameras or directional antennas and feature-based localization where visual or geometric landmarks serve as reference points.

Sensor fusion algorithms combine these data sources for improved accuracy. Additionally, cooperative localization leverages inter-agent communication to share and refine position estimates, reducing individual uncertainty through distributed computation.

4.3.2 Mapping Approaches

Mapping in swarm robotics focuses on creating spatial representations of the environment to support navigation and task planning. Approaches vary from occupancy grid maps, which divide space into discrete cells marked as free or occupied, to feature-based maps that represent key landmarks or structures. Swarms often use Simultaneous Localization and Mapping (SLAM) techniques to build maps while localizing themselves relative to these maps. Collaborative mapping allows multiple agents to contribute sensor data, accelerating map construction and improving coverage. Efficient data sharing and map merging strategies are critical to maintain a consistent, up-to-date global map within the swarm.

4.3.3 Applications

Relative localization and mapping enable swarms to perform coordinated exploration, search and rescue, environmental monitoring and construction tasks in complex, GPS-denied environments. For instance, indoor drone swarms use relative localization to maintain formations and navigate corridors, while underwater swarms map submerged structures collaboratively. In disaster zones, relative mapping helps swarms identify hazards and safe pathways without external infrastructure. The shared maps generated support dynamic task allocation, obstacle avoidance and collective decision-making. These capabilities make relative localization and mapping indispensable for robust and scalable swarm autonomy.

4.3.4 Challenges and Limitations

Relative localization and mapping face challenges such as sensor noise, drift and the complexity of data association when multiple agents observe similar landmarks. Maintaining consistency and accuracy over time requires sophisticated algorithms to correct cumulative errors. Communication constraints can limit data sharing necessary for cooperative localization and map merging. In dynamic or feature-sparse environments, reliable landmark detection becomes difficult, reducing localization accuracy. Furthermore, computational and energy resources are often limited on individual agents, making real-time processing challenging. Despite these limitations, advances in sensor fusion, decentralized algorithms and distributed computing continue to improve the effectiveness of relative localization and mapping in swarms.

4.4 SENSOR FUSION AND NOISE HANDLING

Sensor fusion is the process of integrating data from multiple sensors to obtain a more accurate and reliable understanding of the environment or the system's state. However, sensor data often contain noise and uncertainties caused by sensor imperfections, environmental conditions and signal interference. Noise handling techniques are essential to filter out inaccuracies and improve the quality of fused data. In swarm robotics, effective sensor fusion combined with robust noise handling enhances perception, localization and decision-making, enabling swarms to operate reliably in complex, dynamic environments.

4.4.1 Sources of Noise in Sensors

Noise in sensor measurements can arise from various sources including intrinsic hardware limitations, environmental interference and operational conditions. For example, vision sensors may be affected by poor lighting or motion blur, ultrasonic sensors by echo and reverberation and RF sensors by multipath effects and signal fading. Additionally, temperature fluctuations, electromagnetic interference and mechanical vibrations can introduce measurement errors. Understanding the specific noise characteristics of each sensor type is crucial for designing appropriate filtering and fusion strategies to mitigate their impact on swarm performance.

4.4.2 Sensor Fusion Techniques

Several mathematical models and algorithms are used to combine noisy sensor data into a coherent estimate. Kalman filters and their variants (Extended Kalman Filter, Unscented Kalman Filter) are popular for real-time fusion of data with Gaussian noise characteristics, providing optimal estimates by weighing measurements according to their uncertainty. Particle filters handle non-linear and non-Gaussian noise by representing probability distributions with samples. Bayesian fusion methods probabilistically combine data sources based on their reliability. Machine learning approaches, including deep learning, are increasingly applied to learn complex noise patterns and fuse heterogeneous sensor data adaptively, especially in high-dimensional sensing scenarios like vision.

4.4.3 Noise Handling Methods

Noise reduction methods aim to filter or correct raw sensor data before or during fusion. Common techniques include low-pass filters to remove high-frequency noise, median filters to eliminate spurious outliers and moving average filters for smoothing. Adaptive filters dynamically adjust parameters based on changing noise conditions. Robust statistical methods detect and discard faulty measurements or outliers. Sensor calibration and periodic recalibration help reduce systematic errors. Additionally, sensor redundancy in swarms enables cross-validation of measurements, where inconsistent data can be identified and corrected, improving overall robustness against noise.

4.4.4 Applications in Swarm Robotics

Effective sensor fusion and noise handling are fundamental to enabling swarms to achieve accurate localization, obstacle detection and environmental perception despite noisy measurements. These techniques allow agents to maintain stable formations, navigate cluttered or GPS-denied environments and collaboratively build reliable maps. In multi-agent systems, fusion of distributed sensor data helps reduce individual sensor uncertainty and improves collective situational awareness. Noise handling also enhances fault tolerance, allowing swarms to continue functioning even when some sensors degrade or fail. Overall, robust fusion and noise management are key enablers for scalable, autonomous swarm operation.

4.4.5 Challenges and Limitations

Handling noise and performing sensor fusion in swarms face challenges including the computational overhead of complex filtering algorithms on resource-constrained agents. Synchronizing data from multiple sensors and agents requires precise timing and communication, which can be disrupted by network delays or packet loss. The non-stationary nature of noise, especially in dynamic environments, demands adaptive fusion methods that can recalibrate on-the-fly. Overfitting or underfitting in machine learning-based fusion models can lead to inaccurate estimates. Designing scalable fusion frameworks that maintain accuracy while minimizing latency and energy consumption remains an active area of research in swarm robotics.

4.5 ENVIRONMENT INTERACTION AND ADAPTATION

Environment interaction and adaptation refer to a swarm's ability to perceive, respond and adjust its behaviour based on the changing conditions of the surroundings. Effective interaction enables swarms to perform tasks such as exploration, resource collection, or disaster response more efficiently by dynamically modifying their strategies. Adaptation ensures that the swarm remains resilient against unexpected obstacles, environmental changes, or internal failures, thereby enhancing robustness and autonomy. This capability relies heavily on sensor data, real-time processing and decentralized decision-making within the swarm.

4.5.1 Mechanisms of Environment Interaction

Swarm agents use diverse sensors to detect physical features such as obstacles, terrain texture, temperature and chemical presence. Interaction mechanisms include collision avoidance through proximity sensors, terrain adaptation by assessing surface properties with tactile sensors and environmental monitoring via specialized sensors for gases or radiation. Communication among agents supports cooperative responses like collective obstacle circumnavigation or coordinated task reallocation. Physical interaction with the environment also involves manipulation, such as moving objects or modifying structures, requiring precise force and tactile sensing integrated with control algorithms.

4.5.2 Adaptation Strategies

Adaptation in swarms can be both reactive and proactive. Reactive adaptation involves immediate responses to sensed changes, such as rerouting around obstacles or adjusting formations to maintain connectivity. Proactive adaptation entails learning from past experiences or environmental models to predict future changes and optimize behaviour. Techniques include behavioural plasticity, where agents modify their decision rules and machine learning, where swarms evolve strategies based on performance feedback. Adaptation may also be enabled by morphological changes, such as drones adjusting wing configurations or ground robots altering gait patterns to navigate rough terrain.

4.5.3 Applications

Environment interaction and adaptation empower swarms to perform complex real-world tasks. For instance, in search and rescue missions, swarms adapt to debris fields by reconfiguring movement patterns and sharing hazard information. Agricultural swarms adjust coverage based on soil moisture detected through sensors, optimizing irrigation and pesticide application. In environmental monitoring, swarms adapt sampling density or routes based on detected pollution gradients. Industrial swarms modify assembly sequences if obstacles or malfunctions occur. Such dynamic adaptability enhances efficiency, safety and mission success across diverse domains.

4.5.4 Challenges and Limitations

Implementing effective environment interaction and adaptation faces several challenges. Real-time processing of large volumes of sensor data can strain computational resources onboard small agents. Ensuring robust communication for coordinated adaptation is difficult in cluttered or noisy environments. Predictive adaptation requires accurate environmental models, which may be unavailable or incomplete. Balancing exploration and exploitation—deciding when to adapt versus maintaining a stable strategy—remains a complex trade-off. Physical constraints, such as limited actuator precision or energy reserves, can restrict adaptation capabilities. Despite these challenges, ongoing advances in distributed algorithms, machine learning and sensor technology continue to improve swarm adaptability.

5 Chapter ALGORITHMS AND CONTROL STRATEGIES

5.0 INTRODUCTION: AN OVERVIEW

Algorithms and control strategies are central to realizing the potential of swarm robotics. They provide the mechanisms through which simple individual agents achieve complex, coordinated behaviours necessary for effective collective operation. Advances in algorithm design continue to push the boundaries of what swarms can accomplish, making them increasingly capable, scalable, and adaptive to real-world challenges. As the field evolves, integrating emerging technologies like artificial intelligence, advanced sensing, and bio-inspired computing will further enhance swarm capabilities and expand their application horizons.

Algorithms and control strategies form the backbone of swarm robotics, enabling large groups of relatively simple agents to work together cohesively and efficiently. Unlike traditional centralized robotic systems, swarms rely on decentralized control where individual agents operate based on local information and interactions with neighbours. This decentralized nature demands robust algorithms that can ensure collective behaviour emerges reliably without direct oversight. The design of such algorithms is inspired heavily by natural systems such as ant colonies, bird flocks and fish schools, which demonstrate remarkable coordination and adaptability despite limited individual complexity. Control strategies in swarms address multiple core challenges: maintaining formation, achieving task allocation, ensuring collision avoidance and adapting to dynamic environments. These strategies often involve feedback loops where agents continuously adjust their actions based on sensed data and communication with peers. Because swarm agents are typically resource-constrained, control algorithms must be computationally lightweight yet effective. Furthermore, the algorithms must scale gracefully as the number of agents increases, preserving the swarm's performance and robustness.

Swarm robotics algorithms can be broadly categorized into behaviour-based, rule-based, optimization-based and learning-based approaches. Behaviour-based algorithms use simple reactive rules to generate complex global patterns, relying on local sensing and inter-agent interactions. Rule-based approaches implement predefined protocols for coordination, such as leader election or consensus mechanisms. Optimization-based methods apply mathematical techniques to find efficient solutions for tasks like coverage or path planning. More recently, machine learning and reinforcement learning are being explored to enable swarms to adaptively improve their performance in uncertain and evolving environments (Fig. 1).

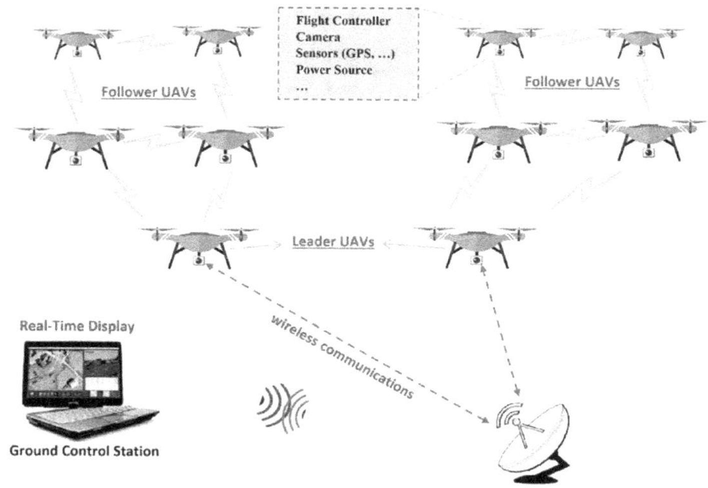

Fig. 1 Trends in robotic swarm coordination and control of swarm robots

A crucial aspect of swarm control is ensuring that individual actions contribute positively to the swarm's collective goals. This often involves designing control laws that promote cohesion and alignment while avoiding overcrowding and collisions. Techniques such as potential fields, flocking models and graph theory-based consensus algorithms are widely used to manage spatial organization and motion coordination. Additionally, distributed decision-making algorithms allow swarms to dynamically allocate tasks, reconfigure formations, or select leaders based on environmental feedback and mission requirements. Robustness is another fundamental consideration, as real-world conditions introduce noise, failures and unpredictability. Algorithms must be fault-tolerant, capable of maintaining functionality even if some agents malfunction or communication links break. This resilience is often achieved through redundancy, probabilistic decision models and adaptive re-planning. Moreover, many swarm systems integrate sensor fusion techniques to enhance perception accuracy, providing reliable inputs for control algorithms despite uncertain sensory data. Communication plays a critical role in control strategies by enabling information sharing and consensus building. However, communication constraints such as limited bandwidth, latency and range must be accounted for within the algorithmic design. Swarms employ various communication topologies—ranging from fully connected to nearest-neighbour graphs—each influencing the choice and performance of control strategies. Balancing communication overhead with control effectiveness is an ongoing research focus. Applications of swarm algorithms and control strategies span diverse domains, including environmental monitoring, agriculture, search and rescue and military operations. Each application presents unique requirements and challenges, driving the development of specialized algorithms tailored for specific tasks. For example, in search and rescue, algorithms emphasize exploration and victim detection under time constraints, whereas agricultural swarms prioritize coverage and resource management.

5.1 RULE-BASED AND BEHAVIOUR-BASED CONTROL

5.1.2 Rule-Based Control

Rule-based control in swarm robotics operates on a foundation of simple, predefined rules that determine how each agent behaves in response to sensory inputs and interactions with nearby agents. These rules are usually expressed as straightforward if-then conditions that govern basic actions, such as maintaining a minimum distance from neighbours to avoid collisions, following a designated leader, or moving toward a goal location. Because the rules are local and simple, they allow agents to operate without needing global knowledge or complex computations. This simplicity enables easy implementation and fast real-time decision-making, which is crucial for swarms composed of resource-limited agents. Rule-based control often yields surprisingly sophisticated group behaviours through the collective effect of individual agents following these local rules. For instance, flocking, dispersion and aggregation behaviours naturally emerge without explicit central control. Moreover, rule-based systems are predictable and transparent, making them easier to debug, verify and maintain. However, the rigid nature of fixed rules can limit flexibility and adaptability when the environment changes unpredictably or when agents encounter novel situations outside the scope of the rules. These limitations necessitate careful design and sometimes manual tuning of the rules to ensure robustness across different scenarios. Despite this, rule-based control remains a foundational technique due to its effectiveness, efficiency and conceptual simplicity (Fig. 2).

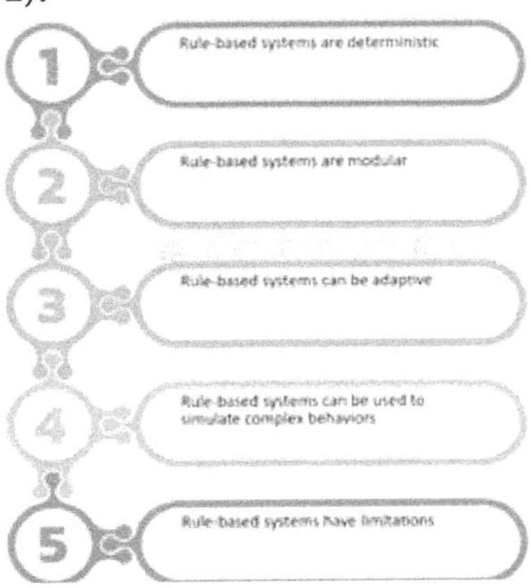

Fig. 2 Rule-Based Control System

5.1.3 Behaviour-Based Control

Behaviour-based control builds on the idea of modularizing an agent's actions into multiple concurrent behaviour components, each dedicated to achieving specific goals such as obstacle avoidance, goal seeking, or maintaining formation. Instead of rigid if-then rules, these behaviours run in parallel and compete or cooperate to influence the agent's overall action, often through weighted prioritization or arbitration mechanisms. This architecture offers greater flexibility, allowing agents to dynamically blend behaviours based on changing environmental conditions and internal states. For example, an agent might prioritize obstacle avoidance when near a barrier but switch to goal-seeking when the path is clear. This reactivity and adaptability make behaviour-based control well suited for complex, dynamic environments where unpredictable events frequently occur. Inspired by biological systems such as insect colonies or bird flocks, behaviour-based models foster emergent coordination through decentralized interactions, without requiring global knowledge or central control. Moreover, this modular approach enhances scalability, since new behaviours can be added or existing ones adjusted without redesigning the entire system. By enabling agents to respond fluidly and simultaneously to multiple stimuli, behaviour-based control provides robustness and resilience, supporting sustained operation even in noisy or partially observable environments. Its capacity to handle real-world complexities makes it a widely favoured approach in swarm robotics research and applications (Fig. 3).

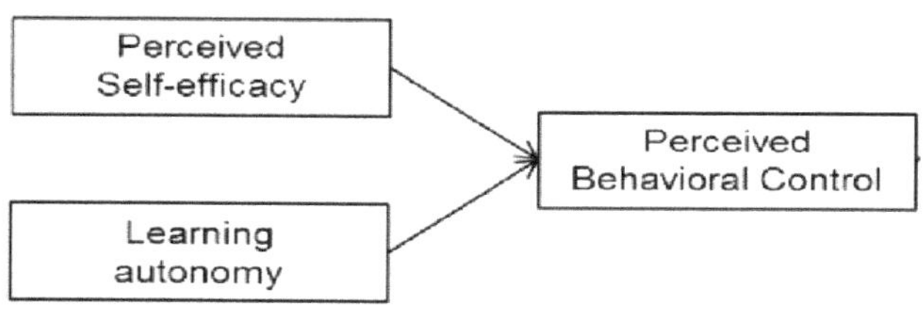

Fig. 3 Behaviour-based control

5.1.4 Comparison and Integration

Rule-based and behaviour-based control strategies each offer unique strengths and address different aspects of swarm coordination challenges. Rule-based control shines in its simplicity, clarity and predictability, providing a straightforward framework for designing agent responses through explicit rules. This makes it easier to implement and reason about but often at the cost of reduced adaptability to unforeseen or highly dynamic conditions. On the other hand, behaviour-based control excels in flexibility and adaptability by enabling agents to execute multiple behaviours concurrently and adjust priorities based on context. This supports more nuanced and sophisticated responses, allowing swarms to cope better with environmental uncertainty and complexity. Recognizing the complementary nature of these methods, many swarm robotics systems integrate rule-based triggers to activate or modulate behaviour modules dynamically. This hybridization leverages the benefits of both: the structure and interpretability of rule-based logic, together with the rich, emergent properties of behaviour-based control. Such integration enhances the overall robustness, allowing swarms to handle diverse tasks and environments effectively. By emphasizing local interactions and decentralized decision-making, both strategies maintain scalability—a critical feature for large-scale swarms. The synergy between rule-based clarity and behaviour-based adaptability forms the core of many advanced swarm control frameworks today.

5.1.5 Applications

Rule-based and behaviour-based control approaches have proven essential across a wide range of swarm robotics applications, demonstrating their practical utility in enabling coordinated collective behaviours. For example, in collective movement tasks such as flocking, simple local rules governing spacing, alignment and cohesion allow agents to move as a cohesive unit, mimicking natural flocking patterns seen in birds or fish. Similarly, in area coverage tasks, these controls enable swarms to spread out efficiently to monitor environments, optimize sensor coverage, or perform surveillance. Obstacle avoidance is another key application, where reactive behaviours ensure agents safely navigate cluttered or dynamic spaces while maintaining group integrity. Foraging behaviours in swarms, inspired by ant colonies, use a combination of exploration and exploitation strategies driven by behavioural modules or rule sets to efficiently locate and collect resources. The power of these approaches lies in their ability to generate complex, adaptive and emergent phenomena from relatively simple individual rules or behaviours, enabling swarms to operate effectively without centralized control. Their versatility allows deployment in domains ranging from environmental monitoring and agriculture to disaster response and military reconnaissance. As foundational control strategies, rule-based and behaviour-based methods continue to inspire innovative designs and enhance the autonomy of robotic swarms.

5.2 CONSENSUS AND VOTING ALGORITHMS

In decentralized multi-agent systems and swarm robotics, consensus and voting algorithms are fundamental mechanisms that enable agents to reach collective decisions without relying on centralized coordination. These algorithms form the backbone of distributed decision-making, allowing agents to align on shared values, beliefs, or actions through local communication and iterative information exchange. In environments where agents have only partial or noisy observations, consensus protocols facilitate agreement on critical variables such as position estimates, task priorities, or the identity of detected objects. Consensus algorithms are designed to ensure that all participating agents asymptotically converge to a common value, even in the presence of communication delays, dynamic topologies, or partial information. Common methods include average consensus, gossip protocols and distributed Kalman filters, which are particularly useful for continuous-valued estimation. For discrete decisions or categorical choices, voting algorithms are employed. These allow agents to collectively select options based on majority, plurality, ranked preferences, or quorum-based thresholds. Robust consensus mechanisms support a wide range of swarm behaviours, including coordinated movement, formation control, target tracking and group classification. They are also critical in fault-tolerant systems, where agreement must be achieved despite the presence of malfunctioning or adversarial agents. Additionally, consensus ensures coherence in scenarios where agents must synchronize timing, roles, or execution of complex strategies. Voting schemes, on the other hand, provide structured ways for swarms to resolve conflicts, prioritize objectives, or choose among multiple hypotheses. These schemes are often embedded within finite-state machines or decision trees, where agent votes influence state transitions. The design of such algorithms must consider fairness, convergence speed, communication overhead and resilience to manipulation or misinformation. Together, consensus and voting algorithms represent essential tools for achieving shared understanding and coordinated action in distributed autonomous systems. They enable swarms to behave intelligently, adaptively and reliably in real-world applications where uncertainty and decentralization are inherent.

5.2.1 Consensus Algorithms

Consensus algorithms are foundational in swarm robotics for enabling groups of agents to agree on shared decisions or values using only local communication. These algorithms operate iteratively: each agent exchanges information with its neighbours and updates its own state based on those inputs, progressively refining its value until the group converges to a consistent solution. This process is critical for tasks like synchronizing movement direction, maintaining cohesive formations, determining global states (e.g., majority observation) and distributing workloads. Common types include average consensus (where agents average values), max/min consensus (to agree on extremal values) and weighted consensus (prioritizing certain agents based on reliability or role). The beauty of consensus lies in its fully distributed nature—there is no central authority, yet the group still collectively makes unified decisions. These algorithms also exhibit strong fault tolerance, meaning that they can still function even when individual agents fail or produce noisy data. Robustness in dynamic environments is another strength, as consensus methods can adapt to changing swarm topologies caused by mobility or communication loss. Efficient consensus is critical in large-scale swarms and current research explores faster convergence, minimal bandwidth use and resilience to adversarial conditions. In essence, consensus is what allows simple, locally aware agents to act as a single intelligent entity.

5.2.2 Voting Algorithms

Voting algorithms empower a swarm to collectively choose among multiple alternatives—such as a leader, path, goal, or area to explore—through individual agent input aggregation. Each agent evaluates the options based on its local knowledge or sensor readings and casts a vote accordingly. Depending on the system, votes can be equal, weighted, or based on multiple preferences. Simple methods like majority voting are easy to implement but may be insufficient when there is no clear favourite or in the presence of noise. More sophisticated approaches such as plurality voting, Borda count and ranked-choice voting allow agents to express nuanced preferences and help avoid ties or suboptimal selections. Voting is particularly useful when swarms must choose between conflicting strategies, allocate resources, or elect temporary leaders in distributed systems. What distinguishes voting from consensus is its focus on discrete selection rather than continuous agreement. This makes it ideal for categorical decisions, such as "which of these three doors should we investigate first?" In swarm systems, voting promotes a democratic and fair decision-making process without central authority, fostering system adaptability and autonomy. Researchers continue to refine voting models to be lightweight, resilient to manipulation and capable of real-time resolution even with partial participation from the swarm.

5.2.3 Applications

Consensus and voting algorithms are widely applied across multiple domains of swarm robotics, underpinning key functionalities in both movement coordination and decision-making. In formation control, consensus ensures that agents align their positions and headings to form and maintain a desired spatial structure. During target tracking, consensus helps swarms agree on object location and movement direction, especially when individual observations vary. In task assignment, agents may use consensus to estimate global workload and distribute subtasks evenly. Conversely, voting mechanisms are particularly useful in leader election, where agents nominate and elect a temporary leader based on criteria like proximity to goal or energy level. These techniques are also deployed in exploration tasks, where swarms vote on promising areas based on sensor input or signal strength. Additionally, in multi-scenario mission planning, swarms use consensus to synchronize plans or collectively switch tasks. These algorithms enhance scalability, fault tolerance and coordination efficiency, making swarms capable of autonomous, synchronized action even in environments with limited communication or agent dropouts. Their versatility has made them essential components of modern multi-agent robotic systems.

5.2.4 Challenges and Enhancements

Despite their usefulness, consensus and voting algorithms in swarm robotics come with significant challenges, especially in large or highly dynamic swarms. Communication delays and packet loss can cause inconsistent data propagation, leading to slow or failed convergence. Asynchronous updates—where not all agents communicate at the same time—can further complicate synchronization, particularly in fast-changing environments. Additionally, scalability poses a challenge, as more agents mean more communication overhead and potential congestion. Maintaining data consistency across agents with differing views of the environment requires smart filtering and timestamping. Moreover, faulty, noisy, or malicious agents can disrupt agreement processes, necessitating fault-tolerant or Byzantine-resilient algorithms. To address these issues, researchers are developing enhancements such as asynchronous consensus protocols, event-triggered communication (to reduce bandwidth) and reputation-weighted voting (to prioritize reliable agents). Machine learning techniques are also being integrated to allow swarms to learn voting patterns and consensus dynamics over time, improving adaptability. With these ongoing advancements, consensus and voting remain active areas of innovation that aim to make swarms more robust, autonomous and efficient in complex real-world deployments.

Understanding of consensus and voting algorithms are depicted in Table-1.

Table-1: Understanding of Consensus and Voting Algorithms

S.No.	Topic	Details
1.	Consensus Algorithms	- Enable agents to agree on shared decisions using local communication. - Iterative process: agents exchange information, update state. - Used for synchronizing movement, forming structures, estimating global states, workload distribution. - Types include: • Average Consensus • Max/Min Consensus • Weighted Consensus - Fully distributed with no central control. - High fault tolerance and robust in dynamic environments. - Key research areas: faster convergence, low bandwidth use, resilience to failures/adversaries.

2.	Voting Algorithms	- Used to choose among discrete alternatives (e.g., leader, path, goal). - Agents vote based on local knowledge or sensor input. - Voting types: • Majority voting (simple) • Plurality voting • Borda count • Ranked-choice voting - Supports nuanced decisions and avoids ties. - Ideal for categorical decisions. - Promotes fairness and autonomy. - Challenges addressed: real-time resolution, manipulation resistance, partial participation.
3.	Applications	- Formation Control: consensus aligns agents' position and heading. - Target Tracking: consensus on object location/movement. - Task Assignment: global workload estimation and task distribution. - Leader Election: voting based on energy level, goal proximity. - Exploration: voting on areas based on sensor data or signal strength. - Mission Planning: consensus for synchronized task switching. - Improves scalability, fault tolerance, autonomy and coordination.
4.	Challenges & Enhancements	- Challenges: • Communication delays and packet loss. • Asynchronous updates. • Scalability and bandwidth overhead. • Data inconsistency from varying local views. • Faulty/malicious agents. - Enhancements: • Asynchronous consensus protocols. • Event-triggered communication. • Reputation-weighted voting. • Integration of machine learning for adaptive behavior. - Goal: improved robustness, efficiency and autonomy in real-world use.

5.3 PATH PLANNING AND OBSTACLE AVOIDANCE

Path Planning and Obstacle Avoidance are core functionalities in autonomous multi-agent systems, enabling individual agents and swarms to navigate complex, dynamic environments safely and efficiently. Path planning refers to the process of determining an optimal or feasible route from a starting point to a destination, considering various constraints such as distance, energy consumption, time, or task-specific goals. Obstacle avoidance, closely intertwined with planning, involves detecting and responding to static or dynamic hazards in real-time to prevent collisions and maintain mission continuity. In swarm systems, path planning must be decentralized and scalable. Each agent must make local decisions while ensuring global coherence with the group's objectives and behaviours. This is often achieved using distributed algorithms, potential fields, graph-based methods (like A*, D*, or RRT variants) and bio-inspired approaches such as ant colony optimization or particle swarm techniques. These algorithms allow agents to explore the environment, evaluate multiple paths and adapt plans based on new sensory inputs. Obstacle avoidance complements planning by incorporating reactive mechanisms. Using sensors like LiDAR, sonar, vision systems, or proximity detectors, agents continuously monitor their surroundings and adjust their trajectories in real time. Techniques such as vector field histograms, dynamic window approaches and velocity obstacles are commonly used to navigate around moving and static obstructions. When implemented effectively, the integration of path planning and obstacle avoidance enables agents to operate autonomously in cluttered, uncertain, or adversarial environments. For swarms, these capabilities ensure cohesive group movement, formation maintenance and collision-free navigation, even in confined or dynamic settings. These systems must also account for inter-agent interactions to prevent traffic congestion or deadlocks during high-density operations. Ultimately, robust path planning and obstacle avoidance are vital for achieving autonomy, safety and adaptability in applications such as autonomous driving, drone navigation, warehouse automation, search and rescue and planetary exploration. Their continued development is central to the evolution of intelligent, resilient swarm robotics and multi-agent systems.

5.3.1 Path Planning

Path planning in swarm robotics involves computing feasible and optimized routes for each agent to move from its current location to a target destination while satisfying constraints like minimal distance, energy usage, safety and time. Unlike centralized systems, swarms operate under a distributed architecture, where each agent plans locally and collaborates through limited communication with nearby peers. This ensures scalability and robustness to failure. Popular approaches include grid-based search algorithms such as A*, which are effective for well-mapped environments but can be computationally intensive. Sampling-based algorithms like Rapidly-exploring Random Trees (RRT) and Probabilistic Roadmaps (PRM) work better in high-dimensional or partially unknown spaces by building probabilistic graphs of navigable paths. Another common method involves artificial potential fields, where agents are attracted to goals and repelled from obstacles or other agents. In dynamic environments, agents continuously re-evaluate their paths in response to moving goals, new hazards, or agent losses. Effective path planning is key to ensuring mission completion with minimal resource waste, while maintaining swarm cohesion and responsiveness. Research continues to focus on improving the real-time efficiency, adaptability and coordination of decentralized path planning systems across large swarms.

5.3.2 Obstacle Avoidance

Obstacle avoidance is a critical capability in swarm robotics, ensuring that agents can safely navigate cluttered, unpredictable, or unknown environments without collisions. Each agent must detect nearby obstacles using onboard sensors (e.g., IR, ultrasonic, vision, or LiDAR) and respond in real time. Reactive strategies such as the Bug algorithm allow agents to follow the perimeter of an obstacle until a path is cleared. Artificial potential fields are widely used, where obstacles generate repulsive forces and goals generate attractive forces, guiding agents away from danger and toward objectives. However, such methods can cause issues like local minima, which require enhancements or hybrid solutions. Velocity and heading adjustments based on sensor feedback also allow for smoother real-time motion and are particularly useful in formation-keeping scenarios. In swarm systems, obstacle avoidance is more complex due to the need to preserve group cohesion and communication. Therefore, agents often coordinate their avoidance manoeuvres to maintain formations or avoid breaking task-related roles. This interplay between autonomy and cooperation is essential for tasks such as indoor mapping, disaster response and surveillance. Obstacle avoidance must be both fast and reliable, adapting to dynamic threats while preserving overall swarm objectives.

5.3.3 Integration of Planning and Avoidance

In practical swarm missions, path planning and obstacle avoidance must work in tandem for agents to navigate efficiently and safely. While path planning offers a global view by finding optimal paths to goals, obstacle avoidance delivers local reactivity, allowing agents to respond immediately to sudden changes in the environment. The integration of these two components enables agents to follow planned trajectories while adapting in real time to new or unforeseen obstacles. This is achieved through hierarchical architectures, where high-level planners suggest goals and low-level controllers handle real-time adjustments. Some systems use predictive models to anticipate obstacle movements (e.g., a moving human or vehicle) and modify trajectories before collisions become likely. Agents may also share environmental updates to inform neighbours of new hazards, thereby enhancing overall swarm awareness. Replanning mechanisms ensure paths are updated continuously as the environment evolves. This seamless integration supports missions in non-static, uncertain terrains such as forests, disaster zones, or crowded urban areas. It also enhances mission resilience, enabling swarms to reroute collectively in case of partial blockage or agent failure. The key challenge lies in balancing global optimization with local responsiveness without overloading computation or communication.

5.3.4 Applications

Path planning and obstacle avoidance are essential in numerous real-world applications where autonomous swarms operate in dynamic and potentially hazardous environments. In search and rescue missions, drones or ground robots must efficiently cover terrain while avoiding debris, collapsed structures and unstable surfaces. In urban surveillance or monitoring, drone swarms navigate between buildings, street poles and power lines, requiring fine-grained obstacle avoidance while maintaining coordinated coverage. Warehouse automation also relies heavily on these functions, as multiple robots move simultaneously through tight aisles, dynamically adjusting their paths to avoid collisions with shelves, humans, or other robots. In agriculture, swarms of robots or UAVs plan paths to inspect crops, while steering clear of trees, irrigation lines, or terrain features. Furthermore, autonomous delivery swarms must calculate optimal delivery routes while avoiding pedestrians, vehicles, or unexpected roadblocks. These applications demand a robust integration of long-term planning and short-term obstacle negotiation. As such, advanced solutions not only boost efficiency and safety but also extend the operational capabilities of swarms in complex, unstructured environments, paving the way for full autonomy in real-world deployments.

5.4 TASK ALLOCATION AND ROLE ASSIGNMENT

Task Allocation and Role Assignment are fundamental processes that enable autonomous multi-agent systems and swarms to function efficiently and cooperatively in dynamic environments. These mechanisms determine how individual agents divide labour, select tasks and assume specific responsibilities based on system goals, capabilities and situational context. In swarm robotics and decentralized systems, where no central controller exists, task allocation must emerge from local interactions, communication and adaptive behaviours. Effective task allocation ensures that agents are neither idle nor overburdened, while role assignment assigns specific functions (e.g., leader, explorer, carrier, observer) to agents based on their current status, expertise, location, or resource availability. Strategies for task allocation include market-based models (e.g., auctions), behavioural rules, threshold-based responses and bio-inspired mechanisms such as ant foraging or bee recruitment. These methods allow agents to make decisions in real time, balancing global objectives with local information. In role assignment, agents may dynamically switch roles in response to environmental changes, agent failures, or mission progress. This flexibility enhances the system's robustness and adaptability. For example, in a search and rescue scenario, a drone swarm might reassign scout drones to transporter roles once victims are located. Task allocation is often complicated by constraints like limited communication, energy restrictions, time-sensitive goals, or heterogeneous agent capabilities. Efficient algorithms must be scalable, fault-tolerant and capable of reassigning tasks on-the-fly to reflect evolving mission demands or unexpected disruptions. Ultimately, task allocation and role assignment are critical to maximizing swarm efficiency, achieving coordinated action and ensuring mission success across a wide range of applications, from environmental monitoring and logistics to exploration and disaster response. These processes form the cognitive infrastructure that transforms a swarm from a collection of autonomous agents into a purposeful, cooperative system (Fig. 2).

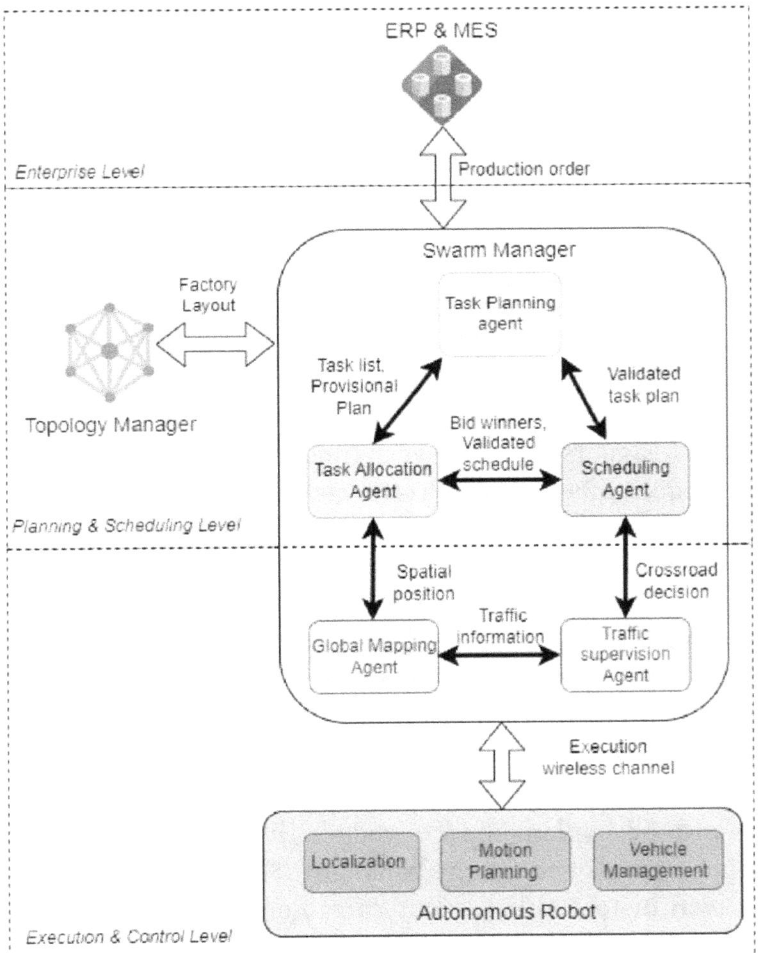

Fig. 2 Swarm Manager conceptual multi-agent framework

5.4.1 Task Allocation

Task allocation in swarm robotics is the process by which multiple autonomous agents distribute a set of tasks among themselves in a way that maximizes efficiency, minimizes redundancy and adapts to real-time environmental changes. This functionality is critical when operating in resource-constrained or time-sensitive environments, where coordination must occur without a central controller. Algorithms for task allocation vary widely, with some inspired by economic models, where agents participate in market-based approaches—placing bids based on internal states (e.g., battery level, proximity to task)—and winning the task based on predefined cost functions. Another biologically inspired approach includes threshold-based allocation, modelled on social insect colonies, where an agent responds to task stimuli only if a certain threshold is exceeded, promoting natural division of labour. Optimization-based methods, including linear programming and distributed constraint optimization, are also used to match tasks to agents by computing the most efficient pairings. Importantly, many of these strategies are designed to be decentralized, allowing each agent to make independent decisions based on local data or shared signals, which enhances fault tolerance and scalability. Real-time task reassignment is also possible, ensuring that if an agent becomes non-functional, its tasks can be seamlessly redistributed. Task allocation serves as the bedrock for ensuring swarm performance in multi-objective operations, enabling autonomous systems to function effectively under uncertainty and partial observability.

5.4.2 Role Assignment

Role assignment in swarm systems involves assigning specific functions or behavioural roles to agents that align with their capabilities, mission objectives, or environmental requirements. Unlike static task allocation, role assignment adds a layer of functional identity to each agent—such as leader, follower, communicator, explorer, or obstacle remover—allowing the swarm to function as a hierarchical or functionally specialized unit. Roles may be fixed, determined at deployment based on hardware capabilities, or dynamic, adapting in response to mission context or agent failures. Dynamic role assignment is particularly powerful in volatile environments where conditions change rapidly or where some agents may lose functionality. Common role assignment mechanisms include voting and consensus algorithms to elect leaders or assign mission-critical functions. Role rotation strategies can also be implemented to reduce the wear on specific agents or to improve mission fairness and energy balancing. Sensor feedback, communication patterns and even historical behaviour can inform which roles are appropriate for which agents at a given moment. This kind of situational role reassignment makes the swarm highly resilient to disruption. Moreover, when combined with learning algorithms, role assignment can become adaptive over time, with agents improving their role selection through past experiences or performance metrics. As swarms scale into the hundreds or thousands of agents, effective and responsive role assignment is key to maintaining structured, intelligent collective behaviour.

5.4.3 Coordination and Adaptability

The true strength of swarm robotics emerges from the tight integration of task allocation and role assignment, enabling seamless cooperation among heterogeneous or homogeneous agents in pursuit of complex objectives. When each agent not only knows what to do (task allocation) but also understands its broader purpose within the team (role assignment), the swarm exhibits higher-order organization akin to biological collectives. This integration allows for multi-level coordination, where agents collaborate on subtasks, monitor role effectiveness and even provide redundancy or backup when another agent fails. Key enablers of this coordination include communication protocols, such as broadcast or peer-to-peer networks, which allow agents to share task status, resource availability and environmental updates. Additionally, sensor fusion techniques enable agents to build shared situational awareness, allowing more informed decisions on task and role transitions. This adaptability allows swarms to respond dynamically to environmental disruptions, unforeseen tasks, or mission goal changes without the need for centralized oversight. Behaviour arbitration systems can be used to prioritize conflicting tasks or switch roles based on urgency or collective demand. Ultimately, this combination fosters a resilient and self-healing system, capable of reorganizing itself in real time to ensure mission continuity. Such adaptability is essential in real-world settings where uncertainty and change are constants.

5.4.4 Applications

Task allocation and role assignment are essential in a broad range of practical swarm robotics applications, offering flexibility, scalability and real-time responsiveness to mission requirements. In search and rescue scenarios, swarm robots can rapidly divide up a disaster zone, with scouts exploring corridors, transporters delivering aid and other agents clearing debris or assisting in evacuation. In precision agriculture, drones and ground robots assume roles such as crop surveyor, pesticide applicator, or health monitor and tasks are dynamically distributed to cover large fields while avoiding overlaps and maximizing sensor efficiency. Military and surveillance operations rely on these mechanisms to assign roles such as patroller, observer, or interceptor, with tasks like perimeter monitoring, target tracking, or communication relay being continuously adjusted based on threats or mission demands. In industrial and warehouse automation, task allocation ensures items are retrieved, transported and sorted efficiently, while role assignment helps manage robot coordination and avoid bottlenecks. These systems have also been deployed in marine and underwater swarms, where acoustic communication is limited and local autonomy is crucial for sample collection or exploration. The ability to allocate tasks and adapt roles in real time ensures that swarms can handle mission diversity, agent heterogeneity and environment variability, greatly enhancing their utility in both structured and unstructured domains.

5.5 FORMATION CONTROL AND SWARM PATTERNING

Formation Control and Swarm Patterning are essential mechanisms in multi-agent systems that govern how agents maintain specific geometric configurations or spatial arrangements while moving collectively. These coordinated behaviours allow a swarm to operate as a coherent unit, enabling tasks such as area coverage, perimeter surveillance, obstacle negotiation and collective transport to be executed with precision and efficiency. Formation control ensures that agents retain relative positions with respect to each other, while swarm patterning involves the dynamic organization of agents into functional or visually meaningful shapes. In formation control, agents must continuously monitor their own state (position, orientation, velocity) and that of their neighbours to maintain a desired spatial structure. This is achieved using distributed control laws, consensus algorithms and relative position tracking techniques. Formations may be fixed (e.g., line, wedge, grid) or adaptive, changing shape based on mission requirements or environmental constraints. Maintaining formations is especially important in applications such as drone fleets, underwater exploration and satellite constellations, where synchronized movement and structure are critical. Swarm patterning extends formation control by focusing on creating and modifying collective patterns, often inspired by biological swarms such as bird flocks or fish schools. These patterns can be dynamic, reactive to external stimuli, or used for signalling and communication. Patterning is influenced by attraction-repulsion dynamics, virtual potential fields, leader-follower models, or decentralized behaviour rules. Robust formation control must account for disturbances like communication loss, agent failure, or unexpected obstacles.

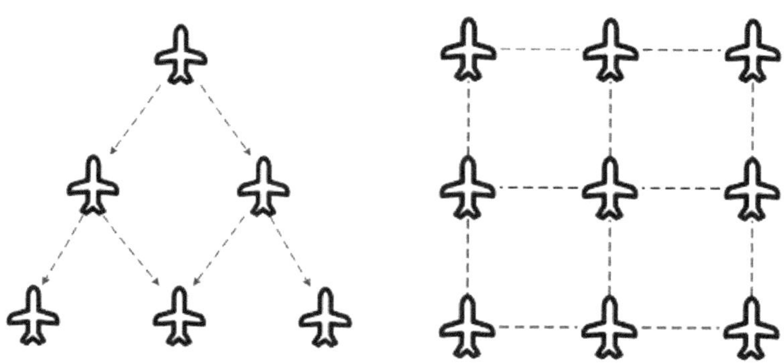

(a) a graph-based model (b) a grid virtual structure model

Fig. 3 UAV (Unmanned Aerial Vehicle) swarm formation representation: (a) a graph-based model with UAVs as vertexes and control links as edges; (b) a grid virtual structure model with UAVs as vertexes of the grid.

Thus, modern approaches incorporate fault tolerance, reconfiguration strategies and local sensing to ensure resilience. Swarm patterning, when combined with environmental awareness, allows the swarm to morph, disperse, regroup, or encircle targets in real time. Together, formation control and swarm patterning provide the structural and behavioural foundation for coordinated motion, enabling autonomous swarms to perform complex group manoeuvres, achieve spatial objectives and adapt to diverse operational scenarios without centralized oversight (Fig. 3).

5.5.1 Formation Control

Formation control is a fundamental capability in swarm robotics that enables agents to maintain specific spatial relationships with one another while navigating through an environment or performing coordinated tasks. The goal is to preserve a desired geometric layout—such as a line, V-shape, grid, or wedge—by dynamically adjusting each agent's position relative to its neighbours. This ensures not only visual order but also task effectiveness, such as maximizing sensor coverage, maintaining communication links, or evenly distributing resources. Popular strategies include the leader-follower approach, where one or more agents lead the group and others maintain fixed offsets relative to them. The virtual structure method treats the entire swarm as a rigid geometric body, controlling each agent's role within that structure. Behaviour-based approaches, like Reynolds' flocking model, use simple local rules—alignment, separation and cohesion—to achieve collective formation without predefined patterns. Formation control supports safe and scalable coordination, as agents avoid collisions while keeping formation integrity. It's especially critical in tasks like multi-drone surveillance, convoy protection, or autonomous transport, where synchronization across agents ensures mission reliability. Advanced systems even allow dynamic formation switching, adapting shape in real time based on mission phase or obstacle encounters. Robust formation control relies heavily on sensor data, relative positioning systems (e.g., GPS, UWB, vision) and local communication to maintain coherence even in partially known or adversarial environments.

5.5.2 Swarm Patterning

Swarm patterning is the process through which a collection of agents self-organizes into meaningful spatial structures or arrangements through decentralized local interactions. Unlike rigid formations, swarm patterns may be flexible, self-adjusting and often emergent—arising without explicit global instructions. These patterns can be geometric (circles, spirals, lattices), functional (barriers, search grids), or biologically inspired (schools of fish or flocks of birds). Patterning enhances a swarm's ability to adapt to changing environments or task demands, especially in missions requiring area coverage, dynamic reconfiguration, or collective signalling (e.g., drone light shows). The underlying mechanisms draw from natural swarm intelligence, where local rules lead to global order. For example, agents may align based on the average heading of neighbours, avoid crowding by maintaining a minimum separation, or follow local gradients. These behaviours enable adaptive, robust and scalable patterning, where even the addition or loss of agents does not compromise overall structure. Patterning is often used in tasks like distributed sensing, formation camouflage, or signal propagation through shape changes. Its decentralized nature makes it resilient to single-point failures and the ability to shift between static and dynamic shapes allows the swarm to react to new information or threats without centralized coordination. Swarm patterning ultimately reflects the power of local decision-making to achieve global order in complex systems.

5.5.3 Techniques and Algorithms

Formation control and swarm patterning rely on a rich set of algorithms that translate local rules and inter-agent sensing into global behaviour. Many of these draw from graph theory, where agents are modelled as nodes with communication or sensing links forming edges; graph-based consensus ensures all agents agree on motion parameters like direction or speed. Artificial potential fields are commonly used, assigning attractive forces to goals and repulsive forces to obstacles or neighbours to maintain spacing. Flocking algorithms, based on alignment, separation and cohesion, offer simple, scalable control over complex swarm shapes. In some systems, virtual physics models are used to simulate spring-like interactions between agents, allowing for elastic and fluid formations. Bio-inspired algorithms—mimicking ants, bees, or birds—provide heuristics for adaptive group behaviour, such as maintaining flow in tight corridors or reconfiguring when blocked. Consensus protocols are essential in synchronizing agent movement or reassigning roles during pattern transitions. Sensor feedback (vision, LiDAR, UWB, GPS) and communication modules (e.g., Bluetooth, RF, mesh networks) are critical for real-time data sharing and coordination. As swarms scale up, algorithms must address challenges of latency, dynamic topology and noise, pushing researchers to develop more robust, energy-efficient and decentralized approaches. Many current trends also integrate machine learning, enabling agents to learn pattern behaviours or optimal formations through trial and error or simulated environments.

5.5.4 Applications

Formation control and swarm patterning are widely applied across sectors where coordinated multi-agent behaviour is essential. In aerial drone displays, such as those seen at public events or light shows, hundreds of drones synchronize precisely to form dynamic shapes and visual effects—requiring real-time formation maintenance and complex transitions. In cooperative object transport, multiple ground or aerial robots position themselves around a payload and apply synchronized force or lift to move it collectively and stably. Environmental monitoring swarms, both aerial and underwater, utilize patterned distributions to efficiently cover terrain or collect evenly spaced sensor data, improving spatial resolution and accuracy. In military operations, formations are used for perimeter surveillance, convoy protection and combat logistics, where structure and spacing influence both safety and effectiveness. Underwater robot formations improve acoustic communication and coordinated exploration in deep-sea missions. Even in space applications, satellite swarms may use virtual formations for coordinated sensing or signal triangulation. Patterning also supports distributed computing tasks, such as spatial load balancing or collaborative signal processing. As the complexity of missions increases, the ability of swarms to dynamically form, hold and transition between formations will continue to expand their role in real-world systems—delivering robust, decentralized solutions to coordination challenges in uncertain environments.

6 Chapter
LEARNING AND ADAPTATION IN SWARMS

6.0 INTRODUCTION: AN OVERVIEW

Learning and adaptation elevate swarm systems from simple reactive entities to intelligent, self-improving collectives. These capabilities enable swarms to operate autonomously over long durations, adjust to unforeseen challenges, and make informed decisions in real-time. By continually refining their behaviour through feedback and experience, swarms become more resilient, flexible, and efficient. This dynamic responsiveness is essential for functioning in complex, unstructured, and evolving environments. The fusion of learning algorithms with decentralized coordination unlocks new levels of swarm intelligence. As the field progresses, such integration will define the future of scalable, robust, and autonomous multi-agent systems.

In swarm robotics, learning and adaptation are critical capabilities that empower collective systems to function autonomously in unpredictable, dynamic and often harsh environments. Unlike traditional robotic systems that rely on pre-programmed behaviour, swarm systems must be capable of adjusting their responses based on experience, sensory input and environmental feedback. Learning enables individual agents and the collective swarm to improve performance over time, while adaptation ensures flexibility in behaviour when confronted with novel scenarios, changes in tasks, or unforeseen challenges. Swarm robotics takes inspiration from nature—especially from biological swarms like ants, bees and birds—which exhibit decentralized learning and adaptation through simple rules and local interactions. In engineered swarms, this translates into agents using distributed algorithms that allow them to refine behaviours without central control. These behaviours include navigation, task allocation, communication, decision-making and coordination. Learning in swarms can occur at multiple levels. At the individual level, an agent can modify its own behaviour based on its past experiences or environmental observations. At the group level, learning involves shared information or emergent patterns that arise from the interactions among agents. This dual-level learning allows swarms to handle noisy data, changing goals and the addition or loss of agents without failure (Fig. 1).

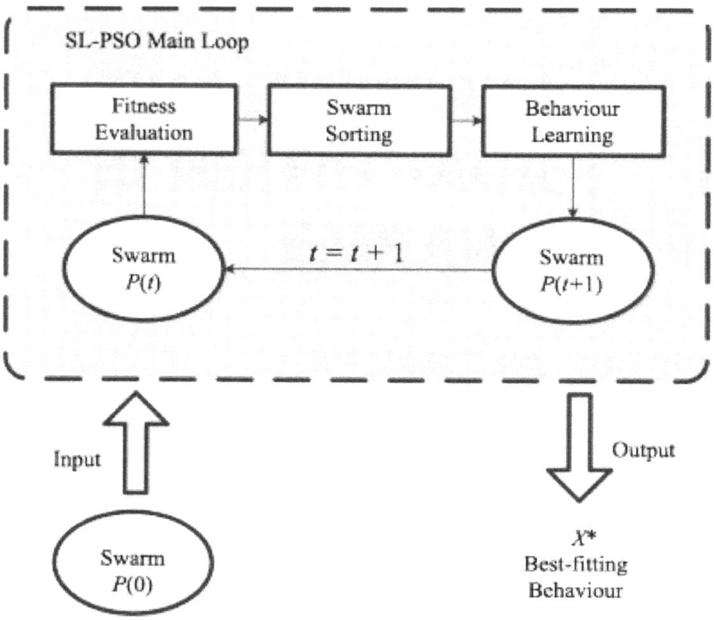

Fig. 1 Social learning particle swarm optimization algorithm

Adaptation mechanisms often rely on feedback loops, where agents continuously sense the environment and adjust their actions accordingly. Reinforcement learning, evolutionary algorithms and neural networks are common methods used to implement adaptive behaviours. These techniques help swarms fine-tune parameters, recognize patterns and evolve strategies over time.

Furthermore, adaptation in swarms includes not only behavioural changes but also structural flexibility, such as reorganizing formations, reallocating tasks, or switching roles. Agents may dynamically change their contribution to the group based on energy levels, environmental proximity, or learned expertise. This ability ensures that swarm systems remain robust and functional even when faced with disturbances, failures, or attacks. A key challenge in learning and adaptation is maintaining decentralization while ensuring that beneficial changes propagate effectively through the swarm. Algorithms must balance local autonomy with global coherence. Communication constraints, partial observability and heterogeneous agent capabilities further complicate the learning process. Recent research has made significant strides in enabling online learning, where agents continuously learn during operation and transfer learning, where experience from one environment can be applied to another. These approaches enhance the swarm's ability to generalize and perform across diverse settings. Applications of learning and adaptation are vast, ranging from environmental monitoring and disaster response to planetary exploration and autonomous farming. In each of these domains, the swarm's ability to learn and adapt directly correlates with its resilience, efficiency and overall mission success.

6.1 REINFORCEMENT LEARNING FOR MULTI-AGENT SYSTEMS

Reinforcement Learning (RL) is a powerful machine learning framework in which agents learn to make sequential decisions by interacting with their environment and receiving evaluative feedback in the form of rewards or penalties. Unlike supervised learning, RL does not require labelled datasets; instead, agents discover optimal behaviours through trial-and-error, gradually improving their decision-making policies over time. This paradigm is particularly well-suited for dynamic, complex, or partially observable environments where adaptability and autonomy are essential. When extended to multi-agent systems, such as robotic swarms, reinforcement learning takes on an added dimension of complexity and opportunity. In such settings, agents are not only influenced by their individual interactions with the environment, but also by the behaviours, strategies and decisions of their peers. This interdependence transforms the learning process into a rich, emergent phenomenon—often described as multi-agent reinforcement learning (MARL)—where cooperation, competition, or coordination dynamics must be accounted for. In swarm robotics, where individual units operate with limited sensing, computation and communication, RL enables agents to learn policies that balance local autonomy with global objectives. Through continuous exploration and feedback, swarm agents can learn to optimize collective behaviours such as formation control, area coverage, target tracking, or cooperative transport (Fig. 2).

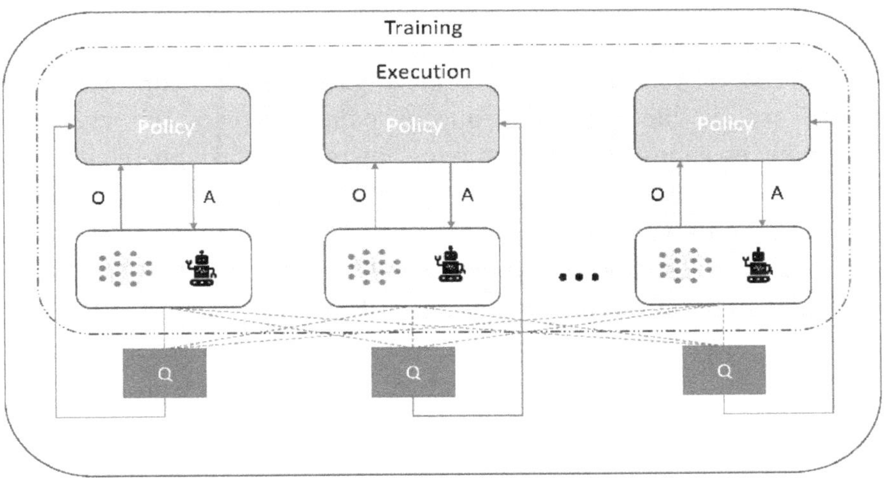

Fig. 2 Multi-Agent Deep Reinforcement Learning for Multi-Robot Applications

RL empowers agents to adapt to unforeseen circumstances, learn new strategies online and improve performance over repeated trials without explicit programming. Moreover, reward structures can be designed to promote desirable group-level behaviours—such as efficiency, safety, or fairness—while discouraging conflicts, collisions, or resource contention. Various architectures, including centralized training with decentralized execution (CTDE), have been proposed to handle the scalability and stability challenges in swarm MARL. Algorithms like Q-learning, policy gradients and actor-critic methods have been adapted to handle continuous action spaces, partial observability and sparse rewards, making them suitable for real-world swarm applications. Recent advances also explore the use of hierarchical RL and meta-learning to enable more abstract planning and rapid adaptation. By integrating RL into swarm systems, researchers and engineers can unlock new levels of intelligence, allowing robotic collectives to self-organize, learn from their collective experience and autonomously evolve behaviours over time. This positions reinforcement learning as a foundational tool for developing truly adaptive, resilient and scalable swarm intelligence in real-world missions ranging from environmental monitoring to search and rescue, exploration and logistics.

6.1.1. Fundamentals of Reinforcement Learning (RL)

Reinforcement Learning (RL) is a type of machine learning where an agent learns optimal behaviour by interacting with an environment, choosing actions and receiving feedback in the form of rewards, aiming to maximize long-term gains through trial and error.

- **Core Concept:** At the heart of Reinforcement Learning lies the concept of learning through interaction. An agent, placed in an environment, observes its current state and selects actions that yield feedback in the form of rewards. Over time, the agent learns a policy—a strategy for choosing the best action in any given state. The goal is to maximize cumulative or long-term reward, rather than immediate gains. Unlike supervised learning, there are no labelled input-output pairs. Instead, the agent explores different possibilities, often making mistakes. Through trial and error, it refines its decision-making. This adaptive learning approach is especially powerful in dynamic or uncertain environments. RL mimics how humans and animals learn from experience. The agent's performance improves through experience accumulation. Ultimately, RL enables autonomous decision-making systems to learn optimal behaviours over time.

Components:

- **Agent:** The agent is the core learner and decision-maker in Reinforcement Learning. It is responsible for choosing actions based on observations of the environment. The agent receives rewards or penalties depending on its choices. Its objective is to learn from experience and improve its behaviour. By interacting repeatedly with the environment, the agent updates its strategy or policy. Initially, it might act randomly, but over time, it begins to favour actions that yield better rewards. The agent encapsulates the intelligence of the system. It uses value functions, models, or direct policy search to guide learning. It can be simple (like a table of values) or complex (like a deep neural network). The design of the agent determines how effectively it can learn. Ultimately, the agent embodies the system's ability to make informed, adaptive decisions.

- **Environment:** The environment represents everything external to the agent that the agent can interact with. It includes the dynamics, constraints and feedback mechanisms the agent must learn to handle. When the agent takes an action, the environment responds by transitioning to a new state and emitting a reward. This interaction loop continues, forming a sequence of experiences. The environment defines the rules of the game the agent must master. It can be simulated (as in games) or real-world (like robotics or finance). The environment might be fully observable or partially observable, deterministic or stochastic. The complexity of the environment impacts how challenging it is for the agent to learn. It provides the structure within which learning occurs. Modeling the environment, when possible, can accelerate learning. Ultimately, the environment tests the agent's ability to generalize and adapt.
- **State (s):** A state is a representation of the agent's current situation in the environment. It encodes all relevant information needed to make a decision. A good state captures enough context to predict the consequences of actions. States can be low-dimensional (e.g., a grid location) or high-dimensional (e.g., an image of a game screen). The state serves as input to the agent's policy or value function. Accurate state representation is critical for effective learning. Poor state design can hinder the agent's ability to learn optimal behaviours. In partially observable settings, the agent may rely on history to approximate the state. Some algorithms learn the state representation automatically. States form the basis of the decision-making loop in RL. Transitions between states occur as a result of agent actions and environmental responses. Understanding the structure of the state space is key to solving RL problems.
- **Action (a):** An action is a decision or move the agent makes in response to its current state. It represents the possible choices available to the agent at any given moment. Actions can be discrete (e.g., move left, right) or continuous (e.g., adjust speed or angle). The chosen action directly affects the next state and the reward received. Selecting the right action is crucial to achieving long-term success. The agent explores different actions to learn their consequences. Over time, it exploits its knowledge to choose better actions. The balance between exploration and exploitation is central to RL. Actions are selected according to the agent's policy, which may

evolve during learning. Action spaces can vary in size and complexity. The design of the action set affects learning performance. Actions are the agent's primary means of influencing the environment.

- **Reward (r):** The reward is a numerical signal given to the agent after taking an action. It tells the agent how good or bad that action was in the current context. Rewards guide the learning process by reinforcing desirable behaviours. A positive reward encourages repetition of an action; a negative one discourages it. The reward function is often handcrafted and must reflect the goals of the task. Immediate rewards may be sparse or deceptive, making long-term planning essential. The agent's objective is to maximize the total cumulative reward over time. Rewards can be scaled, delayed, or noisy, adding to the challenge of learning. The agent estimates expected future rewards using value functions. In complex tasks, shaping the reward properly is key to successful learning. Ultimately, rewards form the feedback loop that drives policy improvement. Without a clear reward signal, effective learning is nearly impossible.
- **Policy (π):** The policy is the agent's strategy for selecting actions based on states. It can be deterministic (one action per state) or stochastic (a distribution over actions). The policy defines the agent's behaviour and is central to reinforcement learning. Learning a good policy is the main goal of most RL algorithms. A policy can be explicitly modelled or implicitly represented in a neural network. The quality of a policy is judged by the rewards it yields over time. As the agent learns, the policy improves through updates based on experience. Some methods learn the policy directly (policy-based), while others derive it from value estimates (value-based). Policies can generalize across similar states for efficiency. A well-optimized policy balances immediate gains with long-term benefits. The ultimate aim is to find an optimal policy that maximizes expected return. In essence, the policy is the brain of the agent.
- **Value Function (V):** The value function estimates how good it is to be in a given state, under a particular policy. It reflects the expected cumulative future reward from that state onward. Value functions help the agent evaluate decisions without immediate rewards. There are two main types: the state-value function (V) and the action-value function (Q). These functions guide the agent in selecting better actions over time. Value-based methods like Q-learning rely heavily on accurate value estimates. The value function is learned from experience using algorithms like Temporal Difference (TD) learning. It helps bridge the gap between short-term rewards and long-term goals. Errors in value estimation can misguide the agent's behaviour. Deep RL methods often use neural networks to approximate complex value

functions. Learning accurate value estimates is critical for effective policy improvement. In summary, value functions quantify the future potential of states or actions.

- **Learning Goal:** The fundamental goal of reinforcement learning is to discover a policy that maximizes long-term cumulative reward. This is achieved through repeated interactions with the environment, using trial and error. The agent learns from its successes and mistakes, refining its strategy over time. Unlike supervised learning, no ground-truth answers are provided; the agent must explore to learn. Balancing exploration (trying new actions) and exploitation (choosing known good actions) is key. The agent must infer which sequences of actions lead to the best outcomes. It builds knowledge of the environment's dynamics, either explicitly or implicitly. This process enables the agent to adapt to changing or uncertain conditions. Learning is often incremental, guided by the feedback encoded in rewards. Success is measured by how well the agent can generalize and perform. The end goal is robust, autonomous decision-making in complex settings. Reinforcement learning, at its core, is about mastering environments through experience..

6.1.2. RL in Multi-Agent Settings

Reinforcement Learning in multi-agent settings extends the classic single-agent framework to environments where multiple agents learn and act simultaneously. Each agent operates with its own goals, observations and actions, interacting not only with the environment but also with other agents. These interactions can be cooperative, competitive, or mixed, depending on the nature of the task. In cooperative settings, agents work together to maximize a shared reward, such as in team-based robotics or swarm intelligence. In competitive scenarios, like games or auctions, agents strive to outperform others, often resulting in adversarial dynamics. Learning becomes significantly more complex due to the non-stationarity introduced by other agents who are also learning and adapting. Policies must account for the evolving behaviours of peers and opponents. Techniques like centralized training with decentralized execution (CTDE) are commonly used to address coordination challenges. Communication protocols and shared representations are often incorporated to enhance cooperation. In competitive domains, strategies such as opponent modelling and self-play are vital. Multi-agent RL (MARL) also raises unique questions about fairness, equilibrium and stability. Applications include autonomous driving, multi-robot systems, finance and distributed control. The field combines elements of game theory, distributed systems and machine learning. As agents learn in parallel, emergent behaviours can arise, making MARL both powerful and unpredictable. Designing scalable, sample-efficient and robust MARL algorithms remains a major research challenge. Nonetheless, it holds promise for solving real-world problems involving decentralized decision-making and dynamic interactions.

Types of Multi-Agent RL (MARL): Multi-Agent Reinforcement Learning (MARL) encompasses a variety of settings based on how agents interact with each other. Broadly, these interactions fall into three categories: cooperative, competitive and mixed. In cooperative MARL, all agents aim to achieve a shared objective, requiring coordination and communication to succeed. Competitive MARL involves agents with opposing goals, where one's gain is another's loss—common in adversarial games and strategic planning. Mixed MARL presents a blend, where agents may cooperate in some situations and compete in others, reflecting more realistic and complex environments. Each type poses unique challenges in learning dynamics, policy optimization and stability. Understanding these distinctions is crucial for designing effective multi-agent systems. The structure of agent interaction defines the strategy space and learning architecture. As a result, the choice of MARL type directly impacts algorithm design and system behaviour.

- **Cooperative:** In cooperative MARL, all agents work together toward a shared objective, aiming to maximize a common reward signal. Collaboration is key and agents often need to coordinate actions to succeed. This setting is common in tasks like multi-robot control, sensor networks and distributed resource allocation. Agents may share observations, policies, or communicate to improve joint performance. Learning stable policies can be challenging due to inter-agent dependencies. Algorithms like QMIX and MADDPG (in cooperative mode) are often applied. Success relies on synchronized behaviour and mutual understanding among agents.
- **Competitive:** In competitive MARL, agents have conflicting goals and success for one may mean failure for another. This setting models adversarial environments such as games, auctions, or security scenarios. Agents aim to outmanoeuvre opponents while adapting to their changing strategies. The environment becomes non-stationary due to simultaneous learning by others. Techniques like self-play, minimax strategies and opponent modelling are used. Competitive learning fosters strategic behaviour and robust decision-making. Game theory concepts like Nash equilibrium often underpin policy evaluation and design.
- **Mixed:** Mixed MARL environments feature a blend of cooperation and competition, where agents might align or clash depending on the situation. This setting mirrors many real-world scenarios like traffic systems, trading markets, or multiplayer games. Agents must adaptively decide when to cooperate and when to act selfishly. This dual nature increases

the complexity of learning and strategy formulation. Policies must be flexible and context-aware, often requiring sophisticated coordination and negotiation mechanisms. Mixed settings challenge both individual and collective intelligence. Achieving balanced, stable behaviour is a key research focus in this domain.

Learning Approaches:

- **Independent Learners:** In this approach, each agent learns its own policy independently, treating other agents as part of the environment. It simplifies the learning process by reducing complexity and decentralizing control. However, because other agents are also learning and changing, the environment appears non-stationary, which can destabilize learning. Despite this, it scales well and is easy to implement. It works better in low-interaction or weakly coupled scenarios. Coordination is typically poor unless emergent behaviour arises. Algorithms like independent Q-learning fall under this category.
- **Centralized Training with Decentralized Execution (CTDE):** CTDE offers a balanced framework where agents are trained with access to global information (e.g., full state, other agents' actions), but must act independently during execution. This allows for better coordination during learning without violating real-world constraints like communication limits. It combines the benefits of centralized optimization and decentralized scalability. Many modern MARL algorithms, like MADDPG and COMA, follow this paradigm. CTDE mitigates non-stationarity during training by treating agents' policies as fixed. It's widely used in cooperative and mixed settings. Effective in high-stakes environments like autonomous driving and robotics.
- **Joint Action Learners:** Joint Action Learners explicitly model the actions of other agents during learning. Agents attempt to predict or observe the joint action space to make better decisions. This approach promotes coordination and strategic reasoning but faces scalability challenges as the number of agents increases. It assumes that agents can observe or infer others' actions, which isn't always feasible. Joint action learning is effective in tightly coupled environments. It supports richer interaction modelling compared to independent learners. Algorithms in this category often rely on joint Q-values or strategy modelling.

6.1.3. Relevance to Swarm Robotics

- **Decentralization:** Swarm robotic systems are inherently decentralized, relying on local sensing, limited communication and individual decision-making. Reinforcement Learning (RL) aligns naturally with this paradigm, particularly in decentralized or distributed RL frameworks. Each robot (agent) can independently learn from its own experiences, adapting its policy based on local observations and rewards. This reduces reliance on a central controller, which is often a bottleneck or single point of failure in large-scale systems. Distributed RL enables robots to operate robustly in environments where communication is sparse or unreliable. Moreover, by limiting the need for global knowledge, systems become more resilient to dynamic conditions and partial observability. Decentralized learning also allows for flexible deployment, where robots can be added or removed without retraining the entire system. Techniques such as independent Q-learning or decentralized actor-critic methods are applicable here. Importantly, decentralization enhances robustness and fault tolerance in swarm behaviour. It also supports scalability, since each agent maintains only its local policy and observations. This approach mirrors how social insects or natural swarms operate—autonomously but with collective intelligence. The success of swarm RL depends on designing local learning rules that, when scaled, lead to desirable global behaviour. Decentralization remains a cornerstone in aligning MARL with swarm robotics objectives.

- **Adaptability:** Adaptability is critical for swarm robotic systems, as they often operate in dynamic, unpredictable environments. Reinforcement Learning provides a powerful mechanism for enabling this adaptability. Through continuous interaction with the environment, each agent can adjust its behaviour to cope with changing conditions, obstacles, or task requirements. For instance, if an agent encounters a new terrain or a failure in its team, RL allows it to re-learn or adjust its strategy without explicit reprogramming. This adaptability extends to structural changes within the swarm, such as fluctuating team sizes or role switching. Policies learned via RL are not static—they evolve with experience, enabling long-term improvement and resilience. Multi-agent variants of RL also allow agents to adapt to the behaviour of their peers, essential for maintaining coordination in non-stationary multi-agent settings. This is especially useful in applications like disaster response, environmental monitoring, or planetary exploration, where pre-programmed responses may fall short. Meta-RL and lifelong learning approaches further enhance an agent's ability to generalize and adapt across tasks. Adaptability via RL ensures that swarm systems remain functional and efficient even when facing unexpected challenges. It leads to more autonomous, self-sustaining teams of robots. Ultimately, adaptability through RL empowers swarms with real-time learning capabilities, crucial for long-term autonomy.

- **Scalability:** Swarm robotics often involves deploying dozens, hundreds, or even thousands of agents, making scalability a non-negotiable requirement. Reinforcement Learning, when carefully designed, can scale to large agent populations with minimal central oversight. One of the core challenges is ensuring that as more agents are added, performance does not degrade due to interference or coordination bottlenecks. Distributed and decentralized RL approaches tackle this by allowing agents to learn and operate independently, or by leveraging local interactions. Shared policies, parameter sharing, or role-based learning are common strategies to reduce training overhead in large swarms. Algorithms like multi-agent PPO and value decomposition methods can be modified to handle increasing agent counts efficiently. Scalability is also supported by communication-efficient learning protocols, where only necessary information is exchanged between agents. Importantly, scalable RL methods reduce training time and computational requirements, making them practical for real-world swarm systems. In scenarios such as area coverage, cooperative transport, or collective surveillance, scalable learning ensures that task performance remains high regardless of swarm size. Moreover, scalable RL contributes to swarm redundancy and robustness—if some agents fail, others continue the task with minimal disruption. Ultimately, RL's scalability enhances the practicality and reliability of deploying intelligent, learning-based swarm systems in diverse environments.
- **Behaviour Emergence:** One of the most fascinating aspects of swarm robotics is the emergence of complex, intelligent behaviours from simple, individual rules. Reinforcement Learning plays a key role in enabling such emergent behaviour. Agents trained with simple reward structures can collectively develop sophisticated group dynamics, such as flocking, foraging, area coverage, or obstacle avoidance. These behaviours are not explicitly coded but arise from the interplay of local policies and interactions over time. RL facilitates this emergence by allowing agents to discover strategies through trial and error, guided only by reward signals. For example, a swarm of robots might independently learn to spread out to maximize area exploration, resulting in efficient coverage as an emergent property. Emergent behaviour is particularly valuable in unknown or dynamic environments where centralized planning is impractical. Even with minimal communication, RL can enable coordination through behaviour shaping and environment-mediated signals. Techniques like reward shaping, curriculum learning, or multi-agent credit assignment enhance the emergence of desirable patterns. Behaviour emergence reduces the need for extensive manual design and programming. It also improves

generalization and adaptability across different tasks or environments. Ultimately, RL fosters autonomous coordination where global goals are achieved through decentralized, self-organized learning. This makes it a powerful tool in scaling up intelligent swarm systems.

6.1.4. Common RL Algorithms in Swarm Systems

- **Q-Learning:** Q-Learning is one of the foundational RL algorithms where agents learn a Q-value function that estimates the expected future reward of taking a given action in a specific state. It is model-free and uses a simple update rule to iteratively improve the value estimates. In swarm robotics, Q-learning enables individual agents to learn optimal behaviours such as navigation, obstacle avoidance, or target tracking through trial and error. Since it's lightweight and easy to implement, Q-learning is suitable for resource-constrained robots. However, it can struggle in multi-agent settings due to non-stationarity caused by other learning agents. Still, with appropriate modifications—like independent Q-learning—it remains a popular choice for decentralized learning in swarms. It performs well in discrete action spaces and can lead to emergent coordination when designed carefully. Q-learning is a solid baseline for simple swarm tasks where environment complexity is manageable.
- **SARSA (State-Action-Reward-State-Action):** SARSA is a variation of Q-learning that updates the value function based on the actual action taken by the agent, rather than the maximum estimated value. This on-policy learning makes SARSA more cautious, which can be beneficial in safety-critical swarm applications such as cooperative flying or formation control. In swarm systems, SARSA helps agents learn more conservative or stable policies, especially when their actions might interfere with others. Like Q-learning, it is simple to implement and works well in environments with discrete actions and limited state spaces. SARSA can be particularly effective in tight, high-density swarm formations where the cost of exploration is high. Its performance depends on careful tuning of exploration strategies like ε-greedy policies. While less aggressive than Q-learning, its on-policy nature often results in smoother collective behaviour among agents.
- **Deep Q-Networks (DQN):** DQN extends Q-learning by using deep neural networks to approximate the Q-value function, enabling learning in high-dimensional or continuous state spaces. This makes DQN highly relevant in swarm robotics applications that involve rich sensory inputs, such as vision-based navigation or aerial mapping. DQN's use of experience replay and target networks helps stabilize learning, which is essential in dynamic multi-agent environments. For swarm systems, DQNs can be deployed

on more capable robots to manage complex perception and decision-making tasks. However, applying DQN in multi-agent scenarios requires adjustments to handle non-stationarity and interference among agents. Techniques such as parameter sharing and multi-agent experience replay can help adapt DQN to swarm settings. DQN has been used in simulated drone swarms, coordinated exploration and distributed surveillance tasks. Despite its power, computational demands can be a limiting factor for real-time embedded swarm systems.

- **Policy Gradient Methods:** Policy gradient methods take a direct approach by optimizing the agent's policy instead of estimating value functions. They use gradient ascent to update policy parameters in the direction that increases expected reward. This makes them suitable for environments with continuous or stochastic action spaces, which are common in swarm robotics tasks like cooperative manipulation or adaptive flocking. Unlike value-based methods, policy gradients can learn smooth and probabilistic behaviours, which leads to more natural coordination in swarms. These methods are often used in continuous control problems where discrete actions are not expressive enough. Their main drawback is high variance in updates, which can lead to unstable training. Nonetheless, techniques like baseline subtraction and entropy regularization can mitigate these issues. Policy gradient algorithms encourage exploration and can generalize well in complex, partially observable swarm scenarios.
- **Actor-Critic Methods:** Actor-Critic methods combine the strengths of both value-based and policy-based learning. The actor updates the policy directly, while the critic estimates the value function to provide feedback. This dual structure leads to more stable and sample-efficient learning. In swarm robotics, actor-critic methods are especially useful when dealing with continuous and cooperative control, such as synchronized drone flying or underwater robot coordination. The critic helps reduce the variance in policy updates, which is crucial when multiple agents interact in a noisy environment. Algorithms like A2C and A3C (Asynchronous Advantage Actor-Critic) are popular for their scalability and parallelism. These methods are also compatible with CTDE, making them well-suited for training agents in multi-agent swarm scenarios. Actor-critic architectures allow swarms to learn nuanced, coordinated behaviours while retaining decentralized decision-making during deployment.
- **Multi-Agent Deep Deterministic Policy Gradient (MADDPG):** MADDPG is a powerful RL algorithm specifically designed for multi-agent environments with continuous action spaces. It is based on the CTDE (Centralized Training with Decentralized Execution) framework, where each agent

learns a deterministic policy (actor) and shares a centralized critic during training. This setup helps each agent learn stable policies by accounting for other agents' actions during training. In swarm robotics, MADDPG is ideal for tasks like formation control, collective pushing, or swarm-level coordination where actions are smooth and interdependent. By modelling the actions of other agents, MADDPG can facilitate emergent cooperation even in competitive or mixed settings. It handles scalability well through shared network architectures and selective communication. While it requires centralized data during training, the learned policies can operate independently during execution. MADDPG has shown success in simulated robotic swarms and is considered state-of-the-art for continuous multi-agent control tasks (Table-1).

Table -1 : Common RL Algorithms in Swarm Systems with their features and relevance

Algorithm	Features	Relevance in Swarm Systems
Q-Learning	Learns Q-values for state-action pairs using a value iteration update rule.	Simple and efficient for discrete actions; suitable for decentralized agents.
SARSA	On-policy method that updates Q-values based on the action actually taken by the agent.	More cautious than Q-learning; useful in safety-critical swarm tasks.
Deep Q-Networks (DQN)	Uses neural networks to approximate Q-values, enabling learning in high-dimensional spaces.	Handles complex sensory input; suitable for advanced perception tasks in swarms.
Policy Gradient Methods	Directly optimize the policy using gradient ascent, allowing stochastic and continuous actions.	Effective for continuous control tasks and smoother coordinated behaviors.
Actor-Critic Methods	Combines value function estimation (critic) with policy optimization (actor) for stable learning.	Enhances sample efficiency and stability in continuous multi-agent environments.
Multi-Agent Deep Deterministic Policy Gradient (MADDPG)	CTDE-based algorithm for continuous actions; centralized critic, decentralized actors.	Supports multi-agent coordination with continuous actions; widely used in swarm robotics.

6.1.5. Challenges in multi-Agent RL

- **Non-Stationarity:** One of the fundamental challenges in Multi-Agent Reinforcement Learning is non-stationarity—the environment changes as each agent learns. Unlike single-agent RL, where the environment is typically fixed, in MARL every agent is simultaneously adapting its behaviour. As a result, an agent's past experience may no longer be relevant because the dynamics it learned from have changed. This makes learning unstable and convergence difficult. Algorithms that assume a stationary environment, such as basic Q-learning, often perform poorly in these conditions. Addressing non-stationarity requires mechanisms like opponent modelling, where agents try to predict others' behaviours, or learning robust policies that perform well across variations. Another solution is to stabilize training using centralized critics or population-based training. Curriculum learning can also help by gradually increasing complexity. Temporal credit assignment becomes harder, as effects of actions can depend on evolving policies of others. Ultimately, the non-stationary nature of MARL adds a layer of complexity that demands specialized architectures and careful algorithm design to ensure convergence and reliability.

- **Scalability:** Scalability is a critical challenge in MARL, especially for swarm robotics and large-scale systems. As the number of agents increases, the joint state and action spaces grow exponentially, making it computationally infeasible to model or learn directly from the entire joint space. This phenomenon, known as the curse of dimensionality, leads to slower learning, degraded performance and difficulties in coordination. Communication, computation and storage requirements also increase with swarm size. Strategies like parameter sharing, decentralized training and hierarchical learning can help alleviate these issues. Additionally, using local observations and interactions reduces dependency on global state knowledge. However, ensuring that agents still coordinate effectively under these constraints remains a challenge. Scalable algorithms like value decomposition networks or CTDE frameworks have shown promise, but often require compromises in precision or generalization. Designing algorithms that remain sample-efficient and stable as swarm size increases is a pressing area of MARL research. Scalability is essential for deploying MARL in real-world, large-scale autonomous systems.
- **Credit Assignment:** The credit assignment problem in MARL involves determining which agent (or agents) contributed to the observed outcome or reward. In cooperative settings, rewards are often global or shared, making it unclear how much each individual agent's action influenced success or failure. Without proper credit assignment, agents may learn suboptimal or even conflicting behaviours. This challenge is especially prominent in swarm robotics, where collective tasks like foraging or formation flying depend on the synchronized efforts of many agents. Techniques such as difference rewards, counterfactual reasoning (as in COMA), or attention-based critics have been developed to address this issue. These methods attempt to isolate the impact of individual actions within a joint outcome.

However, these approaches can be computationally expensive or limited by the observability of other agents. Accurate credit assignment improves learning efficiency, promotes cooperation and accelerates convergence. Without it, agents might receive misleading feedback, resulting in unstable or ineffective policies. It remains a major bottleneck in designing effective multi-agent learning systems.

- **Communication Constraints:** Effective coordination often depends on communication, but communication constraints—such as limited bandwidth, latency and signal range—pose major challenges in MARL. Especially in swarm robotics, where agents may operate in remote, cluttered, or adversarial environments, communication can be intermittent or costly. These constraints limit the amount and quality of information agents can exchange, making joint decision-making harder. Some MARL frameworks rely on centralized training that assumes full observability, which may not be feasible at deployment. Designing communication-efficient algorithms becomes essential. Techniques like message gating, selective communication and emergent communication protocols can help. Learning when and what to communicate is a growing research area in MARL. Communication also adds latency and noise, which can degrade coordination if not handled properly. Decentralized approaches that reduce dependency on communication—by leveraging local policies and observations—are often more robust. Balancing communication overhead with task performance is critical in real-time, resource-constrained swarm systems.
- **Exploration vs. Exploitation:** In MARL, the classic exploration-exploitation dilemma becomes even more complex. Each agent must explore new actions to improve its policy while also exploiting known strategies for immediate reward. However, in multi-agent settings, exploration by one agent can disrupt the learning process of others, introducing noise and instability. Conversely, if all agents exploit too early, the system may converge to suboptimal joint behaviours. Coordinated exploration is especially challenging, as independent exploration can lead to inefficient or redundant behaviour. Approaches like shared experience buffers, curiosity-driven learning, or randomized policy initialization can improve exploration strategies. Some systems also use role-based exploration, where certain agents specialize in exploring while others exploit. The difficulty is magnified in high-dimensional or partially observable environments where safe and effective exploration is hard to define. Balancing this trade-off is crucial for convergence, performance and policy generalization.

Poorly managed exploration can lead to instability, oscillating behaviour, or deadlock in swarm systems. Solving this challenge is key to unlocking robust, scalable MARL deployments (Table-2).

Table- 2 : The Challenges in Multi-Agent Reinforcement Learning (MARL) along with brief descriptions

Challenge	Description
Non-Stationarity	Environment changes dynamically as all agents learn simultaneously, causing instability in learning.
Scalability	Exponential growth of joint state and action spaces as the number of agents increases.
Credit Assignment	Difficulty in determining which agent's actions contributed to collective rewards or outcomes.
Communication Constraints	Limited bandwidth, range and reliability of communication restrict information sharing among agents.
Exploration vs. Exploitation	Balancing the need to explore new strategies while exploiting known successful behaviours.

6.1.6. Solutions and Enhancements

- **Reward Shaping:** Reward shaping involves carefully designing reward functions to provide more informative and frequent feedback to agents during learning. In multi-agent and swarm settings, simple global rewards can be sparse or delayed, making it difficult for agents to understand which actions contribute to success. By incorporating intermediate or shaped rewards that capture sub-goals, such as proximity to a target or maintaining formation, agents receive clearer guidance. This accelerates learning and improves policy quality. Reward shaping also helps mitigate the credit assignment problem by attributing rewards to more immediate, agent-specific behaviours. However, poorly designed rewards can lead to unintended behaviours or gaming of the system, so balance and domain expertise are crucial. Techniques like potential-based shaping ensure that reward modifications do not alter the optimal policy. In swarm robotics, reward shaping can encourage cooperative behaviour such as coordinated foraging or collision avoidance. By aligning local rewards with global objectives, reward shaping facilitates emergent, efficient swarm strategies. It remains a practical and widely adopted method to enhance learning speed and stability in MARL.
- **Role Differentiation:** Role differentiation assigns specific roles or responsibilities to agents within a swarm to simplify coordination and reduce learning complexity. Instead of all agents learning the same policy, specialized roles—like leader, scout, or transporter—enable

division of labour, making large-scale coordination more manageable. This specialization can improve efficiency by focusing learning on distinct sub-tasks, allowing agents to optimize behaviours relevant to their roles. Role differentiation also aids scalability by limiting the action and state spaces each agent must consider. It encourages modular policy design, where role-specific policies can be independently developed and updated. Furthermore, dynamic role assignment can enable adaptability, where agents switch roles in response to environmental changes or team needs. Role differentiation reflects natural systems, such as ant colonies or bee hives, where specialized castes perform dedicated tasks. In swarm robotics, implementing roles improves robustness and task allocation, particularly in complex missions involving heterogeneous agents. Challenges include defining roles clearly and enabling effective communication between roles. When done well, role differentiation dramatically enhances swarm coordination and learning efficiency.

- **Curriculum Learning:** Curriculum learning gradually increases task complexity during training, allowing agents to build foundational skills before tackling harder challenges. This approach mimics human learning, where mastering basic concepts first supports understanding of more difficult tasks. In MARL, curriculum learning can help agents cope with the complexity of multi-agent interactions and high-dimensional state spaces. For example, agents might first learn simple navigation before progressing to cooperative exploration or adversarial scenarios. Breaking down complex problems into sequenced stages prevents agents from being overwhelmed, reducing training instability and speeding up convergence. Curriculum designs can be manual or automatic, adapting dynamically based on agent performance. This is especially useful in swarm robotics where tasks may require multiple coordinated behaviours—exploration, formation and foraging—each introduced progressively. Curriculum learning supports transferability and generalization, preparing agents for real-world deployment. However, designing effective curricula requires domain knowledge and experimentation. When implemented effectively, curriculum learning improves sample efficiency, robustness and final policy quality in multi-agent settings.
- **Shared Experience Replay Buffers:** Shared experience replays buffers allow agents to learn not only from their own experiences but also from those of their peers. This cooperative learning mechanism accelerates training by increasing the diversity and volume of experience data available during updates. In multi-agent environments, sharing experiences helps agents adapt to the behaviours of others more quickly and reduces sample

inefficiency. Replay buffers store past interactions, allowing agents to reuse valuable data multiple times and stabilize training. In swarm robotics, shared buffers can enable faster collective learning, especially when agents encounter rare but critical events. However, care must be taken to balance shared information, as over-sharing can lead to correlated updates and loss of policy diversity. Techniques like prioritized experience replay help focus learning on important transitions. Additionally, decentralized implementations limit communication overhead by selectively sharing key experiences. Overall, shared replay buffers are an effective enhancement to multi-agent RL that improve learning speed and promote more coherent swarm behaviours by leveraging collective knowledge.

- **Attention Mechanisms:** Attention mechanisms allow agents to selectively focus on the most relevant parts of their input—be it sensory data or other agents' behaviours—improving decision-making efficiency and accuracy. In multi-agent systems, attention helps filter out irrelevant information and prioritize critical interactions, which is crucial when dealing with many agents and high-dimensional observations. By learning to attend to key neighbours or environmental features, agents can better coordinate actions and avoid information overload. This leads to more scalable and robust policies, as agents adaptively allocate their limited computational resources. Attention mechanisms have been integrated into neural network architectures in MARL, enabling agents to dynamically weigh contributions from peers or state elements. This fosters better communication, cooperation and even emergent leadership in swarms. In practical terms, attention reduces noise and distractions, improving performance in cluttered or dynamic environments. It also enhances interpretability by highlighting decision drivers. In swarm robotics, attention enables agents to maintain focus on task-relevant cues like obstacles, targets, or team members, thereby improving collective efficiency and safety.
- **Communication Learning:** Communication learning empowers agents to learn not only how to act but also when and what to communicate with peers to improve coordination and task performance. In MARL, explicit communication can significantly enhance cooperation, especially in partially observable or dynamic environments. However, communication comes at a cost—bandwidth, latency and potential interference—so learning efficient protocols is critical. Agents can be trained to generate compact, meaningful messages that convey essential information like intentions, observations, or requests. End-to-end differentiable communication learning integrates message generation and policy learning, allowing communication strategies to evolve naturally. This adaptive communication enables

swarms to coordinate complex tasks such as distributed sensing, dynamic role assignment, or joint planning. Learning when to communicate avoids excessive messaging and reduces network congestion. Moreover, emergent communication protocols discovered through learning can be robust and flexible, surpassing handcrafted rules. In swarm robotics, communication learning enhances resilience and scalability, enabling large teams to operate effectively in challenging environments. This area continues to grow rapidly, opening new frontiers in autonomous multi-agent coordination.

6.1.7. Applications in Swarm Robotics

- **Foraging and Resource Gathering:** In swarm robotics, foraging and resource gathering tasks involve agents learning to efficiently search for, collect and transport valuable items or materials within an environment. Reinforcement learning enables individual agents to develop policies that optimize their paths, reducing redundancy and overlap in coverage. As agents explore the environment, they can adapt to dynamically changing resource locations and competition from other agents. Collective intelligence emerges as agents share learned strategies, leading to improved overall efficiency. RL also helps agents balance exploration of unknown areas with exploitation of known resource-rich zones. This adaptive behaviour is crucial when resources are scarce or randomly distributed. Additionally, agents can learn to coordinate transportation, such as carrying large items cooperatively or optimizing drop-off points. Foraging behaviours inspired by natural systems, like ant colonies, show how simple RL rules at the agent level can lead to robust, scalable resource collection. This application demonstrates the power of decentralized learning for complex, multi-step tasks in unpredictable environments.
- **Exploration and Mapping:** Exploration and mapping are fundamental tasks in many swarm robotics applications, where agents must collaboratively navigate and construct representations of unknown environments. Reinforcement learning enables agents to learn effective exploration strategies, balancing coverage and efficiency while avoiding redundant movements. Agents can develop policies that prioritize unexplored or high-value regions, enhancing map completeness. Collaborative RL facilitates information sharing, allowing agents to merge partial maps and update shared knowledge. This is critical in environments where GPS or centralized control is unavailable, such as underground, underwater, or disaster zones. RL also equips agents to adapt to dynamic or hazardous conditions, learning to avoid obstacles or dangerous areas while maximizing exploration. The emergence of coordinated behaviours such as boundary

tracing or frontier detection arises naturally from local policies. Ultimately, RL-driven exploration and mapping improve swarm autonomy, robustness and situational awareness, making it invaluable for search-and-rescue, environmental monitoring and surveillance tasks.

- **Formation Control:** Formation control tasks require agents to maintain specific geometric configurations while adapting to dynamic environmental conditions and internal changes within the swarm. Reinforcement learning enables agents to learn policies that balance maintaining formation shape, avoiding collisions and responding to external disturbances like wind or obstacles. Unlike traditional control methods that rely on precise modelling, RL allows agents to adaptively handle uncertainties and nonlinearities. Each agent uses local observations to adjust its position relative to neighbours, promoting scalable and decentralized formation maintenance. RL also supports dynamic formation changes, enabling swarms to morph shapes for specific tasks or constraints. For example, agents can learn to spread out for area coverage or cluster tightly for obstacle traversal. Through repeated interactions, agents develop robust coordination strategies that maintain formation integrity even with communication delays or failures. This application highlights the strength of MARL in achieving precise, adaptive collective motion in complex, real-world settings.
- **Target Tracking:** Target tracking involves swarms adaptively following and monitoring moving targets of interest, such as wildlife, vehicles, or environmental phenomena. Reinforcement learning equips agents with the ability to predict target trajectories and adjust their policies accordingly. Agents coordinate to surround or shadow targets, maximizing tracking accuracy while minimizing energy consumption and collision risks. RL helps agents learn how to distribute themselves spatially, ensuring coverage without overcrowding. The decentralized nature of the swarm allows continued tracking even if some agents fail or lose communication. Additionally, agents can learn to share tracking responsibilities dynamically, responding to changes in target speed or manoeuvring. Target tracking in swarms has applications in security, wildlife monitoring and environmental data collection. Reinforcement learning's ability to handle partial observability, noisy sensors and adversarial targets makes it especially suited for these complex, real-time tasks. This results in highly adaptable, resilient multi-agent tracking systems.
- **Collision Avoidance:** Collision avoidance is critical in swarm robotics to ensure safe movement in crowded or cluttered environments, preventing damage and mission failure. Reinforcement learning enables agents to develop reactive policies that dynamically adjust their trajectories based on

local sensory input. Agents learn to predict the movements of neighbours and obstacles, negotiating shared space with minimal communication. This decentralized approach allows scalability to large swarms, where centralized collision avoidance would be infeasible. RL can incorporate constraints like speed limits or energy budgets, optimizing movement for safety and efficiency simultaneously. By training in diverse simulated environments, agents generalize to new scenarios, including dynamic obstacles and complex terrain. Collision avoidance policies also contribute to smoother, more natural swarm behaviours, reducing bottlenecks and congestion. These capabilities are essential for real-world applications like warehouse automation, urban drone delivery, or autonomous traffic management. Overall, RL-driven collision avoidance enhances swarm robustness and operational safety in unpredictable settings.

- **Dynamic Task Allocation:** Dynamic task allocation enables swarms to self-organize and assign tasks in real time, adapting to changing environmental demands and agent capabilities. Reinforcement learning allows agents to learn policies for deciding when to take on new tasks, when to relinquish current ones and how to collaborate efficiently. This decentralized decision-making increases swarm flexibility and responsiveness without the need for central control. Agents can prioritize urgent or high-value tasks, balance workloads and manage resources effectively. Dynamic allocation supports heterogeneous swarms where agents have different abilities, ensuring tasks match agent strengths. RL also facilitates fault tolerance, allowing the swarm to reassign tasks if agents fail or conditions change. This is crucial in unpredictable or hostile environments like disaster response, where tasks and priorities evolve rapidly. Through learning, agents develop coordination protocols that minimize idle time and maximize overall swarm productivity. Dynamic task allocation exemplifies the power of MARL to achieve autonomous, adaptive and scalable multi-agent teamwork (Table-3).

Table-3 : Concise summary of the Applications in Swarm Robotics with their descriptions

Application	Description
Foraging and Resource Gathering	Agents learn to efficiently search for, collect and transport resources within an environment.
Exploration and Mapping	Reinforcement Learning enables agents to collaboratively explore and create maps of unknown areas.
Formation Control	Agents learn to maintain specific formations while adapting to dynamic and changing conditions.

Application	Description
Target Tracking	Swarms use RL to adaptively follow, monitor and track moving targets in real time.
Collision Avoidance	Agents develop policies to navigate safely through crowded or cluttered spaces, avoiding collisions.
Dynamic Task Allocation	RL allows agents to self-organize and dynamically assign tasks based on current demands and priorities.

6.2 EVOLUTIONARY AND GENETIC ALGORITHMS

Evolutionary Algorithms (EAs), including Genetic Algorithms (GAs), are optimization techniques inspired by the process of natural selection. These algorithms are especially well-suited for swarm robotics due to their ability to handle high-dimensional, non-linear and dynamic environments without the need for gradient-based learning or precise models. They enable the evolution of agent behaviours, communication strategies and control policies by simulating the principles of biological evolution such as selection, crossover, mutation and inheritance.

6.2.1. What are Evolutionary and Genetic Algorithms?

- **Evolutionary Algorithms (EAs):** Evolutionary Algorithms (EAs) are a broad class of optimization methods inspired by the principles of natural evolution and biological adaptation. They solve complex problems by iteratively improving a population of candidate solutions through mechanisms akin to natural selection, reproduction and mutation. Unlike gradient-based methods, EAs do not require gradient information and are effective for problems with noisy, discontinuous, or multi-modal search spaces. These algorithms maintain a diverse set of potential solutions, exploring the search space broadly to avoid premature convergence. EAs have been widely applied in engineering, machine learning, robotics and many other fields where traditional optimization techniques struggle. Their ability to handle multi-objective problems and constraints makes them particularly versatile. The evolutionary process mimics survival of the fittest, promoting individuals with higher quality solutions across generations. By leveraging randomness and selection pressures, EAs balance exploration and exploitation to converge on near-optimal solutions.
- **Genetic Algorithms (GAs):** Genetic Algorithms (GAs) are a well-known subtype of Evolutionary Algorithms that represent candidate solutions as chromosomes—strings of genes encoding problem variables. These genetic representations allow biologically inspired operations such as crossover (recombination) and mutation to create new offspring solutions. The core idea is to evolve a population of solutions over successive generations,

guided by a fitness function that quantitatively evaluates solution quality. Selection mechanisms favour individuals with higher fitness, increasing their chance to contribute genes to the next generation. Crossover mixes genetic material from two parents to explore new regions of the solution space, while mutation introduces random changes to maintain genetic diversity and avoid stagnation. GAs have proven successful across a variety of domains, including scheduling, machine learning hyperparameter tuning and robotic control. Their flexible encoding schemes and population-based search provide robustness against local optima and noisy environments. Genetic Algorithms exemplify the power of evolutionary principles to tackle complex, nonlinear optimization problems.

Basic Elements:

- **Population:** The population is a collection of candidate solutions, often called individuals or chromosomes, that represent different points in the solution space. Maintaining a diverse population helps the algorithm explore multiple regions simultaneously and reduces the risk of premature convergence to suboptimal solutions. Populations typically have fixed sizes and evolve over generations through selection, crossover and mutation. Initial populations can be randomly generated or seeded with domain-specific heuristics. Diversity within the population is crucial for effective search, enabling the algorithm to adapt and discover new, high-quality solutions. In swarm robotics or RL contexts, populations may represent policies, neural network weights, or control parameters. Effective population management balances exploration of new areas and exploitation of promising regions in the search space.
- **Fitness Function:** The fitness function quantitatively assesses how well each candidate solution solves the problem at hand. It acts as a measure of quality or performance, guiding selection and reproduction. Designing an effective fitness function is critical, as it directly influences the evolutionary search's direction and speed. The fitness function can be a single scalar value or a vector for multi-objective optimization. It may incorporate domain-specific constraints and penalties to ensure feasible solutions. In dynamic or noisy environments, fitness evaluations may be stochastic or involve averaging multiple trials to ensure reliability. For example, in swarm robotics, fitness might measure task completion rate, energy efficiency, or collective behaviour quality. A well-crafted fitness function encourages the emergence of desirable traits and avoids unintended optimization artifacts.
- **Selection:** Selection is the process of choosing individuals from the current population to serve as parents for the next generation. The goal is to

favour better-performing solutions while maintaining genetic diversity. Common selection methods include roulette wheel (fitness proportionate), tournament and rank-based selection. Selection pressure determines how strongly the algorithm favours fitter individuals; too high pressure may cause premature convergence, while too low pressure slows progress. By balancing exploitation of good solutions with exploration through diversity preservation, selection drives the evolutionary process. In multi-agent or swarm systems, selection helps refine populations of policies or parameters by promoting promising behaviours. Effective selection ensures that high-quality traits propagate, increasing the overall population fitness over generations.

- **Crossover:** Crossover, or recombination, is a genetic operator that combines parts of two parent chromosomes to produce offspring. This operation mimics biological reproduction, where offspring inherit genetic material from both parents, potentially mixing beneficial traits. Different crossover techniques exist, including single-point, multi-point and uniform crossover, each varying in how genes are exchanged. Crossover promotes exploration by creating novel solutions that may outperform their parents. It exploits existing good building blocks and assembles them into better combinations. In evolutionary robotics, crossover can recombine neural network parameters or control sequences to generate new behaviours. The effectiveness of crossover depends on the problem representation and the compatibility of parental genes. Properly designed crossover operators enhance the diversity and convergence speed of the algorithm.
- **Mutation:** Mutation introduces random changes to individual genes within chromosomes, ensuring genetic diversity and preventing premature convergence. By occasionally altering parts of a solution, mutation allows the algorithm to explore new areas of the search space that might be unreachable through crossover alone. Mutation rates must be carefully chosen; too high a rate turns the search into a random walk, while too low risks stagnation. Mutation can involve flipping bits in binary encodings, perturbing real-valued parameters, or modifying discrete elements. In multi-agent or swarm applications, mutation helps maintain robustness by encouraging policy variety. It also provides resilience against noisy fitness landscapes and dynamic environments. Mutation is essential for escaping local optima and sustaining long-term evolutionary progress.
- **Generations:** Generations represent discrete iterations of the evolutionary cycle, where a new population is created from the old through selection, crossover and mutation. Each generation ideally improves the overall

population fitness by producing better candidate solutions. The number of generations needed depends on the problem complexity, population size and algorithm parameters. Evolution proceeds until a stopping criterion is met, such as a fitness threshold, a maximum number of generations, or convergence detection. Throughout generations, the population ideally moves closer to optimal or near-optimal solutions, with diverse individuals exploring promising areas. In swarm robotics, generations can correspond to training cycles for evolving control policies or behaviours. Monitoring generational progress helps tune parameters and detect issues like premature convergence or loss of diversity.

6.2.2. Relevance to Swarm Robotics

- **Controller Design:** In swarm robotics, one of the core challenges is designing low-level controllers that govern individual agent behaviour. Genetic Algorithms (GAs) offer a powerful method for evolving these controllers automatically. Instead of manually crafting rules or tuning parameters, GAs can optimize control strategies—such as rule-based systems or neural network weights—based on performance in a simulated or real-world task. This is particularly useful when designing controllers for tasks like obstacle avoidance, flocking, or path following, where explicit programming may be complex or inflexible. The controller's genotype (e.g., a vector of neural weights) can evolve through generations, with selection based on task success. This approach allows rapid prototyping of behaviours without domain-specific programming. Furthermore, controller evolution can be task-specific (e.g., object retrieval) or general (e.g., adaptive locomotion). Since GAs are model-free and population-based, they are well-suited for nonlinear, high-dimensional problems, making them ideal for designing decentralized controllers in swarm systems. They also support optimization in environments with partial observability or noise, common in real-world swarm deployments.
- **Behaviour Evolution:** Beyond low-level control, GAs can also drive the evolution of high-level behaviours in swarm agents. Behaviour evolution involves developing strategies for navigation, aggregation, dispersion, foraging, or cooperative decision-making, often encoded as finite-state machines, behaviour trees, or rule sets. Agents can be evolved to achieve specific objectives, such as forming geometric patterns or exploring unknown environments. Fitness functions are designed to reward collective effectiveness, efficiency, or task completion. Over time, emergent strategies can arise that outperform manually engineered solutions. For example, agents might evolve efficient path coordination in a cluttered environment

or intelligent target pursuit through cooperative tracking. Since behaviour design in swarms is often non-intuitive, evolutionary methods excel by exploring solution spaces that human designers might overlook. These evolved behaviours can be modular, reusable across tasks and robust to environmental changes. This makes behaviour evolution a key tool for developing autonomous, flexible swarm systems that can adapt and scale in diverse operational contexts.

- **Decentralized Evolution:** A major advantage of using evolutionary methods in swarm robotics is their natural compatibility with decentralization. Traditional machine learning methods often rely on centralized training or control, but swarm systems require distributed decision-making due to scale, communication limits, or environmental constraints. With decentralized evolution, each agent—or small local group—evolves independently or shares partial information with neighbours. This setup mirrors biological systems, where adaptation occurs at the individual or group level through local interactions. Agents can adapt to local conditions, specialize in roles, or even develop complementary behaviours through co-evolution. Decentralized evolution enables online learning, allowing swarms to adapt in real-time to dynamic tasks or environments without external intervention. Algorithms like embodied evolution or evolutionary robotics frameworks support this local adaptation process. Additionally, decentralized evolution reduces bottlenecks, increases robustness to individual failures and scales well to large numbers of agents. It also allows for heterogeneity within the swarm, as different agents may evolve different strategies suited to their operational context.
- **Emergent Behaviour:** One of the most compelling reasons to apply evolutionary algorithms in swarm robotics is their ability to generate emergent behaviours—complex collective dynamics that arise from simple local interactions and rules. Rather than programming specific group outcomes, evolutionary processes discover agent-level strategies that, when executed in parallel by many agents, produce sophisticated global behaviours. Examples include self-organizing formations, coordinated area coverage, collective decision-making, or synchronized movement. These behaviours are often difficult to engineer directly due to the complexity of multi-agent interactions. Evolutionary algorithms enable the discovery of such patterns through simulation-based trial and error, guided by fitness functions that reward desirable system-level performance. Emergence is especially valuable in unpredictable environments where predefined strategies may fail. It also contributes to flexibility and resilience, as the swarm can adapt or reconfigure itself in response to changing conditions.

The ability of evolution to harness emergent dynamics makes it a powerful tool for designing scalable, adaptable and intelligent swarm systems.

- **Robustness:** Robustness is a critical requirement in swarm robotics, where agents must operate in noisy, dynamic, or partially observable environments, often with limited sensing, communication, or processing. Evolutionary methods, particularly GAs, tend to produce robust solutions because they explore a wide range of behaviours and optimize across diverse scenarios. During training, stochastic variations and random mutations encourage agents to develop policies that are not overfitted to a specific configuration or condition. As a result, the evolved behaviours generalize better and can withstand real-world uncertainties, such as sensor errors, communication delays, or hardware malfunctions. Moreover, evolutionary algorithms naturally support redundancy: multiple agents may evolve similar or complementary capabilities, ensuring that the system continues functioning even if some agents fail. This fault tolerance is essential for deploying swarms in mission-critical settings like disaster zones, deep-sea exploration, or space missions. Robustness achieved through evolutionary learning translates into higher reliability, flexibility and autonomy in swarm-based systems, making it a cornerstone of practical, long-term deployment.

6.2.3. Genetic Representation in Swarms

Genetic representation in swarms involves encoding potential solutions as chromosomes. These chromosomes can take various forms, such as binary strings, where sequences like 101010 represent sets of rules governing agent actions. Alternatively, real-valued vectors may be used, encoding parameters like weights that influence behaviour. In neuroevolutionary approaches, chromosomes often consist of neural network parameters that define how agents process information and respond to their environment. A crucial aspect of genetic representation is the phenotype mapping, where the encoded chromosomes are translated into actual agent behaviours or strategies within the swarm. This mapping is essential because it determines how the genotype—the encoded information—influences the overall swarm behaviour and performance. Effective phenotype mapping ensures that genetic variations lead to meaningful changes in swarm dynamics, enabling optimization and adaptation. Through this process, the swarm evolves by selecting and refining chromosomes that yield desirable collective behaviours. Thus, genetic representation and phenotype mapping together form the foundation for evolving complex swarm intelligence.

Chromosome Structure:

- Binary strings (e.g., 101010) representing rule sets.
- Real-valued vectors (e.g., weights for behaviour parameters).
- Neural network parameters (in neuroevolutionary approaches).

Phenotype Mapping:

- Chromosomes are translated into agent behaviours or strategies.
- The mapping defines how genotype influences swarm behaviour.

6.2.4. Fitness Evaluation in Multi-Agent Systems

- **Individual Fitness:** In multi-agent systems, individual fitness evaluation measures the performance of each agent independently based on its own actions and outcomes. This method is simple to implement and computationally efficient, especially in decentralized systems. It is useful when agents operate with minimal interaction or pursue loosely coupled objectives, such as local resource collection or obstacle avoidance. The fitness score may be calculated from metrics like distance travelled, tasks completed, or energy consumed. However, when cooperation or coordination is necessary, purely individual fitness can be problematic—it may ignore the value of collaborative behaviour and lead to selfish policies that harm group performance. For example, an agent might block others to maximize its own score, reducing overall efficiency. Despite this, individual fitness remains valuable for encouraging specialization or role differentiation in heterogeneous swarms. To improve fairness and promote cooperative dynamics, individual fitness is often complemented with team-based metrics or modified with penalties for behaviours that conflict with group goals.
- **Group Fitness:** Group fitness evaluates performance at the swarm or team level by considering how well all agents perform collectively. This approach is essential in tasks where coordination and synergy are crucial, such as formation control, area coverage, cooperative transport, or search-and-rescue missions. Group fitness might include metrics like total resources gathered, coverage uniformity, formation accuracy, or time to task completion. By rewarding collective outcomes, this evaluation encourages agents to cooperate, align strategies and contribute to the shared objective. One challenge, however, is the credit assignment problem—figuring out which agents contributed most to success or failure. This can reduce evolutionary pressure on individual agents, especially in large teams, potentially slowing adaptation. To address this, hybrid

methods may combine group-level assessment with agent-level statistics or introduce difference rewards that estimate individual contributions within the team context. Group fitness is a powerful driver of emergent coordination but needs careful design to avoid promoting passive or dependent behaviours.

- **Shared Fitness:** Shared fitness strategies aim to balance cooperation and individual accountability by distributing the group's overall fitness among its members in a way that reflects each agent's contribution. This method addresses issues like freeloading, where some agents benefit from group success without actively contributing. In shared fitness systems, each agent's reward is a function of its involvement in achieving the team's objectives. For example, in a foraging task, agents that collect more resources may receive a larger share of the group reward. Alternatively, shared fitness can be designed to equalize incentives and encourage synchronized behaviour, depending on the task. This approach promotes fairness, strengthens cooperation and mitigates the credit assignment problem. It is particularly effective in heterogeneous swarms, where agents may have different capabilities or roles. Implementing shared fitness requires careful calibration to ensure it neither penalizes cooperation nor inadvertently promotes selfishness. It is commonly used in multi-agent reinforcement learning (MARL) and evolutionary swarm robotics to encourage both individual initiative and group cohesion.
- **Co-Evolution:** Co-evolution involves evolving multiple agents simultaneously, where the fitness of each agent depends on the behaviours or adaptations of others in the population. This dynamic process reflects real-world multi-agent interactions, where success is context-dependent and shaped by the strategies of peers or opponents. Co-evolution can be competitive, as seen in predator-prey models or adversarial games, or cooperative, such as evolving partner strategies for collaborative tasks. The evolutionary pressure constantly shifts, pushing agents to adapt to one another, which can lead to an evolutionary arms race—a cycle of mutual improvement. Co-evolution is especially powerful in swarm systems with role specialization, emergent teamwork, or adaptive communication strategies. However, it comes with challenges such as maintaining stability, avoiding cyclic behaviours and ensuring sufficient diversity to prevent convergence to mediocre equilibria. Techniques like shared archives, diversity preservation, or hall-of-fame tracking are used to address these issues. Co-evolution is central to the development of adaptive, context-aware swarm intelligence.

6.2.5. Types of Evolutionary Techniques in Swarms

- **Standard Genetic Algorithms (GAs):** Standard Genetic Algorithms are the foundational approach in evolutionary computation, inspired by natural selection. They work by evolving a population of candidate solutions, where each individual (chromosome) encodes a potential solution—often represented as binary strings, real-valued vectors, or other compact forms. In swarm robotics, these individuals may represent control rules, behaviour parameters, or coordination strategies. The algorithm proceeds through cycles of selection (favouring fitter individuals), crossover (combining parts of two parents) and mutation (randomly modifying genes) to generate new offspring. Over successive generations, the population ideally converges toward more optimal behaviours. GAs is particularly effective for tasks requiring broad exploration of the search space, such as evolving navigation rules or optimizing distributed decision-making. Their simplicity and flexibility make them well-suited for decentralized swarm scenarios. However, without diversity-preserving mechanisms or task-specific enhancements, standard GAs may suffer from premature convergence or slow adaptation in complex swarm environments.
- **Neuroevolution (e.g., NEAT, HyperNEAT):** Neuroevolutionary refers to the use of evolutionary algorithms to optimize artificial neural networks (ANNs)—both their weights and, in advanced methods, their architectures. In swarm robotics, neuroevolutionary enables agents to learn complex mappings from sensor inputs to motor outputs without requiring gradient-based learning, which is often infeasible due to partial observability and noisy environments. Approaches like NEAT (NeuroEvolution of Augmenting Topologies) evolve both network structure and parameters, allowing agents to gradually develop more complex behaviour representations. HyperNEAT, an extension of NEAT, exploits geometric regularities by encoding connectivity patterns using compositional pattern-producing networks (CPPNs), making it especially useful for coordinated swarm behaviours like formation control or cooperative exploration. Neuroevolution supports end-to-end learning, accommodates continuous state/action spaces and is robust to noisy inputs—making it ideal for real-world swarm robotics. However, training can be computationally intensive and evolved networks may lack interpretability compared to hand-coded rules or symbolic controllers.
- **Evolution Strategies (ES):** Evolution Strategies (ES) are a class of evolutionary techniques that focus primarily on mutation and selection, with less emphasis on crossover. They typically operate on real-valued vectors and

emphasize self-adaptation, where mutation rates or strategy parameters evolve along with the candidate solutions. In swarm robotics, ES can be used to fine-tune continuous behaviour parameters, such as movement speed, sensing thresholds, or communication frequencies. Modern variants like Covariance Matrix Adaptation ES (CMA-ES) adaptively adjust search distributions, enabling efficient optimization in high-dimensional, non-linear spaces. ES is particularly suitable for evolving controllers in continuous control tasks, such as coordinated motion, obstacle avoidance, or target tracking. Compared to GAs, ES methods are more focused on local refinement and are often more sample-efficient in smooth search spaces. Their deterministic nature also makes them favourable for scenarios where repeatability and convergence speed are important. ES has also gained popularity for being parallelizable and scalable for large population-based search.

- **Genetic Programming (GP):** Genetic Programming evolves entire program structures, often represented as syntax trees, to create interpretable and modular behaviours for agents. In swarm robotics, GP can be used to evolve decision-making logic, reactive rules, or control algorithms composed of logical and arithmetic operations. Each individual in the population is a candidate program and genetic operators like subtree crossover and mutation modify these trees to produce new behaviours. GP is particularly valuable when transparency and modularity are important—e.g., in safety-critical applications or when human operators must understand or modify the learned policies. It also excels in symbolic domains where behaviours can be broken down into rules or conditions. In multi-agent settings, GP has been applied to evolve cooperative behaviours, communication protocols, or condition-based task allocation. However, the search space is vast and can lead to bloat (unnecessarily large programs), requiring pruning or simplification strategies. Overall, GP provides a powerful tool for evolving intelligible, flexible behaviours in swarm contexts.
- **Coevolutionary Algorithms:** Coevolutionary algorithms simulate multiple evolving populations—often agents or subcomponents—that influence each other's evolutionary trajectory. In competitive coevolution, agents are pitted against each other (e.g., predator vs. prey), promoting arms-race dynamics that drive continual improvement. In cooperative coevolution, agents evolve complementary roles or behaviours that enhance overall team performance, such as in division of labour or multi-skill task handling. Coevolution is particularly valuable in swarm robotics for developing adaptive, context-sensitive strategies, as agents must account for the behaviours and adaptations of peers or adversaries. This makes it

suitable for dynamic environments and heterogeneous swarms. However, coevolution introduces complexity: maintaining balance between populations, avoiding cycling behaviours and ensuring diverse exploration are ongoing challenges. Techniques such as shared archives, hall-of-fame selection and fitness shaping help stabilize coevolution. As swarms become more complex and multi-agent learning becomes more interactive, coevolution will play a key role in evolving sophisticated, decentralized intelligence.

6.2.6. Distributed and Embodied Evolution

- **Distributed Evolution:** Distributed evolution is an approach where each agent in a swarm independently evolves its behaviour or control parameters through local interactions, without relying on a central controller. In this model, agents maintain their own "genetic material" (e.g., a controller, a set of parameters, or a behavioural policy) and periodically exchange this information with nearby peers during encounters. These exchanges may involve copying, recombining, or mutating genetic material based on performance feedback or local rules. Distributed evolution is well-suited for large-scale swarms operating in environments where global coordination is infeasible due to communication limits, failure risks, or environmental uncertainty. It mirrors the decentralized nature of biological evolution and supports natural selection within local contexts. The system is inherently scalable and robust—agents continue to evolve even if parts of the swarm are damaged or disconnected. This approach fosters behavioural diversity and adaptation, making it valuable for tasks like decentralized exploration, adaptive flocking, or dynamic task allocation. Its success, however, depends on effective local fitness estimation and sufficient agent interaction frequency for gene exchange.
- **Embodied Evolution:** Embodied evolution brings the evolutionary process directly into the physical or simulated embodiment of the robots, allowing evolution to occur in situ, during operation. Unlike traditional evolution, which is usually done offline in simulation or centralized computation, embodied evolution takes place in real time, using feedback from the agent's actual experience in the environment. This method integrates sensing, acting and adapting, enabling agents to evolve in response to real-world stimuli like sensor noise, physical constraints and dynamic obstacles. Agents periodically evaluate their own performance (e.g., through task success metrics or internal rewards) and may engage in interactions such as reproduction, mutation and crossover based on localized fitness measures. Embodied evolution is ideal for environments where simulation

mismatches reality ("reality gap"), as learning occurs under actual deployment conditions. It is particularly useful for long-duration missions or tasks requiring persistent adaptation. The key challenges include safe mutation during operation, managing evolution without disrupting core tasks and ensuring convergence under noisy or partial feedback.

Advantages of Distributed and Embodied Evolution

- **No Central Controller Needed:** These evolutionary strategies eliminate the need for a centralized controller or external supervisor, which significantly enhances scalability and robustness. This allows swarms to operate autonomously in communication-constrained or infrastructure-less environments, such as disaster zones, deep oceans, or outer space.
- **Better Adaptation to Real-World Conditions:** By evolving behaviours directly through real or simulated experience, agents are naturally exposed to the unpredictability of physical environments—such as actuator noise, sensor errors and terrain variability. This enables them to learn robust, adaptive strategies that are well-suited to real-world deployment, bridging the simulation-to-reality gap.
- **Online Learning and Resilience to Agent Loss:** Distributed and embodied evolution support online adaptation, meaning agents can continuously improve their performance during mission execution. This leads to resilience—if some agents fail or are removed, others can adapt to compensate or take over roles dynamically. Additionally, behaviours can evolve over time as environmental conditions shift or tasks change.
- **Scalability and Autonomy:** These methods scale naturally to hundreds or thousands of agents. Since each agent learns and evolves independently (but locally cooperatively), the computational burden is distributed across the swarm. This enables flexible adaptation without overwhelming centralized systems.
- **Promotes Behavioural Diversity:** Decentralized evolution often results in heterogeneous agent behaviours, as agents evolve under different environmental pressures or initial conditions. This diversity is beneficial for complex swarm tasks that require role differentiation, task specialization, or adaptable group responses (Table-4).

Table:4. Advantages of Distributed and Embodied Evolution

Advantage	Description
No Central Controller Needed	Enables fully decentralized operation, enhancing system robustness, fault tolerance and scalability in communication-limited or infrastructure-free zones.
Better Adaptation to Real-World Conditions	Evolution happens under real sensory and environmental noise, improving robustness and reducing dependency on accurate simulations.
Online Learning	Agents can adapt and improve their behaviours continuously during deployment without needing retraining or reprogramming.
Resilience to Agent Loss	Since learning is distributed, the system can tolerate individual agent failures without disrupting global behaviour.
Scalability	Works well with large numbers of agents as learning and adaptation are localized, reducing the need for global coordination.
Behavioural Diversity	Promotes varied agent behaviours, encouraging specialization and flexible role assignment within the swarm.
Emergent Cooperation	Encourages the development of cooperative behaviours without explicit programming through localized fitness pressures.
Reduced Reality Gap	Learning directly on real robots minimizes the mismatch between simulated and physical performance.

6.2.7. Applications in Swarm Robotics

- **Foraging:** In swarm robotics, foraging refers to the task of autonomously locating, collecting and transporting resources—whether physical objects or data packets—from dispersed locations to a central depot. Evolutionary algorithms are highly effective for developing foraging behaviours, as they can optimize both exploration and retrieval strategies under diverse conditions. Each agent may evolve parameters such as movement speed, turning angle, memory duration, or response thresholds to environmental stimuli. Through fitness-based selection, agents that discover more efficient search patterns—such as spiral sweeps, pheromone-like trails, or flock-assisted collection—are favoured. Evolution can also improve energy efficiency, preventing redundant paths or bottlenecks. In distributed setups, local evolution allows agents to adapt their behaviour based on terrain, obstacle density, or object distribution. Over time, emergent cooperation can arise, with agents evolving complementary roles such as scouts or carriers. These behaviours are especially relevant in environments like disaster zones (e.g., debris removal), agriculture (e.g., fruit collection), or space mining. Evolution-based foraging adapts well to both static and dynamic resource environments.

- **Exploration and Mapping:** Exploration and mapping tasks require agents to navigate and understand previously unknown or changing environments, often under uncertainty and limited sensory information. Evolutionary algorithms help generate behaviours that balance coverage, efficiency and safety during exploration. In particular, distributed and embodied evolution are well-suited for learning decentralized navigation strategies, obstacle response patterns and frontier-following heuristics. Agents evolve control policies that maximize area coverage while minimizing redundancy or collision. Fitness functions may reward the number of newly discovered regions, the speed of mapping, or the completeness of environmental representation. In swarm systems, evolution can also lead to the emergence of specialized roles—such as pathfinders, mappers, or relays—that enhance group performance. Co-evolutionary models allow behaviours to adapt in response to team dynamics or environmental complexity. Evolution-based exploration has practical uses in search-and-rescue missions, planetary reconnaissance, environmental monitoring and warehouse automation. These algorithms allow the swarm to learn from experience and improve map accuracy even as the environment changes.
- **Obstacle Avoidance:** Obstacle avoidance is a fundamental requirement in swarm robotics, especially in dynamic, cluttered, or unstructured environments. Evolutionary algorithms are used to evolve reactive movement strategies that help agents navigate safely while still progressing toward their objectives. These strategies often use sensor inputs (e.g., infrared, LiDAR, vision) to determine velocity, direction, or avoidance manoeuvrers. Evolution can optimize rule-based systems, neural networks, or behaviour trees that respond quickly and reliably to obstacles of varying size, shape, or movement. Fitness functions typically penalize collisions and reward smooth trajectories or time spent in safe motion. In multi-agent systems, avoidance must also consider inter-agent collisions, prompting the evolution of group-aware behaviours that balance personal space with team coordination. Embodied evolution is especially valuable, allowing behaviours to adapt to sensor inaccuracies and environmental noise. These methods are widely applied in applications like autonomous delivery, traffic navigation, warehouse robotics and underwater or aerial swarm systems operating in unpredictable terrain.
- **Formation Control:** Formation control involves coordinating a group of robots to maintain specific spatial arrangements while moving collectively.

Evolutionary algorithms are used to evolve decentralized rules or control policies that govern agent positioning relative to their neighbours, enabling formations like lines, V-shapes, circles, or dynamic morphing patterns. These formations are useful for surveillance, transport and environment sensing tasks. Evolution optimizes behaviours to maintain formation stability, adapt to obstacles and recover from disturbances such as agent loss or environmental change. Fitness functions might evaluate factors like geometric precision, formation cohesion, collision avoidance and target-following efficiency. Approaches such as neuroevolution or genetic programming can produce compact controllers that generalize well across different formation sizes and speeds. Co-evolution may lead to the emergence of leader-follower dynamics or role-specific positioning. Formation control benefits from distributed and embodied evolution, where agents learn to maintain global structure based on only local information. It is especially critical in drone swarms, mobile sensor networks and automated convoy systems.

- **Task Allocation:** In swarm robotics, task allocation refers to dynamically distributing different tasks or roles among agents to optimize system-level performance. Evolutionary algorithms are particularly useful in adaptive task allocation, where agents evolve decision-making strategies based on real-time inputs, task priorities, or environmental context. Agents may evolve parameters or rules to decide when to switch tasks, how to coordinate with others, or how to assess their own suitability for a task based on location, battery level, or skills. Fitness functions often combine task completion rates, response times and overall efficiency metrics. Evolution encourages the development of diverse behaviours across the swarm, leading to emergent role specialization, such as scouts, transporters, or relays. In co-evolutionary systems, task dependencies may drive mutual adaptation across subgroups. Evolution-based task allocation is valuable in environments with fluctuating demands, like disaster response, autonomous maintenance, or logistics. Distributed evolutionary methods allow the swarm to self-organize and rebalance workloads without central oversight, increasing resilience and responsiveness.

6.2.8. Challenges in Evolutionary Approaches

- **Fitness Design:** Designing an effective fitness function is one of the most critical and challenging aspects of evolutionary algorithms applied to swarm robotics. The fitness function acts as a guide, determining which individuals (solutions) are favoured for reproduction and further evolution. If this function is poorly crafted or misaligned with the true objectives of the task, it can lead to undesirable or unintended behaviours. For instance, a fitness function that rewards only speed may encourage reckless navigation, causing collisions or inefficient energy use. Conversely, overly complex or multi-objective fitness functions might confuse the evolutionary process, making it difficult for the swarm to converge on useful behaviours. Another challenge is balancing immediate versus long-term rewards; short-term gains may not lead to sustainable or robust swarm performance. Moreover, in decentralized or embodied evolution scenarios, agents must estimate fitness locally, which may be noisy or incomplete. Hence, designing fitness functions that promote desired behaviours, maintain swarm coherence, encourage cooperation and avoid shortcuts or “gaming” the system requires careful domain knowledge and iterative refinement. The fitness landscape should also foster diversity to prevent early stagnation. Overall, fitness design demands a delicate balance between specificity and generality to ensure evolution produces meaningful, safe and adaptive swarm behaviours.

- **Convergence Speed:** The convergence speed of evolutionary algorithms refers to how quickly the population evolves toward high-performing solutions. In swarm robotics, this can be particularly slow due to the complexity and high dimensionality of the search space. Each agent may have many parameters controlling its behaviour and the interactions between multiple agents can produce a combinatorial explosion of possible strategies. As a result, evolution may require thousands of generations to find optimal or even satisfactory solutions. This slow pace is exacerbated by the need for real-world evaluation or embodied evolution, where physical trials are time-consuming and costly. Slow convergence limits the practical deployment of evolutionary methods in time-sensitive applications. Additionally, evaluating fitness accurately can be computationally expensive, especially when simulating realistic environments or when many agents must be assessed simultaneously. Researchers often use surrogate models or parallelized simulations to accelerate convergence, but these can introduce inaccuracies or the reality gap problem. Balancing exploration (searching broadly) and exploitation (refining good solutions) is crucial for improving convergence speed. Without strategies such as adaptive mutation rates, curriculum learning, or hybrid algorithms combining evolution with reinforcement learning, the evolutionary process may stall or fail to deliver timely, high-quality behaviours for swarms.
- **Premature Convergence:** Premature convergence occurs when an evolutionary algorithm rapidly settles on a suboptimal solution, losing population diversity before thoroughly exploring the solution space.

This is a common and persistent problem in swarm robotics due to the interdependent and nonlinear nature of agent behaviours. Once diversity declines, the evolutionary search loses the ability to discover novel strategies and the population becomes trapped in local optima—solutions that are good but not the best overall. Premature convergence is often driven by overly strong selection pressure, where only a few top-performing individuals dominate reproduction. It can also arise if mutation rates are too low or if crossover operators fail to generate sufficient variability. In multi-agent systems, the challenge intensifies as agents co-evolve and adapt to each other, which can create shifting fitness landscapes that either exacerbate or help prevent premature convergence. Maintaining diversity through methods like fitness sharing, niching, novelty search, or island models (subpopulations evolving semi-independently) is essential. Another approach is to dynamically adjust evolutionary parameters to encourage exploration during stagnation periods. Ultimately, avoiding premature convergence is vital for evolving robust, flexible and innovative swarm behaviours capable of adapting to diverse and dynamic environments.

- **Scalability:** Scalability refers to the ability of evolutionary approaches to effectively handle increasing swarm sizes and the associated complexity. As the number of agents grows, the state and action spaces expand exponentially, making it significantly harder to evaluate and maintain diverse populations. Each agent's behaviour depends not only on its own parameters but also on the evolving behaviours of others, creating a complex web of interactions and dependencies. This can overwhelm traditional fitness evaluation methods, especially those relying on centralized assessments or global metrics. Moreover, maintaining genetic diversity across large populations becomes computationally intensive, requiring sophisticated techniques to prevent genetic drift and premature convergence. Communication overhead between agents during gene exchange or fitness sharing can further burden distributed evolution. Scalability challenges also manifest in physical deployments—testing thousands of robots simultaneously is often infeasible, forcing reliance on simulation, which risks introducing the reality gap. To address these issues, researchers explore hierarchical or modular evolution, decentralized fitness evaluation, parallel computation and hybrid methods that integrate evolutionary algorithms with reinforcement learning or other machine learning techniques. Achieving scalable evolutionary solutions is essential for deploying real-world swarm robotic systems with hundreds or thousands of agents operating collaboratively and autonomously.

- **Reality Gap:** The reality gap is a fundamental challenge in evolutionary robotics where controllers or behaviours evolved in simulation fail to perform adequately when transferred to physical robots. Simulations often simplify or approximate real-world physics, sensor noise, actuator imperfections and environmental variability. As a result, solutions that appear highly effective in simulation can behave unpredictably or degrade significantly when deployed on actual hardware. This gap is particularly problematic in swarm robotics, where the cumulative effects of small discrepancies across many agents can lead to large-scale behavioural failures. The reality gap may cause evolved behaviours to rely on unrealistic assumptions, overfit simulated conditions, or ignore real-world constraints such as communication delays or battery limitations. Bridging this gap requires strategies such as evolving controllers directly on robots (embodied evolution), using more realistic simulators with noise injection, domain randomization (training across diverse simulated environments), or transfer learning techniques. Additionally, continuous online adaptation during deployment can help swarms adjust and refine behaviours based on real-time feedback. Successfully managing the reality gap is critical to ensure that evolutionary algorithms produce robust, reliable and deployable swarm behaviours in complex, unpredictable environments (Table-5).

Table:5 Summarised Challenges in Evolutionary Approaches

Challenge	Description
Fitness Design	Crafting fitness functions that align closely with the desired behaviour is difficult. Poorly designed objectives can result in unintended or unsafe outcomes.
Convergence Speed	Evolutionary algorithms often require many generations to find optimal solutions, especially in high-dimensional or complex behaviour spaces.
Premature Convergence	Populations may quickly converge to suboptimal solutions, losing genetic diversity and the ability to explore alternative strategies.
Scalability	As the number of agents increases, the complexity of evaluating each agent's fitness and maintaining population diversity grows exponentially.
Reality Gap	Controllers evolved in simulation may fail to perform well in the real world due to unmodeled noise, physical inaccuracies, or environmental differences.

6.2.9. Hybrid and Enhanced Approaches

- **Hybrid Methods:** Hybrid approaches combine Evolutionary Algorithms (EAs) with other learning paradigms—most notably Reinforcement Learning (RL), rule-based systems, or supervised learning—to exploit the strengths of each method. EAs excel at global exploration and can find diverse solutions without gradient information, while RL is effective at local policy refinement based on real-time feedback. In hybrid EA-RL systems, EAs may be used to evolve initial policy parameters, network architectures, or behaviour modules, which are later fine-tuned using RL to adapt to specific environmental conditions. Conversely, RL agents can bootstrap populations that EAs further evolve for generalization. In swarm robotics, hybrids are useful for combining the interpretability and modularity of rule-based control with the adaptability of learning systems. For example, rule-based heuristics may handle safety-critical constraints, while evolved components handle high-level task strategies. These combinations offer better convergence, robustness and sample efficiency than either method alone. The challenge lies in designing seamless integration and managing interactions between the learning modules to avoid conflicts or instability.

- **Multi-Objective Optimization:** In real-world swarm robotic applications, agents must often balance competing objectives—such as speed versus energy consumption, or task efficiency versus communication overhead. Multi-objective optimization (MOO) in evolutionary computation allows these trade-offs to be addressed directly by optimizing multiple fitness criteria simultaneously. Instead of finding a single "best" solution, MOO produces a Pareto front—a set of solutions that represent optimal trade-offs among objectives. Swarm agents can then choose policies based on mission-specific constraints or dynamic goals. Algorithms like NSGA-II (Non-dominated Sorting Genetic Algorithm) or MOEA/D (Multi-Objective Evolutionary Algorithm based on Decomposition) are commonly used. MOO is particularly relevant when designing behaviours for long-duration or resource-sensitive missions, such as autonomous exploration with limited battery life. In swarm systems, it may also balance local versus global performance, individual safety versus group success, or task specialization versus flexibility. Future research aims to develop scalable MOO techniques for large agent populations and explore decision-making mechanisms for choosing among Pareto-optimal strategies on the fly.
- **Behavioural Diversity Maintenance:** One of the key challenges in evolutionary systems is premature convergence, where the population quickly collapses to a suboptimal solution, losing exploration potential. Behavioural diversity maintenance techniques, such as novelty search, quality diversity (QD), or fitness sharing, are designed to explicitly encourage exploration of novel behaviours instead of just optimizing for performance. In swarm robotics, where complex group behaviours emerge from simple local interactions, encouraging diversity can lead to the discovery of

innovative coordination strategies that pure performance-based selection might overlook. For example, novelty search rewards individuals that exhibit unique trajectories, formations, or decision patterns, regardless of task success. These techniques also increase robustness, as a diverse swarm is more likely to adapt to changing tasks or failures. Maintaining diversity is especially important in multi-agent settings to prevent behavioural homogeneity that can limit swarm capabilities. Future enhancements may include dynamically switching between novelty and objective-based rewards, or leveraging diversity in co-evolutionary setups to evolve heterogeneous agent roles.

- **Surrogate Models:** Surrogate models are approximations of expensive fitness functions, used to accelerate the evolutionary process by reducing the number of real evaluations required. In swarm robotics, evaluating a candidate policy might involve time-consuming simulations or real-world trials. Surrogate models—often built using regression techniques, Gaussian processes, or neural networks—learn to predict fitness values based on previously evaluated candidates. These models guide the search by filtering or pre-selecting promising individuals, drastically reducing computational overhead. In some systems, active learning strategies help balance between surrogate use and real evaluation, minimizing error accumulation. Surrogates are especially useful in hardware-in-the-loop evolution, where testing on physical robots is slow, costly, or risky. However, maintaining surrogate accuracy across a diverse population and dynamic environments remains a challenge. Hybrid systems may use uncertainty quantification to decide when to trust the surrogate. As simulation fidelity improves and data-efficient learning advances, surrogate-assisted evolution is poised to become a core enabler of scalable, real-time evolutionary optimization in swarm robotics.

- **Memetic Algorithms:** Memetic algorithms enhance traditional EAs by combining global evolutionary search with local refinement techniques, inspired by the concept of memes—units of cultural transmission and adaptation. In this approach, each individual solution (or a selected subset) undergoes additional fine-tuning using local optimization strategies such as hill climbing, gradient descent, or reinforcement learning. This hybrid of exploration and exploitation leads to faster convergence and higher-quality solutions. In swarm robotics, memetic algorithms are especially effective in optimizing both global group behaviours and fine-grained agent-level control. For example, a memetic framework might evolve the structure of a neural controller while refining its weights through local learning. This layered optimization is also useful in multi-objective settings, where local tuning helps balance competing criteria. A key advantage is the ability to rapidly adapt high-performing individuals to specific task conditions or environmental changes. Challenges include managing computational cost and ensuring that local search does not bias the population too narrowly. Memetic strategies are gaining traction for real-time applications where both speed and precision matter..

6.2.10. Future Trends and Research Directions

- **Self-Evolving Swarms:** Self-evolving swarms represent a future in which agents can autonomously adapt and evolve their behaviours during deployment, without offline training or human intervention. This concept pushes the boundaries of embodied evolution, where evolutionary processes occur in real-time as agents interact with their environment and each other. The agents continually evaluate their performance, exchange successful traits and mutate behaviours to adapt to new tasks or conditions. This allows the swarm to handle unforeseen challenges, such as novel terrains, dynamic obstacles, or mission shifts. Self-evolution enables on-site learning, critical for missions in remote or inaccessible environments like deep sea or space, where pre-training is insufficient. The key challenges include maintaining safety during learning, managing communication and memory constraints and avoiding catastrophic failures from poorly adapted mutations. Advances in on-board computation, sensor miniaturization and distributed evolutionary algorithms are making this vision increasingly practical. In the future, self-evolving swarms could exhibit lifelike adaptability, making them ideal for long-term, autonomous operations in uncertain settings.
- **Human-in-the-Loop Evolution:** Human-in-the-loop (HITL) evolution integrates human insight into the evolutionary process by allowing experts—or even non-experts—to influence selection, reward shaping, or constraint imposition. Rather than relying solely on predefined fitness functions, this approach leverages human intuition to guide evolution toward solutions that are not just efficient, but also interpretable, safe, or aligned with mission goals. For example, a human operator might reward behaviours that appear cooperative or penalize those that are erratic or unsafe, even if they score well on an automated metric. HITL evolution bridges the gap between black-box optimization and real-world usability, making evolved behaviours more acceptable and trustworthy in critical applications. It also enables rapid prototyping and fine-tuning of swarm behaviours in interactive design loops. The challenge lies in designing intuitive interfaces and efficient feedback integration methods without

overwhelming the user or slowing down evolution. Future developments in explainable AI and interactive machine learning are expected to enhance the effectiveness of HITL systems in swarm robotics.

- **Scalable Co-Evolution:** As swarms grow larger and tasks become more complex, future evolutionary algorithms must handle scalable co-evolution—the simultaneous evolution of behaviours across thousands of agents with potentially diverse roles, capabilities, or goals. Traditional approaches often struggle with computational cost and coordination overhead at this scale. Co-evolution introduces additional complexity by having agents evolve not just in isolation, but in response to each other's behaviours, fostering specialization, competition, or collaboration. In large-scale swarms, this may involve evolving leader-follower dynamics, heterogeneous agent roles, or communication protocols. Efficient co-evolution requires smart encoding, parallelized simulations and fitness functions that reflect both individual and group performance. Novel representations like modular genomes or distributed neural controllers can help manage complexity. Additionally, hierarchical or layered evolution schemes may be used, where macro-level strategies evolve over micro-level controllers. The ability to scale co-evolution effectively will be key to deploying large, intelligent and adaptive swarms in real-world applications such as smart cities, precision agriculture, or environmental monitoring.
- **Robust-to-Failure Evolution:** Robust-to-failure evolution focuses on developing agents and swarm behaviours that can withstand individual failures, harsh environmental changes, or loss of communication. In future deployments—where agents might face unpredictable terrain, adversarial interference, or hardware degradation—robustness cannot be an afterthought. Evolutionary algorithms can explicitly prioritize resilience by incorporating penalties for fragility or rewards for redundancy and graceful degradation. This includes evolving fallback behaviours, self-repair routines, or decentralized coordination strategies that tolerate partial system failures. For example, if a subset of drones in a swarm is disabled, the remaining agents must dynamically redistribute tasks and adapt formations without collapsing mission performance. Robustness is also crucial in safety-critical applications, where the cost of failure is high. Simulated evolution across diverse and adverse conditions helps generalize agent responses. Future work may integrate robustness metrics directly into multi-objective evolutionary frameworks, combining performance with survivability. Robust-to-failure evolution is central to ensuring the long-term reliability and operational safety of autonomous swarm systems in the wild.

- **Hardware-Efficient Evolution:** As swarm robots are typically small, low-power and resource-constrained, hardware-efficient evolution is an essential research direction. It aims to evolve control policies that are lightweight, fast and compatible with limited computational, memory and energy resources of embedded platforms. This involves optimizing not just behaviour, but also computational efficiency—such as minimizing the number of neural network parameters, reducing sensing overhead, or compressing control logic. Methods like neuroevolutionary of spiking neural networks, symbolic controller evolution, or compact decision trees are being explored for this purpose. Real-time applicability is key: evolved controllers must run with low latency and reliability under tight energy budgets. Additionally, simulations must accurately model hardware constraints to ensure transferability of evolved behaviours to real robots (bridging the "sim-to-real" gap). Research in this area is critical for practical deployment in large-scale outdoor swarms, wearable robotics, or embedded IoT-based agents. Hardware-efficient evolution will enable more capable, scalable and affordable robotic swarms across a range of industries.

6.3 ADAPTIVE BEHAVIOUR AND ONLINE LEARNING

Swarm robotics systems operate in dynamic, uncertain environments where pre-programmed behaviours may not suffice. Adaptive behaviour refers to the swarm's ability to modify its actions in response to changes in the environment, tasks, or internal system conditions. Online learning enables this adaptability by allowing agents to learn continuously during operation, rather than relying solely on prior training. Together, these capabilities are vital for long-term autonomy, robustness and intelligent coordination in real-world deployments (Fig. 3).

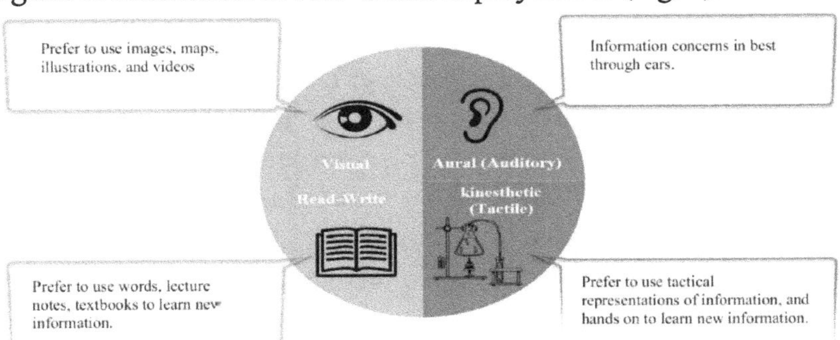

Fig. 3 Adaptive e-learning environment based on learning styles

6.3.1. Adaptive Behaviour

Definition: The capacity of an agent or swarm to alter its behaviour based on experience, feedback, or environmental changes.

Features:

- **Reactivity:** Immediate response to external stimuli.
- **Flexibility:** Ability to change strategies or tasks as needed.
- **Resilience:** Continued functionality despite failures or perturbations.

Mechanisms:

- Behaviour switching (rule-based or learned).
- Dynamic parameter tuning (e.g., speed, formation size).
- Experience-based modifications to control laws.

6.3.2. Online Learning

Definition: A learning paradigm where agents update their knowledge and policies continuously while interacting with the environment.

Difference from Offline Learning:

- Offline learning occurs in a simulated or pre-collected data environment.
- Online learning happens in real-time during deployment.

Advantages:

- Real-time adaptation to changing conditions.
- No need for complete environment knowledge beforehand.
- Continuous improvement of performance over time.

6.3.3. Online Learning Methods in Swarm Systems

- **Incremental Reinforcement Learning:** Incremental Reinforcement Learning enables agents to adapt continuously by updating their policies based on real-time reward feedback. A classic example is Q-learning with online updates, where the agent refines its value estimates with each interaction in the environment. This approach allows learning to proceed in dynamic, non-stationary settings without needing full episodes or batch data. The agent balances exploration (trying new actions) and exploitation (choosing known best actions), improving decision-making over time. Incremental updates help reduce memory requirements compared to batch learning. It is highly suited for robotics, games and adaptive control systems. The real-time nature supports responsiveness to environmental changes or unexpected scenarios. However, stability and convergence can be challenging in noisy environments. Techniques like experience replay or learning rate decay are often applied to enhance performance.

- **Online Evolutionary Algorithms:** Online Evolutionary Algorithms operate continuously, allowing agents to evolve and adapt as they interact with their environment. Unlike traditional evolutionary algorithms that rely on discrete generations, this approach supports ongoing selection, mutation and recombination during runtime. Agents may perform local mating, share information, or mutate their internal parameters while still operating in the environment. This leads to distributed adaptation, where populations evolve gradually without centralized control. The method is useful in multi-agent systems, swarm robotics and environments where performance must improve on the fly. It allows for adaptation to environmental shifts or agent failures. Online evolution avoids the cold start problem by enabling learning from partial solutions. The challenge lies in managing the balance between exploration (diversity) and exploitation (refinement). It's particularly effective in open-ended or non-deterministic environments.
- **Bayesian Learning:** Bayesian Learning empowers agents to maintain and update probabilistic beliefs about the world based on new sensor data or observations. This continuous learning process helps agents handle uncertainty, noise and partial observability more robustly than deterministic models. When new data is received, the agent applies Bayes' Theorem to refine its prior beliefs, resulting in an updated posterior distribution. This dynamic updating allows for real-time decision-making under uncertainty. Bayesian approaches are often used in robotics, perception systems and adaptive filtering (e.g., Kalman filters). They offer a principled way to incorporate both prior knowledge and new evidence. Computational cost and scalability can be a concern, especially with large data or complex models. However, approximations like Bayesian networks, particle filters, or variational inference help manage complexity. Bayesian learning excels in environments requiring probabilistic reasoning and confidence estimation.
- **Online Supervised Learning:** Online Supervised Learning enables agents to learn continuously from real-time labelled data or immediate feedback. Unlike batch learning, where training occurs on large static datasets, online methods update model parameters incrementally as new data points arrive. This makes them suitable for streaming applications, dynamic environments and personalization tasks. Algorithms like stochastic gradient descent (SGD) are commonly used to adjust weights efficiently after each data instance. Online supervised learning supports fast adaptation to changes in data distribution, such as concept drift. It's widely applied in spam filtering, recommendation engines and adaptive user interfaces. Challenges include ensuring stability and avoiding overfitting to noisy or

sparse data. Regularization techniques and sliding window methods are often employed to maintain generalization. This approach is ideal where continuous feedback is available or real-time decisions are critical.

- **Neural Network Tuning:** Neural Network Tuning involves adjusting the weights of a neural network in real-time, allowing it to refine its behaviour as new data becomes available. This can be achieved through online backpropagation, where gradient updates are made after each sample, or through Hebbian learning, which strengthens connections based on correlated activity. These methods allow networks to adapt to changing environments without retraining from scratch. Online tuning is particularly valuable in applications like adaptive control, real-time prediction and autonomous navigation. While effective, it requires mechanisms to avoid catastrophic forgetting—where learning new patterns causes the network to lose old knowledge. Techniques such as replay buffers, elastic weight consolidation, or meta-learning are used to mitigate this. Neural network tuning supports flexible and responsive learning, but maintaining stability and computational efficiency remains a challenge in resource-constrained environments.

6.3.4. Triggers for Adaptation in Swarms

- **Environmental Change:** Swarm systems often operate in dynamic and unpredictable environments, making environmental change a key trigger for adaptation. This includes the sudden appearance of new obstacles, alterations in terrain, moving or shifting targets and weather-related changes like wind, rain, or temperature fluctuations. Such variations can affect navigation, sensing accuracy, or mission objectives. Adaptive swarm behaviour allows agents to reconfigure formations, change strategies, or switch sensors based on external stimuli. For instance, drones may need to fly lower in strong winds or avoid rain-prone areas to protect electronics. Timely detection and response to these changes are crucial for maintaining task performance and swarm safety. The use of onboard sensors, shared environment maps and environmental models enables context-aware adaptation. Swarm intelligence ensures the group responds collectively and efficiently to environmental shifts.
- **Agent State Changes:** Individual agents within a swarm may experience internal state changes that necessitate collective adaptation. These include low battery levels, sensor degradation, physical damage, or complete agent failure. When such changes are detected, the swarm can dynamically redistribute roles or reassign tasks to maintain performance. For example, an agent running low on power may withdraw from active roles and return

to a charging station, while nearby agents take over its responsibilities. Swarm-level redundancy allows the system to continue functioning even if individual agents fail. This adaptability enhances robustness and resilience, which is essential in high-stakes applications like search and rescue or military surveillance. Monitoring internal states requires local sensors and continuous communication with the rest of the swarm. Real-time self-assessment at the agent level enables prompt adaptation without disrupting overall coordination.

- **Mission Phase Shift:** Swarm behaviour often follows phased mission structures, where goals and strategies evolve over time. A mission phase shift—such as transitioning from exploration to tracking, or from searching to rescuing—triggers a reconfiguration of the swarm's roles, formations and communication protocols. For example, during exploration, agents may spread out to cover a large area, while in tracking mode, they cluster to follow a moving target. This flexibility allows the swarm to align with changing objectives and situational demands. Successful adaptation depends on shared mission awareness, phase-specific behaviours and effective coordination. Swarm members must detect and interpret phase changes—sometimes autonomously, or through leader agents or external commands. These shifts often require real-time learning, task reallocation and behavioural synchronization. Mission adaptability ensures the swarm remains efficient and purpose-driven throughout all phases.
- **Interaction Dynamics:** Swarm systems are highly dependent on inter-agent interactions and changes in these dynamics can trigger adaptation. For instance, variations in group size, caused by the addition or loss of agents, demand redistribution of roles and path planning adjustments. Communication loss, due to range limitations or interference, may require agents to switch to decentralized decision-making or adjust formations to re-establish links. External interference, like jamming or competing signals, can disrupt coordination and navigation, prompting the swarm to activate fallback strategies. Adaptation to these scenarios ensures that collaborative tasks such as mapping, patrolling, or coverage remain effective despite internal disruptions. Resilient swarm algorithms often include redundancy, consensus protocols and local autonomy to maintain function when global coordination breaks down. Overall, flexible interaction handling allows the swarm to continue functioning under uncertain or degraded conditions.

6.3.5. Applications of Adaptive Behaviour

- **Formation Control:** Adaptive formation control enables swarms to dynamically adjust their size, shape and positioning in response to environmental factors like obstacles, terrain irregularities, or mission demands. For instance, a swarm of drones navigating through a narrow canyon may shift from a wide to a single-file formation to avoid collisions. Similarly, in open areas, the formation can expand to maximize coverage. These adjustments are made autonomously based on sensor inputs and real-time communication between agents. The ability to adapt formations improves navigational efficiency, collision avoidance and task effectiveness in diverse and dynamic environments. Formation control also helps maintain line-of-sight communication and optimizes energy usage. Swarm coordination algorithms ensure smooth transitions between formation states. This adaptability is vital for surveillance, agriculture and disaster response operations.

- **Target Tracking:** In target tracking, swarms must respond to unpredictable changes in target movement, such as sudden shifts in direction, speed, or visibility. Adaptive behaviour allows agents to modify their pursuit strategies, redistribute themselves and adjust sensing focus based on real-time target data. For example, if a target accelerates, some agents may increase tracking resolution, while others anticipate its path to cut off escape. When multiple targets are detected, swarm agents may autonomously split into sub-groups. Adaptation ensures consistent tracking performance even under uncertainty or partial data loss. Reinforcement learning and predictive models often aid in anticipating target behaviour. This application is critical in surveillance, wildlife monitoring and defence systems. Flexibility and responsiveness improve mission success and resource efficiency.
- **Task Allocation:** Task allocation in adaptive swarms involves redistributing agents in response to changing mission priorities, resource availability, or individual agent status. For example, if a drone in a search-and-rescue mission runs low on battery, another drone may automatically take over its area. Adaptive algorithms allow agents to assess local and global needs, volunteering or requesting tasks as required. Dynamic reallocation ensures balanced workload, minimizes idle time and improves mission completion rates. Agents may consider factors like proximity, capability and urgency during reassignment. This adaptability is essential in unpredictable scenarios where conditions evolve rapidly. Task allocation mechanisms often leverage utility-based models, market-based systems, or consensus protocols. Effective adaptation ensures the swarm remains mission-effective despite internal or external disruptions.
- **Exploration:** Adaptive exploration allows swarm agents to modify their search patterns to maximize environmental coverage while conserving

energy and avoiding redundancy. In unknown or dynamic terrains, agents may spread out or concentrate based on signal strength, environmental cues, or terrain difficulty. For instance, in hazardous zones, agents may slow down and tighten formation, while in safe areas, they may fan out for broader coverage. Agents also adapt to avoid overlapping search paths, improving efficiency. Energy-aware exploration strategies adjust agent behaviour based on battery life or solar charging opportunities. Such adaptive methods are key in planetary exploration, environmental monitoring and archaeological surveys. Exploration efficiency is enhanced through learning from past search results and dynamically changing behaviour. The balance between coverage and conservation is crucial for mission longevity.

- **Collective Decision-Making:** Adaptive collective decision-making allows swarms to change how decisions are made based on environmental complexity, urgency, or internal disagreement. For instance, in a calm situation, agents may use a slow consensus approach, while under threat, a faster leader-based decision may be adopted. The swarm can switch between voting, averaging, or decentralized methods depending on the context. Adaptation helps maintain robustness even when communication is degraded or some agents provide unreliable data. Context-aware adjustments to decision rules improve the swarm's responsiveness and resilience. This is especially important in tasks like route selection, threat avoidance, or target identification. Algorithms inspired by social insects or game theory often guide such decisions. Flexibility in decision-making enhances autonomy and overall mission reliability.

6.3.6. Design Principles for Adaptive Systems

Modularity: Modularity is a foundational design principle in adaptive systems, allowing behaviours or subsystems to be developed, activated, or deactivated independently. By compartmentalizing functions—such as navigation, obstacle avoidance, or communication—systems become more flexible and scalable. This separation makes it easier to update or replace individual modules without affecting the entire architecture. In swarm robotics, for example, different behaviour modules can be engaged depending on the mission phase or external triggers. Modularity also improves fault isolation, allowing a system to continue functioning even if one module fails. It supports reusability, enabling designers to deploy proven modules across different applications. This principle enhances maintainability, simplifies testing and accelerates innovation. A modular approach is critical for managing the complexity of real-time, multi-agent adaptive systems.

Context Awareness: Context awareness enables adaptive systems to perceive and interpret changes in their environment or internal state to make informed decisions. Agents gather contextual data through sensors, GPS, or internal diagnostics—such as battery level, obstacle proximity, or temperature. By understanding their situation, agents can adapt behaviours to better fit real-time conditions. For example, a drone may reduce its altitude in strong winds or conserve energy when battery levels are low. Context awareness is essential for avoiding hazards, optimizing resource use and maintaining mission goals. Systems often employ sensor fusion and machine learning to extract meaningful context from noisy or partial data. Context-aware adaptation allows systems to behave more intelligently and responsively, increasing their autonomy and robustness in uncertain environments. It forms the perceptual backbone of adaptive behaviour.

Feedback Loops: Feedback loops are vital mechanisms that allow adaptive systems to adjust behaviour in real time based on performance outcomes or environmental feedback. These loops involve monitoring, evaluating and modifying behaviour continuously, creating a self-correcting system. For example, if a robot's path is blocked, sensory feedback triggers a change in navigation strategy. Feedback can be positive (reinforcing certain behaviours) or negative (correcting errors or inefficiencies). Control systems, reinforcement learning and adaptive filtering often rely on such loops to ensure responsiveness and goal alignment. Effective feedback loops enhance system stability, accuracy and resilience to disturbances. Delays or noise in feedback can impair performance, so robust signal processing is often required. Well-designed feedback systems enable real-time learning and continual improvement in both single-agent and swarm systems.

Behaviour Arbitration: Behaviour arbitration is the process by which adaptive systems resolve conflicts between competing or simultaneous behaviours. In complex environments, an agent may face conflicting objectives—such as avoiding an obstacle while tracking a target. Arbitration mechanisms prioritize or blend behaviours based on the current context, system goals, or predefined rules. This may involve hierarchical decision trees, priority levels, or subsumption architectures, where higher-level goals can override lower-level ones. Arbitration ensures that only the most appropriate behaviours are active at any given time, preventing erratic or contradictory actions. In swarm systems, arbitration may also manage coordination among agents to avoid duplication or interference. Effective behaviour arbitration leads to coherent, goal-oriented and safe operations, especially in unpredictable environments. It's essential for managing complexity in adaptive, autonomous systems (Fig. 4).

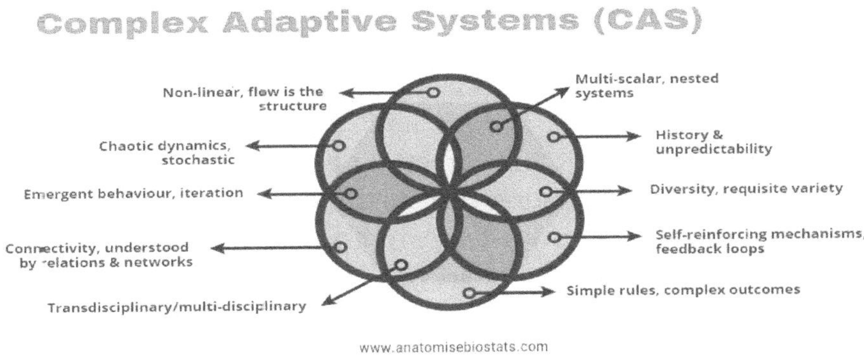

Fig. 4 Complex Adaptive Systems (CAS)

6.3.7. Online Learning Architecture

Sensing: Sensing is the first layer of an online learning architecture, responsible for continuous data collection from the environment and nearby agents. This includes inputs like temperature, location, velocity, visual data, or signals from peers. High-quality sensing enables the system to maintain an up-to-date picture of its surroundings. These sensors provide the raw data needed to detect patterns, identify anomalies, or recognize changes that require adaptation. In swarm systems, inter-agent communication also acts as a form of sensing, allowing individual agents to learn from group behaviour. The accuracy and responsiveness of sensing directly affect the system's ability to adapt in real time. Redundant or multimodal sensing improves robustness, especially in noisy or uncertain environments. Efficient preprocessing often filters or compresses sensor data before further analysis, reducing computational overhead.

Processing: Processing involves the real-time evaluation of sensory inputs and the execution of learning algorithms to update internal models. This stage translates raw data into meaningful representations that inform decision-making. Techniques like feature extraction, signal processing, or anomaly detection are commonly used here. Online learning requires low-latency processing to ensure that adaptation can occur without delays. In adaptive systems, this component often includes lightweight versions of machine learning algorithms such as incremental neural networks, decision trees, or Bayesian inference. The goal is to identify actionable changes or trends and update behavioural outputs accordingly. Processing must strike a balance between speed and accuracy, especially in resource-constrained environments like embedded systems or mobile robots. This stage acts as the "thinking" part of the architecture, turning perception into understanding.

Memory: Memory in online learning systems retains past observations, actions and outcomes to support learning over time. It provides historical context, allowing agents to recognize patterns, remember previously encountered states, or avoid repeating mistakes. Depending on the system, memory can be short-term (e.g., recent sensor readings) or long-term (e.g., accumulated knowledge or policies). Some systems use experience replay, storing key data points to refine learning in off-peak times. Memory helps manage non-stationary environments, where knowledge must be updated without forgetting earlier important information. Efficient memory management ensures that storage constraints do not overwhelm the system, often using prioritization or compression techniques. It also enables meta-learning and transfer learning, where previous experience can inform future tasks. In essence, memory gives online learning systems a sense of continuity and progression.

Policy Update: The policy update stage governs how the system adjusts its behaviour rules or control strategies based on newly processed data and stored experiences. These updates can happen immediately in response to significant changes, or periodically to refine performance over time. Reinforcement learning systems use policy updates to improve decision-making by maximizing cumulative rewards. Supervised or unsupervised learners may revise internal models or rule sets as new labelled or unlabelled data becomes available. In swarm systems, policy updates may also include coordination strategies or role adjustments. Updates must be efficient and stable to avoid erratic behaviour or overfitting to recent events. Constraints are often applied to ensure safety, reliability and convergence. This component closes the learning loop, enabling the system to act more intelligently in the next cycle. It's the critical final step in achieving true adaptivity (Fig. 5).

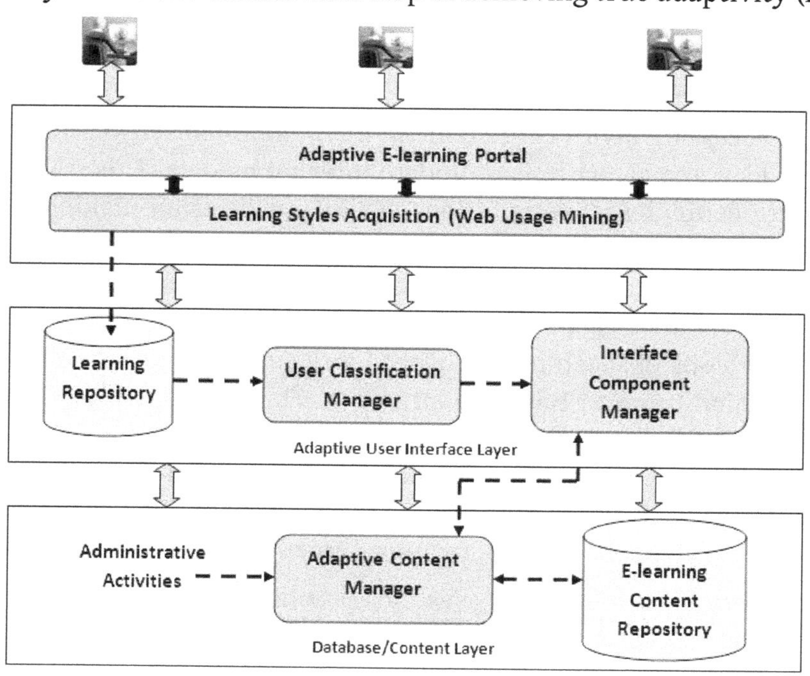

Fig. 5 Architecture diagram of E-learning System

6.3.8. Challenges in Adaptive and Online Learning

- **Resource Constraints:** In adaptive and online learning systems, especially within distributed or embedded agents, limited resources pose a critical bottleneck. Agents often operate with constrained processing power, memory and energy, particularly in edge devices or sensor networks. This limits the complexity of algorithms they can run in real time. Efficient learning thus requires lightweight, computationally frugal models that still deliver robust performance. Trade-offs between model accuracy and resource use must be carefully managed. Moreover, resource constraints may inhibit large-scale data processing or storing long-term histories. Adaptive compression, pruning, or federated learning approaches help reduce overhead. Ultimately, scalable learning solutions must be resource-aware by design.
- **Stability vs. Plasticity:** Adaptive systems must constantly update in response to new data, but this flexibility risks instability. The stability–plasticity dilemma highlights the need to balance learning new patterns (plasticity) without forgetting or corrupting existing knowledge (stability). Excessive plasticity may cause the agent to overfit transient changes or noise, leading to erratic or unreliable behaviour. Conversely, too much stability makes the agent slow or unable to respond to critical environmental shifts. Techniques like dual-memory models, meta-learning, or dynamic learning rate adaptation attempt to maintain this balance. Ensuring consistent performance across non-stationary tasks is key. Robustness must not come at the cost of stagnation.
- **Non-Stationarity:** In online learning, environments are rarely static — they evolve due to internal dynamics or external factors. This non-stationarity means that data distributions, task objectives and optimal policies may change unpredictably over time. For multi-agent systems or swarms, the behaviour of other agents further alters the learning context. Models trained under the assumption of stationarity quickly become outdated, leading to performance degradation. Continual learning methods, context-aware models and recurrent architectures can help agents adapt to such shifts. However, detecting when changes occur remains a key challenge. Resilience to non-stationarity is essential for long-term autonomy and effectiveness.
- **Delayed Rewards:** Delayed rewards complicate the learning process by creating a temporal disconnect between actions and outcomes. In reinforcement learning scenarios, agents may perform a sequence of actions before receiving any evaluative feedback. This delay makes it hard to assign credit or blame to specific decisions, slowing convergence and

increasing variance in learning. Effective credit assignment strategies, like eligibility traces or reward shaping, are crucial to address this issue. Additionally, long time horizons exacerbate exploration challenges, making trial-and-error learning inefficient. Agents must maintain robust memory and planning capabilities to bridge the reward gap. Managing reward delay is vital for real-time adaptation.

- **Partial Observability:** In many real-world environments, agents operate with limited sensory information and can only perceive part of the state space. This partial observability impairs their ability to make fully informed decisions. For swarm or multi-agent systems, lack of insight into others' internal states or strategies adds another layer of uncertainty. As a result, the agent must infer hidden variables or beliefs about the environment to act effectively. Probabilistic models, belief tracking and recurrent neural networks can mitigate this challenge. Communication and coordination protocols also help reduce uncertainty. Nonetheless, operating reliably with incomplete data remains a central hurdle in adaptive learning.
- **Safety:** Safety is a critical concern, particularly in high-stakes or real-world adaptive learning applications. During learning, agents may explore actions that lead to unsafe or undesirable states, especially when faced with unknown or poorly modelled environments. Unlike supervised systems, online learners continuously adapt and may lack pre-defined bounds on behaviour. Ensuring safety requires a combination of fail-safe mechanisms, formal verification, or constrained optimization techniques. Safe exploration methods, such as shielding or using conservative policies, can limit risky actions. Embedding safety into the learning objective itself is a growing area of research. Balancing exploration with constraint adherence is non-trivial but essential.

6.3.9. Solutions and Enhancements

- **Meta-Learning:** Meta-learning, or "learning to learn," enables agents to improve their learning strategies over time by leveraging past experiences. Instead of starting from scratch for every new task, agents develop higher-order learning mechanisms that allow rapid adaptation with minimal data. This is especially useful in non-stationary or resource-constrained environments. Meta-learning frameworks, such as Model-Agnostic Meta-Learning (MAML), optimize initial parameters that can be fine-tuned quickly for new challenges. It supports both online and few-shot learning scenarios. By embedding adaptability into the learning architecture, agents become more resilient and efficient. Meta-learning accelerates convergence while reducing computational load over repeated tasks.

- **Transfer Learning:** Transfer learning enables an agent to apply knowledge gained in one domain to improve performance in a different but related domain. This significantly reduces the data and time required to learn new tasks, especially in environments where labelled data is scarce or changes frequently. It is particularly valuable in multi-agent and swarm systems where environments share structural similarities. Transfer learning helps mitigate cold-start problems and enhances robustness in dynamic conditions. Techniques include fine-tuning pre-trained models, domain adaptation and feature re-use. Careful alignment of source and target domains is crucial to avoid negative transfer. Overall, it promotes scalable, lifelong learning.
- **Event-Triggered Learning:** Event-triggered learning reduces unnecessary computation by activating the learning process only when meaningful changes occur in the environment or agent behaviour. This strategy optimizes resource usage, making it well-suited for real-time and embedded systems with limited energy or processing power. It prevents overfitting to noise and ensures that updates are made only when needed. Event detection mechanisms can be based on statistical thresholds, anomaly detection, or dynamic system monitoring. By focusing learning on impactful moments, agents become more efficient and responsive. This approach supports fast adaptation while preserving long-term stability. It strikes a balance between vigilance and economy.
- **Imitation Learning:** Imitation learning allows agents to acquire skills by observing demonstrations from expert agents or humans, reducing the need for trial-and-error exploration. This is particularly useful in complex environments where unsafe exploration is not acceptable. By learning from successful trajectories, agents can quickly replicate competent behaviour, accelerating initial learning phases. Techniques include behaviour cloning, inverse reinforcement learning and generative adversarial imitation. Imitation can serve as a foundation for further reinforcement learning, where the agent refines its strategy over time. It is also valuable for transferring human expertise to autonomous systems. Overall, it enables safer, faster and more human-aligned learning.
- **Decentralized Learning Frameworks:** Decentralized learning frameworks distribute learning processes across multiple agents, allowing each to learn locally while coordinating with others to maintain a coherent global strategy. This approach improves scalability, fault tolerance and privacy, as raw data need not be shared centrally. It is ideal for multi-agent systems, sensor networks and edge computing applications. Techniques like federated learning, consensus algorithms and gossip protocols help

synchronize local models efficiently. Despite being decentralized, these systems strive for convergence and collaboration. Such frameworks reduce latency and energy consumption, while enhancing adaptability in dynamic settings. They empower agents to learn in parallel, yet harmoniously.

6.3.10. Future Trends and Research Directions

- **Self-Adaptive Swarms:** Self-adaptive swarms represent a future where collective systems can autonomously learn, coordinate and adapt without human intervention, even in unpredictable or hostile environments. These swarms dynamically reconfigure themselves in response to internal failures, environmental shifts, or new objectives. Learning happens at both the individual and group level, enabling emergent intelligence. Reinforcement learning, evolutionary algorithms and swarm intelligence principles guide adaptation. A key challenge is achieving scalable coordination while preserving decentralization. Applications include disaster response, deep-sea exploration and planetary missions. Research is moving toward increasing autonomy, resilience and task versatility. The goal is long-term, real-world deployment with minimal oversight.
- **Behavioural Diversity Promotion:** Promoting behavioural diversity ensures that not all agents converge on the same strategy, which can be risky in dynamic or adversarial settings. Diversity leads to greater robustness, better exploration and increased fault tolerance across the swarm. It also enables the swarm to tackle a wider range of tasks or respond to unforeseen challenges. Techniques such as novelty search, population-based training and evolutionary strategies help maintain diversity during learning. This contrasts with standard optimization approaches that push all agents toward a single optimum. Encouraging varied behaviours enhances adaptability and creativity. It prepares agents to handle edge cases and rare events effectively.
- **Online Learning with Minimal Data:** In the future, agents will need to adapt rapidly using only a handful of examples — a major shift from traditional data-hungry models. Few-shot and one-shot learning approaches are gaining traction as environments become more dynamic and labelled data becomes scarce. These methods rely on prior experience or meta-learned models to generalize quickly from limited input. Online, data-efficient learning is especially critical in scenarios with communication constraints or time-sensitive decisions. Innovations include attention mechanisms, memory-augmented networks and Bayesian optimization. The aim is to reduce sample complexity without sacrificing performance. Quick, intelligent adaptation becomes the new standard.

- **Safety-Aware Learning:** As learning systems become more autonomous, embedding safety into the learning process is essential. Safety-aware learning integrates risk mitigation directly into the adaptation loop, ensuring that agents avoid dangerous actions even during exploration. This involves formal safety guarantees, constraint-based optimization and real-time monitoring. Techniques like safe reinforcement learning, shielding and reachability analysis are key enablers. These frameworks allow systems to learn flexibly while always operating within predefined safety bounds. Especially critical in human-interactive or mission-critical environments, safety-aware learning paves the way for broader deployment of adaptive systems. It balances innovation with reliability.
- **Human-Swarm Interaction:** The next generation of swarm systems will not operate in isolation but interact closely with humans, adapting to feedback, preferences, or commands in real time. Human-swarm interaction (HSI) research focuses on building intuitive interfaces and adaptive mechanisms that let swarms understand and respond to human intent. Learning from demonstration, preference modelling and shared control are key techniques. This collaboration enhances trust, usability and effectiveness in tasks like search and rescue, agriculture, or smart manufacturing. A major challenge is aligning swarm behaviour with ambiguous or evolving human goals. Bridging cognitive gaps between humans and AI swarms is a crucial frontier.
- **Hardware-Level Learning:** Future adaptive systems will integrate learning mechanisms directly into hardware, enabling faster, more efficient on-device adaptation. Neuromorphic chips, FPGA-based learning circuits and ASICs for online learning allow real-time decision-making with low energy consumption. This hardware-level integration reduces latency, supports edge intelligence and increases robustness in the field. Unlike traditional architectures where learning occurs in the cloud or on general-purpose processors, embedded learning brings intelligence closer to sensors and actuators. It's particularly promising for small-scale robots, drones and IoT devices. Research is focusing on co-designing algorithms and circuits for learning at the silicon level. This paves the way for truly autonomous, self-improving machines.

6.4 DECENTRALIZED AND FEDERATED LEARNING APPROACHES

As swarm robotic systems grow in scale and complexity, centralized learning methods become impractical due to communication bottlenecks, privacy concerns and single points of failure. Decentralized learning and federated learning have emerged as powerful frameworks that enable multiple agents to collaboratively learn models or policies without relying on a central coordinator. These approaches are essential for maintaining autonomy, scalability and robustness in distributed multi-agent systems (Fig. 6).

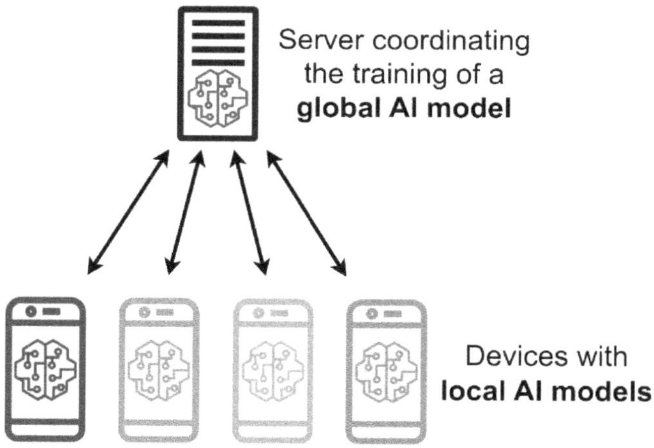

Fig. 6 Federated Learning

6.4.1. Decentralized Learning

Learning paradigm where agents independently train models using local data and share information only with neighbours or nearby peers.

- **Characteristics:** Swarm systems operate without a central server or coordinator, allowing agents to function independently. This decentralization means no single point of failure, enhancing system resilience. Learning is distributed across agents, with each one adapting based on local data and experience. Such distribution enables real-time responses to environmental changes. Agents don't require global awareness to be effective. Instead, they rely on local communication, like signals or short-range messaging. This approach mirrors biological systems such as insect colonies or bird flocks. Each agent contributes to the overall behaviour through simple interactions. Coordination arises organically from these localized exchanges. The result is an adaptive, scalable and robust system functioning as a unified whole.
- **Advantages:** One key advantage of swarm systems is their ability to scale with the number of agents. Adding more agents enhances capabilities without requiring architectural redesign. Local communication greatly reduces system-wide data exchange, minimizing bandwidth use. This reduces communication overhead and simplifies infrastructure requirements. Fault tolerance is also significantly improved—if one agent fails, others can continue the task. Redundancy among agents ensures system stability in unpredictable environments. Robustness is a natural

result of distributed control and localized processing. Swarms can recover quickly from disruptions and continue functioning. These traits make swarm-based systems ideal for dynamic, large-scale applications. Their efficiency and resilience stem directly from nature-inspired principles.

6.4.2. Federated Learning

A learning framework where multiple agents collaboratively train a shared global model while keeping their data locally.

- **Process:** In decentralized learning systems, each agent trains a model locally using its own private data. This local training allows agents to tailor models to their specific data without sharing sensitive information. At regular intervals, agents send only their model updates—such as weights or gradients—to a central server or aggregator. These updates do not include the raw data, preserving confidentiality. The server collects and combines updates from all participating agents. It then creates a refined global model by averaging or aggregating these contributions. This updated global model is redistributed back to all agents. Each agent then continues training using the new model and its own data. This cycle repeats, leading to a gradually improving global model. The process allows collaboration without compromising individual data ownership or privacy.
- **Privacy and Security:** One of the key strengths of this approach is that raw data never leaves the agent's device. This significantly enhances data privacy, especially in sensitive domains like healthcare or finance. Since only model updates are shared, the risk of exposing personal information is minimized. Privacy can be further strengthened by applying techniques like differential privacy, which adds noise to updates. Encryption methods, such as homomorphic encryption, can also secure communications. These layers of protection ensure that even if updates are intercepted, the data remains unintelligible. Moreover, localized data training reduces attack surfaces for hackers. Users maintain control over their information at all times. The system balances collaboration and confidentiality effectively. It's a privacy-preserving method ideal for modern, data-driven applications.

6.4.3. Differences and Similarities

As intelligent systems scale across networks of devices and agents, both Decentralized Learning and Federated Learning have emerged as prominent frameworks for distributed model training. While they share the core principle of preserving data privacy by keeping data local, they differ significantly in their architecture, coordination mechanisms and fault tolerance. Federated Learning relies on a central server to aggregate model updates from distributed clients, making it more structured but vulnerable to single points of failure. In contrast, Decentralized Learning removes the central coordinator, enabling peer-to-peer communication and improving scalability and robustness. Both aim to optimize learning without compromising user data privacy. However, their communication patterns, synchronization methods and system resilience reflect distinct trade-offs. Understanding these differences is essential for designing efficient and reliable distributed AI systems (Table-6) .

Table-6 Comparison between Decentralized Learning and Federated Learning

Aspect	Decentralized Learning	Federated Learning
Coordination	Fully distributed, peer-to-peer	Centralized aggregation server
Data Privacy	Data remains local, shared info is model params or gradients	Data remains local, only model updates sent
Communication Pattern	Local communication only	Periodic global synchronization
Scalability	High, no single bottleneck	Scalable but depends on central server capacity
Fault Tolerance	High, no single point of failure	Dependent on central server availability

6.4.4. Decentralized Learning Techniques

- **Consensus-Based Algorithms:** Consensus-based algorithms enable a group of agents to iteratively share and update their model parameters until they reach agreement. Each agent begins with its own local model and communicates only with neighbours in the network. Through repeated averaging or weighted updating of parameters, all agents gradually converge toward a common model. This method ensures consistent decision-making across the swarm without a central controller. It's robust against network changes and can tolerate delayed or missing updates. Consensus mechanisms are often used in distributed learning and coordination tasks. They help synchronize models in federated or decentralized setups. The approach scales well and maintains privacy since only model parameters are exchanged. Consensus algorithms reflect how natural swarms achieve harmony through repeated local adjustments. Ultimately, they provide a strong foundation for collective intelligence in distributed systems.
- **Gossip Protocols:** Gossip protocols are decentralized, randomized methods where agents exchange information with randomly selected peers. In the context of model learning, each agent shares its model parameters with one or a few neighbours during each round. Over time, information spreads through the network similarly to how gossip travels in social settings. This

process enables the gradual propagation and mixing of knowledge across all agents. Gossip-based communication is lightweight and highly scalable. It avoids the need for synchronized or global communication structures. The randomness adds resilience to failures and delays, making it well-suited for dynamic or unreliable networks. These protocols reduce congestion and communication overhead. Their simplicity and fault tolerance make them ideal for large-scale distributed learning. Gossip protocols mimic natural information diffusion and are effective in both structured and unstructured environments.

- **Distributed Optimization:** Distributed optimization focuses on solving a global objective function collaboratively across multiple agents. Each agent works with its own local data and contributes partial insights to a shared problem. Through coordinated updates and communication, the agents iteratively improve the global solution. This method reduces the computational burden on any single node. Techniques like gradient descent are adapted for parallel use across the network. Agents can optimize tasks such as minimizing loss functions or improving model accuracy. Distributed optimization is essential for training large models efficiently and privately. It allows for real-time learning in decentralized settings. The method is flexible and can incorporate constraints, heterogeneity and asynchrony. Its power lies in transforming local effort into global intelligence.
- **Graph Neural Networks (GNNs):** Graph Neural Networks (GNNs) extend neural learning to structured data represented as graphs. In distributed systems, agents are nodes in a graph and edges represent communication links. GNNs leverage this topology to enable agents to aggregate features from their neighbours during training. This results in context-aware learning that captures both node attributes and network structure. Each layer in the GNN allows agents to learn from increasingly distant neighbours. This is ideal for scenarios where relational or spatial information is critical. GNNs are powerful in domains like sensor networks, transportation and social systems. They support localized computation and message passing, which aligns well with swarm and multi-agent systems. Distributed GNN training enables scalability and resilience. The architecture naturally supports decentralized and asynchronous learning. GNNs offer a principled way to model complex inter-agent dependencies.
- **Multi-Agent Reinforcement Learning (MARL):** Multi-Agent Reinforcement Learning (MARL) allows agents to learn by interacting with their environment and one another. Each agent follows a policy that maps observations to actions, which it updates over time to maximize cumulative

reward. In MARL, agents are not isolated—they consider the presence and actions of others during learning. Local experiences are used to adjust policies, while shared information helps align behaviours. This enables coordination, competition, or cooperation among agents depending on the task. MARL systems are well-suited for complex environments like robotics, traffic control and games. The decentralized nature supports scalable and adaptive behaviour. Agents can learn to specialize or generalize based on their roles. Combining MARL with communication protocols enhances performance and robustness. Ultimately, MARL equips agents with autonomy and intelligence in dynamic multi-agent ecosystems.

6.4.5. Federated Learning in Swarm Robotics

- **Applications:** Federated learning in swarm robotics enables collaborative intelligence without requiring raw data sharing, making it ideal for tasks like collective perception. For example, multiple robots can individually train models for object recognition or environment mapping using their local sensory inputs. These locally trained models are then aggregated to form a more robust, swarm-level perception model. This approach helps the swarm understand its surroundings more accurately, even in dynamic or unknown environments. Another major application is shared policy learning for coordinated tasks such as formation control, area coverage, or cooperative transport. Each robot learns from its experiences while benefiting from the collective knowledge of the group. Additionally, federated learning supports distributed anomaly detection, allowing robots to recognize abnormal behaviours or environmental hazards collectively. This enhances safety and operational efficiency. The framework allows swarm members to update their models continuously and adapt to changes in real time. Federated learning maintains privacy, improves generalization across agents and supports on-the-fly learning. It promotes decentralized autonomy, critical in large-scale or bandwidth-constrained swarm deployments. Applications span agriculture, disaster response, surveillance and industrial automation. By enabling localized learning with global coordination, federated learning brings scalable intelligence to robot swarms.
- **Challenges:** Despite its promise, applying federated learning in swarm robotics presents several technical and operational challenges. One major issue is communication latency and synchronization delays, especially in large or mobile swarms. Coordinating model updates across many agents in real time can become computationally expensive and prone to packet loss or delay. Furthermore, data collected by individual robots is often non-

i.i.d.—that is, each robot may experience different environments, leading to heterogeneous data distributions. This inconsistency can slow down or destabilize the global learning process. Balancing model accuracy with communication efficiency is another critical challenge. Frequent model updates may improve accuracy but increase bandwidth usage and energy consumption. Conversely, less frequent updates risk model divergence. Swarms must also handle partial participation, where some agents may be offline or in low-connectivity zones. Designing robust aggregation strategies that tolerate noisy, sparse, or biased updates is essential. Additionally, ensuring security and privacy during model exchanges—especially in adversarial settings—is vital. Hardware limitations on processing and storage can restrict the complexity of models that individual agents can support. Managing resource constraints while maintaining learning performance remains an ongoing research challenge. Addressing these issues is key to making federated learning truly practical in real-world swarm robotics systems.

6.4.6. Communication and Computation Trade-Offs

- **Decentralized Learning:** In decentralized learning, agents communicate directly with their neighbours to exchange model updates or parameter information in frequent, iterative rounds. This form of local interaction enables real-time adaptation and quick convergence within nearby clusters of agents. Because updates happen at a fine-grained level, decentralized learning typically exhibits lower latency and better responsiveness to environmental changes. However, this comes at the cost of increased message passing across the network, which can burden communication bandwidth, especially in large-scale systems. Each agent needs to process multiple updates frequently, leading to a higher cumulative communication load even if the individual messages are small. The system must handle dynamic topology changes and possible message delays or dropouts. Moreover, there is often no centralized coordinator, which can make achieving global consensus more complex and slower. The frequent updates also increase energy consumption, a significant concern in mobile or battery-powered agents like drones or ground robots. On the upside, this method enhances robustness: if a node fails, the rest of the network can continue learning. Decentralized approaches are well-suited to systems where real-time collaboration and fault tolerance are prioritized over bandwidth efficiency. The communication-computation balance leans toward constant local computation with distributed, incremental knowledge sharing. Scalability depends heavily on network density and connectivity patterns. While flexible and adaptive, careful design is required to prevent communication bottlenecks and update noise.

- **Federated Learning:** Federated learning minimizes frequent communication by allowing agents to train models locally for extended periods before sending updates to a central aggregator. This approach dramatically reduces the communication frequency, making it especially efficient for systems with bandwidth constraints. Updates are sent in bulk—often after multiple local training epochs—thereby lowering the overall communication load. However, this results in higher latency between learning rounds and can slow down convergence, especially in highly dynamic environments. The global model is refined through periodic aggregation, which assumes the central server is available and trusted. To further optimize communication, techniques like update sparsification, quantization and compression are commonly applied. These reduce the size of transmitted model updates while preserving learning accuracy. Federated learning supports heterogeneous devices, as each agent can operate asynchronously and on non-identical data. However, stragglers (slower agents) can introduce delays in aggregation, requiring strategies like partial participation or weighted averaging. This architecture also introduces a computational trade-off: each agent performs more local training, which increases its processing load but reduces reliance on constant communication. Privacy is enhanced as raw data stays local, though security risks remain in model inference or poisoning attacks. Federated learning excels in scenarios prioritizing privacy, scalability and reduced communication, but it needs robust aggregation and synchronization schemes to ensure model stability. The approach is increasingly favoured in real-world applications, from mobile devices to swarm robotics and industrial IoT networks.

6.4.7. Privacy and Security Concerns

- **Data Privacy:** Data privacy is a central concern in distributed machine learning approaches such as Federated Learning (FL) and other decentralized models. A major benefit of these methods is that raw data remains on users' devices rather than being sent to a central server. This inherently reduces the risk of data breaches or misuse, especially when dealing with sensitive information like health records or personal communications. In Federated Learning, only model updates (such as gradients) are shared, rather than the data itself. To further enhance privacy, techniques like Differential Privacy can be applied. Differential Privacy introduces random noise to the model updates before they are sent, making it statistically impossible to determine whether a specific individual's data contributed to the model. This balances the trade-off between model utility and privacy protection. Moreover, encryption techniques such as Secure Multiparty Computation (SMPC) and Homomorphic Encryption may be employed to ensure that updates remain secure during transmission. However, while these strategies increase privacy, they also come with computation and communication overhead. The design challenge lies in maximizing privacy while maintaining acceptable performance. Ultimately, both FL and privacy-enhancing techniques are gaining traction in privacy-sensitive industries like healthcare, finance and mobile applications.

- **Security Threats:** Security threats in Federated Learning and similar decentralized systems pose significant challenges. Among the most common threats are poisoning attacks, where malicious agents intentionally send corrupted model updates to degrade overall model performance or mislead it into making incorrect predictions. These attacks can be targeted (focusing on specific outcomes) or untargeted (general model degradation). Another serious threat is the Sybil attack, where an adversary creates multiple fake clients (or "sybils") to influence the learning process disproportionately. These fake agents can flood the system with misleading data, skewing the model's learning trajectory. To combat these threats, researchers have developed robust aggregation techniques, such as median and trimmed mean, which can reduce the influence of outlier updates. Another promising defence is reputation-based systems, which assign trust scores to clients based on their past behaviour, reducing the weight of potentially malicious actors. Some systems also use anomaly detection to flag unusual update patterns. However, designing secure federated systems is inherently difficult because the server typically has no access to the raw data and limited observability. This makes it challenging to differentiate between benign variations and malicious intent. Therefore, continual research and adaptation are crucial to ensure secure, trustworthy federated learning environments.
- **Mitigations:** To safeguard Federated Learning systems from security threats such as poisoning and Sybil attacks, several mitigation strategies have been developed. One effective approach is the use of robust aggregation techniques. Traditional averaging of model updates is vulnerable to outliers and malicious data, so alternatives like the median and trimmed mean are used to reduce the impact of anomalous updates. The median selects the middle value of updates for each model parameter, resisting extreme values. The trimmed mean excludes a fixed percentage of the highest and lowest updates before averaging, further increasing robustness. These methods

ensure that even if some clients submit malicious data, the final model remains stable and accurate. Another line of defence involves reputation systems, which evaluate and track the reliability of each participating client. Clients that consistently submit useful and aligned updates receive higher trust scores and their contributions are given more weight in aggregation. Conversely, suspicious or erratic behaviour leads to reduced influence or exclusion. Some reputation systems incorporate historical performance, while others use anomaly detection or cryptographic proofs. Together, these mitigations enhance system resilience, helping federated learning maintain integrity even in the presence of adversarial agents and noisy environments.

6.4.8. Integration with Consensus and Voting

In decentralized learning environments, where a central authority is absent or minimal, ensuring consistent and trustworthy model updates across participating agents becomes challenging. To address this, consensus algorithms—widely used in blockchain and distributed systems—can be integrated into the learning framework. These algorithms help align model parameters across nodes by ensuring that updates are agreed upon by a majority or a quorum before they are accepted. Examples include Proof of Stake (PoS), Byzantine Fault Tolerance (BFT) variants and Raft, each offering different trade-offs in terms of speed, scalability and fault tolerance. By reaching consensus on updates, the system can guard against conflicting or malicious inputs, thus enhancing model integrity.

In addition to consensus, voting mechanisms can be utilized during the model aggregation phase. Instead of naïvely averaging all updates, voting-based strategies allow agents to vote on the validity or quality of peer updates. For example, clients may evaluate the impact of others' updates on their own local models, casting votes that reflect alignment or divergence. The system can then weigh contributions according to how well they conform to the majority or expected behaviour. This discourages adversarial behaviour and promotes fairness, as outlier or malicious contributions naturally receive less influence. Some systems even use weighted voting, where the weight is determined by a client's past performance, reputation, or similarity to consensus.

Combining consensus protocols with voting strategies introduces an additional layer of fault tolerance and transparency in federated learning. These integrations enable decentralized networks to self-regulate, minimizing reliance on centralized oversight and increasing resilience to attacks. They also support fair representation, ensuring that no single participant—whether benign or adversarial—dominates the learning process. While such systems introduce computational and communication overhead, their benefits in terms of robustness, security and democratic governance are becoming increasingly attractive. As decentralized AI systems evolve, these consensuses and voting mechanisms will likely become foundational components in ensuring trust, accuracy and equitable participation in distributed learning environments.

6.4.9. Practical Applications

- **Distributed Environmental Monitoring:** In distributed environmental monitoring, networks of swarm sensors are deployed across large or remote regions to collect data such as temperature, humidity, air quality, or seismic activity. Rather than sending all raw data to a central server, which may be infeasible due to bandwidth constraints or privacy concerns, these sensors employ decentralized learning to collaboratively build accurate environmental models. Each node learns from local observations and periodically exchanges model updates with neighbouring nodes or aggregators. Over time, these shared updates converge into a global model that captures region-wide environmental dynamics. This approach is highly scalable and energy-efficient, particularly important for battery-powered sensors. It also supports real-time adaptation to environmental changes, enabling early detection of anomalies such as wildfires, pollution spikes, or flood risks. Privacy is preserved since sensitive data, such as information from protected ecosystems or private lands, never leaves the local device. Federated averaging, robust update sharing and consensus mechanisms help maintain model integrity even in harsh conditions. The decentralized approach allows continuous monitoring with resilience to node failures or disconnections. This makes swarm-based environmental learning ideal for climate research, urban planning and ecological conservation.
- **Search and Rescue Operations:** Search and rescue missions often involve autonomous agents such as drones, ground robots, or sensor-equipped vehicles operating in uncertain and hazardous environments. In such scenarios, decentralized learning allows agents to adaptively learn navigation and search policies from localized experiences without waiting for centralized command updates. For instance, a drone encountering debris patterns or blocked paths can learn optimal avoidance strategies and share its policy updates with nearby agents. Over time, the swarm collectively refines a robust policy that generalizes across different terrain and conditions. This collaborative learning approach is especially valuable in dynamic environments, such as disaster zones where conditions change rapidly. By leveraging federated reinforcement learning, agents improve their strategies without exposing sensitive data such as survivor identities, geographic vulnerabilities, or classified infrastructure details.

The system remains operational even with partial connectivity, as agents communicate locally. Consensus and voting strategies can be used to filter out potentially harmful or misleading updates from malfunctioning units. This decentralized intelligence ensures timely decisions, improves mission efficiency and maximizes the chances of locating survivors in time-critical operations.

- **Agricultural Robotics:** In modern agriculture, fleets of autonomous robots and drones are being deployed for tasks such as crop monitoring, pest detection, irrigation planning and automated harvesting. These robots operate across vast farmlands and experience varied conditions depending on soil type, weather and crop species. Through decentralized learning, agricultural robots can learn from their local conditions and share insights with others to build robust predictive models. For example, one robot may detect early signs of a disease in a specific crop variety and transmit model updates that help others anticipate similar issues in nearby plots. Federated learning enables this knowledge transfer without requiring centralized storage of sensitive farm data, ensuring data privacy for individual farmers. Coordinated learning also enhances efficiency in harvesting, where robots must adapt to varying ripeness levels and field layouts. As each robot refines its policy through local trial and error, the aggregated knowledge benefits the entire swarm. Voting mechanisms can be used to weigh updates based on crop health feedback or yield accuracy. This approach minimizes redundancy, increases productivity and supports precision agriculture that is both sustainable and responsive to real-world variability.
- **Military and Surveillance:** Military and surveillance applications often require rapid, confidential and accurate decision-making across distributed agents operating in sensitive or hostile environments. Decentralized learning provides a powerful framework for enabling collaborative intelligence without centralized data aggregation, which may pose security and latency risks. Surveillance drones, radar systems, or patrol units can locally process visual, auditory, or electromagnetic signals to detect patterns indicative of threats such as intrusions, weapon activity, or cyberattacks. Instead of transmitting raw data, agents share encrypted or differentially private model updates that contribute to a collective situational awareness model. This ensures sensitive intelligence—like troop positions or classified sensor readings—remains protected. Additionally, consensus protocols help ensure only trustworthy agents influence the shared model, reducing vulnerability to misinformation or adversarial manipulation.

Voting systems can prioritize updates from units with high confidence or proximity to the threat zone. The resulting distributed threat detection system is resilient, fast and scalable across borders or terrains. It reduces reliance on satellite links or command centres and enables coordinated responses to emerging threats with minimal human intervention.

6.4.10. Future Directions

- **Hybrid Learning Architectures:** As distributed learning systems mature, a promising direction lies in hybrid learning architectures that blend the strengths of both federated learning (FL) and fully decentralized approaches. Federated learning centralizes the aggregation of updates, making it easier to manage and enforce privacy but potentially limiting scalability and fault tolerance. On the other hand, decentralized learning distributes responsibility entirely across peers, improving resilience but sometimes lacking coordination. A hybrid model can dynamically switch between centralized aggregation and peer-to-peer learning based on application needs, network topology, or privacy requirements. For example, agents in close proximity could use decentralized protocols for real-time collaboration, while periodically syncing with a central aggregator for global optimization. This flexibility enhances performance in heterogeneous environments, such as smart cities or industrial IoT networks. Hybrid systems can also implement hierarchical learning, where local groups of agents first consolidate updates before contributing to a global model, thus reducing communication overhead and improving scalability. Additionally, combining centralized trust mechanisms with decentralized verification (e.g., through blockchain or reputation systems) could offer enhanced security. The future of AI in edge networks, swarm robotics and multi-agent coordination may well depend on such adaptive, hybrid models that intelligently balance control, performance and resilience.
- **Edge Computing Integration:** The integration of edge computing into distributed learning frameworks is transforming how models are trained and deployed. In traditional settings, data is transmitted to centralized servers for processing—a model that suffers from latency, bandwidth limitations and privacy concerns. With edge computing, data processing, model training and inference happen closer to the data source, such as smartphones, IoT sensors, surveillance cameras, or drones. This enables faster response times and reduces the need for constant connectivity to cloud infrastructure. In federated learning, edge devices can locally train models using their own data and contribute updates, preserving privacy while reducing cloud dependency. As AI workloads become more intensive, offloading computation to the edge also alleviates server bottlenecks.

Moreover, edge devices can act as intelligent nodes that filter, preprocess, or even summarize data before sharing, improving both efficiency and relevance. Challenges such as device heterogeneity, energy limitations and hardware failures can be addressed through lightweight models, adaptive algorithms and intermittent communication strategies. The fusion of edge computing with federated or decentralized learning will be vital in applications like real-time health monitoring, autonomous driving, industrial automation and smart infrastructure—where low latency and high reliability are critical. This convergence represents a major leap toward sustainable, scalable and secure AI ecosystems.

- **Adaptive Communication Protocols:** In distributed learning systems, communication efficiency is crucial, especially in bandwidth-constrained or intermittently connected environments. As models become more complex and deployments scale across mobile and edge devices, transmitting frequent, large updates can lead to network congestion, delays, or data loss. Adaptive communication protocols offer a solution by dynamically adjusting the frequency, size and content of exchanged messages based on current network conditions, device capabilities, or task urgency. For example, devices might reduce the frequency of updates during network congestion, send compressed or sparsified gradients, or selectively share only high-impact parameters. Techniques like event-triggered communication, update quantization and gradient sparsification help reduce overhead while maintaining model performance. Additionally, asynchronous update mechanisms allow agents to contribute at different intervals, preventing stragglers from stalling the system. These adaptive strategies also support fairness, allowing low-power or low-bandwidth devices to participate meaningfully without being overwhelmed. Furthermore, edge-aware routing protocols can prioritize communication within clusters of nearby devices to minimize latency and energy usage. By integrating adaptive communication into federated and decentralized learning, systems become more robust, scalable and energy-efficient. This is especially important for real-time applications such as drone swarms, mobile health systems and sensor networks operating under uncertain conditions.
- **Federated Meta-Learning:** Federated meta-learning is a cutting-edge extension of federated learning that equips distributed agents with the ability to rapidly adapt to new tasks using previously acquired meta-knowledge. Traditional federated learning involves training a single global model across diverse clients, which may not generalize well to new or evolving tasks. Meta-learning, often described as "learning to learn," focuses on building models that can quickly adapt with minimal data. In

a federated setting, each client trains on its local task and contributes updates that encapsulate not only task-specific knowledge but also patterns useful across tasks. This shared meta-knowledge forms the basis of a meta-model, which can be fine-tuned locally for new challenges. In swarm systems—like autonomous drones, rescue robots, or collaborative sensors—this enables agents to adapt rapidly to unfamiliar environments, such as a new terrain, target behaviour, or task configuration. The approach is particularly powerful in scenarios with non-i.i.d. data, where local experiences vary widely. By focusing on adaptability rather than just accuracy, federated meta-learning allows systems to remain effective under dynamic conditions. Challenges include ensuring efficient aggregation of heterogeneous updates and preserving privacy. However, its potential for continual learning, cross-task transfer and quick personalization makes it a promising frontier in distributed intelligence.

- **Blockchain for Trust:** Trust is a persistent concern in federated and decentralized learning, where potentially untrusted or anonymous agents contribute to a shared model. Blockchain technology offers a compelling solution by introducing a transparent, immutable ledger that records all model updates, agent interactions and decision-making processes. By leveraging blockchain, every contribution—whether a model update, policy suggestion, or metadata exchange—is timestamped, traceable and verifiable. Smart contracts can be employed to enforce rules around participation, aggregation, or incentive distribution without requiring a central authority. This prevents malicious behaviour such as data poisoning, Sybil attacks, or update forgery, since any anomaly can be detected and audited on-chain. Additionally, agents can be rewarded through tokens or credits for valuable contributions, encouraging honest participation. Blockchain also supports decentralized governance, allowing participating nodes to vote on key decisions, such as model updates or policy changes. When combined with federated learning, blockchain can facilitate secure multi-party collaboration across industries like finance, healthcare and defense—where transparency, data ownership and auditability are critical. Although blockchain introduces computational overhead, emerging lightweight and scalable consensus protocols (e.g., Proof of Stake, DAG-based chains) are mitigating these challenges. The synergy of federated learning and blockchain marks a major step toward secure, trustworthy and democratized AI.

6.5 BIO-INSPIRED LEARNING MODELS

Bio-inspired learning models in swarm robotics draw profound inspiration from the remarkable behaviours and adaptive strategies observed in natural systems, including social insects like ants and bees, coordinated animal groups such as bird flocks and fish schools and the intricate workings of biological neural networks. These natural systems demonstrate extraordinary capabilities for learning, adaptation and self-organization, all achieved through simple, localized interactions rather than centralized control. By emulating these principles, swarm robotics researchers develop algorithms that empower robotic agents to collectively solve complex tasks in a decentralized manner. The foundation of these models lies in evolutionary and ecological concepts, where processes like natural selection, mutation and survival of the fittest guide the gradual improvement and adaptation of behaviours across the swarm. Collective intelligence plays a pivotal role, enabling individual agents to contribute to the swarm's overall decision-making and problem-solving abilities by following straightforward local rules and responding to environmental stimuli. Through mechanisms such as stigmergy—where agents communicate indirectly via changes to their environment, like pheromone trails—bio-inspired models facilitate efficient coordination without explicit messaging. Feedback loops, both positive and negative, allow the swarm to reinforce beneficial behaviours while diminishing ineffective or harmful ones, fostering a robust self-organizing system. These emergent behaviours manifest as complex global patterns, such as dynamic foraging, obstacle avoidance, formation control and adaptive task allocation, all arising from the interactions of relatively simple agents. The decentralized nature of these models ensures high scalability, as the addition of new agents does not significantly increase the complexity of coordination. Moreover, bio-inspired approaches imbue swarms with remarkable robustness, enabling them to withstand individual agent failures, environmental noise, or unforeseen perturbations without catastrophic breakdown (Fig. 7).

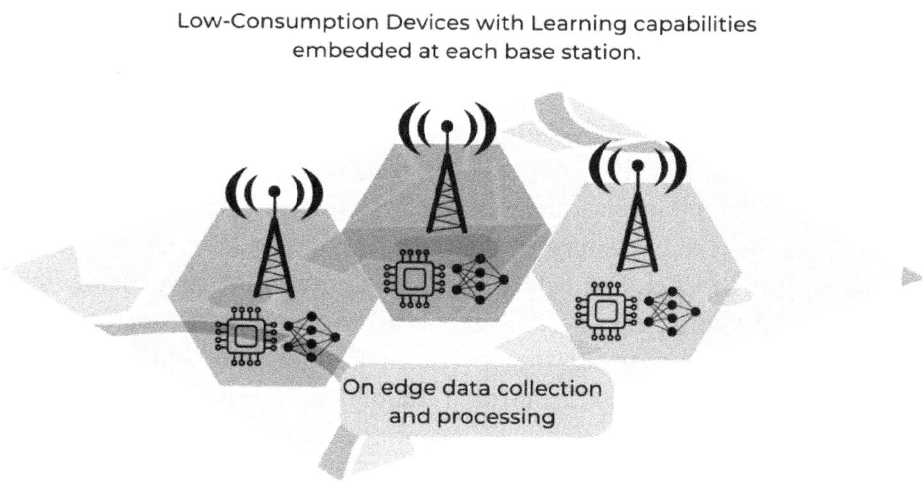

Fig. 7 Evaluation of Bio-Inspired Models under Different Learning Settings For Energy Efficiency in Network Traffic Prediction

Beyond robustness and scalability, the adaptability of bio-inspired models is a key advantage. Swarms can learn and modify their strategies in real-time, adjusting to changes in their environment, task requirements, or internal state. This adaptability is critical for deployment in dynamic, uncertain, or partially known environments, were rigid, pre-programmed behaviours would fail. The simplicity of local rules also reduces computational and communication overhead, allowing swarms to operate efficiently with limited resources. Despite these strengths, challenges remain, such as tuning parameters for optimal performance, ensuring convergence speed and translating simulated behaviours to real-world robotic platforms. To address these, researchers often integrate bio-inspired models with machine learning, evolutionary algorithms and optimization techniques, creating hybrid systems that leverage the best of both worlds. Looking forward, bio-inspired learning models continue to evolve by incorporating insights from multiple biological scales, from the neural to the ecosystem level and exploring emerging fields such as deep bio-inspired learning and bio-hybrid systems that combine living organisms with robots. These advances promise to make swarm robotics more intelligent, autonomous and capable of tackling increasingly complex real-world problems, ultimately bridging the gap between natural collective intelligence and artificial multi-agent systems.

6.5.1. Overview of Bio-Inspired Learning: Learning mechanisms derived from observing biological organisms and ecosystems.

Traits:

- **Decentralized decision-making:** In swarm systems, there is no central authority guiding every agent's action. Instead, each agent makes decisions based on local information and its internal rules. This decentralization enhances robustness, as the system doesn't collapse if a single unit fails. It also fosters parallelism, enabling the swarm to perform multiple tasks simultaneously. Coordination emerges from simple, distributed interactions rather than top-down control. This mirrors decision-making in natural swarms like ant colonies or bird flocks. Decentralized systems tend to be more scalable since adding new agents doesn't overburden a central node. Moreover, such systems are often more adaptable to dynamic environments. Local autonomy allows agents to quickly respond to local changes. As a result, the swarm operates efficiently even under uncertainty and noise
- **Local interactions among agents:** Swarm intelligence is fundamentally driven by local interactions among agents. Each agent responds to its immediate environment and the behaviour of nearby peers. There's no need for a global overview or full system awareness. Through simple local

rules, complex global behaviours emerge naturally. For instance, birds in a flock align with neighbours to maintain formation. In artificial systems, local communication reduces bandwidth and processing needs. It also enables faster reaction times and fault tolerance. These interactions are often governed by rules like alignment, cohesion and separation. As agents interact repeatedly, patterns such as clustering or pathfinding develop. This principle ensures scalability and resilience in the swarm. It is a key enabler of emergent intelligence in decentralized systems

- **Adaptation through feedback from the environment:** Swarm systems adapt based on continuous environmental feedback. Agents observe their surroundings and modify their actions accordingly. This loop enables the system to self-correct and improve over time. For instance, ants adjust their foraging paths based on pheromone trails. In artificial swarms, sensors gather environmental data to guide behaviour. This allows agents to optimize performance in changing conditions. Feedback loops help distribute resources efficiently and avoid obstacles. As conditions evolve, agents adapt without external reprogramming. This ability supports resilience and long-term operation in unpredictable settings. Learning from the environment enables swarms to solve complex, dynamic problems. Ultimately, adaptation ensures survival and success in real-world applications.

Motivation: Natural swarms, like those of bees or fish, display extraordinary coordination without central control. These systems handle disruptions with ease and adapt seamlessly to change. Such traits—robustness, scalability and flexibility—are highly desirable in engineered systems. Emulating these features can enhance robotics, logistics and communication networks. Robustness ensures the system continues functioning even when parts fail. Scalability allows the swarm to grow or shrink without redesign. Flexibility enables adaptation to new tasks or environments. These principles reduce design complexity and increase operational efficiency. Artificial swarms inspired by nature can tackle distributed tasks like search-and-rescue or environmental monitoring. By learning from biology, we design systems that are both efficient and resilient. This biomimicry bridges the gap between nature's wisdom and technological innovation.

6.5.2. Types of Bio-Inspired Learning Models

- **Swarm Intelligence Algorithms:** Swarm intelligence algorithms are inspired by the collective behaviour of social animals such as ants, bees, birds and fish, which achieve complex tasks through simple local interactions without centralized control. These algorithms mimic natural processes like foraging, flocking and nest building, enabling robotic swarms to perform coordinated actions such as searching for resources, forming formations and optimizing paths. They rely on decentralized communication mechanisms such as stigmergy, where agents indirectly influence one another through environmental markers, similar to pheromone trails in ants. The emergent global behaviour results from agents following basic behavioural rules, which collectively lead to efficient problem-solving. Examples include Ant Colony Optimization (ACO) for route finding and Particle Swarm Optimization (PSO) for optimization tasks. These algorithms are scalable, fault-tolerant and adaptive, making them well-suited for dynamic and uncertain environments. By leveraging distributed intelligence, swarm algorithms can rapidly adapt to changes and maintain robustness even with agent failures. Their simplicity allows for easy implementation in resource-constrained robotic systems, enabling real-world applications such as environmental monitoring, search and rescue and collective construction.

- **Neural Models:** Neural models in swarm robotics are inspired by the structure and function of biological brains, particularly how neurons process and transmit information. Artificial Neural Networks (ANNs) mimic this by creating interconnected layers of nodes (neurons) that transform input data into meaningful outputs through weighted connections. These networks enable swarms to perform complex pattern recognition, decision-making and control tasks. In swarm systems, neural models can be distributed among agents to support collective learning and adaptation. Techniques such as deep learning, reinforcement learning and neuroevolutionary enhance the swarm's ability to generalize from experiences, optimize policies and handle noisy or incomplete data. Neural models allow individual robots to process sensory inputs and learn from interactions with their environment, improving autonomy and responsiveness. They also support emergent coordination by enabling agents to predict and align behaviours based on local observations. While powerful, neural models require careful design to balance computational demands with real-time operation in distributed settings. Integrating neural models with other bio-inspired approaches fosters more intelligent and flexible swarm behaviours.

- **Evolutionary Models:** Evolutionary models draw from the principles of natural evolution, such as selection, mutation and reproduction, to iteratively improve swarm behaviours and control policies over generations. In these models, each robotic agent or a group of agents represents an individual solution encoded as a set of parameters or strategies. The fitness of these individuals is evaluated based on their performance in tasks like navigation, task allocation, or formation control. The most successful individuals are selected to reproduce, often combining their traits through crossover, while random mutations introduce variability to explore new solutions. This process drives the swarm population toward optimized collective behaviours without explicit programming. Evolutionary algorithms are particularly useful for discovering novel strategies in complex, poorly understood environments where analytical solutions are unavailable. They enable automatic adaptation to changing conditions by continuously evolving solutions during deployment or in simulation. However, evolutionary models can require significant computational resources and time to converge, especially in large swarms. Hybrid approaches often combine evolutionary models with online learning for faster adaptation and real-world applicability.

- **Immune System Models:** Immune system models in swarm robotics are inspired by the adaptive and distributed nature of biological immune responses, which detect and respond to pathogens through a network of specialized cells. These models simulate mechanisms such as antigen recognition, immune memory and immune network interactions to enable swarms to detect anomalies, adapt to threats and maintain system health. Robots can be programmed with immune-inspired algorithms that recognize unusual patterns or faults within the swarm or environment and trigger appropriate responses to mitigate risks. For example, an immune system model might help identify malfunctioning agents or external disturbances and initiate self-healing or reconfiguration behaviours. These models contribute to the robustness and resilience of swarms by ensuring sustained performance despite internal or external challenges. They also support distributed fault detection and isolation without central control, making them suitable for large-scale, long-duration missions. Immune-inspired approaches often incorporate learning to improve recognition capabilities over time, adapting to evolving threats. Their biological basis provides a rich framework for designing autonomous, self-protective multi-agent systems.
- **Behavioural Models:** Behavioural models in swarm robotics emulate animal learning processes such as habituation, sensitization and conditioning to shape agent responses based on experience. Habituation allows agents to reduce responses to repetitive, non-threatening stimuli, conserving energy and attention. Sensitization, in contrast, increases responsiveness following significant or novel stimuli, preparing agents to act when necessary. Conditioning involves associating specific environmental cues with rewards or punishments, enabling agents to learn adaptive

behaviours through trial and error. These simple yet powerful learning mechanisms enable individual robots to adjust their actions dynamically and contribute to collective swarm intelligence. Behavioural models facilitate flexible and context-sensitive decision-making, allowing swarms to respond appropriately to changing environments or mission goals. They also support emergent behaviours through local interactions, reinforcing cooperation or competition as required. By incorporating biologically grounded learning rules, behavioural models enhance the autonomy and adaptability of robotic swarms without heavy computational requirements. Their use is widespread in navigation, exploration, obstacle avoidance and communication protocols within swarm systems.

6.5.3. Bio-Inspired Algorithms

- **Ant Colony Optimization (ACO):** Ant Colony Optimization mimics the natural foraging behaviour of ants, which use pheromone trails to communicate and find the shortest paths between their nest and food sources. In ACO, robotic agents simulate this behaviour by depositing virtual pheromones on paths they traverse, with stronger pheromone concentrations indicating better routes. Over time, agents preferentially choose paths with higher pheromone levels, reinforcing efficient routes and allowing the swarm to collectively discover optimal or near-optimal solutions. This indirect communication through the environment, called stigmergy, enables decentralized coordination without explicit messaging. ACO is widely applied in routing, path planning and task allocation within swarms. Its ability to adapt dynamically to changing environments makes it robust against obstacles or failures. Furthermore, ACO algorithms balance exploration and exploitation, ensuring continual search for better solutions while consolidating known good routes.
- **Particle Swarm Optimization (PSO):** Particle Swarm Optimization is inspired by the collective movement patterns of bird flocks and fish schools, where individuals adjust their velocity and position based on both their own best-known location and the best-known positions of their neighbours. In PSO, each agent (particle) represents a potential solution in a search space and updates its trajectory iteratively by combining personal experience with social influence. This cooperative learning allows the swarm to converge on optimal or near-optimal solutions efficiently. PSO is widely used in optimization problems such as formation control, resource allocation and parameter tuning in swarm robotics. The simplicity of the update rules and the minimal communication required between agents make PSO attractive for distributed systems. Its continuous adaptation

ensures resilience to dynamic changes in the environment or mission objectives.

- **Artificial Immune Systems (AIS):** Artificial Immune Systems emulate the biological immune system's ability to detect and respond to pathogens in a distributed, adaptive manner. AIS algorithms model immune processes such as antigen recognition, immune memory and clonal selection to enable robotic swarms to identify anomalies, faults, or threats within themselves or their surroundings. Agents collaboratively monitor system health and environmental conditions, triggering defensive or corrective behaviours when irregularities are detected. AIS contributes to fault tolerance, robustness and self-healing capabilities in multi-agent systems. By learning to recognize and remember harmful patterns, AIS enhances long-term adaptability. These models are particularly useful in security-sensitive applications like surveillance, where early detection of faults or intrusions is critical.
- **Neuroevolution:** Neuroevolution combines neural networks with evolutionary algorithms to evolve control policies and decision-making strategies for robotic swarms. Instead of hand-crafting network parameters, neuroevolutionary iteratively improves neural architectures and weights through genetic operators such as mutation and crossover. Each individual in the evolutionary population represents a neural network whose fitness is evaluated based on performance in simulated or real tasks. Over generations, this process leads to increasingly effective control strategies that can handle complex, nonlinear behaviours. Neuroevolutionary enables swarms to autonomously develop robust behaviours for navigation, coordination and adaptation without explicit programming. It is particularly powerful in environments with incomplete information or noisy data. By merging learning and evolution, neuroevolutionary promotes scalable and flexible swarm intelligence.
- **Honeybee-Inspired Algorithms:** Honeybee-inspired algorithms simulate the foraging behaviour and communication patterns of honeybees, especially the waggle dance used to share information about food sources. In swarm robotics, these algorithms model how agents explore environments, assess resource quality and recruit other agents to promising locations through indirect signalling. This approach optimizes resource allocation, task distribution and exploration efficiency. Honeybee-inspired methods balance exploration and exploitation by dynamically adjusting recruitment intensity based on environmental feedback. Their distributed nature enhances scalability and fault tolerance, as decisions emerge from collective

interactions rather than centralized commands. These algorithms have been successfully applied to problems like area coverage, environmental monitoring and multi-robot task allocation. By mimicking natural bee behaviour, swarms achieve adaptive, efficient and robust collective performance

6.5.4. Learning Mechanisms in Bio-Inspired Models

- **Stigmergy:** Stigmergy is a form of indirect coordination where agents communicate and coordinate their actions by modifying the environment rather than through direct interaction. A classic example is pheromone trails laid by ants to guide others toward food sources. In swarm robotics, agents leave markers or signals in the environment, which influence the behaviour of other agents that encounter them. This mechanism enables decentralized control, allowing swarms to self-organize and solve complex tasks such as path finding, resource gathering, or construction. Stigmergy is highly robust to failures since no single agent controls the process and it naturally adapts to environmental changes. It also reduces communication overhead because agents rely on environmental cues rather than continuous messaging.
- **Positive and Negative Feedback:** Positive and negative feedback mechanisms regulate swarm behaviour by reinforcing effective actions and discouraging ineffective or harmful ones. Positive feedback amplifies successful behaviours — for example, more agents following a well-marked trail increase its pheromone strength, attracting even more agents. Negative feedback acts to suppress overused or suboptimal behaviours, preventing the swarm from converging prematurely or over-exploiting a resource. This dynamic balance between amplification and inhibition helps swarms adaptively explore their environment and avoid stagnation. Feedback loops are fundamental to self-organization and collective decision-making, ensuring that the swarm remains flexible and responsive.
- **Self-Organization:** Self-organization is the process where global order and complex patterns emerge from local interactions among agents without centralized control. In swarm robotics, individual agents follow simple rules based on local information, but their collective behaviour leads to coordinated formations, task allocation, or efficient exploration. This emergent order is scalable and robust, as it relies on redundancy and distributed control rather than single points of failure. Self-organization allows swarms to adapt quickly to changing environments and recover from disruptions. It is a key principle behind natural phenomena such as flocking birds, schooling fish and colony formation in social insects.

- **Distributed Learning:** Distributed learning refers to the process where individual agents learn from their own experiences and observations while simultaneously contributing to the swarm's collective knowledge. Each agent adapts its behaviour based on local data and interactions, but the aggregation of these adaptations leads to improved swarm performance over time. This decentralized approach enhances scalability, as learning does not depend on a central unit and robustness, as it tolerates agent failures. Distributed learning supports dynamic environments by allowing the swarm to continuously update strategies and share insights implicitly or explicitly. It forms the foundation for adaptive and autonomous swarm systems capable of real-time decision-making.

6.5.5. Applications in Swarm Robotics

- **Path Planning and Navigation:** Swarm robots use bio-inspired algorithms like Ant Colony Optimization (ACO) and Particle Swarm Optimization (PSO) for efficient and adaptive path planning. ACO enables agents to find optimal routes by reinforcing frequently travelled paths with pheromone-like markers, while PSO allows agents to adjust their trajectories based on both individual and group experience. These methods help swarms navigate complex, dynamic environments with obstacles, varying terrain, or moving targets. The decentralized nature of these algorithms ensures that the system remains functional even if some agents fail or become isolated. Together, they enable robust, flexible and scalable navigation strategies without central control.
- **Task Allocation:** In dynamic environments, bio-inspired swarm systems handle task allocation through local interaction and environmental feedback. Inspired by behaviours like division of labour in insect colonies, agents evaluate local task demands (e.g., object transport, area scanning) and self-assign roles accordingly. This decentralized mechanism ensures efficient resource use, balancing workload across the swarm. Algorithms like honeybee foraging models or neural-based decision frameworks allow agents to dynamically switch tasks based on changing conditions or swarm needs. Task allocation is key for autonomous operation in complex missions, ensuring that no area or task is neglected while avoiding redundant efforts.
- **Environmental Monitoring:** Swarm robotics excels in environmental monitoring due to its ability to deploy large numbers of simple, sensor-equipped agents that can adaptively respond to real-time changes. Bio-inspired learning allows agents to explore, detect and map environmental features such as pollution, temperature anomalies, or structural damage. Feedback-based learning ensures that the swarm focuses on areas of interest,

while distributed learning and stigmergy facilitate information sharing and coordinated data collection. This approach is useful for applications like agriculture, disaster management and habitat monitoring, where broad coverage, adaptability and robustness are critical.

- **Search and Rescue:** In search and rescue missions, bio-inspired swarms use coordinated exploration strategies to locate victims or assess hazards in unknown or collapsed environments. Inspired by insect foraging and animal search patterns, agents explore in a distributed yet purposeful manner, often guided by scent gradients, heat signatures, or sound. Algorithms like ACO support efficient area coverage, while feedback and learning models help prioritize promising regions. Swarms adapt to terrain changes, navigate debris and maintain connectivity through local rules. The decentralized design allows partial swarm failure without mission collapse, making this approach ideal for high-risk, uncertain scenarios.
- **Formation Control:** Formation control involves the creation and maintenance of spatial structures by the swarm using only local sensing and communication. Inspired by flocking birds and schooling fish, robots follow simple rules related to separation, alignment and cohesion to form coordinated geometric patterns. These behaviours are reinforced through bio-inspired learning to maintain formations during movement, obstacle avoidance, or environmental disruptions. Neural models and PSO-based methods help optimize formation parameters and enable reconfiguration as needed. This capability is essential for tasks requiring synchronized actions, such as surveillance, payload transport, or boundary monitoring.

6.5.6. Advantages of Bio-Inspired Learning

- **Scalability:** Bio-inspired learning models are inherently scalable, making them ideal for systems involving hundreds or thousands of agents. Since decisions and behaviours emerge from local interactions rather than centralized coordination, adding more agents does not significantly increase system complexity. Each agent operates independently based on simple rules, ensuring that the swarm's performance grows proportionally with its size. This characteristic allows the swarm to cover larger areas, handle more complex tasks, or increase redundancy without redesigning the control logic. Swarm performance often improves with scale, as more agents provide more data, redundancy and flexibility. This makes bio-inspired approaches perfect for large-scale applications like environmental monitoring or disaster response.
- **Robustness:** One of the core strengths of bio-inspired learning is its robustness to individual agent failure, sensor noise, or communication loss.

Since no single agent is essential to the swarm's functionality, the system can continue operating effectively even when some units malfunction or drop out. This mirrors nature, where insect colonies or animal groups continue functioning despite individual losses. Redundancy in behaviour and distributed decision-making ensure that tasks are reallocated or compensated for by other agents. Furthermore, feedback mechanisms and environmental cues help the swarm recover or re-stabilize after disruptions. This robustness is especially important in harsh or unpredictable environments where reliability is crucial.

- **Adaptability:** Bio-inspired swarms are highly adaptive, continuously learning from their environment and modifying behaviours in real-time. Agents adjust to dynamic conditions, such as changing terrain, task requirements, or unexpected obstacles, through feedback-based learning and decentralized sensing. Evolutionary models allow the swarm to evolve improved strategies over time, while behavioural models enable individual agents to learn from experience. This capacity for self-modification ensures long-term autonomy and effectiveness in missions with incomplete or evolving knowledge. Adaptability is vital for real-world scenarios like exploration, search and rescue and autonomous agriculture, where static behaviour models would quickly become obsolete.
- **Simplicity:** Despite enabling complex group behaviours, bio-inspired learning relies on simple local rules that are easy to implement and require minimal computational resources. Each agent only needs to sense its immediate surroundings and follow straightforward protocols, such as moving toward a signal or avoiding collisions. This simplicity reduces development time, lowers hardware requirements and facilitates real-time operation, even in resource-constrained robots. It also enhances interpretability and ease of debugging, as system behaviour can often be traced back to a few core rules. The power of these systems lies in emergent behaviour — where coordinated, intelligent group dynamics arise from individually basic agents.

6.5.7. Challenges and Limitations

- **Parameter Tuning:** Bio-inspired learning algorithms often rely on carefully chosen parameters to function effectively. These include values like pheromone evaporation rate in Ant Colony Optimization, learning rates in neural models, or mutation probabilities in evolutionary algorithms. The performance of the swarm can vary drastically with even slight changes to these parameters. This sensitivity can make fine-tuning difficult, particularly because optimal values may depend heavily on the environment, task complexity and swarm size. Moreover, parameters that work well in one context may fail in another, necessitating dynamic adjustment or adaptive tuning mechanisms. Manual tuning is time-consuming and impractical for large systems or real-time operations. In some cases, automated methods like meta-optimization or reinforcement learning are used to tune parameters on the fly, but these add additional computational cost. Additionally, tuning is even more complicated in decentralized settings, where agents may need to individually adapt without global knowledge. Poorly chosen parameters can lead to instability, slow learning, or convergence to suboptimal behaviours. Therefore, parameter sensitivity remains a key bottleneck in the reliability and generalizability of bio-inspired algorithms in real-world deployments.

- **Convergence Speed:** A major challenge of bio-inspired learning in swarm robotics is the relatively slow convergence speed of many algorithms. Because swarm behaviour relies on the accumulation of local interactions and indirect communication, such as pheromone trails or imitation of neighbours, it can take many iterations for the system to reach a stable and effective solution. This delay is especially problematic in time-sensitive tasks like search and rescue, where immediate responsiveness is crucial. Algorithms like evolutionary strategies or distributed reinforcement learning may require thousands of simulation steps before learning effective behaviours. Additionally, the lack of centralized control means that convergence depends on how efficiently information spreads across the swarm, which can be hindered by communication noise, spatial dispersion, or asynchrony. In dynamic environments, slow convergence may cause the swarm to adapt too late, rendering its behaviour ineffective. Researchers are exploring ways to accelerate convergence through mechanisms like event-triggered updates, adaptive learning rates, or incorporating short-term memory. However, achieving a balance between fast learning and stable, reliable behaviour remains a significant technical hurdle.
- **Real-World Transfer:** One of the most persistent challenges in swarm robotics is transferring bio-inspired algorithms from simulation to physical robots. Simulations often make idealized assumptions—such as perfect sensing, noise-free communication and uniform environments—that do not hold in real-world settings. Physical robots face issues like hardware imperfections, battery constraints, sensor noise and environmental unpredictability, all of which can disrupt carefully tuned learning models. Furthermore, bio-inspired algorithms often rely on large populations of agents and long learning periods, which may not be feasible or safe in physical trials. As a result, behaviours that work flawlessly in simulation

can perform poorly or unpredictably when deployed in real hardware. Synchronizing learning across decentralized agents in real-time and managing environmental variability without centralized oversight adds further complexity. To address this, researchers are developing robust simulation-to-reality transfer techniques, such as domain randomization, calibration with real-world data, or hybrid testing environments. Nevertheless, bridging the gap between digital models and physical embodiment remains a major barrier to large-scale, real-world adoption of bio-inspired swarm systems.

- **Complexity of Emergent Behaviour:** Emergent behaviour is both a strength and a challenge of bio-inspired swarm systems. While local rules can give rise to powerful global coordination, predicting or controlling these emergent outcomes is often extremely difficult. Small changes in individual agent behaviour or environmental conditions can lead to disproportionately large and unexpected system-wide effects. This non-linearity makes debugging, validation and safety assurance complex. Engineers often struggle to design or verify swarms that behave reliably under all possible scenarios. Moreover, emergent behaviours can sometimes conflict with task objectives or lead to inefficient or unstable outcomes, such as clustering, deadlocks, or infinite loops. The lack of transparency in how individual decisions aggregate into collective patterns limits our ability to enforce constraints or ensure goal alignment. Researchers are actively working on tools and models to better understand and guide emergent behaviour, such as using formal methods, simulation-based verification, or rule synthesis algorithms. However, fully mastering the complexity of emergence remains one of the grand challenges in the field of swarm robotics.

6.5.8. Enhancements and Hybrid Models

- **Hybrid Algorithms:** Hybrid algorithms represent a significant advancement in swarm robotics, combining the strengths of bio-inspired approaches with modern machine learning, control theory and optimization techniques. These systems leverage the adaptability and distributed intelligence of models like ACO, PSO, or neural evolution, while enhancing performance with reinforcement learning, deep learning, or gradient-based optimization. For instance, neuroevolutionary can evolve neural networks that are later fine-tuned using supervised learning, resulting in highly adaptive and generalizable behaviours. Similarly, combining ACO with heuristic optimization can speed up convergence while preserving robustness. These hybrid models allow for both emergent behaviour and fine-grained control, enabling agents to learn policies that adapt to both known and unknown scenarios. This integration also improves decision-making in complex, multi-agent environments where purely bio-inspired models may struggle to generalize. Furthermore, hybrid systems can operate across different layers of the swarm, where some agents focus on learning and others on maintaining structural cohesion or coordination. By fusing multiple techniques, hybrid algorithms achieve a balance of flexibility, precision and scalability.

- **Adaptive Parameter Control:** Adaptive parameter control addresses one of the core limitations of traditional bio-inspired algorithms: their sensitivity to static parameter settings. Instead of using fixed values for critical factors like learning rates, pheromone decay, or mutation probabilities, adaptive models adjust these parameters dynamically based on the swarm's performance or environmental feedback. For example, an ant-inspired system might increase pheromone evaporation during high congestion or noise to encourage exploration, while reducing it when stable paths are needed. Evolutionary algorithms can self-tune mutation rates based on fitness progression, optimizing the exploration-exploitation balance. Reinforcement learning agents can use meta-learning to adapt their learning strategies in real-time. These mechanisms improve convergence speed, robustness and adaptability, especially in non-stationary or unpredictable environments. Adaptive control also supports transferability across scenarios by allowing the system to calibrate itself to new conditions without manual intervention. It brings greater autonomy and resilience, making swarms more effective in long-term, real-world deployments.
- **Multi-Objective Optimization:** Real-world swarm applications often require balancing multiple competing objectives—such as energy efficiency, task performance, risk avoidance and communication overhead. Multi-objective optimization (MOO) methods enable swarm systems to find solutions that trade-off between these goals rather than optimizing a single criterion. Bio-inspired approaches like multi-objective PSO or evolutionary strategies allow the swarm to explore a diverse set of solutions along the Pareto front, providing a range of optimal choices instead of a single fixed solution. For example, in a surveillance task, the swarm may need to maximize area coverage while minimizing battery usage. MOO enables agents to weigh these factors contextually, making better-informed decisions. These models also support priority adjustments during mission execution, such as shifting focus from speed to accuracy in critical situations. Integrating MOO into bio-inspired learning fosters more intelligent and context-aware behaviours, allowing swarms to perform robustly under real-world constraints. It also enhances decision-making in

dynamic and uncertain conditions, where static trade-offs are ineffective.

- **Learning from Nature at Multiple Scales:** One of the most promising frontiers in bio-inspired robotics is learning from nature across multiple biological scales—individual, social and ecological. At the individual level, agents learn from personal experience using models inspired by neural plasticity, habituation, or conditioning. At the group level, they engage in social learning and collective decision-making, modelled after flocks, herds, or insect colonies. At the ecosystem level, swarm behaviours reflect long-term evolutionary adaptation and population-level resilience, inspired by species diversity, predator-prey dynamics and resource competition. Integrating learning mechanisms across these scales allows for rich, layered intelligence in swarms, where agents can switch between reactive, learned and evolved behaviours based on context. This multi-scale learning supports adaptability not just over time but also across complexity levels—handling simple navigation tasks as well as high-level mission coordination. It fosters holistic system design, where swarm behaviour emerges from the interplay between immediate stimuli, social interactions and evolutionary memory. Such a layered approach promises robust, scalable and ecologically intelligent swarm systems capable of thriving in complex real-world environments.

6.5.9. Future Research Directions

- **Deep Bio-Inspired Learning:** Deep bio-inspired learning envisions the convergence of deep learning with the principles of swarm intelligence, aiming to create systems that possess both powerful pattern recognition and robust decentralized behaviour. While traditional swarms operate using simple, local rules, integrating deep neural networks allows agents to interpret complex sensory data—such as vision or audio—and make context-aware decisions. For instance, an agent could use a convolutional neural network (CNN) to detect obstacles or victims in a disaster zone and then use swarm rules to coordinate exploration or rescue. This fusion also enables end-to-end learning, where swarms can be trained to perform tasks from raw input to action without explicit rule encoding. Deep reinforcement learning (DRL) combined with swarm principles allows for learning coordinated policies that scale to dynamic, high-dimensional environments. This direction holds promise for enabling swarms to perform intelligent behaviours in real-world, unpredictable scenarios—blending adaptability, autonomy and collective cognition.
- **Bio-Hybrid Systems:** Bio-hybrid systems explore the direct integration of biological organisms with robotic swarms, creating systems that blend

natural and artificial intelligence. These can take the form of robots guided by animal signals, robotic systems that influence insect behaviour, or mixed collectives where living and robotic agents interact cooperatively. For example, robotic bees might interact with real bees to influence foraging patterns, or fish-like robots could guide schools of real fish for environmental monitoring. These systems enable a new class of applications—such as bio-monitoring, behavioural studies and eco-robotics—where robots act not just in artificial environments but also within ecosystems. Challenges remain in safety, communication and ethical implications, but the potential for bio-robot symbiosis opens the door to previously unthinkable applications. Moreover, studying these interactions can inform better robot design, inspired by how biological systems handle complexity, adaptability and learning.

- **Self-Healing and Self-Replication:** Inspired by biological regeneration, self-healing and self-replication represent two of the most futuristic yet critical capabilities in swarm robotics. Self-healing swarms would allow agents to detect internal damage or external disruption and autonomously reconfigure or repair themselves without halting mission execution. This could involve rerouting internal systems, reprogramming behaviours, or redistributing responsibilities among neighbouring agents. Self-replication, on the other hand, involves the ability for robots to construct new agents from raw materials or modular parts—much like cellular mitosis or regeneration in organisms like starfish. Together, these capabilities would drastically enhance mission longevity, autonomy and resilience, especially in remote or hostile environments such as space exploration or deep-sea monitoring. Implementing these features requires breakthroughs in modular hardware, material science and autonomous construction algorithms, making this a rich area for interdisciplinary research.
- **Cross-Disciplinary Insights:** The future of bio-inspired swarm robotics is deeply tied to cross-disciplinary insights from fields such as biology, neuroscience, ecology and cognitive science. Understanding how ants communicate using minimal information, how birds coordinate mid-flight, or how neurons form adaptive networks provides foundational principles for new algorithms and architectures. For instance, studying synaptic plasticity in brains may inspire more nuanced learning models, while ecological studies on resource distribution could inform energy-efficient task allocation strategies in robotic swarms. Collaborations with ecologists could also lead to swarms that interact sustainably with natural habitats, minimizing ecological disruption. These cross-domain influences not only

broaden the scope of what swarm systems can do but also ensure that future technologies are grounded in the tested wisdom of natural systems. Interdisciplinary frameworks are vital for pushing the boundaries of autonomy, intelligence and resilience in collective robotic systems.

7 Chapter

SIMULATION AND MODELING TOOLS

7.0 INTRODUCTION: AN OVERVIEW

Simulation and modelling tools are fundamental to the design, testing and validation of swarm robotic systems. Before deploying a swarm in real-world environments, researchers rely heavily on simulations to prototype behaviours, evaluate algorithms and study emergent phenomena under controlled, repeatable conditions. These tools enable developers to create virtual environments where hundreds or even thousands of agents can be modelled, each with realistic sensing, actuation and communication capabilities. Given the decentralized and dynamic nature of swarms, simulation environments must also support scalability, real-time feedback and the emulation of complex interactions between agents and their surroundings. Swarm systems are inherently nonlinear and stochastic, making their analysis challenging without the aid of computational tools. Modelling platforms help researchers observe how simple local rules can produce complex global behaviours, such as flocking, foraging and formation maintenance. They also allow for fine-tuning of parameters and exploration of edge cases that would be too time-consuming, costly, or dangerous to test physically. With modern simulation frameworks, one can simulate diverse terrains, sensor noise, communication delays and even physical damage, providing a comprehensive platform for stress-testing algorithms under a wide range of conditions. These tools play a vital role in the iterative development process. Developers can simulate multiple scenarios, measure performance metrics (like coverage, convergence time, energy use) and analyse swarm responses before committing to physical trials. Furthermore, simulations facilitate collaborative development by offering open-source platforms where researchers across the world can test and compare algorithms using shared benchmarks. Many tools also support integration with machine learning libraries, allowing for training and testing of adaptive behaviours directly within simulated environments (Fig. 1).

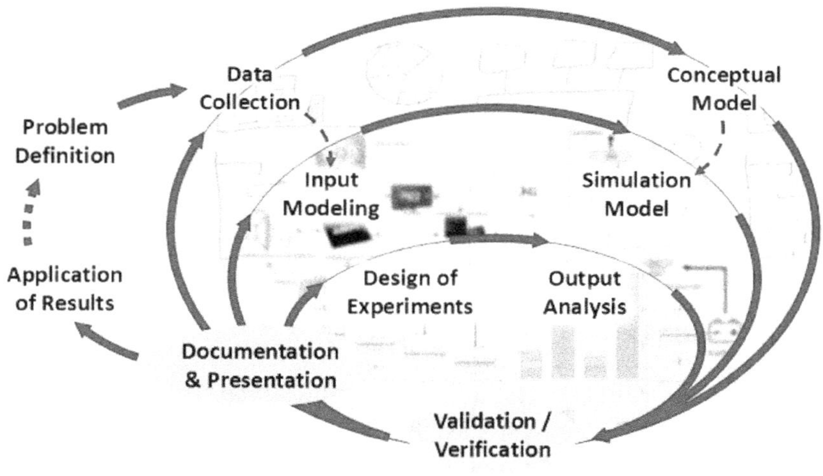

Fig. 1 Simulation and Modeling

As swarms grow in size and complexity, so too do the requirements for their simulation. Tools must be both computationally efficient and highly configurable, capable of modelling heterogeneity among agents and real-time communication constraints. Additionally, many modern simulators now offer 3D visualizations, physics engines and support for hardware-in-the-loop testing, narrowing the gap between simulation and deployment. Some even enable transfer learning, where behaviours learned in virtual environments can be transferred directly to physical robots with minimal re-tuning.

Simulation is not only a testing tool but also a research instrument. It allows for the exploration of theoretical models of coordination, communication and control, often revealing emergent dynamics that inspire new algorithmic strategies. Simulations support education and training, helping students and practitioners visualize and experiment with swarm behaviours in an accessible, risk-free manner. Moreover, modelling enables rapid prototyping of swarm configurations tailored for specific applications—from environmental monitoring and warehouse automation to planetary exploration and defence. The importance of simulation is further emphasized in multi-disciplinary research, where robotic behaviours must be coordinated with models from biology, physics, or environmental science. This makes simulation tools essential not only for robotics engineers but also for ecologists, cognitive scientists and systems theorists studying collective behaviour. As robotics continues to shift toward autonomy at scale, simulation will remain central to designing, predicting and refining intelligent swarms capable of operating in complex, uncertain environments. Simulation and modelling tools form the backbone of swarm robotics development. They provide a virtual laboratory where ideas can be tested, refined and matured—ultimately enabling the creation of more robust, efficient and intelligent swarm systems. As new challenges arise and technology evolves, these tools will continue to adapt, incorporating advances in AI, physics modelling and cloud computing to support the next generation of swarm robotics research and applications.

7.1 SIMULATION ENVIRONMENTS (E.G., ARGOS, WEBOTS, GAZEBO)

Simulation environments serve as essential platforms for designing, testing and refining swarm robotics algorithms before deployment in the real world. The most effective tools provide scalability, physics realism, support for multi-agent interaction and flexibility for custom behaviour scripting. Below is a detailed head wise description of three widely adopted simulation environments in swarm robotics:

7.1.1 ARGoS (Autonomous Robots Go Swarming)

ARGoS is a high-performance, open-source simulation framework specifically designed for large-scale swarm robotics experiments. Developed by the Swarmanoid and Swarm-bots projects, it is optimized for simulating thousands of agents with efficiency and precision.

Characteristic Features:

Highly Scalable: One of the key strengths of advanced simulation platforms is their ability to handle high scalability, enabling the real-time simulation of thousands of agents. This makes them ideal for modelling large-scale systems like drone swarms, autonomous vehicles, or IoT devices. These platforms use optimized scheduling and lightweight representations to ensure that even as the number of agents grows, the simulation remains stable and responsive. Developers and researchers can observe emergent behaviours at scale, test load balancing strategies and evaluate algorithm performance under dense deployment scenarios. This scalability is crucial for validating theories that only manifest in large populations, such as decentralized decision-making or network dynamics.

- **Multi-Engine Architecture:** Simulation frameworks with multi-engine architecture can integrate various physics engines—like fast 2D engines for rapid prototyping and detailed 3D engines like ODE (Open Dynamics Engine) for realistic interaction. This flexibility allows users to tailor simulations based on accuracy, speed and computational cost. For instance, a developer may run a quick test in 2D, then switch to a full-physics 3D environment to fine-tune robot movement or collision behaviour. Multiple engines can even operate simultaneously for hybrid scenarios. This architecture ensures that simulations are both efficient and realistic, supporting applications from simple control systems to complex multi-body dynamics and terrain interactions.

- **Customizable Plugins:** A modular plugin system enables users to customize and extend simulation functionality through sensors, actuators and control modules. This allows developers to plug in custom algorithms, interface real-world data streams, or simulate unique robot configurations. For example, plugins can emulate LIDAR, GPS, cameras, or manipulators, each with adjustable noise and parameters. Control architectures—like PID controllers, neural networks, or swarm behaviour scripts—can also be modularly integrated. This flexibility supports rapid prototyping, iterative testing and comparative evaluation across different designs. A well-designed plugin system fosters innovation by encouraging community-contributed modules and simplifying adaptation to diverse research needs.
- **Parallelization:** Modern simulators leverage parallel computing to distribute tasks across multiple processor cores, dramatically accelerating the simulation of complex environments and large agent populations. Instead of running agent behaviours sequentially, actions such as sensor processing, physics calculations and control updates are computed in parallel threads. This enables more frequent simulation steps and greater realism without sacrificing speed. Parallelization is especially beneficial when running computationally intensive algorithms or simulating physical interactions in 3D. It allows researchers to run long experiments in a fraction of the time and supports real-time interaction or visualization. Efficient parallel processing is essential for bridging the gap between simulation and real-world deployment timelines.
- **Swarm-Optimized:** Simulation platforms optimized for swarm intelligence are designed to evaluate and benchmark distributed algorithms involving coordination among many agents. These include key swarm behaviours such as consensus formation, flocking, formation control and cooperative exploration. Built-in tools and metrics allow researchers to measure performance indicators like convergence speed, energy efficiency and robustness to failure. Swarm-optimized simulators support agent-to-agent communication, dynamic network topologies and decentralized decision-making models. Real-time visualization helps monitor emergent group behaviours, while built-in disturbance models test system resilience. Such platforms are invaluable for advancing research in distributed AI, multi-agent systems and real-world robotic swarm deployments.
- **Use Cases:** Ideal for academic and research scenarios focused on swarm coordination, control strategies and algorithm performance under high agent density. It's also used in education due to its scripting flexibility and visualization capabilities.

7.1.2 Webots

Webots is a professional-grade, open-source robot simulator developed by Cyberbotics. It provides a user-friendly interface and robust physics simulation for modelling individual and multi-agent robotic systems, including swarms.

Characteristic Features:

- **Realistic Physics Engine:** The simulation platform utilizes the Open Dynamics Engine (ODE) to provide a highly realistic and accurate physics environment. ODE simulates rigid body dynamics with precise handling of collisions, friction and joint constraints, making it suitable for modelling real-world robotic motion. This high-fidelity physics support enables researchers to test and validate locomotion strategies, grasping, balancing and multi-body interactions under realistic constraints. Robots react authentically to terrain, gravity and obstacles, allowing for more reliable transfer of simulation results to real-world deployments. Whether it's a drone stabilizing mid-air or a humanoid navigating uneven surfaces, the engine ensures credible motion behaviour.
- **Wide Robot Library:** A diverse and pre-configured robot library comes bundled with the simulator, covering a wide range of platforms including quadcopters, differential-drive robots, humanoid figures and robotic arms. Each model is equipped with realistic sensors such as LIDAR, GPS, IMUs and cameras, enabling complex scenario development straight out of the box. These models serve as excellent starting points for testing algorithms like navigation, SLAM, or object recognition without building robots from scratch. The modularity of these robot templates allows for easy customization and integration of new components. This comprehensive library drastically shortens development cycles and enhances simulation realism.
- **Intuitive GUI:** The platform features an intuitive graphical user interface (GUI) that supports drag-and-drop world building, object placement and scene customization in a 3D space. Users can easily assemble simulation environments by adding terrain, robots and obstacles without writing code. Real-time visualization tools provide performance metrics, robot telemetry and live video feeds from simulated sensors. The GUI also supports interactive debugging, parameter tuning and scenario playback, making it user-friendly for both beginners and experts. With its accessible interface, the simulator encourages rapid prototyping and easier teaching or demonstration of robotics concepts.

- **Support for Popular Languages:** To cater to a broad community of developers and researchers, the simulator supports controller development in widely used programming languages such as C, C++, Python, Java and MATLAB. This flexibility ensures that users can leverage their existing expertise and libraries without needing to switch languages. For instance, machine learning models written in Python can directly control robot behaviour, while engineers using MATLAB for signal processing can integrate their tools seamlessly. The multi-language support also promotes collaborative development across interdisciplinary teams, making the platform a powerful bridge between AI research, robotics engineering and system integration.
- **Remote API & ROS Integration:** The simulator includes a remote API and tight ROS (Robot Operating System) integration, enabling easy interaction with external tools and frameworks. Through the remote API, users can send commands, retrieve sensor data, or adjust simulation parameters from external applications—ideal for real-time control, multi-agent coordination, or distributed computing setups. With ROS compatibility, the simulator can plug directly into existing robotic software stacks, allowing developers to test their ROS nodes in simulation before deploying them on physical robots. This dual interface greatly enhances flexibility and is especially beneficial for hybrid systems where physical and virtual components must interact continuously.
- **Use Cases:** Used in swarm robotics for visualizing multi-robot interactions, training learning-based agents and prototyping real-world deployment scenarios. It is especially favoured in education and rapid prototyping environments due to its accessible interface.

7.1.3 Gazebo

Gazebo is a powerful, open-source 3D robotics simulator developed by Open Robotics, often used alongside the Robot Operating System (ROS). Known for its realistic environments and physics modelling, Gazebo is a preferred choice for real-world-oriented swarm robotic experiments.

Characteristic Features:

- **Realistic 3D Simulation:** The platform provides a highly realistic 3D simulation environment that replicates physical interactions and environmental dynamics with great detail. It includes support for real-world elements like lighting conditions, varying terrain topographies, material-based friction and aerodynamic forces such as air resistance—crucial for aerial robotics and ground locomotion. In addition, sensor noise models replicate the imperfections of real-world sensing, making AI and control algorithms more robust when transitioning from simulation to reality. This realism allows for rigorous testing of perception, control and navigation systems under unpredictable and noisy conditions, closely mimicking the challenges faced in physical deployments.

- **Extensive ROS Support:** The simulator offers extensive ROS (Robot Operating System) integration, allowing robots in the simulation to publish and subscribe to ROS topics just like their real-world counterparts. This enables seamless prototyping, testing and debugging of robotics applications using the existing ROS ecosystem. Developers can simulate everything from simple control loops to full autonomous systems, including SLAM, object tracking and multi-robot communication. ROS bags can be recorded and played back and real-time data streams can be analysed as if they came from real hardware. This deep compatibility bridges the gap between simulation and deployment, significantly accelerating development timelines.
- **Sensor Simulation:** Accurate sensor simulation is a core strength of this platform, enabling virtual testing of robotic systems that rely on perception and localization. It supports detailed modelling of key sensors such as RGB and depth cameras, LIDAR, GPS, IMUs and even ultrasonic or infrared devices. Each sensor can be configured with realistic noise profiles, data rates and field-of-view parameters to match specific hardware models. The ability to simulate multiple, heterogeneous sensors allows for complex data fusion and perception tasks, including vision-based navigation, obstacle avoidance and sensor redundancy analysis. This empowers developers to build resilient, sensor-aware AI systems entirely in simulation.
- **Plugins and Customization:** With its modular design, the simulator supports custom plugins for users to extend core functionality. Developers can create or modify robot models, sensor modules, environment objects and control algorithms through well-documented APIs. Custom control plugins enable real-time interaction with the simulation using neural networks, PID controllers, or reinforcement learning agents. External systems—such as MATLAB, TensorFlow, or remote ROS nodes—can be integrated directly for advanced behaviour modelling. This flexibility makes the platform highly adaptable for academic research, industrial prototyping and education. Whether simulating unique hardware or experimenting with novel control architectures, users can tailor every aspect of the simulation.
- **Multi-Robot Capability:** The platform is built to handle multi-robot simulations with efficiency and scalability. Users can simulate dozens to

hundreds of robots operating simultaneously within a shared virtual world. These robots can interact with each other and the environment, enabling the study of swarm behaviour, formation control, task allocation and decentralized coordination strategies. Each robot can run an independent controller or share synchronized tasks, supporting complex experiments in collaborative autonomy. The system also supports inter-robot communication, conflict resolution and collision detection in real-time. This multi-robot capability is essential for advancing research in swarm robotics, warehouse automation and distributed AI systems.

Use Cases: Ideal for simulating complex outdoor or indoor environments involving navigation, localization, SLAM (Simultaneous Localization and Mapping) and multi-robot communication. Frequently used in competitions, industrial projects and research requiring ROS compatibility. Comparison features of ARGoS, Webots and Gazebo is depicted in Table-1.

Table 1:Comparison features of ARGoS, Webots and Gazebo

Feature	ARGoS	Webots	Gazebo
Focus Area	Swarm robotics, large-scale	Educational, general-purpose	Realistic ROS-based robotics
Scalability	Very high (1000+ agents)	Moderate	Moderate
Physics Realism	Medium to high (configurable)	High	Very high
Interface	Scripting & plugins	GUI & code	Plugin-based + ROS tools
Programming Languages	C++, Lua	C, C++, Python, Java, MATLAB	C++, Python via ROS
ROS Integration	Limited	Partial	Full

7.2 PHYSICS ENGINES AND ENVIRONMENT MODELLING

In swarm robotics, accurate physical interaction with the environment is critical for testing and validating behaviours such as navigation, object manipulation, obstacle avoidance and formation control. Physics engines simulate real-world dynamics—like gravity, collisions, friction and inertia—while environment modelling creates the virtual surroundings in which the swarm operates. Together, these components allow developers to test how robots respond to physical stimuli and environmental complexities before real-world deployment.

7.2.1 Role of Physics Engines

Physics engines are responsible for modelling how objects move and interact based on physical laws. In swarm simulations, this ensures realistic behaviour in scenarios where precise motion, contact dynamics, or terrain interaction are involved.

Functions of Physics Engines in Swarm Robotics:

- **Rigid body dynamics:** Simulate physical interactions between agents and obstacles.
- **Collision detection and response:** Ensure that agents avoid or bounce off objects realistically.
- **Friction and drag modeling:** Crucial for locomotion in different environments (e.g., land, air, water).
- **Joint simulation:** Useful for articulated robots or modular swarm agents.
- **Sensor emulation:** Simulate realistic readings from lidar, cameras, GPS, or inertial sensors.

Popular Physics Engines Used:

- **ODE (Open Dynamics Engine):** Lightweight, often used in Webots and ARGoS for fast simulation.
- **Bullet Physics:** Real-time physics simulation with soft body support; used in CoppeliaSim (V-REP).
- **DART (Dynamic Animation and Robotics Toolkit):** High-fidelity simulation with articulated models.
- **PhysX (NVIDIA):** GPU-accelerated, highly realistic engine often used in high-end robotics research.
- **Gazebo's internal physics plugins:** Interface with ODE, Bullet, DART, or Simbody as backends.

7.2.2 Environment Modelling

Environment modelling refers to the creation of the virtual world in which robotic agents operate. This includes terrain, obstacles, buildings, weather conditions and other dynamic elements that affect robot behaviour.

Essential Aspects of Environment Modelling:

- **Static Elements:** Static elements form the structural foundation of any simulation. These include walls, floors, buildings, terrain features and landmarks that robots use for navigation, localization and collision testing. Accurately modelled static elements are crucial for path planning, mapping and obstacle avoidance. Their geometry, material properties and spatial layout influence robot perception and movement. These elements serve as reference points in SLAM and play a key role in evaluating robustness to environmental layout changes.

- **Dynamic Elements:** Dynamic elements introduce real-world unpredictability into simulations. These can be moving obstacles, swinging doors, elevators, or even terrain that shifts or deforms over time. They force robots to make real-time decisions and adapt to changing contexts, testing reactivity and fault tolerance. This is essential for training and evaluating adaptive behaviours, especially in autonomous navigation, human-robot interaction, or rescue operations. Realism in dynamics boosts transferability to real-world environments.
- **Sensor Fidelity:** High sensor fidelity ensures that the simulated perception system behaves like its physical counterpart. This involves modelling sensor noise, signal attenuation, occlusion effects and communication latency. Adding these imperfections is crucial to developing algorithms that are resilient to uncertainty. Realistic sensor modelling helps avoid overfitting to ideal conditions and improves deployment success. It also allows testing sensor fusion algorithms under more accurate, multi-modal data conditions.
- **Environmental Conditions:** Simulating diverse environmental conditions such as lighting variations, fog, rain, snow, or different times of day helps test system robustness in unpredictable settings. These factors impact visibility, traction and even sensor performance, especially for vision-based systems. Dynamic weather scenarios prepare robots for real-world deployment where conditions are not controlled. This aspect is vital for outdoor robotics, delivery drones and autonomous vehicles operating in all-weather environments.
- **Scalability:** Scalability ensures that the simulation platform can support a range of scenarios—from small test environments to vast, realistic arenas. Whether it's a simple maze, a factory floor, or a forest trail, the simulator must maintain performance and realism. Efficient memory and compute handling allows for complex simulations without performance bottlenecks. Scalability is essential for testing algorithms at both the unit and swarm levels, helping validate performance at scale.

Modelling Tools and File Formats:

- **URDF (Unified Robot Description Format):** URDF is widely used in ROS and Gazebo to define the kinematic structure of robots, including links, joints, sensors and visuals. It allows developers to model robots using XML-based syntax, specifying physical and visual properties like mass, inertia and collision boundaries. Though primarily for robots, URDF can also represent static environmental objects. It integrates well with ROS packages for simulation, control and visualization. URDF is ideal for creating reproducible and structured robot models in robotic software pipelines.

- **SDF (Simulation Description Format):** SDF builds upon URDF to describe more complex simulation environments in Gazebo. It supports not just robots but also lights, terrain, fluids and dynamic objects with fine-grained detail. SDF includes richer features like pose hierarchies, advanced physics parameters and nested models, making it ideal for building entire worlds. It also allows for plugins that define custom behaviours or sensors. SDF is essential for users needing high-fidelity simulation environments beyond what URDF can support.
- **PROTO Files in Webots:** In Webots, PROTO files are used to create modular, reusable components like wheels, grippers, sensors, or full robot models. They encapsulate object definitions using Webots' scene description language and allow parameterization, so models can be customized without duplicating code. This enables efficient development and consistency across projects. PROTO files support 3D visuals, physical properties and embedded control logic. They're crucial for simplifying complex robot designs and managing large simulation projects in Webots.
- **Custom Plugin Systems in ARGoS:** ARGoS offers a flexible plugin architecture that allows users to define robots, sensors, actuators and even terrain programmatically in C++. Unlike file-based modelling, ARGoS plugins enable fine-grained control over simulation logic and performance optimization. Users can implement custom physics, communication protocols, or behavioural logic tailored to specific experiments. This makes ARGoS especially powerful for swarm robotics research, where novel algorithms and hardware abstractions often require bespoke simulation capabilities.

7.2.3 Integration of Physics and Environment

The power of simulation lies in combining realistic physics with a well-designed environment:

- Enables testing of swarm algorithms like flocking, coverage, or exploration in realistic terrain.
- Validates control algorithms under environmental constraints like uneven surfaces or moving barriers.
- Ensures that agents can still perform under sensor noise, communication delays and real-world dynamics.

For example, a swarm simulation might involve:

- A rescue scenario in a debris-filled environment.
- A foraging task in a terrain with slopes and obstacles.
- A surveillance mission with limited line-of-sight and dynamic weather.

7.2.4 Challenges and Opportunities

Challenges:

- **Computational Cost:** High-fidelity physics simulations demand substantial CPU and GPU resources to accurately model motion, collisions and sensor feedback in real time. As simulation complexity grows—through more agents, detailed environments, or advanced physics—the computational load increases exponentially. This can limit simulation speed or scale, requiring powerful hardware or cloud resources. Balancing simulation fidelity and performance remains a critical challenge, especially for real-time applications or large-scale swarm testing.
- **Simulation-Reality Gap:** The simulation-reality gap refers to differences between simulated models and real-world behaviour, often caused by simplifications or inaccuracies in physics, sensor models, or environmental conditions. Algorithms that perform well in simulation may fail when deployed due to unmodeled noise, hardware imperfections, or unexpected dynamics. Bridging this gap requires continuous refinement, domain randomization and real-world validation to improve simulation fidelity and ensure effective transfer of learned policies.
- **Complex Environment Design:** Designing rich, interactive environments that realistically mimic real-world settings is a time-consuming and labour-intensive process. It involves modelling diverse elements like terrain, objects, dynamic obstacles, lighting and weather, each requiring detailed geometry, textures and physics parameters. Creating scenarios that are both realistic and computationally efficient demands significant expertise and development effort. This complexity can slow down prototyping and reduce iteration speed in simulation-based research.

Opportunities:

- **GPU Acceleration:** GPU acceleration leverages the parallel processing power of graphics cards to handle the intense computations required for simulating large-scale swarms and complex physical interactions. By offloading physics calculations, collision detection and sensor simulations to the GPU, the platform can run real-time or faster-than-real-time simulations involving thousands of agents. This not only improves scalability but also enables more detailed and accurate modelling of dynamics without sacrificing performance. GPU acceleration is critical for supporting high-fidelity swarm robotics experiments and training AI models efficiently.
- **Procedural Environment Generation:** Procedural generation techniques automatically create varied and complex simulation environments by

algorithmically defining terrain features, obstacles, lighting and weather conditions. This approach saves time compared to manual design and provides a virtually unlimited set of test scenarios. Diverse environments generated procedurally help test the robustness and adaptability of swarm behaviours and control algorithms under different, unpredictable conditions. Procedural generation also supports domain randomization, which is key for bridging the simulation-to-reality gap by exposing agents to wide-ranging environmental variations.

- **Physics-Based Learning:** Physics-based learning integrates reinforcement learning directly within high-fidelity physics simulations, allowing swarms to train policies that account for realistic dynamics, collisions and sensor noise. By incorporating the physical constraints and uncertainties present in the real world, agents develop more robust and transferable behaviours. This method enhances the reliability of learned control strategies when deployed on physical robots, reducing costly trial-and-error in real environments. Physics-aware learning is especially important for complex multi-agent coordination, where subtle interactions significantly impact performance.

7.3 REALISM VS. SCALABILITY IN SIMULATIONS

One of the central trade-offs in swarm robotics simulation is realism versus scalability. While high-fidelity simulations offer precise and detailed representations of the physical world, they often demand substantial computational resources. On the other hand, highly scalable simulations that can model thousands of agents efficiently often do so at the cost of environmental and physical realism. Understanding this trade-off is crucial when selecting simulation platforms or designing custom tools for swarm robotics.

7.3.1 Understanding the Trade-Off

- **Realism:** Realism in simulation aims to faithfully replicate the physical world by modelling detailed sensor outputs, precise collision detection and accurate terrain and environmental dynamics. It includes simulating actuator behaviours, friction and environmental factors like lighting or weather, ensuring that virtual agents respond as they would in reality. This high-fidelity modelling is crucial for developing algorithms that transfer effectively from simulation to physical robots. However, achieving such realism often demands intensive computation and limits scalability. The benefit is a rich testing ground where subtle nuances of robot-environment interactions are captured, enhancing the reliability of experimental results.

- **Scalability:** Scalability prioritizes the ability to simulate large populations of agents simultaneously, enabling researchers to study collective behaviours like swarm coordination or multi-robot task allocation. To achieve this, simulators often simplify physics, use abstract models, or reduce sensor detail to save computational resources. This trade-off allows real-time interaction and experimentation at scale but may sacrifice some accuracy in individual agent dynamics. Scalability is essential for exploring emergent phenomena and stress-testing algorithms in diverse scenarios, though it requires balancing model fidelity to ensure meaningful insights while maintaining performance.

Striking the right balance between the two depends on the application goals. For early-stage algorithm development or studying emergent behaviours, scalability may be prioritized. For deployment-level testing or hardware validation, realism becomes more critical.

7.3.2 Dimensions of Realism

Realism in swarm simulations includes:

- **Physical Interactions:** Physical interactions are fundamental to realistic swarm simulations, encompassing accurate modelling of motion dynamics, frictional forces, gravity and collisions between agents and their environment. Realistic physics ensure that robot movements and contacts behave as they would in the real world, affecting stability, energy consumption and maneuverability. This allows researchers to test locomotion algorithms, obstacle avoidance and formation control under authentic constraints. High-fidelity physics models help identify potential failure modes early, improving safety and performance before physical deployment.
- **Sensor Fidelity:** Sensor fidelity involves replicating the imperfections and characteristics of real-world sensing devices in simulation. This includes adding noise, latency, distortion and limited resolution to simulated readings from cameras, lidars, GPS and inertial measurement units. By mimicking these inaccuracies, algorithms trained in simulation learn to cope with uncertainty and unreliable data. Sensor fidelity is critical for perception, localization and mapping tasks, ensuring that models remain robust when transferred to physical robots operating in noisy or challenging conditions.
- **Communication Modelling:** Communication modelling captures the realistic constraints of wireless data exchange among swarm agents, such as message delays, packet loss, interference and limited communication range. These factors can significantly impact distributed decision-making,

coordination and consensus-building in multi-robot systems. Including communication imperfections in simulation helps test fault tolerance and protocol resilience under adverse network conditions. Accurate communication models enable developers to design robust algorithms capable of functioning effectively in real-world environments with unreliable connectivity.

- **Environmental Complexity:** Environmental complexity refers to simulating diverse and dynamic settings that robots encounter, including varied terrain features, weather effects like rain or fog and moving obstacles such as humans or vehicles. These complexities affect navigation, sensor performance and overall mission success. Incorporating such details in simulations provides a realistic context for evaluating swarm adaptability and robustness. Rich environmental modelling prepares systems for deployment in unpredictable or unstructured environments, enhancing their practical utility and safety.
- **Hardware-in-the-Loop (HIL):** Hardware-in-the-loop (HIL) integration bridges simulation with physical hardware by incorporating real robot components—such as sensors, actuators, or controllers—into the simulation loop. This hybrid approach allows final-stage validation of algorithms under controlled yet realistic conditions, combining the flexibility of simulation with real-world fidelity. HIL testing helps uncover issues related to hardware-software interaction, timing and signal processing that pure simulations may miss. It serves as a critical step before full deployment, ensuring system reliability and performance.

Simulators prioritizing realism: Gazebo, Webots, CoppeliaSim.

7.3.3 Dimensions of Scalability

Scalability includes:

- **Number of Agents:** A key measure of scalability is the capacity to simulate hundreds or thousands of agents simultaneously without causing significant slowdowns. Large swarm sizes enable the study of collective behaviours, emergent phenomena and robustness under dense population scenarios. Achieving this requires efficient data management, memory usage and optimized algorithms to handle interactions and state updates. The ability to scale agent count while maintaining real-time or near-real-time performance is essential for validating swarm algorithms intended for real-world deployments.
- **Efficiency of Updates:** Efficiency in simulation updates is crucial to managing computational load, especially as agent numbers increase.

Using simplified physics models—such as basic kinematics instead of full dynamics—or employing event-driven update mechanisms helps reduce unnecessary calculations. This selective updating focuses resources on meaningful changes in agent states rather than redundant processing. Efficient update schemes strike a balance between realism and speed, enabling faster simulations without drastically compromising the accuracy needed for effective swarm behaviour analysis.

- **Parallelism:** Parallelism harnesses multi-threaded CPUs and GPU acceleration to distribute the workload of physics calculations, sensor simulations and communication updates across multiple processing units. This concurrent execution allows simulations to handle more agents or complex interactions without bottlenecks. Effective parallelism requires careful synchronization and workload balancing to avoid race conditions or idle cores. By fully leveraging modern hardware capabilities, parallelism significantly enhances the scalability and responsiveness of swarm simulations.
- **Minimalist Representations:** Minimalist representations simplify agent models using basic kinematics, discrete-time steps, or 2D abstractions instead of complex 3D physics. This reduction in detail decreases computational overhead and memory consumption, allowing simulations to run faster and scale to larger populations. While minimalist models sacrifice some physical realism, they remain sufficient for studying high-level swarm dynamics, communication protocols and strategic behaviours. These abstractions are especially useful in early-stage algorithm development and large-scale exploratory experiments.

Simulators prioritizing scalability: ARGoS, Breve, NetLogo (for abstract agent-based modeling).

7.3.4 When to Prioritize Realism

Choose high realism when:

- Testing deployment-ready behaviours on real-world terrain and sensors.
- Evaluating system robustness under realistic sensor/actuator noise.
- Verifying compliance with hardware constraints.
- Preparing for real-time missions like search & rescue, UAV operation, or manipulation tasks.

7.3.5 When to Prioritize Scalability

Choose scalability when:

- Studying emergent behaviour, consensus, or distributed learning.

- Evaluating algorithm performance across thousands of agents.
- Prototyping early-stage behaviour in conceptual environments.
- Testing fault tolerance, communication strategies, or load balancing in large networks.

7.3.6 Bridging the Gap

Modern research increasingly focuses on bridging realism and scalability:

- **Hierarchical Simulation:** Hierarchical simulation strategically applies high-fidelity models to a critical subset of agents while using simplified, abstract representations for the remainder. This balance allows detailed analysis where precision is essential, such as for leader agents or robots in complex tasks, while maintaining computational efficiency. By focusing resources selectively, hierarchical methods enable scaling to large swarms without sacrificing critical physical accuracy. This approach supports both detailed behaviour modelling and broad emergent phenomena study within a unified simulation framework.
- **Hybrid Simulation Layers:** Hybrid simulation layers integrate high-fidelity physics in important regions or tasks with lightweight approximations in less critical zones. For example, close to obstacles or in areas requiring precise control, detailed physics ensure accurate interactions, whereas distant regions use simplified dynamics to save computational power. This layered approach optimizes resource allocation, improving simulation speed and enabling real-time performance for large environments. It also allows flexible adjustments depending on the scenario's requirements, balancing accuracy with scalability.
- **Adaptive Fidelity:** Adaptive fidelity dynamically modulates the level of simulation detail based on factors like spatial location, task importance, or available computational resources. The simulation can increase detail in high-priority areas or during critical maneuvers while reducing it elsewhere to conserve resources. This technique maintains overall performance and realism where it matters most, ensuring efficient use of processing power. Adaptive fidelity is especially beneficial for large-scale swarm experiments, where workload and precision demands vary constantly.
- **Multi-Core and GPU Utilization:** Exploiting multi-core CPUs and GPUs accelerates the execution of high-fidelity physics and sensor models across large swarms. Parallel processing distributes computational tasks, allowing simultaneous simulation of multiple agents and complex environments without bottlenecks. GPU utilization is particularly effective for physics calculations and sensor data processing, drastically reducing runtime. This

hardware-aware approach enhances scalability without compromising realism, enabling real-time, large-scale swarm simulations that were previously infeasible.

Sim-to-Real Transfer Techniques: Sim-to-real transfer methods train robotic policies in simulation before fine-tuning them on physical hardware, addressing discrepancies between virtual and real-world conditions. Techniques like domain randomization expose agents to a wide range of simulated environmental variations and sensor noise, improving robustness and generalization. This approach reduces the need for costly and time-consuming real-world data collection. By systematically bridging the simulation-reality gap, sim-to-real strategies enable faster, safer and more reliable deployment of swarm robotics systems. Realism vs. Scalability is described in Table-2.

Table-2: Realism vs. Scalability

Aspect	Realism Focused Simulations	Scalability Focused Simulations
Agent Detail	High (physical and sensory)	Low (abstracted behaviour)
Number of Agents	Limited (10s–100s)	High (1000s+)
Computation Cost	High	Low
Suitable For	Deployment, validation, HIL	Algorithm development, emergent behaviour
Examples	Gazebo, Webots, CoppeliaSim	ARGoS, NetLogo, Breve

In swarm robotics, the choice between realism and scalability is not absolute—it's contextual. Effective simulation strategies often combine both ends of the spectrum to allow iterative development, from abstract behaviour design to real-world deployment readiness.

7.4 MODEL VALIDATION AND EXPERIMENTAL REPRODUCIBILITY

In swarm robotics, model validation and experimental reproducibility are critical components for ensuring the credibility, reliability and scientific rigor of simulation-based studies. While simulations offer a powerful tool for testing and development, their usefulness hinges on how accurately they reflect real-world behaviour and how consistently their results can be replicated by other researchers or across different runs.

7.4.1 Model Validation

Model validation refers to the process of ensuring that a simulation accurately represents the physical, behavioural and environmental dynamics it is intended to replicate. It bridges the gap between theoretical models, simulation behaviour and real-world system performance.

Objectives of model validation:

- Confirm that agent behaviours align with actual robot hardware capabilities.
- Ensure sensor and actuator models reflect real-world noise, latency and precision.
- Validate environmental conditions such as terrain, obstacles and communication range.
- Match simulation outcomes with empirical data from real-world experiments.

Approaches to validation:

- **Cross-validation with physical experiments on hardware platforms:** Cross-validation through real-world deployment on hardware platforms is a robust way to assess an algorithm's practical viability. It involves implementing the system on actual physical components—such as sensors, actuators, or robots—to observe real-time behaviour. This approach uncovers hardware-induced noise, latency and other constraints often missed in simulations. It tests the integration fidelity between software and hardware. The results reflect real environmental factors, making this validation highly realistic. By repeating trials under various physical conditions, reliability and robustness can be evaluated. It also helps refine system tuning for deployment-readiness.
- **Data-driven modelling using recorded real-world traces (e.g., sensor logs):** This method utilizes historical data, such as sensor logs or operational traces, to model system behaviour. It allows algorithms to be validated under conditions previously encountered in the field. The replaying of real-world data ensures that edge cases and anomalies are included in testing. This can highlight limitations in predictive performance or adaptation capabilities. It's a cost-effective alternative to repeated field testing. When integrated with simulations, it bridges the gap between idealized models and complex real-world dynamics. The approach supports iterative refinement without requiring live experimentation.
- **Analytical comparisons with expected algorithmic performance:** Analytical validation involves comparing the algorithm's output to theoretical benchmarks or mathematically derived expectations. It provides insight into the correctness and efficiency of the method under ideal assumptions. This approach can highlight algorithmic soundness, complexity bounds and convergence properties. It's especially useful in early development phases before deployment. Analytical checks can catch errors in logic, formulation, or numerical stability. The method strengthens

confidence in performance guarantees, particularly in safety-critical systems. It also serves as a reference point for evaluating deviations seen in practical implementations.

- **Benchmarking against known behaviours or standardized test scenarios:** Benchmarking uses established datasets, simulation environments, or defined tasks to assess algorithm performance. It allows comparisons across different methods using consistent criteria. This is essential for determining relative strengths, weaknesses and trade-offs. Benchmarks often involve well-characterized scenarios with known expected outcomes. They provide repeatability, transparency and community-accepted standards. This type of validation encourages adherence to best practices and facilitates peer evaluation. It also enables developers to track improvements over time and measure against state-of-the-art results.

7.4.2 Importance of Reproducibility

Experimental reproducibility is a cornerstone of scientific validity and technological reliability. It refers to the ability to consistently replicate results using the same setup, parameters and conditions. In swarm systems—where behaviours often emerge from interactions among numerous agents—randomness, non-determinism and environmental variability can significantly influence outcomes. These systems may exhibit stochastic behaviours even when underlying algorithms are deterministic. As a result, without reproducibility, it's difficult to distinguish between true system capabilities and artifacts of randomness. Reproducible experiments allow researchers to isolate the impact of algorithmic design from accidental successes. They ensure that observed performance is not the result of overfitting, biased parameter tuning, or hidden dependencies. This is critical in fields like robotics, autonomous systems and AI, where deploying non-robust solutions can lead to failure or unsafe behaviour. Reproducibility also promotes transparency and trust in research findings, allowing peers to independently verify results. It facilitates iterative development, debugging and performance benchmarking. Moreover, it supports meaningful comparisons across different research works and implementation platforms. Documenting experimental conditions, random seeds and software versions becomes essential for this purpose. Ultimately, reproducibility transforms experimental research from anecdotal demonstration into scientifically grounded evidence.

Challenges in swarm reproducibility:

- Random initial positions, sensor noise and agent failures introduce stochasticity.
- Time-dependent variables and asynchronous communication may cause different outcomes.

- Differences in hardware or OS environments can subtly alter simulation behavior.

Best practices to improve reproducibility:

- Fixed random seeds to control randomness in simulations.
- Clear documentation of software versions, simulation parameters and scenario configurations.
- Code and data sharing through open-source platforms (e.g., GitHub, ROS packages).
- Use of containers or virtual machines to ensure consistent execution environments (e.g., Docker).
- Statistical analysis over multiple runs to report average and variance-based results, not single outcomes.

7.4.3 Evaluation Techniques for Validation

Evaluation techniques are essential for assessing the performance, robustness and reliability of computational systems, especially in complex domains like robotics, AI and swarm intelligence. Validation ensures that a system behaves as intended, meets design requirements and performs well under varying conditions. As systems grow more autonomous and adaptive, evaluation must go beyond simple functionality checks to include behaviour under uncertainty, edge-case performance and real-world applicability. Techniques used for validation range from controlled simulations to full-scale physical deployment. Simulation-based evaluations allow rapid, repeatable testing across many scenarios with adjustable parameters. Hardware-in-the-loop testing brings the evaluation closer to real-world dynamics, capturing issues like latency, sensor noise and actuation delays. Data-driven validation uses real-world logs to test responsiveness to environmental variation. Analytical validation techniques compare algorithm performance against theoretical expectations, offering insights into correctness and efficiency. Benchmarking against standardized datasets or test scenarios facilitates comparative analysis across different approaches. Cross-validation methods improve confidence in generalization by testing performance across subsets of data or conditions. Together, these evaluation techniques form a multi-layered strategy that balances theoretical rigor with empirical realism. Selecting the right combination of techniques is key to building trust in complex systems. Thorough evaluation not only validates the system but also guides further refinement and innovation.

To verify both the correctness and reliability of simulations, researchers use:

- **Comparative metrics:** Compare simulated results to real-world experiment data.
- **Trace analysis:** Track trajectories, sensor inputs and control outputs for debugging.
- **Error quantification:** Measure deviation between expected and observed behaviour (e.g., path error, consensus accuracy).
- **Replay mechanisms:** Re-execute past runs for verification or teaching.
- **Scenario benchmarking:** Test under known conditions and compare to published results.

7.4.4 Tools and Frameworks Supporting Validation

Effective validation of complex systems relies heavily on the availability and use of specialized tools and frameworks. These tools help automate testing, ensure repeatability and provide accurate measurements of system performance under controlled and varied conditions. In simulation-based validation, environments like Gazebo, Webots and CoppeliaSim offer physics-accurate, customizable platforms to test robotic and swarm behaviours. For real-world testing, platforms such as ROS (Robot Operating System) provide middleware support for integrating sensors, actuators and logging mechanisms. Data analysis and visualization tools like MATLAB, Python (with libraries like NumPy, Pandas, Matplotlib) and R are essential for interpreting experimental results. For swarm systems, frameworks like ARGoS or Buzz allow scalable, parallel execution of agent behaviours with configurable noise models and sensor uncertainty. Benchmarking tools like OpenAI Gym or PyBullet support standardized testing across multiple algorithms and environments. Version control systems (e.g., Git) and containerization technologies (e.g., Docker) contribute to reproducibility by tracking code changes and encapsulating dependencies. Logging and monitoring tools further support debugging and validation by capturing detailed runtime information. Collectively, these tools enhance the reliability, transparency and scalability of validation efforts. Choosing appropriate frameworks depends on the system's domain, scale and desired evaluation depth. Ultimately, they serve as the backbone of rigorous experimental research and development.

Several modern simulation platforms and frameworks support model validation and reproducibility:

- **Gazebo + ROS:** Enables hardware-in-the-loop (HIL) testing and real-world calibration.
- **Webots:** Offers accurate physical modeling and consistent reproducible execution.

- **ARGoS:** Provides plugin flexibility for modeling real sensor/actuator behaviors and supports reproducible batch testing.
- **CoppeliaSim (V-REP):** Includes recording, replay and scripting tools for behaviour comparison.

7.4.5 The Role of Standardization

Standardization plays a pivotal role in ensuring consistency, comparability and reliability in the validation of complex systems. It establishes agreed-upon protocols, formats and metrics that enable researchers and developers to evaluate and compare results in a uniform manner. In fields such as robotics, AI and swarm systems, where implementations can vary widely, standardization ensures that different approaches are assessed under equivalent conditions. Standardized datasets, testing scenarios and evaluation metrics remove ambiguity and subjectivity from performance claims. This fosters transparency, repeatability and peer verification, which are essential for scientific integrity. Standardization also accelerates progress by reducing redundant work and enabling benchmarking across platforms and institutions. In industrial contexts, it ensures regulatory compliance, safety certification and interoperability among components. Frameworks like IEEE standards for autonomous systems and standardized APIs (e.g., ROS messaging protocols) provide common ground for integration and validation. Moreover, standardized documentation and reporting practices help disseminate knowledge effectively. As systems become more interconnected and collaborative, standardization supports scalable and modular development. Ultimately, it acts as a foundation for building trust in technology—ensuring that validated performance is not only credible but also universally interpretable.

Standardization efforts improve validation and reproducibility:

- **Benchmarking datasets:** Public repositories (e.g., OpenSwarm, Duckietown) provide standard scenarios and metrics.
- **Community frameworks:** Open-source libraries and simulation models reduce variability.
- **Publishing standards:** Many conferences and journals now require code, data and seed disclosure for replicability.

Summary of Key Concepts and Their Importance is given in Table -3.

Table-3 Summary of Key Concepts and Their Importance

Concept	Description	Importance
Model Validation	Matching simulation behaviour to real-world performance	Ensures simulation reliability
Reproducibility	Consistent results under identical simulation settings	Supports scientific rigor and fairness
Best Practices	Fixed seeds, clear documentation, containerization	Enables others to replicate your work
Tools Supporting It	ARGoS, Gazebo, Webots, CoppeliaSim, ROS	Provide simulation and validation support
Standardization Benefits	Benchmark scenarios, shared models, consistent metrics	Promotes comparability and trust

Validation and reproducibility are not just academic ideals—they are essential to building trust in simulation results and ensuring that developed algorithms can transition from simulation to real-world application. In swarm robotics, where complex interactions and emergent behaviors dominate, rigorous validation ensures that the system performs as expected under varied, unpredictable conditions. Reproducibility enables cumulative scientific progress, collaborative development and broader community engagement.

7.5 METRICS FOR SWARM PERFORMANCE EVALUATION

Evaluating the performance of swarm robotic systems demands a nuanced and multidimensional approach, rooted in metrics that go beyond traditional single-agent evaluations. Unlike centralized systems, swarm robotics emphasizes decentralized control, local interactions and the emergence of global behaviour from simple individual rules. Therefore, performance metrics must account for both the microscopic (individual agent-level) and macroscopic (group-level) dynamics that define swarm intelligence. Metrics such as task completion rate, time efficiency, scalability and fault tolerance are commonly employed to assess the effectiveness and robustness of the swarm as a whole.

At the agent level, key indicators include responsiveness, energy usage and communication overhead, which influence the system's sustainability and efficiency. Group-level metrics—such as cohesion, dispersion, consensus time and adaptability—are crucial for capturing the emergent properties of the swarm. In addition, robustness metrics evaluate the swarm's ability to maintain performance under failures, environmental changes, or agent loss. Scalability metrics test how well the system performs as the number of agents increases. To support fair and reproducible comparisons, quantitative performance metrics must be defined clearly and measured consistently across experiments. This includes defining environmental complexity, initial conditions and stochastic factors that can influence outcomes. Evaluations should also consider mission-specific criteria—for instance, foraging efficiency, area coverage, or formation stability—depending on the application domain. Simulation tools often integrate automated metric logging, enabling rapid iteration and evaluation of swarm algorithms. However, transitioning from simulation to physical experiments introduces new variables, such as sensor noise or imperfect actuation, requiring adjustments in metric interpretation. Comparative analysis using standardized benchmarks further helps position new approaches within the broader research landscape. Ultimately, well-chosen and well-understood performance metrics are essential not only for validating swarm behaviour but also for driving algorithmic improvements, fostering reproducibility and building systems that are both efficient and resilient in real-world conditions.

7.5.1 Dimensions of Performance

The performance of swarm robotic systems is inherently multi-dimensional, encompassing several interrelated aspects that together determine the system's overall effectiveness. One of the core dimensions is effectiveness, which measures how well the swarm achieves its intended task—be it area coverage, object transport, or collective decision-making. Closely linked is efficiency, often quantified by the time taken, energy consumed, or resources used to complete a task. Efficiency is particularly important in real-world deployments where power and operational time are limited. Scalability is another critical dimension, assessing how well the swarm's performance holds as the number of agents increases. A well-designed system should maintain or improve performance without requiring major algorithmic changes. Robustness, meanwhile, evaluates how the swarm performs under uncertainties, such as sensor noise, communication delays, or the failure of individual agents. Swarm systems are expected to degrade gracefully rather than collapse entirely when disrupted. Adaptability captures the swarm's ability to adjust its behaviour in response to dynamic environments or unexpected conditions. Cohesion and dispersion metrics help assess how agents maintain formation or spread appropriately across the environment. Responsiveness measures how quickly the swarm reacts to changes, which is vital for real-time applications. Together, these dimensions provide a comprehensive view of system behaviour, guiding both development and validation toward more resilient, scalable and mission-capable swarm robotic solutions.

Swarm performance metrics generally fall into the following categories:

- **Effectiveness:** How well does the swarm achieve the desired task?
- **Efficiency:** What resources (time, energy, communication) does the swarm use?

- **Robustness:** How resilient is the swarm to failures or environmental changes?
- **Scalability:** How does performance change as the number of agents increases?
- **Flexibility/Adaptability:** How well does the swarm adapt to new tasks or changing conditions?

7.5.2 Commonly Used Metrics

Swarm robotic systems are evaluated using a range of metrics that aim to capture both individual agent performance and collective system behaviour. Task completion rate is one of the most fundamental metrics, measuring whether and how efficiently the swarm achieves its goal. Time to completion tracks how quickly the swarm finishes the task, often used to assess temporal efficiency. Energy consumption per agent or per task is critical, especially for battery-powered systems or long-duration missions. Coverage measures how effectively the swarm explores or occupies a given area, often used in surveillance or environmental monitoring tasks. Cohesion evaluates how well agents stay together, which is vital for formation control or safety. Conversely, dispersion assesses the agents' ability to spread out when needed, such as in search-and-rescue or area mapping. Communication overhead reflects the amount of inter-agent communication required, influencing scalability and energy use. Fault tolerance is measured by how well the swarm continues to function after agent failure or environmental disruption. Scalability metrics track performance changes as the number of agents increases. Redundancy is sometimes evaluated to determine how many agents are doing unnecessary or duplicate work. Other specialized metrics include consensus time (in decision-making tasks), path efficiency, obstacle avoidance rate and resource collection rate. These metrics provide a versatile toolkit to quantitatively assess performance, optimize algorithms and ensure robustness in both simulated and real-world deployments.

- **Task Completion Time:** Task completion time measures how quickly the swarm can successfully complete a given mission, such as area exploration, target search, or object transport. It serves as a primary indicator of operational efficiency. Lower completion times typically reflect better coordination and decision-making among agents. However, speed must be balanced with accuracy and safety. In time-sensitive applications, such as emergency response or surveillance, fast task execution is critical. This metric is also useful for comparing the performance of different algorithms or configurations. It often serves as a baseline for optimization efforts.
- **Coverage Ratio:** Coverage ratio refers to the percentage of an environment that the swarm has explored or monitored during a mission. This metric

is particularly important in tasks such as environmental monitoring, surveillance and search-and-rescue. Higher coverage indicates better spatial distribution and effectiveness. It reflects the swarm's ability to collectively plan, spread and avoid redundant effort. Metrics can be fine-tuned by considering overlap or critical zones. Dynamic environments may require continuous updates to maintain high coverage. It is often paired with time and energy metrics to assess trade-offs.

- **Energy Consumption:** Energy consumption measures the total or average energy used by agents throughout a task. In resource-constrained or battery-powered systems, this is a key metric. Minimizing energy usage extends mission duration and operational range. Energy can be consumed in locomotion, sensing, processing and communication. Efficient swarm behaviours reduce unnecessary movements and idle communication. Monitoring this metric helps identify agents or behaviours that disproportionately drain resources. It is often used in sustainability analysis and long-term autonomy planning.
- **Communication Overhead:** Communication overhead refers to the volume or frequency of data exchanged among swarm agents. Excessive communication can congest the network, introduce delays and consume energy. In large-scale systems, managing overhead is critical for maintaining real-time responsiveness and scalability. This metric helps evaluate the efficiency of distributed coordination protocols. Low communication overhead is desirable in bandwidth-limited or noisy environments. It also reflects how well agents can operate autonomously with minimal centralized input. Balancing information sharing and independence is key.
- **Consensus Accuracy:** Consensus accuracy measures the degree of agreement reached by agents in tasks requiring a collective decision, such as target selection or direction voting. High consensus accuracy indicates that agents have successfully aligned on a shared goal or state. This is essential for coordinated actions, especially in decentralized systems. Poor accuracy may lead to fragmented behaviour and task failure. Evaluating this metric helps assess the reliability of consensus algorithms under noise and uncertainty. It's particularly relevant in systems that rely on majority voting, leader election, or collective estimation.
- **Robustness to Failures:** Robustness to failures evaluates how well the swarm performs in the presence of agent malfunctions, environmental changes, or communication losses. It's measured by task success rate despite such disruptions. A robust system continues to function effectively even when some agents drop out or behave unpredictably. This metric is

crucial in real-world deployments where perfect conditions are rare. It reflects the system's fault tolerance and self-healing capabilities. Designers aim for graceful degradation, where performance declines slowly—not catastrophically—under stress.

- **Scalability:** Scalability measures how the swarm's performance evolves as the number of agents increases. It determines whether algorithms and protocols can handle small and large swarms without major modifications. Ideally, performance should improve or remain stable with larger swarms. Key sub-metrics include changes in task completion time, success rate and communication overhead across different swarm sizes. Poor scalability may lead to coordination breakdowns, excessive congestion, or inefficiency. It is vital for applications requiring deployment of tens, hundreds, or even thousands of agents.
- **Formation Stability:** Formation stability assesses the swarm's ability to maintain specific spatial arrangements during movement or operation. This is especially relevant in tasks requiring synchronized formations, such as drone swarms or underwater fleets. The metric is typically quantified by deviations in inter-agent distances or from a predefined formation pattern. Stable formations indicate strong coordination and control fidelity. Instability may arise from delayed responses, environmental disturbances, or poor sensing. Maintaining formations enhances safety, aesthetics and functional coherence in multi-agent systems.
- **Adaptation Speed:** Adaptation speed refers to how quickly a swarm can respond to changes in the environment or shifts in task objectives. This is crucial in dynamic or unpredictable scenarios like disaster zones or rapidly evolving missions. A fast adaptation rate reflects a flexible, resilient control architecture. It involves rapid reallocation of roles, reconfiguration of paths, or changes in decision-making strategies. This metric often complements robustness and responsiveness evaluations. High adaptation speed allows the swarm to remain effective in uncertain, real-world settings. It supports continuous autonomy and mission success.

7.5.3 Composite and Scenario-Specific Metrics

While individual performance metrics offer valuable insights, real-world swarm robotic applications often require composite metrics that integrate multiple performance dimensions into a single evaluative framework. These composite metrics help balance trade-offs—such as speed versus energy efficiency or accuracy versus communication overhead—by weighting and aggregating various factors into a unified score. For example, a mission success index might combine task completion time, energy consumption and robustness under failure conditions. This approach enables more holistic evaluation and better aligns with mission priorities. In addition, scenario-specific metrics are tailored to particular tasks or operational domains. For instance, in a foraging task, the rate of item retrieval and the efficiency of transport paths might be key metrics. In search-and-rescue operations, metrics like time to locate targets, false positive rates and adaptability to dynamic environments take precedence. These tailored evaluations ensure relevance and accuracy in performance assessment. By aligning metrics with specific mission goals, researchers and engineers can design, optimize and validate swarm systems more effectively. Ultimately, both composite and scenario-specific metrics provide deeper insights than generic indicators alone and help bridge the gap between abstract performance evaluation and real-world operational success.

Some applications require combining multiple metrics or tailoring metrics to the task:

- **Search and Rescue:** May use a weighted combination of coverage ratio, victim detection rate and completion time.
- **Foraging:** Combines collection rate with energy efficiency.
- **Distributed Mapping:** Accuracy and completeness of the generated map.

Composite metrics often incorporate trade-offs, such as balancing speed with energy consumption or robustness with communication cost.

7.5.4 Data Collection and Analysis

Accurate evaluation of swarm robotic systems relies heavily on systematic data collection and thorough analysis. During both simulation and real-world experiments, it is essential to log detailed agent-level data, including positions, sensor inputs and communication events. This granular data capture enables researchers to reconstruct system behaviours and diagnose performance issues. Because swarm behaviours often involve randomness and variability, statistical aggregation methods such as computing means, medians and variances over multiple experimental runs are crucial. These statistics help account for stochastic effects and ensure that conclusions are robust rather than anecdotal. Additionally, visualization tools play a vital role in interpreting complex datasets. Heatmaps can illustrate spatial coverage and density, while communication graphs reveal interaction patterns and network load. Timelines and progress charts track task execution over time, highlighting phases of efficiency or delay. Combining quantitative metrics with intuitive visualizations enables deeper insights into system dynamics. Together, careful data collection and analysis form the foundation for validating, refining and benchmarking swarm robotic algorithms under diverse conditions.

To evaluate these metrics, simulation and real-world experiments must include:

- **Logging agent states:** Positions, sensor readings, communication events.
- **Statistical aggregation:** Mean, median, variance over multiple runs to account for stochasticity.
- **Visualization tools:** Heatmaps for coverage, graphs of communication patterns and timelines of task progress.

7.5.5 Challenges in Metric Selection

- **Task Specificity:** Metrics used for evaluating swarm robotic systems must be closely aligned with the specific mission objectives and the overarching goals of the swarm. Different tasks—such as search-and-rescue, environmental monitoring, or cooperative transport—require distinct performance indicators. A one-size-fits-all approach risks overlooking critical success factors unique to each mission. For instance, while speed might be crucial in emergency response, energy efficiency could be paramount in long-term monitoring. Carefully tailoring metrics ensures that evaluations accurately reflect the swarm's real-world effectiveness and relevance. This alignment guides algorithm design toward meeting practical needs, not just theoretical performance. It also helps prioritize resources during development and testing.
- **Emergent Behaviour Complexity:** Swarm robotic systems often exhibit emergent behaviours—complex patterns and outcomes arising from simple local interactions. These emergent phenomena can be difficult to quantify directly using standard metrics. Some behaviours, like spontaneous formation, self-healing, or adaptive clustering, defy straightforward measurement because they evolve dynamically and nonlinearly. Capturing their value may require composite or qualitative assessments alongside quantitative metrics. Moreover, emergent behaviours might only become apparent under certain environmental conditions or scales. Developing metrics that reflect the richness of emergent dynamics remains a research challenge but is essential for understanding the full capabilities of swarm systems.
- **Balancing Multiple Criteria:** Swarm system evaluation frequently involves balancing multiple, sometimes conflicting, criteria. For example, improving task completion speed often comes at the cost of increased energy consumption or reduced robustness. Similarly, enhancing communication to improve coordination might raise overhead, limiting scalability. Optimizing for one metric without considering others can lead to suboptimal or even detrimental outcomes. Effective evaluation

frameworks acknowledge these trade-offs and seek a balanced approach that meets mission priorities holistically. Multi-objective optimization and weighted composite metrics are common strategies to navigate these conflicts, ensuring that no critical aspect is sacrificed unduly for marginal gains in another.

- **Consistency:** Consistency in metrics is vital to enable meaningful comparisons across different simulation environments, hardware platforms and experimental setups. Variability in sensor models, environmental complexity, or communication protocols can skew results if metrics are not standardized or carefully calibrated. Ensuring consistent definitions, measurement procedures and reporting formats helps maintain the integrity of validation efforts. It also facilitates reproducibility, allowing other researchers to verify findings independently. Without consistency, it becomes difficult to assess progress, benchmark against other systems, or generalize conclusions. Establishing community-wide standards and best practices supports this goal and strengthens the scientific foundation of swarm robotics research.

8 Chapter SWARM ROBOTIC PLATFORMS AND HARDWARE

8.0 INTRODUCTION: AN OVERVIEW

Swarm robotics involves coordinating multiple simple robots to perform complex tasks collectively, inspired by natural systems like ant colonies and bird flocks. These robots rely on decentralized control, local sensing, and limited communication to work together effectively. Hardware design focuses on simplicity, scalability, and cost-efficiency to enable large-scale deployment. Advances in microcontrollers, sensors, and wireless communication have made such platforms more feasible. Key challenges include power management, communication reliability, and real-time sensing. Bio-inspired strategies enhance adaptability and fault tolerance. Popular platforms like Kilobots and E-Pucks support research and real-world applications.

Swarm robotics is an emerging and rapidly growing field within robotics that draws inspiration from the collective behaviour of social organisms such as ants, bees and birds. Unlike traditional single-robot systems, swarm robotics involves the coordination of multiple autonomous robots that interact with one another and their environment to accomplish tasks that are often too complex or dynamic for a single robot to handle efficiently. These robotic swarms offer advantages such as scalability, robustness and flexibility, making them highly suitable for a variety of applications ranging from environmental monitoring and search-and-rescue operations to agriculture, logistics and space exploration. At the core of any swarm robotics system lies the hardware platform that supports decentralized control, local sensing, limited communication and cooperative behaviour. Swarm robotic hardware typically emphasizes simplicity, modularity and cost-efficiency to enable deployment at scale. Unlike high-end, sophisticated standalone robots, swarm robots often operate with minimalistic sensors, processors and actuators, relying on collective intelligence to perform tasks. The physical embodiment of swarm intelligence requires thoughtful design decisions in robot morphology, energy management, mobility mechanisms and sensor integration. Recent technological advances in microcontrollers, embedded systems and wireless communication have significantly contributed to the feasibility of developing low-cost, efficient swarm robotic platforms. Additionally, developments in materials science and manufacturing techniques, such as 3D printing and flexible electronics, have accelerated prototyping and customization of swarm robot hardware. These trends have facilitated the creation of both academic research platforms and commercial systems that demonstrate the power of distributed robotic intelligence. Designing effective swarm robotic platforms involves overcoming various hardware-level challenges. These include achieving reliable inter-robot communication, ensuring robust localization in GPS-denied environments, enabling real-time sensing and data fusion and maintaining swarm cohesion in dynamic and unpredictable conditions. Battery life, mechanical durability and computational limitations also impose critical constraints on platform design. To mitigate these issues, many swarm robots incorporate energy-efficient components, minimalistic mechanical designs and decentralized control algorithms that allow them to operate independently yet harmoniously (Fig. 1).

Fig. 1 Swarm Robotic Platform

Swarm robotic systems often adopt bio-inspired strategies to replicate the self-organizing and adaptive capabilities found in nature. These strategies are embedded into both the hardware configuration and the control architecture, enabling the swarm to dynamically reconfigure in response to environmental changes or internal failures. For example, redundancy in hardware allows for fault-tolerance, while the use of simple infrared, ultrasonic or visual sensors permits basic yet effective perception of the environment and neighbouring robots. Various platforms have been developed to support swarm robotics research, each with unique strengths tailored to specific domains. Notable examples include Kilobots, E-Puck robots, GRITSBots and Crazyflie drones—each designed with scalability, programmability and robustness in mind. These platforms provide standardized yet flexible frameworks for researchers to study emergent behaviours, collective decision-making and swarm coordination in both simulated and real-world environments. The evolution of swarm robotics hardware continues to be driven by interdisciplinary collaboration between robotics, biology, electronics and computer science. As the demand for autonomous multi-robot systems grows, the development of reliable and affordable swarm robotic platforms becomes increasingly critical. From ground-based micro-robots to aerial drone swarms, the diversity of hardware architectures reflects the vast potential and adaptability of swarm robotics. The convergence of hardware design and swarm intelligence opens new frontiers in automation, enabling machines to collectively achieve what individuals cannot. This chapter explores the key hardware platforms and technologies underpinning swarm robotic systems, offering insights into their design principles, components, challenges and future directions.

8.1 MINIATURE ROBOTS AND MODULAR DESIGNS

8.1.1. Concept of Swarm Robotics

Swarm robotics is a subfield of multi-robot systems that focuses on coordinating large numbers of relatively simple, autonomous robots. Inspired by collective behaviours in nature—such as ant foraging, bird flocking or fish schooling—swarm robots work together without a central command unit. Each robot acts based on local rules, sensing its environment and neighbouring robots to contribute to the group's goal. This self-organizing behaviour allows the swarm to be highly adaptable, scalable and fault-tolerant. Whether the task is exploring an unknown environment, performing surveillance or coordinating in disaster response, swarm robotics offers a flexible and robust solution. The key lies in the collective intelligence emerging from local interactions, not individual sophistication.

8.1.2. Core Operating Principles

Swarm robotic systems operate on the principle of decentralization—meaning no single robot controls the group. Instead, each unit processes local information from sensors and communicates with nearby robots using simple signals. These interactions lead to emergent behaviours that allow the swarm to accomplish complex objectives as a whole. Robots typically follow simple behavioural rules such as obstacle avoidance, alignment or attraction, which collectively lead to path formation, object clustering or area coverage. Communication is often minimal—through infrared, radio or visual cues—ensuring robustness and energy efficiency. This decentralized architecture makes swarms highly resilient to failure, as the loss of a few units doesn't affect the overall system performance significantly.

8.1.3. Hardware Design Focus

The design of swarm robotic hardware centres around creating compact, low-cost and energy-efficient platforms that can be deployed in large numbers. Components are often modular and interchangeable, allowing easy scaling and maintenance. Typical swarm robots are small in size, with minimal sensing and actuation capabilities. Mobility systems (like wheels, legs or propellers) are optimized for short-range movement and power systems are designed for lightweight energy sources such as Li-Po batteries. Processing is handled by low-power microcontrollers capable of basic computation and communication tasks. Simplicity is key: instead of equipping each robot with expensive sensors or processors, swarm design leverages the collective power of multiple units working together to achieve high-level functionality.

8.1.4. Technological Advancements

Recent advances in microelectronics, communication protocols and materials have greatly improved the feasibility and performance of swarm robotic platforms. Microcontrollers have become more powerful and energy-efficient, enabling onboard processing of sensor data and decentralized decision-making. Wireless communication technologies, such as Bluetooth Low Energy (BLE), Zigbee or custom RF protocols, allow real-time inter-robot coordination. Advances in sensors—including IMUs, proximity sensors, cameras and microphones—enable better situational awareness. 3D printing and low-cost PCB manufacturing have also made rapid prototyping more accessible, allowing researchers to experiment with diverse robot forms. Collectively, these technological improvements have lowered the cost barrier and accelerated the development and deployment of swarm robotics systems.

8.1.5. Challenges

Despite its promise, swarm robotics faces significant hardware and operational challenges. Power management is a major concern; robots must operate for extended periods on small batteries, requiring energy-efficient components. Communication within large swarms is also difficult, especially in environments with noise or interference. Achieving accurate localization—especially in indoor or GPS-denied areas—is another hurdle, often requiring vision-based or RF-based solutions. Sensing the environment and nearby robots in real-time demands reliable sensors and fast processing. Mechanical robustness is critical, particularly for outdoor or hazardous deployments. Additionally, ensuring the swarm maintains coordinated behaviour without central oversight requires robust algorithms that can handle delays, failures or dynamic obstacles.

8.1.6. Bio-Inspired Strategies

Swarm robotic systems frequently incorporate bio-inspired design strategies to enhance adaptability and collective behaviour. Just as insects follow simple local rules to achieve complex group tasks, robots in a swarm operate based on predefined behaviour sets that mimic natural systems. For instance, flocking algorithms inspired by birds allow coordinated movement, while ant-like foraging algorithms support efficient resource gathering. These behaviours are often encoded in lightweight, distributed software that requires minimal computational overhead. Additionally, evolutionary algorithms and artificial immune systems are sometimes used for adaptive learning within the swarm. Redundancy and minimalism ensure that even if individual robots fail, the swarm continues functioning—just like in biological colonies (Table 1).

Table 1: Miniature Robots and Modular Designs in swarm robotics

S. No.	Title	Key Points
1	Concept of Swarm Robotics	- Focuses on coordination of many simple robots - Inspired by natural systems (ants, birds, fish) - No central control; robots act based on local rules - Enables adaptability, scalability, fault tolerance - Ideal for exploration, surveillance, disaster response
2	Core Operating Principles	- Based on decentralized control and local interactions - Robots use simple signals for communication (IR, radio, visual) - Behaviours include obstacle avoidance, alignment, attraction - Emergent collective behaviour enables complex tasks - Resilient to individual failures
3	Hardware Design Focus	- Emphasis on compact, low-cost, modular hardware - Minimal sensors and actuators - Lightweight power sources (e.g., Li-Po batteries) - Low-power microcontrollers for basic tasks - Focus on collective function over individual sophistication
4	Technological Advancements	- Improvements in microcontrollers and sensors - Enhanced communication (BLE, Zigbee, RF) - Use of IMUs, cameras, proximity sensors - 3D printing and low-cost PCBs for rapid prototyping - More feasible and affordable swarm deployment
5	Challenges	- Power constraints for extended operations - Communication issues in noisy environments - Difficulty with localization in GPS-denied areas - Real-time sensing and processing needs - Physical robustness and decentralized coordination are critical
6	Bio-Inspired Strategies	- Mimicry of insect behaviour (e.g., foraging, flocking) - Use of simple local rules to achieve global goals - Lightweight, distributed software control - Inclusion of evolutionary and adaptive algorithms - Redundancy ensures system robustness even with individual failures

8.1.7. Popular Research Platforms

Several standardized platforms have emerged to support research in swarm robotics. Kilobots, developed at Harvard, are small, affordable robots designed to demonstrate swarm behaviours like clustering and pattern formation. They use vibration-based movement and IR communication. E-Puck robots, developed in Switzerland, are more capable platforms featuring wheels, proximity sensors, cameras and Bluetooth, ideal for advanced coordination tasks. Crazyflie drones, on the other hand, enable aerial swarm experiments, offering lightweight flight capabilities and onboard processing. GRITSBots and Swarm Drones are other examples that offer scalable, programmable and modular systems. These platforms allow researchers to test control algorithms, simulate real-world scenarios and advance the field through reproducible experiments.

8.2 UAV SWARMS (QUADCOPTERS AND FIXED-WING)

8.2.1 Unmanned Aerial Vehicle (UAV) swarms

Unmanned Aerial Vehicle (UAV) swarms are networks of autonomous flying robots—often quadcopters or fixed-wing aircraft—that coordinate in real time to perform tasks collaboratively. Similar to ground-based swarm robots, UAV swarms operate without centralized control, relying on local sensing, onboard processing and wireless communication to maintain cohesion and achieve mission goals. They are used in a wide range of applications including aerial surveillance, environmental monitoring, precision agriculture, search and rescue and military reconnaissance.

8.2.2 Quadcopter-Based Swarms

Quadcopters or quadrotor drones, are the most common platform for UAV swarms due to their vertical take-off and landing (VTOL) capabilities, stability and maneuverability. Each quadcopter typically includes:

- Four rotors for lift and directional control
- IMUs, GPS and cameras for navigation and sensing
- Onboard microcontrollers for decentralized control
- Communication modules (Wi-Fi, RF, BLE) for inter-UAV coordination Quadcopter swarms can perform tasks like formation flying, distributed mapping, cooperative surveillance and payload delivery. Their ability to hover makes them ideal for precision tasks in confined or complex environments.

8.2.3 Fixed-Wing UAV Swarms

Fixed-wing UAVs offer greater energy efficiency and longer flight ranges compared to quadcopters, making them suitable for large-area missions like environmental monitoring, border patrol or disaster assessment. They rely on:

- Lift generated by fixed wings and forward motion
- Higher airspeeds and longer battery or fuel life
- Advanced path-planning and terrain-following capabilities

Swarming fixed-wing UAVs often operate in loose formations and require sophisticated flight control algorithms for collision avoidance, altitude synchronization and energy management.

8.2.4 Communication and Coordination

Effective swarm operation requires real-time communication and coordination. Common communication technologies include:

- **RF Modules for Short-Range Communication:** Radio Frequency (RF) modules are widely used for short-distance communication between UAVs in a swarm. These modules operate in standard frequency bands (e.g., 2.4 GHz, 433 MHz) and enable peer-to-peer messaging with low latency. RF communication is ideal for local coordination, such as maintaining formations, avoiding collisions or sharing sensory data. Due to their simplicity and energy efficiency, RF modules are commonly embedded in lightweight drone platforms. However, they may face interference in noisy or urban environments and their range is typically limited to a few hundred meters.
- **Mesh Networking for Robust and Redundant Data Sharing:** Mesh networks enhance swarm communication by allowing each UAV to act as a node that can relay messages to others, forming a decentralized and self-healing network. If one link fails or a UAV exits the network, the data is automatically rerouted through other nodes. This structure greatly improves robustness, especially in large or dispersed swarms operating in complex terrains. Mesh networking supports distributed control, synchronization and collective decision-making across the swarm, ensuring that no single point of failure disrupts operations.
- **Cloud-Based Coordination for Long-Range Control and Data Aggregation:** For extended operations, especially in beyond-visual-line-of-sight (BVLOS) missions, cloud-based systems are used to coordinate and manage swarm activities from a centralized interface. UAVs transmit telemetry, sensor data and mission status to the cloud via cellular networks, satellite links or 5G infrastructure. Operators can then issue commands, monitor progress and update mission parameters in real time. Cloud platforms also enable large-scale data storage, AI-based analysis and

collaborative mission planning. This method supports strategic oversight and post-mission analysis, though it depends on network availability and may introduce latency.

Coordination algorithms are used to handle leader-follower models, consensus protocols and behaviour-based control. These allow the swarm to maintain formations, adapt to dynamic environments and reassign tasks in response to failures or environmental changes.

8.2.5 Sensing and Navigation

Navigation in UAV swarms is typically achieved through a combination of:

- **GPS for Global Positioning:** Global Positioning System (GPS) is the most widely used method for determining a UAV's absolute position in outdoor environments. It allows each UAV in the swarm to determine its latitude, longitude and altitude in real time, facilitating coordinated movements, geofencing and path planning. GPS is essential for missions requiring wide-area coverage or waypoint-based navigation. However, GPS accuracy may degrade in urban canyons, forests or during signal jamming, making it less reliable in certain contexts.
- **IMUs for Orientation and Movement Tracking:** Inertial Measurement Units (IMUs) are onboard sensors that measure acceleration, angular velocity and sometimes magnetic fields using accelerometers, gyroscopes and magnetometers. IMUs provide vital information about a drone's orientation (pitch, roll, yaw), enabling stabilization and flight control. Although IMUs do not provide absolute positioning, they are critical for short-term motion estimation, especially during fast maneuvers or GPS outages. When fused with GPS data (via sensor fusion algorithms), IMUs help produce smoother and more accurate navigation.
- **Vision-Based Systems (e.g., Optical Flow, SLAM) for GPS-Denied Environments:** In indoor or GPS-denied environments (e.g., tunnels, caves or dense urban areas), vision-based navigation becomes essential. Optical flow systems use downward-facing cameras to detect pixel shifts between frames, estimating the drone's movement relative to the ground. Simultaneous Localization and Mapping (SLAM) techniques allow UAVs to map their surroundings while simultaneously determining their position within that map. SLAM can use cameras (visual SLAM), LiDAR (LiDAR-SLAM) or depth sensors.

These systems allow drones to navigate autonomously in complex, unstructured spaces where GPS is unavailable or unreliable. Additional sensors like LiDAR, ultrasonic altimeters or infrared cameras help in obstacle avoidance and terrain mapping. Fusion of multi-sensor data allows the swarm to navigate autonomously and respond to environmental stimuli.

8.2.6 Swarm Applications

UAV swarms are increasingly used across various sectors:

Agriculture: UAV swarms are revolutionizing modern farming through:

- **Crop Monitoring:** Drones fly in formation to capture multispectral or thermal imagery, helping detect diseases, nutrient deficiencies and irrigation issues early.
- **Pesticide Spraying:** Coordinated swarms can cover large areas quickly and uniformly, improving efficiency and reducing human exposure to chemicals.
- **Yield Estimation:** Drones use visual data to analyse plant health and predict crop yield, aiding in more accurate forecasting and resource planning.

Disaster Response: Swarm drones significantly enhance emergency operations by:

- **Search and Rescue:** Swarms can divide and scan large areas simultaneously, identifying survivors with thermal cameras or AI-based object detection.
- **Damage Assessment:** After disasters like earthquakes or floods, UAVs rapidly map affected regions, helping prioritize rescue and recovery efforts.
- **Supply Drops:** In inaccessible or dangerous zones, drone swarms can deliver critical supplies like medicine, food or communication devices.

Military and Défense: UAV swarms are being developed for various strategic roles:

- **Surveillance and Reconnaissance:** Swarms perform persistent monitoring over hostile or remote areas, collecting real-time intelligence without risking human lives.
- **Decoy Tactics:** Multiple drones can be used to distract or confuse enemy radar and defense systems.
- **Threat Neutralization:** Armed or kamikaze-style swarms can engage enemy targets autonomously, supporting offensive or defensive operations.

Environmental Monitoring: Environmental agencies utilize UAV swarms to collect ecological data efficiently:

- **Air Quality Measurement:** Drones equipped with gas sensors can monitor pollutants across large urban or industrial areas.
- **Wildlife Tracking:** Swarms help track animal populations or migration routes using thermal or optical cameras without disturbing habitats.

- Forest Fire Detection: Early-stage fire outbreaks can be detected using infrared imaging, allowing faster response before large-scale damage occurs.

Construction and Infrastructure: In civil engineering and urban planning, UAV swarms play a growing role:

- 3D Mapping and Surveying: Coordinated flights generate detailed digital elevation models (DEMs) for land surveying or construction planning.
- Structural Inspection: Swarms inspect bridges, towers and pipelines simultaneously from multiple angles, reducing inspection time and increasing safety.
- Progress Monitoring: Drones capture site images over time to monitor construction progress, detect anomalies and verify work against plans.

8.2.7 Advantages of UAV Swarms

- **High Scalability and Redundancy:** UAV swarms can be scaled up easily by adding more units without major changes to the system architecture. Since each drone operates semi-independently, the swarm can grow or shrink based on the mission's complexity or coverage needs. Redundancy ensures that if one or several drones fail, the remaining units can compensate, maintaining mission continuity without system collapse.
- **Faster Task Execution Through Parallelism:** Swarm drones operate simultaneously, dividing large tasks into smaller, manageable units executed in parallel. For example, during an area scan or search-and-rescue mission, each UAV can cover a different zone, significantly reducing the overall time required compared to a single drone or a centralized system.
- **Greater Coverage in Less Time:** Due to their distributed operation, swarms can cover wide geographic areas more efficiently. This is particularly beneficial in missions like agricultural surveying, disaster mapping or border patrol, where large territories must be analysed quickly and frequently.
- **Flexibility in Deployment (Urban, Rural, Hostile Terrains):** UAV swarms are adaptable to a variety of environments—be it dense urban centres with signal interference, rural areas lacking infrastructure or dangerous zones such as disaster-hit regions or military zones. Their decentralized nature and autonomous navigation systems allow for real-time path adjustments and dynamic task reassignment.
- **Resilience to Individual UAV Failures:** The swarm's behaviour does not depend on any single unit. If one UAV experiences a mechanical failure,

communication loss or environmental interference, others adjust their roles dynamically. This fault tolerance increases mission reliability and minimizes disruption due to localized failures.

8.2.8 Challenges and Limitations

- **Communication Interference and Bandwidth Limitations:** In large UAV swarms, inter-drone communication can suffer from signal congestion, interference or limited bandwidth—especially when using RF or Wi-Fi-based links in crowded frequency bands. This can lead to delayed commands, dropped packets or loss of synchronization, severely impacting real-time coordination and control.
- **Short Battery Life in Quadcopters:** Quadcopters are typically constrained by small onboard batteries, limiting flight duration to 15–30 minutes in many cases. High energy demands from rotors, sensors and communication systems further reduce operational time. Frequent battery swaps or recharging infrastructure becomes a logistical challenge during long missions or large deployments.
- **Complex Flight Dynamics in Changing Weather Conditions:** Environmental factors like wind gusts, rain, snow and temperature variations complicate flight stability, path planning and sensor reliability. Swarm algorithms must account for varying conditions across different areas of the swarm, requiring robust adaptive control systems to maintain formations and avoid accidents.
- **Legal and Regulatory Constraints:** Many countries impose strict regulations on UAV operations, particularly concerning:
  - Beyond Visual Line of Sight (BVLOS) missions
  - Altitude and area restrictions
  - Swarm size and number of UAVs under a single operator
  - Airspace sharing with manned aircraft

Compliance requires special permits, air traffic integration and often limits real-world deployment of fully autonomous swarms.

- **Safety and Collision Avoidance in Dense Swarms:** As swarm density increases, the risk of mid-air collisions or close encounters grows. Real-time collision avoidance systems are necessary but add computational and sensory overhead. Ensuring spatial separation while maintaining coordination is a core challenge, particularly during high-speed or close-formation missions.
- **Coordination Overhead with Increased Swarm Size:** Larger swarms increase the complexity of coordination, decision-making and data sharing.

Without efficient distributed control algorithms, the system can become sluggish or unstable. Managing computational load, role distribution and latency becomes critical to maintain cohesive swarm behaviour as size scales up.

8.2.9 Research Trends and Future Directions

- **Integration of AI/ML for Adaptive Flight and Decision-Making:** Artificial Intelligence (AI) and Machine Learning (ML) are increasingly being integrated into UAV swarms to enable autonomous, real-time decision-making. These technologies allow drones to learn from environmental data, predict obstacles or threats and adapt flight behaviour accordingly. For example, reinforcement learning can help swarms optimize flight paths dynamically, while neural networks can be used for object detection, target tracking and formation control. AI enables UAVs to make decisions independently in unpredictable environments, reducing reliance on human operators or pre-programmed behaviours.
- **Use of 5G and Satellite Communication for Extended Coordination:** The adoption of 5G networks and Low Earth Orbit (LEO) satellite communication systems is revolutionizing how UAVs communicate over long distances. 5G offers ultra-low latency, high bandwidth and dense connectivity—ideal for large swarms operating in urban or industrial zones. Satellite links extend this capability to remote and unconnected areas, allowing seamless, beyond-visual-line-of-sight (BVLOS) operations. These technologies facilitate real-time video streaming, swarm-wide updates and cloud-based control, enabling complex, distributed missions with high data throughput.
- **Bio-Inspired Flight Patterns and Energy-Efficient Algorithms:** Researchers are increasingly drawing inspiration from birds, insects and bats to develop bio-inspired flight strategies. These include techniques for formation flying (like V-formations in geese), adaptive flocking and energy-saving maneuvers based on fluid dynamics. Such designs can reduce drag, minimize energy consumption and improve flight endurance. Additionally, bio-inspired control algorithms—such as stigmergy or swarm heuristics—enhance collective behaviour, allowing drones to self-organize and adapt to dynamic conditions with minimal computation and communication overhead.
- **Development of Hybrid UAVs (VTOL + Fixed-Wing Capabilities):** Hybrid UAVs combine the vertical take-off and landing (VTOL) advantages of quadcopters with the long-range efficiency of fixed-wing aircraft. This

dual-mode capability allows UAVs to operate in tight spaces and hover when needed while also covering long distances at higher speeds. These platforms are ideal for complex missions such as terrain mapping, border patrol or maritime surveillance, where both precision and range are required. Future research focuses on improving aerodynamic transition mechanisms, energy efficiency and flight control algorithms for seamless mode switching.

- **Increased Autonomy for Swarm-Level Planning and Reconfiguration:** Next-generation UAV swarms aim for at the swarm level, enabling drones to plan missions collectively, allocate tasks dynamically and reconfigure formations without human intervention. This includes features like autonomous target recognition, real-time formation change and automatic fault management (e.g., reassigning roles when a drone fails). Research is directed at swarm intelligence frameworks, distributed decision-making models and robust reconfiguration strategies that ensure mission continuity, adaptability and resilience under varying operational conditions.

8.3 GROUND ROBOTS AND AQUATIC SWARMS

8.3.1 Overview of Ground Robots and Aquatic Swarms

Swarm robotics is not limited to aerial systems. Ground-based and aquatic robot swarms are becoming increasingly important in various fields, from environmental exploration to infrastructure inspection. Like their aerial counterparts, these robots operate on decentralized control, local sensing and distributed decision-making. Their designs are typically adapted for movement over rugged terrain or through water bodies, with emphasis on durability, stability and energy efficiency.

8.3.2 Ground Robot Swarms

Ground-based swarm robots are autonomous mobile systems that navigate over surfaces using wheels, tracks or legs. They are used in:

- **Agriculture (Soil Monitoring, Precision Seeding):** Ground robot swarms are transforming agriculture by enabling data-driven, precision farming. Small, autonomous ground robots equipped with soil sensors and multispectral cameras can traverse large fields to monitor soil moisture, pH, nutrient levels and plant health in real time. By operating as a swarm, these robots can divide the field into zones and cover the area in parallel, greatly improving efficiency and accuracy. In precision seeding, robots can follow GPS-defined paths to plant seeds at optimal depths and spacing, adapting in real time to terrain or soil quality. Swarm coordination ensures uniform coverage while avoiding overlaps or gaps, reducing resource waste and increasing crop yield.

- **Search and Rescue (Collapsed Buildings, Tunnels):** In disaster scenarios such as earthquakes, building collapses or underground accidents, ground robot swarms offer a non-invasive, rapid-response solution for search and rescue. These robots are typically small, rugged and equipped with thermal cameras, microphones, gas sensors and proximity detectors. Their collective deployment allows for simultaneous exploration of multiple entry points and efficient mapping of hazardous environments. Unlike single large robots, swarms can navigate through tight spaces, debris or narrow tunnels. If some units are lost or damaged, the others continue operating—ensuring high mission reliability. They can also relay information back to first responders in real-time, enabling informed decisions about victim location and rescue strategy.
- **Military Operations (Terrain Scouting, Mine Detection):** Ground robot swarms are being increasingly researched for combat support and reconnaissance missions in military applications. For terrain scouting, autonomous ground units can map unfamiliar landscapes, detect hidden enemy positions or monitor troop movements without exposing soldiers to danger. In mine detection, sensor-equipped robots move in distributed formations to scan for buried explosives or IEDs using ground-penetrating radar, metal detectors or chemical sensors. Swarm coordination ensures fast, large-scale area coverage, with overlapping paths to verify anomalies. Their decentralized nature makes the system robust against interference, while real-time communication allows dynamic route adjustments in response to threats or terrain.
- **Industrial Inspection (Pipelines, Warehouses):** In industrial environments, ground robot swarms are utilized for routine inspection and maintenance, particularly in hard-to-access or dangerous areas. In pipelines, small robots equipped with cameras and leak sensors can crawl through conduits to detect corrosion, pressure drops or blockages. For warehouses and factories, ground swarms can perform inventory tracking, equipment inspection and environmental monitoring (e.g., temperature, gas levels). Multiple units working together reduce downtime and improve inspection frequency without requiring human labour. Autonomous path planning, RFID integration and real-time data streaming enhance the scalability of such systems in logistics, energy and manufacturing industries.

Features include:

- Onboard sensors (e.g., ultrasonic, LIDAR, infrared) for obstacle detection
- Local path planning and terrain adaptation

- Mesh communication for coordination
- Power-efficient locomotion to maximize uptime
- Modular design for rapid deployment and maintenance

8.3.3 Aquatic Swarms

Aquatic swarm robots operate in underwater or surface-level environments such as lakes, oceans and rivers. They include:

- **Autonomous Surface Vehicles (ASVs):** Autonomous Surface Vehicles (ASVs) are robotic systems designed to operate on the surface of water bodies such as lakes, rivers and oceans. These vehicles navigate autonomously using onboard GPS, inertial measurement units (IMUs) and, in some cases, vision-based systems. ASVs are typically equipped with solar panels or rechargeable batteries, enabling long-duration missions with minimal human intervention. They communicate using wireless technologies such as 4G/5G, satellite or short-range radio, allowing real-time data exchange and fleet coordination. Structurally, ASVs are rugged and waterproof, built to endure harsh weather and water conditions. In swarm configurations, multiple ASVs can coordinate to perform large-area tasks more efficiently. Their most common applications include environmental monitoring—measuring parameters like water temperature, salinity, pH and pollutant levels across wide zones. They are also used in bathymetric mapping, helping researchers and engineers understand underwater topography. In maritime security, ASVs assist in coastal surveillance, detecting unauthorized vessels or activities. During natural disasters such as floods or oil spills, ASVs can collect situational data, assist in damage assessments or carry lightweight relief supplies. Thanks to their modular design and scalable architecture, ASVs can be rapidly deployed in swarms for distributed data collection and patrolling missions. Their decentralized coordination models, often inspired by natural behaviours like flocking or schooling, make them highly adaptive to dynamic environments. With advancements in AI, sensor integration and marine autonomy, ASVs are becoming an essential tool for sustainable ocean management, autonomous shipping support and climate research.
- **Autonomous Underwater Vehicles (AUVs):** Autonomous Underwater Vehicles (AUVs) are self-contained robotic platforms that operate beneath the surface of oceans, lakes or reservoirs without the need for tethers or real-time human control. Designed for subaquatic exploration, AUVs use inertial navigation systems (INS), Doppler Velocity Logs (DVL), sonar and acoustic positioning systems to move and localize themselves in GPS-denied

underwater environments. These vehicles are pressure-resistant and watertight, engineered to withstand extreme depths and fluctuating currents. Propelled by thrusters or bio-inspired mechanisms (e.g., fins), AUVs can travel autonomously for extended periods while collecting and processing large volumes of environmental and structural data. AUV swarms are increasingly used for cooperative seabed mapping, underwater infrastructure inspection and marine environmental monitoring. Equipped with sonar arrays, cameras, CTD (Conductivity, Temperature, Depth) sensors and chemical detectors, they can explore vast, difficult-to-reach underwater zones, such as deep-sea trenches or offshore oil platforms. In Défense applications, they perform tasks like underwater mine detection, stealth surveillance or route reconnaissance for naval operations. AUVs in swarm configurations can distribute tasks, share data through acoustic modems and reconfigure their behaviour based on mission status or detected anomalies. The absence of GPS and the challenges of underwater communication make AUV coordination complex, but advances in AI, SLAM (Simultaneous Localization and Mapping) and acoustic networking have significantly enhanced their autonomy. With their ability to operate silently and persistently in hazardous or unexplored environments, AUVs are becoming indispensable in oceanography, climate research, offshore construction and national security. Future AUV systems are expected to be smaller, smarter and more cooperative, functioning as intelligent marine teams capable of self-organization and adaptive mission execution (Fig. 2).

Fig. 2 Free Underwater Fish Swarm

Applications include

- **Marine Life Monitoring and Mapping:** AUV swarms are playing a vital role in marine biodiversity research and ecosystem mapping. Equipped with cameras, hydrophones, sonar and environmental sensors, they can silently track fish schools, monitor coral reefs and record whale or dolphin migrations without disturbing the natural habitat. By operating in coordinated formations, these robots can cover large, ecologically sensitive areas simultaneously, collecting synchronized data on temperature, salinity, plankton levels and animal behaviour. This data is crucial for studying ocean health, migratory patterns and the impacts of climate change or human activity on marine life.

- **Pollution Detection (e.g., Oil Spills, Chemical Leaks):** Swarm AUVs are highly effective for early detection and monitoring of underwater pollution events. Outfitted with chemical sensors, fluorometers and turbidity detectors, they can detect oil dispersions, heavy metals or chemical leaks from pipelines and shipping lanes. Unlike single large submersibles, swarms allow real-time tracking of pollutant spread over vast underwater regions. Their ability to dive to specific depths and follow contamination gradients enables more accurate 3D mapping of pollutants, which is essential for rapid environmental response, cleanup planning and regulatory reporting.
- **Underwater Archaeology and Inspection:** In underwater archaeology, AUV swarms assist in locating and documenting submerged historical sites such as shipwrecks, sunken cities and ancient artifacts. Using high-resolution sonar, 3D imaging and magnetometers, they can survey the seafloor without physical contact, preserving delicate structures. For inspection tasks, AUVs are used in examining underwater infrastructure like pipelines, cables, offshore platforms or dam walls. Swarm deployment ensures quick, detailed and redundant coverage of structures from multiple angles, detecting corrosion, damage or biofouling with precision and minimal human risk.
- **Naval Operations (Stealth Reconnaissance, Surveillance):** Military and Défense sectors deploy AUV swarms for covert underwater operations, including reconnaissance of hostile waters, surveillance of enemy vessels and detection of underwater mines or intrusion attempts. Their low acoustic signature and autonomous navigation make them suitable for stealth missions where conventional submarines or manned units would be detectable or vulnerable. AUVs can also support maritime border patrols, track submarines or establish underwater sensor networks. With increasing autonomy and AI-powered decision-making, future AUVs are expected to coordinate in real-time combat environments, acting as autonomous naval scouts or decoys.

These robots face unique challenges like:

- Pressure tolerance and waterproofing
- Limited GPS underwater (often use sonar or acoustic localization)

- Communication via underwater modems or acoustic signalling
- Energy-efficient propulsion (propellers, fins or gliders)

8.3.4 Communication and Navigation

- **Ground Robot Swarms:** Ground robots typically rely on radio-frequency (RF) communication systems such as Bluetooth, Zigbee or Wi-Fi to exchange data with nearby units and coordinate behaviours. These short- to mid-range protocols are sufficient for most terrestrial environments, especially indoors or within line-of-sight ranges. For navigation, ground robots often use Global Positioning System (GPS) in outdoor settings, while visual markers (e.g., AprilTags or QR codes), LIDAR and camera-based localization are used indoors or in GPS-denied environments. Advanced systems may also integrate wheel encoders, IMUs or magnetometers for dead reckoning and motion estimation.
- **Aquatic Robot Swarms:** Communication and navigation in aquatic environments present unique challenges due to the absence of GPS underwater and signal attenuation in water. Aquatic robots, particularly AUVs, use acoustic modems for inter-robot communication. These low-bandwidth systems allow basic coordination, such as sharing location, sensor data or task updates. For navigation, aquatic swarms rely on technologies like inertial navigation systems (INS), Doppler Velocity Logs (DVL), compasses and depth sensors to estimate position. Some also use optical beacons, SLAM algorithms or ultra-short baseline (USBL) systems for relative or absolute localization when operating near known landmarks or surface stations.

8.3.5 Swarm Behaviours and Control

Ground and aquatic robotic swarms are designed to perform complex tasks by exhibiting emergent collective behaviours, which arise from simple, local rules followed by each individual robot. These behaviours are often inspired by natural systems—such as flocks of birds, schools of fish or insect colonies—and are implemented through bio-inspired algorithms or behaviour-based control architectures. Below are the key behaviours commonly observed in robotic swarms:

- **Flocking (Maintaining Formation):** In flocking, robots align their movements to maintain relative positions within a group, ensuring coordinated navigation across space. This is critical in applications like area scanning or group travel, where maintaining shape and cohesion is necessary. Flocking is typically based on three simple rules:
  - Separation: Avoid crowding neighbours
  - Alignment: Match velocity with neighbours

- Cohesion: Move toward the average position of nearby robots

This behaviour ensures smooth, group-level motion and is used extensively in formation control for both land and aquatic swarms.

- **Aggregation (Gathering at Specific Locations):** Aggregation enables the swarm to converge at a target location—for example, when robots need to recharge, share data or respond to detected signals. It is typically triggered by environmental cues such as sound, light or chemical gradients. Ground and aquatic robots use sensors to detect these cues and localize hotspots, coordinating with nearby peers to minimize redundancy while ensuring convergence.
- **Dispersion (Evenly Covering Areas):** Dispersion involves robots spreading out uniformly across a region to maximize area coverage. This is particularly useful in applications such as environmental monitoring, mine detection or pollution tracking. Dispersion algorithms often use repulsion forces or virtual fields to prevent clustering, ensuring optimal sensor deployment and minimal blind spots. Robots adjust their positions based on proximity to neighbours and boundaries, achieving efficient spatial distribution.
- **Foraging (Searching and Collecting Samples or Data):** Foraging mimics the behaviour of ants or bees—robots search for targets (e.g., specific samples, leaks or objects), collect data or payload and return it to a base or aggregation zone. Robots operate independently or in small groups, often using stigmergy (indirect coordination through environmental signals like virtual pheromones) or probabilistic search patterns. This is particularly useful in unknown or hazardous environments where exploration must be distributed and redundant.

Control Approaches

These swarm behaviours are often managed by:

- Bio-inspired algorithms: such as Ant Colony Optimization (ACO), Particle Swarm Optimization (PSO) and Artificial Immune Systems
- Behaviour-based robotics: where robots switch between behaviour modules (e.g., avoid, follow, explore) based on sensor input
- Finite State Machines (FSM) or Subsumption Architectures for lightweight control logic.The simplicity of individual behaviours, combined with robust local interaction rules, enables complex global outcomes to emerge without the need for centralized control.

8.3.6 Technical Challenges

- **Terrain Variability for Ground Robots (Rocks, Stairs, Mud):** Ground robots frequently encounter a wide range of terrain types in both urban and natural environments, making mobility and stability a major challenge. Uneven surfaces like rocky paths can hinder wheel or track movement, while loose soil and mud can lead to slippage or entrapment. Stairs and vertical steps are particularly problematic for robots without adaptive legged or climbing mechanisms. The variability in terrain friction, hardness and geometry requires dynamic adjustment of locomotion strategies in real time. Traditional wheeled platforms often struggle with elevation changes or obstacles beyond a few centimeters in height. Sensor systems must also be capable of detecting and interpreting terrain types ahead of time to allow for predictive motion planning. Additionally, dust, water and mud can obscure or damage critical components such as cameras and motors. Effective navigation over diverse terrain demands a fusion of mechanical robustness, real-time terrain classification and adaptive control algorithms. The integration of compliant actuators or hybrid wheel-leg mechanisms can provide enhanced versatility. Simultaneously, machine learning techniques can be employed to help robots "learn" terrain traversability from past experiences. Energy consumption also increases significantly when dealing with difficult terrain, putting more pressure on power systems. Without high-fidelity terrain mapping and mobility planning, robots risk immobilization. Thus, terrain adaptability remains one of the most demanding aspects of autonomous ground mobility.

- **Fluid Dynamics and Drag for Aquatic Robots:** Aquatic robots operate in complex and highly dynamic environments where fluid dynamics play a pivotal role in vehicle control and energy efficiency. Unlike aerial or ground robots, they must constantly overcome the resistance of water, which is nearly 800 times denser than air, resulting in substantial drag forces. Changes in water temperature, salinity and current direction can affect buoyancy and maneuverability. Additionally, aquatic robots must account for laminar and turbulent flow conditions, both of which impact the effectiveness of propulsion and control surfaces. Precise modelling of these hydrodynamic forces is critical but computationally intensive. Turbulence around hulls and propellers can introduce noise in sensor data, particularly for sonar systems. Marine biofouling — the accumulation of organisms like algae and barnacles — can increase drag and degrade performance over time. Design choices such as streamlined shapes, adaptive fins or distributed thrusters can help mitigate these effects. However, they must be balanced against space, weight and energy constraints. Real-time response to changing water currents is also essential for tasks like underwater mapping, pipeline inspection or search and rescue. Accurate control under these conditions requires advanced algorithms and low-latency feedback loops. Thus, mastering fluid dynamics is fundamental to enhancing the reliability and operational lifespan of aquatic robots.

- **Battery Limitations in Long-Duration Missions:** Battery technology remains a primary bottleneck in the deployment of autonomous robots for extended missions. Most current battery systems provide limited energy density, meaning that mission duration and capabilities are directly constrained by onboard power reserves. This is particularly problematic for applications in remote or hazardous environments where recharging or swapping batteries is infeasible. High-performance actions such as locomotion, sensor data processing and communication all draw significant power, leading to rapid depletion. Environmental conditions like extreme temperatures can further degrade battery efficiency and lifespan. For aerial and underwater drones, weight constraints severely limit battery capacity, while ground robots may carry more but still face endurance ceilings. To address this, researchers explore hybrid power systems, energy harvesting (solar, kinetic or thermal) and sleep-mode scheduling to conserve energy. Software optimization for task prioritization and power-aware planning can also extend operational periods. Advanced battery chemistries like lithium-sulphur or solid-state batteries are promising but not yet widely commercialized. Autonomous docking and recharging stations represent another possible solution, though they require precise navigation and localization. Without breakthroughs in energy management or storage, long-term autonomy across platforms remains a significant hurdle in robotics. Ultimately, improving battery reliability, capacity and efficiency is essential for enabling persistent, untethered robotic operations.
- **Sensor Noise and Drift in GPS-Denied Environments:** Operating in environments where GPS signals are unavailable or unreliable — such as indoors, underwater, underground or in dense urban areas — poses serious localization and navigation challenges for autonomous robots. In such scenarios, robots must rely on internal sensors like IMUs, magnetometers, LiDAR, vision systems and odometry to estimate their position. However, these sensors are prone to various forms of error. Inertial sensors, for instance, suffer from cumulative drift over time, gradually leading to significant inaccuracies in localization. Visual sensors can be affected by poor lighting, featureless surfaces or occlusions, while magnetometers may be influenced by local electromagnetic interference. LiDAR-based SLAM (Simultaneous Localization and Mapping) can provide high accuracy but is computationally demanding and may struggle in visually or structurally ambiguous environments. Data fusion techniques such as Extended Kalman Filters (EKF) or particle filters are used to combine multiple sensor inputs

to reduce error, but they cannot fully eliminate noise or drift. Additionally, the robot must frequently recalibrate or correct its position through loop closure or external references when possible. Ensuring reliable navigation in GPS-denied environments often requires sophisticated algorithms, redundancy in sensors and robust error-checking methods. Without these, a robot can easily become disoriented, jeopardizing mission success and safety.

- **Coordination Difficulties in Real-Time Dynamic Conditions:** Coordinating multiple robots in real-time, especially in environments that are fast-changing or unpredictable, introduces a layer of complexity that extends beyond individual autonomy. Robots must maintain constant communication, share situational awareness and adapt to new information in milliseconds — all without causing interference or collision. Real-time coordination is especially critical in missions involving search and rescue, military operations or industrial automation, where the environment or task requirements can evolve rapidly. Communication bandwidth limitations, signal interference and latency can disrupt coordination protocols. Moreover, decentralized decision-making requires that each robot make context-aware choices while still achieving a global objective. Distributed consensus algorithms and multi-agent reinforcement learning are being explored to address these challenges, but scalability and reliability remain concerns. Task allocation must also account for the heterogeneous capabilities of different robots and changing task priorities. In swarm robotics, emergent behaviours can be harnessed, but they are difficult to control precisely. Real-time coordination must also consider external dynamics, such as moving obstacles or human presence, demanding high levels of perception and reactivity. Ultimately, seamless collaboration under dynamic conditions demands robust frameworks for communication, negotiation and synchronization — areas still under active research in robotics.

8.3.7 Research Trends and Future Directions

- Hybrid Ground-Aquatic Robots (e.g., Amphibious Crawlers): A major trend in robotics research is the development of hybrid ground-aquatic robots capable of operating across both land and water environments. These robots are often inspired by amphibious organisms like frogs, crabs or turtles, combining legs, wheels or tracks with fins or propellers to enable seamless transitions between terrains. This dual capability significantly enhances mission flexibility, particularly in areas with mixed terrain such as coastal zones, flood-prone regions or disaster-struck urban environments. Key challenges include developing robust waterproofing, adaptive propulsion systems and flexible control architectures to accommodate the vastly different dynamics of land versus water movement. Researchers are also focusing on energy efficiency to ensure that such robots can maintain long-duration missions without recharging. Bioinspired designs such as fin-like actuators or compliant limbs have shown promise for improving maneuverability in soft ground and shallow water. Advances in materials science are playing a critical role, enabling the construction of lightweight, corrosion-resistant and pressure-tolerant structures. Control algorithms must handle a wider range of sensory input and motion dynamics, requiring sophisticated multi-modal planning. As the technology matures, hybrid robots are likely to be deployed in areas such as environmental monitoring, military reconnaissance and humanitarian aid — providing unparalleled reach across traditionally segmented domains.

- Soft-Bodied Aquatic Swarms Inspired by Jellyfish or Fish Schools: Soft robotics is gaining momentum as researchers look to mimic the flexible, efficient and adaptive movement of marine life like jellyfish, octopuses or schools of fish. These robots often use silicone, elastomers or fluidic actuators that allow for smooth, compliant movement in underwater environments. When deployed in coordinated swarms, these soft-bodied robots can perform tasks such as ocean sensing, pollutant detection, coral reef monitoring and underwater exploration with minimal ecological disruption. Swarm behaviour takes inspiration from biological phenomena like flocking, schooling and gradient-following, enabling distributed intelligence and robust performance even if individual units fail. The non-rigid design also allows soft robots to navigate through narrow crevices or sensitive habitats without causing damage. However, challenges remain in integrating onboard power, communication modules and navigation systems within deformable structures. Researchers are exploring wireless energy transfer and bio-hybrid systems where living cells power or guide robotic behaviour. Such systems promise high redundancy, fault tolerance and adaptability. The convergence of soft robotics and swarm intelligence is pushing boundaries in how we design autonomous systems for complex and fragile ecosystems. These robotic collectives may soon serve as persistent, low-impact tools for oceanographic data collection and marine conservation efforts.
- Use of AI/ML for Adaptive Terrain and Current Navigation: Artificial intelligence and machine learning are increasingly being leveraged to enhance robotic autonomy in unpredictable environments. For terrain and current navigation, AI algorithms can analyze sensory data in real-

time to detect patterns, predict environmental changes and adjust movement strategies accordingly. For instance, reinforcement learning allows robots to improve performance over time by learning from trial-and-error in simulated or real-world conditions. Deep learning models can process visual or sonar input to classify terrain types, detect obstacles and identify optimal paths. In aquatic environments, AI can model and predict current flows, enabling underwater vehicles to exploit or resist them for energy-efficient travel. Adaptive control frameworks also allow robots to reconfigure their behaviour in response to sensor noise, hardware degradation or mission changes. The integration of AI not only improves navigation but also enhances decision-making, allowing for dynamic task allocation, obstacle avoidance and cooperative strategies in multi-robot systems. However, training robust models requires large datasets and extensive computational resources, especially for edge computing on embedded systems. To overcome this, transfer learning and online learning methods are being researched to reduce dependency on prior data. As AI capabilities advance, we can expect more resilient and intelligent robots that thrive in challenging, data-sparse environments.

- 3D Mapping and Data Fusion from Multi-Modal Sensors: High-fidelity environmental understanding is fundamental for effective robotic operation, particularly in unstructured or GPS-denied environments. A growing research direction focuses on integrating data from multiple sensor modalities — such as LiDAR, sonar, visual cameras, inertial measurement units (IMUs) and radar — to generate comprehensive 3D maps in real-time. Data fusion techniques combine the strengths of each sensor type while mitigating their individual weaknesses; for example, LiDAR provides accurate range data but may struggle underwater, while sonar excels in aquatic contexts but offers lower resolution. The fused data allows for more robust localization, object detection and obstacle avoidance. Advances in SLAM (Simultaneous Localization and Mapping), both classical and deep learning-based, are helping robots construct dynamic maps even as the environment changes. 3D reconstruction is also essential for tasks like inspection, navigation in cluttered spaces and environmental monitoring. The integration of semantic labelling adds contextual information to the map, enabling higher-level reasoning such as identifying terrain features or classifying obstacles. Real-time processing of such rich data remains computationally intensive, but edge computing, parallel processing and lightweight algorithms are helping address this. Ultimately, multi-modal 3D mapping enables smarter, more aware robots capable of functioning in environments that were once too ambiguous or dynamic to navigate autonomously.

- **Swarm-Cloud Integration for Data Aggregation and Mission Control:** One of the emerging directions in robotics is the seamless integration between decentralized robotic swarms and centralized cloud-based infrastructure. In this model, individual robots operate locally with autonomy while intermittently communicating with the cloud for high-level coordination, data aggregation and mission planning. The swarm-cloud approach enables massive data sharing across units, allowing robots to collectively build global maps, share situational updates and optimize collective strategies. This fusion of edge and cloud computing supports scalable missions involving hundreds or even thousands of agents. Real-time synchronization is enhanced by cloud services that can process large datasets, run computationally expensive models (e.g., for object recognition or prediction) and send back distilled instructions or updates. Additionally, cloud infrastructure can coordinate logistics such as task delegation, resource management and emergency re-routing. The challenge lies in ensuring robust and secure communication, particularly in bandwidth-limited or delay-sensitive environments like underwater or disaster zones. Research is focusing on efficient data compression, fault-tolerant networking protocols and cloud-edge orchestration. With proper integration, the swarm-cloud model transforms distributed robotic systems into a highly coordinated, adaptable force — applicable to everything from large-scale environmental surveys to collaborative construction and planetary exploration.

8.4 ENERGY MANAGEMENT AND CHARGING SOLUTIONS

8.4.1 Introduction to Energy Management

Energy management refers to the process of monitoring, controlling and conserving energy in a system or facility. In the context of electric vehicles (EVs) and smart grids, energy management ensures optimal usage of electrical energy for propulsion, battery charging and auxiliary systems. The aim is to enhance energy efficiency, reduce losses and integrate renewable energy sources effectively. Good energy management improves the lifecycle of batteries, reduces operational costs and supports grid stability.

8.4.2 Components of Energy Management Systems (EMS)

An effective Energy Management System (EMS) includes several components such as:

- **Energy Storage Systems (Batteries):** Energy Storage Systems (ESS) are critical in modern EMS as they store excess energy generated from renewable sources or during off-peak hours for use during peak demand.

Batteries help balance supply and demand, improve power quality and provide backup during outages. Lithium-ion, lead-acid and flow batteries are common types used depending on the application. ESS enhances energy efficiency by minimizing reliance on grid power. They also support grid stability by enabling frequency and voltage regulation. Integration with renewable energy sources like solar or wind further maximizes system utility. Advanced systems can be modular and scalable, offering flexibility for both residential and industrial needs. Proper sizing and management of these batteries are crucial for safety and performance. ESS also plays a key role in demand response strategies.

- **Battery Management Systems (BMS):** A Battery Management System (BMS) is the intelligence behind battery packs, ensuring safe and optimal operation. It monitors individual cell voltages, temperatures and state of charge (SoC). The BMS prevents overcharging and over-discharging, extending battery life and reducing safety risks. It also performs balancing to ensure all cells operate uniformly. Modern BMS can communicate with other EMS components, enabling real-time control and data exchange. Diagnostic features help identify failing cells or abnormal conditions early. In large installations, centralized or distributed BMS architectures may be used. The BMS is essential for performance optimization, especially in renewable and EV applications. Its firmware can often be updated for better algorithms and integration capabilities. A well-designed BMS boosts system efficiency, safety and reliability.
- **Load Controllers:** Load controllers manage the distribution and prioritization of electrical loads within a system. They can shed non-critical loads during peak times to prevent overloads or reduce energy costs. These devices operate based on pre-set rules, demand levels or real-time energy availability. They are crucial in off-grid and hybrid systems where energy resources are limited. Smart load controllers can respond dynamically to price signals or grid conditions. Integration with user preferences and automation systems enhances comfort and energy savings. In commercial settings, load control helps reduce demand charges on utility bills. These systems also contribute to peak shaving and load shifting strategies. Programmable and adaptive load controllers add resilience and flexibility. Properly configured, they ensure uninterrupted power for essential services.
- **Energy Monitoring Tools:** Energy monitoring tools collect, display and analyse data from various sources in the EMS. These tools provide insights into energy consumption patterns, generation levels, storage status and

system performance. They enable real-time tracking and historical analysis for better decision-making. Monitoring can be done at device, circuit or system levels depending on the resolution required. Dashboards present data in user-friendly formats, including charts and alerts. These tools often support remote access via web or mobile apps. Energy audits and benchmarking are facilitated through accurate monitoring. Anomalies such as energy waste or equipment malfunctions can be quickly identified. Monitoring also ensures compliance with energy efficiency standards and sustainability goals. Integration with analytics and reporting systems completes the feedback loop for continuous improvement.

- **Software for Predictive Analytics and Control:** Predictive analytics software uses data from sensors, historical trends and AI models to forecast energy demand, supply and performance issues. These insights enable proactive control strategies that enhance efficiency and reduce costs. For example, the software might predict when to charge batteries or curtail loads based on forecasted prices or weather. It supports intelligent automation by adjusting system behaviour without manual intervention. Control algorithms can prioritize renewable usage, balance loads and extend equipment lifespan. These tools often include machine learning capabilities that improve accuracy over time. Integration with IoT devices and cloud platforms enables scalable and adaptive solutions. Predictive analytics help identify maintenance needs before failures occur, reducing downtime. In microgrids or smart buildings, they play a key role in optimization. Overall, such software is the brain of modern EMS, enabling data-driven, efficient energy management.

These systems communicate with each other via sensors and data links, enabling real-time decision-making for energy distribution and load balancing.

8.4.3 Role in Electric Vehicles

In electric vehicles, Energy Management Systems (EMS) play a vital role in maximizing battery efficiency and overall vehicle performance. The EMS ensures optimal use of stored energy by intelligently managing power distribution between the motor, battery and auxiliary systems (like air conditioning, lighting, etc.). Regenerative braking systems are integrated to recover energy during deceleration and feed it back into the battery, improving range. Real-time monitoring of driving conditions and battery status allows the EMS to adjust power output dynamically. The system also manages charging strategies to extend battery lifespan and reduce energy loss. Efficient coordination between the powertrain and support systems ensures minimal energy waste. Thermal management is included to maintain battery temperature within optimal ranges. EMS in EVs also supports eco-driving modes, enhancing driving efficiency. Additionally, it facilitates connectivity with charging infrastructure for smart charging. Overall, EMS is central to delivering better range, safety and performance in EVs.

The EMS ensures:

- Minimum energy wastage
- Efficient torque and speed control
- Smart energy distribution across vehicle subsystems Moreover, predictive algorithms are often used to estimate range, optimize driving patterns and control HVAC systems to minimize power consumption.

8.4.4 Smart Charging Solutions

Smart charging solutions enable electric vehicles (EVs) to charge in a way that is both efficient and grid-friendly. These systems adjust charging times and rates based on real-time electricity prices, grid load and availability of renewable energy. By charging during off-peak hours or when clean energy is abundant, smart charging reduces costs and carbon footprint. It helps prevent grid overload by distributing demand more evenly throughout the day. Integration with home energy systems or solar panels allows for even smarter, localized energy use. Smart chargers often include communication capabilities (V2G-ready), enabling two-way interaction between EVs and the grid. Users can schedule charging via mobile apps or let the system decide the best time automatically. In fleet operations, smart charging optimizes vehicle readiness and reduces operational expenses. These solutions are essential for scaling EV adoption without straining existing grid infrastructure. Ultimately, smart charging supports a more sustainable and resilient energy ecosystem. Key types include:

- **Scheduled Charging:** Scheduled charging allows EV owners to set specific times for charging, typically during off-peak electricity hours. This helps reduce energy costs by taking advantage of lower rates when demand is low. It also eases pressure on the grid during peak times, supporting overall grid stability. Users can program charging sessions through mobile apps or vehicle interfaces. This method is especially beneficial for residential users and fleet operators looking to optimize energy use. Scheduled charging contributes to a more predictable and manageable load profile for utilities. It also reduces the need for infrastructure upgrades by shifting demand. Integrating with time-of-use (TOU) tariffs maximizes savings. This simple yet effective strategy enhances both user convenience and system efficiency. Scheduled charging is a foundational feature in most smart charging systems.

- **Dynamic Charging:** Dynamic charging adjusts the EV's charging rate in real-time based on current grid conditions, energy prices and renewable energy availability. This ensures that EVs draw power when it is most sustainable and affordable. Charging slows down or speeds up automatically to balance grid demand, helping avoid overloads and blackouts. It enables utilities to respond flexibly to fluctuating energy supply, especially with intermittent renewables. Dynamic charging is often controlled through smart meters and communication protocols between the EV, charger and grid. It provides grid operators with a valuable tool for demand-side management. For EV owners, it enhances efficiency without compromising convenience. Dynamic charging is key to integrating EVs into a flexible, future-ready energy system. It supports real-time energy optimization at scale.
- **Vehicle-to-Grid (V2G):** Vehicle-to-Grid (V2G) technology enables electric vehicles to discharge stored energy back into the grid when needed. This transforms EVs into mobile energy storage units, helping stabilize the grid and support peak demand. V2G allows for bi-directional energy flow, where EVs both charge and supply electricity. It benefits EV owners through incentives or reduced energy costs in exchange for grid services. V2G supports the integration of renewable energy by filling in supply gaps with stored energy. It can also provide backup power to homes or buildings during outages. Successful V2G systems require advanced communication protocols and compatible charging infrastructure. While still emerging, V2G holds vast potential for enhancing energy resilience and sustainability. It represents a shift toward more interactive, decentralized energy systems. As adoption grows, V2G can play a critical role in the smart grid of the future.

These methods reduce stress on the grid and allow integration of renewable energy like solar or wind.

8.4.5 Charging Infrastructure

Charging infrastructure forms the backbone of the electric vehicle (EV) ecosystem, enabling convenient and reliable energy access for EV users. It includes both public and private charging stations, strategically deployed in homes, workplaces, commercial areas and highways. These stations are categorized based on charging speed and technology: AC Level 1 and 2 chargers offer slow to moderate charging for daily use, while DC fast chargers provide rapid charging for quick top-ups. Emerging technologies like wireless (inductive) charging add convenience by eliminating cables. Modern charging stations incorporate advanced energy management systems to handle load balancing, preventing grid overload. Features like user authentication, real-time billing and remote diagnostics ensure efficient and secure operation. IoT and smart grid integration enable intelligent communication and automation across the network. Together, these elements create a scalable and responsive charging infrastructure. As EV adoption grows, robust and smart charging networks are essential for sustainable mobility.

The charging infrastructure includes public and private charging stations, categorized as:

- AC Level 1 and 2 Chargers (slow to moderate speed)
- DC Fast Chargers (rapid charging)
- Wireless Charging (inductive technology)

Energy management at these stations includes load balancing, user authentication, billing and remote diagnostics. Smart grids and IoT technologies are increasingly embedded in modern charging setups.

8.4.6 Integration with Renewable Energy

Integrating renewable energy sources into EV charging systems is a key step toward sustainable and low-carbon transportation. Energy Management Systems (EMS) play a vital role in coordinating energy flow between renewables like solar or wind and EV chargers. Solar-powered charging stations are increasingly common in residential and commercial settings, while wind-powered solutions are being explored in areas with high wind potential. These systems help reduce reliance on fossil fuels and lower greenhouse gas emissions. However, the intermittent nature of renewables requires careful planning, often supported by energy storage systems such as batteries. EMS uses advanced scheduling and load management to ensure stable and efficient energy use. AI and machine learning algorithms are applied to predict energy demand, optimize charging times and balance supply with availability. This smart integration allows EVs to charge when clean energy is abundant, enhancing grid reliability. Overall, combining renewables with EMS supports greener, smarter and more resilient charging networks.

8.4.7 Challenges in Energy Management and ChargingDespite advancements, several challenges remain

- **High Initial Cost of Infrastructure:** Setting up advanced EV charging infrastructure and energy management systems requires significant capital investment. Costs include not only chargers and hardware but also installation, grid upgrades, software and maintenance. For businesses and municipalities, these upfront expenses can be a barrier to deployment. In residential settings, homeowners may be discouraged by the cost of home chargers and electrical modifications. Although operational savings and incentives can offset costs over time, the payback period remains a concern. The expense is even higher for fast-charging networks or smart systems with integrated renewable energy. Financing options, subsidies and public-private partnerships are essential to accelerate adoption. Without broader support, high costs can slow down the transition to electric mobility.

- **Lack of Standardized Protocols:** The EV charging ecosystem still suffers from a lack of universal standards in hardware, software and communication protocols. Different manufacturers often use proprietary systems, making interoperability a challenge for users and operators. This fragmentation affects everything from plug types and charging speeds to billing and authentication systems. It also complicates integration with energy management platforms and grid systems. For fleet operators and public charging networks, the lack of standardization increases complexity and operational costs. As the EV market grows globally, harmonizing standards is critical for ensuring scalability and user convenience. Regulatory bodies and industry alliances are working toward common frameworks, but full alignment remains a work in progress. Standardization will be key to creating a seamless and future-proof EV ecosystem.
- **Grid Instability During Peak EV Charging:** Mass charging of electric vehicles, especially during peak hours, can place significant strain on the electrical grid. Sudden demand spikes can cause voltage drops, overload substations and even lead to localized outages. Without smart energy management, utilities may struggle to maintain grid stability and reliability. This challenge is particularly critical in densely populated areas or during events where many EVs charge simultaneously. To mitigate this, demand response strategies, time-of-use tariffs and controlled charging schedules are essential. Integration with renewable energy and distributed storage can help balance loads. However, real-time coordination requires robust EMS and advanced grid infrastructure. Without proper planning, widespread EV adoption could outpace the grid's ability to handle new demand.
- **Cybersecurity Risks in Connected Systems:** As charging systems and EMS become increasingly connected through IoT and cloud technologies, cybersecurity becomes a major concern. Unauthorized access, data breaches and system tampering can compromise both user privacy and grid stability. Threats can range from simple malware attacks to complex intrusions targeting infrastructure. Smart chargers and EMS platforms collect sensitive data such as user identities, location and billing information, making them attractive targets. A compromised charger or EMS could also serve as a gateway to other critical systems. Ensuring security requires

end-to-end encryption, regular software updates and robust authentication mechanisms. Industry standards and best practices must be followed to minimize vulnerabilities. Without adequate cybersecurity, the trust and safety of smart energy systems are at risk.

- **Battery Degradation Due to Improper Charging Cycles:** Improper charging practices, such as frequent fast charging or full discharges, can accelerate battery degradation in EVs. Over time, this reduces the battery's capacity, efficiency and overall lifespan, leading to higher replacement costs and decreased vehicle performance. Charging habits, ambient temperature and state-of-charge limits all influence battery health. Energy management systems need to incorporate battery-friendly algorithms that balance charging speed with longevity. Smart EMS can optimize charging cycles by recommending ideal charging windows and limiting extremes. Predictive analytics can also identify patterns that may harm battery health early on. Educating EV users on best charging practices is equally important. Addressing battery degradation is essential for maintaining consumer confidence and maximizing the value of EV ownership. Solutions include policy support, incentive programs, standardized frameworks (like OCPP) and investment in R&D for fast-charging batteries.

8.4.8 Future Trends

The future of energy management and EV charging is rapidly evolving, driven by the need for smarter, faster and more sustainable solutions. One of the most anticipated developments is ultra-fast charging, which aims to reduce charging times to just a few minutes—making EVs more convenient and comparable to traditional refuelling. These high-power chargers will require advanced cooling systems and grid support to function efficiently. AI-based energy distribution is also gaining momentum, where machine learning algorithms will optimize energy flow between EVs, the grid and renewable sources. These intelligent systems will predict demand, identify optimal charging windows and even forecast renewable generation, enhancing efficiency and grid reliability. Bi-directional charging technologies, including Vehicle-to-Grid (V2G) and Vehicle-to-Home (V2H), are expected to become mainstream. These allow EVs to not only consume energy but also supply it back to homes or the grid, turning vehicles into mobile energy storage units. This supports grid resilience, emergency power supply and greater energy flexibility.

Another emerging trend is the integration of EV charging with smart home energy systems, where EVs interact with solar panels, home batteries and energy management platforms. This creates a seamless, self-sustaining ecosystem that maximizes energy use efficiency at the household level. Additionally, blockchain technology is being explored for secure, transparent and decentralized energy transactions. Through blockchain, peer-to-peer energy trading between EVs, homes and microgrids becomes possible, reducing dependence on centralized utilities. Overall, these innovations point toward a future where EVs are not just transportation tools but integral components of a smart, green energy ecosystem. As these technologies mature, they will play a pivotal role in accelerating the transition to a more sustainable and electrified world.

8.5 FABRICATION AND COST CONSIDERATIONS

8.5. 1. Introduction to Fabrication and Cost Analysis

Fabrication and cost analysis form a critical foundation in the development of modern energy systems such as electric vehicles (EVs), batteries and solar panels. Fabrication involves the systematic process of designing, selecting materials, manufacturing, assembling and testing components to create efficient, durable and scalable products. It includes precision techniques like machining, coating, moulding and integration of electronics, especially in high-tech systems like EVs and battery packs. Alongside fabrication, cost analysis plays a crucial role in evaluating the total financial investment across the product's lifecycle—from raw material procurement, manufacturing and labour to packaging, transportation and maintenance. Strategic material selection, modular design and automation in fabrication can significantly reduce costs while improving performance and reliability. Additionally, adherence to environmental and safety standards often adds regulatory costs, making it essential to optimize every stage of the fabrication process. For energy technologies, cost efficiency determines market adoption, making affordability a top priority without compromising quality. Lifecycle cost analysis goes beyond production, accounting for usage, servicing, energy consumption and end-of-life recycling. As technologies advance, reducing total cost of ownership (TCO) through innovative design and sustainable practices becomes central to achieving economic feasibility, environmental responsibility and mass deployment. Ultimately, effective fabrication and cost planning enable the production of reliable, affordable and sustainable energy solutions.

8.5.2 Factors in Fabrication

Fabrication is influenced by various technical and economic parameters, including:

- **Material Selection:** Material selection plays a critical role in the performance, efficiency and sustainability of energy and electric vehicle systems. High-efficiency and lightweight materials—such as lithium for batteries, aluminium for EV frames and silicon for solar cells—are favoured due to their superior energy density and structural benefits. These materials contribute to improved range, reduced energy consumption and enhanced durability. However, availability, cost and geopolitical factors can influence their supply chain stability. Recyclability is becoming a key consideration to promote circular economy practices and reduce environmental impact. Sustainable sourcing of raw materials like rare earth elements and lithium is essential. Alternatives such as solid-state battery materials or carbon fibre composites are also under active research. The goal is to strike a balance between performance, affordability and ecological responsibility. Material innovation continues to be a driving force in making green technologies viable at scale.

- **Manufacturing Processes:** Advanced manufacturing processes are essential for producing high-quality, reliable energy systems and EV components. Precision techniques such as automated assembly lines, CNC machining and 3D printing enhance accuracy, speed and repeatability in production. These methods reduce human error and support mass customization. In battery manufacturing, complex steps like electrode coating, cell stacking, electrolyte filling and sealing are highly sensitive and often performed in clean-room environments. These steps are capital- and energy-intensive, contributing significantly to the final cost of EVs and energy storage systems. Quality control is vital, especially to prevent defects that could lead to safety risks or performance degradation. Additive manufacturing is also being explored for creating lightweight and geometrically complex parts. Efficiency in these processes directly affects scalability and profitability. Continuous innovation in manufacturing is key to reducing costs and increasing adoption of sustainable technologies.
- **Design for Manufacturability (DFM):** Design for Manufacturability (DFM) focuses on optimizing product designs to simplify and streamline the manufacturing process. By reducing the number of components, minimizing assembly steps and standardizing parts, DFM lowers production time and tooling costs. This approach helps in cutting down material waste and improving consistency in output. Modular and scalable design strategies allow products to be easily customized or upgraded without overhauling the entire system. DFM also facilitates maintenance and repairs, making it easier and more cost-effective to service products post-sale. For EVs and energy systems, DFM ensures that innovations can be produced efficiently at industrial scale. Close collaboration between design and manufacturing teams is essential in this process. Simulation tools are often used to test design feasibility before production begins. Ultimately, DFM contributes to faster time-to-market, lower costs and higher quality in sustainable technology solutions.

8.5.3 Fabrication in Specific Technologies

- **Electric Vehicles (EVs):** Electric vehicles involve complex and cost-intensive fabrication processes, largely driven by advanced materials and precision components. The chassis and body often use lightweight materials like aluminium and carbon fibre to improve efficiency and range by reducing overall vehicle weight. While these materials offer performance advantages, they significantly increase fabrication costs due to expensive raw material and specialized manufacturing processes. Power electronics—including inverters, converters and motor controllers—are precisely engineered components that require tight tolerances and robust thermal management, contributing further to costs. The battery pack is the most expensive part of an EV, involving intricate cell arrangements, cooling systems and rigorous safety testing. Battery integration also demands advanced battery management systems (BMS) to ensure performance, longevity and safety. Altogether, the combination of materials, precision and safety protocols makes EV fabrication a high-cost, high-complexity endeavour, although costs are gradually decreasing with scale and innovation.
- **Battery Systems:** Battery system fabrication, especially for lithium-ion batteries, is a multi-step, resource-intensive process. It begins with the mining and refining of raw materials like lithium, nickel and cobalt—minerals that are both geopolitically sensitive and environmentally taxing to extract. These materials are processed into electrodes during cell fabrication, where components like anode, cathode, separator and electrolyte are assembled with high precision. Cells are then grouped into modules and packs, requiring robust casings, thermal management systems and electrical interconnections. The final battery pack must undergo rigorous safety testing, thermal validation and BMS integration to ensure reliable operation under varying conditions. Clean-room environments, advanced machinery and skilled labour contribute heavily to the overall cost. Given that batteries define an EV's range, performance and safety, the stakes in manufacturing are incredibly high. Despite this, innovations in chemistry and automation are gradually driving down costs.
- **Solar Panels and Renewable Systems:** The fabrication of solar panels and renewable systems involves high-precision processes and multiple layers of materials and components. A typical solar panel starts with crystalline silicon wafer fabrication, a process requiring pure silicon, high-temperature furnaces and precision cutting. These wafers are then treated with anti-reflective coatings to improve light absorption and sealed with glass lamination to protect against weather and damage. While the panel itself is the most visible part, the Balance of System (BOS) components add

substantial complexity and cost. These include inverters (for converting DC to AC), wiring, mounting structures and monitoring systems. BOS components must be carefully selected and integrated to ensure system efficiency, safety and durability. Installation and maintenance add to total lifecycle costs. As with EVs and batteries, solar systems benefit from economies of scale and improved manufacturing technologies, gradually improving affordability and performance.

8.5.4 Cost Components

Cost considerations are broadly divided into the following categories:

- **Capital Cost (CAPEX):** Capital costs represent the significant upfront investment needed to establish manufacturing facilities and production capabilities. This includes expenses for plant infrastructure, machinery, specialized tools and technology acquisition. For industries like electric vehicle production and battery manufacturing, CAPEX tends to be particularly high due to the complexity and precision required. Setting up clean rooms, automated assembly lines and quality control systems adds to these costs. Such investments are often necessary to achieve economies of scale and meet regulatory standards. Capital costs also include the cost of integrating renewable energy sources or advanced manufacturing technologies. While these costs are substantial, they are foundational for long-term operation and competitiveness. Financing, subsidies and government incentives can play a critical role in offsetting CAPEX. Effective capital planning helps companies balance risk and growth potential.
- **Operational Cost (OPEX):** Operational costs cover the recurring expenses involved in running manufacturing plants and energy systems daily. These include energy consumption, labour wages, routine maintenance, waste disposal and logistics such as transportation and inventory management. Optimizing OPEX is crucial for maintaining profitability over the long term, especially in industries with tight margins like EV and battery manufacturing. Efficient energy use, predictive maintenance and process automation can help reduce operational costs. Supply chain management also influences OPEX by minimizing delays and excess inventory. Environmental compliance and quality assurance activities add to operational expenses but are necessary for sustainable and safe production. Monitoring and controlling OPEX enables businesses to adapt to market fluctuations and improve competitiveness. Smart energy management systems further contribute to lowering operational costs.
- **Raw Material Costs:** Raw material costs fluctuate significantly depending on global supply and demand dynamics. Critical materials such as lithium,

cobalt, nickel and rare earth elements are subject to price volatility influenced by mining capacity, geopolitical tensions and regulatory policies. Import dependencies often introduce additional costs such as tariffs, transportation fees and customs duties, further complicating cost management. Securing stable, ethical and sustainable supply chains is a growing concern for manufacturers. Material scarcity can also drive innovation in recycling and alternative materials. Efficient inventory management and long-term contracts help mitigate some price risks. Since raw materials constitute a substantial portion of the total product cost, careful sourcing strategies directly impact profitability. Industry trends towards circular economy models aim to reduce raw material demand and environmental impact.

- **Labor and Automation:** Labor costs vary widely based on regional wage standards, skill availability and labour market conditions. Skilled labour is essential for specialized manufacturing processes such as battery assembly, quality control and system integration. However, labour-intensive operations can increase production costs and limit scalability. To address this, many manufacturers invest heavily in automation technologies, including robotics, AI-driven inspection and automated material handling. While automation reduces long-term labour costs and improves precision, it requires substantial upfront capital investment and ongoing maintenance. A balanced approach often involves combining skilled labour with automation to optimize efficiency. Workforce training and development remain critical to ensure smooth operation of advanced manufacturing systems. As technology evolves, labour roles shift towards more supervisory and technical expertise, impacting cost structures.
- **Environmental and Compliance Costs:** Environmental and regulatory compliance costs are integral to modern manufacturing and energy production. These expenses include meeting emission standards, managing hazardous waste, implementing safety protocols and adhering to industry-specific regulations. Obtaining and maintaining certifications such as ISO, UL and CE involves fees, audits and continuous monitoring, which add to operational costs. Non-compliance can result in fines, legal liabilities and reputational damage. As governments worldwide tighten environmental laws, companies must invest in cleaner technologies and robust waste management systems. Sustainable manufacturing practices may initially raise costs but offer long-term benefits through reduced risk and improved market acceptance. Environmental compliance also influences supply chain decisions and product design. Proactive engagement with regulators

and adoption of best practices help control these costs while supporting sustainability goals.

8.5.5 Cost Optimization Strategies

To improve cost efficiency:

- **Localization:** Localization involves sourcing raw materials and conducting manufacturing processes closer to the end market. This strategy helps reduce transportation costs, import duties and delivery lead times, which can significantly lower overall expenses. By relying on local suppliers and production facilities, companies can improve supply chain resilience, reducing vulnerability to international disruptions or geopolitical tensions. It also supports faster response to market demand changes and enhances collaboration between design and manufacturing teams. Localization can create regional economic benefits, such as job creation and development of local expertise. However, setting up local operations requires initial investments and evaluation of supplier capabilities. Balancing cost savings with quality and capacity is essential. As global logistics face increasing challenges, localization gains strategic importance for cost efficiency.
- **Standardization and Modularity:** Standardization and modularity focus on designing products using common parts and interchangeable modules. This approach reduces the need for custom components, which are often expensive to design, produce and maintain. Using standardized modules simplifies manufacturing processes, lowers tooling and setup costs and facilitates faster assembly. It also streamlines inventory management by minimizing the variety of spare parts required. Modularity enables easier upgrades, customization and repairs, extending product lifecycle and reducing total cost of ownership. Furthermore, it supports scalability by allowing manufacturers to produce multiple product variants without significant redesign. This strategy is especially beneficial in industries like EVs and energy systems where rapid innovation and product diversity are common. Standardization promotes efficiency, consistency and quality control across production lines.
- **Supply Chain Optimization:** Supply chain optimization involves improving logistics, vendor relationships and procurement strategies to reduce costs and increase efficiency. Bulk purchasing of raw materials or components can secure better pricing and reduce unit costs. Efficient vendor management ensures reliability, quality and timely deliveries, preventing production delays and excess inventory. Streamlining logistics by optimizing transport routes, warehousing and order fulfilment cuts unnecessary expenses and environmental impact. Advanced supply chain analytics help forecast

demand accurately, minimizing stockouts or overstock situations. Digital tools and automation improve visibility and coordination among supply chain partners. A well-optimized supply chain reduces working capital needs and operational risks. Overall, it supports smoother production cycles and contributes to competitive pricing.

- **Process Innovation:** Process innovation focuses on adopting new manufacturing techniques and technologies that enhance efficiency and reduce costs. For example, energy-efficient methods such as dry electrode coating in battery production minimize material waste and reduce energy consumption compared to traditional wet coating processes. Similarly, laser cutting offers precision and speed with less material loss than mechanical cutting. These innovations not only lower raw material and energy costs but also improve product quality and reduce defect rates. Automation and digitalization in fabrication can further streamline workflows, reduce labour dependency and shorten production times. Process innovation requires upfront investment in research, equipment and training but leads to long-term savings and competitive advantage. Continuous improvement in manufacturing techniques is vital to meet evolving market demands sustainably.
- **Recycling and Reuse:** Recycling and reuse are central to circular economy strategies aimed at reducing dependence on virgin raw materials. In industries like electric vehicles and energy storage, recycling battery components and other materials can significantly cut costs and environmental impact. Advanced recycling technologies recover valuable metals such as lithium, cobalt and nickel from spent batteries, allowing them to be reintroduced into new production cycles. Reusing components or modules where possible extends product life and reduces waste. Implementing recycling programs requires investment in collection, sorting and processing infrastructure, but growing regulatory pressure and sustainability goals drive adoption. Recycling also mitigates supply chain risks linked to material scarcity and price volatility. By closing material loops, companies can improve resource efficiency, lower production costs and enhance their environmental credentials (Table-2). Cost Comparison: Conventional vs. Sustainable Systems is given in Table-3.

Table: 2 Concise Summary of Optimization Strategies

Strategy	Description
Localization	Sourcing materials and manufacturing locally to reduce transportation costs, import duties and lead times. This improves supply chain resilience and lowers overall expenses.
Standardization and Modularity	Reducing the use of custom parts by adopting standardized components and modular designs across products. This simplifies manufacturing, lowers tooling costs and eases maintenance.
Supply Chain Optimization	Streamlining logistics through bulk purchasing, better vendor management and efficient inventory control. This reduces delays, cost fluctuations and operational complexity.
Process Innovation	Introducing advanced, energy-efficient fabrication techniques such as dry electrode coating or laser cutting to reduce waste, speed up production and lower energy consumption.
Recycling and Reuse	Implementing circular economy approaches by recycling raw materials, battery cells and components. This reduces dependency on raw materials and lowers environmental impact.

Table:3 Cost Comparison: Conventional vs. Sustainable Systems

Parameter	Conventional Systems	Sustainable (EV/Battery/Solar)
Initial Cost	Lower	Higher
Operating Cost	Higher (fuel, service)	Lower (electricity, fewer parts)
Maintenance Cost	Moderate to High	Low to Moderate
Lifecycle Cost	Often higher overall	Competitive with incentives
ROI (Return on Investment)	Variable	Improving with tech advancements

8.5.6 Government Incentives and Policies

To accelerate the global shift toward sustainability, many governments are implementing proactive policies and financial incentives to promote green technologies. These measures aim to reduce environmental impact while strengthening local economies and innovation ecosystems. Key incentives include subsidies, tax credits, reduced GST/VAT and preferential procurement policies, all designed to lower the financial barriers associated with adopting clean energy and eco-friendly solutions. For instance, India's FAME II scheme supports electric mobility through subsidies on EVs and charging infrastructure. The USA's Inflation Reduction Act offers significant tax benefits for renewable energy and domestic manufacturing. Meanwhile, the EU Green Deal channels investment into climate-friendly industries and technologies across Europe. These policies not only reduce upfront fabrication and deployment costs but also encourage local R&D, job creation and industrial self-reliance. By aligning economic incentives with environmental goals, governments play a crucial role in accelerating the green transition.

- Many countries offer subsidies, tax credits and reduced GST for green technologies.
- Examples include:
  - FAME II (India)
  - Inflation Reduction Act (USA)
  - EU Green Deal (Europe)

These reduce upfront fabrication costs and encourage local manufacturing.

8.5.7 Emerging Trends and Technologies

- **Gigafactories for Batteries (e.g., Tesla, CATL):** Gigafactories are large-scale, highly automated manufacturing facilities designed to produce batteries and energy storage systems at unprecedented volumes. Companies like Tesla (USA) and CATL (China) have pioneered this model to achieve economies of scale, reduce per-unit battery cost and secure global supply chains. These factories streamline the entire battery production process—from cell fabrication to module assembly—within a single location, minimizing logistics costs and time. By localizing supply chains and automating production, gigafactories significantly drive down the cost per kWh and improve production efficiency, playing a crucial role in making EVs and renewable energy systems more affordable.
- **Flexible Solar Cells Using Perovskite Materials:** Perovskite solar cells represent the next generation of photovoltaic (PV) technology. They are made using a class of materials with a unique crystal structure that allows for high light absorption and efficiency, while being inexpensive and easy to fabricate. Unlike traditional silicon-based panels, perovskite solar cells can be produced using low-temperature solution processing, making them suitable for roll-to-roll printing on flexible substrates like plastic. This drastically reduces the manufacturing cost and opens up new applications such as wearable solar tech, curved surfaces and building-integrated photovoltaics (BIPV). However, stability and durability are ongoing research challenges.
- **Solid-State Batteries:** Solid-state batteries replace the liquid or gel electrolyte used in conventional lithium-ion batteries with a solid electrolyte, resulting in batteries that are safer, more energy-dense and longer-lasting. These batteries are expected to reduce the cost per kWh by 30–50% due to higher efficiency, less need for complex battery management systems (BMS) and potential use of cheaper materials. Additionally, solid-state batteries are more compact and have the potential to revolutionize not only EVs but also portable electronics and grid storage. However,

challenges like scalable manufacturing techniques, interface resistance and cost of solid electrolytes must be addressed.

- **Digital Twins and AI-Driven Manufacturing:** Digital twins are virtual replicas of physical systems used to simulate, analyse and optimize manufacturing processes in real time. When combined with AI (Artificial Intelligence) and machine learning algorithms, they allow manufacturers to predict equipment failures, optimize energy usage, reduce material waste and improve product design before physical prototypes are even made. AI-driven manufacturing can also assist in cost forecasting, quality control and process automation, significantly reducing overall production costs and downtime. In energy system fabrication, such as EVs and battery packs, this leads to better precision, reliability and cost-efficiency across the production lifecycle.

8.5.8 Challenges in Fabrication and Cost Control

- **High Capital Requirement for Advanced Technologies:** Modern energy systems like EVs, battery storage and solar modules require sophisticated manufacturing infrastructure, including precision machinery, cleanrooms and automation tools. Setting up these facilities involves substantial capital investment in land, equipment, safety systems and R&D. The cost is even higher for emerging technologies such as solid-state batteries or perovskite solar cells, which require specialized environments. This becomes a barrier for small and mid-sized enterprises and slows down market entry, innovation and scaling.
- **Global Material Shortages and Supply Chain Disruption:** Fabrication heavily depends on the availability of critical raw materials like lithium, cobalt, nickel, rare earth metals and silicon. These resources are unevenly distributed across the globe and often subject to geopolitical tensions, export restrictions or mining limitations. Events like the COVID-19 pandemic, wars or trade wars (e.g., US-China tensions) have exposed the fragility of global supply chains, leading to delays, price hikes and production halts. Ensuring a stable and ethical supply chain remains a major challenge in cost planning.
- **Rapid Technology Changes Leading to Obsolescence:** The field of energy systems is evolving rapidly, with new technologies, materials and manufacturing techniques emerging every few years. This makes current tools and processes quickly outdated or incompatible, forcing manufacturers to regularly upgrade machinery, retrain staff and discard old inventory. Such frequent changes not only increase cost but also pose

risks to long-term investments, as today's cutting-edge technology could become tomorrow's legacy system.

- **Need for Skilled Workforce and Automation:** Advanced fabrication systems require a highly skilled workforce capable of operating automated machines, handling high-precision tasks and maintaining quality control. However, there is often a shortage of trained technicians and engineers, especially in developing countries. At the same time, automation, while essential for reducing human error and long-term cost, demands significant upfront investment in robotics, sensors, software and training. Balancing human expertise and automation remains a key challenge in controlling fabrication costs.

9 Chapter

APPLICATIONS OF SWARM ROBOTICS

9.0 INTRODUCTION: AN OVERVIEW

Swarm robotics stands at the dynamic intersection of biology, robotics, and artificial intelligence, offering groundbreaking solutions to some of the world's most complex and large-scale challenges. Inspired by the collective behaviour of social organisms, swarm systems leverage distributed intelligence, enabling large numbers of simple robots to cooperate seamlessly without centralized control. This decentralized architecture provides unparalleled resilience, scalability, and adaptability, making swarm robotics ideal for unpredictable or harsh environments. Its applications span a wide range of domains—from disaster response and spaceexploration to healthcare, agriculture, and urban management.

Swarm robotics is an emerging field inspired by the collective behaviour of social insects like ants, bees and termites, where large numbers of relatively simple agents work together to accomplish complex tasks. Unlike traditional robotics, which often relies on centralized control and sophisticated individual units, swarm robotics leverages decentralized coordination, local communication and emergent behaviour to achieve robust, scalable and flexible systems. This paradigm is especially powerful in environments that are dynamic, unpredictable or too hazardous for human intervention. The core principles of swarm robotics—autonomy, scalability, redundancy and self-organization—make it ideally suited for a wide range of real-world applications. From search and rescue missions in disaster zones to environmental monitoring across vast terrains, swarm robotic systems offer a highly adaptable solution. These systems function effectively even with partial failure, as the collective behaviour is not dependent on the success of any single agent. This redundancy ensures resilience and fault tolerance, crucial in mission-critical applications. Swarm robotics also plays a transformative role in sectors such as agriculture, space exploration, military operations, infrastructure inspection and healthcare. For instance, in precision agriculture, swarms of autonomous robots can collaborate to plant, monitor and harvest crops efficiently, reducing labour costs and improving yield. In outer space missions, swarm robots can collectively explore planetary surfaces, construct habitats or maintain equipment in extreme conditions without centralized oversight. One of the key strengths of swarm systems is their ability to dynamically adapt to changing environments and objectives. Through simple rules and local interactions, swarm robots can reconfigure themselves, navigate unknown terrain and complete tasks without pre-defined pathways. This decentralized intelligence reduces vulnerability to central points of failure and allows for real-time problem-solving (Fig. 1).

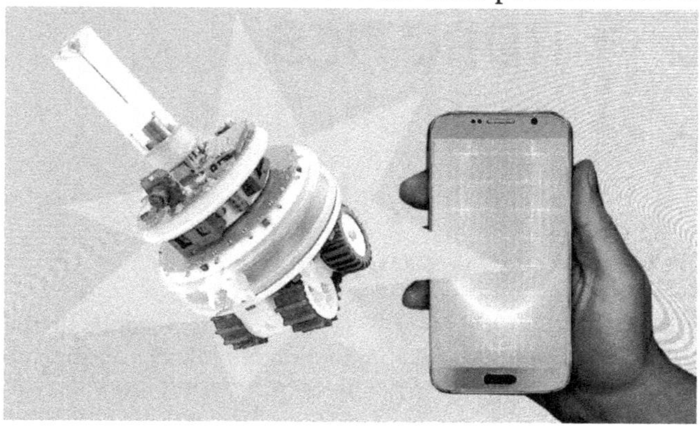

Fig. 1 Real Applications for Swarm Robotics

Furthermore, swarm robotics is increasingly finding applications in urban management and infrastructure maintenance, such as automated traffic control, distributed waste collection and bridge or pipeline inspection. Swarm drones, for example, can survey large areas collaboratively, identifying cracks or weak points more efficiently than traditional methods. These applications highlight the potential of swarm systems to improve operational efficiency while reducing human exposure to risk. In the healthcare domain, micro and nano-scale swarm robots are being developed for targeted drug delivery, non-invasive surgeries and internal diagnostics. These bio-inspired machines can navigate through the human bloodstream to perform precise medical tasks, representing a major leap forward in personalized medicine and minimally invasive treatments. Industrial automation is another promising area, where swarm robots are deployed on factory floors for tasks such as material handling, assembly and quality inspection. Their ability to collaborate, self-organize and function continuously without fatigue enhances productivity and lowers operational costs. Additionally, their modularity allows manufacturers to easily scale operations by simply adding more units to the system. Despite the promising capabilities, real-world deployment of swarm robotics still faces technical challenges, including robust communication in noisy environments, efficient energy management and reliable decision-making in the presence of incomplete or uncertain information. However, advances in artificial intelligence, edge computing and low-power sensors are steadily bridging these gaps. As technology evolves, the integration of machine learning, meta-learning and edge intelligence is enabling more sophisticated swarm behaviours. These advances allow swarm systems to not only adapt but also learn from experience, optimizing their performance over time. Governments and industries are recognizing this potential, with increasing investments in R&D and pilot projects across sectors.

9.1 ENVIRONMENTAL MONITORING AND DISASTER RESPONSE

Environmental Monitoring and Disaster Response are vital for sustainable development and reducing disaster risks. They involve the continuous observation of environmental indicators such as air and water quality, weather patterns and land use changes. This data helps predict and prepare for natural disasters like floods, earthquakes, hurricanes and wildfires. Timely monitoring enables early warning systems that can save lives and reduce property damage. It also supports better planning and resource management during emergencies. Disaster response includes coordinated actions by governments, NGOs and communities to provide relief and recovery. Effective communication and infrastructure are essential for rapid response. Integrating technology like remote sensing, GIS and AI improves accuracy and efficiency. Ultimately, these efforts build community resilience and support long-term environmental sustainability.

9.1.1 Environmental Monitoring

Environmental Monitoring refers to the systematic collection of data over time to assess the quality and health of the environment. It involves tracking various environmental parameters such as air and water quality, soil conditions, noise levels and radiation. This data helps identify pollution sources, detect environmental changes and ensure compliance with environmental regulations. Governments, researchers and environmental agencies use this information to make informed decisions for environmental protection and policy-making. Environmental monitoring plays a crucial role in early warning systems for natural disasters like floods, droughts and wildfires. It also supports biodiversity conservation by tracking habitat conditions and species populations. Advances in remote sensing, satellite imagery and IoT sensors have improved the accuracy and efficiency of monitoring. Regular monitoring helps measure the impact of human activities and climate change. Ultimately, it contributes to sustainable development and the preservation of natural resources for future generations.

9.1.2 Objectives

- Detect changes in environmental conditions.
- Identify pollution levels and sources.
- Provide data for policymaking and planning.
- Predict potential environmental risks.

9.1.3 Types of Environmental Monitoring

- **Air Quality Monitoring:** Air quality monitoring involves measuring the concentration of airborne pollutants such as carbon dioxide (CO_2), sulphur dioxide (SO_2), nitrogen oxides (NOx) and particulate matter like PM2.5 and PM10. These pollutants can have harmful effects on human health and the environment. Monitoring helps detect pollution sources and assess the effectiveness of air quality regulations. Data collected is used to issue public health advisories and guide policy decisions. Advanced sensors and satellite systems now provide real-time air quality information.
- **Water Quality Monitoring:** Water quality monitoring assesses the physical, chemical and biological characteristics of water in rivers, lakes, oceans and groundwater. It includes parameters like pH, temperature, turbidity, dissolved oxygen and presence of pathogens or toxic substances. This monitoring is essential for ensuring safe drinking water, protecting aquatic life and supporting agriculture. Regular testing helps detect contamination from industries, agriculture and sewage. It also aids in managing water resources sustainably.
- **Soil Monitoring:** Soil monitoring involves analysing soil for contaminants, nutrient levels, moisture content and signs of erosion or degradation. This information is vital for maintaining soil health, supporting agriculture and preventing land pollution. Monitoring helps detect heavy metals, pesticides and other pollutants that can harm crops and human health. It also guides the use of fertilizers and soil conservation techniques. Sustainable land management relies heavily on accurate soil data.
- **Noise Monitoring:** Noise monitoring measures sound levels in urban, industrial and sensitive areas to assess exposure and potential impacts. It focuses on identifying harmful noise sources such as traffic, construction and factories. Long-term exposure to high noise levels can lead to hearing loss, stress and other health issues. Monitoring ensures compliance with noise regulations and supports urban planning to reduce noise pollution. It also helps create quieter and healthier living environments.
- **Biodiversity Monitoring:** Biodiversity monitoring tracks changes in ecosystems, species populations and habitat conditions over time. It helps identify threats such as habitat destruction, invasive species and climate change. Conservationists use this data to develop strategies for protecting endangered species and maintaining ecosystem balance. It also contributes to global biodiversity databases and environmental impact assessments. Monitoring is crucial for preserving the planet's biological diversity and ecological resilience.

- **Climate Monitoring:** Climate monitoring involves recording long-term data on temperature, precipitation, sea level, humidity and atmospheric conditions. It helps detect trends in global warming, climate variability and extreme weather events. Accurate data is essential for climate modelling, forecasting and forming climate action plans. It supports international agreements like the Paris Climate Accord and informs national climate policies. Monitoring also raises awareness about the impacts of climate change on ecosystems and societies.

9.1.4 Tools and Techniques

- **Satellite Remote Sensing (e.g., Landsat, MODIS):** Satellite remote sensing involves collecting data about the Earth's surface from space using sensors aboard satellites like Landsat and MODIS. These tools monitor land use changes, deforestation, water bodies, temperature and atmospheric conditions on a global scale. They provide continuous, large-scale data that is invaluable for tracking environmental changes over time. Remote sensing is especially useful in inaccessible or hazardous areas. It supports disaster response, climate studies and ecosystem monitoring.
- **Geographic Information Systems (GIS):** GIS is a powerful tool used to capture, store, analyse and visualize spatial and geographic data. It allows integration of various environmental datasets, including maps, satellite imagery and field data, into a single platform. GIS helps identify patterns, trends and relationships in environmental processes. It supports decision-making in urban planning, disaster management and conservation efforts. GIS is essential for modelling environmental scenarios and impact assessments.
- **Drones and UAVs:** Drones and Unmanned Aerial Vehicles (UAVs) offer high-resolution, real-time aerial imagery and data collection. They are ideal for monitoring small-scale areas like forests, coastlines and agricultural lands. Drones can assess damage after disasters, track wildlife and detect illegal activities like logging or mining. They provide flexibility, reduce monitoring costs and can access remote or dangerous locations. Equipped with sensors, they gather data on temperature, vegetation, pollution and more.
- **Internet of Things (IoT) Sensors:** IoT sensors are smart devices deployed in the environment to collect real-time data on parameters such as air quality, temperature, humidity, noise and water levels. These interconnected sensors transmit data to central systems for immediate analysis and action. IoT enables continuous and remote monitoring with high precision. It plays a crucial role in early warning systems and rapid disaster response. The

scalability and automation of IoT make it highly efficient for environmental surveillance.

- **Environmental Impact Assessment (EIA):** EIA is a formal process used to predict the environmental consequences of proposed projects or developments before they are carried out. It evaluates potential impacts on air, water, soil, biodiversity and human health. The assessment includes public consultation and ensures that decision-makers consider environmental factors. EIA helps avoid or mitigate environmental damage and promotes sustainable development. It is a legal requirement in many countries for large infrastructure projects.
- **Real-time Monitoring Stations:** Real-time monitoring stations are fixed installations equipped with sensors to continuously record environmental data like air and water quality, radiation and weather conditions. These stations provide up-to-the-minute information crucial for early warnings and immediate action during environmental emergencies. They are used in urban areas, industrial zones and ecologically sensitive regions. The data supports regulatory compliance, research and public awareness. Their accuracy and reliability make them a backbone of environmental monitoring systems

9.1.5 Types of Disasters

- **Natural Disasters:** Natural disasters are extreme events caused by natural processes of the Earth, such as earthquakes, floods, cyclones, droughts and tsunamis. These events can lead to massive loss of life, destruction of infrastructure and long-term environmental damage. Effective environmental monitoring helps in forecasting and early warning to minimize their impact. Preparedness, resilient infrastructure and emergency response systems are critical to managing these disasters. Climate change is increasing the frequency and severity of many natural disasters.
- **Man-made Disasters:** Man-made disasters result from human activities and negligence, including industrial accidents, nuclear leaks, oil spills and acts of terrorism. These disasters often cause significant environmental pollution, health hazards and economic losses. Monitoring hazardous activities and enforcing safety regulations are essential preventive measures. Quick response and containment efforts can reduce long-term damage. These incidents highlight the need for stricter environmental and safety management systems.
- Biological Disasters: Biological disasters involve the spread of diseases and organisms that can harm humans, animals and crops—examples include

epidemics, pandemics and infestations. They can be triggered by pathogens like viruses, bacteria or invasive species disrupting ecosystems. Environmental monitoring helps detect early signs of outbreaks through water quality, air sampling and vector surveillance. Preparedness includes vaccination, sanitation and rapid public health response. Global coordination is vital to control large-scale biological threats (Fig. 2).

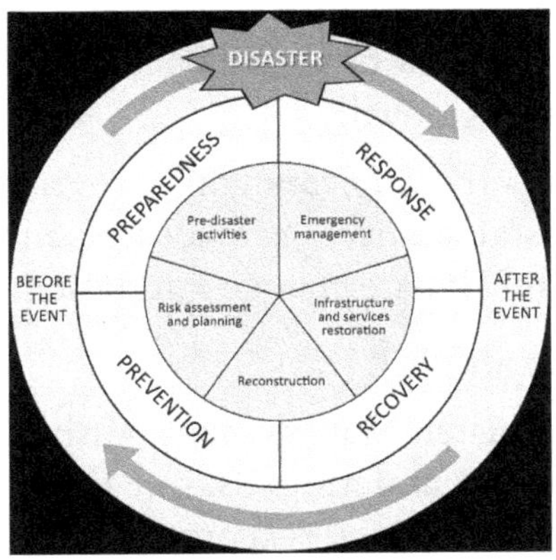

Fig.2 Disaster management cycle

9.1.6 Role of Technology in Monitoring and Response

- Satellite and Remote Sensing provide real-time imaging that is crucial for disaster management activities such as flood mapping, detecting forest fires and monitoring land-use changes. These technologies allow for wide-area surveillance and early identification of environmental hazards.
- GIS (Geographic Information Systems) plays a vital role in mapping disaster-prone and affected zones, helping authorities plan evacuation routes and allocate resources efficiently. It provides layered data visualization for better situational awareness during crises.
- Early Warning Systems, including earthquake sensors, cyclone alerts and tsunami buoys, offer critical lead time to take protective measures and evacuate vulnerable populations. These systems save lives by triggering timely emergency responses.
- Drones and UAVs are used to assess damage in disaster-hit areas and provide high-resolution imagery for rescue planning. They are also effective in delivering emergency supplies to remote or inaccessible regions where traditional methods fail.
- AI and Big Data technologies help predict the likelihood of disasters by analysing vast amounts of historical and real-time environmental data. These tools can identify patterns and trends, supporting faster decision-making and risk reduction strategies.

9.1.7 Institutional Framework

International Organizations:

- UNDRR (United Nations Office for Disaster Risk Reduction) leads global efforts in reducing disaster risks and building resilient communities through policy guidance, awareness and international cooperation.
- WMO (World Meteorological Organization) provides authoritative weather, climate and water-related data, supporting early warning systems and forecasting capabilities globally.
- UNEP (United Nations Environment Programme) focuses on global environmental sustainability, promoting environmental monitoring, pollution control and climate change mitigation.

National Bodies (India Example):

- NDMA (National Disaster Management Authority) is the apex body in India responsible for formulating disaster management policies, ensuring preparedness and coordinating response activities during emergencies.
- IMD (India Meteorological Department) provides weather forecasts, cyclone warnings and climate data essential for early warning and disaster risk management.
- NDRF (National Disaster Response Force) is a specialized force trained for quick response to natural and man-made disasters, including rescue, relief and recovery operations.
- CPCB (Central Pollution Control Board) monitors air and water quality across India and enforces environmental regulations to reduce pollution and ensure ecological balance.

9.1.8 Case Studies

- **Indian Ocean Tsunami (2004):** The 2004 tsunami caused massive destruction across several countries, with over 230,000 lives lost. A major factor in the scale of devastation was the absence of an early warning system in the Indian Ocean region. This tragedy led to the establishment of the Indian Ocean Tsunami Warning System (IOTWS) and improved international cooperation in disaster preparedness. Regional governments began investing in seismic monitoring and community awareness. It highlighted the critical need for global coordination in early warning mechanisms.
- **Uttarakhand Floods (2013):** Heavy rainfall triggered devastating floods and landslides in Uttarakhand, causing severe loss of life and property. Remote sensing and satellite imagery played a vital role in assessing the extent of damage and guiding relief efforts. The disaster emphasized the

importance of real-time monitoring of river levels and better management of hydroelectric projects. It also underlined the vulnerability of ecologically sensitive zones and the need for sustainable development in hilly terrains.

- **Bhopal Gas Tragedy (1984):** One of the world's worst industrial disasters, the Bhopal gas leak exposed severe gaps in industrial safety and environmental monitoring. Thousands lost their lives due to the release of toxic methyl isocyanate gas from a pesticide plant. The tragedy highlighted the urgent need for stricter environmental regulations, corporate accountability and rapid emergency response systems. It remains a stark reminder of the dangers of negligence in hazardous industries.

9.1.9 Challenges

- Inadequate infrastructure in rural and remote areas.
- Lack of trained personnel.
- Data inaccessibility and fragmentation.
- Coordination gaps between agencies.
- Public unawareness and misinformation.

9.1.10. Recommendations and Way Forward

- Strengthening real-time monitoring systems.
- Integrating disaster risk reduction in development planning.
- Promoting community-based disaster preparedness.
- Enhancing international cooperation.
- Investing in advanced technologies (AI, ML, IoT).

9.2 PRECISION AGRICULTURE AND LIVESTOCK MANAGEMENT

Precision agriculture is a farming management concept that uses digital technology to monitor and optimize agricultural production processes. The goal is to ensure efficiency, sustainability and increased productivity by tailoring interventions to specific locations, times and crop/livestock needs.

9.2.1 Core Technologies in Precision Agriculture

- Global Positioning System (GPS) is used in precision agriculture to map fields accurately, guide machinery and track equipment movements. This allows for efficient planting, fertilizing and harvesting, reducing input waste and improving productivity.
- Geographic Information Systems (GIS) analyze spatial and temporal variability within fields, enabling farmers to apply site-specific treatments and manage land more effectively.

- Remote Sensing through satellites and drones provides valuable imagery for monitoring crop health, detecting stress, assessing soil conditions and optimizing irrigation. It supports timely interventions and better resource management.
- Internet of Things (IoT) integrates sensors in fields to collect real-time data on key parameters like soil moisture, temperature and nutrient levels. This data feeds into smart farming systems for automated and responsive decision-making.
- Big Data Analytics and Artificial Intelligence (AI) process massive datasets from these technologies to predict crop diseases, forecast yields and optimize farming practices. AI-driven insights help farmers make informed, data-backed decisions for sustainable agriculture.

9.2.2 Benefits of Precision Agriculture

- **Increased Productivity:** By precisely optimizing planting, fertilizing and irrigation, precision agriculture boosts crop yields and resource efficiency.
- **Cost Efficiency:** It reduces the use of unnecessary inputs like fertilizers, water and pesticides, lowering overall costs and minimizing waste.
- **Environmental Sustainability:** Targeted application minimizes chemical overuse, helping to preserve soil health and protect surrounding ecosystems.
- **Real-Time Decision Making:** Continuous monitoring allows farmers to respond quickly to changing field conditions, improving crop management and reducing risks.

9.2.3 Introduction to Precision Livestock Management

Precision Livestock Farming (PLF) is an advanced approach that utilizes technology to monitor and manage livestock at the individual or group level. It integrates tools like sensors, wearable devices, cameras and data analytics to continuously track animal behaviour, health, reproduction and feeding patterns. The goal is to enhance productivity while ensuring the welfare and ethical treatment of animals. Real-time data allows farmers to detect illnesses early, reduce antibiotic use and optimize nutrition. PLF also supports sustainable farming by minimizing waste, improving feed efficiency and reducing the environmental footprint of livestock operations. Automated systems reduce labour demands and improve consistency in animal care. The data-driven approach enables informed decision-making and improves traceability across the supply chain. As consumer demand grows for ethically produced animal products, PLF plays a crucial role in aligning production with welfare standards. Ultimately, it combines animal science and smart farming to ensure both economic viability and environmental responsibility.

9.2.4 Technologies in Livestock Management

- **Wearable Sensors & RFID Tags:** Wearable sensors and RFID (Radio Frequency Identification) tags are used to monitor individual animals' movement, location and health in real time. These devices can detect abnormal behaviours, such as reduced movement or feeding, which may indicate illness or stress. RFID tags also assist in identifying and tracking animals across large herds. This improves farm management, biosecurity and traceability. The continuous monitoring helps in early diagnosis and timely intervention.
- **Automated Feeding Systems:** Automated feeding systems deliver precise amounts of feed tailored to each animal's age, weight and health status. These systems use sensors and data to adjust feed composition and timing, ensuring optimal nutrition. This reduces feed waste and enhances growth rates and milk or meat production. It also ensures that animals get consistent and balanced diets without overfeeding. Automation improves efficiency and reduces manual labour on farms.
- **Climate-Controlled Housing:** Climate-controlled systems regulate temperature, humidity and ventilation within animal housing to maintain ideal living conditions. These systems are especially important in extreme climates where animals may suffer from heat stress or cold-related illnesses. Proper housing conditions improve animal comfort, health and productivity. Sensors continuously adjust environmental conditions based on real-time data. This leads to healthier animals and better overall farm performance.
- **Image and Sound Recognition:** Advanced cameras and microphones use AI-based image and sound recognition to monitor animal behaviour and health. These systems can detect unusual vocalizations, changes in posture or movement patterns that may signal stress, pain or illness. This non-invasive method provides early alerts for veterinary attention. Continuous monitoring also supports welfare assessment and compliance with animal welfare standards. It allows for more humane and responsive livestock management.
- **Reproductive Monitoring Tools:** Reproductive technologies track estrus (heat) cycles, monitor pregnancies and predict calving events using sensors and ultrasound tools. This helps farmers breed animals at the optimal time and improve reproductive efficiency. Early detection of complications during pregnancy or birth reduces animal mortality. These tools also support genetic planning and livestock improvement. Automated alerts ensure timely veterinary support and minimize losses.

9.2.5 Benefits of Precision Livestock Management

Precision livestock management offers numerous benefits by integrating technology into daily animal care. It ensures improved animal health and welfare through early detection of illness, stress or abnormal behaviour, allowing for timely treatment and reduced mortality. The system enables efficient resource utilization by optimizing feed, water and energy use, thereby lowering operational costs and environmental impact. With real-time monitoring and automated systems, it supports enhanced productivity, leading to better growth rates, improved reproduction and higher yields in milk, meat or eggs. Additionally, PLF promotes traceability and food safety, as each animal can be tracked from farm to fork, ensuring transparency and building consumer trust. These combined advantages contribute to more sustainable, ethical and profitable livestock farming.

- **Improved Animal Health & Welfare:** Early detection of illness or stress.
- **Efficient Resource Utilization:** Optimizes feed, water and energy usage.
- **Enhanced Productivity:** Leads to better growth rates and reproduction.
- **Traceability & Food Safety:** Enables tracking from farm to fork.

9.2.6 Challenges and Limitations

- **High Initial Investment:** Implementing precision technologies requires significant upfront costs for equipment, software, sensors and infrastructure. Small and medium-scale farmers may find it difficult to afford these investments without financial assistance or subsidies. Maintenance and upgrades further add to the expense over time. This financial barrier can slow adoption, especially in developing regions. Government support and affordable tech solutions are essential to bridge this gap.
- **Data Management Issues:** Precision farming generates massive volumes of data that require skilled professionals to analyse, interpret and convert into actionable insights. Many farmers lack access to data scientists or agritech consultants. Poor data integration or analysis can lead to incorrect decisions, reducing the effectiveness of the technology. Ensuring data security and privacy is another growing concern. Training and support in digital literacy and data handling are crucial for success.
- **Connectivity Problems:** Reliable internet connectivity is a basic requirement for operating cloud-based systems, IoT devices and real-time monitoring tools. However, many rural and remote areas still face poor network coverage or no internet access at all. This limits the functionality of digital solutions and delays communication or updates. Lack of infrastructure also affects remote software support and troubleshooting. Expanding rural broadband access is key to widespread tech adoption.

- **Farmer Training:** Many farmers are unfamiliar with modern digital tools, software and automated systems, making training essential. Without proper education, the full potential of precision technologies cannot be realized. Resistance to change and digital illiteracy further hinder adoption. Practical, hands-on training and ongoing technical support are needed to build confidence and capability. Farmer-friendly interfaces and local language support can also enhance usability.

9.2.7 Future Prospects

The future of agriculture and livestock management is rapidly evolving with the integration of AI and machine learning, enabling predictive analysis, early disease detection and intelligent automation of farm operations. Robotics in agriculture will play a major role, with machines performing tasks like automated harvesting, precision milking and feed distribution, reducing labour dependency. Emphasis on sustainable practices will grow, as precision technologies align with climate-smart agriculture to optimize resource use and minimize environmental impact. The concept of smart farms is emerging, where technologies like IoT, drones, AI and robotics work together in a fully integrated system for real-time, end-to-end farm management. These advancements promise to increase productivity, enhance food security and make agriculture more resilient, efficient and environmentally responsible.

- **Integration of AI and Machine Learning:** For predictive analysis and automation.
- **Robotics in Agriculture:** Automated harvesting, milking and feeding.
- **Sustainable Practices:** Precision methods will support climate-smart agriculture.
- **Smart Farms:** Fully integrated farms using IoT, drones, AI and robotics for end-to-end management.

9.3 SEARCH AND RESCUE OPERATIONS

Search and Rescue (SAR) operations are critical, life-saving efforts aimed at locating, assisting and recovering individuals who are lost, injured or in immediate danger. These missions are carried out in diverse and often challenging environments, including mountains, seas, forests, disaster zones and conflict-affected regions. SAR operations are typically coordinated by specialized teams involving trained personnel, emergency responders and sometimes military forces. Advanced technologies such as GPS, drones, thermal imaging and communication tools greatly enhance the speed and efficiency of these missions. SAR plays a vital role during natural disasters like earthquakes, floods and landslides where time is crucial. They are equally essential in industrial accidents, transportation crashes and humanitarian emergencies. International cooperation often supports cross-border SAR operations during large-scale crises. The ultimate goal is to minimize fatalities, provide timely medical aid and ensure the safety and recovery of affected individuals. As disasters become more frequent, SAR operations continue to evolve with smarter tools and global collaboration.

9.3.1 Types of Search and Rescue Operations

- **Urban Search and Rescue (USAR):** Urban Search and Rescue operations are conducted in densely populated areas affected by disasters such as earthquakes, explosions or building collapses. These missions involve locating survivors trapped under debris, stabilizing structures and providing emergency medical care. USAR teams are equipped with tools like thermal imaging cameras, acoustic sensors and search dogs. Coordination with local emergency services is critical for quick response. Specialized training in confined space rescue and debris navigation is essential. These operations are time-sensitive and require rapid deployment to save lives.
- **Mountain and Wilderness SAR:** Mountain and wilderness SAR operations are carried out in remote, rugged or forested terrains where individuals may be lost, injured or stranded. Rescuers often face extreme weather, difficult terrain and limited access, requiring advanced navigation and survival skills. Helicopters, drones and GPS devices are commonly used to locate victims. Teams may include mountaineers, medics and canine units trained for backcountry environments. These missions often involve long durations and high physical demands. Timely action is crucial to prevent hypothermia, dehydration or worsening injuries.
- **Maritime Search and Rescue:** Maritime SAR focuses on rescuing individuals in distress at sea, including sailors, fishermen and passengers of capsized or sinking vessels. Operations are coordinated by coast guards, naval forces or maritime rescue coordination centres. They often involve the use of helicopters, lifeboats and surveillance aircraft. Harsh weather, strong currents and limited visibility make these missions challenging. Communication with vessels and nearby ports is vital for effective response. These rescues are crucial for saving lives during shipwrecks, offshore accidents or severe storms.
- **Air Search and Rescue:** Air SAR operations aim to locate and rescue downed aircraft, lost pilots or missing passengers in both civil and military aviation incidents. These missions require aerial reconnaissance, radar tracking and ground coordination to identify crash sites. Often conducted in remote

or mountainous regions, air SAR involves helicopters, drones and rescue planes. Teams may parachute into inaccessible areas to reach survivors. Weather and terrain significantly affect search visibility and access. Quick response is essential to treat injuries and prevent further loss of life.

- **Combat Search and Rescue (CSAR):** Combat Search and Rescue is a specialized military operation designed to recover personnel isolated behind enemy lines or in hostile territories. These missions are high-risk and involve coordination between air, ground and special forces units. Stealth, speed and advanced intelligence are critical for success. Equipment includes armoured vehicles, helicopters, night-vision gear and encrypted communication systems. CSAR teams are trained to extract, stabilize and evacuate personnel while minimizing engagement with enemy forces. These operations reflect a nation's commitment to leaving no soldier behind.

9.3.2 Technologies Used in SAR

- **Unmanned Aerial Vehicles (Drones):** Drones have revolutionized SAR operations by providing rapid aerial surveillance in areas that are difficult or dangerous to access. Equipped with high-resolution cameras and sensors, drones can scan vast terrains, identify movement and locate victims with precision. They are particularly useful in mountainous, flooded or densely forested regions where ground teams may struggle to navigate. Drones can also deliver essential supplies like water, food or medical kits to stranded individuals. Night-vision and thermal-capable drones extend operational hours beyond daylight. Their agility and cost-effectiveness make them indispensable tools in both urban and remote SAR missions. Drones reduce risks to human rescuers and speed up search efforts. Real-time video feeds help command centres make quick, informed decisions during emergencies.
- **Thermal Imaging and Infrared Cameras:** Thermal imaging and infrared (IR) cameras detect heat signatures emitted by human bodies, making them crucial for finding victims in low-visibility environments. These tools are effective during night operations, in heavy smoke, dense forests or after structural collapses. Mounted on drones, helicopters or handheld devices, they help locate trapped individuals under debris or snow. IR technology also aids in identifying heat leaks from damaged buildings, helping assess structural safety. Rescue teams can use this data to prioritize areas with higher chances of survival. It significantly reduces the time spent searching manually in dangerous areas. Thermal imaging improves the speed and safety of SAR operations. This technology is especially valuable in disaster zones where seconds matter.

- **GPS and GIS Systems:** Global Positioning System (GPS) and Geographic Information Systems (GIS) are essential for accurate navigation and mapping during SAR missions. GPS helps locate victims and guide rescue teams with precision, even in vast or remote areas. GIS integrates satellite data, terrain maps and environmental conditions to support real-time decision-making. These systems enhance coordination among SAR teams by sharing geospatial information instantly. They also help identify hazards, blocked routes and safe zones. GPS/GIS tools are used to track the movement of rescuers and manage logistics. Their use in planning and executing missions improves operational efficiency. Digital maps allow dynamic updates as situations evolve on the ground. Together, they provide a vital backbone for organized and effective SAR efforts.
- **Robots and Ground Vehicles:** Robots and remote-controlled ground vehicles are deployed in hazardous SAR environments, such as collapsed buildings, tunnels or minefields, where human entry is too dangerous. Equipped with cameras, microphones and sensors, these robots can navigate narrow passages and transmit live data to rescue teams. They are often used in earthquake aftermaths, bomb sites and toxic environments. Some advanced robots are capable of lifting debris or carrying emergency supplies. Their small size and maneuverability allow them to search under rubble or inside confined spaces. Ground robots reduce the risk to rescuers and increase the chances of locating survivors quickly. Certain models can even assess structural stability before human teams enter. These innovations are becoming increasingly vital in modern SAR operations.
- **Communication Systems:** Effective communication is the backbone of any successful SAR mission. Technologies such as satellite phones, handheld radios and mobile apps enable real-time coordination between teams on the ground and central command. In disaster zones where cellular networks are down, satellite communication ensures uninterrupted contact. Advanced systems also allow victims to send SOS signals or share their locations using smartphones or wearable devices. Radio networks with encrypted channels ensure secure coordination in sensitive operations. Apps integrated with GPS can guide rescuers directly to victims. Communication tools also relay weather updates and hazard warnings to teams in the field. Reliable connectivity speeds up response times and ensures that efforts are synchronized. Without it, even the best equipment and trained personnel may be ineffective.

9.3.3 SAR Equipment and Tools

- **Rescue Helicopters and Boats:** Rescue helicopters and boats are essential for reaching victims in inaccessible areas such as mountains, oceans or flood zones. Helicopters offer rapid evacuation, aerial surveillance and supply drops in emergencies. Boats are used for maritime SAR and flood rescues, equipped with life-saving gear and trained crews. Both are crucial for transporting injured individuals to safety or medical facilities. Their speed and versatility make them vital assets in time-sensitive operations.

- **Search Dogs (K9 Units):** Search dogs or K9 units, are trained to locate missing persons by scent, making them incredibly effective in rubble, forests and snow-covered areas. Their acute sense of smell allows them to detect survivors much faster than human teams. K9 units are often deployed in earthquake zones, avalanches and wilderness rescues. They work closely with handlers and can also detect deceased individuals, aiding recovery missions. Their loyalty, speed and efficiency are unmatched in SAR efforts.
- **Medical Kits and Stretchers:** Medical kits and stretchers are essential for providing immediate care to injured individuals during SAR operations. Kits include first-aid supplies, trauma gear and emergency medications to stabilize victims before transport. Stretchers, including collapsible and air-liftable versions, help safely move patients from hazardous areas. Timely medical support increases survival chances, especially in remote locations. These tools ensure that victims receive care even before reaching hospitals.
- **Cutting and Lifting Tools:** Cutting and lifting tools are used to remove debris, break through collapsed structures and free trapped individuals. These include hydraulic cutters, spreaders, saws and jacks designed for high-stress, precision rescue work. They are commonly used in urban search and rescue after earthquakes or accidents. Proper use of these tools reduces rescue time and improves safety for both victims and rescuers. Their strength and portability are critical in difficult environments.
- **Emergency Beacons and Signal Devices (PLBs, EPIRBs):** Personal Locator Beacons (PLBs) and Emergency Position Indicating Radio Beacons (EPIRBs) transmit distress signals and GPS coordinates to rescue authorities. They are vital for individuals in remote or high-risk areas like mountains or open seas. Once activated, they send location data to satellites, enabling fast and accurate SAR deployment. These devices drastically reduce search times and improve survival rates. Compact and reliable, they are essential gear for adventurers and emergency teams alike.

9.3.4 Phases of a SAR Operation

- **Preparation and Planning:** This initial phase involves developing strategic rescue plans, training personnel and ensuring all equipment is operational. Risk assessments are conducted based on the terrain, weather and nature of the emergency. Coordination between agencies, such as police, fire services and medical teams, is established. Pre-planned response protocols are reviewed and updated. Effective preparation ensures rapid organized action when a SAR mission is triggered.

- **Alert and Mobilization:** In this phase, SAR teams are alerted through distress calls, beacon signals or incident reports. Based on the situation, the appropriate personnel and equipment are quickly mobilized. Time is critical, so rapid communication and decision-making are essential. Teams are deployed to staging areas near the incident site. Mobilization also includes setting up command centres and securing transportation logistics.
- **Search Phase:** The goal in this phase is to locate the missing or distressed individuals using all available resources. Techniques may include drone surveillance, GPS tracking, thermal imaging and search dogs. Search areas are divided into sectors and prioritized based on clues or last known positions. This phase may take hours or days depending on the terrain and conditions. Coordination and real-time updates help optimize the search effort.
- **Rescue Phase:** Once the victims are located, the focus shifts to safely reaching and stabilizing them. This includes providing first aid, assessing injuries and extracting individuals from dangerous or confined areas. Rescue may involve lifting equipment, cutting tools or rope systems in challenging terrain. Rescuers work quickly but carefully to prevent further harm. Communication with medical teams is essential to ensure proper treatment.
- **Evacuation and Recovery:** In the final phase, victims are transported to safe zones or medical facilities for advanced care. Evacuation may involve helicopters, ambulances or boats depending on the environment. Recovery efforts also include securing the area, collecting data for reports and debriefing teams. Post-mission assessments help improve future SAR readiness. In large-scale operations, this phase may extend to psychological support and community recovery.

9.3.5 Organizations Involved

- **National Disaster Response Forces (e.g., NDRF, FEMA):** National Disaster Response Forces are specially trained units dedicated to responding to emergencies and disasters within their countries. Organizations like India's NDRF and the U.S. FEMA coordinate large-scale rescue, relief and rehabilitation efforts. They possess expertise in urban search and rescue, medical aid and logistics management. These forces are often the first responders during natural disasters such as earthquakes and floods. Their preparedness and rapid deployment capabilities are critical to minimizing casualties.

- **Military and Coast Guard:** The military and coast guard play a crucial role in Search and Rescue, especially in combat zones and maritime environments. The military provides highly trained personnel, advanced equipment and logistical support for complex rescue operations. The coast guard specializes in maritime SAR, patrolling seas and responding to shipwrecks, floods and coastal emergencies. Their ability to operate in hostile or remote locations makes them indispensable partners in national and international SAR efforts. Coordination with civilian agencies ensures comprehensive coverage during crises.
- **Police and Fire Departments:** Local police and fire departments are often the first responders during emergencies within urban and suburban areas. Police coordinate evacuations, maintain security and support search efforts, while fire departments specialize in rescue operations involving fires, structural collapses and hazardous materials. They provide vital on-ground manpower, equipment and medical assistance. Their close connection to the community enables swift mobilization. Training and collaboration with other SAR agencies improve overall response efficiency.
- **Volunteer Rescue Teams and NGOs:** Volunteer rescue teams and non-governmental organizations (NGOs) contribute valuable manpower, specialized skills and local knowledge to SAR operations. These groups often assist in community-based rescues, medical aid and relief distribution. Many NGOs provide training and resources to strengthen grassroots disaster preparedness. Volunteers play a crucial role during large-scale disasters where official agencies may be overwhelmed. Their dedication and flexibility enhance the reach and effectiveness of SAR efforts.
- **International Bodies (e.g., UN Search and Rescue Teams):** International organizations like the United Nations coordinate multinational SAR missions, especially during large-scale disasters that exceed national capacities. They provide technical expertise, funding and personnel through agencies such as the UN Office for Disaster Risk Reduction (UNDRR). These bodies facilitate cooperation among countries, share best practices and mobilize rapid response teams across borders. International SAR support is essential in humanitarian crises, conflicts and natural catastrophes. Their efforts promote global solidarity and disaster resilience.

9.3.6 Challenges in SAR Operations

- **Adverse Weather Conditions:** Search and Rescue (SAR) operations often face significant challenges due to adverse weather conditions such as heavy rain, snow, fog or extreme winds. These conditions can severely limit visibility and hamper the use of aerial support like helicopters or drones. Additionally, bad weather can put rescuers at risk and slow down ground movements, making it harder to reach victims quickly. The unpredictability of weather requires SAR teams to be flexible and well-prepared with specialized gear. Despite these challenges, maintaining safety for both victims and rescuers remains a top priority.
- **Difficult Terrain and Accessibility:** Many SAR missions occur in remote, rugged or otherwise difficult terrain, such as mountains, dense forests or flooded areas. These environments often lack proper roads or pathways, making it difficult for vehicles to reach the scene and forcing teams to travel on foot or use specialized equipment. Accessibility issues can increase the time needed to locate and evacuate victims, sometimes requiring technical climbing or water rescue skills. The physical demands on rescuers are high, necessitating thorough training and physical fitness. Overcoming terrain challenges requires careful planning and sometimes innovative approaches to transportation and communication.
- **Limited Resources and Manpower:** SAR operations frequently operate under constraints of limited personnel, equipment and funding. Given that emergencies can arise suddenly and simultaneously in different locations, allocating sufficient resources becomes a major challenge. Specialized tools such as thermal imaging cameras, rescue dogs and medical supplies might be in short supply. Moreover, volunteer rescuers often play a critical role but may lack full-time availability or specialized training. Efficient resource management and prioritization are essential to maximize the effectiveness of the response.
- **Time Sensitivity – The First 24–48 Hours Are Critical:** The initial 24 to 48 hours following an incident are crucial for SAR operations, as the chances of finding survivors diminish rapidly over time. Swift action is necessary to locate victims, provide medical assistance and evacuate them to safety. Delays due to any factor—such as weather, terrain or communication issues—can drastically reduce survival rates. SAR teams must work efficiently, often under intense pressure, to optimize the use of every minute. This urgency demands high coordination, preparedness and resilience from all involved.

- **Coordination Between Agencies:** Effective SAR operations often require the collaboration of multiple agencies, including local law enforcement, fire departments, medical teams, military units and volunteer groups. Each agency may have different protocols, communication systems and areas of expertise, which can complicate coordination efforts. Establishing clear roles, unified command structures and interoperable communication channels is essential to prevent duplication of efforts and confusion. Joint training exercises and pre-established agreements can enhance cooperation during real emergencies. Strong inter-agency coordination ultimately leads to faster and more effective rescue outcomes.

9.3.7 Innovations

- **AI-Powered Victim Detection:** Artificial Intelligence (AI) is revolutionizing SAR operations by enabling faster and more accurate victim detection. AI algorithms analyse images and sensor data from drones, satellites and ground units to identify signs of life or movement. This technology reduces the time rescuers spend searching large areas and increases the chances of locating survivors. Machine learning models continuously improve detection accuracy by learning from previous missions. Integrating AI into SAR enhances operational efficiency and allows responders to focus efforts where they are most needed.
- **Drone Swarms for Large Area Coverage:** Deploying drone swarms allows SAR teams to quickly cover vast and difficult terrains that would be time-consuming or dangerous to search on foot. These drones can communicate with each other to divide the search area, optimizing coverage and reducing redundancy. Equipped with cameras, thermal sensors and communication relays, drone swarms provide real-time data and high-resolution imagery. Their ability to operate autonomously or semi-autonomously ensures continuous operation even in challenging conditions. This technology significantly speeds up search operations and expands situational awareness for command centers.
- **Wearable Emergency Transmitters:** Wearable emergency transmitters are small, portable devices worn by individuals that can send distress signals and location data during emergencies. These devices use GPS and satellite communication to provide real-time tracking, even in remote or signal-poor environments. When activated, they alert SAR teams immediately, drastically reducing response times. Integration with smartphones and other wearable tech increases accessibility and usability. This innovation empowers at-risk populations like hikers, climbers and remote workers to call for help quickly and reliably.

- **Real-time Mapping and Analytics:** Real-time mapping and data analytics have transformed SAR operations by offering up-to-date visualizations of search areas and victim locations. Advanced Geographic Information Systems (GIS) integrate data from various sources, such as drones, satellites and ground teams, to create dynamic maps. Analytics tools help prioritize search zones based on terrain, weather and last known positions of victims. Command centers can make informed decisions rapidly, optimizing resource deployment and improving overall mission effectiveness. These technologies enhance coordination and situational awareness throughout the operation.
- **Virtual and Augmented Reality for Training:** Virtual Reality (VR) and Augmented Reality (AR) provide immersive, realistic training environments for SAR personnel without the risks or costs of field exercises. Trainees can experience a wide range of scenarios, including natural disasters, urban rescues and technical extractions, with real-time feedback and performance analysis. AR enhances on-site operations by overlaying critical information, such as maps or victim vitals, onto rescuers' field of view. These technologies improve preparedness, decision-making skills and coordination among team members. Incorporating VR and AR into training programs leads to more effective and confident SAR teams._

9.3.8 Importance of Training and Drills

Regular Mock Drills Ensure Preparedness: Conducting regular mock drills is essential for maintaining a high level of preparedness among SAR teams. These simulated exercises replicate real-life scenarios, helping responders practice their skills under realistic conditions. Drills expose potential weaknesses in planning, communication and execution, allowing teams to improve continuously. Regular practice ensures that all members are familiar with their roles and can respond quickly and effectively during actual emergencies. Ultimately, consistent drills build confidence and readiness, which are crucial for saving lives.

Training in First Aid, Navigation and Technical Rescue Techniques: Comprehensive training in first aid, navigation and technical rescue techniques forms the backbone of effective SAR operations. First aid skills enable rescuers to provide critical medical support to victims before professional medical help arrives. Navigation training ensures teams can efficiently traverse challenging terrain and avoid getting lost themselves. Technical rescue training equips personnel with specialized skills such as rope rescue, water rescue and extrication from confined spaces. Continuous education and certification updates keep teams proficient and adaptable to evolving rescue demands.

Inter-agency Coordination and Standard Operating Procedures (SOPs): Effective SAR missions rely heavily on seamless coordination between multiple agencies, including police, fire departments, medical services and volunteers. Training that emphasizes inter-agency cooperation helps break down communication barriers and fosters teamwork. Standard Operating Procedures (SOPs) provide a clear framework for roles, responsibilities and workflows, minimizing confusion during high-pressure situations. Joint drills involving all stakeholders reinforce these protocols and improve interoperability. Strong collaboration supported by well-defined SOPs enhances overall mission efficiency and success.

9.4 SURVEILLANCE AND MILITARY APPLICATIONS

Surveillance and military applications involve the use of advanced technologies to monitor, detect, analyze and respond to threats or strategic situations. These systems play a crucial role in national defense, intelligence gathering, border security and tactical warfare.

9.4.1 Objectives of Surveillance in Military Context

- **Monitoring Enemy Movement and Activity:** One of the primary objectives of military surveillance is to continuously monitor enemy forces to detect their movements, deployments and operational activities. This information allows commanders to anticipate potential threats and prepare defenses accordingly. Surveillance systems, including radar, satellites and reconnaissance drones, provide real-time data on troop concentrations and logistics. Keeping track of enemy maneuvers helps prevent surprise attacks and ensures timely counteractions. Maintaining constant vigilance over adversaries is critical to maintaining battlefield advantage.
- **Ensuring Border and National Security:** Surveillance plays a vital role in safeguarding national borders by detecting unauthorized crossings, smuggling activities or infiltration attempts by hostile elements. Border surveillance includes the use of sensors, cameras, patrols and aerial reconnaissance to monitor vast and often remote areas. Effective surveillance strengthens national security by providing early warning of potential incursions. It also aids in the enforcement of immigration and customs laws. Protecting territorial integrity through continuous monitoring is a fundamental military responsibility.
- **Intelligence Gathering and Reconnaissance:** Surveillance is essential for collecting intelligence on enemy capabilities, intentions and weaknesses. Reconnaissance missions gather critical information about terrain, infrastructure and enemy installations that influence military decision-making. This intelligence supports the development of detailed operational

plans and the identification of high-value targets. Surveillance tools like signals interception, imagery analysis and human intelligence complement each other to create a comprehensive picture. Accurate intelligence reduces uncertainties and enhances mission success rates.

- **Supporting Strategic and Tactical Planning:** The data obtained from surveillance activities directly supports both strategic-level and tactical-level military planning. Strategically, it informs policymakers about broader security threats and force posturing. Tactically, it assists commanders on the ground by providing situational awareness, targeting information and updates on changing battlefield conditions. Real-time surveillance feedback enables rapid adjustments to plans, maximizing effectiveness. Integration of surveillance intelligence into planning processes is critical for informed and adaptive operations.
- **Counter-terrorism and Anti-insurgency Operations:** Surveillance is a cornerstone in counter-terrorism and anti-insurgency efforts by helping identify, track and disrupt hostile networks and activities. Monitoring communications, movements and gatherings of suspected terrorists or insurgents enables timely interventions. Surveillance technologies also support covert operations and the protection of civilian populations. These operations often require specialized surveillance methods tailored to urban environments and asymmetrical threats. Persistent surveillance helps dismantle hostile groups before they can carry out attacks.

9.4.2 Types of Military Surveillance

- **Aerial Surveillance:** Aerial surveillance employs drones, helicopters and manned aircraft to observe enemy movements, terrain features and specific targets from above. These platforms provide flexibility and rapid deployment, covering areas that might be difficult or dangerous to access on the ground. Equipped with cameras, infrared sensors and radar, aerial units can conduct day-and-night operations. Drones, in particular, offer cost-effective, persistent monitoring without risking pilot lives. This type of surveillance is critical for real-time intelligence and battlefield awareness.
- **Satellite Surveillance:** Satellite surveillance utilizes orbiting satellites equipped with high-resolution cameras and sensors to monitor large geographic areas over extended periods. It allows military forces to track troop deployments, infrastructure changes and logistical movements across borders and remote regions. Satellites provide strategic-level intelligence, offering broad perspectives impossible to obtain from ground or aerial means alone. They can operate in all weather conditions and gather data

continuously, making them invaluable for long-term surveillance and reconnaissance missions.

- **Ground Surveillance:** Ground surveillance involves the use of radar systems, motion detectors, cameras and sometimes human patrols to monitor borders, military bases and critical infrastructure. It is particularly effective for detecting unauthorized intrusions and suspicious activities in fixed or controlled areas. Ground sensors can alert forces to movements in remote or difficult terrain, providing early warnings. Integration with other surveillance types enhances situational awareness. Ground surveillance remains vital for maintaining security in sensitive or high-risk zones.
- **Naval Surveillance:** Naval surveillance focuses on monitoring maritime environments to detect and track surface and underwater threats. Tools include sonar systems for underwater detection, radar for tracking surface vessels and underwater drones for reconnaissance and mine detection. These capabilities protect naval assets, shipping lanes and coastal regions from hostile submarines, ships or underwater mines. Maritime surveillance supports both defensive and offensive naval operations. It is essential for maintaining control over critical waterways and ensuring maritime security.
- **Cyber Surveillance:** Cyber surveillance involves monitoring digital communications, internet traffic and network activity to identify cyber threats, espionage and hacking attempts. It plays a crucial role in protecting military networks, gathering intelligence on adversaries' cyber capabilities and disrupting hostile cyber operations. Advanced software tools and algorithms analyse vast amounts of data in real-time, identifying suspicious patterns and intrusions. Cyber surveillance is increasingly important in modern warfare, where cyberattacks can disrupt command and control systems or critical infrastructure.

9.4.3 Technologies in Surveillance and Military Operations

- **Unmanned Aerial Vehicles (UAVs)/Drones:** UAVs, commonly known as drones, have become indispensable tools in modern military surveillance and operations. They provide real-time video feeds for reconnaissance, allowing forces to monitor enemy positions without exposing personnel to danger. Beyond observation, armed drones can carry out precise targeted strikes, minimizing collateral damage. Their versatility and relatively low operational cost make them valuable for both intelligence gathering and combat missions. Drones also enhance battlefield awareness by operating in hostile or inaccessible areas.

- **Radar and Sonar Systems:** Radar systems are crucial for detecting and tracking aircraft, vehicles and ships by emitting radio waves and analysing their reflections. Sonar systems, on the other hand, use sound waves to detect submarines and underwater objects. Both technologies enable early warning and situational awareness in air, land and maritime domains. Advances in radar and sonar have improved detection range, accuracy and the ability to identify stealthy or fast-moving targets. These systems form the backbone of surveillance in military defence.
- **Thermal and Infrared Imaging:** Thermal and infrared imaging technologies allow military forces to see heat signatures emitted by people, vehicles or equipment. This capability is essential for night operations or in conditions with poor visibility such as smoke, fog or dense foliage. Thermal sensors can detect hidden enemies or equipment that would otherwise be invisible to the naked eye or conventional cameras. These imaging technologies enhance target identification and threat assessment, increasing the effectiveness of surveillance and combat missions under challenging conditions.
- **Artificial Intelligence and Machine Learning:** AI and machine learning are transforming military surveillance by automating data analysis, pattern recognition and threat prediction. These technologies process vast amounts of sensor data, identifying anomalies or suspicious behaviours faster than human analysts. Predictive analytics help anticipate enemy movements or potential attacks, enabling proactive responses. AI also supports decision-making by providing actionable insights and prioritizing information. The integration of AI enhances efficiency, reduces human error and strengthens situational awareness on the battlefield.
- **Satellite Communication and GPS:** Satellite communication systems provide secure, reliable and long-range data transmission essential for coordinating military operations globally. GPS technology enables precise real-time tracking of troops, vehicles and equipment, improving navigation and operational planning. Together, these technologies facilitate seamless communication between units, command centers and allied forces, even in remote or hostile environments. Satellite links are vital for command and control, intelligence sharing and emergency response coordination in modern warfare.
- **Robotics and Autonomous Systems:** Robotics and autonomous systems are increasingly deployed in military operations for tasks such as bomb disposal, perimeter surveillance and combat support. These systems can operate in hazardous environments, reducing risk to human personnel. Autonomous

ground vehicles and drones can conduct patrols, gather intelligence or even engage targets with minimal human intervention. Advances in robotics improve precision, endurance and operational flexibility. Their integration into military strategy enhances force multiplication and operational safety.

9.4.4 Weapons Systems with Integrated Surveillance

- **Smart Missiles and Guided Bombs:** Modern smart missiles and precision-guided bombs incorporate GPS, laser guidance and advanced imaging systems to accurately strike targets with minimal collateral damage. These weapons rely on real-time data and surveillance inputs to adjust their flight paths and improve targeting accuracy. Some systems are equipped with onboard sensors and cameras that verify targets before impact. Integration of surveillance enhances mission effectiveness and reduces the risk to non-combatants. These weapons are key components in surgical strikes and high-value target elimination.
- **Combat Drones:** Combat drones are dual-purpose platforms that combine advanced surveillance capabilities with offensive firepower. Equipped with high-resolution cameras, infrared sensors and data links, they perform real-time reconnaissance over enemy territory. Simultaneously, they can be armed with missiles or bombs for precision attacks. Their ability to loiter over an area for extended periods provides persistent surveillance and immediate strike capabilities when needed. Combat drones reduce risk to personnel while maintaining a powerful presence in contested zones.
- **Tanks and Armored Vehicles:** Modern tanks and armored vehicles are outfitted with integrated surveillance systems including 360-degree cameras, thermal imaging, radar and laser rangefinders. These technologies assist in target detection, threat assessment and battlefield awareness, even in low-visibility conditions. Advanced fire control systems link surveillance data directly to weapon systems for faster and more accurate engagement. Some vehicles also share surveillance feeds with command units, improving coordination. These upgrades transform armored vehicles into mobile surveillance and combat platforms.

9.4.5 Cybersecurity and Electronic Warfare

- **Cyber Surveillance:** Cyber surveillance is a critical aspect of military cybersecurity, focusing on monitoring digital systems to detect unauthorized access, cyber espionage and data breaches. It involves the use of advanced software tools and network monitoring systems to track suspicious activity across military and Défense networks. Cyber surveillance helps identify vulnerabilities, trace intrusions and prevent the compromise of sensitive information. In modern warfare, protecting communication, control systems and classified data is vital. This proactive monitoring forms the first line of Défense against cyber threats.

- **Electronic Warfare (EW):** Electronic Warfare refers to the strategic use of electromagnetic energy to disrupt, deceive or disable enemy electronics and communication systems. EW operations commonly involve jamming enemy radar, radio and GPS signals, thereby blinding or confusing their situational awareness and targeting capabilities. It can also include spoofing, where false signals are sent to mislead the adversary. EW plays a crucial role in denying the enemy access to key information while protecting friendly systems from interference. It is increasingly decisive in high-tech combat environments.
- **Signal Intelligence (SIGINT):** Signal Intelligence or SIGINT, involves intercepting and analysing communication signals—such as radio, satellite and cellular transmissions—to gather military intelligence. This form of surveillance provides insights into enemy intentions, capabilities and movements. SIGINT operations support strategic planning, threat assessment and early warning systems. It often works alongside other intelligence disciplines like cyber and electronic intelligence to form a comprehensive information picture. Effective SIGINT can neutralize threats before they materialize and shape the outcome of operations (Fig. 3).

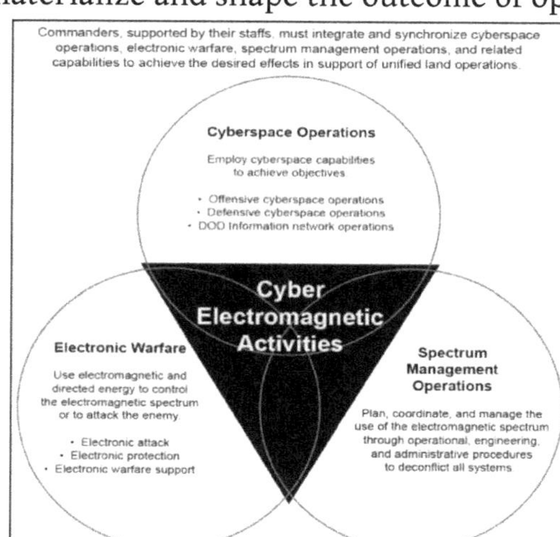

Fig. 3 Cyber Magnetic Activities

9.4.6 Role of Surveillance in Modern Warfare

- **Real-time Intelligence:** Surveillance provides real-time intelligence that is vital for operational decision-making on the battlefield. Live data from drones, satellites and sensors give commanders immediate insights into enemy movements, terrain conditions and unfolding threats. This continuous flow of information enhances situational awareness and allows for faster, more informed responses. Real-time intelligence reduces uncertainty and enables dynamic adaptation during missions. It is a cornerstone of modern, technology-driven military operations.

- **Force Protection:** Surveillance plays a key role in safeguarding military personnel, assets and installations by identifying threats before they strike. Ground sensors, perimeter cameras, UAVs and radar systems detect hostile activity, intrusions or ambushes in advance. Early detection allows defensive actions such as repositioning troops, deploying countermeasures or initiating evacuation. Surveillance also assists in monitoring convoy routes and patrolling hostile areas. This proactive threat detection dramatically improves troop safety and mission success rates.
- **Target Acquisition and Tracking:** Integrated surveillance systems help identify, verify and track high-value targets with precision, reducing the likelihood of errors or collateral damage. Technologies such as thermal imaging, laser range finding and AI-assisted recognition enable pinpoint accuracy in hostile environments. Continuous target tracking also ensures real-time updates on enemy position and status, even after initial detection. This capability is essential for the effectiveness of guided weapons and precision strikes. Accurate targeting increases mission efficiency while minimizing unintended consequences.
- **Strategic Planning:** Accurate and timely surveillance data supports long-term strategic planning by providing insights into enemy capabilities, infrastructure and potential threat zones. It enables military leaders to analyse trends, assess risks and develop effective operational plans. Surveillance also informs resource allocation, troop movements and contingency strategies. When combined with intelligence from other sources, it allows for comprehensive situational assessments. Strategic use of surveillance strengthens national Défense and shapes the outcome of future conflicts.

9.5 SPACE EXPLORATION AND AUTONOMOUS PROBES

Space exploration involves the investigation of outer space through manned and unmanned spacecraft. Autonomous probes play a crucial role by traveling to distant planets, moons, asteroids and beyond, gathering valuable data without direct human control (Fig. 4).

Fig.4 Examples of Robots in Space

9.5.1 Role of Autonomous Probes in Space Exploration

Autonomous probes play a vital role in space exploration by conducting scientific experiments and collecting data in environments that are too distant or hazardous for humans to reach. These probes operate independently, using onboard sensors and artificial intelligence to make real-time decisions without needing constant input from Earth. This autonomy is crucial for missions where communication delays, caused by vast distances, make remote control impractical. By functioning without direct human intervention, autonomous probes enable long-duration missions that can span years or even decades. They significantly reduce the risks to human life and lower the costs associated with manned space missions. Additionally, these probes can explore harsh environments such as the surface of Mars, icy moons or the outer edges of the solar system where human survival would be impossible. Their ability to transmit valuable scientific data back to Earth has expanded our understanding of the universe. Through continuous advancements in AI, robotics and sensor technology, autonomous probes are becoming increasingly capable and sophisticated. They are essential for future deep space missions and the search for life beyond Earth. Overall, autonomous probes are indispensable tools that drive space exploration forward, opening new frontiers and enabling humanity to uncover the mysteries of the cosmos safely and efficiently..

9.5.2 Technologies in Autonomous Space Probes

- **Artificial Intelligence (AI):** Artificial Intelligence plays a critical role in autonomous space probes by enabling advanced navigation, data analysis and autonomous decision-making. AI algorithms allow probes to interpret complex environmental data, detect anomalies and adjust mission parameters in real time. This capability is especially important for deep space missions where communication delays make remote control impossible. AI also helps optimize resource use, such as power management and instrument deployment. By learning from their surroundings, AI-driven probes can adapt to unforeseen challenges during exploration. Overall, AI significantly increases the autonomy, efficiency and success rates of space missions.

- **Robotics:** Robotics technology equips space probes with manipulators and mobility systems designed for sample collection, surface exploration and interaction with extraterrestrial environments. These robotic arms and wheels enable probes to perform tasks like drilling, scooping and analysing soil or rock samples. Mobility systems, including wheels or legs, allow rovers to navigate rough terrains, slopes and obstacles safely. Robotics extend the range and scope of scientific investigations, allowing detailed study of planetary surfaces without human presence. They also increase mission flexibility by enabling remote adjustments and repairs. Advancements in robotics continue to enhance the versatility and effectiveness of space exploration.
- **Onboard Sensors and Instruments:** Autonomous space probes carry a variety of sophisticated sensors and scientific instruments such as cameras, spectrometers, magnetometers and radiation detectors. These devices gather critical data about the physical, chemical and magnetic properties of celestial bodies and their atmospheres. Cameras capture high-resolution images for geological and atmospheric analysis, while spectrometers identify mineral compositions and chemical signatures. Magnetometers measure magnetic fields, offering insights into planetary interiors and solar interactions. Together, these instruments provide a comprehensive understanding of the probe's surroundings. Constant innovations make these sensors more sensitive, durable and energy-efficient for long-term missions.
- **Communication Systems:** Communication systems onboard autonomous probes are essential for transmitting scientific data and telemetry back to Earth. They typically use radio frequency transmitters and receivers, often supported by relay satellites to maintain contact over vast distances. These systems must operate reliably under extreme conditions and ensure secure, high-bandwidth data transfer. Due to the enormous distances, probes rely on delayed and low-bandwidth communication, which necessitates efficient data compression and error correction protocols. Innovations such as laser communication are being developed to increase data rates and reduce transmission times. Effective communication systems enable mission control teams to monitor probe status and receive vital scientific information promptly.

- **Power Systems:** Power systems provide the necessary energy for all operations of autonomous space probes, including instruments, communication and mobility functions. Common power sources include solar panels, which convert sunlight into electricity, making them ideal for missions near the Sun. For deep space missions where sunlight is weak or unavailable, probes use radioisotope thermoelectric generators (RTGs) that generate power through the decay of radioactive materials. Batteries store energy and provide backup power during periods of low sunlight or high demand. Efficient power management systems optimize energy usage to maximize mission longevity. The choice and design of power systems are critical for the success of long-duration space explorations.

9.5.3 Types of Autonomous Space Probes

- **Flyby Probes:** Flyby probes are spacecraft designed to pass close to celestial bodies, gathering valuable data without entering orbit or landing. These missions are typically shorter and less complex, allowing for quick surveys of planets, moons or asteroids. An example is the Voyager missions, which conducted flybys of the outer planets and continue to send data from interstellar space. Flyby probes use onboard instruments to capture images, measure magnetic fields and analyse atmospheres during their brief encounters. Their trajectories are carefully planned to maximize data collection while conserving fuel. Flybys provide initial reconnaissance and pave the way for more detailed missions.
- **Orbiters:** Orbiters are spacecraft that enter into stable orbits around planets, moons or other celestial bodies to conduct long-term observations. By circling their targets orbiters can collect continuous data on atmospheric conditions, surface geology and climate changes over time. For example, the Mars Reconnaissance Orbiter has provided high-resolution imagery and climate data on Mars since 2006. Orbiters carry a suite of scientific instruments that allow detailed mapping and environmental monitoring. They often serve as communication relays for landers and rovers on the surface. Orbiters are essential for understanding planetary systems and planning future missions.
- **Landers:** Landers are probes engineered to touch down gently on the surfaces of planets or moons to perform in-depth scientific experiments. Unlike orbiters or flybys, landers provide a stationary platform for direct analysis of soil, rocks and atmospheric samples. The Viking landers on Mars, for instance, conducted chemical experiments searching for signs of life. Landers typically carry cameras, drills and environmental sensors to study the geology and weather conditions of their landing sites. They face

challenges such as safe descent and stable operation in harsh environments. Landers offer detailed insights into surface composition and processes.

- **Rovers:** Rovers are mobile robotic landers capable of traversing planetary surfaces to explore diverse terrains and perform scientific experiments over wide areas. Equipped with wheels or tracks, rovers like NASA's Curiosity navigate rocky, sandy or uneven landscapes to analyse soil, rocks and atmospheric samples. Their mobility allows them to visit multiple locations, increasing the scope and depth of exploration. Rovers carry sophisticated instruments including spectrometers, cameras and weather stations. They send data back to Earth and often receive updated commands to explore specific targets. Rovers have greatly expanded our understanding of Mars and other celestial bodies.
- **Sample Return Probes:** Sample return probes are advanced spacecraft designed to collect extraterrestrial materials such as soil, rock or dust and safely bring them back to Earth for detailed laboratory analysis. These missions offer the highest level of scientific insight by allowing direct study with sophisticated Earth-based instruments. For example, Japan's Hayabusa and NASA's OSIRIS-REx missions have successfully returned samples from asteroids. Sample return missions face complex challenges including precise landing, sample collection and safe re-entry. They help answer key questions about the origins of the solar system, planetary formation and the possibility of life beyond Earth. These probes represent a major leap forward in space exploration capabilities.

9.5.4 Notable Autonomous Space Missions

- **Voyager 1 and 2:** Voyager 1 and 2 are iconic space probes launched in 1977 to explore the outer planets of our solar system. They provided groundbreaking data on Jupiter, Saturn, Uranus and Neptune, revealing new moons, rings and atmospheric details. After completing their planetary missions, both Voyagers entered interstellar space, sending back information about the heliosphere and cosmic environment beyond our solar system. They continue to communicate with Earth, farthest human-made objects in space. Their success has greatly expanded humanity's understanding of the solar system's outer reaches. The missions exemplify long-term autonomous space exploration.
- **Mars Rovers (Spirit, Opportunity, Curiosity, Perseverance):** The Mars rover missions have transformed our knowledge of the Red Planet by exploring its surface in detail. Spirit and Opportunity, launched in 2003, discovered evidence of past water activity. Curiosity, operational since 2012,

has analysed soil chemistry and assessed Mars' habitability. Perseverance, the most recent rover, landed in 2021 with advanced instruments to search for signs of ancient microbial life and collect samples for future return to Earth. These rovers operate autonomously but receive updated instructions from Earth. Their discoveries help prepare for potential human missions to Mars. They highlight the capabilities of mobile autonomous probes in planetary exploration.

- **Cassini-Huygens:** The Cassini-Huygens mission was a joint NASA/ESA/ASI project that extensively studied Saturn and its moons from 2004 to 2017. Cassini orbited Saturn, providing detailed images and data on its rings, atmosphere and magnetic environment. The Huygens probe detached and landed on Titan, Saturn's largest moon, sending back the first surface images and data about its dense atmosphere and methane lakes. The mission greatly expanded knowledge about the complexity of Saturn's system and potential habitability of its moons. Cassini-Huygens demonstrated the power of combined orbiter-lander missions in deep space exploration.
- **New Horizons:** New Horizons is a NASA mission launched in 2006 with the goal of conducting a flyby study of Pluto and the Kuiper Belt. In 2015, it became the first spacecraft to provide close-up images and scientific data of Pluto's surface, atmosphere and moons, revealing a surprisingly complex and active world. After the Pluto flyby, New Horizons continued its journey into the Kuiper Belt, studying other distant objects and expanding our knowledge of the solar system's outer frontier. The mission showcased the capabilities of long-distance autonomous navigation and data collection. It marked a milestone in exploring previously unseen regions of space.
- **Rosetta:** The Rosetta mission by the European Space Agency was the first to orbit and land a probe on a comet, specifically Comet 67P/Churyumov-Gerasimenko. Launched in 2004, Rosetta entered orbit around the comet in 2014, studying its surface and environment in detail. The lander, Philae, performed the first-ever soft landing on a comet, conducting experiments on its composition and activity. Despite challenges during landing, the mission provided unprecedented insight into the nature of comets, which are considered primordial building blocks of the solar system. Rosetta expanded our understanding of cometary science and early solar system history (Fig. 5).

Fig. 5 The most important space missions

9.5.5 Challenges Faced by Autonomous Probes

- **Communication Delays:** One of the most significant challenges for autonomous probes is the communication delay between Earth and the spacecraft. Due to vast distances, signals can take anywhere from several minutes to hours to travel one way, making real-time remote control impossible. This necessitates the development of highly autonomous systems capable of making decisions independently without waiting for instructions from mission control. Probes must analyse situations, execute maneuvers and handle unexpected events on their own. Communication delays also impact the speed at which data and commands are exchanged, requiring efficient prioritization and compression of information. Overcoming these delays is critical for mission success, especially in deep space exploration.
- **Harsh Space Environment:** Space probes operate in extremely harsh environments that can severely affect their performance and longevity. They face wide temperature extremes, ranging from intense heat near the Sun to freezing cold in shadowed regions or deep space. High levels of cosmic radiation and solar particle events can damage electronics and sensors, causing system malfunctions or data corruption. Micrometeoroids and space debris pose physical threats by potentially puncturing or damaging the probe's structure. Designing probes with robust shielding, radiation-hardened components and thermal control systems is essential to survive these conditions. The harsh environment demands durable hardware and intelligent fault management to ensure mission continuity.
- **Limited Power Supply:** Autonomous probes often rely on limited power sources, which presents a significant challenge for long-duration space missions. Solar panels are effective near the Sun but provide less energy as distance increases and may be affected by dust or shadowing on planetary surfaces. For missions far from the Sun, probes depend on radioisotope

thermoelectric generators (RTGs), which provide steady but finite energy. Batteries store energy but must be carefully managed to avoid depletion during high-demand activities. Power constraints force careful planning of instrument usage, communication windows and mobility operations to optimize energy consumption. Ensuring a reliable power supply is crucial to keep all systems functional throughout the mission lifespan.

- **Complex Navigation and Landing:** Navigating and landing autonomously on unfamiliar celestial bodies is one of the most complex challenges for probes. Without human intervention, probes must use onboard sensors and algorithms to identify safe landing zones, avoid hazards and execute precise descent trajectories. Unknown terrain features such as rocks, cliffs and uneven surfaces increase the risk of mission failure. Probes need advanced guidance, navigation and control (GNC) systems that can adapt to real-time conditions. Additionally, landing maneuvers must account for varying gravitational fields and atmospheric properties. Success in this area is vital for missions involving surface exploration and sample collection.
- **Data Transmission Limits:** Data transmission from autonomous probes is limited by bandwidth constraints and long communication delays. Deep-space probes can only send data at relatively low bit rates due to weak signal strength and distance, restricting the volume of information transmitted to Earth. The long delay also means that data cannot be monitored or corrected in real time. Compression techniques and onboard data processing help optimize the data sent, prioritizing the most valuable information. Communication windows can be short and depend on probe orientation and Earth's position. Managing these limits requires intelligent scheduling and efficient use of communication resources to maximize scientific return.

9.5.6 Future Prospects and Innovations

- **Increased AI Capabilities:** Future autonomous probes will benefit from significantly enhanced artificial intelligence, enabling smarter onboard problem-solving and greater adaptability. With more advanced AI, probes can better interpret complex data, diagnose system faults and autonomously adjust mission plans in response to unexpected conditions. This will reduce reliance on Earth-based control, allowing missions to operate more efficiently and safely in distant, communication-delayed environments. Machine learning algorithms will enable probes to improve their performance over time. Enhanced AI will also facilitate better coordination in multi-probe missions and optimize resource use. These advances will push the boundaries of autonomous exploration.

- **Swarm Probes:** Swarm probes represent a new frontier where coordinated groups of small, inexpensive spacecraft work together to explore space. By distributing tasks among multiple units, swarm systems increase redundancy and resilience—if one probe fails, others continue the mission. These probes can communicate and collaborate to map large areas, perform simultaneous measurements and share data. Swarm technology enables exploration of complex environments, such as asteroid fields or planetary atmospheres, that would be difficult for a single probe. The collective intelligence of swarms can overcome challenges in navigation, data collection and communication. This innovation promises more flexible and scalable space missions.
- **Advanced Propulsion Systems:** Advancements in propulsion technology are crucial for reducing travel time and expanding mission capabilities. Future probes may use ion thrusters, which provide efficient and continuous thrust by accelerating ions, allowing for longer missions with less fuel. Nuclear propulsion, including nuclear thermal and nuclear electric systems, promises higher speeds and greater power output for deep space travel. These propulsion methods could enable faster journeys to distant planets, moons and even interstellar space. Improved propulsion reduces mission durations, which can decrease costs and risks. Continued research will refine these technologies for reliable, long-term spaceflight.
- **Sample Return Missions:** Sample return missions will continue to expand beyond asteroids to more challenging targets like Mars, moons and comets. Returning extraterrestrial materials to Earth allows scientists to perform detailed analyses using advanced laboratory equipment unavailable on probes. These missions face complex engineering challenges, including safe sample collection, containment and re-entry. Future missions aim to bring back diverse materials that could reveal the origins of life, planetary formation processes and potential habitability. Advances in autonomous landing, ascent vehicles and rendezvous techniques will make sample return increasingly feasible. This approach offers unparalleled scientific returns.
- **Interstellar Probes:** Concepts for interstellar probes envision spacecraft capable of traveling beyond our solar system to explore nearby stars and their planetary systems. These probes would require revolutionary propulsion methods, such as light sails pushed by powerful lasers or advanced nuclear propulsion. Interstellar missions must be highly autonomous due to extreme communication delays, potentially spanning decades or centuries. Probes would gather data on exoplanets, interstellar medium and cosmic phenomena. Although still theoretical, these missions

could provide humanity's first direct look at other star systems. Ongoing research into miniaturization, AI and propulsion will pave the way for these ambitious explorations.

9.6 INDUSTRIAL AUTOMATION AND WAREHOUSE MANAGEMENT

Industrial automation involves the integration of advanced control systems, including computers, robots and software, to manage and operate industrial processes and machinery with minimal human intervention. This technology enhances efficiency, consistency and productivity by automating repetitive, precise or hazardous tasks, thereby reducing errors and operational costs. Automation enables real-time monitoring and control, allowing industries to optimize production workflows and respond quickly to changing demands. Complementing this, warehouse management focuses on streamlining the storage, retrieval and inventory control functions through the use of sophisticated technologies like barcode scanning, RFID, automated guided vehicles (AGVs) and warehouse management systems (WMS). Together, these solutions improve accuracy, reduce human labor and increase the speed of goods handling. By integrating industrial automation with warehouse management, companies achieve seamless coordination between manufacturing and supply chain logistics, enhancing overall operational efficiency. This combination also supports data-driven decision-making, enabling better forecasting, resource allocation and inventory optimization. Ultimately, industrial automation and warehouse management drive innovation, scalability and competitiveness in today's fast-paced market environments.

9.6.1 Technologies in Industrial Automation

- **Programmable Logic Controllers (PLCs):** Programmable Logic Controllers (PLCs) are specialized industrial computers designed to control machinery and automate complex processes reliably and efficiently. They monitor inputs from sensors and execute programmed logic to operate machines, conveyors, motors and other equipment in real time. PLCs are highly robust, able to withstand harsh industrial environments like extreme temperatures, dust and vibrations. Their flexibility allows easy reprogramming to accommodate process changes or upgrades. Widely used in manufacturing, energy and infrastructure sectors, PLCs serve as the backbone of many automation systems. They ensure precise control, reduce human error and improve safety by automating critical tasks.
- **Robotics:** Robotics technology plays a pivotal role in industrial automation by performing repetitive, hazardous or precision-based tasks that are difficult or unsafe for humans. Robots can handle tasks such as welding, assembly, packaging and material handling with high speed and accuracy.

They are equipped with advanced sensors and actuators to adapt to variations in the environment and maintain consistent quality. Robotics also enhances workplace safety by taking over dangerous operations, reducing workplace injuries. Collaborative robots or cobots, work alongside humans to increase productivity without compromising safety. Continuous advancements in robotics improve flexibility, intelligence and integration with other automated systems.

- **Sensors and Actuators:** Sensors and actuators are fundamental components of industrial automation systems, enabling real-time data collection and execution of control commands. Sensors detect physical parameters like temperature, pressure, proximity or motion, converting them into electrical signals for monitoring and analysis. Actuators respond to control signals by performing physical actions such as opening valves, moving robotic arms or adjusting conveyor speeds. Together, they create a feedback loop that allows automated systems to respond quickly and accurately to changing conditions. The precision and reliability of sensors and actuators directly impact process efficiency and product quality. Their integration with control systems supports smart manufacturing and adaptive automation.
- **Human-Machine Interfaces (HMIs):** Human-Machine Interfaces (HMIs) provide the crucial link between operators and automated industrial systems, allowing real-time monitoring, control and diagnostics. Through graphical displays, touchscreens or control panels, HMIs present complex data in an understandable format, enabling operators to oversee machine status and performance easily. HMIs facilitate quick responses to alarms, system faults or production adjustments, enhancing operational safety and efficiency. Modern HMIs incorporate advanced features like data logging, remote access and customizable dashboards. They improve collaboration between human operators and automated systems, ensuring seamless interaction and effective decision-making in dynamic industrial environments.
- **Industrial Internet of Things (IIoT):** The Industrial Internet of Things (IIoT) connects machines, sensors and devices within industrial environments to enable seamless data exchange and comprehensive system integration. IIoT networks collect vast amounts of real-time operational data, which can be analyzed to optimize workflows, predict equipment failures and improve maintenance schedules. By linking physical assets to cloud platforms and analytics tools, IIoT facilitates smarter decision-making and enhances productivity. It also enables remote monitoring and control, reducing

downtime and operational costs. IIoT promotes interoperability across diverse equipment and systems, driving innovation in smart factories and Industry 4.0 initiatives.

- **Artificial Intelligence (AI) and Machine Learning:** Artificial Intelligence (AI) and Machine Learning technologies are transforming industrial automation by enabling intelligent process optimization and predictive maintenance. AI algorithms analyse historical and real-time data to detect patterns, predict equipment failures and recommend corrective actions before breakdowns occur. This reduces unplanned downtime and extends the lifespan of machinery. Machine learning models continuously improve by learning from new data, enhancing accuracy and adaptability. AI-driven automation also optimizes production schedules, quality control and supply chain management. Integrating AI with automation systems creates more resilient, efficient and self-optimizing industrial processes that adapt to changing conditions and demands.

9.6.2 Applications of Industrial Automation

- **Assembly Lines and Manufacturing Processes:** Industrial automation plays a crucial role in assembly lines by streamlining manufacturing processes and increasing production speed and consistency. Automated machinery and robots handle repetitive tasks such as welding, painting and component assembly with high precision, reducing human error and improving product quality. Automation allows for continuous operation, boosting throughput and minimizing downtime. It also enables customization and flexibility in production, adapting quickly to changes in product design. Automated assembly lines improve worker safety by taking over hazardous tasks. Overall, automation enhances efficiency, reduces costs and supports mass production in diverse industries.
- **Quality Control and Inspection:** Automation is widely used for quality control and inspection to ensure products meet strict standards without slowing production. Vision systems, sensors and AI-driven software inspect parts and assemblies for defects such as cracks, misalignments or surface imperfections. Automated inspection systems provide consistent, unbiased evaluations that surpass human capabilities in speed and accuracy. This real-time monitoring enables immediate correction of errors, reducing waste and rework. Integration with data analytics helps identify trends and improve manufacturing processes over time. Automated quality control increases customer satisfaction by delivering reliable, high-quality products.

- **Material Handling and Packaging:** Material handling and packaging benefit greatly from automation through the use of conveyors, robotic arms, automated guided vehicles (AGVs) and sorting systems. These technologies streamline the movement, sorting and packing of raw materials and finished goods within warehouses and production lines. Automation speeds up loading and unloading, reduces manual labour and minimizes damage during handling. It also enhances inventory management by tracking items precisely. Automated packaging systems ensure consistent sealing, labelling and palletizing, improving product presentation and shipping efficiency. Together, these solutions reduce costs and improve supply chain responsiveness.
- **Predictive Maintenance to Reduce Downtime:** Predictive maintenance uses automated monitoring tools and AI algorithms to analyse equipment health and predict potential failures before they occur. Sensors collect data on vibration, temperature and other parameters, allowing systems to identify abnormal patterns. This proactive approach reduces unexpected breakdowns, minimizes costly downtime and extends the lifespan of machinery. Automated alerts and maintenance scheduling improve planning and resource allocation. Predictive maintenance also enhances workplace safety by preventing accidents caused by equipment failure. Overall, it leads to more reliable operations and lower maintenance costs.
- **Energy Management and Environmental Control:** Automation systems play a vital role in optimizing energy consumption and maintaining environmental conditions in industrial facilities. Sensors and control algorithms regulate lighting, heating, ventilation and air conditioning (HVAC) to reduce energy waste and maintain optimal working environments. Automated energy management helps monitor usage patterns, identify inefficiencies and implement energy-saving strategies. In manufacturing, automation controls emissions and waste treatment processes to comply with environmental regulations. These systems support sustainability goals while lowering operational costs. Integrating energy management with industrial automation promotes greener, more efficient production facilities.

9.6.3 Warehouse Management Systems (WMS)

Warehouse Management Systems (WMS) are advanced software solutions designed to optimize and control daily warehouse operations. They manage inventory tracking order fulfilment and logistics processes with high accuracy and efficiency. WMS integrates with technologies like barcode scanners, RFID and mobile devices to enable real-time data capture and visibility. This allows accurate location tracking of goods and minimizes errors in stock handling. The system automates key tasks such as replenishment, picking, packing and shipping, improving overall productivity. By streamlining operations, WMS enhances supply chain performance and customer satisfaction.

- Software solutions that manage inventory tracking order fulfilment and logistics.
- Integration with barcode scanners, RFID and mobile devices.
- Real-time inventory visibility and location tracking.
- Automation of replenishment, picking, packing and shipping tasks.

9.6.4 Automation Technologies in Warehousing

- **Automated Guided Vehicles (AGVs):** Automated Guided Vehicles (AGVs) are robotic transport systems designed to move goods autonomously within warehouses. They follow predefined paths or use advanced navigation technologies like lasers and sensors to navigate complex layouts safely. AGVs reduce the need for manual labour in transporting heavy or bulky items, increasing efficiency and minimizing workplace injuries. These vehicles can operate continuously, optimizing workflow and reducing bottlenecks in busy warehouses. AGVs integrate with warehouse management systems to coordinate tasks and improve inventory handling. Their flexibility allows easy reprogramming to adapt to changing warehouse configurations or priorities.
- **Automated Storage and Retrieval Systems (AS/RS):** Automated Storage and Retrieval Systems (AS/RS) are mechanized systems that automatically store and retrieve inventory items from designated storage locations. These systems use cranes, shuttles or robotic arms to efficiently handle goods, minimizing human error and speeding up order fulfilment. AS/RS optimize warehouse space by enabling high-density storage and precise inventory control. They improve accuracy and reduce labour costs associated with manual storage and picking. Integration with warehouse management software ensures real-time tracking and efficient inventory management. AS/RS enhance operational productivity and are particularly valuable in high-volume distribution centres.
- **Robotic Picking Systems:** Robotic picking systems use advanced robotics and vision technology to identify, pick and sort items in warehouses. These robots can handle a wide range of product shapes, sizes and weights with precision and speed, outperforming manual picking in consistency and productivity. They reduce human fatigue and errors in order fulfilment

processes, leading to faster shipping times and improved customer satisfaction. Robotic pickers are often integrated with conveyor belts and automated packing stations for seamless workflow. Continuous advancements in AI and machine learning enhance their ability to adapt to new items and complex picking scenarios. These systems are transforming warehousing by enabling scalable, flexible operations.

- **Conveyor Systems:** Conveyor systems are fundamental automation tools that efficiently transport goods through different areas of warehouses and distribution centres. They reduce the need for manual carrying and movement, speeding up material flow and minimizing handling damage. Conveyors can be customized to fit various warehouse layouts and include features like sorting, merging and accumulation. Integration with automated picking and packing systems creates a smooth, continuous process from inventory storage to shipping. Conveyors improve throughput, reduce labour costs and enhance workplace safety by minimizing manual transport. They are essential for large-scale warehousing operations aiming for high efficiency.
- **Drones:** Drones are increasingly used in warehouses for inventory audits and stocktaking, offering a fast and accurate alternative to manual counting. Equipped with cameras and barcode or RFID scanners, drones can access hard-to-reach storage areas and quickly scan large volumes of inventory. They provide real-time data to warehouse management systems, improving inventory accuracy and reducing discrepancies. Drones help identify misplaced or missing items and support safety inspections by monitoring warehouse infrastructure. Their use reduces labour costs and the time required for inventory checks, enabling more frequent and reliable stock audits. As drone technology advances, their role in warehousing is expected to expand further.

9.6.5 Benefits of Industrial Automation and Warehouse Automation

- Increased efficiency and throughput.
- Reduction in human errors and workplace injuries.
- Lower operational costs over time.
- Improved accuracy in inventory management.
- Faster order processing and delivery.
- Enhanced scalability to meet demand fluctuations.

9.6.6 Challenges in Implementation

- **High Initial Investment and Maintenance Costs:** Implementing industrial automation and warehouse technologies often requires significant upfront capital for purchasing equipment, software and infrastructure upgrades. Beyond the initial purchase, ongoing maintenance and system updates add to the total cost of ownership. Smaller businesses may find these financial barriers challenging, slowing adoption rates. Budget constraints can also impact the scale and speed of automation deployment. However, long-term benefits like increased productivity and reduced labour costs often justify the investment. Careful planning and phased implementation can help manage expenses and maximize return on investment.
- **Integration with Existing Legacy Systems:** One of the major challenges is integrating new automation technologies with pre-existing legacy systems that may lack compatibility or standardized interfaces. Legacy equipment and software may not support modern communication protocols or data formats, complicating seamless data exchange. This can lead to inefficiencies, increased downtime or the need for costly custom solutions. Successful integration requires thorough system analysis, careful planning and often, upgrading or replacing outdated components. Ensuring interoperability is crucial to harness the full benefits of automation and maintain smooth operations.
- **Workforce Training and Change Management:** Transitioning to automated systems demands substantial workforce training to equip employees with the skills needed to operate, monitor and maintain new technologies. Resistance to change from staff accustomed to manual processes can hinder implementation. Effective change management strategies, including communication, involvement and ongoing support, are essential to foster acceptance and collaboration. Upskilling workers not only improves productivity but also enhances job satisfaction by empowering employees to work alongside advanced technologies. Companies must invest in continuous learning programs to keep pace with evolving automation tools.
- **Cybersecurity Risks Related to Connected Systems:** As industrial automation increasingly relies on interconnected devices and networks, cybersecurity risks become a critical concern. Connected systems are vulnerable to cyberattacks that could disrupt operations, steal sensitive data or damage equipment. Protecting automated environments requires robust security measures, including firewalls, encryption, intrusion detection and regular security audits. Employee awareness and adherence

to cybersecurity protocols are also vital. Failure to address these risks can lead to costly downtime, reputational damage and regulatory penalties. Securing automation systems is an ongoing and evolving challenge.

- **Ensuring System Reliability and Minimizing Downtime:** Automation systems must maintain high reliability to avoid costly interruptions in production and warehousing processes. Unexpected system failures or downtime can disrupt supply chains and lead to significant financial losses. Designing resilient systems with redundancy, predictive maintenance and real-time monitoring helps detect issues before they escalate. Quick troubleshooting and repair capabilities are also necessary to minimize downtime. Continuous improvement and regular updates ensure that automation infrastructure remains robust and responsive to operational demands. Maintaining reliability is critical to realizing the full advantages of automation.

9.6.7 Future Trends

Future trends in industrial automation and warehousing are rapidly evolving with technology advancements. There will be greater adoption of AI and machine learning, enabling more accurate predictive analytics for maintenance, inventory forecasting and process optimization. Collaborative robots or cobots, will increasingly work alongside human operators to enhance productivity and safety without replacing the workforce. Autonomous vehicles and drone-based inventory systems will expand, streamlining the movement and tracking of goods within warehouses. Cloud-based warehouse management systems will provide real-time analytics and improved data accessibility, supporting faster decision-making. Additionally, blockchain technology is expected to be widely used for enhancing supply chain transparency, security and traceability, reducing fraud and errors. Together, these innovations will create smarter, more efficient and resilient industrial and warehouse operations in the near future.

10 Chapter

CHALLENGES AND LIMITATIONS

10.0 INTRODUCTION: AN OVERVIEW

Swarm robotics is an emerging and highly promising field that draws inspiration from the collective behaviour of social insects such as ants, bees and termites. By deploying large numbers of relatively simple, autonomous robots that interact locally with one another and their environment, swarm robotics systems aim to achieve complex tasks in a distributed and scalable manner. Despite the potential for high robustness, flexibility and adaptability, the development and deployment of swarm robotics face a range of significant challenges and limitations. These issues span across technological, computational, communication, design, ethical and operational dimensions. One of the primary technical challenges lies in achieving reliable and scalable coordination among robots. As the size of the swarm increases, so does the complexity of maintaining consistent behaviour without centralized control. Moreover, ensuring fault tolerance and preventing cascading failures becomes a daunting task. Communication is another critical hurdle. Most swarm systems rely on limited-range, low-bandwidth, peer-to-peer communication, which can be unreliable in real-world environments due to interference, latency or signal loss. Designing effective decentralized algorithms that allow for robust cooperation despite these limitations is still an active area of research. Additionally, localization and mapping are non-trivial problems in swarm robotics, especially in GPS-denied or unstructured environments. While individual robots may lack advanced sensing capabilities, the system as a whole must still construct and respond to spatial information. Hardware constraints also pose limitations; swarm robots must be small, energy-efficient, low-cost and easy to mass-produce—characteristics that often restrict their processing power, sensor quality and mobility. The trade-off between simplicity and functionality is a fundamental challenge. Power consumption and battery life become major concerns, particularly in tasks requiring long operation times or remote deployment. Moreover, the physical durability of the robots is often tested in rough or dynamic terrains, where mobility and recovery from failure are difficult to manage autonomously.

On the software side, algorithmic challenges include designing distributed control systems that are scalable, adaptive and capable of learning from the environment. Despite the success of many bio-inspired algorithms in simulations, transferring those models to real-world robotic swarms remains difficult due to noise, variability and unforeseen interactions. There's often a significant reality gap between what works in controlled laboratory settings versus unpredictable real-world environments. Testing and validation of swarm systems at scale is another critical limitation. Creating real-time, large-scale experimental setups is resource-intensive and logistically complex. Simulations can model thousands of robots, but they cannot fully replicate the unpredictable dynamics of real-world deployment. From an operational perspective, deploying and managing a swarm in real scenarios (e.g., disaster recovery, agriculture, exploration) requires robust interfaces and control mechanisms, often necessitating some form of human oversight, which contradicts the ideal of full autonomy. Furthermore, ethical and safety concerns are becoming increasingly relevant. Questions about swarm behaviour in populated areas, risk of uncontrolled actions and accountability in case of malfunctions or harm are yet to be fully addressed. Data privacy, surveillance concerns and compliance with legal frameworks also limit where and how swarms can be used. Lastly, cost and accessibility remain significant barriers. While individual robots may be inexpensive, the cumulative cost of producing, programming, testing and maintaining a swarm at scale can be substantial. The lack of standardized platforms and open-source tools further complicates development. As research advances, many of these challenges will be mitigated, but a full realization of swarm robotics in practical applications will require interdisciplinary solutions. This section aims to provide an in-depth overview of these challenges and limitations, offering context for the technical discussions that follow and highlighting the critical areas where further innovation is needed.

10.1 SCALABILITY AND COORDINATION OVERHEAD

Scalability is one of the most significant advantages of swarm robotics, enabling large groups of relatively simple robots to work together and accomplish complex tasks that would be difficult or impossible for a single robot. However, as the size of the swarm increases, the complexity of coordinating these robots grows exponentially. This coordination overhead can create bottlenecks in communication, processing and decision-making, ultimately limiting the overall system performance. Managing interactions among numerous robots requires efficient algorithms to ensure smooth cooperation without excessive delays or conflicts. Without proper coordination strategies, the benefits of scaling up the swarm can be outweighed by increased complexity and resource demands. Therefore, balancing scalability with manageable coordination overhead remains a critical challenge in swarm robotics research and applications. Addressing this challenge is essential to unlock the full potential of large-scale robotic swarms.

10.1.1 Scalability Challenges

- **Exponential Complexity:** As the size of a robotic swarm increases, the number of possible interactions between individual robots grows exponentially. This rapid growth in interactions makes managing communication and coordination increasingly difficult. Each robot must continuously exchange information with multiple neighbours, leading to a complex web of data flows that can overwhelm the system. Decision-making processes become slower and more error-prone due to the sheer volume of inputs and dependencies. Furthermore, the dynamic nature of the environment and robot behaviours adds layers of unpredictability, complicating coordination even more. Without efficient management, this exponential complexity can cause delays, conflicts and failures within the swarm. Researchers face the challenge of designing algorithms that scale gracefully despite this complexity. Failure to address exponential growth in interactions risks limiting swarm size and reducing the overall effectiveness of the system. Thus, balancing complexity and performance is vital for practical applications of swarm robotics.
- **Resource Constraints:** Swarm robotics often relies on small, low-cost robots with limited onboard computational power and energy resources. As the swarm size increases, the demand for processing capability and communication bandwidth also rises significantly. However, the hardware limitations inherent in these simple robots restrict their ability to handle intensive computations or maintain high-frequency communication. Power consumption becomes a critical concern, as frequent messaging and processing drain batteries quickly, reducing mission duration. Communication channels may become congested, leading to data loss or delays, especially in dense swarms. These resource constraints limit the complexity of algorithms that can be implemented and the amount of data that can be shared. Managing limited resources effectively is essential to maintaining reliable coordination and system robustness. Innovations in energy-efficient hardware and optimized communication protocols are crucial to overcoming these constraints and enabling larger swarms.
- **Algorithmic Limitations:** Many of the control algorithms developed for swarm robotics work well for small to medium-sized groups but struggle to maintain performance at scale. As the number of robots increases into the hundreds or thousands, these algorithms can become inefficient or unstable. Challenges include ensuring consistent global behaviour based

on local interactions, avoiding deadlocks and preventing unintended emergent behaviours. Some algorithms rely on assumptions that break down in large swarms, such as perfect communication or synchronization, which are difficult to guarantee in real-world conditions. Additionally, algorithms must adapt to dynamic environments and robot failures, which becomes increasingly complex with scale. The computational overhead of running complex algorithms on simple robots further restricts feasibility. Developing scalable, robust algorithms that are both lightweight and adaptable remains an active research area. Overcoming these limitations is key to unlocking the full capabilities of large robotic swarms.

10.1.2 Coordination Overhead

- **Communication Load:** Effective coordination within a swarm requires frequent exchanges of information, where each robot shares its current state, intentions and environmental observations with neighbouring robots. As the number of robots increases, the volume of messages being sent grows rapidly, putting a significant strain on the communication network. This increased communication load can lead to network congestion, causing delays, message collisions and even loss of critical information. Limited bandwidth and interference in real-world environments exacerbate these challenges. To maintain effective coordination, the system must balance the frequency and size of messages with the available communication capacity. Inefficient communication protocols can drain energy quickly, further reducing operational time. Thus, minimizing unnecessary communication while ensuring timely data sharing is a vital design consideration. Researchers are exploring adaptive communication schemes and message compression techniques to manage this load efficiently. Overcoming communication bottlenecks is essential for enabling larger, more reliable robotic swarms.

- **Synchronization Issues:** Maintaining synchronization among a large number of robots in a swarm is a complex and ongoing challenge. Synchronization involves ensuring that robots share a consistent view of the environment and coordinate their actions in time. In large swarms, differences in communication delays, processing speeds and local decision-making can cause synchronization discrepancies. These delays lead to inconsistencies in shared data, causing some robots to act on outdated or incomplete information. As a result, the overall responsiveness of the swarm decreases and coordinated group behaviour may degrade. Attempts to enforce strict synchronization can introduce additional overhead and latency, further complicating the issue. Designing synchronization methods that are resilient to these delays while remaining efficient is critical. Techniques like asynchronous updating, local synchronization or event-driven coordination are actively researched. Balancing synchronization needs with practical constraints helps maintain swarm coherence without sacrificing scalability or speed.

- **Conflict Resolution:** As the number of robots in a swarm increases, the likelihood of conflicting actions among robots also rises. Conflicts may arise when multiple robots attempt to occupy the same space, perform contradictory tasks or interfere with one another's objectives. Without effective conflict detection and resolution mechanisms, these conflicts can lead to collisions, wasted effort and overall task failure. Designing robust strategies for conflict management is essential to ensure smooth and efficient swarm operation. Approaches include priority-based task assignment, negotiation protocols and real-time conflict avoidance algorithms. However, implementing these mechanisms in a decentralized, resource-constrained swarm presents unique challenges. Conflict resolution must be fast and lightweight to avoid adding excessive overhead or delays. Additionally, it should accommodate dynamic changes in the environment and the swarm itself. Continuous improvement of conflict management techniques is critical for achieving safe, scalable and reliable swarm robotics systems.

10.1.3 Impact on Performance

- **Reduced Efficiency:** Coordination and communication overhead in large robotic swarms can significantly reduce overall efficiency. As more time and resources are devoted to exchanging information and synchronizing actions, the swarm's ability to make rapid decisions and complete tasks diminishes. Delays caused by message congestion or processing bottlenecks can slow down responses to environmental changes, reducing the system's agility and adaptability. When individual robots wait for updated information or conflict resolutions, idle time increases, which lowers productivity. This inefficiency becomes more pronounced as the swarm size grows, potentially negating the benefits of having many cooperating robots. Hence, achieving an optimal balance between coordination and autonomous action is critical. Efficient protocols and lightweight algorithms help mitigate these issues but often involve trade-offs. Maintaining high performance while managing overhead remains a core design challenge for scalable swarm robotics.
- **Increased Energy Consumption:** Frequent communication and intensive coordination efforts impose a heavy energy burden on small, battery-

powered swarm robots. Each message transmission and reception consume precious energy, as does the continuous processing required for interpreting and responding to incoming data. In larger swarms, the cumulative effect of these activities drastically shortens the operational lifespan of individual robots, limiting mission duration. Energy consumption not only affects battery life but can also lead to overheating or component wear in some cases. Since many swarm applications require long periods of autonomy, optimizing energy efficiency is paramount. Strategies such as minimizing communication frequency, using energy-efficient hardware and adopting event-driven communication protocols are actively researched to address this challenge. Balancing energy usage without compromising coordination quality is vital for practical deployment.

- **Risk of Failure Propagation:** In swarm robotics, the interconnected nature of the system means that faults or failures in one robot or subgroup can quickly propagate through the entire swarm. For example, communication errors or incorrect decisions by one robot can mislead others, causing cascading failures or widespread disruption of tasks. This risk increases with swarm size and complexity, where monitoring and isolating faults become more difficult. Without effective fault-tolerant mechanisms, a small issue can escalate, reducing the robustness and reliability of the entire system. Researchers develop methods such as redundancy, decentralized decision-making and real-time fault detection to contain and mitigate failure propagation. Ensuring that the swarm can gracefully handle individual robot failures without compromising the collective mission is essential for trustworthy and resilient swarm deployments.

10.1.4 Mitigation Strategies

- **Decentralized Control:** Utilizing local rules and neighbour-based communication minimizes communication overhead and significantly enhances the system's scalability. Each agent makes decisions based on local information, which allows the swarm to operate efficiently without a central controller.
- **Hierarchical Structures:** Implementing leader roles or organizing agents into clusters can help manage the complexity of large swarms. Hierarchical organization balances the benefits of decentralization with some level of coordination, improving overall system performance and robustness.
- **Adaptive Algorithms:** Algorithms that dynamically adjust communication frequency and coordination intensity based on the current task requirements and swarm size can optimize resource use. This adaptability ensures

efficient operation across varying conditions, improving responsiveness and energy efficiency (Table-1).

Table: 1 Concise Mitigation Strategy

Mitigation Strategy	Description
Decentralized Control	Utilizing local rules and neighbour-based communication minimizes communication overhead and significantly enhances scalability. Each agent makes decisions based on local information, allowing efficient operation without a central controller.
Hierarchical Structures	Implementing leader roles or organizing agents into clusters helps manage the complexity of large swarms. This balances decentralization with coordination, improving performance and robustness.
Adaptive Algorithms	Algorithms dynamically adjust communication frequency and coordination intensity based on task requirements and swarm size, optimizing resource use and improving responsiveness and energy efficiency.

10.2 HARDWARE CONSTRAINTS AND FAILURES

In swarm robotic systems, hardware limitations and potential failures pose significant challenges to overall performance, reliability and coordination. Since individual robots are typically designed to be low-cost and minimalistic, they often operate with constrained processing power, limited sensing capabilities and basic communication hardware. These constraints can lead to imprecise movements, reduced situational awareness and delayed responses. Additionally, the likelihood of hardware failure increases with the number of agents, making fault tolerance a critical design requirement. A single malfunctioning robot may not disrupt the system, but widespread failures can degrade swarm efficiency. Therefore, swarm systems must be designed with redundancy and robustness in mind. Adaptive behaviours, local autonomy and decentralized decision-making help mitigate the effects of individual failures. Furthermore, lightweight, efficient algorithms are necessary to operate within limited computational resources. Ultimately, building resilience into both the hardware and the swarm coordination strategy is key to ensuring reliable operation in dynamic and unpredictable environments.

10.2.1 Limited Processing Power

Swarm robots are typically designed with minimal onboard computational resources to maintain low cost, reduce power consumption and ensure scalability. While this design choice makes large-scale deployment feasible, it also imposes significant constraints on each robot's ability to process complex data or run computationally intensive algorithms. Tasks such as advanced path planning, image recognition or high-level decision-making become impractical at the individual level. As a result, swarm systems must rely on highly efficient, lightweight algorithms that enable basic decision-making using local information. Additionally, responsibilities are often distributed across the swarm, leveraging collective intelligence rather than individual processing strength. This trade-off between performance and simplicity necessitates careful algorithmic design to ensure responsiveness and coordination without overloading limited hardware.

10.2.2 Sensor and Actuator Limitations:

- **Low-Resolution Sensors:** In swarm robotic systems, sensors are typically low-cost and compact, which often results in limited resolution, sensitivity and range. These constraints directly impact the robot's ability to accurately perceive its environment, detect obstacles and identify neighbouring agents. Poor environmental perception can lead to misinterpretation of surroundings, delayed reactions or failed obstacle avoidance. In swarm contexts, where coordination heavily depends on spatial awareness and proximity sensing, such limitations can cause errors in collective behaviours like flocking or aggregation. Low-resolution sensors also struggle in complex or dynamic environments, especially where detailed perception is crucial. The reduced data fidelity demands the use of simplified perception algorithms that must work under uncertainty. Additionally, the lack of advanced sensor fusion limits the swarm's ability to make informed decisions. To mitigate these issues, strategies such as redundancy, shared information and cooperative sensing are often used. These compensate for individual sensor weaknesses through collective perception.
- **Actuator Precision:** Actuators in swarm robots are usually selected for affordability and energy efficiency, often at the expense of mechanical accuracy and reliability. Low-precision actuators can result in inconsistent or jittery movements, which pose challenges for tasks requiring smooth navigation or tight formation control. Even minor inaccuracies in movement can compound over time, causing robots to drift from planned paths or misalign with their neighbours. In coordinated swarm behaviours such as synchronized motion, shape formation or object transport, this lack of precision can significantly disrupt group dynamics. Additionally, the inability to perform fine motor actions limits the swarm's effectiveness in tasks requiring delicate manipulation or tight-space operations. These limitations necessitate control algorithms that are tolerant to mechanical error and capable of self-correction. Feedback-based navigation, dead-reckoning and local recalibration are common techniques used to counteract these inaccuracies. Despite their shortcomings, low-precision

actuators remain viable through collective compensation and adaptive control strategies.

10.2.3 Communication Constraints

- **Limited Range:** Swarm robots commonly use short-range wireless communication technologies such as Bluetooth or RF modules to maintain cost-effectiveness and energy efficiency. However, this results in limited communication range, meaning robots can only exchange information with immediate neighbours. As a result, global awareness of the system is constrained and messages must propagate through multi-hop communication, which can introduce delays or distort information. This limitation hinders fast swarm-wide coordination and may impact responsiveness in large or spatially dispersed environments. Moreover, in highly dynamic scenarios, changing neighbour relationships further complicate reliable communication. To cope with range limitations, many swarm algorithms are designed to rely solely on local interactions and emergent behaviours. This ensures robustness, but often comes at the expense of precision or efficiency in task execution. Strategies such as relay-based communication or mobile hubs are sometimes employed to extend effective range. Overall, designing communication-efficient and locally aware behaviours is essential for swarm robustness.
- **Bandwidth Limitations:** Due to the use of simple and low-power communication hardware, swarm robots operate under strict bandwidth constraints. This limits the amount and frequency of data that can be exchanged between agents, making it impractical to transmit large payloads such as high-resolution images or complex sensor data. Communication protocols must therefore be lightweight, minimalistic and optimized for speed and efficiency. These limitations can affect coordination in tasks that require real-time data sharing, such as cooperative mapping or target tracking. Bandwidth restrictions also increase the risk of message loss or congestion when too many agents attempt to transmit simultaneously. To address these issues, swarm systems often use event-driven or priority-based communication, where only critical or time-sensitive messages are exchanged. Data compression, token-based communication and pre-shared behaviour models also help reduce dependency on bandwidth. Ultimately, designing with bandwidth constraints in mind ensures scalability and operational stability.
- **Signal Interference:** In densely populated swarm environments, multiple robots operating in close proximity can cause significant wireless signal interference. As communication channels become saturated, data packets

may collide, leading to transmission errors, delays or complete message loss. Environmental factors such as physical obstructions, electromagnetic noise or even weather conditions can further degrade signal quality. These disruptions can severely affect coordination, especially in tasks that depend on real-time message exchange or synchronization. In worst-case scenarios, communication blackouts may lead to behavioural instability or unsafe actions. Mitigation strategies include using frequency-hopping techniques, channel diversity and collision-avoidance protocols. Additionally, spatial or temporal message scheduling can help reduce congestion by staggering transmissions. In some systems, fallback mechanisms allow robots to continue operating autonomously if communication is lost. Ensuring communication robustness under interference conditions is crucial for reliable swarm operation in real-world, noisy environments.

10.2.4. Energy Constraints

- **Battery Life:** One of the most significant limitations in swarm robotic systems is the restricted battery capacity of individual robots. Designed for affordability and compactness, these robots typically use small batteries that limit operational time, especially during energy-intensive tasks such as movement, sensing or communication. In long-duration missions or in environments where recharging is not feasible, limited battery life becomes a critical bottleneck. This constraint can reduce mission effectiveness, cause early dropout of agents and ultimately affect the swarm's overall performance and reliability. Uneven battery drain among agents may also lead to unbalanced swarm behaviour or communication breakdowns. To address these issues, energy-efficient hardware and behaviour-based energy conservation techniques are vital. Additionally, incorporating energy-aware algorithms that prioritize essential actions and reduce non-critical processes can help extend operational lifespan. In some advanced systems, energy harvesting (e.g., solar) or mobile charging stations are explored to sustain swarm longevity.
- **Power Management:** Effective power management is essential to maximize the operational lifespan of swarm robots, especially in resource-constrained settings. Given the tight energy budgets, robots must intelligently balance their power consumption across sensing, computation, movement and communication. This requires adaptive behaviour strategies that scale activity levels based on task urgency, proximity to other agents or available battery levels. For instance, a robot may reduce its communication frequency or disable non-essential sensors when power is low. Algorithms must be designed to be computationally lightweight to prevent unnecessary

processing overhead. Furthermore, task allocation can be optimized to delegate energy-heavy tasks to robots with higher charge, improving overall swarm efficiency. Real-time monitoring of power usage and battery health enables dynamic adjustments and fault prevention. By embedding power-awareness into both software and hardware design, swarm systems can operate more sustainably and reliably in energy-limited environments.

10.2.5 Hardware Failures

- **Component Degradation:** Over time, the hardware components in swarm robots—such as sensors, motors and actuators—undergo natural wear and tear. This gradual degradation can lead to reduced accuracy in sensing, decreased mobility and less reliable performance. For example, worn-out motors may cause inconsistent motion, while aging sensors may provide faulty data, affecting local decision-making and swarm coordination. In long-term deployments or harsh environments, component degradation is inevitable and without proper maintenance or self-assessment, it may go unnoticed until performance drops significantly. Unlike high-end robots, swarm agents are often not designed for frequent maintenance due to cost and scale, so resilience must be built into the system from the start. Calibration routines, simplified self-checks or behaviour-based health monitoring can help detect subtle signs of degradation early. Designing the swarm to tolerate a certain level of performance variation ensures that even slightly degraded units can still contribute meaningfully to the collective goal.
- **Node Failures:** In swarm robotic systems, individual robots—also known as nodes—may completely fail due to hardware malfunctions, energy depletion or environmental damage. These failures are more likely in large-scale swarms using low-cost hardware, where reliability trade-offs are made to keep the system affordable. When a node fails, it may stop moving, responding or communicating, which can disrupt swarm behaviours that rely on distributed roles or collaborative actions. If critical nodes fail in leader-based or cluster-based configurations, the effect can be more severe. However, swarm systems are generally designed with redundancy in mind, meaning the failure of a few robots should not jeopardize the entire mission. Mechanisms such as reallocation of tasks, dynamic formation changes and route replanning help ensure continued functionality. Ultimately, the swarm's ability to tolerate node failures is a key advantage over centralized systems, provided failure handling is properly implemented.

10.2.6 Impact on Swarm Behaviour

Hardware limitations and failures in swarm robotic systems can have significant and sometimes cascading effects on the swarm's overall behaviour. The collective intelligence and performance of the swarm rely heavily on the functioning of individual agents. When robots degrade or fail, the swarm's ability to maintain robustness, coordination and task execution can be compromised in the following key ways:

- **Reduced Redundancy:** One of the core strengths of swarm robotics is redundancy—multiple robots working together to provide fault tolerance and adaptability. However, when individual robots fail due to hardware issues, the swarm's redundancy is diminished. Each failed robot represents a loss in sensing, communication or actuation capability, making the system less resilient to further failures or environmental disruptions. In tasks requiring mass cooperation—such as area coverage, object transport or formation control—this loss can lead to noticeable performance degradation. The ability to reassign roles or redistribute the workload becomes critical in maintaining effectiveness. If the rate of failures exceeds the swarm's redundancy threshold, the system may become unstable or incapable of completing the task.
- **Coordination Errors:** Swarm behaviours are typically emergent, relying on local sensing and neighbour-to-neighbour communication. Hardware issues in sensors or communication modules can lead to inaccurate or missing data, which disrupts these local interactions. For instance, a robot with a faulty proximity sensor may fail to maintain correct formation spacing or one with impaired communication may not relay critical status updates. Such discrepancies can propagate through the swarm, leading to coordination errors like misalignments, desynchronization or conflicting behaviours. In densely packed swarms or complex tasks, even minor coordination errors can escalate, causing the swarm to lose structure, direction or efficiency. Designing systems that tolerate small local errors without compromising global behaviour is essential.
- **Task Incompletion:** When hardware failures affect critical components or occur in a high number of agents, the swarm may be unable to complete its assigned task. For example, if too many robots lose mobility, a transport task may become infeasible. Similarly, failure in leader agents or cluster heads in hierarchical swarms can leave subordinate units without guidance. Tasks that depend on specific sensor readings, timing synchronization or physical manipulation may fail outright if the involved robots malfunction. In mission-critical scenarios such as search and rescue or hazardous

environment monitoring, task incompletion due to hardware failure can have serious consequences. To mitigate this, swarm systems must be designed to detect critical failure conditions early and either adapt the mission plan or initiate recovery protocols.

10.2.7 Mitigation Strategies

To ensure robust and reliable performance in the presence of hardware failures and limitations, swarm robotic systems must incorporate strategies that enhance resilience, adaptability and fault tolerance. The following approaches play a crucial role in mitigating the impact of individual robot failures and maintaining overall system functionality:

- **Redundancy in Numbers:** One of the fundamental principles of swarm robotics is leveraging large populations of simple, inexpensive agents. By deploying a high number of robots, the system gains natural redundancy, allowing it to tolerate multiple individual failures without significant loss in performance. If one or more robots malfunction, others can seamlessly take over their roles or cover their area of responsibility. This redundancy reduces the risk of mission failure and enhances system robustness in dynamic or unpredictable environments. However, redundancy also increases the complexity of coordination and communication, which must be managed efficiently. Properly designed swarm behaviours can ensure that this large population remains coordinated and effective despite losses.
- **Robust Algorithms:** Swarm control algorithms must be designed to be inherently fault-tolerant. This means that behaviours such as aggregation, dispersion, flocking or task allocation should not depend on the flawless performance of every individual agent. Robust algorithms are decentralized, reactive and often probabilistic, allowing the swarm to self-organize and adapt even when some agents behave unexpectedly or drop out. These algorithms can absorb minor local failures without compromising global objectives. For example, task reallocation algorithms can automatically redistribute work from failed agents to active ones. The use of simple rules based on local interactions also helps prevent error propagation throughout the swarm.
- **Self-Diagnosis and Recovery:** To improve long-term reliability and autonomy, individual robots in the swarm should be capable of detecting and responding to their own internal faults. Self-diagnosis involves monitoring components such as sensors, motors, battery levels and communication modules for anomalies. Once a fault is detected, a robot can engage in recovery strategies such as switching to a low-power mode, alerting neighbouring agents or gracefully withdrawing from active participation.

More advanced approaches may include self-healing behaviours or system-wide adaptations triggered by reported failures. Incorporating self-awareness into each agent not only prevents the spread of dysfunction but also enhances the swarm's ability to recover dynamically and continue its mission with minimal disruption.

10.3 REAL-TIME PROCESSING AND LATENCY

Real-time processing and low-latency communication are critical for effective coordination in swarm robotic systems. Delays in decision-making or data transmission can lead to synchronization issues, degraded performance or failure to respond to dynamic environments (Fig. 1).

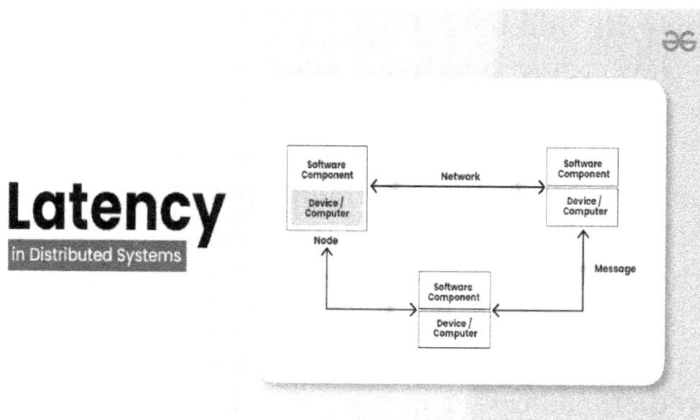

Fig. 1 Latency in Distributed Systems

10.3.1 Importance of Real-Time Processing

- **Immediate Decision-Making:** Swarm robots need to rapidly process sensory data and make decisions in real time to maintain effective coordination within the group. Delays in processing can lead to missed cues, causing collisions or breakdowns in collective behaviour. Because of limited onboard computation, algorithms must be highly efficient to enable quick responses. Immediate decision-making is essential for dynamically adapting to unpredictable environments. This responsiveness ensures smooth interactions among agents and continuous task progress.
- **Task Responsiveness:** Many swarm applications, such as search and rescue or environmental monitoring, operate in dynamic, time-sensitive environments where conditions can change rapidly. Robots must respond promptly to new information, obstacles or emergencies to maximize effectiveness. Delays could result in missed opportunities or unsafe situations. Hence, responsiveness in task execution is critical for success, requiring streamlined sensing, processing and communication pipelines.

Fast reaction times enable swarms to adapt and perform reliably under pressure.

- **Synchronization:** Maintaining synchronized actions is vital for collective behaviours like flocking, formation control and cooperative transport. Synchronization depends heavily on real-time processing and consistent communication among agents to align movements and decisions. Without tight coordination, the swarm risks fragmentation or inefficiency. Achieving synchronization is challenging given hardware constraints and communication delays but is crucial for preserving swarm coherence and accomplishing shared goals. Robust timing and update mechanisms help maintain this collective rhythm.

10.3.2 Sources of Latency

- **Sensor Delays:** Time taken to capture and process sensor data.
- **Processing Delays:** Limited onboard computational power can cause lags in executing control algorithms.
- **Communication Latency:** Delay in transmitting and receiving data between agents, which may be worsened by:
    - Network congestion
    - Distance between nodes
    - Signal interference
- **Actuation Delay:** Time between issuing a command and the robot physically acting on it.

10.3.3 Impacts of Latency on Swarm Behaviour

- **Desynchronization:** When timing coordination breaks down among swarm agents, the overall formation and behaviour can become unstable and erratic. This loss of synchronization leads to fragmented group movement, causing the swarm to lose cohesion and effectiveness. Such instability can result in collisions, gaps in coverage or failure to maintain desired patterns. Desynchronization reduces the reliability of collective tasks that depend on precise timing. Maintaining synchronization is therefore critical for preserving orderly swarm behaviour.
- **Inaccurate Responses:** Delayed reactions to sensory input cause robots to miss fast-moving targets or fail to avoid sudden obstacles, compromising mission success. In dynamic environments, even small timing lags can result in poor decision-making and misaligned actions. These inaccuracies increase the risk of collisions, inefficient paths and lost opportunities. Ensuring prompt and accurate responses is essential to maintain safety and

effectiveness. Robust real-time processing helps minimize such response errors.

- **Inefficiency:** Poor coordination and timing issues often cause swarm tasks to take longer than necessary and consume more energy. Robots may duplicate efforts, travel inefficient routes or idle unnecessarily while waiting for updates. This inefficiency reduces mission endurance, increases wear on hardware and lowers overall productivity. Optimizing coordination and synchronization helps conserve resources and speeds task completion. Efficient swarm operation relies heavily on well-timed interactions and streamlined workflows.

10.3.4 Mitigation Strategies

- **Lightweight Algorithms:** Utilizing efficient and streamlined control and communication algorithms minimizes processing time on resource-constrained robots. These lightweight algorithms reduce computational load, enabling faster responses and conserving energy. By simplifying decision rules and optimizing code execution, swarms maintain high-speed interactions without overburdening hardware. This approach is crucial for real-time operation and scalability. Efficient algorithms form the backbone of responsive swarm behaviour.
- **Local Decision-Making:** Minimizing reliance on global information helps reduce communication bottlenecks and latency issues in swarm systems. By enabling robots to make decisions based primarily on local sensory data and neighbour interactions, the system achieves faster response times. This decentralization enhances robustness, as agents operate independently without waiting for global commands. Local decision-making fosters scalability and fault tolerance. It supports emergent behaviours critical for complex swarm tasks.
- **Predictive Models:** Implementing predictive models allows robots to estimate future states of themselves and their neighbours, compensating for communication and processing delays. By forecasting movements or environmental changes, robots can proactively adjust their actions, reducing errors caused by latency. This foresight enhances coordination and smoothness in collective behaviours. Predictive modelling improves task accuracy and helps maintain formation integrity. It is especially valuable in dynamic and time-sensitive environments.
- **Priority Scheduling:** Assigning higher priority to critical, time-sensitive processes like collision avoidance ensures that these functions receive immediate attention from the robot's processor. Priority scheduling helps

prevent delays in essential safety-related actions even when the system is busy handling less urgent tasks. By managing task execution order efficiently, the swarm maintains operational safety and responsiveness. This approach balances multiple processes without compromising critical performance. It enhances real-time reliability in complex scenarios.

- **Latency-Aware Protocols:** Designing communication protocols that adapt dynamically to current network latency conditions helps maintain effective information flow within the swarm. Latency-aware protocols can adjust message frequency, transmission power or routing paths based on observed delays or interference. This adaptability reduces data loss and prevents communication overload. By responding to network conditions, these protocols improve synchronization and coordination under varying environmental challenges. They are key to sustaining robust swarm communication.

10.3.5 Real-World Considerations

- **Hardware Constraints:** Swarm robots typically use low-cost, lightweight sensors and processors to keep the system affordable and energy-efficient. However, these components often lack the capacity for high-speed data processing and complex computations. This hardware limitation restricts the ability to perform intensive real-time analysis, slowing down decision-making and responsiveness. The trade-off between cost and performance necessitates careful algorithm design to operate within these constraints. Addressing hardware limitations is crucial for maintaining swarm effectiveness in time-sensitive tasks.
- **Environmental Factors:** Wireless communication in swarm robotics is vulnerable to environmental influences such as physical obstacles, electromagnetic interference and signal attenuation. These factors can cause delays, data loss or reduced communication quality, leading to unreliable message exchanges among agents. In cluttered or noisy environments, maintaining consistent connectivity is challenging, impacting synchronization and coordination. Robust communication protocols and adaptive behaviours are needed to mitigate these environmental effects. Understanding deployment conditions is essential for reliable swarm operation.
- **Scalability Challenges:** As the number of agents in a swarm grows, the communication demand increases exponentially, making it harder to maintain low latency and efficient data exchange. Large swarms face challenges such as network congestion, increased message collisions and

bandwidth limitations. These issues can degrade overall performance and slow down collective decision-making. Scalability requires scalable communication architectures and protocols that can handle growth without sacrificing responsiveness. Designing swarms with scalable, latency-aware solutions is key to effective large-scale deployment.

10.4 CYBERSECURITY AND COMMUNICATION JAMMING

In swarm robotic systems, secure and reliable communication forms the backbone of effective coordination and mission success. Given their decentralized architecture and reliance on wireless networks, these systems are particularly vulnerable to a range of cyber threats, including hacking, data interception and denial-of-service attacks. Communication jamming—where adversaries intentionally disrupt signal transmission—poses a serious risk to maintaining continuous connectivity among agents. Protecting against such vulnerabilities is critical to preserving the integrity and confidentiality of exchanged information. Robust cybersecurity measures, including encryption, authentication and intrusion detection, are essential. Additionally, implementing resilient communication protocols that can detect and recover from jamming attempts ensures operational continuity. Together, these safeguards enable swarms to perform reliably even in contested or hostile environments (Fig. 2).

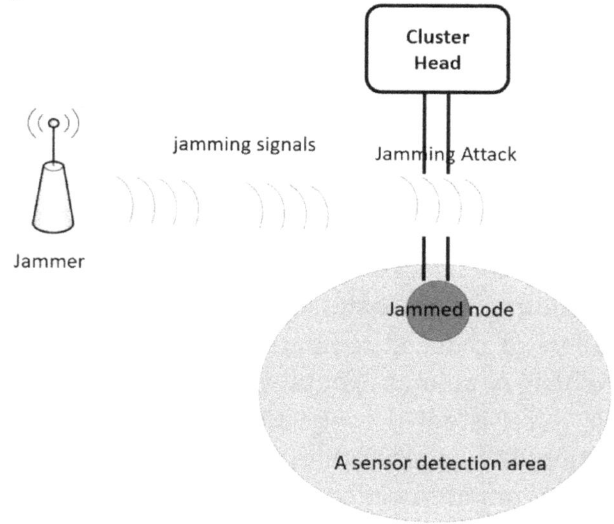

Fig. 2 Jamming attack in wireless communications of cyber physical systems

10.4.1 Cybersecurity Threats:

Swarm systems can be exposed to various cyber threats, including:

- **Unauthorized Access:** Unauthorized access occurs when attackers breach the swarm's security defenses to take control of individual robots or intercept sensitive data. By compromising a single agent, adversaries can manipulate its actions or gain insight into the swarm's operations. This breach threatens the entire system's integrity, as a hijacked robot might disrupt coordination or leak confidential information. Preventing unauthorized access requires strong authentication protocols and secure communication channels. Robust access controls are essential to safeguard the swarm from external and internal threats.

- **Data Manipulation:** Data manipulation involves malicious actors altering sensor readings, control signals or communication messages within the swarm. Such tampering can mislead robots, causing them to make incorrect decisions or behave erratically. For example, falsified location data might cause the swarm to scatter or collide, undermining mission objectives. Protecting data integrity through encryption, message validation and anomaly detection helps mitigate these risks. Ensuring the accuracy of exchanged information is critical for reliable and safe swarm operation.
- **Replay Attacks:** Replay attacks happen when adversaries capture legitimate communication messages and resend them later to confuse or disrupt the swarm. These repeated messages can cause robots to perform outdated or conflicting actions, leading to coordination breakdowns or task failures. Detecting and preventing replay attacks requires implementing time-stamping, sequence numbers or nonce-based protocols in communication. By ensuring that messages are fresh and non-repetitive, the swarm maintains correct situational awareness and decision-making.
- **Spoofing:** Spoofing involves impersonating legitimate swarm members or external signals to deceive the robotic system. Attackers may inject false identities or mimic trusted agents to send misleading commands or disrupt communication. This can cause the swarm to trust malicious inputs, potentially leading to erratic behaviour or security breaches. Strong identity verification methods and cryptographic authentication are necessary to defend against spoofing attempts. Maintaining trust among swarm members is vital for coordinated and secure operations..

10.4.2 Communication Jamming

Communication jamming refers to deliberate interference with the swarm's wireless communication channels. This can include:

- **Signal Jamming:** Signal jamming involves intentionally blocking or overwhelming the wireless communication channels used by the swarm. By saturating the frequency bands with noise or false signals, attackers prevent robots from exchanging critical messages. This disruption can cause loss of coordination, delayed responses and fragmented swarm behaviour. Defending against signal jamming requires frequency hopping, spread spectrum techniques or adaptive channel selection. Maintaining communication integrity despite jamming attempts is crucial for swarm resilience.

- **Selective Jamming:** Selective jamming targets specific nodes or communication frequencies within the swarm to disrupt key agents or critical links selectively. This targeted approach is more subtle and harder to detect, as it does not affect the entire network uniformly. By focusing on leaders, cluster heads or nodes with unique roles, attackers can cripple swarm functionality disproportionately. Countermeasures include dynamic routing, node redundancy and monitoring for abnormal packet loss patterns. Selective jamming poses a strategic threat to swarm operations requiring sophisticated Défense mechanisms.
- **Denial-of-Service (DoS) Attacks:** Denial-of-Service (DoS) attacks flood the swarm's communication network with excessive, unnecessary data, overwhelming the system's capacity. This overload can degrade network performance, increase latency and ultimately cause communication failures. In swarm robotics, DoS attacks disrupt synchronization and decision-making, leading to mission degradation or failure. Effective mitigation involves traffic filtering, rate limiting and anomaly detection to identify and block malicious data floods. Ensuring network availability under attack is vital for continuous swarm operation.

10.4.3 Impacts on Swarm Systems

- **Loss of Coordination:** Disrupted communication channels cause the swarm to lose synchronization and coordination among agents. Without reliable message exchange, robots may act based on outdated or incomplete information, leading to fragmented or conflicting behaviours. This breakdown in collective control reduces the swarm's effectiveness and increases the risk of collisions or task failure. Maintaining continuous communication is therefore essential to preserve cohesive swarm operation. Coordination loss directly threatens mission success.
- **Mission Failure:** When critical data cannot be shared promptly due to communication disruptions, the swarm's ability to complete its assigned tasks is jeopardized. In missions like search and rescue or environmental monitoring, missing real-time updates can prevent timely responses to changing conditions. Communication breakdowns may cause agents to work at cross-purposes or abandon objectives entirely. Ensuring robust and secure communication pathways is crucial to prevent mission-critical failures. Failure to do so undermines the core value of swarm robotics.

- **Security Breach:** Compromised communication channels or agents open the door to security breaches within the swarm. Attackers gaining control over or misleading individual robots can inject false data, manipulate swarm behaviour or leak sensitive information. This not only endangers mission integrity but may also expose confidential or proprietary data. Protecting communication networks and enforcing strict authentication protocols are vital to defend against such breaches. Maintaining trust in swarm members is fundamental to system security.
- **Increased Latency:** Attacks or environmental interference causing delays in communication increase system latency, impairing the swarm's real-time responsiveness. Higher latency means slower reactions to dynamic changes, missed deadlines and delayed decision-making. In time-critical operations, such delays can cascade into failures or unsafe conditions. Optimizing communication protocols and mitigating sources of latency are essential for preserving operational efficiency. Low latency supports precise coordination and rapid adaptation (Table-2).

Table 2–Brief Impact on Swarm

Impact	Cause	Effect	Mitigation
Loss of Coordination	Disrupted communication channels	Desynchronization, conflicting behaviours, task failure	Ensure reliable, real-time communication
Mission Failure	Inability to share critical data promptly	Incomplete tasks, cross-purpose actions, objective abandonment	Use secure and redundant communication systems
Security Breach	Compromised agents or communication channels	False data injection, manipulation, data leakage	Enforce encryption, authentication and intrusion detection
Increased Latency	Attacks or environmental interference	Delayed responses, missed deadlines, reduced efficiency	Optimize communication protocols, reduce interference

10.4.4 Mitigation Strategies

Cybersecurity Measures

- **Authentication Protocols:** Authentication protocols verify that messages exchanged within the swarm originate from trusted and legitimate sources. By confirming the identity of each communicating agent, these protocols prevent unauthorized entities from injecting malicious commands or data. Strong authentication mechanisms help maintain the integrity of inter-robot communication and safeguard against impersonation attacks. This trust framework is essential for coordinated and secure swarm operation. Implementing robust identity verification is a first line of defence against cyber threats.

- **Encryption:** Encryption ensures that data transmitted between swarm robots remains confidential and protected from eavesdropping or interception by malicious actors. By encoding messages, encryption prevents unauthorized parties from reading or tampering with sensitive information. This safeguard maintains privacy and trust within the swarm, especially when operating in adversarial environments. Using strong cryptographic standards balances security with the limited processing power of swarm agents. Encryption is critical for preserving data integrity and operational secrecy.
- **Secure Boot and Firmware Updates:** Secure boot processes and verified firmware updates prevent unauthorized or malicious code from running on individual swarm members. By ensuring that only authenticated software is executed, these mechanisms protect the system from rootkits, malware or corrupted firmware that could compromise robot behaviour. Regular, secure updates also allow patching of vulnerabilities without risking system integrity. Maintaining a trusted software environment is key to resilient and safe swarm operations. This foundation helps prevent internal breaches and preserves system reliability.
- **Anomaly Detection:** Anomaly detection uses behavioural models and monitoring tools to identify swarm agents exhibiting unusual or suspicious actions that may indicate compromise or malfunction. By isolating or removing these agents, the swarm prevents the spread of errors or malicious influence. This proactive approach enhances the system's resilience against cyber-attacks and hardware failures. Effective anomaly detection relies on continuous analysis of communication patterns and agent behaviours. Early identification of threats is vital for maintaining swarm security and mission success.

Anti-Jamming Techniques

- **Frequency Hopping Spread Spectrum (FHSS):** Frequency Hopping Spread Spectrum (FHSS) involves continuously changing communication frequencies in a predetermined pattern to avoid jamming. By rapidly switching channels, the swarm makes it difficult for attackers to block or interfere with signals consistently. This technique enhances communication resilience and reduces the risk of prolonged disruptions. FHSS also complicates interception attempts, improving security. It is a widely used method to maintain robust wireless connectivity in hostile environments.

- **Multi-Channel Communication:** Multi-channel communication uses multiple redundant communication channels simultaneously to ensure connectivity even if some frequencies are jammed or blocked. This redundancy allows swarm agents to switch to alternative channels seamlessly, maintaining continuous data exchange. It minimizes the impact of targeted or broad-spectrum jamming attacks by distributing communication load. Multi-channel systems increase reliability and fault tolerance in the swarm's network infrastructure. This approach supports stable operations in challenging or contested conditions.
- **Local Autonomy:** Local autonomy enables individual robots to operate independently when communication with the rest of the swarm is disrupted or lost. By relying on onboard sensors and pre-programmed behaviours, agents can continue essential tasks without centralized coordination. This capability ensures partial mission progress even during jamming events or network failures. Local autonomy reduces vulnerability by decreasing dependency on continuous communication. It enhances swarm resilience and adaptability in unpredictable environments.
- **Signal Strength Monitoring:** Signal strength monitoring involves continuously analysing communication signals to detect anomalies that may indicate jamming attempts. Sudden drops, fluctuations or irregular patterns in signal strength can trigger alerts for potential interference. Early detection enables the swarm to activate countermeasures such as frequency hopping or channel switching. This proactive approach helps maintain communication integrity and prevents prolonged outages. Monitoring signal quality is crucial for real-time jamming mitigation.

10.5 ETHICAL CONSIDERATIONS AND PUBLIC ACCEPTANCE

As swarm robotic systems become increasingly integrated into societal functions—from agriculture and logistics to surveillance and disaster response—ethical considerations and public acceptance emerge as critical factors. Designing and deploying these systems responsibly is essential to ensure trust, safety and alignment with societal values.

10.5.1 Ethical Considerations

- **Privacy Concerns:** Swarm robots equipped with cameras and sensors can inadvertently collect sensitive information, raising significant privacy issues. There is a risk of surveillance and monitoring of individuals without their knowledge or consent. How data is stored, shared and protected becomes critical to prevent misuse. Transparent policies and strict regulations are needed to safeguard personal privacy. Addressing these concerns is vital to gain public trust and acceptance.

- **Accountability and Responsibility:** As swarm robots often operate with a high degree of autonomy, assigning responsibility when malfunctions or harm occur is complex. It remains unclear whether developers, manufacturers or operators should be held liable for unintended consequences. Clear legal frameworks and ethical guidelines are necessary to define accountability. This clarity ensures justice and encourages responsible innovation. Accountability is fundamental to ethical deployment and societal acceptance.
- **Safety and Human Interaction:** Ensuring operational safety is paramount, particularly when swarm robots function near humans in dynamic or public environments. Robots must be designed to avoid causing harm and respond safely to unexpected situations. Incorporating fail-safe mechanisms, such as emergency shutdowns or safe failure modes, is essential for risk mitigation. Ethical design prioritizes human well-being alongside technological advancement. Safe human-robot interaction fosters confidence and widespread adoption.
- **Dual-Use Technology:** Swarm robotics technology holds potential for both beneficial civilian applications and harmful military uses. Preventing the weaponization or misuse of these systems poses significant ethical and regulatory challenges. Balancing innovation with safeguards against malicious deployment requires international cooperation. Ethical frameworks must address dual-use concerns to guide responsible development. Managing this duality is crucial for the technology's positive impact on society.

10.5.2 Public Acceptance

- **Trust and Transparency:** For swarm robotic systems to gain public trust, their behaviours must be understandable, predictable and easy to interpret. People need to feel confident that swarms act in consistent, rational ways. Open communication about how decisions are made, what data is collected and who controls the swarm is crucial. Transparency builds accountability and fosters acceptance. Clear explanations reduce fear and promote responsible use.
- **Inclusivity and Accessibility:** Inclusive design ensures that a diverse range of stakeholders—communities, users, regulators—are involved from the start. This collaborative approach helps address ethical, cultural and practical concerns early in the deployment process. Making swarm systems accessible and beneficial to various social groups promotes fairness and equity. Accessibility also ensures that marginalized populations are not

excluded from the advantages of emerging technology. Ethical design must reflect diverse needs and values.

- **Media Influence and Perception:** The public's perception of swarm robotics is strongly shaped by how media portray these technologies—often highlighting fears of loss of control or dystopian futures. Misleading narratives can generate resistance or fear, hindering real-world adoption. Providing accurate, balanced information through education and outreach is essential to combat misconceptions. Transparency about capabilities and limitations helps the public form informed opinions. Proactive communication can shift perceptions toward trust and informed engagement (Table-3).

Table: 3 Mitigation Strategies for Ethical Deployment

Issue	Strategy
Privacy Invasion	Implement strict data anonymization, limit data collection and enforce clear usage policies.
Lack of Accountability	Define legal frameworks for autonomy and ensure traceability of actions.
Safety Risks	Design robust fail-safe protocols and conduct thorough safety testing.
Public Distrust	Promote transparency, provide user education and ensure community involvement.
Misuse Potential	Enforce usage licenses and include tamper-proof hardware/ software safeguards.

10.5.3 Regulatory and Ethical Frameworks

- **Existing Guidelines:** Several internationally recognized frameworks provide a foundation for the ethical and responsible deployment of swarm robotics. Standards such as the IEEE's Ethically Aligned Design and the European Union's AI Act offer concrete principles covering transparency, accountability, privacy and human-centric design. These guidelines help developers align technological advancements with societal values and legal norms. They emphasize safeguards like explainability, fairness and human oversight in autonomous systems. By referencing such established ethical frameworks, swarm robotics can be guided toward safe and socially acceptable implementation. These documents encourage interdisciplinary collaboration and stakeholder inclusion during development. Importantly, they help ensure that systems are not only effective but also respectful of human rights. While they do not offer prescriptive rules for every scenario, they serve as essential ethical compasses. Adhering to these guidelines lays the groundwork for public trust and long-term acceptance of swarm technologies.

- **Need for Policy Development:** Despite the value of existing frameworks, the pace of innovation in swarm robotics often far outstrips current regulatory systems. As robots become more autonomous and widespread, new challenges emerge that are not fully addressed by existing laws, particularly in areas like liability, cybersecurity and data protection. There is a growing need for adaptive, forward-thinking policies that can evolve alongside the technology. Policymakers must work proactively with engineers, ethicists and communities to anticipate risks and close regulatory gaps. These policies should be dynamic, allowing for continuous revision based on real-world deployments and technological changes. Furthermore, laws must balance innovation with public safety and ethical integrity, avoiding overly restrictive measures that stifle progress. Public input and global cooperation will be essential to developing coherent, inclusive policies. As swarm robotics matures, comprehensive legal and ethical frameworks will be crucial to guide its safe integration into society. Policy evolution must keep pace with technological advancement to ensure responsible and beneficial use.

11 Chapter HUMAN-SWARM INTERACTION (HSI)

11.0 INTRODUCTION: AN OVERVIEW

Human-Swarm Interaction (HSI) is an emerging field at the intersection of robotics, human-computer interaction and systems engineering. It focuses on how humans can effectively interact with, guide and collaborate with large groups of autonomous robots—or "swarms"—that exhibit collective behaviour inspired by natural systems like flocks of birds or colonies of ants. Unlike traditional human-robot interaction, which often involves one-on-one control or supervision, HSI involves managing complex, decentralized systems where individual robots operate autonomously but coordinate their actions collectively. The challenge in HSI lies in bridging the cognitive and operational gap between human decision-making and swarm autonomy. Humans must be able to influence swarm behaviour without micromanaging each agent, requiring new paradigms of control, communication and feedback. Interfaces must translate high-level human intent into distributed swarm actions and in turn, provide intuitive feedback about the swarm's state, goals and environmental context.

HSI has applications across many domains, including environmental monitoring, search and rescue, military operations, agriculture and medical nanorobotics. In each case, effective human oversight and adaptability are essential to ensure safety, reliability and mission success. Furthermore, the scalability of swarm systems introduces unique complexities for human operators—such as managing uncertainty, trust, workload and situational awareness. As technology advances, HSI is increasingly becoming a key area of research to unlock the full potential of swarm robotics. It requires interdisciplinary contributions from AI, robotics, cognitive science and human factors engineering. Ultimately, well-designed human-swarm interaction will allow swarms to remain autonomous yet responsive to human goals—creating systems that are not only intelligent but also controllable, transparent and trustworthy (Fig. 1).

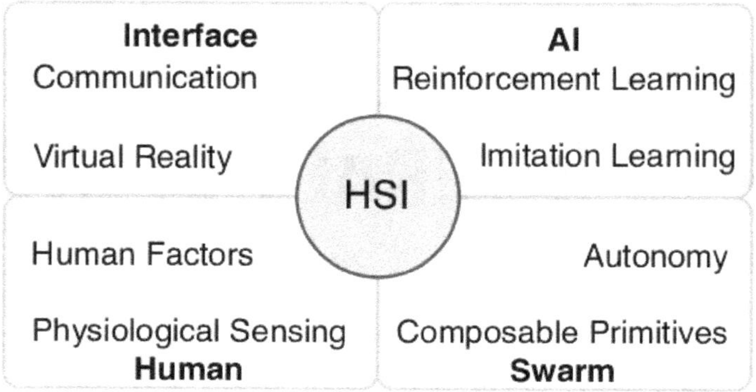

Fig. 1 The tetrad of human-swarm interaction (HSI)

11.1 INTERFACES AND COMMAND STRUCTURES

Human-Swarm Interaction requires intuitive and effective interfaces that allow humans to communicate with and control large groups of autonomous agents. Because of the decentralized nature of swarms, traditional one-to-one control methods are inadequate. Instead, interfaces must support high-level commands that influence collective behaviour rather than individual robots. The command structures must balance autonomy with human oversight, allowing for scalable control across varying swarm sizes and mission complexities. Below are key interface types and command paradigms used in HSI:

11.1.1 Graphical User Interfaces (GUIs)

GUIs provide visual feedback about the swarm's state, position and tasks through maps, dashboards or simulation environments. They allow operators to issue commands such as target locations or behavioural modes. Effective GUIs support situational awareness and mission planning with minimal cognitive load. Features like zoom, filtering and clustering help manage large numbers of agents. GUIs are especially useful in mission-critical applications like surveillance and rescue.

11.1.2 Gesture and Motion-Based Interfaces

In field operations, human gestures, hand signals or body movements can be interpreted by nearby robots using vision or wearable sensors. These interfaces allow intuitive, real-time control without traditional input devices. This method is useful in noisy or hands-busy environments where voice or GUI input is impractical. The system must reliably map human motion into swarm-level commands. This interface is especially relevant for Défense or emergency scenarios.

11.1.3 Voice and Natural Language Commands

Voice-based interaction allows users to command swarms using spoken language, supported by natural language processing (NLP). It enables intuitive communication, especially for non-experts. However, reliability may be impacted by background noise or ambiguity in phrasing. These systems must translate human intent into formal instructions that swarms can execute. Combining voice input with other interfaces can improve robustness and control fidelity.

11.1.4 Haptic and Wearable Interfaces

Haptic feedback devices (e.g., gloves, vests) or wearable controllers provide tactile feedback and allow users to feel swarm dynamics or environmental data. These interfaces enhance immersion and enable bi-directional communication. Wearables can also track movement or physiological data, which can be used to adjust swarm behaviour in response to operator stress or intent. Haptic interaction is useful for tasks requiring fine control or feedback without relying on visuals.

11.1.5 Command Structures

Centralized vs. Distributed: In centralized command structures, the human issues direct commands to the entire swarm or designated leaders, which propagate instructions. This offers higher control but lower scalability. In distributed command models, the human provides high-level goals and the swarm self-organizes to fulfil them, offering flexibility and resilience. Hybrid models combine both to allow strategic oversight with tactical autonomy. Choosing the right command structure depends on the task, environment and desired autonomy level.

11.2 SUPERVISORY CONTROL AND TRUST MODELS

In Human-Swarm Interaction (HSI), the human operator typically acts as a supervisor, guiding swarm behaviour at a high level rather than controlling individual agents. This approach, known as supervisory control, enables scalability and leverages the swarm's autonomous capabilities. However, for this model to work effectively, the operator must trust the swarm to act reliably and within acceptable boundaries. Trust becomes a central factor influencing decision-making, engagement and overall system performance.

11.2.1 Supervisory Control

Supervisory control allows humans to issue high-level goals or mission parameters, while the swarm autonomously handles execution details. The operator monitors swarm behaviour, intervening only when needed—such as during system errors or critical decisions. This reduces operator workload and improves responsiveness in large-scale operations. However, maintaining situational awareness is a challenge, especially as swarm size and complexity grow. Effective supervisory control depends on informative interfaces and well-calibrated autonomy.

11.2.2 Trust in Automation

Trust in swarm systems is the human's willingness to rely on the swarm's autonomous decisions. Too little trust leads to excessive intervention, reducing efficiency; too much trust may result in complacency and safety risks. Trust must be calibrated based on the swarm's reliability, transparency and previous performance. Factors such as false alarms, unclear feedback or unpredictable behaviour can erode trust. Therefore, swarm systems should be designed to foster appropriate levels of trust through transparency and consistency.

11.2.3 Dynamic Trust Models

Dynamic trust models adapt the level of human trust over time, based on ongoing interaction and system performance. These models use real-time data such as system reliability, task success rates or even physiological indicators (e.g., stress, fatigue) to adjust autonomy or interface behaviour. For example, if trust drops, the system may provide more explanations or request confirmation before taking action. Dynamic trust management ensures that operator engagement matches system capabilities and risk levels.

11.2.4 Shared Authority and Human-in-the-Loop:

hared authority means both the human and the swarm contribute to decision-making, allowing flexibility in who takes the lead based on context. In human-in-the-loop systems, the operator is kept actively involved during critical decisions or uncertain scenarios. This ensures that humans remain informed and capable of taking control when necessary. Balancing autonomy and control prevent over-reliance on automation and keeps the operator's skills sharp and situationally aware.

11.2.5 Building Trust Through Transparency

For trust to develop, swarm systems must be transparent—explaining what they're doing, why and what they plan to do next. This can be achieved through status indicators, intent visualization or explanation generation. When the swarm's decisions are understandable, operators feel more confident in allowing the system to operate autonomously. Transparency reduces uncertainty and increases user satisfaction, especially during unexpected behaviour or mission-critical operations.

11.3 TRANSPARENCY AND EXPLAINABILITY IN SWARMS

In swarm robotic systems, transparency and explainability are critical for enabling effective and safe human-swarm interaction. Due to the distributed and often emergent nature of swarm behaviour, it can be challenging for human operators to understand why certain actions are taken. Without clear insight into swarm intent and decision-making processes, operators may struggle to trust or effectively supervise the system. Transparency involves making the swarm's status, goals and behaviours visible and understandable in real time. Explainability goes a step further, providing justifications or reasons for those actions in a human-friendly manner. These elements help users interpret swarm behaviour, anticipate future actions and intervene appropriately when needed. In complex or mission-critical tasks, a lack of transparency can lead to confusion, errors or even mission failure. Well-designed interfaces and algorithms are essential to bridge the cognitive gap between humans and autonomous swarms. As HSI evolves, enhancing transparency and explainability remains a top priority.

11.3.1 Importance of Transparency in HIS

Transparency refers to how clearly a system reveals its status, intentions and reasoning to human operators. In swarm robotics, where behaviour emerges from local interactions among many agents, understanding the swarm's collective intent can be challenging. Transparent systems enable operators to predict and interpret swarm actions, reducing confusion and hesitation. In high-stakes environments—like search and rescue or Défense—this clarity is vital for timely and confident decisions. A transparent interface helps the human maintain situational awareness and control without micromanaging. Transparency also plays a central role in fostering calibrated trust, as users are more likely to rely on systems they understand. In HSI, transparency must be scalable—conveying useful insights about swarm behaviour without overwhelming the user with raw data. Visual cues, mission summaries and event logs are common tools for enhancing swarm transparency. Ultimately, transparency improves usability, confidence and collaborative performance between human and swarm.

11.3.2 Explainability of Swarm Behaviour

Explainability in HSI refers to the swarm's ability to justify its decisions, actions or outcomes in a way that is understandable to a human operator. Since swarm systems often use decentralized algorithms, their behaviour may appear unpredictable or even irrational without proper context. Explainability mechanisms break down this complexity by providing simplified yet meaningful explanations of why certain movements, formations or tasks occurred. For instance, if a swarm changes direction, the system might explain that it's avoiding a detected obstacle or optimizing coverage. This helps prevent operator confusion and reduces the risk of unnecessary intervention. Explainable swarms can also be audited more easily, improving accountability. AI-based techniques, such as behaviour summarization, trajectory rationalization and causal tracing, support this capability. By demystifying autonomous behaviour, explainability bridges the gap between human cognition and algorithmic logic, ensuring alignment between human expectations and swarm actions.

11.3.3 Techniques to Achieve Transparency and Explainability

Several interface and algorithmic techniques are employed to make swarm systems both transparent and explainable. Visual overlays (like heatmaps or swarm trails) allow users to see areas of focus or movement patterns in real time. Intent visualization tools display what the swarm is planning to do next, enhancing predictability. Behaviour tagging and logs can track specific agents or clusters to analyse decision flow. Natural language generation (NLG) systems can convert swarm status into simple statements like, "The swarm is scanning high-risk zones." Machine learning models can also detect and highlight deviations from normal swarm behaviour. In addition, modular swarm designs that separate navigation, task allocation and threat avoidance make it easier to trace cause-and-effect relationships. Effective techniques ensure that users are informed, not overwhelmed. The goal is to offer just the right amount of information at the right time to support situational awareness, learning and responsive control.

11.4 VISUALIZATION TOOLS FOR MONITORING SWARMS

Effective visualization tools are essential in Human-Swarm Interaction (HSI) to support operators in monitoring, understanding and controlling large groups of autonomous robots. Due to the complexity and scale of swarms, raw data from individual agents can be overwhelming and difficult to interpret. Visualization helps translate this data into intuitive, actionable insights by presenting swarm states, behaviours and environmental interactions in a clear and concise manner. By leveraging graphical representations, operators can maintain situational awareness, detect anomalies and make timely decisions. These tools vary widely in design and functionality depending on the mission context, swarm size and user needs. Below, we explore some of the primary visualization techniques used in swarm robotics and how they enhance human understanding and interaction.

11.4.1 Spatial and Geographical Visualizations

Spatial visualizations map the physical locations and movements of swarm agents onto a 2D or 3D environment, often using maps or simulated terrains. These tools allow operators to track swarm distribution, formations and navigation paths in real time. Heatmaps or density maps indicate areas of high activity or coverage, helping to identify gaps or overlaps in the swarm's operational field. Geographical visualizations can integrate sensor data such as temperature, chemical concentrations or radiation levels, providing a multi-layered environmental context. This spatial awareness is crucial for applications like search and rescue, environmental monitoring or military reconnaissance, were precise positioning impacts mission success. Effective spatial visualization enables operators to issue location-based commands and quickly assess swarm progress against objectives.

11.4.2 Behaviour and State Indicators

Behavioural visualizations focus on displaying the internal states and activities of swarm members or groups. These indicators might include color-coding agents based on roles, status (e.g., idle, active, damaged) or current tasks (e.g., exploring, communicating). State indicators help operators quickly gauge swarm health and performance without needing to monitor individual robots. They can highlight anomalies, such as agents deviating from expected paths or failing to respond to commands. Visualization of communication links and network topology also informs operators about connectivity and potential bottlenecks. By abstracting complex behaviours into simple visual cues, these tools reduce cognitive load and facilitate rapid decision-making, especially in high-pressure or time-sensitive environments.

11.4.3. Temporal and Predictive Visualizations

Temporal visualization tools provide insights into how swarm behaviour evolves over time, often using timelines, activity charts or playback features. This allows operators to review past actions, identify patterns and predict future states. Predictive models integrated with visualization can forecast swarm movements, potential collisions or task completion times, enabling proactive intervention. For example, trajectory prediction overlays can help anticipate the swarm's path through dynamic or hazardous environments. Temporal visualizations support training, debugging and post-mission analysis, offering a deeper understanding of swarm dynamics. Incorporating these tools into real-time monitoring enhances responsiveness and allows operators to better manage uncertainties inherent in autonomous swarm operations.

11.5 COLLABORATIVE HUMAN-ROBOT TEAMS

In modern robotics, collaborative human-robot teams combine the unique strengths of humans and autonomous swarms to achieve complex goals that neither can accomplish alone. These teams leverage the swarm's scalability, speed and resilience alongside human creativity, strategic thinking and ethical judgment. Collaboration requires seamless communication, shared understanding and adaptive coordination mechanisms that support flexible division of labour. By working together, human operators and robotic swarms can tackle diverse applications such as disaster response, industrial automation, environmental monitoring and military operations with increased efficiency and safety. Successful collaboration depends on well-designed interfaces and mutual trust to synchronize efforts and manage dynamic environments effectively.

11.5.1 Complementary Strengths of Humans and Swarms

Humans excel in abstract reasoning, ethical decision-making and handling unexpected situations, while swarms provide rapid, parallel processing, distributed sensing and redundancy through large numbers of agents. Swarms can cover vast areas quickly and persistently, collecting data and performing routine tasks autonomously. Humans guide overall mission goals, intervene during uncertainties and provide contextual interpretation that is difficult for robots to replicate. This synergy allows teams to adapt dynamically to evolving scenarios, combining machine efficiency with human judgment to optimize task outcomes. Understanding these complementary roles is essential to designing effective collaboration frameworks.

11.5.2 Communication and Coordination

Efficient communication protocols are vital to maintain alignment between human operators and robotic swarms. This involves not only transmitting commands but also conveying feedback, swarm status and environmental updates in real time. Coordination mechanisms enable the team to divide tasks appropriately, delegate authority and reassign roles dynamically as conditions change. Visual and auditory cues, haptic feedback and augmented reality interfaces can enhance situational awareness and reduce cognitive load. Multi-modal communication ensures that humans remain informed and engaged without being overwhelmed by the swarm's complexity. Effective coordination also includes conflict resolution strategies and error recovery to maintain operational continuity.

11.5.3 Challenges and Future Directions

Despite advances, several challenges persist in achieving truly seamless collaboration. These include managing cognitive overload for human operators, ensuring trust and transparency and developing adaptive autonomy that can shift control based on context. Integrating heterogeneous robot types and scales within swarms further complicates coordination. Future research focuses on improving machine learning algorithms for better understanding human intent, enhancing natural language interfaces and developing ethical guidelines for shared decision-making. The ultimate goal is to create resilient, flexible teams that can operate autonomously yet synergize smoothly with humans across diverse and unpredictable environments.

12 Chapter REGULATORY AND ETHICAL PERSPECTIVES

12.0 INTRODUCTION: AN OVERVIEW

In today's rapidly evolving global environment, the significance of regulatory and ethical perspectives has never been more pronounced. As industries expand, technologies advance and societies become increasingly interconnected, the need for clearly defined frameworks governing behaviour, practices and accountability grows. Regulatory and ethical perspectives serve as foundational pillars that guide the operations of governments, businesses, healthcare systems, educational institutions and virtually all facets of society. Regulations are structured systems of rules enforced by governing bodies to ensure compliance with the law, maintain order, protect public interests and promote fair practices. Ethics, on the other hand, delve into moral philosophy—exploring what is right or wrong, just or unjust, fair or unfair—and represent the collective conscience that influences human decisions and institutional policies. While regulations are often codified and legally binding, ethics represent broader societal values that may or may not be legislated but are nonetheless powerful in shaping behaviour. Ethical considerations often precede regulatory measures and play a critical role in highlighting the need for new laws and reforms. Together, they provide a dual framework that fosters integrity, trust, transparency, accountability and social responsibility across all sectors. In industries such as healthcare, finance, information technology and scientific research, the interplay between ethics and regulation determines the boundaries of acceptable practice and helps in safeguarding human rights, data privacy, patient welfare and environmental sustainability (Fig. 1).

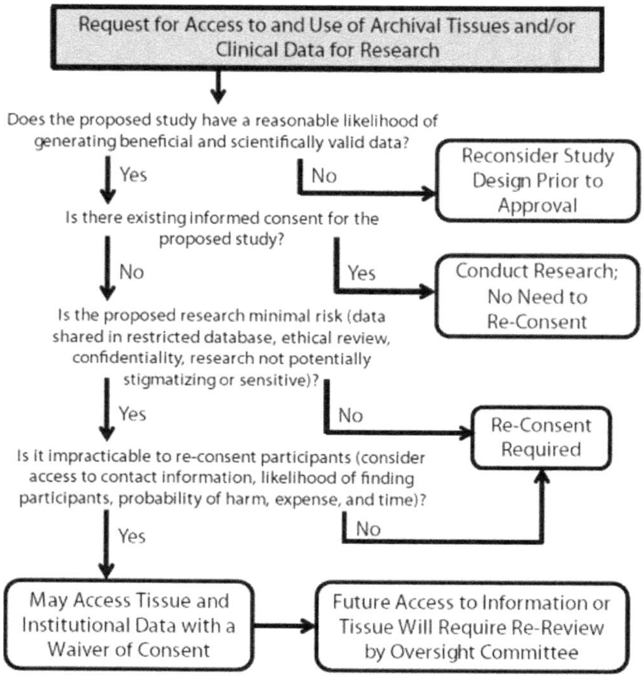

Fig. 1 Ethical, Legal and Regulatory Considerations

For instance, the healthcare sector must navigate both the ethical obligation to "do no harm" and comply with medical regulations governing patient care and data confidentiality. Similarly, the financial industry is bound by regulatory frameworks designed to prevent fraud, insider trading and market manipulation, while simultaneously being guided by ethical standards concerning honesty, equity and client trust. In the realm of artificial intelligence and data science, rapidly advancing innovations are outpacing regulatory frameworks, posing urgent ethical dilemmas surrounding privacy, algorithmic bias, surveillance and autonomy. This highlights the ongoing need for adaptive regulations and ethical foresight to ensure that technological progress aligns with societal values and human dignity. Regulatory bodies such as the Food and Drug Administration (FDA), Securities and Exchange Commission (SEC) and General Data Protection Regulation (GDPR) represent some of the many institutional mechanisms established to enforce compliance and protect public welfare. However, regulations alone are insufficient without an internalized ethical commitment by individuals and organizations. Ethical leadership and a culture of integrity are essential in promoting compliance not just out of obligation, but from a shared sense of purpose and societal good. Additionally, ethical theories—such as utilitarianism, deontology, virtue ethics and rights-based approaches—provide frameworks for evaluating moral dilemmas and informing policy decisions. Understanding the regulatory and ethical perspectives is crucial not only for policymakers and corporate leaders but also for employees, students, consumers and citizens at large. In an age of social media scrutiny, global activism and instant communication, the consequences of ethical lapses and regulatory failures are more visible and far-reaching than ever. Therefore, integrating ethics and regulation into organizational strategies, educational curricula and public discourse is essential to building resilient, equitable and sustainable systems. This chapter explores the multifaceted relationship between regulation and ethics, their applications across various sectors and the challenges and opportunities that lie ahead. As we delve deeper, we will examine how regulatory and ethical considerations shape decision-making, influence behaviour and ultimately contribute to the development of a just and responsible global society.

12.1 SAFETY AND RISK ASSESSMENT

Safety and risk assessment refers to the systematic process of identifying potential hazards, analysing associated risks and implementing measures to reduce or eliminate harm. It is a foundational practice across various sectors including healthcare, manufacturing, engineering, construction, information technology and public services. The goal is to protect individuals, assets and the environment from potential damage or injury.

12.1.1 Importance of Safety in Organizational Contexts

- **Protecting Human Life:** The foremost priority in any organization is safeguarding the health and safety of its employees, customers and the broader public. Effective safety measures prevent workplace injuries, illnesses and fatalities, fostering a secure environment. By prioritizing human well-being organizations demonstrate ethical responsibility and care. A safe workplace enhances employee morale and productivity, reducing absenteeism. Ultimately, protecting human life builds a foundation of trust and respect essential for long-term success.
- **Legal Compliance:** Organizations must adhere to various laws and regulations designed to protect workers and communities from harm. Compliance with these legal requirements helps avoid penalties, fines and lawsuits that can arise from safety violations. It also ensures alignment with government standards and industry best practices. Meeting legal obligations safeguards the company's operational license and market position. Moreover, proactive compliance reflects an organization's commitment to ethical and responsible conduct.
- **Financial Implications:** Investing in safety programs can significantly reduce costs associated with workplace accidents, such as medical expenses, compensation claims and legal fees. Accidents often lead to operational

disruptions and downtime, which negatively impact productivity and profitability. Insurance premiums may also increase following incidents, adding to financial strain. Conversely, a strong safety record can attract business and reduce overall risk exposure. Thus, effective safety management is a sound financial strategy that protects both assets and revenues.

- **Reputation Management:** An organization's reputation is closely tied to how well it manages safety and risk. A strong safety culture builds public confidence, making customers, partners and investors more likely to engage and support the business. Conversely, safety failures can lead to negative publicity, loss of trust and damaged relationships. Maintaining a solid reputation requires transparent communication and consistent adherence to safety standards. Ultimately, protecting reputation through safety fosters brand loyalty and competitive advantage.

12.1.2. Understanding Risk

Definition of Risk: The possibility of harm or loss resulting from exposure to a hazard.

Types of Risks:

- Physical Risks (e.g., machinery hazards)
- Chemical Risks (e.g., toxic exposure)
- Biological Risks (e.g., infections in healthcare)
- Cybersecurity Risks (e.g., data breaches)
- Psychological Risks (e.g., stress and burnout)

12.1.3 Risk Assessment Process

A structured risk assessment typically includes the following steps:

- **Hazard Identification:** Hazard identification is the foundational step in the risk assessment process, focused on recognizing any potential sources of harm within the workplace or system. This involves a thorough examination of the environment, equipment, procedures and human factors that could lead to injury or damage. Tools such as checklists, past incident reports, safety audits and employee feedback are instrumental in uncovering hazards. Identifying hazards early helps prevent accidents and lays the groundwork for effective risk management. It requires collaboration among safety experts, workers and management to ensure no risks are overlooked. Comprehensive hazard identification enhances overall workplace safety culture.

- **Risk Analysis:** Once hazards are identified, risk analysis evaluates the likelihood that each hazard will cause harm and the potential severity of that harm. This step uses both quantitative methods, such as statistical data and probability models and qualitative approaches like expert judgment and scoring systems. The goal is to understand how risks manifest and their possible impacts on people, property and operations. Accurate risk analysis helps prioritize risks and allocate resources efficiently. It also highlights areas requiring urgent attention or further investigation. By quantifying risk organizations can make informed decisions on control measures.
- **Risk Evaluation:** Risk evaluation compares the assessed risks against predefined criteria or acceptable thresholds to determine their significance. This step helps prioritize risks based on factors like urgency, frequency and potential impact, allowing organizations to focus on the most critical issues first. Risks deemed unacceptable must be addressed immediately, while lower-priority risks may be monitored or controlled over time. Risk evaluation requires clear benchmarks, often derived from legal standards, industry guidelines or organizational policies. Effective evaluation supports strategic planning and resource allocation. It ensures that risk management efforts are targeted and aligned with overall safety goals.
- **Risk Control Measures:** After evaluating risks, appropriate control measures are implemented to eliminate or reduce them to acceptable levels. Controls follow a hierarchy: first, eliminating the hazard entirely; if that's not possible, substituting it with something safer; then applying engineering controls to isolate people from the hazard. Administrative controls, such as updated procedures and training, help minimize exposure. Finally, personal protective equipment (PPE) acts as the last line of Défense when other controls are insufficient. This layered approach maximizes safety by addressing hazards from multiple angles. Regular assessment of these controls ensures they remain effective over time.
- **Monitoring and Review:** Monitoring and review are ongoing activities that ensure risk control measures continue to be effective and relevant. Regular inspections, audits and feedback loops help detect changes in the workplace or emerging hazards that may affect risk levels. This continuous process allows for timely updates to risk assessments and control strategies based on new data, technological advancements or regulatory changes. Employee involvement in monitoring encourages a proactive safety culture. Effective review prevents complacency and adapts risk management to evolving conditions. Ultimately, it sustains long-term safety and resilience.

12.1.4 Tools and Techniques for Risk Assessment

Risk assessment relies on a variety of tools and techniques designed to identify, analyse and manage potential hazards effectively. SWOT analysis helps evaluate internal strengths and weaknesses alongside external opportunities and threats, providing a broad overview of risk factors. FMEA focuses on identifying possible failure modes within a system and their potential effects to prioritize mitigation efforts. HAZOP is a detailed, systematic study that examines how deviations from normal operation can lead to hazards. Risk matrices visually categorize risks by likelihood and impact to aid decision-making. Bowtie diagrams offer a clear representation of risk causes and controls in a single view. Incident investigation reports provide valuable lessons by analysing past failures. Together, these tools enable comprehensive and proactive risk management.

- SWOT Analysis (Strengths, Weaknesses, Opportunities, Threats)
- FMEA (Failure Mode and Effects Analysis)
- HAZOP (Hazard and Operability Study)
- Risk Matrices
- Bowtie Diagrams
- Incident Investigation Reports

12.1.5 Regulatory Frameworks and Standards

Safety and risk assessment practices are guided by a range of regulatory frameworks and standards established at both global and national levels. These regulations provide structured approaches to identifying, evaluating and managing risks across industries. ISO 31000 offers universal guidelines for risk management, promoting a systematic and consistent methodology. In the United States, OSHA ensures workplace safety through enforceable regulations, while the UK follows the Health and Safety at Work Act to protect employees and the public. Environmental protection laws mandate responsible practices to minimize ecological harm. Additionally, industry-specific frameworks—such as FDA regulations for healthcare, aviation authority standards or cybersecurity guidelines—address unique risks in specialized sectors. Adhering to these frameworks not only ensures legal compliance but also promotes ethical, safe and efficient operations.

Various global and national regulations govern safety and risk assessment practices:

- ISO 31000 – Risk Management Guidelines
- OSHA (Occupational Safety and Health Administration – USA)
- Health and Safety at Work Act (UK)
- Environmental Protection Laws

- Industry-Specific Guidelines (e.g., FDA, Aviation Authorities, Cybersecurity Frameworks)

12.1.6 Ethical Considerations in Safety and Risk

Ethical considerations play a vital role in safety and risk management, going beyond regulations and technical standards. Ensuring the safety of workers, the public and the environment is not just a legal duty—it is a moral responsibility that reflects an organization's core values. Ethical safety practices demonstrate respect for human life and dignity, reinforcing a culture of care and accountability. Transparency in communicating risks is essential for building trust among employees, stakeholders and the public. Concealing or downplaying hazards for the sake of reputation or convenience can have serious ethical and legal consequences. In many cases, ethical dilemmas arise when organizations are pressured to choose between cost savings and comprehensive safety measures. Profit should never come at the expense of human well-being. Decision-makers must be guided by integrity, empathy and a long-term vision. Ethical frameworks also help navigate uncertainties, especially in emerging industries or high-risk environments. Ultimately, ethical safety management fosters a sustainable, trustworthy and socially responsible operation.

- Ensuring worker and public safety is not only a legal requirement but a moral obligation.
- Transparency in risk communication fosters trust.
- Ethical dilemmas may arise when balancing profit and safety—prioritizing human well-being must be central.

12.1.7 Challenges in Safety and Risk Assessment

Safety and risk assessment is a critical component of any operational or technological system, ensuring potential hazards are identified, evaluated and mitigated. However organizations often face significant challenges in conducting accurate and comprehensive assessments. A common issue is the lack of complete data or absence of historical incident records, making it difficult to predict future risks. Additionally, resistance to change and high implementation costs can hinder the adoption of improved safety measures. As technologies rapidly evolve, new and unforeseen risks emerge, requiring continuous reassessment and adaptation. Balancing the push for innovation with the need for precaution adds another layer of complexity. These challenges highlight the need for proactive, flexible and well-informed risk management strategies. Without addressing them, both safety and progress may be compromised.

- Incomplete data or lack of historical incidents.
- Resistance to change or implementation costs.

- Dynamic and evolving risks, especially with new technologies.
- Balancing innovation with precaution.

12.2 STANDARDIZATION AND COMPLIANCE

Standardization and compliance are key pillars in maintaining quality, safety and consistency across industries and organizations. Standardization refers to the process of developing and implementing technical standards based on consensus and best practices, while compliance involves adhering to those established standards, regulations and laws. Together, they ensure that products, services and operations meet required benchmarks, reduce risks and promote trust among consumers, stakeholders and regulators.

12.2.1 Importance of Standardization

- **Uniformity and Consistency:** Uniformity and consistency in standards ensure that processes, products and services deliver predictable and reliable outcomes every time. This minimizes errors and variations, helping organizations maintain high-quality performance across different locations and teams. Consistent application of standards simplifies training and quality control efforts. It also fosters trust internally among employees and externally with customers and partners. Ultimately, this leads to smoother operations and reduced risk of defects or failures.
- **Interoperability:** Interoperability guarantees that different systems, components or technologies can communicate and work together effectively without compatibility issues. This is especially critical in complex engineering, IT and manufacturing environments where multiple subsystems must integrate seamlessly. Standards promoting interoperability enable flexibility in choosing suppliers and upgrading components without major disruptions. It also supports innovation by allowing new technologies to fit into existing infrastructures. Ensuring interoperability reduces downtime and enhances overall system performance.
- **Efficiency and Productivity:** Implementing standardized procedures helps streamline workflows by reducing unnecessary variability, redundancies and waste. This leads to faster production cycles and optimized use of resources, including time, materials and labour. Consistent processes also make it easier to identify and eliminate bottlenecks or inefficiencies. As a result organizations can increase output quality while lowering costs. Enhanced efficiency and productivity give businesses a competitive edge in rapidly changing markets.
- **Global Trade Facilitation:** Standards play a key role in enabling international trade by ensuring products and services meet universally

recognized criteria. This reduces technical barriers between countries and simplifies regulatory approvals, making it easier to export and import goods. Harmonized standards foster mutual trust among trading partners and consumers worldwide. They also help companies access new markets by complying with global expectations. Overall, standards act as a bridge supporting smoother, safer and more efficient global commerce.

- **Customer Confidence:** Adherence to recognized standards signals to customers that an organization is committed to quality, safety and reliability. This transparency builds trust and enhances the company's reputation, encouraging customer loyalty and repeat business. When customers know that products or services meet rigorous standards, their perceived risk decreases, leading to higher satisfaction. It also differentiates companies from competitors who may have less stringent controls. Strong customer confidence is essential for long-term success and brand strength.

12.2.2 Importance of Compliance

- **Legal Obligation:** Avoids legal penalties, sanctions and shutdowns by following mandatory regulations.
- **Risk Mitigation:** Helps prevent accidents, data breaches, fraud and other operational risks.
- **Reputation Management:** A compliant organization gains respect from customers, investors and partners.
- **Operational Excellence:** Encourages ethical practices and responsible behaviour across the organization.
- **Employee and Consumer Protection:** Ensures a safe and secure environment for all stakeholders. The summary of the importance of compliance is presented in Table-1.

Table 1: Summary of the Importance of Compliance presented

Aspect	Importance
Legal Obligation	Prevents legal penalties, sanctions or shutdowns by adhering to regulations.
Risk Mitigation	Reduces risks such as accidents, data breaches and fraud.
Reputation Management	Enhances trust and credibility with customers, investors and partners.
Operational Excellence	Promotes ethical conduct and responsible organizational behaviour.
Employee & Consumer Protection	Ensures safety and security for employees, customers and other stakeholders.

12.2.3 Types of Standards

- **International Standards:** Developed by organizations like ISO, IEC and ITU (e.g., ISO 9001 for quality management).
- **National Standards:** Defined by local governing bodies (e.g., BIS in India, ANSI in the U.S.).
- **Industry-Specific Standards:** Tailored to particular sectors such as healthcare, IT, finance, construction, etc.
- **Regulatory Standards:** Mandated by law (e.g., GDPR for data protection in Europe, FDA standards for food and drugs).

12.2.4 Regulatory and Standardization Bodies

ISO (International Organization for Standardization)

IEC (International Electrotechnical Commission)

FDA (Food and Drug Administration)

GDPR (General Data Protection Regulation)

OSHA (Occupational Safety and Health Administration)

SEBI, FSSAI, NABH, BIS (in India)

12.2.5 Standardization Process

- **Identification of Need:** Stakeholders propose a need for standardization in a specific area.
- **Development and Drafting:** Technical committees draft standards based on research and industry consensus.
- **Review and Approval:** Drafts are reviewed by stakeholders and finalized after public feedback.
- **Publication and Implementation:** Approved standards are published and adopted by industries or governments.
- **Periodic Revision:** Standards are updated to reflect technological advancements and societal needs.

12.2.6 Compliance Management System

To ensure continuous adherence to standards and regulations, many organizations adopt a compliance management system (CMS) which includes:

- Policy Development
- Internal Audits
- Employee Training

- Monitoring and Reporting
- Corrective Actions
- Compliance Officer or Team Oversight

12.2.7 Challenges in Standardization and Compliance

- **Rapid Technological Change:** Standards may lag behind innovations, causing compliance gaps.
- **Complex Regulatory Landscapes:** Varying regulations across regions can complicate international operations.
- **High Implementation Costs**: Especially for SMEs, the cost of adopting and maintaining standards may be a barrier.
- **Lack of Awareness or Training:** Employees or management may not fully understand the importance or methods of compliance.

12.2.8 Ethical Considerations

- **Beyond Legal Compliance:** Ethical organizations strive not just to follow rules but to act with integrity.
- **Transparency:** Openly communicating about compliance status and challenges.
- **Fair Enforcement:** Avoiding selective or discriminatory application of standards.
- **Responsibility to Society:** Ensuring standards protect public welfare, privacy and environmental sustainability.

12.2.9. Case Examples

- **ISO 27001 (Information Security):** Widely adopted to protect sensitive data across industries.
- **GDPR (General Data Protection Regulation):** A strict compliance requirement for organizations handling EU citizen data.
- **NABH Accreditation (Healthcare in India):** Encourages hospitals to maintain high clinical standards.
- **ROHS & WEEE (Electronics):** Ensures sustainable and safe disposal of electronic waste.

12.2.10 Benefits of Achieving Compliance

- **Competitive Advantage:** Certified organizations are more likely to gain client trust and win contracts.

- **Access to Global Markets:** Many standards are prerequisites for international trade.
- **Reduced Risk Exposure:** Proactively identifying and correcting non-compliance reduces future liabilities.
- **Cultural Strengthening:** Encourages a workplace culture built on accountability, ethics and improvement.

12.3 ETHICAL USE IN CIVILIAN AND MILITARY CONTEXTS

Ethics play a pivotal role in both civilian and military applications of technology, power and decision-making. As the boundaries between civilian and military spheres blur—especially with advancements in artificial intelligence, surveillance and dual-use technologies—the importance of ethical frameworks becomes increasingly crucial. While both sectors aim to protect and serve society, the methods, consequences and moral considerations behind their actions often differ. This section explores the ethical dimensions involved in both civilian and military contexts, highlighting their similarities, differences and the growing challenges in maintaining ethical integrity.

- **Human Rights and Dignity:** In civilian contexts, ethics are fundamentally centered on upholding human rights and respecting individual dignity. This includes safeguarding privacy and ensuring the confidentiality of personal information, especially in healthcare and research. Ethical practices demand equality, rejecting any form of discrimination based on race, gender or other factors. Informed consent is crucial, guaranteeing individuals fully understand and agree to any interventions or data use affecting them. Protecting these rights promotes trust and fairness in societal interactions.
- **Accountability and Transparency:** Civil institutions such as governments, corporations and public services are entrusted with public resources and responsibilities, making transparency essential. Accountability means that these entities must openly report decisions, actions and outcomes to the public and accept responsibility for their conduct. Transparent operations help prevent corruption, build public trust and foster democratic engagement. Clear communication and honest disclosure empower citizens to hold institutions accountable. This principle is vital for maintaining legitimacy and ethical governance.
- **Public Welfare and Justice:** Ethical decision-making in civilian life prioritizes the well-being of the entire community while safeguarding the rights of vulnerable groups. Policies and actions should aim to maximize public benefit, addressing social inequalities and minimizing harm. Justice

requires fair treatment for all, including equitable access to resources, services and opportunities. Ethical frameworks encourage inclusivity and seek to balance diverse interests to promote social cohesion. Protecting public welfare is the cornerstone of sustainable and ethical societal development.

- **Corporate and Technological Ethics:** Modern civilian ethics increasingly focus on the responsibilities of corporations and technology developers in society. Responsible AI development emphasizes fairness, transparency and avoiding biases in algorithms affecting people's lives. Ethical data use involves protecting user privacy and securing sensitive information. Environmental sustainability has become a core ethical concern, urging companies to minimize ecological impact. Ethical marketing ensures truthful communication and protects consumer rights. Together, these principles guide the responsible integration of technology in daily life.

12.3.1 Ethical Principles in Military Contexts:

- **Just War Theory:** Just War Theory provides a moral framework for evaluating when and how war can be ethically justified. It consists of two main parts: jus ad bellum (the right to go to war) and jus in bello (right conduct in war). Jus ad bellum focuses on legitimate reasons for war, such as self-defence or protecting innocent lives. Jus in bello ensures that military actions during war are proportional and discriminate between combatants and non-combatants. The theory aims to prevent unnecessary violence and uphold justice even in times of conflict. It serves as a guide for ethical decision-making in military strategy.
- **Rules of Engagement and International Law:** Rules of Engagement (ROE) define the conditions under which military personnel may engage in combat. These rules are shaped by international law, including treaties like the Geneva Conventions and national military policies. ROE ensure actions taken in conflict align with legal and ethical obligations. They limit excessive force, protect human rights and prevent unlawful actions. Military leaders and soldiers are trained to understand and apply these rules in real-time decisions. ROE maintain discipline and accountability, reinforcing legitimacy in military operations.
- **Protection of Non-Combatants:** Protecting non-combatants is a core ethical principle in military operations. International humanitarian law requires that civilians not directly involved in fighting be spared from harm. Discrimination between combatants and non-combatants is essential to avoid unnecessary suffering. Strategies like precision targeting and evacuation protocols are used to minimize civilian casualties. Violating this

principle can result in serious legal and moral consequences. Upholding it reflects a commitment to human rights even amid warfare.

- **Responsibility and Obedience:** Military personnel are expected to follow lawful orders, but they also bear responsibility for their actions. Ethical military conduct involves balancing obedience with moral judgment. Blindly following unlawful or unethical orders is not acceptable under international law. Soldiers are trained to recognize when an order may violate legal or ethical standards. Accountability mechanisms ensure that individuals are held responsible for misconduct. This principle reinforces the idea that integrity and discipline are vital to ethical military service.

12.3.2 Dual-Use Technologies- Ethical Dilemmas

Many modern technologies serve both civilian and military purposes. Examples include:

- Drones: Used for commercial delivery or targeted military strikes
- AI and Machine Learning: Applied in healthcare diagnostics and autonomous weapon systems
- Satellite Surveillance: Aids in environmental monitoring or military reconnaissance

These dual-use capabilities raise difficult ethical questions:

- How should control and access be managed?
- Can one justify development if misuse is likely?
- Where do ethical responsibilities lie—developers, users or governments?

12.3.3 Case Studies and Examples

- **Civilian Ethics- Data Privacy:** The misuse of personal data by corporations or governments (e.g., Facebook-Cambridge Analytica scandal) demonstrates the ethical risks in civilian systems when transparency is lacking.
- **Military Ethics- Autonomous Weapons:** Lethal autonomous weapon systems (LAWS) pose ethical risks by removing human decision-making from life-and-death scenarios. Concerns include accountability, bias and civilian casualties.
- **Ethical Whistleblowing:** Cases such as Edward Snowden (NSA surveillance) and Chelsea Manning (military leaks) highlight ethical conflicts between institutional loyalty and public interest.

12.3.4. Differences Between Civilian and Military Ethical Frameworks

Civilian and military ethical frameworks differ significantly due to their distinct roles, responsibilities and environments. Civilian ethics are rooted in the principles of public welfare, justice and the protection of individual rights. In contrast, military ethics prioritize national Défense, security and the success of missions, sometimes requiring difficult decisions in high-stakes situations. Decision-making in civilian contexts typically involves democratically accountable bodies such as courts, legislatures and public institutions, ensuring transparency and accountability. In the military, decisions are made within a hierarchical chain of command, emphasizing obedience, discipline and strategic leadership. While civilian ethics uphold the minimal harm principle, striving to avoid harm to individuals or communities, military ethics accept that some harm may be unavoidable, especially in combat or conflict zones.

Transparency also differs sharply between the two. Civilians expect openness in decision-making processes, with public access to information being a cornerstone of democratic accountability. The military, however, often operates under confidentiality due to the sensitive nature of its operations, where certain information must remain classified to protect national interests. Furthermore, the use of force is a key area of divergence. In civilian life, the use of force is heavily restricted and typically regarded as unacceptable unless under clear legal justification. Conversely, in military contexts, force may be conditionally permitted, such as during warfare, peacekeeping missions or Défense operations, where it is a tool of state power exercised under specific legal and ethical frameworks.

Despite these differences, both ethical systems aim to uphold integrity, responsibility and respect for human dignity. Military ethics are guided by codes such as the Law of Armed Conflict and Rules of Engagement, which provide boundaries for conduct in warfare. Civilian ethics are shaped by legal frameworks, professional standards and societal values. Ultimately, while their methods and tolerances may differ, both civilian and military ethics are crucial to the functioning of society and the protection of fundamental values. Understanding these distinctions helps foster mutual respect and informed dialogue between civilian and military communities.

12.3.5 Converging Ethical Challenges

In the 21st century, some ethical issues are becoming common to both contexts:

- **Cybersecurity:** Cybersecurity is a growing concern for both civilian and military institutions as they face constant threats from hacking, data breaches, surveillance and digital warfare. These attacks can compromise critical infrastructure, disrupt services and endanger national security. Civilians face risks like identity theft and privacy violations, while militaries must protect classified systems and operational integrity. Ethical considerations include respecting privacy, avoiding overreach in surveillance and ensuring transparency in data use. Both sectors must collaborate to develop secure systems and ethical frameworks. Cyber Défense is now a shared responsibility across society.

- **AI Bias:** Artificial Intelligence is increasingly used in decision-making systems, including criminal justice tools and military targeting algorithms. However, these systems can unintentionally reinforce existing social biases if not properly designed and tested. In civilian life, biased AI can lead to unjust legal outcomes or discriminatory policing. In military contexts, flawed AI can cause misidentification or wrongful targeting with serious consequences. Ethical use of AI requires transparency, accountability and fairness in data and design. Ensuring AI systems are unbiased is essential for justice and operational credibility in both sectors.
- **Climate Change:** Climate change poses an ethical challenge for both civilian and military organizations, as both contribute to environmental degradation. Civilian sectors must reduce emissions, promote sustainability and support vulnerable populations. Militaries, while often heavy energy users, are also increasingly recognizing their role in reducing environmental harm. Ethical responsibility includes minimizing ecological footprints and preparing for climate-driven conflicts and disasters. Both institutions must lead by example in environmental stewardship. Addressing climate change is a shared moral duty that affects global stability and human welfare.

12.3.6 The Role of International and National Ethics Bodies

To address complex ethical challenges across civilian and military domains, various international and national bodies work to promote and uphold ethical standards. Organizations like UNESCO and the United Nations Human Rights Council advocate for global human rights and ethical governance. The International Committee of the Red Cross (ICRC) plays a key role in guiding military ethics, particularly during armed conflict. National ethics commissions and professional boards help regulate practices in fields like medicine, science and defence, ensuring accountability and integrity. Additionally, multilateral treaties focus on critical issues such as arms control, cyber warfare and AI safety. These collective efforts aim to establish shared ethical norms, reduce harm and support global stability. Through collaboration, these bodies help align policies with fundamental human values.

12.3.7 Ethical Education and Training

Ethical behaviour is not automatic—it must be taught and reinforced. Both civilians (e.g., corporate leaders, scientists, public servants) and military personnel benefit from:

- **Ethics Courses in Professional Education:** Ethics courses are essential in shaping responsible professionals across all sectors. These courses introduce foundational principles, ethical dilemmas and critical thinking tools. In both civilian and military institutions, they foster awareness of moral responsibilities. By learning case studies and real-world implications, individuals develop a framework for sound judgment. Such education builds a culture of integrity and accountability.

- **Scenario-Based Training:** Scenario-based training helps individuals apply ethical principles in realistic, high-pressure situations. Through simulations and role-playing, participants learn to navigate complex decisions. This method enhances problem-solving and moral reasoning skills, especially in unpredictable environments. Military personnel, public officials and corporate leaders all benefit from experiential learning. It prepares them to act ethically when it matters most.
- **Institutional Ethics Committees:** Institutional ethics committees provide oversight and guidance on difficult ethical issues within organizations. These bodies review decisions, offer consultations and set ethical policies. In medicine, defence, research and government, they ensure actions align with accepted standards. They serve as a check against unethical behaviour and foster transparency. Their presence strengthens institutional trust and ethical culture.
- **Whistleblower Protection Laws:** Whistleblower protection laws safeguard individuals who report unethical or illegal actions. These laws encourage accountability by ensuring safety from retaliation. In both civilian and military settings, they empower people to speak up without fear. Protecting whistleblowers promotes transparency and deters misconduct. Such laws are vital to upholding justice and ethical governance.

12.4 LEGAL FRAMEWORKS FOR AUTONOMOUS AGENTS

12.4.1. Introduction

As artificial intelligence (AI) and autonomous systems become increasingly integrated into civilian, commercial and military applications, the need for clear legal frameworks to govern their behaviour and accountability is becoming urgent. Autonomous agents—systems capable of making decisions and acting independently—present both opportunities and challenges in terms of legality, ethics and regulation. This section explores the current and emerging legal frameworks that aim to manage the use of autonomous agents, focusing on areas such as liability, accountability, rights and international regulation.

12.4.2 Autonomous Agents

An autonomous agent is a system—typically software or a robot—that can:

- Perceive its environment
- Make decisions or perform actions
- Learn or adapt based on data
- Operate with minimal human intervention

Examples include:

- Self-driving vehicles
- AI customer service bots
- Military drones
- Algorithmic trading systems

Key Characteristics

- Autonomy (independent operation)
- Adaptability (learning from data)
- Interactivity (engaging with humans or environments)

12.4.3 Why Legal Frameworks Are Necessary

- **Accountability:** Accountability in the age of autonomous systems is a complex but critical issue. When an AI or autonomous agent causes harm—be it physical, financial or psychological—determining liability becomes challenging. Is the fault with the developer, the operator, the user or even the data used for training? Without clear legal standards, responsibility can become diffused or denied altogether. Robust frameworks are needed to ensure someone remains accountable for system behaviour. This promotes justice for victims and incentivizes responsible design. Accountability is the foundation of trust and ethical governance in automation.
- **Transparency:** Transparency refers to the clarity and explainability of how autonomous systems make decisions. Many AI models, particularly deep learning systems, operate like "black boxes," making it hard even for developers to trace how an outcome was reached. This lack of visibility can undermine trust and complicate regulation, oversight and legal scrutiny. Transparent systems allow users and auditors to understand how and why certain decisions were made. This is essential for debugging, correcting biases and ensuring fairness. Transparency not only enhances trust but also supports informed consent and ethical use.
- **Rights and Protections:** As autonomous systems become more involved in everyday life, protecting human rights is essential. People interacting with or being affected by these systems must be safeguarded from

discrimination, privacy violations and unjust treatment. There is a growing need to enshrine legal protections in areas like automated decision-making, biometric surveillance and AI-driven public services. Ensuring the dignity, autonomy and safety of individuals must be prioritized over technological convenience. Ethical innovation requires that systems be designed and deployed in ways that respect universal human rights. These protections are key to inclusive and equitable AI integration.

- **Prevention of Abuse:** Preventing abuse of autonomous systems is a major ethical concern, particularly in high-stakes fields like surveillance, military operations and criminal justice. These technologies can be exploited to oppress, manipulate or discriminate, especially when operated without oversight. For example, biased algorithms may reinforce systemic injustice, while autonomous weapons raise existential risks. Effective safeguards, such as strict regulations, human-in-the-loop mechanisms and ethical audits, must be implemented to prevent misuse. Developers and governments alike must ensure these systems are not repurposed for harm. Abuse prevention is a moral imperative in responsible technology deployment.

12.4.4 Current Legal Approaches

- **Traditional Legal Principles:** In most legal systems, autonomous agents—such as AI-driven systems or robots—are treated as tools rather than independent legal entities. This means that humans, including owners, operators, manufacturers or developers, are held responsible for their actions or failures. Tort law addresses issues of negligence or harm caused by these systems, ensuring that those affected can seek redress. Product liability holds manufacturers accountable for defective systems or poor designs that result in damage. Contract law becomes relevant when autonomous systems act on behalf of users, such as executing financial transactions or service agreements. Though these systems make decisions independently, legal frameworks currently do not assign them agency. Instead, liability traces back to the human or corporate entities involved in their deployment or creation.
- **Data Protection and Privacy Laws:** Autonomous systems also raise significant concerns around data protection and privacy, especially given their capacity to collect, process and act on vast amounts of personal data. The General Data Protection Regulation (GDPR) in the European Union enforces strict controls over automated decision-making, requiring transparency, consent and the right to an explanation. Individuals must be informed when data is collected and have the right to object or request human review. Similarly, the California Consumer Privacy Act (CCPA)

and other national regulations seek to empower users by limiting how companies and autonomous agents handle personal information. These laws emphasize accountability, consent and secure data handling practices. As AI becomes more embedded in daily life, privacy laws will continue evolving to address the ethical and legal implications of machine autonomy.

12.4.5 Emerging Legal Concepts

- **Electronic Personhood (Proposed in EU):** Electronic personhood is a controversial concept proposed within the EU to grant certain AI systems a form of limited legal personhood. The idea is to assign legal and financial responsibilities directly to autonomous systems, especially those capable of acting independently. This could relieve developers or owners from full liability in specific contexts. While still theoretical, it has sparked intense debate among legal, ethical and technological communities. Critics argue it could dilute accountability and human responsibility. Supporters claim it may be necessary for dealing with highly autonomous agents. Questions about the moral status, rights and duties of AI remain unresolved. The proposal challenges traditional definitions of personhood and legal agency.
- **AI Liability Directive (EU Proposal):** The EU's proposed AI Liability Directive aims to modernize liability rules by making it easier for victims to claim compensation for harm caused by AI systems. A key aspect of the directive is the shift of burden of proof, meaning victims wouldn't always need to prove exactly how an AI system failed. Instead, under certain conditions, developers or operators must demonstrate they were not at fault. This is especially relevant for complex or opaque systems, like machine learning models. The directive aligns with the broader EU push for trustworthy AI. It seeks to close legal gaps where existing laws struggle to assign responsibility. If enacted, it could become a model for AI liability worldwide.
- **Algorithmic Accountability Acts (Various Countries):** Several countries have introduced or proposed Algorithmic Accountability Acts to regulate the development and use of AI systems. These laws require transparency in AI decision-making, ensuring that people understand how outcomes are generated. They also mandate fairness audits to detect and correct biases within algorithms, particularly in sensitive areas like hiring, lending or law enforcement. Human oversight is emphasized to prevent fully autonomous decisions without accountability. These acts aim to balance innovation with protection of rights. Governments and private entities are being pushed to document, test and justify their AI systems. The focus is on ethical deployment, avoiding harm and ensuring public trust in AI technologies.

12.4.6 Sector-Specific Legal Considerations

- **Autonomous Vehicles:** Autonomous vehicles are regulated under frameworks like UN Regulation No. 157, which governs automated lane-keeping systems globally. Countries such as the US, Germany and the UK have introduced their own national laws to guide the testing, deployment and commercial use of self-driving cars. Key legal and ethical concerns include insurance liability, determining who is responsible in the event of an accident and how traffic law violations by autonomous systems are addressed. Another major issue is ethical decision-making—for example, how a vehicle should respond in an unavoidable crash scenario. Policymakers must balance innovation with public safety. Regulations continue evolving as technology advances. Public trust hinges on transparent rules and responsible deployment.
- **Military Drones and Autonomous Weapons:** Autonomous weapons, including military drones, fall under the scope of International Humanitarian Law (IHL) and the Geneva Conventions, which govern conduct during armed conflict. A central concern is the emergence of Lethal Autonomous Weapon Systems (LAWS), which can select and engage targets without human intervention. Their legality and morality are subjects of intense international debate. Critics argue these systems may violate principles of distinction and proportionality, core to IHL. The UN and various NGOs have called for a global treaty to ban or restrict fully autonomous weapons before they become widespread. Advocates for regulation stress the need for human oversight in life-or-death decisions. The issue reflects deep ethical and strategic challenges in modern warfare.
- **Healthcare and AI Diagnosis:** AI systems in healthcare are increasingly used for diagnosis, treatment planning and medical decision support. In the US, such technologies must comply with FDA regulations, while in the EU they fall under the Medical Device Regulation (MDR). Legal and ethical challenges include ensuring informed patient consent, assigning liability in cases of misdiagnosis and protecting sensitive medical data from breaches. These systems must be transparent and explainable to earn clinician and patient trust. Regulatory bodies demand rigorous testing to ensure safety and accuracy. While AI can enhance efficiency and accuracy, mistakes can have life-altering consequences. Thus, legal safeguards must evolve in parallel with technological capabilities.

12.4.7 Challenges in Legal Regulation

- **Attribution of Responsibility:** When AI systems act autonomously, assigning legal responsibility becomes a complex issue. Traditional models of liability assume a clear human actor, but with AI, many parties may be involved—developers, end users, data trainers and manufacturers. If harm occurs, determining which party is at fault is often unclear. For example, was the error due to flawed design, poor training data or user misuse? This ambiguity complicates legal claims and accountability. Without clear frameworks, victims may struggle to receive justice. Legal systems must adapt to distribute liability fairly in cases involving autonomous agents.

- **Cross-border Jurisdiction:** AI systems and autonomous agents frequently operate across international borders, especially in digital contexts like online bots, cloud AI services and cross-border data flows. This creates significant challenges for legal jurisdiction—who governs and enforces the law when a system developed in one country causes harm in another? Differences in national regulations, privacy laws and legal standards can lead to conflicts or enforcement gaps. Victims may find it difficult to seek redress or even identify responsible parties. International cooperation and harmonization of AI-related laws are urgently needed. Without it, regulatory inconsistencies could allow harmful AI use to go unchecked.
- **Rapid Technological Advancement:** AI technology evolves faster than the legal frameworks designed to regulate it. As new capabilities emerge—such as generative AI, autonomous decision-making or real-time data processing—existing laws often become outdated or insufficient. Policymakers struggle to keep pace, resulting in legal grey zones where regulation is unclear. This lag can hinder innovation, reduce public trust or allow unethical uses to flourish. A proactive, flexible approach to legislation is required. Governments must engage with technologists and ethicists to anticipate future risks and build adaptable legal systems.
- **Explainability:** Many AI systems, particularly those based on deep learning, function as "black boxes", making their internal decision-making processes difficult to understand. This lack of explainability poses serious legal challenges, especially were laws demand transparency, accountability or a right to explanation (e.g., under GDPR). In high-stakes areas like healthcare, finance or criminal justice, not understanding how an AI made a decision can erode trust and prevent meaningful oversight. Legal standards must balance performance with interpretability. Enhancing AI explainability is essential to ensuring that systems remain subject to human control and democratic accountability.

12.4.8 International Efforts and Guidelines

- **OECD Principles on AI:** The OECD Principles on AI serve as a foundational international framework to guide the responsible development and deployment of artificial intelligence. These principles emphasize the importance of trustworthy AI that upholds human rights, democratic values and transparency. They call for systems that are robust, secure and accountable, ensuring that AI benefits society while minimizing risks. The principles also stress the need for ongoing risk assessments and public engagement. As non-binding guidelines, they help shape national AI strategies and influence policy alignment across OECD member states and beyond. They represent one of the first global efforts to set ethical boundaries for AI.

- **UNESCO Recommendations on AI Ethics:** UNESCO's Recommendation on the Ethics of Artificial Intelligence is a landmark agreement adopted by nearly all member states to establish a global ethical framework for AI. It underscores the need for human oversight, ensuring that AI systems remain under meaningful human control. The recommendations highlight values such as fairness, non-discrimination, privacy and cultural diversity. It calls for regulatory mechanisms to prevent bias, exclusion and human rights violations. UNESCO also promotes inclusive development and equitable access to AI technologies. The recommendation is intended to guide national legislation and corporate practices worldwide. It marks a major step toward ethical AI governance on a global scale.
- **G20 and UN AI Initiatives:** The G20 and United Nations have launched several initiatives aimed at fostering international cooperation on AI ethics and regulation. These initiatives recognize the cross-border nature of AI challenges and aim to create shared standards for safety, fairness and accountability. The G20 focuses on responsible innovation, digital inclusion and AI for sustainable development, while UN agencies emphasize human rights protection and capacity building in developing countries. These global platforms encourage dialogue among nations to align ethical frameworks and promote peaceful, beneficial uses of AI. Their collective work helps prevent fragmentation in global AI governance and reinforces ethical consistency across borders.

12.4.9 Ethical Dimensions of Legal Frameworks

Legal frameworks regulating AI must closely align with core ethical principles to ensure just and responsible use. Fairness and non-discrimination are crucial, requiring laws that prevent biased outcomes in AI decisions which could unfairly disadvantage individuals or groups. Emphasizing human-centered design, legal standards should guarantee that humans remain in control of AI systems, maintaining accountability and moral oversight. The principle of proportionality ensures AI applications do not expose individuals or society to excessive or unacceptable risks. Additionally, transparency and the right to explanation are fundamental; users and those impacted by AI decisions must have clear, accessible information on how those decisions are made. Together, these ethical dimensions foster trust, protect rights and support equitable AI governance Legal frameworks must also align with ethical principles:

- **Fairness and Non-Discrimination:** Avoiding bias in AI decisions
- **Human-Centered Design:** Keeping humans in control
- **Proportionality:** Ensuring the use of AI does not exceed acceptable risk levels
- **Transparency and Right to Explanation:** Users and affected parties should understand how AI decisions are made (Table-2).

Table: 2 Concise forms of Ethical Dimensions of Legal Frameworks

Ethical Dimension	Description
Fairness and Non-Discrimination	Laws must prevent biased AI decisions that could unfairly disadvantage individuals or groups.
Human-Cantered Design	Legal standards should ensure humans remain in control of AI systems, maintaining accountability and moral oversight.
Proportionality	AI use should not expose individuals or society to risks beyond what is considered acceptable.
Transparency and Right to Explanation	Users and affected parties have the right to clear, accessible information on how AI decisions are made.

12.5 SOCIETAL IMPACT AND RESPONSIBLE INNOVATION

As technological advancements accelerate, the intersection between innovation and society becomes increasingly significant. While innovation drives progress, improves quality of life and solves complex challenges, it also carries the potential for unintended consequences that may disrupt social structures, widen inequalities or threaten ethical values. Responsible innovation seeks to guide scientific and technological progress in ways that align with societal needs, ethical standards and long-term sustainability. This section explores the societal impact of innovation and outlines the principles and practices that define responsible innovation.

12.5.1 Understanding Societal Impact

Societal impact refers to the broad effects that innovations have on individuals, communities, institutions and the environment. These impacts may be:

- **Positive Impacts:** Innovations can bring transformative positive impacts across various sectors, significantly improving quality of life. For instance, AI-assisted diagnostics are revolutionizing healthcare by enabling faster, more accurate disease detection, potentially saving lives and optimizing treatments. Assistive technologies—such as speech-to-text software or mobility aids—are enhancing accessibility for people with disabilities, promoting inclusion. In the energy sector, sustainable technologies like solar panels and smart grids contribute to reducing carbon emissions and combating climate change. Additionally, digital tools improve efficiency in education, allowing personalized learning and global access to resources. Communication technologies also foster real-time collaboration and global connectivity. Overall, when ethically guided, innovation can be a powerful force for human progress and social good.

- **Negative or Unintended Impacts:** Despite their benefits, innovations may also lead to negative or unintended impacts that require critical attention. One major concern is job displacement due to automation and AI, especially in manufacturing, transportation and customer service sectors, potentially increasing unemployment and economic instability. Surveillance technologies raise serious issues around privacy erosion, as individuals may be constantly monitored without consent. Additionally, the digital divide can worsen, where rural or low-income communities lack access to technology, deepening social inequality. Environmental consequences also arise, such as e-waste and pollution from tech manufacturing and data centres. These issues highlight the importance of foresight and responsibility in innovation to ensure harm is minimized and justice is upheld.

12.5.2 Responsible Innovation

Responsible Innovation (RI) is an approach that actively anticipates, reflects on and evaluates the broader social, ethical and environmental consequences of scientific and technological advancements. It emphasizes the need to align innovation with public values, human rights and sustainability from the earliest stages of development. RI encourages inclusive dialogue among stakeholders—scientists, policymakers, industry and the public—to ensure diverse perspectives are considered in shaping outcomes. By promoting principles like anticipation, inclusiveness, reflexivity and responsiveness, Responsible Innovation ensures that emerging technologies do not cause unintended harm and remain adaptable to societal needs. It aims to build public trust, promote fairness and guide innovation toward long-term benefits for all. Ultimately, RI is about shaping technology not just for what it can do, but for what it should do in a just and equitable society. Responsible Innovation (RI) is an approach that anticipates and evaluates the broader consequences of innovation, ensuring that technologies are developed:

- Ethically
- Sustainably

- Socially inclusive
- Aligned with public values and democratic principles

RI emphasizes not just what is possible, but what ought to be pursued.

12.5.3 Principles of Responsible Innovation

- **Anticipation:** Anticipation involves identifying and analysing potential risks and societal impacts early in the innovation process before technologies are widely deployed. This proactive approach helps prevent negative consequences by forecasting ethical, social and environmental challenges. For example, assessing the risks of using AI in sensitive areas like policing or hiring practices allows developers and policymakers to implement safeguards before harm occurs. Early anticipation supports informed decision-making and responsible governance. It encourages innovators to consider long-term effects rather than focusing solely on short-term gains. By integrating anticipation into development stages, technologies are better aligned with public values and safety concerns. This principle fosters a culture of foresight and precaution.
- **Inclusiveness:** Inclusiveness ensures that innovation processes engage a broad and diverse range of stakeholders, including scientists, citizens, policymakers, industry experts and ethicists. This participation guarantees that multiple perspectives, experiences and values are considered, reducing blind spots and biases. Public involvement in decision-making increases transparency and democratic legitimacy. Inclusive innovation promotes social justice by giving marginalized or vulnerable groups a voice. It also helps identify unforeseen impacts by tapping into local knowledge and lived experiences. By fostering dialogue and collaboration, inclusiveness strengthens societal trust in new technologies. This principle encourages co-creation and shared responsibility in innovation outcomes.
- **Reflexivity:** Reflexivity encourages innovators to critically examine their own values, assumptions and responsibilities throughout the development process. This self-awareness promotes humility, openness to feedback and a willingness to reconsider initial goals or methods. Reflexivity helps uncover hidden biases or ethical dilemmas that might otherwise be overlooked. It fosters ethical mindfulness and continuous learning, enabling innovators to navigate complex societal contexts more thoughtfully. By regularly reflecting on the broader implications of their work, innovators can align their practices with evolving social norms and expectations. Reflexivity supports responsible adaptation and ethical integrity in innovation.

- **Responsiveness:** Responsiveness is the capacity to adapt innovation practices based on public feedback, ethical concerns or new scientific knowledge. It involves being flexible and willing to modify or halt projects when unintended harms or risks emerge. This principle underscores the importance of ongoing monitoring and engagement with affected communities. Responsiveness ensures that innovation remains aligned with societal needs and values, even as conditions change. It fosters trust by demonstrating accountability and commitment to ethical standards. Adopting a responsive approach allows innovators to correct course and improve technologies for the common good. It reflects a dynamic, iterative process of responsible development.

12.5.4 Areas of Societal Concern

- **Employment and Economic Disruption:** The rise of automation and AI technologies is transforming the labour market, potentially causing significant job losses in traditional sectors like manufacturing, retail and transportation. This disruption challenges economies to adapt quickly to changing employment landscapes. To address this, there is a critical need for reskilling and upskilling programs that prepare workers for new roles created by technological advances. Governments and industries must collaborate to design policies that support workforce transitions, such as social safety nets and lifelong learning opportunities. Without proactive measures, economic disparities may widen, causing social instability. Responsible innovation requires balancing technological progress with protection and empowerment of affected workers. Ensuring fair economic transitions promotes social cohesion and shared prosperity.
- **Equity and Access:** Innovation often risks benefiting primarily privileged groups, leaving rural populations, low-income individuals and marginalized communities behind. This digital divide exacerbates existing inequalities in access to healthcare, education and economic opportunities. Addressing these gaps requires intentional digital inclusion initiatives that expand infrastructure, affordability and digital literacy. Policies must focus on equitable distribution of technological benefits and resources. Inclusive innovation ensures that no community is excluded from the advantages of progress. Promoting access to emerging technologies also strengthens social justice and economic resilience. Bridging these divides is essential for a fair and just society where innovation uplifts all members.
- **Privacy and Surveillance:** The proliferation of data-driven technologies, including facial recognition, social media platforms and Internet of Things (IoT) devices, raises serious concerns about privacy and surveillance.

These technologies collect and analyse vast amounts of personal data, often without full user awareness or consent. This creates risks of misuse, unauthorized surveillance and erosion of individual freedoms. To protect privacy, strong legal and ethical safeguards must be implemented and enforced, including data protection laws, transparency requirements and user control mechanisms. Responsible innovation demands balancing technological capabilities with respect for human dignity and rights. Upholding privacy is critical to maintaining public trust in digital systems.

- **Misinformation and Trust:** Innovations such as deepfakes, generative AI and sophisticated content manipulation tools challenge the reliability of information in public discourse. These technologies can spread misinformation and disinformation rapidly, undermining democratic processes and social cohesion. Rebuilding public trust requires concerted efforts to promote transparency, accountability and media literacy. Platforms and developers must develop tools to detect and limit harmful content, while governments and civil society engage in educating users. Responsible innovation involves anticipating the societal impact of new technologies on truth and communication. Ensuring accurate and trustworthy information is foundational to informed citizenry and effective governance.
- **Environmental Sustainability:** Innovation has the potential either to worsen environmental challenges or to be a powerful force for climate action and sustainable development. Emerging technologies must be designed with environmental sustainability in mind, minimizing resource consumption, waste and emissions. Concepts such as green technology and the circular economy promote efficient use of materials and energy throughout the product lifecycle. Innovations should align with global efforts to combat climate change and preserve natural ecosystems. Responsible innovation integrates environmental goals into research, design and deployment stages. By prioritizing sustainability, technology can support resilient economies and healthier societies for future generations.

12.5.5 The Role of Stakeholders

- **Governments:** Governments play a crucial role in shaping the environment for responsible innovation by creating regulatory frameworks that both encourage technological advancement and protect the public interest. They must balance supporting innovation with ensuring safety, fairness and ethical standards. Beyond regulation, governments invest in public infrastructure and promote equitable access to new technologies to reduce digital divides and social inequalities. They also fund research and development initiatives that align with societal goals such as sustainability and health. By fostering collaboration among different sectors and setting clear legal boundaries, governments help guide innovation in ways that benefit society broadly. Their leadership is essential for establishing trust and accountability in emerging technologies.

- **Industry and Corporations:** Industry and corporations are at the forefront of developing and deploying new technologies and thus carry significant responsibility for ethical innovation. They must adopt ethical design principles, conduct thorough risk assessments and implement sustainability metrics to minimize harm and promote long-term benefits. Corporate Social Responsibility (CSR) practices encourage businesses to consider social and environmental impacts beyond profit, fostering transparency and accountability. Engaging stakeholders, including customers and communities, helps companies better understand societal concerns and expectations. By integrating ethics into their innovation strategies, corporations can build public trust and contribute to sustainable development. Industry leadership is vital for setting practical standards and scaling responsible technologies.
- **Academia and Research Institutions:** Academia and research institutions provide foundational knowledge and drive innovation through interdisciplinary approaches that combine technology, ethics, social sciences and environmental studies. These institutions have a key role in promoting responsible innovation by embedding ethics and sustainability into STEM education and research practices. By training future innovators to think critically about the societal impacts of technology, academia helps build a culture of responsibility. Research institutions also serve as independent evaluators of emerging technologies, conducting ethical impact assessments and fostering public dialogue. Collaboration with industry and governments amplifies their influence in shaping policies and standards. Overall, academia acts as both a knowledge hub and an ethical compass for innovation.
- **Civil Society and Media:** Civil society organizations and the media act as essential watchdogs and advocates in the innovation ecosystem. They promote transparency, hold powerful actors accountable and push for fairness in the development and deployment of new technologies. By raising public awareness about the societal, ethical and environmental consequences of emerging technologies, they empower communities to engage in informed debates. Civil society groups often represent marginalized voices, ensuring diverse perspectives shape innovation policies. The media plays a critical role in disseminating information,

exposing risks or abuses and fostering dialogue between stakeholders. Together, they help create a more inclusive and democratic innovation process that aligns with public values.

12.5.6 Tools and Frameworks for Responsible Innovation

- **RI Frameworks (e.g., from the EU Horizon 2020 programme):** Responsible Innovation (RI) frameworks, such as those developed under the EU Horizon 2020 programme, provide structured approaches to embedding ethics and responsibility into research and innovation processes. These frameworks emphasize four key dimensions: anticipation (forecasting potential impacts), inclusivity (engaging diverse stakeholders), reflexivity (reflecting on underlying assumptions) and responsiveness (adapting to societal needs and concerns). The goal is to ensure that innovations align with societal values, ethical standards and sustainable development. Horizon 2020's RI guidelines encourage transparency and accountability in project planning and implementation. By integrating these principles, researchers and developers can better manage risks and build public trust. These frameworks help bridge the gap between technology advancement and social responsibility. They are widely adopted in EU-funded research initiatives.
- **Technology Assessment (TA):** Technology Assessment (TA) is a systematic process for evaluating the broader implications of new and emerging technologies before they are widely deployed. It examines the social, economic, environmental and ethical consequences of technological innovation. TA involves multidisciplinary analysis and stakeholder consultations to identify potential benefits, risks and unintended side effects. By forecasting both positive and negative outcomes, TA informs policymakers, industry leaders and the public to make more informed decisions. It helps prevent harm by highlighting areas where regulation or further research is needed. Technology Assessment supports responsible innovation by encouraging precaution and transparency. It has been applied across sectors including energy, biotechnology and AI. TA serves as an early warning tool for societal impacts.
- **Ethical Impact Assessments (EIA):** Ethical Impact Assessments (EIA) focus specifically on the ethical dimensions of new technologies, identifying potential risks related to human rights, privacy, fairness and accountability. Unlike general risk assessments, EIAs evaluate moral and societal values affected by innovation. They help developers and regulators anticipate dilemmas, such as bias in AI, data misuse or unequal access to benefits. EIAs often involve stakeholder engagement to capture diverse perspectives

and values. The process supports transparent decision-making and fosters ethical responsibility throughout a technology's lifecycle. By integrating EIA early in design and policy development organizations can address concerns before harm occurs. EIAs are increasingly recognized as essential for technologies with profound societal impact. They complement other assessment tools like TA and legal reviews.

- **AI Ethics Guidelines (OECD, UNESCO, IEEE, etc.):** Several international organizations have developed AI Ethics Guidelines to promote trustworthy and responsible AI development. The OECD Principles on AI emphasize transparency, human rights and accountability. UNESCO's Recommendations on AI Ethics stress fairness, inclusiveness and human oversight. The IEEE offers standards for ethical AI design, focusing on safety, privacy and social good. These guidelines provide practical frameworks for developers, policymakers and users to navigate complex ethical issues in AI, such as bias, explainability and autonomy. Although non-binding, they influence national regulations and corporate policies globally. By encouraging adherence to shared principles, these guidelines foster interoperability and public trust. They also help harmonize approaches to AI governance across countries. Collectively, they serve as reference points for ethical AI innovation.
- **Sustainable Development Goals (SDGs) as a reference for global priorities:** The Sustainable Development Goals (SDGs), established by the United Nations, provide a universal framework to guide innovation toward addressing global challenges. With 17 goals covering poverty, health, education, equality, climate action and more, the SDGs offer clear social and environmental priorities for responsible innovation. Aligning technological development with these goals encourages solutions that promote equity, environmental sustainability and inclusive growth. Innovators are urged to consider how their products and services contribute to or hinder progress toward these targets. Using the SDGs as a reference helps balance economic objectives with broader societal needs. It fosters a holistic approach where innovation supports long-term planetary health and human well-being. Many funding bodies and corporations now integrate SDGs into their strategic planning. This alignment strengthens the ethical foundation of technological advancement globally.

12.5.7 Challenges to Responsible Innovation

- **Balancing Innovation Speed with Careful Evaluation:** One of the main challenges in responsible innovation is finding the right balance between rapidly developing new technologies and ensuring thorough evaluation of their ethical, legal and social impacts. Speed is often prioritized to maintain competitive advantage and meet market demands, but this can lead to insufficient testing and oversight. Rushing innovations risks unintended consequences, such as safety issues, biased outcomes or privacy breaches. Careful evaluation requires time, expertise and resources, which may slow down deployment. However, neglecting this step can undermine public trust and long-term sustainability. Thus, innovators, regulators and stakeholders must collaborate to create processes that support both innovation and responsibility.

- **Global Disparities in Regulation and Enforcement:** Regulatory frameworks for emerging technologies like AI vary widely across countries and regions, creating significant global disparities. Some nations have advanced laws and robust enforcement mechanisms, while others lack comprehensive rules or the capacity to implement them effectively. These inconsistencies can lead to regulatory arbitrage, where companies move operations to regions with lax oversight. Such disparities complicate international cooperation, cross-border data flows and accountability for harm caused by technology. They also risk creating uneven benefits and harms globally, exacerbating inequalities. Addressing this challenge requires global dialogue and harmonization of standards to ensure equitable and consistent governance worldwide.
- **Profit-Driven Models May Overlook Social Concerns:** Many technological innovations are developed and deployed within profit-driven business models that prioritize financial returns over social responsibility. This focus can lead companies to overlook ethical issues such as data privacy, bias or long-term societal impact. Market pressures may incentivize shortcuts on safety, transparency or inclusivity to reduce costs or accelerate time to market. Without strong external regulation or internal ethics commitments, commercial interests may clash with public good. This tension highlights the need for ethical frameworks that integrate social values into innovation processes. Encouraging corporate social responsibility and stakeholder engagement can help align profit motives with ethical outcomes.
- **Resistance to Public Involvement or Ethical Constraints:** Another barrier to responsible innovation is resistance from some stakeholders to involve the public or to accept ethical constraints. Innovators, companies or governments may perceive public input as slowing progress or complicating decision-making. Ethical constraints might be seen as burdensome regulations that limit creativity or competitiveness. However, excluding public voices risks alienating communities and ignoring diverse perspectives, which can result in technologies that fail to meet societal

needs or cause harm. Genuine public engagement and adherence to ethical standards can enhance legitimacy and trust. Overcoming this resistance requires demonstrating how ethics and inclusivity contribute to sustainable and accepted innovation.

13 Chapter

FUTURE DIRECTIONS IN SWARM ROBOTICS

13.0 INTRODUCTION

Swarm robotics, inspired by the collective behaviour of social insects such as ants, bees and termites, represents a rapidly evolving field in robotics that emphasizes the coordination of large numbers of relatively simple robots to achieve complex tasks. Unlike traditional robotics, which often rely on a single powerful machine, swarm robotics leverages decentralization, redundancy and self-organization to enhance robustness, scalability and flexibility. These characteristics make swarm robotics particularly well-suited for applications in dynamic and unstructured environments where adaptability and resilience are crucial. Over the past decade, significant advancements have been made in algorithms, communication methods, hardware design and task allocation strategies, pushing the boundaries of what swarms can accomplish. Despite these achievements, numerous challenges remain, particularly in areas such as real-time decision making, energy efficiency, fault tolerance and seamless human-swarm interaction. Looking ahead, the future of swarm robotics promises exciting developments that could revolutionize various sectors including agriculture, environmental monitoring, disaster response, infrastructure maintenance and even space exploration. One key direction is the integration of advanced artificial intelligence and machine learning techniques, enabling swarms to learn from their environment and improve their collective behaviours autonomously. Another promising avenue is the enhancement of communication protocols, moving towards more reliable, scalable and energy-efficient methods that support large-scale deployments. Additionally, advances in bio-inspired design and novel materials are expected to produce robots that are more adaptable, lightweight and resilient. The ethical and societal implications of deploying autonomous swarms on a large scale also demand careful consideration, including issues of privacy, security and accountability. As research continues to push the frontiers, collaboration between multidisciplinary fields such as robotics, computer science, biology and ethics will be essential to realize the full potential of swarm robotics. This introductory overview sets the stage for exploring these future directions in detail, highlighting how ongoing innovations could transform swarm robotics from experimental prototypes to indispensable tools in everyday life.

13.1 SELF-HEALING AND MORPHOGENETIC SWARMS

- **Self-Healing Swarms:** Self-healing in swarm robotics refers to the ability of the swarm to detect, isolate and recover from faults or damage within individual robots or parts of the system without external intervention. This capability enhances the swarm's robustness and reliability, ensuring continuous operation even in hostile or unpredictable environments. When a robot fails or gets damaged, self-healing swarms dynamically reconfigure themselves by redistributing tasks and adapting their formation, maintaining overall functionality. Techniques for self-healing include decentralized fault detection, redundancy in roles and cooperative repair strategies, often inspired by biological systems like tissue regeneration in living organisms.
- **Morphogenetic Swarms:** Morphogenetic swarms take inspiration from the biological process of morphogenesis—the development of an organism's shape and structure. These swarms can autonomously change their spatial configuration and physical form to adapt to different tasks and environments. Through local interactions and simple rules, the swarm members collectively build and reorganize complex structures, allowing the swarm to optimize task performance, navigate obstacles or form temporary tools and shapes. This ability to self-assemble and morph makes morphogenetic swarms highly versatile and capable of tackling multi-functional applications.
- **Key Challenges:** Achieving effective self-healing and morphogenetic behaviours requires advanced sensing, communication and decision-making capabilities within individual robots, as well as scalable coordination algorithms. Managing energy consumption during continuous adaptation, ensuring stability in dynamic reconfiguration and handling partial system failures are major challenges. Additionally, balancing autonomy with controllability remains an ongoing research focus.
- **Future Outlook:** Future research in self-healing and morphogenetic swarms aims to develop smarter, more resilient swarms capable of long-term autonomous operation in complex, real-world scenarios. Integrating machine learning for adaptive behaviour, improving material science for self-repairing hardware and enhancing swarm intelligence through bio-inspired mechanisms are promising directions. These advancements could lead to swarm systems that not only survive damage but also thrive by evolving their morphology and functions in response to changing environments.

13.2 NANO-ROBOTIC SWARMS IN MEDICINE

Nano-robotic swarms represent a groundbreaking frontier in medical technology, where vast numbers of microscopic robots operate collaboratively within the human body. These nano-scale robots, often just a few nanometres to micrometres in size, work collectively to perform precise diagnostic, therapeutic and monitoring tasks that are otherwise impossible with conventional medical tools. By leveraging swarm robotics principles, nano-robots can coordinate to navigate complex biological environments, target specific cells or tissues and respond dynamically to changes within the body.

13.2.1 Applications

- **Targeted Drug Delivery:** Nano-robotic swarms can deliver medication directly to diseased cells, such as tumours, minimizing side effects and improving treatment efficacy. The swarm's collective behaviour ensures accurate localization and controlled release of drugs.
- **Minimally Invasive Surgery:** Coordinated nano-robots can perform delicate surgical procedures at the cellular or molecular level, reducing trauma and speeding recovery times.
- **Disease Detection and Diagnostics:** Nano-swarms can continuously monitor biochemical markers, detect early signs of diseases and relay real-time data for prompt medical intervention.
- **Tissue Repair and Regeneration:** By working together, nano-robots can facilitate tissue repair processes, assist in wound healing and promote regeneration by delivering growth factors or assembling scaffold materials (Table-1).

Table: 1 Applications of Nano-Robotic Swarms in Medicine

Application	Description
Targeted Drug Delivery	Nano-robotic swarms can deliver medication directly to diseased cells (e.g., tumours), minimizing side effects and improving treatment efficacy through precise targeting.
Minimally Invasive Surgery	Coordinated nano-robots can perform delicate surgical tasks at the cellular or molecular level, reducing physical trauma and promoting faster recovery.
Disease Detection and Diagnostics	Nano-swarms can monitor biochemical markers in real time, detect early signs of diseases and transmit data for prompt medical intervention.
Tissue Repair and Regeneration	Working collectively, nano-robots can aid in tissue repair by delivering growth factors, assisting in wound healing or assembling scaffold structures for regeneration.

13.2.2 Challenges

Despite their immense potential, nano-robotic swarms in medicine face significant challenges. Precise control and navigation within the complex, dynamic and fluidic environment of the human body require advanced sensing and communication strategies. Biocompatibility and safety are paramount concerns, demanding the development of materials that are non-toxic and can be safely broken down or removed after completing their tasks. Energy supply for sustained operation at the nano-scale remains an ongoing research challenge. Additionally, ensuring the security and privacy of medical data collected and transmitted by nano-robots is critical.

13.2.3 Future Directions

Future research is focused on improving the autonomy and intelligence of nano-robotic swarms by integrating advanced algorithms, including machine learning, to enable real-time adaptation and decision-making. Innovations in nanomaterials and bioengineering aim to create more efficient, biocompatible and self-powered nano-robots. Development of robust communication protocols that function effectively at the nano-scale inside the body will enhance coordination among swarm members. Ethical considerations and regulatory frameworks will also evolve to ensure safe and responsible deployment of these technologies in clinical settings. As these advancements mature, nano-robotic swarms hold the promise of transforming personalized medicine, offering highly precise, minimally invasive and adaptive healthcare solutions.

13.3 AI-ENHANCED SWARM AUTONOMY

13.3.1 Introduction

AI-enhanced swarm autonomy refers to the use of artificial intelligence (AI) to manage and coordinate multi-agent systems—often called "swarms"—that operate autonomously in a decentralized manner. These systems are inspired by collective behaviours observed in nature (e.g., flocks of birds, schools of fish, ant colonies), where individual agents follow simple rules yet produce complex, intelligent group behaviours. AI technologies such as machine learning, reinforcement learning and neural networks dramatically improve the efficiency, adaptability and decision-making capabilities of such swarms. This advancement holds transformative potential across civilian, industrial and military domains.

13.3.2 Characteristics of Swarm Autonomy

a. Decentralization

- No central controller; each agent makes decisions based on local information.
- Enhances robustness and fault tolerance.

b. Scalability

- Easily expandable by adding more agents without redesigning the system architecture.

c. Redundancy

- System performance is not heavily reliant on any single unit, ensuring high resilience.

d. Self-Organization

- Agents can dynamically adapt to changes in the environment or mission without external commands.

13.3.3 Role of AI in Enhancing Swarm Autonomy

AI algorithms provide swarm systems with the ability to:

- Learn from past missions or simulations.
- Make real-time decisions under uncertainty.
- Adapt to new environments without human intervention.
- Coordinate complex tasks through emergent behavior.

Common AI methods used include:

- **Reinforcement Learning:** Agents learn optimal behavior through trial and error.
- **Evolutionary Algorithms:** Systems evolve over time to enhance performance.
- **Neural Networks:** Used for perception, pattern recognition and decision-making.
- **Multi-Agent Systems (MAS):** Frameworks to manage inter-agent communication and cooperation.

13.3.4 Applications of AI-Enhanced Swarm Autonomy

a. Civilian and Industrial Use

- **Search and Rescue:** Drones collaboratively scan disaster zones for survivors.
- **Agriculture:** Autonomous swarms of robots for planting, harvesting and monitoring crops.
- **Environmental Monitoring:** Swarms collect data on pollution, climate and biodiversity.

- **Infrastructure Inspection:** Swarms of aerial or underwater drones inspect pipelines, bridges and offshore rigs.
- **Delivery Services:** Coordinated drone delivery networks improve logistics in urban environments.

b. Military and Defense Applications

- **Surveillance and Reconnaissance:** AI swarms can cover vast areas, adaptively avoid threats and relay information in real time.
- **Electronic Warfare:** Swarms jam or deceive enemy sensors using coordinated signals.
- **Attack Missions:** Autonomous drone swarms capable of offensive actions with minimal human control (highly controversial).
- **Logistical Support:** Autonomous ground or aerial vehicles deliver supplies or construct temporary infrastructure.

13.3.5 Advantages of AI-Driven Swarms

- **High Resilience:** Can continue functioning even when several units fail.
- **Real-Time Adaptation:** AI allows for dynamic re-planning in changing environments.
- **Lower Cost:** Many low-cost units can replace one large and expensive system.
- **Fast Deployment:** Ideal for time-sensitive missions with little preparation time.
- **Reduced Human Risk:** Enables operations in hazardous or hostile environments.

13.3.6 Challenges and Limitations

a. Communication and Coordination

- Maintaining reliable communication in dense or contested environments is difficult .

b. Energy Constraints

- Battery life and power management limit operational time.

c. Security Risks

- Vulnerable to cyberattacks, spoofing or hacking if not properly secured.

d. Ethical and Legal Concerns

- Use of autonomous lethal swarms raises serious moral and legal questions.
- Attribution of responsibility in swarm failures is complex.
- Privacy concerns with mass surveillance using autonomous drones.

e. Algorithmic Transparency

- "Black box" AI systems make it difficult to understand or predict swarm behavior.

13.3.7 Notable Projects and Research

- **DARPA OFFensive Swarm-Enabled Tactics (OFFSET):** US-based research initiative for large-scale tactical drone swarms.
- **SwarmDiver (Aquabotix):** Underwater swarm drones used for environmental monitoring and military reconnaissance.
- **ETH Zurich's Flying Machine Arena:** Demonstrates complex aerial swarm behaviors using quadrotors.
- **European Union's SWARM-TECH project:** Focuses on AI coordination in multi-robot systems for civilian use.

13.3.8 Ethical and Regulatory Perspectives

As AI-enhanced swarms become more autonomous and pervasive, several ethical and legal questions arise:

- Who is responsible if a swarm malfunctions or causes harm?
- Should lethal autonomous swarm systems be banned or limited under international law?
- How can transparency and accountability be built into AI swarms?
- Should civilian swarms be regulated to prevent misuse, especially in surveillance or data collection?

International collaboration is increasingly necessary to develop norms, treaties and frameworks that ensure safe and responsible use of swarm autonomy.

13.3.9 Future Directions

- **Human-Swarm Interaction (HSI):** Developing intuitive interfaces for humans to monitor and influence swarm behavior.
- **Swarm Intelligence + Edge AI:** Deploying onboard AI for real-time decision-making without centralized computation.

- **Interdisciplinary Integration:** Combining biology, robotics, AI and cognitive science to improve swarm capabilities.
- **Swarm-as-a-Service (SaaS):** Emerging model for commercial access to autonomous drone swarms for tasks like mapping or security.

13.4 INTEGRATION WITH IOT AND 6G

13.4.1 Era of hyper-connectivity, the integration of Artificial Intelligence (AI) with the Internet of Things (IoT) and 6G networks

As we move deeper into the era of hyper-connectivity, the integration of Artificial Intelligence (AI) with the Internet of Things (IoT) and 6G networks is poised to revolutionize how systems interact, make decisions and function autonomously. IoT connects physical devices to the internet, allowing them to collect and exchange data. AI enables these systems to make smart decisions based on that data, while 6G—expected to succeed 5G—will provide the ultra-fast, ultra-low latency and highly reliable communication infrastructure necessary to support this integration on a massive scale. Together, these technologies will form the backbone of future smart environments—smart cities, autonomous vehicles, remote healthcare, industry 5.0 and even military operations—by enabling real-time sensing, analysis and action.

- **Internet of Things (IoT):** The Internet of Things (IoT) refers to a vast network of interconnected physical devices that collect, exchange and act on data from their surroundings. These devices range from wearables and home appliances to industrial controllers, vehicles and environmental sensors. IoT enables real-time monitoring, automation and enhanced decision-making across sectors like healthcare, agriculture and urban planning. By bridging the digital and physical worlds, IoT fosters data-driven intelligence in everyday objects. As the number of connected devices grows into the billions, managing this data efficiently becomes increasingly critical. IoT forms the foundational layer for smart systems, feeding both AI and next-gen connectivity like 6G.
- **Sixth Generation (6G) Networks:** 6G represents the next leap in wireless communication, expected to roll out commercially by the early 2030s. It will deliver groundbreaking capabilities, including data rates up to 1 terabit per second (Tbps) and latency under 1 millisecond, enabling near-instant interactions. 6G will offer ubiquitous connectivity, integrating terrestrial, aerial and satellite networks for seamless global coverage. With AI-native architectures, networks will feature built-in intelligence and edge computing for decentralized, low-latency processing. Additionally, terahertz (THz) communication will open vast new bandwidths. 6G is poised

to power highly immersive, intelligent and interconnected ecosystems across all domains.

- **Artificial Intelligence (AI):** Artificial Intelligence (AI) plays a central role in enhancing both IoT and 6G systems by enabling machines to think, learn and adapt autonomously. AI empowers real-time intelligent decision-making, predictive analytics and self-optimization across devices and networks. It allows systems to identify patterns, prevent failures and respond dynamically to changing conditions. AI also supports autonomy in robotics, vehicles and smart infrastructure. When embedded within IoT and supported by 6G's speed and connectivity, AI transforms static data into meaningful actions. This triad—AI, IoT and 6G—forms the backbone of the next technological revolution across all sectors.

13.4.2 Benefits of Integration

- **Real-Time Decision Making:** With the rise of AI at the edge and the advancement of 6G networks, IoT devices are increasingly capable of making instant, autonomous decisions without relying on centralized servers. This shift enables faster response times in critical applications like industrial automation, autonomous vehicles and smart healthcare. By reducing latency and enhancing local processing, AI can analyse data and act in milliseconds. Edge AI also improves privacy by minimizing data transmission. In high-stakes scenarios, such as robotic surgery or emergency response, real-time decision-making can mean the difference between success and failure. This capability is a cornerstone of next-gen intelligent systems. It fosters self-reliant, responsive technology ecosystems.
- **Ultra-Reliable Communication:** 6G networks aim to deliver ultra-reliable and low-latency communication, ensuring that devices exchange data with near-zero delay and minimal disruption. This is crucial for time-sensitive tasks like autonomous driving, where split-second decisions impact safety or remote surgery, where stable connectivity is vital. AI enhances this reliability by predicting and preventing failures in real-time. Together, AI and 6G create networks that are not only fast but also resilient. They support mission-critical applications where data loss or delay is unacceptable. This ultra-reliability opens doors to innovations previously limited by unstable connectivity. It sets the foundation for intelligent, always-available systems.
- **Scalability and Flexibility:** The integration of AI with 6G enables seamless scalability and dynamic management of billions of connected devices across multiple sectors, including healthcare, manufacturing, agriculture and defence. AI helps prioritize and allocate network resources efficiently,

even as the number of devices and applications expands rapidly. 6G's flexible architecture supports varied use cases—from smart homes to industrial IoT—without compromising performance. This adaptability allows networks to evolve in real time, adjusting to changing demands or emergencies. Scalability ensures innovations can be widely deployed without overwhelming infrastructure. It also promotes inclusivity, bringing smart connectivity to remote or underserved areas. The result is a truly connected global ecosystem.

- **Energy Efficiency:** AI-driven optimization combined with 6G innovations leads to significant energy efficiency across networks and devices. Smart algorithms can monitor and adjust energy use in real-time, reducing waste and extending device lifespans. 6G introduces energy-aware protocols and low-power communication technologies that cut power consumption without sacrificing performance. This is especially important in remote or resource-constrained environments. Improved energy efficiency supports sustainability goals and lowers operational costs for businesses and service providers. It also makes large-scale deployments of smart devices more environmentally viable. Together, AI and 6G are shaping a greener digital future with intelligent, energy-conscious systems.

13.4.3 Applications Across Domains

- **Smart Cities:** Smart cities rely on the integration of AI and IoT to manage complex urban systems such as traffic control, waste disposal, energy usage and pollution monitoring. With 6G connectivity, real-time data from millions of sensors enables instantaneous decision-making and automated responses. For instance, AI can adjust traffic lights to reduce congestion or reroute services during emergencies. High-resolution video surveillance, supported by 6G's ultra-fast bandwidth, enhances public safety and disaster response. Infrastructure health—like bridges or pipelines—can also be continuously monitored. Together, these technologies create cities that are more efficient, sustainable and resilient.
- **Healthcare and Telemedicine:** In modern healthcare, wearables and IoT devices collect continuous data on patients' vitals, activity and symptoms. AI algorithms analyse this information to diagnose conditions, detect anomalies or suggest treatments. With 6G's near-zero latency, real-time telemedicine becomes highly advanced, allowing for remote surgeries and specialist consultations across borders. Doctors can interact with patients in immersive, tactile ways using haptic feedback systems. AI also assists in drug discovery and personalized medicine. This trio—AI, IoT and 6G—is

revolutionizing healthcare delivery, making it faster, more precise and more accessible.

- **Autonomous Transportation:** Autonomous vehicles rely on AI for real-time decision-making, from route optimization to obstacle avoidance. Vehicle-to-everything (V2X) communication, enabled by IoT, allows cars to interact with traffic lights, road infrastructure and other vehicles. With the arrival of 6G, ultra-fast, low-latency connections support seamless coordination, safety and control at high speeds. This is essential for platooning, emergency maneuvers and reducing traffic collisions. AI also handles predictive maintenance to avoid mechanical failures. Combined, these technologies pave the way for safer, smarter and more efficient transportation networks.
- **Industry 5.0 / Smart Manufacturing:** Smart factories use IoT sensors to monitor machine performance, environment conditions and supply chain flows in real time. AI systems process this data to detect inefficiencies, predict equipment failures and automate quality control. 6G networks enable ultra-reliable, low-latency communication between robots, human operators and control systems across distributed manufacturing sites. This allows for synchronized operations, even across global facilities. The vision of Industry 5.0 goes beyond automation to human-machine collaboration, enhancing productivity and customization. Together, AI, IoT and 6G redefine manufacturing for flexibility, resilience and intelligence.
- **Military and Defence:** In defence, the fusion of AI, IoT and 6G enables advanced capabilities such as autonomous drone swarms that can coordinate in real time on surveillance or strike missions. AI-driven analytics provide real-time battlefield insights, predicting enemy movements or identifying hidden threats. Cybersecurity benefits from AI threat detection systems that analyse traffic patterns to stop attacks before damage occurs. 6G satellite connectivity ensures global, uninterrupted communication, linking forces across air, land, sea and space. These technologies enhance situational awareness, decision speed and force protection, ushering in a new era of intelligent warfare.
- **Environmental Monitoring:** Large-scale deployment of IoT sensors across forests, oceans and urban environments allows continuous monitoring of climate variables, pollution levels and natural disasters. AI analyses this vast data to predict weather patterns, identify early signs of environmental degradation and support climate modelling. With 6G connectivity, alerts for floods, wildfires or hazardous air quality can be transmitted in real time, enabling swift mitigation responses. Predictive analytics also help

policymakers make informed decisions for sustainability planning. This tech ecosystem plays a vital role in protecting ecosystems and promoting climate resilience worldwide.

13.4.4 Technical Challenges

- **Data Privacy and Security:** With billions of interconnected devices, the potential attack surface expands exponentially, making networks more vulnerable. Ensuring robust encryption, secure authentication and data isolation becomes crucial. Real-time AI-driven threat detection must be implemented to spot anomalies and intrusions proactively. Privacy regulations like GDPR add further complexity in handling sensitive data. Building trust in these systems hinges on resilient, adaptive security frameworks.
- **Network Congestion and Spectrum Management:** As device numbers surge, so does the demand for bandwidth, straining current network infrastructures. Efficient allocation of high-frequency bands like terahertz is essential to prevent congestion. Advanced signal processing and dynamic spectrum sharing technologies are needed. Regulatory frameworks must evolve to support flexible use of spectrum. Without these innovations, latency and performance degradation will become major bottlenecks.
- **Interoperability:** The vast diversity of devices, platforms and protocols makes seamless communication a technical hurdle. Standardization across manufacturers and regions is critical to ensure compatibility. Open APIs and collaborative industry frameworks can support integration. Lack of interoperability limits scalability and innovation. Bridging these gaps is essential for a truly global and unified IoT ecosystem.
- **Edge vs. Cloud AI Processing:** Determining the right balance between edge and cloud computing remains a challenge. Edge devices offer low-latency, real-time processing, while the cloud provides scalable compute power. Factors like data sensitivity, bandwidth limitations and latency requirements must guide decision-making. An optimized hybrid model is often necessary but complex to implement. Strategic distribution of AI workloads is key for efficiency and responsiveness.
- **Energy Constraints:** Connected devices, especially in remote or mobile environments, must operate with limited power resources. Achieving energy efficiency while delivering high-performance computing is a delicate balance. Innovations in low-power hardware, smart energy harvesting and adaptive processing are essential. AI models need to be lightweight yet effective on constrained devices. Sustaining device longevity without frequent recharging or replacement is a core design challenge.

13.4.5 Future Outlook and Innovations

- **AI-Native 6G:** The future 6G networks will be designed with AI integrated at the core, rather than as an add-on. This will allow networks to self-organize, automatically adapting to changes in traffic and demand. AI will enable predictive maintenance, reducing downtime and operational costs. Intelligent traffic optimization will improve latency, reliability and user experience. Faults will be detected and corrected autonomously, enhancing resilience and service quality.
- **Brain-Computer Interfaces (BCI):** Brain-computer interfaces could revolutionize how humans interact with digital systems, bypassing traditional input methods. With the ultra-low latency of 6G and pervasive IoT, real-time neural communication becomes viable. This has transformative implications for assistive technologies, allowing direct control of devices for people with disabilities. In defence and personal computing, BCIs may unlock unprecedented levels of speed and control. Ethical, privacy and security concerns will need to evolve alongside these breakthroughs.
- **Digital Twins:** Digital twins are virtual replicas of physical assets or environments, kept synchronized in real time using IoT and 6G data streams. These models enable advanced monitoring, simulation and optimization in domains like manufacturing, urban planning and healthcare. With ultra-fast and reliable connectivity, decisions can be made instantly based on real-world changes. Predictive analytics within digital twins can prevent failures and improve performance. They will become central to managing complex, data-driven systems of the future.
- **Quantum and Neuromorphic Computing:** Quantum and neuromorphic computing represent a leap in processing capabilities far beyond classical hardware. These technologies promise to handle complex AI tasks more efficiently, especially in energy- or resource-constrained environments. Neuromorphic chips mimic the brain's structure, making them ideal for edge AI that requires low power and high adaptability. Quantum processors, meanwhile, could accelerate optimization and data processing in large-scale networks. Together, they will redefine the limits of AI performance and scalability.

13.4.6 Ethical and Societal Considerations

- **Surveillance and Privacy:** As 6G and IoT technologies enable constant data collection, the risk of intrusive surveillance grows. Safeguarding individual privacy must be a fundamental design principle, not an afterthought. Transparent data practices, robust consent mechanisms and strict regulatory oversight are essential. Balancing public safety with civil liberties will be a persistent challenge. Technology should empower, not monitor or control, individuals without accountability.

- **AI Bias:** AI-driven systems in healthcare, policing and social services must operate without discrimination. Bias in training data or flawed algorithms can lead to unfair outcomes, disproportionately affecting marginalized communities. Ethical AI development requires transparency, diverse datasets and continuous auditing. Inclusive design processes can help ensure fairness and accountability. Without these safeguards, public trust in AI will erode quickly.
- **Digital Divide:** Access to high-speed networks and connected devices remains uneven globally and within nations. Rural areas, low-income communities and developing regions often lag behind in digital infrastructure. 6G must aim to be inclusive, with policies that prioritize equitable rollout. Bridging the digital divide is essential for social progress, economic opportunity and education. True technological advancement must benefit everyone, not just the privileged few.
- **Sustainability:** With billions of devices coming online, the environmental impact of 6G must be addressed from the start. Energy-efficient network design, sustainable materials and circular electronics will be key. AI can help optimize energy use, but the infrastructure itself must be built responsibly. Failure to prioritize sustainability could offset the benefits of connectivity. Green innovation must go hand in hand with digital transformation.

13.5 TOWARD GENERALIZED SWARM INTELLIGENCE

Swarm intelligence, inspired by natural systems like ant colonies, bird flocks and fish schools, refers to the collective behaviour of decentralized, self-organized systems. Traditionally, swarm systems are task-specific—designed to solve narrowly defined problems such as pathfinding, coverage or area exploration. However, the next frontier is Generalized Swarm Intelligence (GSI): the development of swarm systems that can adaptively learn, reason and perform a broad range of tasks across dynamic environments without being explicitly reprogrammed for each one. Generalized Swarm Intelligence aims to merge the flexibility and learning capability of Artificial General Intelligence (AGI) with the distributed robustness and scalability of swarms, resulting in systems that are autonomous, intelligent and versatile at a collective level.

13.5.1 Generalized Swarm Intelligence

Generalized Swarm Intelligence (GSI) refers to a system in which multiple autonomous agents collectively:

- Learn and adapt to unfamiliar tasks
- Coordinate dynamically in real time
- Exhibit emergent intelligence beyond pre-programmed behaviour
- Operate in open, unpredictable environments (Table-2).

Table: 2 Comparison between Traditional Swarm Intelligence

Feature	Traditional Swarm Intelligence	Generalized Swarm Intelligence
Task Scope	Narrow, domain-specific	Broad, cross-domain
Adaptability	Low to moderate	High
Learning Capability	Limited or rule-based	AI-driven (ML, RL, etc.)
Coordination Mechanism	Simple local rules	Dynamic, goal-driven learning
Decision-making	Emergent but task-specific	Context-aware and flexible

13.5.2 Enabling Technologies

Several emerging technologies contribute to the realization of Generalized Swarm Intelligence:

- **Artificial Intelligence (AI):** Reinforcement Learning (RL) and Multi-Agent Reinforcement Learning (MARL) empower swarm agents to develop cooperative behaviours through trial and error. These methods enable the swarm to optimize strategies collectively, adapting to dynamic tasks. Transfer learning further enhances flexibility by allowing swarms to leverage prior knowledge when encountering new environments or challenges. Together, these AI techniques are fundamental to building adaptable and intelligent swarm systems.
- **Edge and Cloud Computing:** Edge computing brings data processing closer to the agents, reducing latency and enabling real-time decision-making at the source. Cloud computing complements this by providing vast computational resources and centralized data storage for complex analysis and long-term learning. The synergy between edge and cloud allows swarms to share collective memories and insights efficiently, improving their overall responsiveness and intelligence. This distributed architecture is critical for scaling generalized swarm intelligence.
- **Neuromorphic and Quantum Computing:** Neuromorphic computing mimics the human brain's neural architecture, offering ultra-efficient, parallel processing ideal for complex swarm decision-making tasks. Quantum computing, with its potential for exponential speed-up in optimization and simulation, could revolutionize how swarms solve

collective problems. Both technologies promise significant gains in energy efficiency and processing power, enabling more sophisticated and faster swarm intelligence in real-world applications. Their integration is an exciting frontier for next-generation autonomous systems.

- **6G and IoT Integration:** The upcoming 6G networks will provide unprecedented data rates, ultra-low latency and seamless connectivity essential for coordinating large-scale swarms. Coupled with IoT, which embeds sensing and actuation capabilities into countless devices, this integration ensures continuous, reliable communication among swarm agents. Such robust networking allows swarms to operate effectively in distributed, dynamic environments, supporting complex collaborative behaviours. Together, 6G and IoT form the communication backbone of generalized swarm intelligence.

13.5.3 Features of a Generalized Swarm Intelligence System

- **Task Generalization:** A generalized swarm intelligence system is designed to adapt seamlessly across various missions without hardware or software reconfiguration. Whether it's mapping terrain, conducting surveillance, delivering supplies or executing rescue operations, the swarm adjusts on the fly. This flexibility greatly enhances deployment efficiency and reduces operational downtime. It enables real-world versatility across civilian, industrial and defence applications. The same swarm can perform diverse roles, improving cost-effectiveness and scalability.
- **Context Awareness:** Swarm agents are capable of sensing and interpreting their surrounding environments to make mission-specific decisions. This includes recognizing terrain changes, weather conditions or shifting objectives in real time. Context awareness allows the swarm to adjust behaviours dynamically, improving efficiency and mission success rates. The system does not rely on centralized control, making it robust to disruption. As a result, the swarm can maintain operational relevance in unpredictable environments.
- **Distributed Learning:** Instead of relying on a central brain, each agent contributes to learning and shares insights with others, building a collective intelligence. As individual agents encounter new challenges or data, the swarm benefits from that localized experience. This decentralized approach enhances adaptability and ensures resilience, even if some agents fail. Over time, the swarm refines its behaviours based on cumulative experience. This continuous, distributed learning mimics biological systems like ant colonies or bird flocks.

- **Autonomy at Multiple Levels:** Each agent in the swarm is capable of making local, real-time decisions based on immediate inputs. Simultaneously, the swarm as a whole exhibit organized, high-level behaviour without direct oversight. This layered autonomy allows for complex coordination and decision-making across large-scale environments. It ensures that the system is both flexible and scalable. Such autonomy reduces the need for constant human intervention, making it ideal for remote or hazardous missions.
- **Emergent Complexity:** Swarm intelligence leverages simple rules and interactions between agents to generate complex behaviours. For example, when basic obstacle avoidance and communication protocols are combined, adaptive pathfinding naturally emerges. These emergent behaviours are not explicitly programmed but arise from local interactions. This makes swarm systems highly adaptive and robust to changing environments. It's a powerful paradigm that mirrors intelligence in biological systems.

13.5.4 Applications of Generalized Swarm Intelligence

- **Disaster Response:** In disaster-stricken areas, swarm systems can simultaneously handle multiple tasks such as search and rescue, terrain mapping, supply delivery and emergency communication setup. Their ability to navigate unstructured and hazardous environments autonomously makes them invaluable in crisis situations. Swarms can adapt to debris, blocked paths or shifting conditions without needing central control. Their distributed nature ensures the mission continues even if some units are lost. This flexibility significantly enhances response speed and effectiveness.
- **Space Exploration:** Autonomous swarm satellites or rovers can collaboratively explore planetary surfaces, offering redundancy and efficiency in unknown terrains. These agents can map terrain, gather samples and share findings, all while adapting to unpredictable environments like Mars or the Moon. Swarms reduce the risk of mission failure by avoiding single points of failure. They can split tasks and self-organize to cover more ground than traditional single-vehicle missions. Such adaptability is crucial for long-duration, unmanned space missions.
- **Environmental Monitoring:** Sensing swarms can be deployed to monitor air and water quality, track wildlife and analyse ecological changes over vast and dynamic environments. These systems can adjust their sensing strategies in real time—for example, intensifying data collection in pollution hotspots. Distributed learning allows the swarm to adapt based on local environmental feedback. They offer a cost-effective, scalable and

continuous monitoring solution. Swarms can play a key role in combating climate change through timely and accurate data collection.

- **Military and Défense:** Swarm systems in defence applications can execute a range of tasks including reconnaissance, electronic warfare (e.g., jamming), surveillance and direct engagement. Their real-time responsiveness to battlefield conditions gives them a tactical advantage. Swarms can operate autonomously or follow high-level commands from human controllers. Redundancy and coordination make them hard to intercept or neutralize. This multi-role capability enhances situational awareness and strategic effectiveness.
- **Smart Infrastructure:** In urban or industrial environments, swarm robots can collaboratively perform construction, inspection, repair and maintenance tasks. Integrated with AI planning systems, they can optimize resource use and adapt to delays or obstacles in real-time. Their ability to operate continuously with minimal human oversight reduces downtime and operational costs. Swarms are ideal for maintaining hard-to-reach infrastructure like pipelines, bridges or skyscrapers. They bring scalability and precision to complex, large-scale engineering efforts.

13.5.5 Challenges and Research Directions

- **Scalability of Learning:** Scaling learning across thousands of swarm agents poses a major computational challenge. As each agent gathers and processes data, maintaining synchronized learning without overwhelming communication networks is complex. Traditional centralized training is impractical at large scales due to latency and bottlenecks. Distributed learning algorithms must be designed to function with limited local data and bandwidth. Techniques like federated learning and swarm reinforcement learning are emerging solutions. However, their efficiency and convergence at massive scales remain under research. Ensuring reliable, efficient learning with minimal resources is key to practical swarm deployment.
- **Coordination Without Centralization:** Swarm systems must coordinate their actions in real time without relying on a central controller. Centralized coordination creates single points of failure and scalability issues. Designing decentralized algorithms that allow agents to cooperate using only local information is critical. These algorithms must remain robust even if communication is delayed, limited or disrupted. Challenges include ensuring task allocation, collision avoidance and convergence to group goals. Recent advances in distributed consensus and swarm robotics offer promising directions. Still, fully autonomous, resilient coordination remains an open area of research.

- **Reward Structures in MARL (Multi-Agent Reinforcement Learning):** In multi-agent settings, aligning individual agents' rewards with the overall swarm objective is a fundamental challenge. If each agent optimizes its own reward, the collective behaviour may diverge from the intended goal. Crafting reward functions that promote cooperation and discourage selfish behaviour is non-trivial. Poorly designed incentives can lead to inefficiencies or instability in swarm dynamics. Solutions include global reward sharing, difference rewards or team-based reinforcement signals. However, these methods often scale poorly or introduce complexity. Research continues into scalable, stable reward structures for dynamic and diverse swarm tasks.
- **Explainability:** Understanding how a swarm arrives at its decisions is difficult due to the emergent and decentralized nature of behaviour. Traditional explainable AI techniques are often insufficient for analysing collective actions. In safety-critical domains like healthcare, defence or transportation, a lack of transparency can be unacceptable. Developing models that offer interpretable insights into swarm dynamics is essential. This includes visualizing behaviour patterns, identifying influence pathways and simplifying decision processes. Explainability also aids in debugging, trust-building and regulatory compliance. It remains a crucial area of ongoing interdisciplinary research.
- **Ethical and Legal Considerations:** Deploying intelligent swarms raises significant ethical and legal concerns. Questions of accountability become complex when decisions are made collectively and autonomously. In military contexts, autonomous swarms may be weaponized, leading to debates about legality under international humanitarian law. Additionally, swarms used in surveillance, policing or crowd control risk infringing on civil liberties. The impact on labour markets also cannot be ignored, as swarm automation may displace human jobs. Regulatory frameworks must evolve to address responsibility, usage limits and societal impact. Ethical swarm design must be prioritized alongside technical advancement (Table-3).

Table: 3 Summarized version of Challenges and Research Directions

Challenge	Summary
Scalability of Learning	Learning across thousands of agents strains computation and communication. Distributed methods like federated or swarm RL are promising but still face scalability and convergence issues.
Decentralized Coordination	Swarms must act without a central controller. Local, robust algorithms are needed for real-time cooperation, especially under limited or disrupted communication.

Challenge	Summary
Reward Structures in MARL	Aligning agent rewards with group goals is complex. Poorly designed rewards can cause selfish behaviour. Solutions exist but often lack scalability.
Explainability	Understanding swarm decisions is difficult due to emergent behaviour. New tools are needed for transparency, especially in critical domains.
Ethical & Legal Issues	Autonomous swarms raise concerns around accountability, military use, surveillance and job loss. Legal and ethical frameworks must evolve accordingly.

13.5.6 Societal and Ethical Implications

- **Jobs & Automation:** As swarm systems become more capable, they may replace human labour in sectors like agriculture, security, logistics and even disaster response. While this improves efficiency and safety, it raises concerns about job displacement and economic inequality. Reskilling programs and inclusive tech policies will be essential to ensure a just transition. The challenge lies in balancing innovation with societal well-being. Without intervention, automation could deepen existing social divides.
- **Surveillance:** The deployment of swarms equipped with cameras and sensors can lead to widespread, continuous surveillance. While useful for security or emergency management, this capability risks infringing on privacy rights. Transparent governance, ethical data usage and public oversight are critical to prevent misuse. The line between public safety and mass surveillance is thin and must be managed carefully. Citizens must retain control over how and when they are monitored.
- **Warfare:** Autonomous drone swarms represent a major shift in the nature of modern warfare, raising serious ethical and legal concerns. These systems can operate without human intervention, challenging accountability in combat decisions. Existing international laws may be insufficient to govern their use. There's a growing need for global treaties and ethical frameworks to regulate autonomous weapons. Left unchecked, swarm warfare could lower the threshold for conflict and civilian harm.
- **Environment:** Swarm technologies offer environmental benefits like pollution tracking and wildlife monitoring, enabling smarter conservation efforts. However, their large-scale deployment could also increase energy use, contribute to e-waste and create noise pollution. Sustainable design and energy-efficient algorithms must be prioritized to minimize harm. Lifecycle impacts—from production to disposal—should be considered. If managed responsibly, swarms can be a powerful force for environmental good.

REFERENCES

Akrour, R.; Schoenauer, M.; Sebag, M. April: Active preference learning-based reinforcement learning. In Proceedings of the Joint European Conference on Machine Learning and Knowledge Discovery in Databases, Bristol, UK, 24–28 September 2012; pp. 116–131.

Albani, D.; IJsselmuiden, J.; Haken, R.; Trianni, V. Monitoring and mapping with robot swarms for agricultural applications. In Proceedings of the 2017 14th IEEE International Conference on Advanced Video and Signal Based Surveillance (AVSS), Lecce, Italy, 29 August–1 September 2017; pp. 1–6.

Ali, S.; Khan, Z.; Din, A.; HASSAN, M.U. Investigation on communication aspects of multiple swarm networked robotics. Turk. J. Electr. Eng. Comput. Sci. 2019, 27, 2010–2020.

Anil, H.; Nikhil, K.; Chaitra, V.; Sharan, B.G. Revolutionizing farming using swarm robotics. In Proceedings of the 2015 6th International Conference on Intelligent Systems, Modelling and Simulation, Kuala Lumpur, Malaysia, 9–12 February 2015; pp. 141–147

Antoun, A.; Valentini, G.; Hocquard, E.; Wiandt, B.; Trianni, V.; Dorigo, M. Kilogrid: A modular virtualization environment for the kilobot robot. In Proceedings of the 2016 IEEE/RSJ International Conference on Intelligent Robots and Systems (IROS), Daejeon, Korea, 9–14 October 2016; pp. 3809–3814.

Arvanitakis, I.; Tzes, A. Collaborative mapping and navigation for a mobile robot swarm. In Proceedings of the 2017 25th Mediterranean Conference on Control and Automation (MED), Valletta, Malta, 3–6 July 2017; pp. 696–700.

Arvin, F.; Krajník, T.; Turgut, A.E.; Yue, S. COSΦ: Artificial pheromone system for robotic swarms research. In Proceedings of the 2015 IEEE/RSJ international conference on intelligent robots and systems (IROS), Vancouver, BC, Canada, 24–28 September 2015; pp. 407–412.

Arvin, F.; Murray, J.; Zhang, C.; Yue, S. Colias: An autonomous micro robot for swarm robotic applications. Int. J. Adv. Robot. Syst. 2014, 11, 113.

Arvin, F.; Samsudin, K.; Ramli, A.R. Development of a miniature robot for swarm robotic application. Int. J. Comput. Electr. Eng. 2009, 1, 436–442.

Ayre, M.; Izzo, D.; Pettazzi, L. Self assembly in space using behaviour based intelligent components. In Proceedings of the TAROS, Towards Autonomous Robotic Systems, London, UK, 12–14 September 2005; pp. 1–8.

Balakirsky, S.; Kootbally, Z. Usarsim/ros: A combined framework for robotic control and simulation. In Proceedings of the International Symposium on Flexible Automation, St. Louis, MI, USA, 18–20 June 2012; Volume 45110, pp. 101–108.

Bayert, J.; Khorbotly, S. Robotic Swarm Dispersion Using Gradient Descent Algorithm. In Proceedings of the 2019 IEEE International Symposium on Robotic and Sensors Environments (ROSE), Ottawa, ON, Canada, 17–18 June 2019; pp. 1–6.

Bayındır, L. A review of swarm robotics tasks. Neurocomputing 2016, 172, 292–321.

Beni, G. From swarm intelligence to swarm robotics. In Proceedings of the International Workshop on Swarm Robotic, Santa Monica, CA, USA, 17 July 2004; pp. 1–9.]

Benotsmane, R.; Kovács, G.; Dudás, L. Economic, Social Impacts and Operation of Smart Factories in Industry 4.0 Focusing on Simulation and Artificial Intelligence of Collaborating Robots. Soc. Sci. 2019, 8, 143.

Blender, T.; Buchner, T.; Fernandez, B.; Pichlmaier, B.; Schlegel, C. Managing a mobile agricultural robot swarm for a seeding task. In Proceedings of the IECON 2016-42nd Annual Conference of the IEEE Industrial Electronics Society, Florence, Italy, 23–26 October 2016; pp. 6879–6886.

Blum, C.; Li, X. Swarm intelligence in optimization. In Swarm Intelligence; Springer: Berlin/Heidelberg, Germany, 2008; pp. 43–85.

Bonabeau, E.; Marco, D.D.R.D.F.; Dorigo, M.; Théraulaz, G.; Theraulaz, G. Swarm Intelligence: From Natural to Artificial Systems; Number 1; Oxford University Press: Oxford, UK, 1999.

Boskovic, J.; Knoebel, N.; Moshtagh, N.; Amin, J.; Larson, G. Collaborative mission planning & autonomous control technology (compact) system employing swarms of uavs. In Proceedings of the AIAA Guidance, Navigation, and Control Conference, Chicago, IL, USA, 10–13 August 2009; p. 5653.

Brambilla, M.; Ferrante, E.; Birattari, M.; Dorigo, M. Swarm robotics: A review from the swarm engineering perspective. Swarm Intell. 2013, 7, 1–41.

Browning, B.; Tryzelaar, E. Ubersim: A realistic simulation engine for robot soccer. In Proceedings of the Autonomous Agents and Multi-Agent Systems, AAMAS'03, Auckland, New Zealand, 9–13 May 2003.

Cambier, N.; Miletitch, R.; Frémont, V.; Dorigo, M.; Ferrante, E.; Trianni, V. Language Evolution in Swarm Robotics: A Perspective. Front. Robot. AI 2020, 7, 12.]

Camci, E.; Kripalani, D.R.; Ma, L.; Kayacan, E.; Khanesar, M.A. An aerial robot for rice farm quality inspection with type-2 fuzzy neural networks tuned by particle swarm optimization-sliding mode control hybrid algorithm. Swarm Evol. Comput. 2018, 41, 1–8.

Caprari, G.; Estier, T.; Siegwart, R. Fascination of down scaling-Alice the sugar cube robot. J. Micromechatron. 2001, 1, 177–189.

Caprari, G.; Siegwart, R. Mobile micro-robots ready to use: Alice. In Proceedings of the 2005 IEEE/RSJ International Conference on Intelligent Robots and Systems, Edmonton, AB, Canada, 2–6 August 2005; pp. 3295–3300.

Carbone, C.; Garibaldi, O.; Kurt, Z. Swarm robotics as a solution to crops inspection for precision agriculture. KnE Eng. 2018, 552–562.

Carpin, S.; Lewis, M.; Wang, J.; Balakirsky, S.; Scrapper, C. USARSim: A robot simulator for research and education. In Proceedings of the 2007 IEEE International Conference on Robotics and Automation, Rome, Italy, 10–14 April 2007; pp. 1400–1405.

Chattopadhyay, I.; Ray, A. Supervised self-organization of homogeneous swarms using ergodic projections of Markov chains. IEEE Trans. Syst. Man, Cybern. Part B (Cybernetics) 2009, 39, 1505–1515.

Chen, W.; Liu, B.; Huang, H.; Guo, S.; Zheng, Z. When UAV swarm meets edge-cloud computing: The QoS perspective. IEEE Netw. 2019, 33, 36–43.

Chen, Y.; Du, Z.; Garcia-Acosta, M. Robot as a service in cloud computing. In Proceedings of the 2010 Fifth IEEE International Symposium on Service Oriented System Engineering, Nanjing, China, 4–5 June 2010; pp. 151–158.

Coppola, M.; Guo, J.; Gill, E.; de Croon, G.C. Provable self-organizing pattern formation by a swarm of robots with limited knowledge. Swarm Intell. 2019, 13, 59–94.

Correll, N.; Hamann, H. Probabilistic modeling of swarming systems. In Springer Handbook of Computational Intelligence; Springer: Berlin/Heidelberg, Germany, 2015; pp. 1423–1432.

Couceiro, M.S.; Figueiredo, C.M.; Luz, J.M.A.; Ferreira, N.M.; Rocha, R.P. A Low-Cost Educational Platform for Swarm Robotics. Int. J. Robot. Educ. Art 2012, 2, 1–15.

Couzin, I.D. Collective cognition in animal groups. Trends Cogn. Sci. 2009, 13, 36–43.

Couzin, I.D.; Krause, J. Self-organization and collective behavior in vertebrates. Adv. Study Behav. 2003, 32, 10–1016.

Dadgar, M.; Couceiro, M.S.; Hamzeh, A. RbRDPSO: Repulsion-Based RDPSO for Robotic Target Searching. Iran. J. Sci. Technol. Trans. Electr. Eng. 2020, 44, 551–563.

De Nicola, R.; Di Stefano, L.; Inverso, O. Multi-agent systems with virtual stigmergy. In Proceedings of the Federation of International Conferences on Software Technologies: Applications and Foundations, Toulouse, France, 25–29 June 2018; pp. 351–366.

Delight, M.; Ramakrishnan, S.; Zambrano, T.; MacCready, T. Developing robotic swarms for ocean surface mapping. In Proceedings of the 2016 IEEE International Conference on Robotics and Automation (ICRA), Stockholm, Sweden, 16–21 May 2016; pp. 5309–5315.]

Di Mario, E.; Navarro, I.; Martinoli, A. Distributed learning of cooperative robotic behaviors using particle swarm optimization. In Proceedings of the Experimental Robotics, Tokyo, Japan, 3–6 October 2016; pp. 591–604.

Dorigo, M.; Birattari, M.; Brambilla, M. Swarm robotics. Scholarpedia 2014, 9, 1463.

Duarte, M.; Silva, F.; Rodrigues, T.; Moura Oliveira, S.; Christensen, A. JBotEvolver: A Versatile Simulation Program for Evolutionary Robotics. In Artificial Life 14; Proceedings of the Fourteenth International Conference on the Synthesis and Simulation of Living Systems, New York, NY, USA, 30 July–2 August 2014; MIT Press: Cambridge, MA, USA, 2014; pp. 210–211

Ebel, H.; Luo, W.; Yu, F.; Tang, Q.; Eberhard, P. Design and Experimental Validation of a Distributed Cooperative Transportation Scheme. IEEE Trans. Autom. Sci. Eng. 2020.

Eshaghi, K.; Li, Y.; Kashino, Z.; Nejat, G.; Benhabib, B. mROBerTO 2.0–An Autonomous Millirobot With Enhanced Locomotion for Swarm Robotics. IEEE Robot. Autom. Lett. 2020, 5, 962–969.

Farooq, M.; Caro, G.A.D. Routing Protocols for Next-Generation Networks Inspired by Collective Behaviors of Insect Societies: An Overview. In Natural Computing Series; Springer: Berlin/Heidelberg, Germany, 2008; pp. 101–160

Farrugia, J.L.; Fabri, S.G. Swarm robotics for object transportation. In Proceedings of the 2018 UKACC 12th International Conference on Control (CONTROL), Sheffield, UK, 5–7 September 2018; pp. 353–358

Firat, Z.; Ferrante, E.; Gillet, Y.; Tuci, E. On self-organised aggregation dynamics in swarms of robots with informed robots. Neural Comput. Appl. 2020, 32, 13825–13841

Florea, A.G.; Buiu, C. Synchronized dispersion of robotic swarms using XP colonies. In Proceedings of the 2016 8th International Conference on Electronics, Computers and Artificial Intelligence (ECAI), Ploiesti, Romania, 30 June–2 July 2016; pp. 1–6.

Gabellieri, C.; Tognon, M.; Sanalitro, D.; Pallottino, L.; Franchi, A. A study on force-based collaboration in swarms. Swarm Intell. 2020, 14, 57–82.

Garattoni, L.; Birattari, M. Swarm robotics. In Wiley Encyclopedia of Electrical and Electronics Engineering; Wiley-Interscience: Hoboken, NJ, USA, 2016.

Garcia-Aunon, P.; Roldán, J.J.; Barrientos, A. Monitoring traffic in future cities with aerial swarms: Developing and optimizing a behavior-based surveillance algorithm. Cogn. Syst. Res. 2019, 54, 273–286

Garnier, S.; Gautrais, J.; Theraulaz, G. The biological principles of swarm intelligence. Swarm Intell. 2007, 1, 3–31.

Gaus, C.C.; Urso, L.M.; Minßen, T.F.; de Witte, T. Economics of Mechanical Weeding by a Swarm of Small Field Robots. In Proceedings of the 57th Annual Conference of the German Association of Agricultural Economists (GEWISOLA), Weihenstephan, Germany, 13–15 September 2017.

Gerkey, B.; Vaughan, R.T.; Howard, A. The player/stage project: Tools for multi-robot and distributed sensor systems. In Proceedings of the 11th International Conference on Advanced Robotics, Coimbra, Portuga, 30 June–3 July 2003; Volume 1, pp. 317–323.

Gerling, V.; Von Mammen, S. Robotics for self-organised construction. In Proceedings of the 2016 IEEE 1st International Workshops on Foundations and Applications of Self* Systems (FAS* W), Augsburg, Germany, 12–16 September 2016; pp. 162–167.

Giardina, I. Collective behavior in animal groups: Theoretical models and empirical studies. HFSP J. 2008, 2, 205–219.

Gregory, C.; Vardy, A. microUSV: A low-cost platform for indoor marine swarm robotics research. HardwareX 2020, 7, e00105.

Gupta, R.; Bayal, R. Source Detection of Oil Spill using Modified Glowworm Swarm optimization. In Proceedings of the 2020 5th International Conference on Computing, Communication and Security (ICCCS), Patna, India, 14–16 October 2020; pp. 1–6.

Hamann, H. Swarm Robotics: A Formal Approach; Springer: Berlin/Heidelberg, Germany, 2018.

Hamann, H.; Schmickl, T. Modelling the swarm: Analysing biological and engineered swarm systems. Math. Comput. Model. Dyn. Syst. 2012, 18, 1–12.

Hao, W.; Qin, S. Multi-objective path planning for space exploration robot based on chaos immune particle swarm optimization algorithm. In Proceedings of the International Conference on Artificial Intelligence and Computational Intelligence, Taiyuan, China, 24–25 September 2011; pp. 42–52.

Harwell, J.; Lowmanstone, L.; Gini, M. Demystifying Emergent Intelligence and Its Effect on Performance In Large Robot Swarms. In Proceedings of the 19th International Conference on Autonomous Agents and MultiAgent Systems, Auckland, New Zealand, 9–13 May 2020; pp. 474–482.]

He, H.; Kamburugamuve, S.; Fox, G.C.; Zhao, W. Cloud based real-time multi-robot collision avoidance for swarm robotics. Int. J. Grid Distrib. Comput. 2016, 9, 339–358.

Hilder, J.; Naylor, R.; Rizihs, A.; Franks, D.; Timmis, J. The pi swarm: A low-cost platform for swarm robotics research and education. In Proceedings of the Conference Towards Autonomous Robotic Systems, Birmingham, UK, 1–3 September 2014; pp. 151–162.

Hinchey, M.G.; Sterritt, R.; Rouff, C. Swarms and swarm intelligence. Computer 2007, 40, 111–113.

Hou, X.; Ren, Z.; Wang, J.; Zheng, S.; Cheng, W.; Zhang, H. Distributed fog computing for latency and reliability guaranteed swarm of drones. IEEE Access 2020, 8, 7117–7130.

Hu, C.; Fu, Q.; Yue, S. Colias IV: The affordable micro robot platform with bio-inspired vision. In Proceedings of the Annual Conference Towards Autonomous Robotic Systems, Bristol, UK, 25–27 July 2018; pp. 197–208.

Hugues, L.; Bredeche, N. Simbad: An autonomous robot simulation package for education and research. In Proceedings of the International Conference on Simulation of Adaptive Behavior, Daejeon, Korea, 9–14 October 2006; pp. 831–842.

Hung, P.D.; La, H.M.; Ngo, T.D. Adaptive hierarchical distributed control with cooperative task allocation for robot swarms. In Proceedings of the 2020 IEEE/SICE International Symposium on System Integration (SII), Honolulu, HI, USA, 12–15 January 2020; pp. 1300–1305.

Hüttenrauch, M.; Adrian, S.; Neumann, G. Deep reinforcement learning for swarm systems. J. Mach. Learn. Res. 2019, 20, 1–31.]

Hüttenrauch, M.; Šošić, A.; Neumann, G. Local communication protocols for learning complex swarm behaviors with deep reinforcement learning. In Proceedings of the International Conference on Swarm Intelligence, Rome, Italy, 29–31 October 2018; pp. 71–83.

Ivanov, D. Fog robotics distributed computing in a monitoring task. In Proceedings of the Computer Science On-line Conference, Zlin, Czech Republic, 24–27 April 2020; pp. 554–562.

Jackson, J. Microsoft robotics studio: A technical introduction. IEEE Robot. Autom. Mag. 2007, 14, 82–87.

Jain, U.; Tiwari, R.; Godfrey, W.W. Multiple odor source localization using diverse-PSO and group-based strategies in an unknown environment. J. Comput. Sci. 2019, 34, 33–47.

Janson, S.; Merkle, D.; Middendorf, M. A decentralization approach for swarm intelligence algorithms in networks applied to multi swarm PSO. Int. J. Intell. Comput. Cybern. 2008, 1, 25–45.

Karydis, Konstantinos, Prasanna Kannappan, Herbert G. Tanner, Adam Jardine, and Jeffrey Heinz. 2016. "Resilience through Learning in Multi-agent Cyber-Physical Systems." Frontiers in Robotics and AI 3:36.

Katz, J.; Mohan, S.; Miller, D. On-orbit assembly of flexible space structures with SWARM. In Proceedings of the AIAA Infotech@Aerospace 2010, Atlanta, GA, USA, 20–22 April 2010; p. 3524.

Kegeleirs, M.; Ramos, D.G.; Birattari, M. Random walk exploration for swarm mapping. In Proceedings of the Annual Conference Towards Autonomous Robotic Systems, London, UK, 3–5 July 2019; pp. 211–222.

Khalastchi, E.; Kalech, M. Fault Detection and Diagnosis in Multi-Robot Systems: A Survey. Sensors 2019, 19, 4019.

Khaldi, B.; Harrou, F.; Cherif, F.; Sun, Y. Improving robots swarm aggregation performance through the Minkowski distance function. In Proceedings of the 2020 6th International Conference on Mechatronics and Robotics Engineering (ICMRE), Barcelona, Spain, 12–15 February 2020; pp. 87–91. [

Khaluf, Y.; Vanhee, S.; Simoens, P. Local ant system for allocating robot swarms to time-constrained tasks. J. Comput. Sci. 2019, 31, 33–44.

Khaluf, Yara, Pieter Simoens, and Heiko Hamann. 2019. "The Neglected Pieces of Designing Collective Decision-Making Processes." Frontiers in Robotics and AI 6:16.

Kit, J.L.; Mateo, D.; Bouffanais, R. A decentralized mobile computing network for multi-robot systems operations. In Proceedings of the 2018 9th IEEE Annual Ubiquitous Computing, Electronics & Mobile Communication Conference (UEMCON), New York, NY, USA, 8–10 November 2018; pp. 309–314.

Koos, Sylvain, Jean-Baptiste Mouret, and Stéphane Doncieux. 2012. "The Transferability Approach: Crossing the Reality Gap in Evolutionary Robotics." IEEE Transactions on Evolutionary Computation 17 (1): 122–145.

Kornienko, S.; Kornienko, O.; Levi, P. Collective AI: Context awareness via communication. In Proceedings of the IJCAI, Scotland, UK, 30 July–5 August 2005; Volume 5, pp. 1464–1470.

Kshemkalyani, A.D.; Molla, A.R.; Sharma, G. Dispersion of Mobile Robots on Grids. In Proceedings of the International Workshop on Algorithms and Computation, Singapore, 31 March–2 April 2020; pp. 183–197.

Kudelski, M.; Gambardella, L.M.; Di Caro, G.A. RoboNetSim: An integrated framework for multi-robot and network simulation. Robot. Auton. Syst. 2013, 61, 483–496.

Kumar, Vignesh, and Ferat Sahin. 2003. "Cognitive Maps in Swarm Robots for the Mine Detection Application." In 2003 IEEE International Conference on Systems, Man and Cybernetics, 3364–3369. New York: IEEE.

Lee, C. Development of an industrial Internet of Things (IIoT) based smart robotic warehouse management system. In Proceedings of the International Conference on Information Resources Management (CONF-IRM), Ningbo, China, 3–5 June 2018.

Lee, W.; Vaughan, N.; Kim, D. Task Allocation Into a Foraging Task With a Series of Subtasks in Swarm Robotic System. IEEE Access 2020, 8, 107549–107561.

Leofante, F.; Ábrahám, E.; Niemueller, T.; Lakemeyer, G.; Tacchella, A. Integrated synthesis and execution of optimal plans for multi-robot systems in logistics. Inf. Syst. Front. 2019, 21, 87–107.

Li, G.; St-Onge, D.; Pinciroli, C.; Gasparri, A.; Garone, E.; Beltrame, G. Decentralized progressive shape formation with robot swarms. Auton. Robot. 2019, 43, 1505–1521.

Li, J.; Tan, Y. A probabilistic finite state machine-based strategy for multi-target search using swarm robotics. Appl. Soft Comput. 2019, 77, 467–483

Li, Y.; Klingner, J.; Correll, N. Distributed camouflage for swarm robotics and smart materials. Auton. Robot. 2018, 42, 1635–1650.]

Limeira, M.A.; Piardi, L.; Kalempa, V.C.; de Oliveira, A.S.; Leitão, P. WsBot: A Tiny, Low-Cost Swarm Robot for Experimentation on Industry 4.0. In Proceedings of the 2019 Latin American Robotics Symposium (LARS), 2019 Brazilian Symposium on Robotics (SBR) and 2019 Workshop on Robotics in Education (WRE), Grande do Sul, Brazil, 22–26 October 2019; pp. 293–298

Liu, X.; Cao, J.; Yang, Y.; Jiang, S. CPS-based smart warehouse for industry 4.0: A survey of the underlying technologies. Computers 2018, 7, 13.

Liu, Y.; Wang, L.; Huang, H.; Liu, M.; Xu, C.Z. A novel swarm robot simulation platform for warehousing logistics. In Proceedings of the 2017 IEEE International Conference on Robotics and Biomimetics (ROBIO), Macau, China, 5–8 December 2017; pp. 2669–2674.

Liu, Z.; West, C.; Lennox, B.; Arvin, F. Local Bearing Estimation for a Swarm of Low-Cost Miniature Robots. Sensors 2020, 20, 3308.

Lončar, I.; Babić, A.; Arbanas, B.; Vasiljević, G.; Petrović, T.; Bogdan, S.; Mišković, N. A Heterogeneous Robotic Swarm for Long-Term Monitoring of Marine Environments. Appl. Sci. 2019, 9, 1388.

Lu, J.; Liu, J.; Couzin, I.D.; Levin, S.A. Emerging collective behaviors of animal groups. In Proceedings of the 2008 7th World Congress on Intelligent Control and Automation, Chongqing, China, 27–25 June 2008; pp. 1060–1065.

Masár, M.; Zelenka, J. Modification of PSO algorithm for the purpose of space exploration. In Proceedings of the 2012 IEEE 16th International Conference on Intelligent Engineering Systems (INES), Lisbon, Portugal, 13–15 June 2012; pp. 51–54.

Mathews, Nithin, Anders Lyhne Christensen, Rehan O'Grady, Francesco Mondada, and Marco Dorigo. 2017. "Mergeable Nervous Systems for Robots." Nature Communications 8 (1): 1–7.

Meinhardt, Hans, and Alfred Gierer. 2000. "Pattern Formation by Local Self-Activation and Lateral Inhibition." Bioessays 22 (8): 753–760.

Melenbrink, N.; Rinderspacher, K.; Menges, A.; Werfel, J. Autonomous anchoring for robotic construction. Autom. Constr. 2020, 120, 103391.

Melenbrink, N.; Werfel, J. Local force cues for strength and stability in a distributed robotic construction system. Swarm Intell. 2018, 12, 129–153.

Michel, O. Cyberbotics Ltd. Webots™: Professional mobile robot simulation. Int. J. Adv. Robot. Syst. 2004, 1, 5.

Millard, A.G.; Ravikanna, R.; Groß, R.; Chesmore, D. Towards a Swarm Robotic System for Autonomous Cereal Harvesting. In Proceedings of the Annual Conference Towards Autonomous Robotic Systems, London, UK, 3–5 July 2019; pp. 458–461.

Minßen, T.; Gaus, C.; Urso, L.; Hanke, S.; Schattenberg, J.; Frerichs, L. Robots for plant-specific care operations in Arable Farming-concept and technological requirements for the operation of robot swarms for plant care tasks. EFITA/WCCA 2011, 11, 1–11.

Mısır, O.; Gökrem, L.; Can, M.S. Fuzzy-based self organizing aggregation method for swarm robots. Biosystems 2020, 196, 104187.

Mondada, F.; Bonani, M.; Raemy, X.; Pugh, J.; Cianci, C.; Klaptocz, A.; Magnenat, S.; Zufferey, J.C.; Floreano, D.; Martinoli, A. The e-puck, a robot designed for education in engineering. In Proceedings of the 9th Conference on Autonomous Robot Systems and Competitions, Branco, Portugal, 7 May 2009; IPCB: Castelo Branco, Portugal, 2009; Volume 1, pp. 59–65.

Mondada, F.; Franzi, E.; Guignard, A. The development of khepera. Experiments with the Mini-Robot Khepera. In Proceedings of the First International Khepera Workshop, Paderborn, Germany, 10–11 December 1999; pp. 7–14.

Mondada, F.; Guignard, A.; Bonani, M.; Bar, D.; Lauria, M.; Floreano, D. Swarm-bot: From concept to implementation. In Proceedings of the 2003 IEEE/RSJ International Conference on Intelligent Robots and Systems (IROS 2003) (Cat. No. 03CH37453), Las Vegas, NV, USA, 27–31 October 2003; Volume 2, pp. 1626–1631.

Navarro, I.; Matía, F. An introduction to swarm robotics. ISRN Robot. 2013.

Nedjah, N.; Junior, L.S. Review of methodologies and tasks in swarm robotics towards standardization. Swarm Evol. Comput. 2019, 50, 100565.

Nehmzow, U. Mobile Robotics: A Practical Introduction; Springer Science & Business Media: Berlin/Heidelberg, Germany, 2012.

Notomista, G.; Mayya, S.; Hutchinson, S.; Egerstedt, M. An optimal task allocation strategy for heterogeneous multi-robot systems. In Proceedings of the 2019 18th European Control Conference (ECC), Naples, Italy, 25–28 June 2019; pp. 2071–2076.

Novischi, D.M.; Florea, A.M. Decentralized Swarm Aggregation and Dispersion with Inter-Member Collision Avoidance for Non-holonomic Multi-Robot Systems. In Proceedings of the 2018 IEEE 14th International Conference on Intelligent Computer Communication and Processing (ICCP), Cluj-Napoca, Romania, 6–8 September 2018; pp. 89–95.

Osaba, E.; Del Ser, J.; Iglesias, A.; Yang, X.S. Soft Computing for Swarm Robotics: New Trends and Applications; Elsevier: Amsterdam, The Netherlands, 2020.

Parker, L.E. ALLIANCE: An architecture for fault tolerant multirobot cooperation. IEEE Trans. Robot. Autom. 1998, 14, 220–240.

Pettinaro, G.C.; Kwee, I.W.; Gambardella, L.M. Definition, Implementation, and Calibration of the Swarmbot3d Simulator; Technical Report No. IDSIA-21-03; IDSIA: Manno, Switzerland, 2003; pp. 7–10.

Pettinaro, G.C.; Kwee, I.W.; Gambardella, L.M. Swarmbot3D User Manual, Technical Report No. IDSIA-22-03; IDSIA: Manno, Switzerland, 2003.

Pinciroli, C.; Trianni, V.; O'Grady, R.; Pini, G.; Brutschy, A.; Brambilla, M.; Mathews, N.; Ferrante, E.; Di Caro, G.; Ducatelle, F.; et al. ARGoS: A modular, parallel, multi-engine simulator for multi-robot systems. Swarm Intell. 2012, 6, 271–295.

Pinto, M.F.; Honorio, L.M.; Melo, A.; Marcato, A.L. A Robotic Cognitive Architecture for Slope and Dam Inspections. Sensors 2020, 20, 4579.

Pugh, J.; Raemy, X.; Favre, C.; Falconi, R.; Martinoli, A. A fast onboard relative positioning module for multirobot systems. IEEE/ASME Trans. Mechatron. 2009, 14, 151–162.

Puliafito, A.; Hufnagel, L.; Neveu, P.; Streichan, S.; Sigal, A.; Fygenson, D.K.; Shraiman, B.I. Collective and single cell behavior in epithelial contact inhibition. Proc. Natl. Acad. Sci. USA 2012, 109, 739–744.

Queralta, J.P.; McCord, C.; Gia, T.N.; Tenhunen, H.; Westerlund, T. Communication-free and index-free distributed formation control algorithm for multi-robot systems. Procedia Comput. Sci. 2019, 151, 431–438.

Queralta, J.P.; Qingqing, L.; Gia, T.N.; Truong, H.L.; Westerlund, T. End-to-end design for self-reconfigurable heterogeneous robotic swarms. In Proceedings of the 2020 16th International Conference on Distributed Computing in Sensor Systems (DCOSS), Marina del Rey, CA, USA, 25–27 May 2020; pp. 281–287.

Renzaglia, A.; Briñón-Arranz, L. Search and Localization of a Weak Source with a Multi-robot Formation. J. Intell. Robot. Syst. 2020, 97, 623–634.

Rizk, Y.; Awad, M.; Tunstel, E.W. Cooperative heterogeneous multi-robot systems: A survey. ACM Comput. Surv. (CSUR) 2019, 52, 1–31.

Rohmer, E.; Singh, S.; Freese, M. Coppeliasim (formerly v-rep): A versatile and scalable robot simulation framework. In Proceedings of the 2013 IEEE/RSJ International Conference on Intelligent Robots and Systems, Tokyo, Japan, 3–7 November 2013.

Rouff, C.A.; Hinchey, M.G.; Truszkowski, W.F.; Rash, J.L. Experiences applying formal approaches in the development of swarm-based space exploration systems. Int. J. Softw. Tools Technol. Transf. 2006, 8, 587–603.

Rubenstein, M.; Ahler, C.; Hoff, N.; Cabrera, A.; Nagpal, R. Kilobot: A low cost robot with scalable operations designed for collective behaviors. Robot. Auton. Syst. 2014, 62, 966–975.

Rubenstein, M.; Ahler, C.; Nagpal, R. Kilobot: A low cost scalable robot system for collective behaviors. In Proceedings of the 2012 IEEE International Conference on Robotics and Automation, Saint Paul, MN, USA, 14–18 May 2012; pp. 3293–3298.

Rusu, R.B.; Maldonado, A.; Beetz, M.; Gerkey, B. Extending Player/Stage/Gazebo towards cognitive robots acting in ubiquitous sensor-equipped environments. In Proceedings of the International Conference on Robotics and Automation (ICRA) Workshop for Network Robot Systems, Roma, Italy, 10–14 April 2007.

Sabatini, M.; Palmerini, G.B. Collective control of spacecraft swarms for space exploration. Celest. Mech. Dyn. Astron. 2009, 105, 229.

Sahin, E. Swarm robotics: From sources of inspiration to domains of application. In Proceedings of the International Workshop on Swarm Robotics, Santa Monica, CA, USA, 17 July 2004; pp. 10–20.

Sànchez, N.D.G.; Vargas, P.A.; Couceiro, M.S. A darwinian swarm robotics strategy applied to underwater exploration. In Proceedings of the 2018 IEEE Congress on Evolutionary Computation (CEC), Rio de Janeiro, Brazil, 8–13 July 2018; pp. 1–6.

Sanchez-Lopez, J.L.; Fernández, R.A.S.; Bavle, H.; Sampedro, C.; Molina, M.; Pestana, J.; Campoy, P. Aerostack: An architecture and open-source software framework for aerial robotics. In Proceedings of the 2016 International Conference on Unmanned Aircraft Systems (ICUAS), Marriott, VA, USA, 7–10 June 2016; pp. 332–341.

Sartoretti, G.; Wu, Y.; Paivine, W.; Kumar, T.S.; Koenig, S.; Choset, H. Distributed reinforcement learning for multi-robot decentralized collective construction. In Distributed Autonomous Robotic Systems; Springer: Berlin/Heidelberg, Germany, 2019; pp. 35–49.

Scholz, C.; Engel, M.; Pöschel, T. Rotating robots move collectively and self-organize. Nat. Commun. 2018, 9, 1–8.

Scott, A.F.; Yu, C. Cooperative multi-agent mapping and exploration in Webots®. In Proceedings of the 2009 4th International Conference on Autonomous Robots and Agents, Wellington, New Zealand, 10–12 February 2009; pp. 56–61.

Secinti, G.; Trotta, A.; Mohanti, S.; Di Felice, M.; Chowdhury, K.R. FOCUS: Fog computing in UAS software-defined mesh networks. IEEE Trans. Intell. Transp. Syst. 2019, 21, 2664–2674. [

Seyfried, J.; Szymanski, M.; Bender, N.; Estaña, R.; Thiel, M.; Wörn, H. The I-SWARM project: Intelligent small world autonomous robots for micro-manipulation. In Proceedings of the International Workshop on Swarm Robotics, Monica, CA, USA, 17 July 2004; pp. 70–83.

Shah, D.; Vachhani, L. Swarm aggregation without communication and global positioning. IEEE Robot. Autom. Lett. 2019, 4, 886–893.

Shi, H.; Li, J.; Li, Z. A distributed strategy for cooperative autonomous robots using pedestrian behavior for multi-target search in the unknown environment. Sensors 2020, 20, 1606.

Singh, P.K.; Singh, R.; Nandi, S.K.; Ghafoor, K.Z.; Rawat, D.B.; Nandi, S. An efficient blockchain-based approach for cooperative decision making in swarm robotics. Internet Technol. Lett. 2020, 3, e140.

Soares, J.M.; Navarro, I.; Martinoli, A. The Khepera IV mobile robot: Performance evaluation, sensory data and software toolbox. In Proceedings of the Robot 2015: Second Iberian Robotics Conference, Lisbon, Portugal, 19–21 November 2015; pp. 767–781.

Su, H.; Zhang, J.; Zeng, Z. Formation-containment control of multi-robot systems under a stochastic sampling mechanism. Sci. China Technol. Sci. 2020, 63, 1025–1034.

Sugawara, K. Object Transportation by Swarm Robots Based on Constraint Granular Convection. In Distributed Autonomous Robotic Systems; Springer: Berlin/ Heidelberg, Germany, 2019; pp. 329–340.

Sun, X.; Liu, T.; Hu, C.; Fu, Q.; Yue, S. ColCOS φ: A multiple pheromone communication system for swarm robotics and social insects research. In Proceedings of the 2019 IEEE 4th International Conference on Advanced Robotics and Mechatronics (ICARM), Toyonaka, Japan, 3–5 July 2019; pp. 59–66.

Talamali, M.S.; Bose, T.; Haire, M.; Xu, X.; Marshall, J.A.; Reina, A. Sophisticated collective foraging with minimalist agents: A swarm robotics test. Swarm Intell. 2020, 14, 25–56.

Tan, Y.; Zheng, Z.Y. Research advance in swarm robotics. Def. Technol. 2013, 9, 18–39.

Tang, Q.; Xu, Z.; Yu, F.; Zhang, Z.; Zhang, J. Dynamic target searching and tracking with swarm robots based on stigmergy mechanism. Robot. Auton. Syst. 2019, 120, 103251.

Tang, Q.; Yu, F.; Zhang, Y.; Ding, L.; Eberhard, P. A stigmergy based search method for swarm robots. In Proceedings of the International Conference on Swarm Intelligence, Fukuoka, Japan, 27 July 2017; pp. 199–209.

Trianni, V.; Campo, A. Fundamental collective behaviors in swarm robotics. In Springer Handbook of Computational Intelligence; Springer: Berlin/ Heidelberg, Germany, 2015; pp. 1377–1394.

Turgut, A.E.; Çelikkanat, H.; Gökçe, F.; Sahin, E. Self-organized flocking in mobile robot swarms. Swarm Intell. 2008, 2, 97–120. [

Turnbull, L.; Samanta, B. Cloud robotics: Formation control of a multi robot system utilizing cloud infrastructure. In Proceedings of the 2013 Proceedings of IEEE Southeastcon, Jacksonville, FL, USA, 4–7 April 2013; pp. 1–4.

Turner, C.J.; Oyekan, J.; Stergioulas, L.; Griffin, D. Utilizing Industry 4.0 on the Construction Site Challenges and Opportunities. IEEE Trans. Ind. Inf. 2020, 17, 746–756. [

Valdastri, P.; Corradi, P.; Menciassi, A.; Schmickl, T.; Crailsheim, K.; Seyfried, J.; Dario, P. Micromanipulation, communication and swarm intelligence issues in a swarm microrobotic platform. Robot. Auton. Syst. 2006, 54, 789–804.

Valentini, G.; Antoun, A.; Trabattoni, M.; Wiandt, B.; Tamura, Y.; Hocquard, E.; Trianni, V.; Dorigo, M. Kilogrid: A novel experimental environment for the Kilobot robot. Swarm Intell. 2018, 12, 245–266.

Vassev, E.; Sterritt, R.; Rouff, C.; Hinchey, M. Swarm technology at NASA: Building resilient systems. IT Prof. 2012, 14, 36–42.

Wai, H.T.; Yang, Z.; Wang, Z.; Hong, M. Multi-agent reinforcement learning via double averaging primal-dual optimization. arXiv 2018, arXiv:1806.00877.

Wan, S.; Gu, Z.; Ni, Q. Cognitive computing and wireless communications on the edge for healthcare service robots. Comput. Commun. 2020, 149, 99–106.

Wang, H.; Rubenstein, M. Shape Formation in Homogeneous Swarms Using Local Task Swapping. IEEE Trans. Robot. 2020, 36, 597–612.

Wei, H.; Chen, Y.; Tan, J.; Wang, T. Sambot: A self-assembly modular robot system. IEEE/ASME Trans. Mechatron. 2010, 16, 745–757.

Werfel, J.; Petersen, K.; Nagpal, R. Designing collective behavior in a termite-inspired robot construction team. Science 2014, 343, 754–758.

Wilson, S.; Gameros, R.; Sheely, M.; Lin, M.; Dover, K.; Gevorkyan, R.; Haberland, M.; Bertozzi, A.; Berman, S. Pheeno, a versatile swarm robotic research and education platform. IEEE Robot. Autom. Lett. 2016, 1, 884–891.

Woolley, A.W.; Aggarwal, I.; Malone, T.W. Collective intelligence and group performance. Curr. Dir. Psychol. Sci. 2015, 24, 420–424.

Yamagishi, K.; Suzuki, T. Collective movement method for swarm robot based on a thermodynamic model. Int. J. Adv. Comput. Sci. Appl. 2017, 8, 513–519.

Yang, H.a.; Cao, S.; Bai, L.; Zhang, Z.; Kong, J. A distributed and parallel self-assembly approach for swarm robotics. Robot. Auton. Syst. 2019, 118, 80–92.

Yu, H.; Shi, P.; Lim, C.C.; Wang, D. Formation control for multi-robot systems with collision avoidance. Int. J. Control 2019, 92, 2223–2234.

Zambon, I.; Cecchini, M.; Egidi, G.; Saporito, M.G.; Colantoni, A. Revolution 4.0: Industry vs. agriculture in a future development for SMEs. Processes 2019, 7, 36.

Zhakypov, Z.; Mori, K.; Hosoda, K.; Paik, J. Designing minimal and scalable insect-inspired multi-locomotion millirobots. Nature 2019, 571, 381–386.

Zhang, J.; Ding, G.; Zou, Y.; Qin, S.; Fu, J. Review of job shop scheduling research and its new perspectives under Industry 4.0. J. Intell. Manuf. 2019, 30, 1809–1830.

Zhao, H.; Liu, H.; Leung, Y.W.; Chu, X. Self-adaptive collective motion of swarm robots. IEEE Trans. Autom. Sci. Eng. 2018, 15, 1533–1545.

Index

www.ingramcontent.com/pod-product-compliance
Lightning Source LLC
LaVergne TN
LVHW081942200926
848484LV00009B/2494
* 9 7 8 1 7 8 7 1 5 6 2 9 6 *